12-14-63

Elements of Investments

SELECTED READINGS

Hsiu-Kwang Wu
Alan J. Zakon

Boston University

HOLT, RINEHART AND WINSTON, INC.
New York, Chicago, San Francisco, Toronto, London

Copyright © 1965 by Holt, Rinehart and Winston, Inc.
All Rights Reserved
Library of Congress Catalog Card Number: 65-10430

29580-0115

Printed in the United States of America

Preface

This book is designed primarily for two groups of readers: first, upper division and graduate students in finance and economics who would like to know "why" as well as "how" in the subjects of investments and capital markets; and secondly, financial practitioners who normally have neither the time nor the technical training to perform original research in these fields. The book does not pretend to cover the entire field; on the contrary, it concentrates only on the theoretical and the empirical materials, which are usually not included in a standard textbook. It is our belief that theoretical deduction and statistical analysis, as so often used in the physical and social sciences, provide more suitable vehicles for the academic learning process in a university business course than that provided by the traditional descriptive approach. The field of finance as well as the general field of business administration has changed drastically in recent years. Institutional materials, which used to comprise the entire field, have been gradually replaced by scientific analyses. We advocate these changes and hope that our book of readings will contribute to this movement by acquainting the reader, the practitioner as well as the student, with some of the recent theoretical and empirical works in these fields.

Part 1 introduces some economic aspects of the capital markets that are usually not discussed in a traditional university-level investments text. To the editors, this common omission is a serious mistake. Without a full understanding of the characteristics of the capital markets, sound investment decisions cannot be made. In an advanced capitalistic economy where saving and investment are carried out separately, capital markets are essential. Their primary purpose is to facilitate the transfer of savings from surplus units wishing to invest to deficit units wishing to borrow. The first reading, by Duesenberry, is concerned with the criteria that should be used in judging the efficiency of the capital markets in performing this task. The Smith reading discusses some of the reasons for the recent deterioration of the competitive position of long-term government securities in the capital markets. Some possible remedies to attract investors are also suggested. The economic effects of mutual funds on the stock market are examined in the reading by Friend and Brown. In addition to the statistical analysis of the impact of mutual funds, some conceptual problems about supply and demand conditions in the stock market are also discussed.

Part 2 deals with the problem of bonds and common stocks as long-term investments. Prior to the mid-nineteen-twenties, the term "investment" was reserved for use in terms of high-quality bonds. Common stocks were considered to be speculative vehicles and, as such, inappropriate for inclusion in conservative portfolios. Prevailing investment philosophy has changed markedly since this period, to the point where such conservative portfolios as pension and trust funds are heavily committed in common stocks. The purpose of this part is to discuss the reasons behind this shift in attitude and to examine the data supporting this changing philosophy of investments. The use of common stocks as long-term investments was originally suggested by Edgar L. Smith in the mid-nineteen-twenties. The classic studies of Smith are recounted and expanded in the Harold reading. In the Kemmerer study, primary attention is paid to the empirical results of long-term investment made in high-grade bonds in comparison with that made in common stocks. The appropriateness of common stocks as true investment vehicles is based upon their historical record of real growth, particularly in times of price-level inflation. The generality of these findings, in the context of secular economic growth and price-level inflation, is examined by Clendenin. Finally, both Solomon and Weston relate the long-term investment characteristics of common stocks to the growth of the American economy. They explore the historical relationship between common-stock values and national income and conclude that common stocks have grown in real terms as a function of the growth of the economy.

Part 3 discusses some of the factors affecting stock and bond prices. From practical experience, we know that individual stock prices fluctuate greatly, and stocks often are sold at prices below the value of the assets of their companies. Stock prices are monetary values determined by short-term conditions in the markets. "Intrinsic value," which is of interest to investors, represents the long-term true value of stocks, which is difficult to ascertain at a point of time. At the present stage of knowledge, there are no operational theories for the determination of absolute and relative share prices. Thus, controversy in this field exists. The first two readings by Williams and Clendenin examine the theoretical basis for the determination of long-term absolute stock prices. The Williams selection is a classic in the field; it defines the investment value or the intrinsic value of a stock as the present worth of all its future dividends. The selection by Graham introduces the problem created by the shift of attitude in stock valuation from yield and asset value considerations to growth considerations. The following two articles by Durand and Holt deal with different aspects of this problem. By applying the celebrated Petersburg Paradox in probability theory, Durand attempts to explain the apparent contradiction between fact and theory in the valuation of growth stocks. Holt, on the other hand, deals with the problem of the influence of growth duration on stock prices and points out that both the duration and the rate of growth are important in valuing a growth stock. In the following three articles by Walter, Gordon, and Miller and Modigliani, theoretical and empirical evidence regarding the prime determinants of stock prices is discussed. These authors try to determine the

Preface

role of dividend payments in the determination of stock prices. The effects of ex-dividend on share price behavior are examined in the Durand and May selection. Bond valuation, on the other hand, is more straightforward, the most complicated problem being the estimation of the risk involved. The problem of estimating risk premiums on corporate bonds is examined theoretically and empirically in the selection by Fisher.

Part 4 deals with the problem of portfolio management. The first two articles introduce some recent developments in the scientific analysis of portfolio selection. Markowitz suggests that a rational investor, in selecting a portfolio, should take both expected return and variation from the average return into consideration. He emphasizes the traditional rule of diversification and shows geometrically that, for given securities, an "efficient" set—the set of securities providing the maximum return for a given variance— can be obtained.[1] In contrast with Markowitz' analytic approach, Clarkson and Meltzer suggest a heuristic approach, using a computer program to simulate the procedures used in selecting portfolios. The next three articles deal with the problem of the inclusion of common stocks in various institutional portfolios. The selections by Buek and Duncan argue for the inclusion of common stocks in trust portfolios. The problem of providing income for the living beneficiary of the trust while safeguarding the purchasing power of the portfolio for the remainderman is discussed. The inclusion of common stocks in pension funds is justified by Howell in terms of the long-term growth in stock values. It is pointed out that since pension funds face long periods of accumulation before the need for disbursements, the growth characteristics of common stocks render them particularly appropriate for pension funds. The final selection in this section is from the Wharton School study of mutual funds. Empirical data with regard to mutual fund portfolios are presented, and the performance of these portfolios is evaluated.

Part 5 deals with the problem of short-term price movements and forecasting. In the short-run, common-stock prices exhibit a high degree of volatility, raising the question of whether profits may be gained from these fluctuations. This section is devoted first to an examination of several forecasting techniques and, second, to the problem of whether forecasting short-term price movements is in fact feasible. The first three readings discuss methods or indicators by which short-term price movements may be anticipated. The Seligman articles discuss the use of charts. Freeman, utilizing the "advance-decline" line, suggests that the future course of the stock market may be indicated by the breadth of the market's recent price behavior. Friend and Parker conclude this part with an article describing the use of anticipations data in stock market forecasting. While investment and consumer anticipations data enjoy wide use in general economic fore-

[1] Readers who are interested in the actual computation technique in obtaining "efficient" sets by quadratic programing should consult his book, *Portfolio Selection: Efficient Diversification of Investments* (New York: John Wiley & Sons, Inc., 1959).

casting, the Friend and Parker selection represents the first attempt to use this type of data in forecasting stock price movements. The second part of this section deals with the question of whether short-term price prediction is feasible. Both Houthakker and Wu, by examining empirical data, try to determine the degree of success of a particular group of speculators in forecasting price movements. In commodity markets, Houthakker finds some evidence that large speculators, to some extent, can forecast prices correctly. Although Wu finds that corporate insiders made substantial profits by trading, there is no sufficient evidence to indicate that they can outperform the stock market averages. The next two articles by Roberts and Alexander discuss the controversy of whether speculative price movements are, in the short-run, random. Should short-term price movements actually be random, the validity of some forecasting techniques, such as charting, may be questioned. In conclusion, the forecasting of bond prices is examined in the Robinson article. Since bonds of a given quality are priced on a yield basis, forecasting of bond prices is synonymous with the forecasting of interest rates.

Boston, Massachusetts
December 1964

H. K. Wu
A. J. Zakon

Acknowledgments

A book of readings such as this one reflects the educational background of the editors. In this connection, we would like to express our deepest appreciation to our teachers, Professor Irwin Friend of the University of Pennsylvania and Professor John C. Clendenin of the University of California, Los Angeles. They inspired us during our difficult years as graduate students and introduced to us the need for scientific analysis in studying finance. Needless to say, we are also greatly indebted to the publishers and the authors who allow us to use their materials. Among them, special thanks are due to Professor James S. Duesenberry for the revision of his original article. Finally, the encouragement of Acting Dean James W. Kelley of Boston University should also be acknowledged.

H. K. Wu
A. J. Zakon

Contents

Contents

Contents

PART I. Introduction: Some Aspects of Capital Markets

Criteria for Judging the Performance of Capital Markets*

James S. Duesenberry

The primary function of the capital markets is to make possible the transfer of funds from household, business or government units with surpluses, i.e. excesses of savings over investment, to units with deficits, i.e. excesses of investment over saving. As a part of that function the capital markets make it possible for households, businesses and governments to readjust their assets and liabilities in accordance with changes in yields and the changing circumstances of the investors. In our society many of the institutions involved in the investment process also carry on other types of service functions, e.g. insuring lives and casualties, safekeeping, check clearing and so on.

In judging the performance of our capital market institutions we have to keep two sets of criteria in mind. These may be called operating efficiency and allocational efficiency.

We may say that the operating efficiency of capital market institutions is satisfactory if they perform their functions at minimum cost. That requires that (1) their expenditures should be as low as possible given the results that they achieve and that (2) profits should be high enough to attract capital in sufficient volume to permit them as a group to expand with the economy but no higher. We have to judge operating efficiency in much the same way as we judge the operating efficiency of any other industry — i.e. by judicious use of [performance and structure] criteria.

Operating efficiency is obviously unsatisfactory if it can be observed that costs are rising (after adjustment for price and wage changes), if it is apparent that the industry lags in taking advantage of changes in technology which would reduce cost or improve service, or if it contains many firms which are obviously too small for maximum efficiency.

*Commission on Money and Credit Memorandum, April 10, 1960. Some minor changes were made by the author. Reprinted by permission of the author.

We judge efficiency from structure by noting the presence or absence of competitive pressure. If it can be seen that there is active competition in pricing and other lending terms and service and that firms which offer more in terms of price and service grow relative to others, we judge that competitive pressure is forcing firms toward cost minimization. On the other hand evidence of restrictive practices, while not necessarily a proof of inefficiency, at least suggests that competition cannot be relied on to insure efficient performance.

Without going further into detail on the question of operating efficiency, it is worth noting that there is very little research on capital markets comparable to the "industry studies" which are so common in the manufacturing field.

The problem of judging "allocational efficiency" requires a more extended discussion. In the notes which follow I have first outlined the traditional or classical view of the way the capital markets should allocate a limited supply of funds among competing users. Since that view is usually expressed in rather theoretical terms I have been at some pains to show how it must be qualified when applied to the complexities of the real world. The traditional view clearly leads to the conclusion that all market imperfections such as ceilings on interest rates of any type should be eliminated.

In general that view is probably correct but I have noted some cases in which some degree of credit rationing is almost inevitable in practice and some cases in which it may even be regarded as desirable.

THE TRADITIONAL VIEW OF CAPITAL MARKET EFFICIENCY

The basic function of the capital markets is to allocate a limited supply of saving among different types of investment.[1] On the assumption that the available uses for capital exceed the available supplies it is desirable that funds should be supplied first to those investment projects yielding the highest potential returns next to those yielding slightly lower ones, and so on until the available funds are exhausted.[2]

In a static world in which conditions do not change or change very slowly an optimum allocation will be achieved if investors compete for funds in a perfect market. The result will be a uniform interest rate which equates the amount of funds supplied with the amount demanded. The interest rate will equal the potential rate of return on the marginal investment, i.e. on the

---

[1] In the event that the supply of saving exceeds investment at full employment levels of income the capital markets need not allocate funds. They need only channel funds from lenders to borrowers in such a way that every investment project yielding a positive return (allowing for risk) can be financed.

[2] Of course, consumer loans do not produce an investment yield. The statement above has to be modified to say that funds should go to those borrowers willing to pay the most for them whether they intend to use them for investment or consumption.

least profitable investment which is actually financed. All the investment projects which are not financed will have potential rates of return which are below the interest rate.

In such a static situation the performance of the capital markets can be judged very simply. They are working perfectly if there is a uniform interest rate to all borrowers and no rationing of credit. The differentials among interest rates and the amount of rationing measure the failure of the capital markets to perform as they should.

That traditional view is obviously not directly applicable to the real world because among other differences it neglects the costs of placement and servicing loans and security purchases and because it takes no account of risk differentials.

The existence of risks and costs in lending operations will obviously justify the existence of some yield differentials even if the capital markets are working perfectly. Nonetheless it may be useful to take the view that the existence of persistent yield differentials or rationing requires explanation. Their existence should be taken as evidence that capital markets are not working perfectly unless there is a fairly clear cut justification in terms of risks and costs. However, the real difficulty in forming judgments on the efficiency of our financial mechanism from the allocation standpoint is precisely in deciding what yield differences are acceptable on the basis of cost and risk considerations.

PLACEMENT AND SERVICING COSTS

The treatment of yield differentials arising from differences in cost of placement or servicing loans should not be very difficult. These costs can be regarded as associated with services rendered the borrower and should naturally be borne by him. It is to be expected that placement and service costs will be higher for small loans than for large ones and small borrowers will therefore have to pay higher interest rates than large ones even if credit markets are functioning perfectly. The same situation applies to many other services and supplies purchased by firms of different sizes. The resulting handicap to small firms may be offset by other factors in which case there is no problem. In those fields in which the small firms' disadvantage is not offset by other factors it must be concluded that from a [short run] efficiency point of view, those firms ought not to exist. It may, however, be considered that small firms ought to be subsidized in the interests of general social policy or the maintenance of competitive conditions.

Differences in placement and service cost also arise for geographical reasons. It is generally cheaper for localized financial institutions such as savings banks and savings and loan associations to place funds in mortgages in their home areas than to place them in distant areas. Even in a perfect

market then we should expect to find somewhat higher interest rates in areas
which import funds than in areas which export funds. The differences, however, should be no greater than the difference in placement and service cost
between placements in the home territory and placements abroad. Those
costs must be conceived to include some extra risk premium for the institution
lending in strange territory and some differential to induce lenders to make the
effort of going far afield for loans.

Geographical differentials higher than necessary may arise from legal
restrictions in the areas in which financial institutions may operate or because
competitive pressures on lenders are not strong enough to make them try to
take advantage of yield differentials whenever possible.

It does not follow that differential yields associated with lending costs
are always justified. Just as in any other field there must be enough competitive pressure on lenders to insure that placement and servicing costs are as
low as possible.

A more serious problem may arise in another way. Some types of
financial institutions, commercial banks in particular, have a comparative
advantage in making and servicing relatively small loans to local businesses.
They have this advantage because of the knowledge of customer situations
gained from their physical presence in the area in which they place loans and
from continuous association with their customers over long periods. If by
reason of credit policy or the channeling of a large proportion of savings
through other types of institutions the share of commercial banks in the total
flow of credit is reduced, small borrowers may not be adequately served by
their cheapest source of funds. In otherwise perfect markets such a situation
would result in a general rise in rates to small borrowers (to a level high enough
to cover the costs of such loans by non-bank lenders) and ultimately to channeling of a larger volume of funds through banks by one device or another.

In fact, however, it may result in rationing of loans by banks and a certain
amount of high cost borrowing by small business from non-institutional
sources. To the extent that rationing of that type does take place the capital
markets are not working as they should.

RISK DIFFERENTIALS

The problem of the appropriateness of risk differentials is a much more
complex and difficult one. Risks of loss to those who supply investment funds
arise from several different sources. Within the context of generally prosperous conditions individual businesses may suffer losses as a result of shifts
in demand, technological changes and other external causes or because of
management failure or a combination of the two. The over-all risk of loss to
those who supply funds whether debt or equity depends, therefore, on the

nature and size of the business (including the marketability of the assets in case of failure as a going concern) and the record and experience of the management. In general the risk of loss sustained by lenders is reduced as the proportion of capital from equity sources is increased and can be still further reduced if specific marketable assets can be pledged. For a given over-all risk the risk taken by equity holders increases as the risk for the lenders is reduced.

In the absence of cyclical problems, lenders of sufficient size could, in principle, by taking a large number of loans diversified by industry, take an essentially actuarial view of the risk problem. That is, they would find it profitable to take any loan so long as the risk premium was high enough to cover average losses on loans of that class plus any costs of acquiring adequately large numbers of separate loans and adequate diversification. In practice institutional lenders would probably refrain from making loans in which very burdensome debt service charges would be required to cover the risk of loss.

The equity market must supply capital to ventures having a high intrinsic risk and must supply enough capital to ordinary businesses so that they can avoid excessive debt equity ratios. Given an adequate supply of equity capital[3] the debt market is working properly if (a) there is no rationing and (b) risk differentials correspond to average loss experience on different classes of loans.

In practice, some degree of rationing is inevitable because some borrowers will not see eye to eye with their bankers on the maximum debt equity ratio appropriate to their business or because loan officers feel that the borrower's management record and experience requires too high a risk premium. In addition, there are practical problems in classifying borrowers by risk.

A more serious difficulty arises from the cycle problem. When there is a prospect of prolonged major depression, a lender can take an actuarial view of risk only if he is prepared to take a very long view of things. Since the losses generated by depressions come in epidemics they cannot be absorbed out of risk premiums in the year in which they occur. Instead lenders would have to build up substantial loss reserves in prosperous years and absorb losses in depressions.

Institutional lenders may be reluctant to show large losses at any time even if they are adequately compensated for them in the long run. They may therefore ration credit to borrowers rather than charge risk premiums sufficiently high to cover average losses. That would not be so serious if the equity market were operating efficiently but if the equity market does not work efficiently for any class of firm, some firms will simply be frozen out of the capital market altogether.

[3]See the following section on Equity Capital Problems for a discussion of the supply of equity capital.

EQUITY CAPITAL PROBLEMS

There has been complaint about the availability of equity capital for many years and some complaint on that score will be heard under the best of circumstances. There are many reasons for such complaints and many of them do not indicate any real failure in the operation of the capital markets.

There will always be individuals who seek backing for projects which everyone else regards as impractical. Persons who propose to develop perpetual motion machines will always say that there is a shortage of equity capital. Unproven managements or managements with poor records will always find difficulty in attracting outside capital.

In addition, some management will seek outside equity capital but will be unwilling to give up any control over the business. Unless they have very strong records they must expect to find difficulty in raising capital no matter how well organized the equity capital market may be.

The real source of difficulty in the equity capital market is probably the cost of bringing potential buyers and sellers of new issues of relatively small firms into contact with one another. Suppose that a firm wishes to sell shares and that there are individuals who would (in view of the firm's prospects) be willing to buy those shares on terms satisfactory to the issuer. If there is no means by which the potential seller and buyer can be brought into contact we may certainly say that the capital market needs improvement. Almost anything can be done for a price so that buyers and sellers can be brought together at some cost. But the cost may be prohibitive.

There may be many situations in which a new issue could be made if there were no flotation cost but cannot be made because of flotation cost. (Flotation cost here has to include not only underwriter's spreads and legal costs but any expenditures of money or effort by the issuing firm in trying to raise capital.) If a large number of such situations exist we must then ask whether the high costs of floating relatively small issues are inevitable or whether the market has failed to develop an efficient set of arrangements for handling those issues.

It seems reasonable to suppose that it must cost more to sell small issues than large ones no matter what the institutional arrangements. It does not follow that the costs of handling those issues are now as low as possible.

I shall not attempt to say whether any improvement in the equity market can be made but will only note that there are three empirical questions at issue. (1) Is it true that a large number of firms would like to raise more equity capital? (2) If so, are they unable to do so because of the high cost of flotation or because no one would want their shares even in the absence of flotation costs? (3) If flotation costs are a significant element in the equity capital problem, can some new set of institutional arrangements (not involving government) be formed which will reduce the cost of equity?

When firms cannot sell equity issues on satisfactory terms they will complain that the capital markets are not working properly. To the extent that the poor market for their equities is due to high flotation costs their complaint is justified. To the extent that their lack of success in the equity market is due to the unattractiveness of their securities to investors or to unavoidable costs of distributing small issues, the fault is with their size or other characteristics.

Some firms who cannot issue equities will seek to borrow more than institutional lenders will supply at any price. The resulting rationing must be put down to the failure to raise equity capital rather than to the organization of the debt market.

The same thing applies to (to some extent at least) the high costs of financing business investment through non-institutional lenders who finance firms turned down by banks and other institutional lenders.

MORTGAGE CREDIT

The problems of the mortgage credit market give a good example of the connections between the supply of equity capital and credit rationing. Prior to the development of government guarantees and insurance, mortgage credit was always rationed because a large number of potential buyers lacked sufficient equity capital (down payment) to satisfy institutional lenders. Those lenders were not in general prepared to substitute high interest rates for down payments. The gap was filled partially by an imperfect market in second mortgages.

By providing mortgage insurance the government in effect provided equity capital to the housing market. Alternatively it might be said that the government was able to cover risks of loss with a very low premium because it was prepared to take a long view of losses during a depression.

By supplying mortgage insurance and guarantees, the government made the credit market more perfect in one respect but by imposing interest ceilings on guaranteed loans another type of imperfection was introduced. Formerly, credit was always rationed to those who lacked the down payments required on conventional loans. Under the present system, mortgage credit is rationed on a down payment basis when market interest rates are high and not when they are low.

The significance of rationing can be made clear by asking what would have happened if the ceiling rates on guaranteed mortgages had been eliminated in 1953. If the government had pursued the same fiscal policy while the monetary authorities had pursued a policy aimed at holding total investment to the same level as was actually achieved, interest rates would have risen substantially more than was actually the case.

It is generally supposed that the shortage of funds for VA and FHA mortgages reduced investment in housing by 2 or 3 billion dollars per year during 1956 and 1957. Had there been no ceiling rates on guaranteed mortgages the demand for credit (at the rates ruling during 1956 and 1957) would have been 2 or 3 billion higher. If the monetary authorities had pursued a sufficiently restrictive policy to prevent that extra demand from becoming effective, interest rates would have risen to much higher levels than those which actually occurred during that period. How high interest would have had to go we cannot say. In the range of variation which we have experienced in recent years the effect of increasing interest rates, as such, on investment has apparently been quite small. That suggests that a rise in rates of at least 2 or 3 percentage points more than actually occurred would have been required to shake off 2 or 3 billion dollars of investment per year in the 1955–57 period. On the other hand, the level of rates required to stimulate housing construction in 1958–59 would have been just as low as those actually reached.

Thus if capital markets are balanced by the "price effects" of interest rates as distinguished from their "rationing" or "availability" effects, the average level of interest rates required to achieve the objectives of monetary policy would have to be higher and the cyclical swings in rates larger than they have been in a world characterized by market imperfections.

On general theoretical grounds a more rational allocation of resources should be achieved if rationing by prices were substituted for rationing through down payments. However, it seems likely that housing would prove more sensitive to interest rates than other types of investment and in that case the effect of the change would be to raise interest rates without doing much else.

In addition such swings in interest rates would introduce speculative elements into the loan markets which might have undesirable side effects.

It may be doubted, therefore, whether there would be any real net gain in making the capital markets less perfect by removing the ceiling on guaranteed mortgages and letting the free market work itself out.

TAX PROBLEMS

The peculiarities of our tax system may create imperfections in the capital markets in various ways. Tax exemption of state and local securities is an obvious example but I shall not discuss it because the issues involved extend far beyond the question of the efficiency of the capital markets.

It is often said that equity capital is especially attracted to those investments whose yield can be reported in capital gain form or in which tax treatment of depreciation and depletion is especially generous. The net effect of tax factors on the system is complicated and depends on what investors would do with their funds in the absence of special tax treatment. To some extent the capital gains differential increases the total supply of equity capital and thereby helps to solve the problems discussed in the section on risk differentials. On the other hand, it may divert funds into investments with relatively low social returns and away from more productive investments.

Differential taxation of financial intermediaries raises another set of problems. The tax status of intermediaries obviously affects their choices between tax exempt and other securities. The more institutions taxed at the full corporate rate the wider the market for state and local securities. That, however, is probably not a consideration of major importance.

Differential taxation of intermediaries has other net effects on the availability of funds to different types of borrowers to the extent that the institutions in question are highly specialized. Suppose an institution which is legally required to invest in mortgages is tax free while an institution which is not permitted to invest in mortgages is taxed. The tax free institutions will have a competitive advantage in attracting funds and this will draw funds into the mortgage market and away from other markets. Mortgage yields will tend to be lower than would otherwise be the case. The importance of that consideration should not be exaggerated. It is significant only to the extent that financial institutions are strongly specialized in certain markets.

SUMMARY

The capital markets may be said to operate in a satisfactory way when borrowers are not rationed except by price and when there are no interest rate differentials except those due to risk differentials and differentials in placement and servicing cost by size and type of loan or borrower and those due to geographical differences. Periodic rationing in the mortgage market is probably not a great defect in the working of the capital markets and does reduce the cyclical variation in interest rates. Some other rationing is justified by the difficulties of classifying borrowers according to risk and by unwillingness of borrowers to provide an adequate equity cushion.

The allocation of available capital among borrowers may be distorted by (1) unnecessarily high costs of distribution of small equity issues, (2) excessive restriction of the growth of bank assets, (3) legal or customary restrictions on the geographical movement of funds, (4) differential taxation of financial intermediaries operating in specialized loan markets, and (5) the effects of the difference between capital gains and ordinary income taxation on the availability of equity capital to different industries.

All of those sources of difficulty will reflect themselves in non-price of rationing of those seeking capital or in yield differentials not based on differentials in risk or placement and servicing cost.

The Competitive Position
of Government Securities*

Warren L. Smith

In recent years, the Treasury has had great difficulty in selling long-term bonds. During the period of nearly 7 years since the present administration came into office with the intention of extending debt maturities, only $9.4 billion of bonds with a maturity of more than 10 years have been sold altogether, both for cash and in exchange offerings. Thus the average is less than $1.5 billion per year. Moreover, such sales as have been made have been entirely in periods of recession or the fairly early stages of recovery. ... nearly all the investor groups—including savings banks, life insurance companies, pension funds, etc.—who have traditionally shown an interest in Treasury bonds—have either been reducing their holdings of Government securities steadily or, at most, increasing them only very slowly. Certainly one important aspect of debt management is the declining popularity of Government securities, particularly of the longer-term variety. Let us now consider some possible explanations of the apparent deterioration of the competitive position of long term Treasury securities.

SOME COMMON MISCONCEPTIONS

One explanation of the Treasury's debt management problems that seems to have a fairly wide acceptance is that the Federal Government is fiscally irresponsible—that it keeps piling deficit on deficit, virtually never having a budget surplus, and that in consequence the debt grows each year by leaps and bounds. While there is certainly plenty of room for improvement in the fiscal policies of the Federal Government, it is the opinion of the present

*From *Debt Management in the United States*, Study Paper No. 19, materials prepared in connection with the study of employment, growth, and price levels for consideration by the Joint Economic Committee, Congress of the United States, 86th Congress, 2d Session, January 28, 1960, pp. 61–72.

writer that this charge, as usually presented, is not only unfounded but recklessly irresponsible.[1] Those who make this charge are almost invariably careless in their use of statistics. To support their claims, they refer to the administrative budget, changes in the gross public debt, and data relating to total offerings of Treasury securities . . . . the administrative budget has been, in most years, strongly biased toward a deficit because it does not include the transactions of the trust funds, which have consistently shown surpluses. Similarly, the gross public debt greatly exaggerates both the true size of the debt at any particular time and its rate of growth over time, due to the fact that it includes a large and, during most periods, rapidly growing portion of essentially fictitious debt held by Government agencies and trust funds and the Federal Reserve System. Thus, for the 13 fiscal years 1947 through 1959, the administrative budget showed a cumulative deficit of $25.2 billion, while the cash budget, which is a much better measure of the fiscal impact of the Government, had a cumulative surplus of $6.3 billion. There were cash surpluses in 7 of the 13 years and cash deficits in 6. During the same 13-year period, the gross debt increased by $14.9 billion from $269.9 billion to $284.8, while the publicly held debt (i.e., excluding securities held by Government agencies and trust funds and the Federal Reserve) declined by $12.8 billion from $217 billion to $204.2 billion. Moreover, . . . both the level of national income and product and the amount of private debt have grown greatly in recent years, so that, in relation to other relevant variables, the public debt has declined even more than the above statistics suggest.

Reference to gross figures on debt operations can be equally misleading. For example, in the calendar year, 1958, total offerings of certificates, notes, and bonds for cash and in exchange for maturing securities amounted to $61.2 billion. However, when sales or exchanges involving Government agencies and trust funds and the Federal Reserve—which are almost entirely automatic (and fictitious) transactions involving no problems of debt management—are eliminated, the total is reduced to the $39.2 billion. . . . Similar large differences are present in other years.[2]

These exaggerated charges of fiscal irresponsibility are frequently couched in terms which seem designed to increase the public's fear of inflation and to undermine public confidence in Treasury securities on the part of the uninformed. Of course, both of these results tend to make the Treasury's debt management difficulties even greater. The exaggeration and confusion is partly the fault of the Treasury itself, since in its own presentations of budget and debt statistics it tends to place undue emphasis on the administrative

[1]For a particularly flagrant example of this kind of distortion and misrepresentation, see the "scare" story headed "Fiscal Crisis," *Wall Street Journal*, Sept. 10, 1959, p. 1.

[2]The gross offerings of certificates, notes, and bonds, including amounts taken by Government agencies and trust funds and the Federal Reserve, in other years . . . are as follows: $43.8 billion in 1953, $59.5 billion in 1954, $48.4 billion in 1955, $33.2 billion in 1956, and $54.6 billion in 1957.

budget and the gross public debt. Surely the problems of fiscal policy and debt management are sufficiently acute without exaggerating them by using the wrong statistics.

It may be noted that there is a perfectly respectable argument that bears a certain superficial similarity to these distortions. This is the argument that the acuteness of the debt management problem is in large part a byproduct of an excessive reliance on monetary as compared with fiscal policy as a means of controlling inflation during prosperous times. A good case can certainly be made for greater reliance on fiscal policy—cash budget surpluses—during inflationary periods. This would lessen the debt management problem in two ways: (1) by making it possible to retire more debt, and (2) by keeping down the level of private credit demands, thus making it unnecessary for credit to tighten and interest rates to rise as much as would otherwise be the case. We shall return to this argument at a later point.

DECLINING ATTRACTIVENESS OF GOVERNMENT SECURITIES

There can be little doubt that the Treasury's debt management difficulties are partly due to a number of developments in recent years which have made Government securities—particularly longer-term securities—less attractive to investors than they used to be relative to other types of investments. Let us consider some of these developments.

1. INCREASED PRICE VARIABILITY

During the Second World War, the Federal Reserve used its powers to buy Government securities in the open market to maintain a fixed pattern of interest rates and security prices. While somewhat greater flexibility in short-term interest rates was permitted beginning in 1947, the basic policy of preventing the prices of long-term Government bonds from falling below par was continued until the Treasury-Federal Reserve accord in March 1951. At the time of the accord, the rigid policy of supporting bond prices was abandoned, and as increased reliance came to be placed on monetary policy as a means of maintaining economic stability, interest rates and security prices began to fluctuate over a wider range.

In the preaccord period, long-term Treasury bonds were really liquid assets, since the holder of these securities could rely upon being able to sell them at any time at a price very close to par, with the Federal Reserve buying them if necessary to prevent their prices from falling. In fact, bonds were practically as liquid as Treasury bills under these conditions, but with a yield curve sloping steeply upward as maturities increased, the returns from bonds greatly exceeded those from shorter-term securities.[3] For this reason, particularly during the war itself, many investors were attracted to purchase Treasury bonds essentially due to their liquidity.[4] This was even true of many basically long-term investors such as insurance companies. During the war, the lack of other available outlets for funds, together with pressures to assist the Treasury to finance the war, led these investors to buy Treasury bonds which offered a relatively attractive rate of return and promised to be salable at a fixed price at a later time if more attractive investment opportunities became available.

When market forces are able to exert important effects on the structure of interest rates, as has been increasingly the case since the accord, the prices of long-term securities fluctuate much more than those of short-term securities. In fact, in the last 4 or 5 years, as flexible monetary policy has been used with increasing vigor, the prices of long-term Treasury bonds have shown very substantial fluctuations. Under these conditions, long-term bonds are not attractive to investors desiring liquidity—these investors now hold bills, certificates, and notes or bonds that are nearing maturity. Moreover, even to the more stable long-term investors, such as insurance companies and mutual savings banks, liquidity is of some significance, and since institutions of this kind are undoubtedly averse to risk and have to be paid for assuming it, the increased liquidity risk means that such investors are now prepared to hold Treasury bonds only at higher yields than formerly relative to other investments. Of course, Government securities are still free from risk of default of principal and interest and therefore possess an element of superiority over corporate bonds. But the superiority of long-term Governments has been reduced as their liquidity has declined. This development has almost certainly tended to reduce the differential between yields on Government securities and private securities of various kinds and thus to make it necessary for the Treasury to pay higher interest rates relative to other borrowers in order to attract funds.

2. CHANGING ATTITUDES TOWARD CORPORATE SECURITIES

At the end of World War II, it seems very likely that, in their evaluation of the risks involved in corporate bonds, investors were strongly influenced by their experiences in the great depression of the 1930's. There was wide-

---

[3]During the war itself, the Federal Reserve maintained a pattern of interest rates on Government securities running from three-eighths percent on 3-month Treasury bills up to 2½ percent on the longest-term bonds. In the postwar period, some flexibility was gradually introduced in the short-term sector, but short-term interest rates continued to be considerably below long-term rates.

[4]One of the problems that plagued the authorities during the late war and early postwar periods was a tendency for investors to sell Treasury bills and other short-term Government securities in order to shift their funds into long-term bonds, which were equally liquid as long as bond prices were supported but offered a considerably better return.

spread fear that after the war ended the economy might revert to its former state of stagnation and unemployment. Defaults of interest and principal on corporate bonds had been fairly common in the 1930's, and this doubtless led investors to place relatively high risk premiums on corporate bonds, thus making Treasury securities, which are completely free of default risk, quite attractive and making it possible for the Government to borrow at interest rates substantially lower than those paid by corporate borrowers.

However, as the years have passed since the end of the war and prosperity has been sustained with only occasional brief and relatively mild recessions and as the conviction has spread that secular inflation rather than secular stagnation is the problem with which we shall be struggling for some time into the future, the attitude toward corporate securities has undoubtedly undergone a substantial change. As a result, the risk premiums on corporate bonds— particularly those of relatively lower quality—have been reduced. This factor has tended to narrow the yield differentials between corporate bonds and Treasury bonds and thus weaken the competitive position of the Treasury as a borrower.

3. THE RISE OF GOVERNMENT-SUPPORTED MORTGAGES

Another development that has probably served to undercut to some extent the competitive position of Treasury securities is the tremendous growth during the postwar period of amortized mortgages insured by the Federal Housing Administration and guaranteed by the Veterans' Administration. The amount of outstanding FHA-insured mortgages on nonfarm one- to four-family properties rose from $4.1 billion at the end of 1945 to $19.7 billion at the end of 1958, an increase of 380 percent, while the amount of outstanding VA-guaranteed mortgages on the same class of properties grew from practically zero to $30.4 billion during the same period.

FHA-insured and VA-guaranteed mortgages have some of the same investment properties as Treasury securities. While these mortgages are not completely free from risk, they are very low-risk investments and in this respect are very close substitutes for Government securities. While the acquisition and management of these investments involves some costs that are not present in the case of Treasury securities, the interest rates on them have been above those on Government bonds in recent years by a large enough margin to make the net returns to the investor higher. While they are typically long-term investments, having maturities in many cases of 20 to 30 years, the amortization feature greatly reduces their effective maturity, and it is further reduced by the pronounced tendency of borrowers to pay the mortgages off in full substantially before maturity. Finally, the market support activities of the Federal National Mortgage Association have helped to develop an increasingly active secondary market in Government-supported mortgages, thus greatly increasing their liquidity. There seems to be little doubt that the rapid expansion of these housing programs has absorbed a considerable volume of funds that might otherwise have gone into—or at least remained invested in—long-term Treasury securities.

4. CONTINUED TAX EXEMPTION OF STATE AND MUNICIPAL SECURITIES

In 1941, the interest on Treasury securities was made fully subject to Federal taxes. While there was some discussion at the same time of repealing the exemption applicable to interest on State and municipal securities, such action was not taken. As a result, Treasury securities are substantially less attractive to investors in high tax brackets today than was the case before the war. The strength of this factor is, of course, reinforced by the fact that tax rates are substantially higher today. The consequence of this situation is that yields on higher quality State and municipal securities are substantially lower than yields on Treasury bonds of equivalent maturity, even though the State and municipal securities are subject to some risk of default.

If we look at developments during the postwar period, however, some qualification of the above statement is necessary. State and local governments have found it necessary to borrow tremendous sums during the postwar period to finance the construction of schools, roads, and other public facilities. As a result the net indebtedness of State and local governments grew from $13.7 billion in 1945 to $50.9 billion in 1958, an increase of 272 percent.[5] In order to raise such large amounts of money, it has been necessary for State and local governments to tap the savings of investors in intermediate tax brackets, for whom the tax exemption is considerably less valuable than it is to investors in the very highest brackets who used to be almost the sole investor in State and municipal securities. Thus, while States and municipalities—at least those with high credit ratings—can still borrow at lower interest rates than the Treasury, the differential has narrowed somewhat in recent years.

5. SUMMARY

All of the factors just discussed, to the extent that they have been present, have presumably weakened the Treasury's position relative to other borrowers and increased the Treasury's difficulties in borrowing, particularly in the long-term market. Other things remaining the same, they would presumably

---

[5]*Survey of Current Business*, May 1957, p. 17; May 1959, p. 12. Net indebtedness of State and local governments is defined as total debt less State and local government securities held by State and local governments.

result in an increase in the yields on Treasury securities relative to other kinds of debt. On this basis, one might expect to find a tendency for yields on Treasury bonds to rise relative to yields on corporate bonds, particularly lower grade corporate bonds. Yields on State and municipal bonds should be lower in relation to Treasury bonds than before the war, but for reasons suggested above, one might expect the differential between the two to have narrowed somewhat since the early postwar period. In a general way, the movements of interest rates during the postwar period do indicate these tendencies, as indicated in Figure 1, which compares movements of yields on

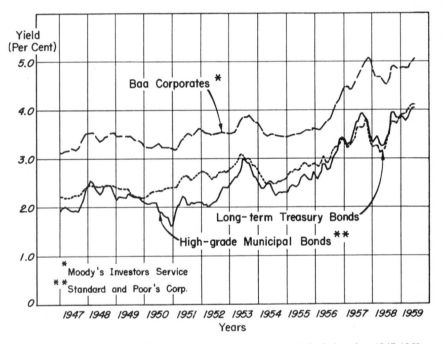

FIGURE 1   Yields on Treasury, corporate, and municipal bonds, 1947-1959. SOURCE: Federal Reserve Board and U.S. Department of Commerce..

long-term Treasury securities, high-grade State and local government bonds, and intermediate grade corporate bonds. The differential between Treasury bonds and intermediate grade corporate bonds was roughly 100 basis points in 1947, and it has been about the same recently. However, due to the general rise in the level of yields, in relative terms corporate yields are only about 25 percent higher than yields on Treasury bonds at the present time, whereas in 1947 they were about 40 percent higher. Yields on high-grade State and local government bonds have been lower than yields on Treasury bonds throughout the postwar period, but since 1951 the differential has declined considerably, presumably reflecting the need to tap the savings of persons and institutions in lower marginal income tax brackets, as suggested above.[6]

While there is thus some indication that yields on Government securities have risen relative to yields on other kinds of debt, it must be admitted that the changes have been rather ragged and irregular and the interpretation is not entirely clear cut. However, there is another factor that must be taken into account. Between the end of 1947 and the end of 1958, the total amount of net corporate debt having an original maturity of over 1 year rose from $46.1 billion to $119.5 billion, an increase of 159 percent, while net State and local government debt grew from $14.4 billion to $50.9 billion, an increase of 253 percent. Total outstanding mortgage debt rose from $48.9 billion at the end of 1947 to $171.4 billion at the end of 1958, an increase of 251 percent. During the same period, the total publicly held marketable Federal debt having an original maturity of more than 1 year (i.e., notes and bonds) fell from $119.7 billion to $98.1 billion, a decline of 18 percent.[7] With the volume of outstanding Treasury securities declining somewhat at the same time that virtually all other kinds of debt were registering huge increases, one might expect that the increased relative scarcity of Treasury securities might have produced some decline in their yields relative to yields on other kinds of debt. If anything, however, as we have seen, the reverse seems to have been the case—yields on Treasury bonds appear to have risen somewhat compared to yields on corporate bonds and have declined only a little relative to yields on State and municipal bonds, despite the fact that there has probably been a substantial decline in the interest saving to State and local government units resulting from the exemption from Federal income taxes. All of this indicates that there has indeed been a decline in the attractiveness to investors of long-term Federal securities relative to other kinds of debt. Probably the chief reasons for this development are the reduced liquidity of Government debt under a flexible monetary policy, the tremendous increase in the outstanding volume of Government-backed mortgages with investment properties somewhat similar to Federal securities and paying higher net yields, and, to a lesser extent, the development of more optimistic views concerning the safety of corporate securities.[8]

[6]Figure 1 also shows that yields on State and municipal securities are subject to unusually wide fluctuations and seem to be especially sensitive to changes in general credit conditions— rising sharply in periods such as early 1953 and 1955–57 when credit was tightening and falling sharply in easy credit periods such as 1953–54 and 1957–58. Part of the explanation for this is probably that banks, which are most directly affected by monetary policy changes, are heavy investors in State and municipal bonds.

[7]Data are taken from various issues of the Survey of Current Business and the Federal Reserve Bulletin.

[8]Another factor sometimes mentioned as partly responsible for the Treasury's difficulties is the growing fear of secular inflation. It is true that an increase in the price level of, say, 2 percent per year means that a 4-percent money rate of interest is in reality only a 2-percent "real" rate of interest. For this reason, prospective inflation may raise the money rates of interest at which given amounts of funds are forthcoming for investment in debt contracts. To the extent that this factor is at work, however, it would affect the cost of funds to all issuers of debt instruments and not merely to the Treasury.

These considerations suggest that the Treasury would have been able to sell a substantial amount of additional long-term bonds in recent years only if it had been willing to pay substantially higher interest rates to overcome the decreasing attractiveness of Government securities. Moreover, to have sold bonds in boom periods such as 1955–57 would have been particularly difficult since, in the case of corporate securities with which the Treasury would have been competing, yields on newly issued securities have shown a tendency to rise sharply above those on outstanding securities. Similarly, it seems certain that the Treasury would have found it necessary to have priced its new issues so as to give the prospective investor a yield substantially higher than the yields on outstanding issues of the same maturity. Thus, an aggressive program of selling long-term bonds would have pushed up the yield curve, especially in the longer maturity range, and also it would have been necessary to pay interest rates on new issues considerably above the yield curve.

SUGGESTED REMEDIES

One hears various suggestions that are designed to restore the Treasury's competitive position and make it easier for the Government to borrow. One possibility might be to restore the tax exemption—that is, to make the interest on Treasury securities exempt from the Federal personal and corporate income taxes, as it was before 1941. However, it is virtually certain that restoration of the exemption would hurt rather than help the Treasury, since it would almost certainly reduce tax receipts more—and probably very much more—than it would reduce interest costs. If the amount of Federal borrowing (together with State and local borrowing which is now tax exempt) were so small that all of the funds could be borrowed from investors in the very highest tax brackets, the savings in interest cost could be expected to be just about equal to the loss of tax revenues. This is because the yield that would have to be paid to the lender would tend to be reduced enough to compensate for the tax loss.[9] However, if, as is obviously the case, the necessary volume of borrowing were large enough to require the Treasury to tap the savings of investors in tax brackets below the highest, the tax losses would tend to exceed the reduction in interest cost. This is because the value of the tax exemption to an investor is lower the lower his marginal tax rate, while the

[9]For example, if the Treasury borrowed $1 billion entirely from investors in the 90 percent tax bracket and if the yield required to induce these investors to buy $1 billion of bonds in the absence of the tax exemption was 3 percent, the required yield should fall to 0.3 percent if the interest were exempted from tax. In the case in which the interest was taxable, the investors would receive $30 million per year in interest and pay back $27 million in taxes on it — the after-tax income of the investors would be $3 million and so would the net cost to the Government. If the interest were exempted from tax, the Government would pay the investors $3 million in interest and receive no taxes on it.

interest rate that must be paid to all investors will be the rate necessary to attract the marginal lender. Consequently, the Treasury will lose more in tax revenues than it will gain through reduced interest cost on the securities it sells to all investors except the marginal ones.[10]

Thus, it is clear that it would be foolish and costly to the Treasury to restore the tax exemption on Federal securities; moreover, it would tend to create a large loophole through which wealthy taxpayers could escape taxation. In fact, a more sensible proposal which would tend to improve the competitive position of Treasury securities would be to remove the exemption from the Federal personal and corporate income tax that is now applicable to State and municipal securities. This exemption is presumably meant to be a subsidy to State and local governments. However, it is a costly and inefficient kind of subsidy. By the same reasoning employed above, if State and local governments borrowed such small amounts that they could obtain the full amount from investors in the highest Federal tax brackets, the reduction in interest cost to States and municipalities would tend to be equal to the loss of tax revenues to the Federal Government. However, as State and local governments increase the scale of their borrowings, they have to appeal to investors in lower Federal tax brackets, and the loss in tax revenues to the Federal Government exceeds the interest savings to States and municipalities. Thus, part of the subsidy, in effect, goes to taxpayers in the higher tax brackets rather than to the State and local governments, who are its intended recipients. It is quite clear that as State and local governments have greatly increased the scale of their borrowings in recent years, they have had to tap the savings of investors in lower tax brackets, with the result that the interest saving to them has been reduced while the benefits of tax exemption have increasingly accrued to wealthy investors.[11] Although there are some problems involved in the removal of the exemption for State and local government borrowing, there are strong arguments for

[10]To take a somewhat oversimplified example, suppose that, in the absence of a tax exemption, the Treasury can sell at a 3 percent interest rate $1 billion of securities to investors in the 90 percent income tax bracket and $1 billion more to investors in the 40 percent tax bracket. If interest is exempted from taxes, it will be necessary to pay an interest rate of 1.8 percent to sell the $1 billion to investors in the 40 percent bracket, since this is the after-tax yield they would have received in the absence of the exemption. By the same reasoning employed in footnote 9, the net cost per year on the $1 billion borrowed from these investors will be $18 million whether interest is tax-exempt or not. However, in the absence of the exemption, the Treasury would have had to pay $30 million in interest on the $1 billion borrowed from investors in the 90 percent bracket but would have received in return $27 million in taxes, reducing the net cost to $3 million. With the tax exemption, however, it would have to pay these investors $18 million and would receive no taxes from them on this interest, so that the net cost would be $18 million. Thus the tax exemption would cost the Treasury $15 million.

[11]It may be noted that if the tax exemption were restored to Federal securities, the result would be a further large increase in the supply of tax-exempt securities. In order to get investors to hold these additional securities, it would be necessary to reach still further down into lower income tax brackets, thus reducing the benefits to State and local governments from tax exemption and providing substantial additional gains to investors in high income tax brackets.

such a step.[12] If it were desired to continue subsidizing State and local government borrowing or capital expenditures, some other more efficient and equitable subsidy could be introduced.[13]

Another possible way of offsetting the attrition that appears to have taken place in the market for Treasury securities would be to establish a captive market for such securities by imposing requirements on some class or classes of investors that a certain portion of their assets must take the form of specified types of Government securities or that they must hold such securities to the extent of a specified proportion of their outstanding claims. For example, commercial banks and perhaps other financial institutions, such as savings and loan associations and mutual savings banks, could be required to hold Government securities to the extent of a certain proportion of their deposit liabilities. Numerous proposals of this kind have been made since World War II. Since, in addition to adding a compulsory element to the demand for Government securities, these proposals have significance in connection with the effectiveness of credit controls, we will postpone our discussion of them until a later point.

A third possible way of increasing the attractiveness of Government securities that has sometimes been suggested is the issuance of purchasing power bonds—i.e., bonds on which the periodic interest payments are tied to an index of the general price level. Such bonds might prove to be very attractive to many investors, since they would combine complete freedom from risk of default with a guaranteed rate of return in real terms. Thus, they would be an ideal hedge against inflation for many types of investors. The merits of the device from the standpoint of Treasury debt management are somewhat more problematical. Presumably to the extent that it is the fear of inflation that has impeded the Treasury's success in selling bonds, the reluctance of the public to invest in its securities could be overcome either by simply paying a sufficiently high contractual rate of interest to compensate the public for the expected inflation or by the institution of a purchasing-power guarantee. Essentially, which of these alternatives would cost the Treasury less would depend upon whether the actual realized rate of inflation was higher or lower than the ex ante rate of inflation expected by investors: If the actual rate turned out to be greater than the ex ante rate, the purchasing power guarantee would be more expensive, while if the ex

[12]The problems have to do mainly with treatment of present holders of outstanding bonds and future buyers of these bonds. For an excellent analysis of the whole problem, see L. C. Fitch, *Taxing Municipal Bond Income* (University of California Press, 1950). See also H. E. Brazer, "Interest on State and Local Bonds and the Federal Income Tax," in *Tax Revision Compendium*, Committee on Ways and Means, House of Representatives (Washington: Government Printing Office, 1959), vol. 1, pp. 721–728.

[13]The problem of devising an appropriate form of subsidy involves many thorny questions of Federal-State relations. It is probably chiefly the difficulties involved in devising an acceptable substitute that have been responsible for the defeat of numerous efforts to remove the tax exemption.

ante rate were higher than the realized rate, the guarantee would be less expensive. However, there is another consideration. If the Treasury's problem arises, as we suggested above, not chiefly as a result of the fear of inflation which makes it necessary for all borrowers to pay higher interest rates, but from a shift in the preferences of investors from Treasury securities to other forms of debt instruments, a purchasing power guarantee might help the Treasury, since it is the only economic entity which is in a position to issue securities which behave like equities but possess no risk of default.[14] By issuing such securities, the Treasury might be able to take advantage of its preferred position as compared with other borrowers to attract funds away from them at an interest saving to itself. Moreover, to the extent that this process restrained private spending by inducing financial institutions to buy—or at least hold onto—Government securities rather than private debt, it would presumably permit a relaxation of the degree of general credit restriction and might thereby allow the Treasury to sell further conventional securities without a purchasing power guarantee at lower interest rates than would otherwise be necessary.

Although a purchasing power guarantee might help the Treasury in its debt management problems by permitting it to sell securities at lower interest cost than would otherwise be possible, the real issues concerning the desirability of purchasing power bonds lie entirely outside the area of debt management. These issues are concerned with the desirability of the Government's providing investors with protection in the form of a hedge against inflation and what the effects of such action would be upon expectations. The opinion appears to be rather widespread that such a policy would be widely interpreted as a sign that the Government had given up on the possibility of controlling inflation and had decided to adapt its policies to the assumption that inflation was inevitable.[15] The present writer is inclined to the view that it would be advantageous to experiment with escalator provisions in savings bonds designed for small investors, but that as a major contribution to the solution of the Treasury's debt management problems, escalation has little to recommend it.[16]

PAYING THE NECESSARY PRICE

In addition to "gimmicks" or special devices to broaden the market for Federal bonds, such as tax exemptions, captive markets, purchasing power bonds, etc., there is a simple, straightforward way to sell more bonds;

[14]Corporations are deterred from issuing equities in any case due to the fact that interest is deductible in computing the corporation income tax while dividends are not and also by the fact that many of the important financial institutions have a strong aversion for risk and therefore prefer to invest in debt instruments.

[15]For a discussion of the alleged evil effects of escalation, see the article entitled "Creeping Inflation," *Federal Reserve Bank of New York Monthly Review* (June 1959), pp. 86–94.

[16]The introduction of escalator clauses in savings bonds is advocated in H. S. Houtthaker, *Protection Against Inflation*, Study Paper No. 8.

namely, pay a sufficiently high interest rate to induce investors to buy them, While, as indicated, it would probably have been necessary to pay considerably higher interest rates, especially during periods of tightening credit conditions, in order to have sold significantly larger amounts of long-term bonds in the last few years, there can be little doubt that if the Treasury is in fact prepared to pay the necessary price it can obtain—at least within reason—any amount of long-term funds it wants. In fact, the "gimmick" approach sometimes seems to miss the whole point about debt management. The proper purpose of debt management is not merely to sell bonds or any other kind of Federal securities—or even to raise money, for that matter. The Government can always create money to finance its expenditures, and this method of financing has the advantage that it involves no interest cost at all. Money can be created not only to meet a current budget deficit but to pay off maturing securities as well.[17] The purpose served by borrowing is therefore not the raising of funds but the production of desirable economic effects—such as the achievement of a more satisfactory level or pattern of private expenditures. Once this point is made clear, it becomes apparent that keeping down the interest rates that the Treasury has to pay for its borrowing is not necessarily a desirable objective. If interest rate variations are an efficient means of controlling the level or the pattern of private expenditures in pursuit of desirable economic objectives, changes in interest rates—for example, increases in time of inflation—may be the very thing that debt management should seek to accomplish. On the other hand, when debt management is considered in terms of its economic effects, the use of "gimmicks" to sell bonds is not necessarily ruled out. However, the test applied in evaluating such devices is not whether they save interest to the Treasury but whether they produce desirable economic effects. For example, in time of inflation, requiring commercial banks to hold government securities may be a more effective way of restraining inflation than offering high interest rates to sell more bonds in a free market. This might be the case if, say, private expenditures were highly inelastic to changes in interest rates, so that offering high rates to obtain funds for the Treasury would do little to curb private spending, while forcing bonds on the banks would effectively reduce their ability to expand loans and contribute considerably to the anti-inflationary program.

Thus, the problems related to the attrition of the market for government securities, discussed above, are often regarded from the narrow point of view of the Treasury as a "money raiser" as the central problems of debt

[17]Actually, this method of financing is a bit difficult to implement under our present institutional arrangements. However, in principle it can be achieved by having the Treasury sell its securities directly to the Federal Reserve, with the System raising member-bank reserve requirements enough to immobilize the excess reserves created when the Treasury uses the funds for current expenditures or the retirement of publicly held debt.

management. However, when debt management is viewed in the proper perspective of general economic policy, the real issue is how to manage the debt so as to produce the most desirable economic effects. In order to arrive at a proper answer to this question, it is necessary to consider the economic effects of changes in the size and composition of the debt. . . .

1·3

Impact of Investment Funds
on the Stock Market*

Irwin Friend and F. E. Brown

. . . This [reading] . . . will be devoted largely to an analysis of the impact of such portfolio activity on stock prices both for the market as a whole and for specific issues. The analysis will consider not only the impact of mutual fund activity on the level of prices but also on the stability or instability of prices, that is, the extent to which fund activity moderates or accentuates market movements. In addition, some attention will be paid to several related technical aspects of the trading behavior of mutual funds as compared with other investors.

The growth in net purchases of common stock by mutual funds, as well as by pension funds and to a much lesser extent other institutional investors, has frequently been cited as one of the major postwar developments explaining the upsurge of stock prices, price-earnings ratios and price-dividends ratios to the highest levels in our history.[1] Though it is extremely difficult to assess the quantitative impact of mutual funds on stock prices, it seems likely that their net injection of money into the market has bolstered stock prices appreciably. Not only are their net purchases substantial, but the fact that initial activity generates additional activity in the direction of the initial change in prices is a well-known market phenomenon.[2] While a significant proportion of money flowing into mutual shares might in their absence have flowed directly into the stock market, presumably largely

*From *A Study of Mutual Funds*, prepared for the Securities and Exchange Commission by the Wharton School of Finance and Commerce, Report of the Committee on Interstate and Foreign Commerce, 87th Congress, 2d Session, August 28, 1962, chap. 6, pp. 359–397.

[1]E.g., Irwin Friend, "New Influences in the Stock Market," *Fortune*, March 1953.

[2]See "Stock Trading on the New York Stock Exchange on Sept. 3, 1946," U. S. Securities and Exchange Commission, 1947, p. 11.

through odd lots (or other small transactions), a significant proportion probably would not have been invested in the stock market either directly or indirectly.[3] Thus there is abundant evidence, including the indirect evidence supplied by the correlation between sales growth and sales charges for individual funds . . . that the intensive sales campaign carried out by mutual funds (in conjunction, of course, with favorable market conditions) is responsible for a substantial proportion of their sales. On the other hand, it is possible that fund buying is more likely than other buying to support the market in a decline rather than to aggravate an advance as a result of a relatively stable inflow of money into mutual shares, policies of dollar averaging and uses of limit orders below the market, but such possibilities have yet to be investigated.

It has been stressed in the financial literature that while stock prices generally have been supported by mutual fund and other institutional buying, high-grade issues might be expected to be particularly affected because most institutional funds channel into such securities. . . . This chapter will attempt to determine to the extent permitted by the data whether there is any evidence of a differential market impact of mutual funds on a sample of market leaders. It should be noted in connection with the effect of mutual fund activity both on stock prices generally and on prices of individual issues that mutual funds to some extent may have the ability to fulfill their own market predictions and in particular to validate their own evaluation of individual issues. It is also possible that, as a result of the insights provided by professional management, the funds have the economically more important ability to channel funds into the companies which are prospectively most profitable.

The basic data available for the analysis of mutual fund portfolio activity, obtained from the replies to the Wharton-SEC questionnaires by 185 mutual funds, consist of monthly purchases and monthly sales of all common stock by the respondents for the periods January–December 1953 and July 1955 to September 1958,[4] corresponding weekly data for four 4-week periods centered around significant market turning points in 1956 and 1957 and daily data for July 1 to September 30, 1958. The daily data include not only total but individual intraday transactions. Similar information was obtained for each of 30 specific stocks which were mutual fund favorites over the period covered. . . . In addition to the portfolio data, monthly and weekly (but not daily) information on the inflow of money to the funds from sales of shares is also available.

---

[3]On the other hand, it might be noted that in some degree mutual funds net out redemptions against sales of their shares and to the probably modest extent that such activity would otherwise have flowed directly into round-lot transactions in the stock market, the funds like the odd lot dealers serve to cut down on the gross volume of such transactions.

[4]Annual data are also available for 1954 and 1955 which permit the filling of the gap in the monthly series.

Some Conceptual Problems

To investigate satisfactorily the impact of mutual funds on the stock market as a whole or on individual stock prices, an operational theory of absolute and relative stock prices is needed. Unfortunately, the theories which exist are not particularly operational. It is, of course, true but not especially useful to say that in the stock market as in other markets supply and demand conditions (or schedules) determine prices. Both the demand for and supply of stock are influenced by such factors as the level and distribution of the national income, money and other assets and liabilities, the public's willingness to save, business' desire to raise new capital, and investors' and businessmen's current preferences as among stocks, bonds, and other assets and liabilities; these preferences reflect not only a reaction to current and past economic variables but also an appraisal of the future. In the short run at least, the supply of outstanding stock issues other than those of mutual funds is likely to be relatively stable but the net demand for such issues is much more volatile.

The demand for stock is determined not only by the expectations of future returns from stock as compared with alternative forms of investment but also by an appraisal of and reaction to the relative risk of stock investment. While objective current and past earnings, dividends, and interest rates are all used by investors in estimating future returns from stock and alternative forms of investment, obviously the psychological or subjective factors associated with shifts in sentiment may play an even more important role both in investors' projections of future returns and in their evaluation of the relative risks of different types of investment. Psychology or sentiment is probably the basic factor in short-run fluctuations in stock prices and may be the dominant factor even in some of the longer run movements.

Mutual funds may be considered to affect the demand for stock in several different ways. First and perhaps most important, to the extent they divert money into stock which otherwise would have been channeled into alternative forms of investment, stock prices must rise, particularly in the short run. Second, just as the entry of new money into the stock market shifts the overall demand schedule for stock in a direction favorable to stock prices, the resulting upward movement in prices probably improves the market sentiment of other investors which brings about a favorable shift in the demand schedule of these investors. Third, the publicity attendant upon both the substantial advertising and other selling effort by the mutual funds and their substantial net purchases of stock may have a similar influence. Not only has the public bought mutual shares heavily but there has been some tendency as a result of the publicity attendant upon fund activities for stock investment as a whole to be viewed more optimistically.

Clearly, it is not possible to ascertain with any precision the extent to which the underlying demand schedules for stock have been affected by the activity of mutual funds. For the postwar period as a whole, in which mutual funds have attained their present importance the only feasible approach to an analysis of their impact on the stock market is essentially qualitative, that is, comparing broad movements in the net inflow of money into mutual funds and through them into the stock market with the corresponding movements in stock prices. For shorter periods, it is possible to make quantitative and somewhat more satisfactory correlation or regression tests relating stock prices for the market as a whole to mutual fund activity. For individual stock issues, even more extensive analysis of the fund impact on market price is possible. However, even if these interrelationships are marked, there may still be formidable problems of the direction of causation. Thus, if there is extremely high intercorrelation of stock prices and fund net purchases, the only methods of determining the direction of causation are, first, by theoretical reasoning (with the theory to the extent possible tested against the facts), and, second, by empirical testing of any leads or lags in timing which may exist in the interrelationships.

For example, if stock prices and fund net purchases move simultaneously in the same direction, theoretical considerations would suggest that stock prices are affected by the net purchases since the decision to make the net purchases could hardly have been dictated by the stock prices not yet realized. On the other hand, this conclusion could be vitiated either by the unrealistic assumption that other investors with an investment pattern highly correlated with that of mutual funds were responsible for the observed stock price movements, or more plausibly by a high intercorrelation not only between stock prices and fund net purchases but between successive values of stock prices and between successive values of fund net purchases. In exploring the economic meaning of any intercorrelation between stock prices and fund net purchases, it will frequently be desirable to hold constant the initial value of such prices or purchases.

If empirical testing points to leads or lags in the interrelationships, say movements in stock prices lag somewhat behind—that is, are led by—movements in fund net purchases, there is more basis for inferring the direction of causation but even here certain limitations should be pointed out. Not only may high intercorrelations between successive values of stock prices and to a lesser extent between successive values of fund net purchases still pose some problem in isolating the correct timing sequence between changes in the two variables, but it is at least theoretically possible that if changes in fund activity precede changes in stock prices it is because the funds correctly anticipate rather than influence the course of stock prices. However, though not conclusive, the analysis of mutual fund performance . . . does not give much support to the thesis that funds as a whole tend to anticipate stock price movements better than the market generally. Finally, if fund net purchases do effect rather than simply anticipate changes in stock prices, it is desirable to disentangle to the extent possible that part of net purchases which reflects the "automatic" reinvestment of the net inflow of money into mutual funds (some of which would presumably have flowed into the stock market in any case) and that part which reflects conscious or independent investment policy by the fund managers.

It is to be expected that the impact of mutual fund activity on stock prices would be a function of the time period involved. In the very long run or secularly, the favorable effect of fund activity on the demand for stock might, at least in large part, be offset by stimulus to supply. In the long run also, expectational or subjective influences should be less important in the determination of the level of stock prices, and the complex of basic economic forces determining the objective rates of earnings, dividends, other prices, and interest rates should exercise the dominant role both on the demand and supply sides. These long-run tendencies, however, might conceivably take many years to be discernible, and there is a considerable degree of indeterminacy in stock prices as compared with other prices in the sense that subjective factors are much more important and may predominate over long periods of time. Technical market factors such as temporary supply-demand imbalances associated with an unusual spurt of new buying or selling are presumably most important in the shortest-run fluctuations of stock prices.

The period covered intensively by the analysis in this chapter consists of only a relatively small number of years, 1953–58, but virtually the entire growth of mutual funds took place after World War II, most of it since 1952. This period—which as a whole may be regarded as part of a postwar secular rise in stock prices—can be broken down into different intervals of time for analyzing the impact of mutual funds on the market. The broadest possible intervals which are meaningful consist of the major stock market rises or declines lasting 5 to 9 months, without any significant turning point, marked by price changes in excess of 10 percent (sometimes termed intermediate market movements). These major market trends are then further divided into monthly, weekly, daily, and within-day movements.

It would be anticipated that the shorter the time period the more marked the impact of a given spurt of new buying on stock prices. Statistically also it may be easier to isolate the short-run than the longer-run effects on the market in view of the multiplicity of factors affecting long-run stock prices, including extremely variable demand conditions, and the small number of long-run observations available.[5] It should be noted therefore that if short-run but not longer-run effects of mutual fund activity on stock prices are detected

---

[5]The high irregular component of very short-term stock price movements would, of course, operate in the opposite direction.

statistically, it may not be possible to infer conclusively whether longer run effects exist. On the one hand, the longer-run effects might easily be submerged statistically by other influences. On the other hand, it cannot be concluded from theoretical considerations that short-run effects necessarily imply a longer-term influence; the short-run effects may either reflect temporary disequilibria which are quickly corrected or more significant changes in demand conditions which induce further changes and hence are self-reinforcing for at least considerable periods of time. In either case, of course, a continuous succession of shortrun stimuli could affect the level of stock prices for a long period of time, or at least until the stimuli were withdrawn.

The following two parts of this chapter will consider the impact of mutual funds separately on the market as a whole and on specific issues. The availability of data on individual issues not only permits an examination of any differential effects of mutual fund activity on various types of stock but also makes possible a more satisfactory analysis of the effects of their activity on the market generally since the number of observations available for testing such overall effects is greatly increased.

IMPACT ON MARKET AS A WHOLE

Table 1 presents for specified periods from 1953 to 1958 the percent change in stock prices, the gross and net common stock purchases of portfolio securities by all mutual funds covered in this study, the net sales of fund shares or net inflow of money, the New York Stock Exchange total volume of sales, and several ratios relating fund portfolio purchases to fund inflow and to exchange volume. The 1953–58 span for which monthly data are available has been divided not only into periods of major market movements but also for each period into three (and to the extent the data permit approximately equal) subperiods so that mutual fund behavior can be analyzed separately in the early, middle, and late stages of market rises and declines. The relevance of the fund net inflow data is, of course, that a substantial portion of this money would normally be expected to be channeled fairly automatically into the stock market, and it is of considerable interest to segregate the apparent influence of such inflow from that of portfolio stock purchases more directly reflecting managerial discretion.

To approximate the proportion of fund inflow that would normally be expected to funnel into common stock, a 60-percent figure has been rather arbitrarily chosen since this is close to the average ratio of net common stock purchases to net inflow in the selected periods covered. . . . However, the precise ratio used as a basis for adjustment is not too important for present purposes. The New York Stock Exchange value of sales has been used as a basis for indicating approximately the relative importance of fund portfolio activity in common stock simply as a matter of convenience, even though the exchange data are not confined to common stock and as an offset not all fund transactions take place on the exchange. The net result is to enhance somewhat the estimated market role played by fund transactions, but again precision in this comparison is not too important.

As table 1 indicates, the monthly net inflow of money into mutual funds went up strongly over the entire period covered though there is some suggestion both in this table and in more current data that the rate of increase has been tapering off.[6] (It might be noted that the second quarter of 1958 in which two large new funds were formed was subject to special influences in net inflow and the third quarter in portfolio purchases.) There is little evidence that the rate of inflow was significantly different during major periods of market decline than during corresponding periods of market rise, or that the rate of inflow varied consistently within the different parts or sub-periods of these major movements.[7] At least during these periods, it would appear that the net inflow of money into mutual funds has been rather stable cyclically in the sense that it has not been affected markedly by market fluctuations. It should be noted, however, that the period as a whole has been one of buoyant stock prices with no catastrophic market declines of the dimensions experienced in earlier decades. On the other hand, mutual fund investors—though relatively unimportant in size until the last decade or so—were fairly consistent net purchasers of fund issues throughout the depressed 1930's even in the face of precipitous market declines. Similarly, odd-lot customers on the New York Stock Exchange who probably are closer than round-lot customers to mutual fund investors generally seemed to exercise a moderating influence on price movements— with substantial purchase balances in the 1929–32 decline and to a lesser extent in the 1937–38 decline.[8]

Portfolio net purchases of common stock by mutual funds have only imperfectly followed the course of the fund net inflow. There is no indication that the funds had a different policy in channeling their inflow into portfolio common stocks in periods of market rise than in periods of market decline. This finding is consistent with the answers given by mutual funds in response to a request to "describe any formula timing or other investment plans which are employed to determine, or as an adjunct to, the company's investment decisions, or which have been so employed during the 10 years

[6]See SEC Statistical Bulletin, July 1961, p. 4.

[7]It was noted . . . [earlier] that annual figures suggest a positive relationship between the percentage changes in stock prices and in inflow while quarterly data for a more limited period suggest an inverse or no relationship.

[8]See "Investment Trust and Investment Companies," pt. 2, U.S. Government Printing Office, 1939, pp. 263–236 and "Selected Statistics on Securities and Exchange Markets," U.S. Securities and Exchange Commission, 1939, p. 91; and "The Course of Odd-Lot Transactions on the New York Stock Exchange—1904–38," U.S. Securities and Exchange Commission, 1939, pp. 1–3, 8, and 27–36.

TABLE 1. *Mutual fund stock market behavior during major market movements, January 1953 to September 1958*

	Percent change in market*		Fund gross purchases of common stock per month§	Fund net purchases of common stock per month§	Fund net inflow per month§	Percent of common net purchases to 60 percent of net inflow (4) ÷ 0.6(5)	New York Stock Exchange volume† per month	Percent of common gross purchases to New York Stock Exchange volume† (3) ÷ (7)	Percent of common net purchases to New York Stock Exchange volume (4) ÷ (7)
	Total	Per month							
	(1)	(2)	(3)	(4)	(5)	(6)	(7)	(8)	(9)
Periods of market decline									
February to September 1953	11.49	1.44	$54.8	$25.9	$35.8	120.7	$1,171	4.68	2.21
February to April	6.67	2.22	67.7	35.2	39.5	148.7	1,443	4.69	2.44
May to June	1.95	.98	48.1	21.4	32.0	111.7	1,016	4.73	2.11
July to September	3.27	1.09	46.5	19.6	34.8	94.0	1,003	4.64	1.95
August 1956 to February 1957	12.41	1.77	123.6	43.4	104.0	69.6	2,311	5.35	1.88
August to September	8.18	4.09	128.8	36.6	74.8	81.7	2,363	5.45	1.55
October to December	2.91‡	.97‡	103.8	37.3	116.9	53.2	2,294	4.52	1.63
January to February	7.31	3.65	148.0	59.2	113.8	86.8	2,284	6.48	2.59
August to December 1957	16.53	3.31	133.8	65.4	93.6	116.7	2,195	6.10	2.98
August to September	11.45	5.72	151.0	83.2	82.9	167.7	1,887	8.00	4.41
October	3.21	3.21	149.6	75.0	108.2	115.7	2,821	5.30	2.66
November to December	2.61	1.30	108.7	42.8	97.1	73.6	2,080	5.23	2.06

*Standard & Poor's composite index, closing.
†SEC data on stock trades cleared during the month, excluding sale of rights and warrants.
‡Market increase not decrease.
§Dollar amounts in millions.

TABLE 1. Mutual fund stock market behavior during major market movements, January 1953 to September 1958 (Continued)

	Percent change in market*		Fund gross purchases of common stock per month§	Fund net purchases of common stock per month§	Fund net inflow per month§	Percent of common net purchases to 60 percent of net inflow (4) ÷ 0.6(5)	New York Stock Exchange volume† per month	Percent of common gross purchases to New York Stock Exchange volume† (3) ÷ (7)	Percent of common net purchases to New York Stock Exchange volume (4) ÷ (7)
	Total	Per month							
	(1)	(2)	(3)	(4)	(5)	(6)	(7)	(8)	(9)
Periods of market rise									
November 1955 to July 1956	16.65	1.85	133.6	47.1	87.0	90.3	2,560	5.22	1.84
November to January	3.50	1.17	107.5	40.6	93.3	72.6	2,445	4.40	1.66
February to April	10.41	3.47	147.3	49.9	96.1	86.7	2,774	5.31	1.80
May to July	2.09	.70	146.0	52.7	71.7	122.7	2,461	5.93	2.14
March to July 1957	10.75	2.15	154.6	49.8	79.2	105.0	2,381	6.49	2.09
March to April	5.73	2.87	143.9	57.0	82.0	116.1	1,985	7.25	2.87
May	3.65	3.65	159.4	46.9	68.4	114.6	2,806	5.68	1.67
June to July	1.02	.51	162.9	44.0	81.8	89.8	2,565	6.35	1.72
January to September 1958	25.18	2.80	195.2	77.1	133.2	96.7	2,388	8.17	3.23
January to March	5.28	1.76	132.1	32.9	94.3	58.3	2,056	6.43	1.60
April to June	7.46	2.49	180.8	65.6	201.1	54.4	2,226	8.12	2.95
July to September	10.65	3.55	272.8	132.9	104.1	213.3	2,882	9.47	4.61

*Standard & Poor's composite index, closing.
†SEC data on stock trades cleared during the month, excluding sale of rights and warrants.
‡Market increase not decrease.
§Dollar amounts in millions.

ended September 30, 1958"; of 145 replies, 134 stated they had never used formula timing or similar investment plans, 2 had used such plans in earlier years but no longer, 7 used investment devices which in some cases might have similar effects though in other cases opposite effects to ordinary formula timing plans, and only 2 used such plans as of the date of reporting.

Within subperiods, however, there is evidence that the net inflow was decreasingly channeled into common stocks during the course of a market decline and to a lesser extent increasingly channeled into common stocks during a market rise. Thus, while the evidence is quite scanty, there is some indication in these data that the discretionary action of the mutual funds may tend to accentuate stock market movements.

The last two columns in table 1 show an impressive increase over this period in the ratio of mutual fund gross and net purchases of stock to New York Stock Exchange volume but also show that even at the peak the ratio for fund gross purchases was well under 10 percent, and for fund net purchases well under 5 percent. Even if member trading is eliminated from exchange volume to estimate the volume of nonmember or public transactions, the ratios of mutual fund to the total of public transactions would be only about one-third higher than the corresponding gross and net ratios presented in the table.[9] Nor do more recent data suggest any increase in these ratios since 1958, with exchange volume up fully as much as fund volume.[10] Nevertheless, the fund net purchases probably are more influential than these figures may suggest. Thus, these net purchases were equivalent to 27 percent of the entire dollar volume of new stock issues by all U.S. corporations (other than mutual funds) over this period, with pension funds and odd-lot investors the only other very substantial net stock buyer groups during these years.[11] This ratio for mutual funds increased fairly steadily from 15 percent in 1953 to 44 percent in 1958. It would also be useful as a basis for comparison to relate net stock purchases by mutual funds to the totality of net stock purchases by all economic units (single individuals or institutions) with purchase balances, but the data for such a comparison do not exist; this ratio would probably be above the ratio of fund gross purchases to total gross purchases but well below the ratio of fund net purchases to new stock issues of U.S. corporations.

Table 2 presents for the seven largest mutual funds the same information as table 1 for all funds. Again there is no evidence that the rate of inflow varied significantly with market fluctuations either among or within the periods covered. Again also there is evidence that the net inflow was de-

[9]See SEC Statistical Bulletins (e.g., February 1961, p. 16) for data on member and nonmember transactions on the New York Stock Exchange.

[10]See Open-End Company Statistics, National Association of Investment Companies, for quarterly data on aggregate portfolio transactions of mutual funds.

[11]See SEC Statistical Bulletins.

creasingly channeled into common stock during the course of a market decline and increasingly into common stock during a market rise. The seven largest mutual funds do not, it will be noted, show the same strong uptrend in their gross and net purchases relative to New York Stock Exchange volume as funds generally. Apart from a stronger growth trend, other mutual funds as a whole experienced about the same relation of net inflow to market fluctuations and of gross and net purchases to net inflow as the seven largest funds.

Table 3 presents for each significant turning point in the market during 1956 and 1957, weekly data for 4 weeks (roughly centered about the turning point) covering the same information shown on a monthly basis for a longer period in table 1. The weekly data permit a closer examination of the behavior of mutual funds around turning points in the market than is possible for the monthly information. Once again, the rate of net inflow around each of the four major turning points in this period did not seem to be correlated with general market price movements. However, unlike the monthly data which indicated some positive correlation between fund net purchases of common stock and stock prices within major market movements there was no such consistent tendency evidenced by the weekly data around these four turning points. There is some indication that fund net purchases were positively correlated with (changes in) stock prices around the August 2, 1956, high which is presumably somewhat destabilizing, but they were negatively correlated with stock prices or stabilizing around the February 12, 1957, low and uncorrelated with stock prices around the July 15, 1957, high and the October 22, 1957, low. When attention is focused on mutual fund discretionary action in channeling inflow into the market, there is some evidence of destabilizing activity around both highs and stabilizing activity around both lows.

The ratio of fund net purchases to New York Stock Exchange volume was substantially higher around the two troughs in the stock market—particularly before the upturn—than around the two peaks; this finding, which cannot be explained by the differential rate of inflow in these periods, again points to a stabilizing influence by mutual funds at the lows in the market. Table 4 shows less evidence both of stabilizing activity at the lows and destabilizing activity at the highs of the market for the seven largest funds as a whole.

MONTHLY ANALYSIS

Several different types of correlation or regression analysis were carried out to examine the monthly aggregate impact of mutual funds on the market for the periods January 1953 to December 1953 and July 1955 to

TABLE 2. *Stock market behavior of 7 largest mutual funds during major market movements, January 1953 to September 1958*

	7 funds' gross purchases of common stock per month†	7 funds' net purchases of common stock per month†	7 funds' net inflow per month†	Percent of 7 funds' common net purchases to 60 percent of net inflow (2) ÷ 0.6(3)	Percent of 7 funds' common gross purchases to New York Stock Exchange volume* (1) ÷ volume	Percent of 7 funds' common net purchases to New York Stock Exchange volume* (2) ÷ volume
	(1)	(2)	(3)	(4)	(5)	(6)
Periods of market decline						
February to September 1953	$20.0	$10.7	$19.5	91.7	1.71	0.91
February to April	25.7	15.6	20.0	130.3	1.78	1.08
May to June	14.1	6.8	17.3	65.6	1.39	.67
July to September	18.3	8.4	20.5	68.5	1.82	.84
August 1956 to February 1957	35.5	10.8	37.5	48.1	1.54	.47
August to September	39.3	12.0	31.5	63.6	1.66	.51
October to December	25.9	10.3	41.0	41.9	1.13	.45
January to February	40.9	10.3	38.2	45.1	1.79	.45
August to December 1957	31.8	17.7	28.5	103.7	1.45	.81
August to September	39.1	23.1	23.7	162.8	2.07	1.22
October	33.8	18.2	32.2	94.4	1.20	.65
November to December	23.5	12.2	31.3	65.1	1.13	.59

*See table 1, col. 7 for New York Stock Exchange volume.
†Dollar amounts in millions.

TABLE 2. Stock market behavior of 7 largest mutual funds during major market movements, January 1953 to September 1958 (Continued)

	7 funds' gross purchases of common stock per month†	7 funds' net purchases of common stock per month†	7 funds' net inflow per month†	Percent of 7 funds' common net purchases to 60 percent of net inflow (2) ÷ 0.6(3)	Percent of 7 funds' common gross purchases to New York Stock Exchange volume* (1) ÷ volume	Percent of 7 funds' common net purchases to New York Stock Exchange volume* (2) ÷ volume
	(1)	(2)	(3)	(4)	(5)	(6)
Periods of market rise						
November 1955 to July 1956	41.0	16.9	35.6	79.3	1.60	.66
November to January	31.3	15.9	34.3	77.5	1.28	.65
February to April	46.8	13.5	39.4	57.3	1.69	.49
May to July	44.8	21.2	33.0	107.2	1.82	.86
March to July 1957	42.2	16.7	23.8	107.2	1.77	.70
March to April	39.9	14.8	25.2	98.0	2.01	.75
May	52.9	26.7	20.7	215.4	1.89	.95
June to July	39.1	13.5	23.9	94.4	1.52	.53
January to September 1958	47.7	18.0	34.5	87.2	2.00	.75
January to March	39.7	13.4	35.9	62.3	1.93	.65
April to June	42.8	15.6	30.3	86.0	1.92	.70
July to September	60.4	25.0	37.3	111.9	2.10	.87

*See table 1, col. 7 for New York Stock Exchange volume.
†Dollar amounts in millions.

TABLE 3. *Mutual fund stock market behavior during specified weeks around turning points,* * 1956–57*

Weekly periods beginning	Percent change in market (1)	Fund net purchases of common stock (2)	Fund net inflow (3)	Percent of common net purchases to 60 percent of net inflow (2) ÷ 0.6(3) (4)	New York Stock Exchange volume per week (5)	Ratio of common net purchases to New York Stock Exchange volume (2) ÷ (5) (6)
1956—July 23	−0.55	$19.7†	$16.9†	194.7	$550†	.036
July 30	+1.14	10.7	16.3	109.6	699	.015
Aug. 6	−1.11	−.7	17.1	−6.8	691	−.001
Aug. 13	−.55	5.9	14.2	69.3	538	.011
1957—Feb. 4	−2.91	20.7	26.7	129.4	321	.065
Feb. 11	+.44	35.0	22.2	263.4	343	.102
Feb. 18	−.07	15.1	20.6	122.4	645	.023
Feb. 25	+.60	−.3	20.9	−2.3	765	−.000
July 1	+2.79	2.4	29.6	13.5	497	.065
July 8	+.80	15.4	10.8	238.1	714	.022
July 15	−1.02	18.1	29.7	101.7	611	.030
July 22	−.27	7.4	19.7	62.8	495	.015
Oct. 7	−4.32	26.7	29.6	150.6	663	.040
Oct. 14	−1.49	12.2	10.8	188.7	576	.021
Oct. 21	+.64	21.5	29.7	120.9	901	.024
Oct. 28	−.37	7.4	19.7	62.8	428	.017

*The peaks were Aug. 2, 1956, and July 15, 1957; the troughs, Feb. 12, 1957, and Oct. 22, 1957.
†Dollar amounts in millions.

TABLE 4. *Stock market behavior of 7 largest mutual funds during specified weeks around turning points,* 1956–57*

Weekly periods beginning	7 funds' net purchases of common stock † (1)	Fund net inflow † (2)	Percent of common net purchases to 60 percent of net inflow (1) ÷ 0.6(2) (3)	Ratio of common net purchases to New York Stock Exchange volume (1) ÷ volume (4)
1956—July 23	$9.9	$7.7	214.8	0.018
July 30	7.0	8.0	146.1	.010
Aug. 6	−2.2	8.6	−43.4	−.003
Aug. 13	2.1	6.2	56.6	.004
1957—Feb. 4	6.3	15.3	68.8	.020
Feb. 11	11.3	7.5	251.7	.033
Feb. 18	6.2	13.9	74.5	.010
Feb. 25	−3.8	6.2	−102.4	−.005
July 1	2.1	6.7	52.3	.004
July 8	7.3	13.7	89.0	.010
July 15	6.2	4.6	225.1	.010
July 22	6.5	5.0	217.1	.013
Oct. 7	8.3	18.4	75.3	.013
Oct. 14	4.0	2.9	230.3	.007
Oct. 21	1.9	9.6	33.1	.002
Oct. 28	.4	4.8	13.9	.001

*The peaks were Aug. 2, 1956, and July 15, 1957; the troughs, Feb. 12, 1957, and Oct. 22, 1957.
†Dollar amounts in millions.

September 1958 as a whole and separately.[12] Stock prices at the end of a month were related to net purchases of common stock by all mutual funds simultaneously for each of the preceding 5 months, to net purchases less adjusted net inflow for each of these months, to net purchases and net inflow separately for each of these months, to net purchases for that month and stock prices at the beginning of the month, to net purchases and net inflow separately for that month and stock prices at the beginning of the month, and to net purchases and net inflow for each of the preceding 3 months and stock prices at the beginning of the 3-month period. Linear, logarithmic, and difference equations were all used. Corresponding relationships were also computed with net purchases as the dependent variable

[12]Rank correlation and chi-square tests were also carried out; these showed very little relationship between changes in stock prices and fund net purchases either on a monthly or daily basis. Simple correlation lead and lag analysis between stock prices and net purchases showed a small positive correlation between month-end prices and net purchases during that same calendar month, and about the same correlation between net purchases and beginning of month prices, but no correlation between month-end prices and net purchases of the preceding calendar month; on a daily basis, virtually no simple correlation is evident between the specific values of the variables indicated.

and with prior movements in stock prices and at times prior net inflow and initial net purchases as the explanatory variables. The logarithmic or linear equations generally gave the highest correlations, and the difference relationships as might be expected from statistical considerations the lowest correlations. The relationships with stock prices as the dependent variable, some of which are presented below, are not demand schedules but may be interpreted as representing the reaction of stock prices to shifts in demand occasioned by mutual fund activity (with the net stock supply but not the net demand schedule assumed relatively stable).

When stock prices as the dependent variable are logarithmically related to net purchases, there is some evidence that higher net purchases in the same month and to a lesser extent in the month before are associated with higher stock prices. However, this evidence disappears if a difference equation is fitted, if the logarithmic relationships are fitted separately to the two periods covered, if net inflow is used directly or indirectly as an additional explanatory variable, or if the initial level of stock prices is introduced into the analysis (as a crude device both to hold constant the host of other influences affecting the market not explicitly included in the analysis and to make possible the disentanglement of the long-run and short-run effects on stock prices of the other explanatory variables explicitly included).[13] In other words, there is no conclusive indication in this analysis that the net purchases by mutual funds significantly affect the month-to-month movements in the stock market as a whole. Three of the simpler linear regressions are presented below:

$$M_t = .272 + .0005P_t + .996M_{t-1} \qquad \overline{R}^2 = .966 \qquad (1)$$
$$ (.008) \qquad (.033)$$

where M_t represents stock prices (Standard and Poor's Composite Index) at the end of the month t; P_t, net purchases (in \$100,000 units) during month t; $\overline{R}^2$, the adjusted coefficient of determination: and the figures in parentheses, standard errors of the regression coefficients.[14] If net purchases of the 2 preceding months are included (1) becomes:

$$M_t = 1.08 + .012P_t + .008P_{t-1} + .005P_{t-2} + .949M_{t-3} \qquad \overline{R}^2 = .905 \qquad (2)$$
$$ (.049) \quad\;\; (.052) \qquad (.050) \qquad (.057)$$

If the cumulative total of net purchases of the same month and the pre-

---

[13]It may be noted that $\overline{R}^2$, the adjusted coefficient of determination between successive month-end stock prices, is extremely high, viz, 0.955 in the simple linear relationship.

[14]Under certain assumptions, which unfortunately are not too realistic for the equations discussed in this chapter, the long-run net purchases effect on stock prices can be obtained by dividing the regression coefficient of P_t (current period net purchases) by the complement of the regression M_{t-1} (lagged price).

ceding months are substituted for the separate monthly purchases, the result is:

$$M_t = 1.06 + .008 \sum_{t-2}^{t} P_t + .950M_{t-3} \qquad \bar{R}^2 = .910 \qquad (3)$$
$$ (.005) (.056)$$

Here there is a little more but still not convincing evidence that higher purchases in the same and preceding months are associated with higher stock prices. A similar result is obtained for the regression coefficient of the cumulative purchases term if (3) is computed for the July 1955–September 1958 period alone, though the regression coefficient of initial market price and the coefficient of determination are substantially reduced.

A similar type of analysis was carried out with fund net purchases as the dependent variable to determine whether the chain of causation in these monthly data went from stock prices to net purchases. There is some evidence from the relationships for the two periods as a whole that net purchases are stimulated by high stock prices in the previous month, but again this result is changed if the two periods are treated separately or if the initial level of net inflow is introduced into the analysis. If the two periods are treated separately, only 1953 shows an apparently significant influence of high stock prices (in the preceding 2 months) on fund net purchases. If monthly net inflow for each of the preceding 4 months is introduced into the analysis, the apparent influence of stock prices in preceding months is further reduced. A typical simple relation among these variables for the two periods as a whole is:

$$P_t = -19.8 + 1.17M_{t-1} + .453P_{t-1}* \qquad \bar{R}^2 = .382 \qquad (4)$$
$$ (.524) \phantom{M_{t-1} + } (.138)$$

If net inflow is also introduced into this relation, it appears that the apparent influence of market prices on net purchases is mainly attributable to the intercorrelation of both with inflow. In other words, there is no indication in this analysis that the monthly net purchases by mutual funds are significantly affected by the prior month's fluctuation in the stock market except insofar as these fluctuations are positively correlated with inflow from net sales of fund shares. Net inflows in each of the preceding 5 months were tested simultaneously for their impact on fund net purchases, and a lead of at least 1 additional month seemed to be needed to properly reflect the influence of inflow on net purchases. The following relation was then computed:

$$P_t = -6.6 - 1.15M_{t-1} + .967M_{t-2}$$
$$ (2.02) (1.99)$$
$$ + .206I_{t-1} + .388I_{t-2} + .257P_{t-2} \qquad \bar{R}^2 = .632 \quad (5)$$
$$ (.091) (.094) (.113)$$

*$\bar{R}^2$ between P_t and P_{t-i} is 0.325.

Here, there is no evidence that market prices affect fund purchases once net inflow (I) and the initial level of purchases are held constant. If inflow is excluded but an additional market price variable included, again there is no significant correlation between net purchases and earlier market prices, viz:

$$P_t = -25.5 + 2.48M_{t-1} + 1.39M_{t-2} - 1.96M_{t-3} - .061P_{t-3} \qquad \bar{R}^2 = .175 \qquad (6)$$
$$(2.96)\phantom{M_{t-1}} (4.35)\phantom{M_{t-2} -} (3.02)\phantom{M_{t-3} -} (.235)$$

WEEKLY ANALYSIS

A correlation or regression analysis of the weekly data on market prices and mutual fund purchases is less satisfactory than either the corresponding monthly and daily analyses, since the weekly data are centered around four significant turning points in 2 years (1956 and 1957) and contain only four weekly observations on fund purchases for each turning point. Thus the weekly data are less typical and have fewer observations than the two other sets of data. The small number of weekly observations on fund purchases pretty much invalidates any regressions with market price as the dependent variable so that the only regressions fitted are those with fund net purchases as the dependent variable. However, the various regressions tested do not show any consistent or significant effects of stock prices in the current and 5 previous weeks on fund net purchases.

DAILY ANALYSIS

Table 5 presents daily data on closing stock market prices, fund net purchases, and New York Stock Exchange volume for the July 1–September 30, 1958, period. Since two large new funds formed in the second quarter of 1958 bought heavily in July, the early part of the third quarter was subject to special influences, and the ratio of fund net purchases of common stock to New York Stock Exchange volume was unusually high (amounting to 13 percent on 2 days). A simple inspection of the table does not show a strong relation on a daily basis between stock prices and fund net purchases.

A more satisfactory indication of the relations between daily stock prices and net purchases is given by correlation analysis. The simplest of these relations which attempts to determine the immediate impact of a day's net purchases (in $100,000 units) on stock prices (Standard & Poor's Composite Index) is the linear regression

$$M_t = .108 + .010P_t + .998M_{t-1} \qquad \bar{R}^2 = .967 \qquad (1)$$
$$(.011) (.029)$$

which suggests a positive but statistically insignificant effect of net purchases. To determine the delayed impact of net purchases of preceding
days as well as of the same day, $P_{t-1} \ldots P_{t-4}$ were introduced in addition
to P_t as explanatory variables in the above regression and M_{t-5} substituted
for M_{t-1}. The findings again suggest a positive impact generally of net
purchases of preceding days as well as of the same day on stock prices,
but once more the regression coefficients are not statistically significant.
However, as a consequence, it seemed desirable to test the relation between
closing stock prices on a given day and the cumulative total of the net
purchases of the same day and the preceding 4 days, with the following
result:

$$M_t = -3.92 + .016 \sum_{t-4}^{t} P_t + 1.08M_{t-5} \qquad \bar{R}^2 = .882 \qquad (2)$$
$$(.006) \qquad\qquad (.06)$$

Equation (2) points to a significant impact of cumulative net purchases
on stock prices.[15] According to this equation, if aggregate net purchases
of mutual funds increase by \$10 million over a 5-day period, or about one-
third of the average 5-day net purchases during the 3 months covered,
the stock market index would be raised in price by 1.6 points by the end of
the 5-day period, or about 3.3 percent of the average index during these
3 months.[16]

The corresponding regressions which relate net purchases to stock
prices in order to analyze the impact of the latter on the former are:

$$P_t = 52.1 - 1.01M_{t-1} + .338P_{t-1} \qquad \bar{R}^2 = .361 \qquad (3)$$
$$(.343) \qquad (.126)$$

and

$$P_t = 72.5 - .287 \sum_{t-5}^{t-1} M_t + .285P_{t-5} \qquad \bar{R}^2 = .422 \qquad (4)$$
$$(.061) \qquad\qquad (.109)$$

These relations imply a statistically significant impact of the preceding
day's and the preceding 5 days' stock prices on daily net purchases, with
an apparent tendency for higher prices to result in lower net purchases.
While the lagged price coefficient in (3) is larger than in (4), the lagged
price variable in (4) is on the average five times as large as in (3), and its

[15]The reduction in the multiple correlation is simply a reflection of the much lower simple
correlation between M_{t-5} and M_t than between M_{t-1} and M_t. The adjusted coefficient of determination between

$$\sum_{t-4}^{t} P_t \text{ and } M_t \text{ is } 0.300 \text{ whereas that between } P_t \text{ and } M_t \text{ is } 0.263.$$

[16]The regression coefficients of the explanatory variables in equations (1) and (2) are not
changed greatly if the two large funds which instituted operations in the second quarter of 1958
are excluded. However, the coefficient of the M_{t-1} term in equation (3) which follows is halved
though still statistically significant at the 2σ level.

TABLE 5. *Mutual fund stock market behavior during specified days,*
July 1–Sept. 30, 1958

Date	Standard & Poor's composite market index	Change in Standard & Poor's	Fund net purchases (millions)	New York Stock Exchange volume (millions)	Ratio of fund net purchases to New York Stock Exchange volume (4) ÷ (5)
(1)	(2)	(3)	(4)	(5)	(6)
July 1	45.28	+0.04	$6.27	$105.9	−0.059
2	45.32	+.04	6.62	96.6	.069
3	45.47	+.15	4.15	107.2	.039
7	45.62	+.15	2.60	102.3	.025
8	45.40	−.22	4.73	99.0	.048
9	45.25	−.15	5.99	107.2	.056
10	45.42	+.17	7.47	102.3	.073
11	45.72	+.30	12.79	97.8	.131
14	45.14	−.58	9.09	103.5	.088
15	45.11	−.03	10.05	125.9	.080
16	45.25	+.14	16.84	132.0	.128
17	45.55	+.30	5.95	129.5	.046
18	45.77	+.22	13.23	136.5	.097
21	46.33	+.56	9.81	140.2	.070
22	46.41	+.08	9.13	139.4	.066
23	46.40	−.01	10.72	144.6	.074
24	46.65	+.25	10.38	152.4	.068
25	46.97	+.32	10.52	180.5	.058
28	47.15	+.18	8.80	160.5	.055
29	46.96	−.19	11.02	134.9	.082
30	47.09	+.13	5.94	149.9	.040
31	47.19	+.10	12.89	180.9	.071
Aug. 1	47.49	+.30	7.00	157.1	.045
4	47.94	+.45	10.83	185.9	.058
5	47.75	−.19	8.61	195.6	.044
6	47.76	+.01	6.56	159.9	.041
7	47.77	+.01	3.46	148.7	.023
8	48.05	+.28	5.85	169.6	.035
11	48.18	+.13	2.96	133.4	.022
12	47.73	−.45	5.54	120.8	.046
13	47.81	+.08	6.19	129.6	.048
14	47.91	+.10	3.75	156.6	.024
15	47.50	−.41	6.30	137.5	.046
18	47.22	−.28	.74	111.1	.007
19	47.30	+.08	3.70	104.6	.035

TABLE 5. *Mutual fund stock market behavior during specified days, July 1–Sept. 30, 1958 (Continued)*

Date	Standard & Poor's composite market index	Change in Standard & Poor's	Fund net purchases (millions)	New York Stock Exchange volume (millions)	Ratio of fund net purchases to New York Stock Exchange volume (4) ÷ (5)
(1)	(2)	(3)	(4)	(5)	(6)
20	47.32	+.02	3.36	114.3	.029
21	47.63	+.31	1.90	116.2	.016
22	47.73	+.10	2.41	123.6	.020
25	47.74	+.01	3.91	121.3	.032
26	47.90	+.16	3.64	139.2	.026
27	47.91	+.01	4.90	151.0	.032
28	47.66	−.25	3.21	118.0	.027
29	47.75	+.09	.42	105.0	.004
Sept. 2	48.00	+.25	3.70	119.0	.031
3	48.18	+.18	4.87	131.6	.037
4	48.10	−.08	2.62	125.9	.021
5	47.97	−.13	1.58	102.4	.015
8	48.13	+.16	2.90	123.1	.024
9	48.46	+.33	7.74	141.3	.055
10	48.31	−.15	3.19	114.5	.028
11	48.64	+.33	3.96	134.0	.030
12	48.53	−.11	9.15	125.9	.073
15	48.96	+.43	−.18	123.5	−.001
16	49.35	+.39	4.04	160.0	.025
17	49.33	−.02	2.85	153.9	.018
18	49.08	−.25	5.02	140.5	.036
19	49.40	+.32	6.49	157.6	.041
22	49.20	−.20	5.97	141.8	.042
23	49.56	+.36	6.01	160.4	.037
24	49.78	+.22	2.97	126.7	.023
25	49.57	−.21	4.28	182.3	.023
26	49.66	+.09	4.22	138.9	.030
29	49.87	+.21	5.54	149.5	.037
30	50.06	+.19	5.98	169.0	.035

coefficient seems to be more statistically reliable. The use of lagged rather than current prices as an explanatory variable reflects of course the belief that it takes time for mutual funds to react to changes in stock prices. However, it is of some interest to test whether net purchases appear to react to price changes the same day, on the theory that extensive use of limit orders by mutual funds might result in a negative relation between net purchases and the same day's price change. The result obtained, which tends to confirm the hypothesis indicated, is:

$$P_t = 47.7 - .918M_t + .363P_{t-1} \qquad \bar{R}^2 = .344 \qquad (5)$$
$$ (.345) \qquad (.126)$$

When M in equations (3) and (5) is replaced by ΔM in one set of regressions, and also P by ΔP in another set, the M coefficients are no longer significant (and not always negative). Inflow data are not available on a daily basis to isolate the influence of market prices on fund purchases when net inflow is held constant.

There are two general comments that should be made in connection with the comparison of equations (1)–(2) with (3)–(5). First, the higher correlations indicated in the former simply reflect the much higher serial correlation between stock prices than between net purchases of successive days. Second, the two sets of daily regressions together suggest that mutual funds as a whole show some tendency to gear or adjust their net purchases inversely to the daily trend in stock prices but that their net purchases do have a significant positive impact on stock prices.

INTRA-DAY ANALYSIS AND CHARACTERISTICS OF ORDERS AND TRANSACTIONS

Since the mutual funds listed separately the details of each transaction within the July 1 to September 30, 1958, period, an attempt was made to analyze the within-day relationship of fund purchases and sales separately in individual stocks to up-ticks or rises, down-ticks or declines, and stability or no change in the market price of the stock involved; the Fitch sheets were used to obtain all individual market transactions in the securities covered. Unfortunately, it was not possible to identify a sufficiently high proportion of the mutual fund transactions on the Fitch sheets to avoid the possibility of substantial bias in the comparison of fund and nonfund transactions. However, a sample of mutual fund transactions, classified by size of transaction and by size of fund, seems to show that large purchase transactions by the funds are more likely to be made on up-ticks than are small purchase transactions and large sales transactions more likely on down-ticks than small sales transactions, a result which it is difficult to interpret without knowing the type of transactor (e.g., public versus professional) on the other side of these transactions. Perhaps more surprising is the indication that fund purchases and sales seem fully as likely to initiate or reinforce a short-run or intra-day market movement (rather than to counter the trend) as nonfund transactions even when size of transaction is held constant, in spite of the evidence to the contrary in the preceding section and the evidence below that funds rely more heavily on limit (as contrasted with market) orders. It seems likely that the biased nature of the fund transactions available for this comparison commented on above is responsible for this result.

The detailed transaction data for the July 1–September 30, 1958, period make possible the derivation of the first reliable information on the characteristics of orders placed by mutual funds and of the resulting transactions effected for them. Table 6 presents for this period a percentage distribution of a random sample of mutual fund transactions[17] in common stock by type of order, place of execution, and size of transaction for purchases and sales separately.[18]

The heavy preponderance in the use of limit orders (day and good-till-canceled) by mutual funds is clearly shown in the table. Thus, of the fund purchases effected on the New York Stock Exchange during this period which could be classified by type of order (i.e., excluding the 13.7 percent of NYSE unclassified, 6.8 percent of other exchange, and 10.6 percent of over-the-counter transactions) 86 percent were attributable to limit orders and only 14 percent to market orders. Similarly, 89 percent of fund sales were attributable to limit orders, and 11 percent to market orders. These are probably much higher proportions of limit orders than those used by other investors generally, but comparable quantitative data for the market as a whole are not available for any recent period.

The only published information on type of order used for the market as a whole relates to a much earlier 1-day period, September 3, 1946, when the market was subject to an unusually large decline in price. On that day, most sellers used market orders, accounting for fully 85 percent of the value of classified sales, and most buyers used limit orders, accounting for close to 65 percent of classified purchases.[19] While the overwhelming importance of market orders on the sales side may have largely reflected the substantial decline in stock prices that day, presumably the importance of limit orders on the purchase side was similarly exaggerated by the same special circumstances. As a result, it seems reasonably clear that mutual funds in the later period were much more likely to use limit orders than the market as a whole in the earlier period. It seems unlikely that this conclusion would be markedly changed if more current data were

[17]A transaction in this table is defined somewhat differently from that in the Fitch sheets; it is the total amount of each security purchased or sold at one price on any 1 day through one broker-dealer in one market.

[18]The place of execution or market channel used by mutual funds . . . is introduced in Table 6 mainly as an additional basis for classification in studying type of order and size of transaction.

[19]See *Stock Trading on the New York Stock Exchange on Sept. 3, 1946*, pp. 63–64. The publisher is U.S. Securities and Exchange Commission.

TABLE 6. *Distribution of mutual fund transactions in purchasing and selling portfolio common stocks, by type of order, place of execution, and size of transaction,* July 1–Sept. 30, 1958*

PURCHASES

Size of transaction	New York Stock Exchange										Over the counter		Other exchange		Total	
	Market		Day		G.T.C.†		Unspecified		Subtotal							
	Num-ber	Per-cent	Num-ber	Per-cent	Num-ber	Per-cent	Num-ber	Per-cent	Num-ber	Per-cent	Num-ber	Per-cent	Num-ber	Per-cent	Num-ber	Per-cent
Less than $1,000	0	0	0	0	1	0.3	0	0	1	0.1	2	1.4	1	1.1	4	0.3
$4,000 to $5,000	22	16.9	70	15.2	52	15.9	35	19.2	179	16.3	22	15.6	21	23.3	222	16.7
$5,000 to $10,000	29	22.3	165	35.7	65	19.9	47	25.8	306	27.8	26	18.4	19	21.1	351	26.4
$10,000 to $25,000	48	36.9	149	32.3	103	31.5	59	32.4	359	32.6	39	27.7	24	26.7	422	31.7
$25,000 to $50,000	21	16.2	61	13.2	64	19.6	28	15.4	174	15.8	24	17.0	16	17.8	214	16.1
$50,000 to $100,000	8	6.2	11	2.4	33	10.1	11	6.0	63	5.7	12	8.5	4	4.4	79	5.9
$100,000 to $500,000	1	.8	5	1.1	8	2.5	2	1.1	16	1.5	15	10.6	5	5.6	36	2.7
$500,000 to $1,000,000	1	.8	0	.0	1	.3	0	0	2	.2	1	.7	0	0	3	.2
$1,000,000 and over	0	0	1	.2	0	0	0	0	1	.1	0	0	0	0	1	.1
Total	130	100.0	462	100.0	327	100.0	182	100.0	1,101	100.0	141	100.0	90	100.0	1,332	100.0
Percent of grand total	9.8		34.7		24.6		13.7		82.7		10.6		6.8		100.0	

*Unit equals transaction. Based on 5 percent sample of common stock transactions by all funds during July to September 1958.
†Good until canceled.

TABLE 6. *Distribution of mutual fund transactions in purchasing and selling portfolio common stocks, by type of order, place of execution, and size of transaction,* July 1—Sept. 30, 1958

SALES

Size of transaction	New York Stock Exchange											Over the counter		Other exchange		Total	
	Market		Day		G.T.C.†		Unspecified		Subtotal								
	Number	Per-cent	Number	Per-cent	Number	Per-cent	Number	Per-cent	Number	Per-cent			Number	Per-cent	Number	Per-cent	Number	Per-cent
Less than $1,000	1	1.6	0	0	1	0.5	0	0	2	0.3	1	1.1	2	3.3	5	0.6
$1,000 to $5,000	12	19.7	56	19.6	37	19.2	13	14.0	118	18.6	9	10.2	19	31.2	146	18.7
$5,000 to $10,000	15	24.6	73	25.5	32	16.6	21	22.6	141	22.3	18	20.5	15	24.6	174	22.3
$10,000 to $25,000	15	24.6	84	29.4	53	27.5	38	40.9	190	30.0	27	30.7	14	23.0	231	29.5
$25,000 to $50,000	11	18.0	51	17.8	35	18.1	19	20.4	116	18.3	20	22.7	9	14.8	145	18.5
$50,000 to $100,000	5	8.2	14	4.9	22	11.4	2	2.2	43	6.8	10	11.4	1	1.6	54	6.9
$100,000 to $500,000	1	1.6	8	2.8	13	6.7	0	0	22	3.5	2	2.3	1	1.6	25	3.2
$500,000 to $1,000,000	1	1.6	0	0	0	0	0	0	1	.2	1	1.1	0	0	2	.3
$1,000,000 and over	0	0	0	0	0	0	0	0	0	0	0	0	0	0	0	0
Total	61	100.0	286	100.0	193	100.0	93	100.0	633	100.0	88	100.0	61	100.0	782	100.0
Percent of grand total	7.8		36.6		24.7		11.9		81.0		11.3		7.8		100.0	

*Unit equals transaction. Based on 5 percent sample of common stock transactions by all funds during July to September 1958.
†Good until canceled.

available for the market as a whole, but in the absence of such data there is no certainty that this is true.

Table 6 also shows the distribution of mutual fund transactions for the July 1–September 30, 1958, period by size of transaction. There were extremely few transactions under $1,000 in size. The most common transaction fell in the $10,000 to $25,000 range, with $5,000 to $10,000 second in frequency. While the size groups from $50,000 up accounted for a relatively small proportion (less than 10 percent) of the number of transactions, they constituted a much more important part (over 50 percent) of the value of transactions. There were no marked consistent differences in the size of transactions effected as a result of market orders as compared with limit orders, although transactions effected as a result of good-till-canceled orders were larger on the average than those resulting from day orders. (Transactions flowing from good-till-canceled limit orders seemed somewhat larger on the average and those from day limit orders somewhat smaller than market orders.) Scattered data available for New York Stock Exchange transactions as a whole point to a much greater concentration of small transactions.[20]

A distribution of the types of orders typically placed by size of fund is presented in table 7. The predominance of limit orders is again evident though it is not so pronounced for funds as for transactions, that is, when a fund rather than a transaction is the unit of observation. The larger funds relied much more heavily on limit orders than the smaller funds. Thus, for the smallest funds, viz, those with assets less than $10 million, market orders seemed fully as important as limit orders.

INDIVIDUAL SECURITIES

MAJOR PRICE MOVEMENTS

Sixty instances of major price movements in specific securities are observable during the 1953–58 span in the monthly data provided for the 30 common stocks selected for special study.[21] Thirty-three of the 60 are cases of price advances and 27 are declines. Each of these periods of price movement was divided into three subperiods in the same manner employed for the earlier analysis of aggregate common stock market

[20] A sample of New York Stock Exchange transactions was compiled from the Fitch sheets for the 3d quarter of 1958; see also a similar sample for May 1953 summarized in Irwin Friend, G. Wright Hoffman, and Willis J. Winn, *The Over-the-Counter Securities Markets*, McGraw-Hill, 1958, p. 28. In addition, more comprehensive data on New York Stock Exchange transactions are available for Dec. 8 and 15, 1954 (and on orders for 6 periods from March 1953 to October 1957), from the *New York Stock Exchange Public Transaction Studies*.

[21] Only sustained price movements in individual securities were classified as major market movement for purposes of this analysis. Periods in which prices were relatively stable were, thus, excluded from this part of the analysis.

movements. The basic data for the analysis of the major price movements are the percentage change in market price of the specific security, net purchases in that security by the investment funds covered in this study, the New York Stock Exchange volume in that security, and the ratio between the latter two. Each of these statistics was computed for the complete price movement and for each of the three subperiods into which these movements were divided, as a total figure and on a per month basis. The fund net purchase figures in the 2 months preceding the movement were also used to obtain a better perspective from which to view activity during that movement. An adjustment for net inflow was made in the aggregate analysis but is not appropriate for the individual securities.[22]

The aggregate data did not indicate that the rate of fund net purchases of common stock during periods of market decline was significantly different from the rate during periods of market advance. The findings for the individual securities are somewhat at variance with this conclusion. The funds were less likely to be net sellers during price increases than during price decreases.[23] As shown in Table 8, the funds were net sellers in only 7 of 32 cases when the price was rising but in 11 of 27 when the price was falling. Although this difference might be regarded as statistically significant, it still shows the funds as net purchasers over half the time in a price decline. Any interpretation from these data that the funds are destabilizing on the downswing must rest on the funds' failure to support the price to the extent they do in an upswing or to the extent warranted by their inflow. The evidence could also be construed as supporting the hypothesis that the funds have been destabilizing in price advances. Again caution must be exercised in this interpretation since the funds have had net purchase balances in general.

Table 9 presents data similar to those of table 8 except that the direction of price movement is related to fund balances in the preceding 2 months. These data suggest that the funds may share partial responsibility for inducing some of these price movements, particularly the declines.[24] This table shows that the funds were net purchasers in 22 of 31 instances in the 2 months preceding a price rise, but net sellers preceding a price decline in 14 of 27. In view of the funds' net purchase balance throughout the study, the latter seems quite striking. Accepting this evidence as consistent with the hypothesis that the funds have been at least partially

[22]The funds were not sellers in individual securities frequently and the ratio of net purchases in a particular security to net inflow was quite small, rarely as high as 1 percent. Any adjustment in view of these relationships would be quite tenuous and none will be employed in any of the analyses based on data for individual securities.

[23]Most of the evidence presented in this section is based on the 30 common stocks in which funds had their largest dollar holdings for the study period. Caution should, thus, be exercised in any generalizations from these 30 issues to other common stocks.

[24]As discussed previously, these data could be interpreted as forecasts rather than activity which was partially responsible for the change.

TABLE 7. *Distribution of mutual funds by types of orders used* in purchasing and selling portfolio common stocks, by size of fund, July 1–Sept. 30, 1958*

	Mainly† market orders		Mainly† day orders		Mainly† g.t.c. orders		COMBINATIONS				Market and g.t.c. More g.t.c.		Subtotal	
							More market		Fairly even					
	Num-ber	Per-cent	Num-ber	Per-cent	Num-ber	Per-cent	Num-ber	Per-cent	Num-ber	Per-cent	Num-ber	Per-cent	Num-ber	Per-cent
All funds	32	27.8	23	20.0	38	33.0	3	2.6	7	6.1	2	1.7	12	10.4
Funds with assets of —														
$300,000,000 and over	1	14.3	2	28.6	1	14.3								
$50,000,000 to $300,000,000	3	9.4	6	18.8	15	46.9	1	3.1	2	6.2	2	6.2	5	15.6
$10,000,000 to $50,000,000	7	20.6	10	29.4	11	32.4	2	5.9	4	11.8			6	17.6
Less than $10,000,000	21	50.0	5	11.9	11	26.2			1	2.4			1	2.4
All common stock funds	16	23.2	14	20.3	27	39.2			4	5.8	2	2.9	6	8.7
All balanced funds	11	28.9	8	21.0	9	23.7	3	7.9	3	7.9			6	15.8

*Unit equals fund.
†Over 90 percent.
‡Good until cancelled.

TABLE 7. Distribution of mutual funds by types of orders used* in purchasing and selling portfolio common stocks, by size of fund, July 1–Sept. 30, 1958 (Continued)

	COMBINATIONS									
	Day and g.t.c.						Subtotal		Total	
	More day		Fairly even		More g.t.c.					
	Num-ber	Per-cent	Num-ber	Per-cent	Num-ber	Per-cent	Num-ber	Per-cent	Num-ber	Per-cent
All funds	5	4.4	2	1.7	3	2.6	10	8.7	115	100
Funds with assets of —										
$300,000,000 and over	3	42.9					3	42.9	7	100
$50,000,000 to $300,000,000	1	3.1	1	3.1	1	3.1	3	9.4	32	100
$10,000,000 to $50,000,000									34	100
Less than $10,000,000	1	2.4	1	2.4	2	4.8	4	9.5	42	100
All common stock funds	3	4.4	2	2.9	1	1.4	6	8.7	69	100
All balanced funds	2	5.3			2	5.3	4	10.5	38	100

*Unit equals fund.
†Over 90 percent.
‡Good until canceled.

TABLE 8. *Relation between direction of major price movement in individual securities and fund net purchases during movement, monthly data, 1953–58*

	Direction of price movement		
Sign of fund net purchases	Increase	Decrease	Total
Positive	25	16	41
Negative	7	11	18
Total	32*	27	59*

*Net purchases were 0 during 1 of the increases.
NOTE. Difference is significant at the 0.1 level.

responsible for some of these major price movements in these issues, their role in the movement after it is started deserves further attention.

Inspecting first the price increases, it is apparent from tables 8 and 9 that the funds had a few more positive net purchases during the upswing

TABLE 9. *Relation between direction of major price movement in individual securities and fund net purchases in 2 months preceding movement, monthly data, 1953–58*

	Direction of price movement		
Sign of fund net purchases 2 preceding months	Increase	Decrease	Total
Positive	22	13	35
Negative	9	14	23
Total	31*	27	58*

*Data not available for 2 of the increases.
NOTE. Difference is significant at the 0.05 level.

than preceding it. This difference is not statistically significant. Moreover, a comparison of net purchases in the 2 preceding months with net purchases during the price movement reveals that net purchases by the funds increased in 15 cases and decreased in 16.[25] These findings give no general indication of increases in the funds' net purchases of specific issues when their price is rising and are more consistent with a hypothesis of no systematic pattern. Comparison within the three subperiods leads to a similar

[25]A comparison among issues that share in the same general market movement is made later in this section. The comparison introduces an automatic adjustment for general market level changes by virtue of the fact that those issues participating in the movement are compared with each other.

conclusion: the funds showed little propensity to increase or decrease their net purchases during the various stages of upward movements in price. Net purchases were increased between the first and second subperiods in only 18 of 33 issues and in only 16 between the second and third subperiods. The tendency of the funds to have positive net purchases during price increases seems to be a continuation of the decisions made in those months preceding the advance rather than a reaction to it. The funds do demonstrate a general refusal to become net sellers during these upswings as shown by a shift from a net purchase role to that of a net seller in only 3 of 22 issues.[26]

Inspecting next the data with respect to price declines, the shift from a majority of net sellers preceding declines to a majority of net purchasers during the decline is in the direction of stabilization, but again not statistically significant. Other evidence during price declines shows that the funds increased their net purchases in 17 of the 26 instances for which data are available and decreased them in 9. This pattern also suggests a stabilizing action although its significance must be modified by the funds' natural tendency to have net purchase balances and the fact that the funds had higher than average net selling balances at the beginning of these declines. Within the subperiods, the funds became destabilizing. The funds exhibited a fairly substantial tendency to decrease their net purchases in the third subperiod, reaching their lowest point at this stage for 14 of 27 observations, and decreasing net purchases between the second and third periods in 19 of 27 instances.

The data available also permit comparisons among various securities in the four different general major market movements (the declines of 1953 and late 1957 and the increases of 1955–56 and 1958). The common stocks that moved in the same direction as the market during these periods were compared in the percentage change in market price (both total and per month) and in fund net purchases for each of the four time intervals previously identified. Fund net purchases were considered on a dollar basis and as a percentage of New York Stock Exchange volume. This analysis introduces an automatic adjustment for price changes in other securities since various issues that participate in the same general price movement are compared with each other. For each of the market movements, various comparisons between fund net purchases and changes in market prices of individual securities were made. None of these attempts suggested an explanation of the differential price movements of these securities in terms of fund net purchases in them.

The aggregate analysis of weekly turning points in 1956 and 1957

---

[26]A wide variety of probability models is available for calculating the expected number of shifts from net purchases to net sales, but all of those employed yielded a greater number than the 3 of 22 which were observed.

revealed no consistent relation between fund net purchases and stock prices at these pivotal dates although fund discretionary action appeared to be destabilizing at the highs and stabilizing at the lows. The analysis for the individual securities does not lend itself to a separation of total net purchases and discretionary activity and only the former is employed. A further difficulty is found because the dates of the turning points for the market average do not coincide with the dates of the turning points for specific issues. Weekly data were provided only for the 4 weeks surrounding the four general turning points so the analysis must be based on them. The actual high (or low) prices for the specific securities were ascertained within each 4-week period and the timing of the price changes was compared to the timing of fund net purchases. Within each 4-week period, rank correlations between net purchases and market prices were computed for each security and various combinations of the coefficients were averaged. With one exception, the results did not indicate the existence of any relationship between fund net purchases and market price in these individual issues at these turning points. The one exception was the trough of October 22, 1957, when the evidence suggests the existence of a slight positive relationship (destabilizing). The evidence was not strong in this one instance, and, in view of the lack of evidence in the rest of the analysis, should probably be attributed to chance.[27]

MONTHLY ANALYSIS

Regression equations based on the monthly data for the 30 mutual fund favorites, contrary to those based on aggregate monthly data, indicate a significant positive correlation between market prices and preceding fund net purchases. The regressions between fund activity and preceding market prices, however, reveal no consistent relationship, a result similar to that obtained from the aggregate data. The analysis for individual securities possesses two inherent advantages not present for the aggregate data. The number of observations is considerably increased, permitting more powerful analysis in terms of statistical tests, and the data can be adjusted for price changes in other securities so that the factors affecting the general level of stock prices are kept constant to a considerable extent.

[27] Of 18 securities in which the funds took positions on opposite sides of the market during this 4-week period (i.e., they had net purchase balances in at least one week and net sales in at least one week), the rank correlation was positive for 10 issues, negative for only 5, and zero for 3. Considering only the 15 cases where the coefficient was nonzero, the difference is significant at the 0.05 level using a nonparametric test of the equal likelihood of positive or negative signs. The number of different comparisons made for this study of weekly turning points would suggest that chance alone might produce this one "statistically significant difference." The funds were net sellers in each of the 4 weeks in 2 of the 30 securities and were not net sellers in any of the 4 weeks in the remaining 10 securities.

The forms of the regressions for individual securities are conceptually quite similar to those used for the aggregate analysis. The initial level of the dependent variable is introduced as a crude attempt to hold other factors affecting relative stock prices constant and to permit the separation of long-run and short-run effects. The explanatory variables of principal interest are employed for each of the three immediately preceding months, the periods found most promising in the aggregate analysis. The stock prices of the specific securities are expressed as a ratio of the Standard & Poor's composite index in order to adjust for any general change in the level of market prices. It is in this form that market price is employed, both as the dependent variable and as an independent variable, on the assumption that the price fluctuations in a particular security vis-a-vis price changes in other securities are more useful than the change by itself in disentangling the impact of funds from other influences.

Changes in basic economic conditions will, of course, generate changes in this ratio, but such changes would be positive for some securities and negative for others and would not be expected to disturb general conclusions which are based on a considerable number of issues. Fund activity, when the dependent variable, is expressed as the ratio of fund net purchases in a specific security to fund net purchases in all common stock. The denominator of this ratio indicates the decision made with respect to common stocks in general. Given this decision, the view of the funds toward any specific security is a relative one that is indicated by this ratio. When fund net purchases are used as the independent variable, one can defend conceptually the use of either the absolute value or the ratio. The dollar figure indicates the actual amount that was invested in the security and is perhaps superior, though the ratio has the advantage of showing the relative importance given by the funds to each security. Equations employing the absolute net purchases were computed for all 30 securities, but equations containing the ratio were computed for only a sample.

The two equations used for the bulk of the analysis were:

$$\frac{M_i}{M_t} = a + b_1 P_{it} + b_2 P_{i(t-1)} + b_3 P_{i(t-2)} + b_4 \frac{M_{i(t-3)}}{M_{(t-3)}} \tag{1}$$

and

$$\frac{P_{it}}{P_t} = a + b_1 \frac{M_{i(t-1)}}{M_{(t-1)}} + b_2 \frac{M_{i(t-2)}}{M_{(t-2)}} + b_3 \frac{M_{i(t-3)}}{M_{(t-3)}} + b_4 \frac{P_{i(t-3)}}{P_{(t-3)}} \tag{2}$$

with the terms defined as before and the subscript "i" referring to an individual security. The constants of the regression equation, the adjusted coefficients of determination (with and without the initial level of the dependent variable), and the mean of the market ratio where it is the dependent variable are presented in appendix tables 1 and 2. The high serial correlation between the market price ratio in time "t" and the same

ratio in time "$t - 3$" is evident in the increase in the coefficients of determination with the introduction of the latter ratio and in the fact that the
regression coefficient of the initial level is more than double its standard
error for every security. The same phenomenon (extremely high serial
correlation) is not observable between the net purchase ratios at "t"
and at "$t - 3$."

The results of the regressions indicate a positive correlation between
net purchases in "t" and market price in "t" for several of these individual securities. The regression coefficient showing this relationship
is statistically significant for 6 of the 30 issues and it is positive in each
of the 6. The evidence also suggests positive relationships between market
prices in "t" and net purchases in periods "$t - 1$" and "$t - 2$," but the
results are not statistically significant.[28]

An inspection of the signs of the regression coefficients suggests a
more widespread positive correlation than indicated by the above comparison. As shown in table 10, 23 of the 30 equations possess positive
regression coefficients for net purchases in "t" when "$t - 1$" and "$t - 2$"
are also included; and 22 of 30, for net purchases in "$t - 1$." These findings
lend strong support to the position that increases by the funds in their
monthly net purchases of a particular security have been followed on the
average by increases in the price of that security relative to general market
prices. Similarly, decreases in their net purchases have been followed
generally by relative decreases in the market price. The data in columns 3
and 4 of table 10 show the same pattern when consideration is given to
only those coefficients that are larger than their own standard error. In
the latter comparison, net purchases in "$t - 2$" also show a significantly
higher portion of positive signs.

The regression coefficients are expressed in units showing the average
change in the ratio of the market price of a specific security to the Standard
and Poor's Composite Index associated with an increase in fund monthly
net purchases of $100,000. The average level of the price ratio is obviously
of some consequence in this relationship, but a division of the coefficient by
that average level converts the figure to a percentage point change in the
price ratio where the base for the computation is the average ratio for
each security. These adjusted regression coefficients were multiplied
separately by the standard deviation and by the arithmetic mean of the
funds' net purchases in that security. The resulting figures permit an

[28]Significance tests are appropriate at two stages in this statement. First, the regression
coefficients are compared to their own standard errors. A 0.05 level of significance was employed
at this stage. Second, consideration must be given to the fact that 30 separate comparisons
have been made. The expected number of "significant differences" due to chance at the 0.05
level is 1.5. The binomial distribution indicates that the six observed for "t" is significantly
greater than expected from chance at a 0.01 level, but the two and three for "$t - 1$" and "$t - 2$"
are not significant at even a 0.1 level.

TABLE 10. *Relation between market price and fund net purchases of 30 individual common stocks, distribution of signs of regression coefficients, monthly data, January 1953–September 1958*

			Coefficient exceeds standard error	
Independent variable	Number of plus signs	Number of minus signs	Number of plus signs	Number of minus signs
Net purchases (t)	23*	7	13*	2
Net purchases ($t - 1$)	22*	8	12*	1
Net purchases ($t - 2$)	19	11	9†	1
Market price ($t - 3$)	30*	0	30*	0

*Significant at the 0.01 level.
†Significant at the 0.05 level.

Equation is $\dfrac{M_{it}}{M_t} = a + b_1 P_{it} + b_2 P_{i(t-1)} + b_3 P_{i(t-2)} + b_4 \dfrac{M_{i(t-3)}}{M_{(t-3)}}$

appraisal of the economic significance of the funds' transactions. The standard deviation introduces a concept which relates the significance of fund activity to differences in fund net purchases from month to month while the arithmetic mean introduces a concept of total influence based upon the level of fund activity. Similar statistics, computed by summing the regression coefficients, provide a crude indication of the cumulative effect. The results thus obtained approximate, under the various assumptions, the percentage point change in the relative market price that is produced by fund activity.

As shown in table 11, the regression coefficients do not assume very large values for net purchases in time "t" when the standard deviation is employed, but values of greater magnitude are recorded as the coefficients are summed or the arithmetic mean is substituted for the standard deviation. Only four securities exceeded 3 percentage points in the first instance (time "t" and standard deviation) and none exceeded 5 percentage points. When the coefficients are summed for all three time periods and the standard deviation is applied, six securities take on values in excess of 5 percentage points with a maximum of 6.3 for United States Steel. The use of the arithmetic mean in time "t" likewise produces an increase in the number of securities for which the result is of an appreciable magnitude with four exceeding 10 percentage points and Amerada reaching a level of 22.7. When the regression coefficients are summed and the arithmetic mean is employed, nine securities exceed 10 percentage points and Amerada reaches 40.8.

Attempts were made to isolate those securities in which the funds

TABLE 11. *Number of individual securities in which adjusted regression coefficients*
exceed given values, monthly data, market price dependent *

		Number of securities with adjusted regression coefficients		
Net purchases regression coefficient(s)	Factor	Exceeding 3 percentage points	Exceeding 5 percentage points	Exceeding 10 percentage points
"t" only	Standard deviation	4	0	0
Do	Arithmetic mean	11	9	4
Σ(t, t − 1, t − 2)	Standard deviation	15	6	0
Σ(t, t − 1, t − 2)	Arithmetic mean	16	13	9

*The original regression coefficients were divided by the arithmetic mean of the dependent variable and were multiplied by the factor indicated in col. 2, i.e., either the standard deviation or the arithmetic mean of the funds' monthly net purchases for the particular security.

seemed to demonstrate a potentially large economic impact and to examine any characteristics common to these securities. Standard Oil
of Indiana, United States Steel, Amerada, Gulf Oil, and Continental Oil
were among the top 10 in all 4 lists and the resulting coefficients were
positive in every instance.[29] Four of these five securities are oils, appreciably more than might be expected even after adjusting for the fact
that 10 of the 30 are oils. The funds' net purchases in each of these securities
exceeded 3 percent of the New York Stock Exchange volume for the time
span of the study,[30] but no general pattern of relationship between the
ratio of exchange volume and the various regression coefficients (in any
of the forms) was disclosed by further study.[31]

The data for the entire study period supply additional evidence
that there is a positive relation between the funds' net purchase of a particular security and the price movement of that security. Table 12 presents
the percentage increase in the market price of the 30 selected issues, the
funds' net purchases in each issue for the major part of the period,[32] and

[29]It should be noted that the values of these various statistics are generated by common factors in several instances.
[30]The ratio of fund net purchases to New York Stock Exchange volume exceeded 3 percent for 16 (or approximately half) of the 30 securities.
[31]A number of rank correlation coefficients were computed relating the above ratio to these adjusted regression coefficients and to various coefficients of determination. The percentage of the New York Stock Exchange volume was also compared to the number of positive regression coefficients. The only statistically significant relationship was between the percentage of New York Stock Exchange volume and the two types ("t" only and "t," "t − 1," plus "t − 2") of coeffi-cients multiplied by the arithmetic mean. The result which is positive is not too informative since dollar net purchases by the funds enter into the numerator of both variables.
[32]The funds supplied purchase and sales data for only 51 months of the 5¾ years. These findings are based on those data which cover January to December 1953 and July 1955 to Sep-tember 1958.

the percentage increase in the Standard & Poor's Composite Index. Of these 30 securities which were investment fund favorites, 18 experienced a percentage increase greater than the market average, and the arithmetic mean increase for all 30 was 126 percent compared to 90 percent for Standard & Poor's. Within these 30 securities, those in which the fund net

TABLE 12. *Percentage increases in market price and fund net purchases of each of 30 individual common stocks, January 1953 to September 1958*

Security	Percentage increase in market price	Fund net purchases*	Fund net purchases as a percent of NYSE volume*
International Business Machines Corp.	450	+$32,714†	4.7
Goodyear Tire & Rubber Co.	249	+21,554	8.8
National Lead Co.	248	−4,439	−1.6
United States Steel Corp.	248	+41,495	3.3
Bethlehem Steel Corp.	243	−10,924	−.9
Firestone Tire & Rubber Co.	194	+12,690	11.6
General Electric Co.	187	+3,683	.5
Armco Steel Corp.	184	+22,606	8.5
The Texas Co.	173	+35,802	8.5
Gulf Oil Corp.	141	+29,478	3.5
Central & South West Corp.	135	+3,931	5.0
Shell Oil Co.	133	+9,191	5.1
Standard Oil Co. (New Jersey)	130	+16,428	1.2
General Motors Corp.	110	−27,426	−2.0
International Paper Co.	109	−1,238	−.4
DuPont (E. I.) de Nemours & Co.	98	+20,220	2.8
Continental Oil Co.	96	+7,797	4.4
Standard Oil Co. (California)	96	+14,546	3.4
Standard & Poor's	90		
Aluminum Ltd.	78	+10,992	2.5
Goodrich (B. F.) Co.	71	−15,451	−8.4
Socony Mobil Oil Co.	69	+13,528	3.1
General Public Utilities Corp.	65	+5,043	6.3
Union Carbide Corp.	56	+5,008	1.1
Phillips Petroleum Co.	48	+1,241	.2
Westinghouse Electric Corp.	42	−4,087	−.6
Atchison, Topeka & Santa Fe Ry. Co.	29	−6,789	−3.0
Amerada Petroleum Corp.	25	+24,331	6.2
Standard Oil Co. (Indiana)	25	+30,449	7.3
Kennecott Copper Corp.	21	−2,130	−.5
American Telephone & Telegraph Co.	20	+17,139	.8

*January to December 1953 and July 1955 to September 1958.
†Dollar amounts in thousands.

purchases accounted for the largest percentage of the New York Stock Exchange volume showed, on the average, the greatest percentage increase. The coefficient of rank correlation between these two variables is +0.37, approximately double its standard error. The rank correlation between the funds' dollar net purchases and the percentage increase in market price is also positive, but somewhat lower at 0.21.

The monthly regression equations in which fund net purchases in each individual security were expressed as a percentage of total fund net purchases in common stocks yielded somewhat similar findings, for a sample of six securities tested, but the results were less significant statistically. A more extensive comparison of the two approaches was made in the daily analysis where the results obtained using dollar figures were again superior to those obtained from the ratios.

The regression equations in which net purchases are the dependent variable disclose very little correlation between these purchases and preceding market prices. As discussed earlier in this section all variables were expressed as ratios, but the distribution of the regression coefficients does not differ significantly from what one would expect from chance forces alone. The coefficients for market price in "$t - 3$" are more than double their standard error for six securities; however two have positive signs and four negative. The data for these six issues as well as the data presented in table 13 disclose no consistent pattern. The switch from a majority of positive signs in "$t - 1$" to a majority of negative signs in "$t - 3$" provides fuel for speculation on a time lag in fund reaction to market prices, but the data do not justify any definite conclusion.

TABLE 13. *Relation between fund net purchases and market prices of 30 individual common stocks, distribution of signs of regression coefficients, monthly data, January 1953–September 1958*

| | | | Coefficient exceeds standard error | |
| | | | --- | --- |
Independent variable	*Number of + signs*	*Number of − signs*	Number of + signs	Number of − signs
Market price ($t - 1$)	17	13	10*	3
Market price ($t - 2$)	17	13	5	5
Market price ($t - 3$)	11	19	2	11*
Net purchases ($t - 3$)	17	13	7*	1

*Significant at the 0.05 level.

NOTE. Equation is $\dfrac{P_{it}}{P_t} = a + b_1 \dfrac{M_{i(t-1)}}{M_{(t-1)}} + b_2 \dfrac{M_{i(t-2)}}{M_{(t-2)}} + b_3 \dfrac{M_{i(t-3)}}{M_{(t-3)}} + b_4 \dfrac{P_{i(t-3)}}{P_{(t-3)}}.$

DAILY ANALYSIS

The individual security regression equations relating daily market prices and daily fund net purchases within the third quarter of 1958 demonstrate the same sort of relationships as those found in the monthly equations, but the results are slightly less significant. The equations employed are of the same form as those in the monthly analysis with the exception that five daily periods are used instead of three monthly periods. The results of the equations are presented in appendix tables 3 and 4 which are symmetric with appendix tables 1 and 2 for the monthly regressions.

Considering first the equations with market price as the dependent variable, the number of statistically significant regression coefficients exceeds the expected number (1.5) for each of the 5 time periods and for all time periods combined there was a total of 18 statistically significant coefficients. This figure of 18 is in contrast to an expected value of $7\frac{1}{2}$, and 14 of the 18 are positive in sign. However, the number of statistically significant coefficients exceeds the expectancy by a significant degree (in a probability sense) for only one time period ($t - 2$) and one of the six coefficients is negative for this period. This evidence is less conclusive than that found in the monthly equations for individual securities, but certainly is consistent with the hypothesis that there is a positive correlation between the two variables. As shown in table 14, the number of

TABLE 14. *Relation between market price and fund net purchases of 30 individual common stocks, distribution of signs of regression coefficients, daily data, 3d quarter 1958*

			Coefficient exceeds standard error	
Independent variable	Number of + signs	Number of − signs	Number of + signs	Number of − signs
Net purchases (t)	20*	10	9	3
Net purchases ($t - 1$)	21*	9	7	2
Net purchases ($t - 2$)	20*	10	9	3
Net purchases ($t - 3$)	22†	8	9*	2
Net purchases ($t - 4$)	20*	10	10	5
Market price ($t - 5$)	29†	1	28†	1

*Significant at the 0.05 level.
†Significant at the 0.01 level.

NOTE. Equation is $\dfrac{M_i}{M_t} = a + b_1 P_{it} + b_2 P_{i(t-1)} + b_3 P_{i(t-2)} + b_4 P_{i(t-3)} + b_5 P_{i(t-4)} + b_6 \dfrac{M_{i(t-5)}}{M_{(t-5)}}.$

positive signs is significantly greater than the number of negative signs for net purchases for each of the five time lags. The figures for the distribution of signs where the coefficient exceeds its own standard error are less impressive. Only one period ("$t - 3$") is statistically significant but all exhibit a positive tendency and the combined results are quite significant.

A comparison of specific securities in the daily and monthly analyses is quite informative. The results indicate that the positive relationships observed between fund net purchases and later market prices hold for these securities in general rather than for specific issues in the group. Only one security, Standard Oil of Indiana, possesses at least one statistically significant regression coefficient (excluding that for initial market price) in both the monthly and daily analyses. Only five securities reveal all positive coefficients in both regression equations: Standard Oil of Indiana, Bethlehem Steel, Goodyear, Phillips Petroleum, and Union Carbide. Both findings coincide almost precisely with the result to be expected if chance forces determined the degree of duplication in the two analyses.

Evidence concerning the economic significance of the regression coefficients is conflicting. Adjustments similar to those employed in the monthly analysis[33] supply the basis for such an appraisal, but negative coefficients appear among the larger values too frequently to justify any generalizations. For example, the summation of the adjusted coefficients multiplied by the standard deviation is greater than 0.02[34] for six securities, but the sign is positive in three cases and negative in the other three. None of the other statistics is as large as 0.02 for any security, and negative signs appear among the highest values for each statistic. In contrast to these findings, the four securities that rank high in each of the four statistics[35] employed have positive signs in every instance. These securities, Firestone, Standard Oil of Indiana, Standard Oil of California, and General Motors, reach their highest level when the adjusted coefficients are summed over the five periods and the standard deviation is employed as the weighting factor. The actual statistics for these four securities vary from 1.6 percentage points for Standard Oil of Indiana to 3.0 for Firestone. Fund net purchases during the third quarter of 1958 were equal to at least 8.0 percent of the New York Stock Exchange volume for each of these four securities, but attempts to establish any general relationship between the apparent significance of the results and percentage of market volume were unsuccessful. The appearance of one issue (Standard Oil of California) on the

---

[33]See that analysis for a discussion of the computations of the statistics employed.

[34]Changes in market prices and the volume of fund activity are naturally much smaller on a daily basis than on a monthly basis. Since this analysis is based on daily data, these figures are much smaller than those of the monthly analysis.

[35]Adjusted coefficients for "t" and for $\sum_{i=0}^{4} (t - i)$ multiplied by arithmetic mean and multiplied by standard deviation.

list for both the monthly and daily data would be expected from chance forces alone and should not be interpreted in any special way with respect to that security.

TABLE 15. *Relation between fund net purchases and market prices of 30 individual common stocks, distribution of signs of regression coefficients, daily data, 3d quarter 1958*

| | | | Coefficient exceeds standard error | |
Independent variable	Number of plus signs	Number of minus signs	Number of plus signs	Number of minus signs
Market price $(t - 1)$	17	13	8	3
Market price $(t - 2)$	14	16	4	6
Market price $(t - 3)$	18	12	8	2
Market price $(t - 4)$	11	19	1	5
Market price $(t - 5)$	16	14	3	2
Net purchases $(t - 5)$	12	18	1	3

NOTE. Equation is $\dfrac{P_{it}}{P_t} = a + b_1 \dfrac{M_{i(t-1)}}{M_{(t-1)}} + b_2 \dfrac{M_{i(t-2)}}{M_{(t-2)}} + b_3 \dfrac{M_{i(t-3)}}{M_{(t-3)}}$
$+ b_4 \dfrac{M_{i(t-4)}}{M_{(t-4)}} + b_5 \dfrac{M_{i(t-5)}}{M_{(t-5)}} + b_6 \dfrac{P_{i(t-5)}}{P_{(t-5)}}.$

The daily regression equation relating fund net purchases in specific issues to preceding market prices in that issue indicate neither a positive nor a negative correlation. There are five securities in which the regression coefficients for market price in $(t - 1)$ are statistically significant, but three are positive and two are negative. Considering the coefficients for all 5 time periods, a total of 14 are statistically significant, but they are divided between 6 positive and 8 negative values. The same sort of pattern can be observed in table 15 which summarizes the signs for all securities. The division between signs is not statistically significant in any comparison, and the pattern fluctuates with respect to which sign is in the majority.

SPECIFIC SECURITIES IN WHICH ONE OR MORE FUNDS HAVE LARGE PERCENTAGE HOLDINGS

Data secured for the analysis of the control of portfolio companies may be useful in the study of impact. Each investment fund was asked to identify all common stocks in which it held 1 percent or more of the outstanding voting securities on either January 1, 1953, or September 30, 1958, and to indicate its purchases or sales in each of the identified securities for every month of the period January–December 1953 and July 1955–September 1958. Many securities were listed by more than one fund and the cumulative percentage holding by all funds listing each security was obtained. A simple random sample of those securities in which the cumulative figure was greater than 10 percent was selected using a sampling fraction of one-third. All securities with fewer than 5 months in which the funds had transactions were discarded, yielding a sample of 20 issues.[36] These data were analyzed in an attempt to show what, if any relationship existed between market price and net purchases by funds with large percentage holdings.

Regression equations similar to those of the preceding section are not particularly useful for these data because net purchases are zero in a large number of instances. A portion of the analysis considered only those months with nonzero net purchases, while a second approach used the months in which net purchases were zero as a standard for comparison. The analyses are based on comparisons between net purchases in a particular month and the change in market price during that month or during the preceding month. Both variables of course refer to a specific security, but the change in market price is expressed relative to the change in the general market level as shown by the Standard and Poor's composite index.

The evidence is not inconsistent with the findings for the market leaders, but it is much more tentative. The inclusion of seven insurance companies tends to obscure the slight suggestion of a positive relationship between the sign of net purchases and the direction of market change. Rank correlation coefficients between change in market price during the month and net purchases of the same month (excluding those months in which net purchases were zero) were computed for each security. If the insurance stocks are not considered, 12 of 13 coefficients are positive although only 1 is statistically significant. Among the insurance stocks five of seven were negative with one of the latter significant. An identification of only those months in which the ratio of the price of the specific security to the market index changed by more than 10 percent revealed no systematic pattern in fund activity either preceding or following the change.[37] Other analyses gave little indication of either a positive or negative relationship between fund net purchases and market price, but the results are inconclusive. An attempt to study the months in which the funds had their largest net purchases (either positive or negative) was equally unproductive. The level of fund net purchases in these analyses is no doubt largely responsible for the inconclusive nature of the results. As

---

[36]None of these 20 securities appeared in the list of 30 market leaders studied in the preceding section.

[37]There were 65 instances of such changes.

already indicated there were many months in which net purchases were zero and the total dollar value was rather small in the other months since it represented activity by only one or two funds.

SOME ECONOMIC ASPECTS OF PREDICTIVE ABILITY

It has been noted that the funds as a whole may have to some extent the ability to fulfill their own market price predictions but that fully as interesting a question from certain points of view relates to their success in channeling funds into issues that subsequently have a favorable trend in per share earnings. The major reason for interest in this question is that one of the economic functions that may be performed by financial intermediaries like mutual funds is to help direct capital into those areas of investment which ultimately turn out to be most profitable. However, since the primary concern of this chapter is with the market impact of mutual funds, only a few simple tests have been made of the relationship between fund stock purchases and subsequent share earnings (adjusted for stock dividends, splits, etc.). These tests were confined to the 30 mutual fund "favorite" stock issues and the 1953–58 period analyzed previously.

The average increase in per share earnings from 1953 to 1958 for the 15 stock issues in which fund net purchases were largest (in dollar amounts) in 1953 amounted to 14.3 percent, while the corresponding increase for the remaining 15 issues with lower initial purchases was 18.7 percent. On the other hand, the coefficient of rank correlation between initial purchases and the subsequent change in earnings was $+0.11$, though neither the difference in the two percentages nor the sign of the rank correlation is statistically significant. These findings do not indicate any significant relationship between fund purchases in individual securities and the later performance of per share earnings.

It is possible of course that the market did not evaluate with sufficient favor the prospective earnings of the 15 issues with largest mutual fund net purchases and the funds moved in to take advantage of this situation. A test of this possibility, though it has many inadequacies, is given by a comparison of the average ratios of 1953 prices to 1958 earnings for the two groups of issues classified by 1953 fund net purchases. The resulting price-earnings ratio was 10.1 for the 15 issues with the largest mutual fund net purchases and 9.8 for the remaining 15 issues, again not a statistically significant difference.

The combined results, while inconclusive without much more extensive testing, do not point to either superior or inferior performance by mutual funds in directing capital into particularly profitable areas of economic investment.

APPENDIX TABLE 1. *Monthly relationships between market price and net purchases for individual common stocks,* constants of regression equations and adjusted coefficients of determination*

Security	Constants					Mean of dependent variable	Adjusted coefficients of determination†	
	a	b_1	b_2	b_3	b_4‡		$\bar{R}^2_{.123}$	$\bar{R}^2_{.1234}$
Aluminum Ltd.	+0.266	−0.021	+0.024	+0.039	+0.864	2.352		0.639
Amerada Petroleum Corp.	+.433	+.240	+.133	+.059	+.868	5.059		.819
American Telephone & Telegraph Co.	−.225	+.009	−.014	−.020	+1.053	4.362		.958
Armco Steel Corp.	+.313	+.011	+.045	+.065	+.837	2.209		.672
Atchison, Topeka & Santa Fe Ry. Co.	+.169	+.130‡	+.051	−.015	+.935	2.950	.057	.899
Bethlehem Steel Corp.	−.190	+.005	+.059	+.105‡	+1.074	3.429	.029	.926
Central & South West Corp.	+.097	+.020	−.003	−.017	+.908	8.644	.084	.657
Continental Oil Co.	+.990	+.116‡	+.059	+.041	+.573	2.381	.087	.569
Du Pont (E. I.) de Nemours & Co	+.945	+.014	+.001	+.032	+.766	4.296	.225	.827
Firestone Tire & Rubber Co.	+.130	+.092	+.045	−.002	+.966	3.601	.373	.833
General Electric Co.	+.694	+.040	+.031	+.034	+.829	3.830	.069	.797
General Motors Corp.	+1.194	−.018	+.006	−.005	+.558	2.747		.361
General Public Utilities Corp.	+.078	+.016	−.012	+.006	+.917	.881	.219	.712
Goodrich (B. F.) Co.	+.650	+.087	−.017	−.022	+.786	3.098		.498
Goodyear Tire & Rubber Co.	+.102	+.071	+.008	+.108	+.961	3.174		.879

*Equation is $\dfrac{M_{it}}{M_t} = a + b_1 P_{it} + b_2 P_{i(t-1)} + b_3 P_{i(t-2)} + b_4 \dfrac{M_{i(t-3)}}{M_{(t-3)}}$

P_i is fund net purchases of security indicated in \$100,000.

M_i is price per share of security indicated, adjusted for stock splits, etc.

M is Standard and Poor's composite stock index.

†See the following: $\bar{R}^2_{.1234}$ is based on all 4 independent variables. $\bar{R}^2_{.123}$ excludes market price as an independent variable.

‡Regression coefficient greater than twice standard error.

APPENDIX TABLE 1. *Monthly relationships between market price and net purchases for individual common stocks,* constants of regression equations and adjusted coefficients of determination (Continued)*

Security	Constants					Mean of dependent variable	Adjusted coefficients of determination†	
	a	b_1	b_2	b_3	b_4‡		$\bar{R}^2._{123}$	$\bar{R}^2._{1234}$
Gulf Oil Corp.	+.671	+.061‡	+.022	+.021	+.698	2.418	.314	.681
International Business Machines Corp.	+1.009	+.042	−.033	+.050	+.991	1.734	.158	.932
International Paper Co.	+.680	−.033	+.008	−.010	+.701	2.307	.256	.588
Kennecott Copper Corp.	+.477	+.121‡	+.060‡	−.016	+.785	2.448	.329	.879
National Lead Co.	+.306	+.041‡	+.019	−.013	+.870	2.093		.859
Phillips Petroleum Co.	+.454	+.039	+.030	+.028	+.776	2.044		.757
Shell Oil Co.	+.726	+.085	+.088	−.011	+.785	3.316	.061	.595
Socony Mobil Oil Co.	+.783	−.005	+.001	+.011	+.457	1.456		.067
Standard Oil Co. (California)	+1.045	−.004	−.026	+.004	+.525	2.184		.228
Standard Oil Co. (Indiana)	−.371	+.070‡	+.039	+.024	+1.106	2.364	.013	.874
Standard Oil Co. (New Jersey)	+.612	−.031	−.020	−.010	+.840	3.556		.739
The Texas Co.	+.425	+.012	+.041	+.022	+.838	2.725	.057	.774
Union Carbide Corp.	+.262	+.041	−.019	+.073‡	+.889	2.443	.129	.687
United States Steel Corp.	+.137	+.027	−.053‡	+.033	+.919	2.543	.183	.903
Westinghouse Electric Corp.	+.092	−.004	+.003	+.057‡	+.929	1.403		.829

*Equation is $\dfrac{M_{it}}{M_t} = a + b_1 P_{it} + b_2 P_{i(t-1)} + b_3 P_{i(t-2)} + b_4 \dfrac{M_{i(t-3)}}{M_{(t-3)}}$

P_i is fund net purchases of security indicated in \$100,000.

M_{it} is price per share of security indicated, adjusted for stock splits, etc.

M is Standard and Poor's composite stock index.

†See the following: $\bar{R}^2._{1234}$ is based on all 4 independent variables. $\bar{R}^2._{123}$ excludes market price as an independent variable.

‡Regression coefficient greater than twice standard error.

APPENDIX TABLE 2. Monthly relationships between net purchases and market prices for individual common stocks,* constants of regression equations and adjusted coefficients of determination

Security	Constants					Adjusted coefficients of determination†	
	a	b_1	b_2	b_3	b_4	$\bar{R}^2_{.123}$	$\bar{R}^2_{.1234}$
Aluminum, Ltd.	−0.002	−0.031	+0.019	+0.015	+0.028		.017
Amerada Petroleum Corp.	−.009	+.015	−.004	−.007	+.153	.024	
American Telephone & Telegraph Co.	−.023	−.005	+.019	−.008	+.166		
Armco Steel Corp.	−.003	−.016	+.019	+.004	−.099		
Atchison, Topeka & Santa Fe Ry. Co.	−.013	+.042‡	+.004	−.042‡	+.137	.187	.186
Bethlehem Steel Corp.	+.076	+.011	−.067	+.033	−.001	.195	.175
Central & South West Corp.	+.031	+.038	−.010	−.062‡	−.120	.180	.174
Continental Oil Co.	+.017	+.012	−.025	+.010	−.043		
Du Pont (E. I.) deNemours & Co.	+.240	+.020	+.027	−.099	−.048	.290	.274
Firestone Tire & Rubber Co.	+.011	−.011	+.005	+.004	−.138‡		
General Electric Co.	+.017	+.019	+.010	−.034	−.348‡		.092
General Motors Corp.	+.347	+.014	−.026	−.117‡	−.089	.461	.459
General Public Utilities Corp.	−.013	−.013	+.045	−.016	+.425‡	.060	.197
Goodrich (B. F.) Co.	−.004	−.016	+.006	−.022	+.128		
Goodyear Tire & Rubber Co.	+.012	−.013	+.022	−.010	+.005		

*Equation is $\dfrac{P_{it}}{P_t} = a + b_1 \dfrac{M_{i(t-1)}}{M_{(t-1)}} + b_2 \dfrac{M_{i(t-2)}}{M_{(t-2)}} + b_3 \dfrac{M_{i(t-3)}}{M_{(t-3)}} + b_4 \dfrac{P_{i(t-3)}}{P_{(t-3)}}$

P is fund net purchases in $100,000; P_i is fund net purchases of security indicated.
M_t is price per share of security indicated, adjusted for stock splits, etc.
M is Standard and Poor's composite stock index.
†See the following:
$\bar{R}^2_{.1234}$ is based on all 4 independent variables. $\bar{R}^2_{.123}$ excludes fund net purchases as an independent variable.
‡Regression coefficient greater than twice standard error.

APPENDIX TABLE 2. Monthly relationships between net purchases and market prices for individual common stocks,* constants of regression equations and adjusted coefficients of determination (Continued)

Security	Constants					Adjusted coefficients of determination †	
	a	b_1	b_2	b_3	b_4	$\bar{R}^2_{.123}$	$\bar{R}^2_{.1234}$
Gulf Oil Corp.	-.069	+.037	+.053	-.057	+.138	.204	.200
International Business Machines Corp.	+.002	-.008	+.015	-.007	-.031	.020	.097
International Paper Co.	+.031	+.020	-.112‡	+.077‡	+.196	.087	.015
Kennecott Copper Corp.	+.007	+.076	-.060	-.016	-.121	.023	.118
National Lead Co.	-.015	+.074	+.017	-.086‡	-.042	.138	.109
Phillips Petroleum Co.	+.023	+.008	+.022	-.041	+.327‡	.007	.034
Shell Oil Co.	+.042	-.005	-.007	+.001	+.183	.022	
Socony Mobil Oil Co.	+.019	-.047	+.049	-.012	+.089		
Standard Oil Co. (California)	+.023	-.029	+.009	+.012	+.084	.091	.077
Standard Oil Co. (Indiana)	+.071	+.086	-.091	-.019	+.095	.116	.113
Standard Oil Co. (New Jersey)	+.004	-.009	-.104	+.115‡	+.153‡		.004
The Texas Co.	-.025	-.018	-.014	+.048	+.206		
Union Carbide Corp.	+.041	+.076	-.053	-.037	-.001	.114	.094
United States Steel Corp.	+.025	+.161‡	-.188‡	+.023	+.048	.012	
Westinghouse Electric Corp.	+.013	-.021	+.123	-.112	-.014		

*Equation is $\dfrac{P_{it}}{P_t} = a + b_1 \dfrac{M_{i(t-1)}}{M_{(t-1)}} + b_2 \dfrac{M_{i(t-2)}}{M_{(t-2)}} + b_3 \dfrac{M_{i(t-3)}}{M_{(t-3)}} + b_4 \dfrac{P_{i(t-3)}}{P_{(t-3)}}$

P is fund net purchases in $100,000; P_t is fund net purchases of security indicated.
M_t is price per share of security indicated, adjusted for stock splits, etc.
M is Standard and Poor's composite stock index.
†See the following:
$\bar{R}^2_{.1234}$ is based on all 4 independent variables. $\bar{R}^2_{.123}$ excludes fund net purchases as an independent variable.
‡Regression coefficient greater than twice standard error.

APPENDIX TABLE 3. Daily relationships between market price and net purchases for individual common stocks,* constants of regression equations and adjusted coefficients of determination

Security	Constants							Mean of dependent variable	Adjusted coefficients of determination†	
	a	b_1	b_2	b_3	b_4	b_5	b_6		$\bar{R}^2_{.12345}$	$\bar{R}^2_{.123456}$
Aluminium Ltd.	+0.546	−0.003	−0.004		+0.0002	−0.004	+0.111	0.621	0.152	0.147
Amerada Petroleum Corp.	+2.306	−.003	−.006	−.005	−.007	−.005	−.007	2.280	.056	.038
American Telephone & Telegraph Co.	+2.414	−.0002	+.0001	+.0004	+.001	+.0002	+.372‡	3.849		.124
Armco Steel Corp.	+.591	+.001	+.001	−.004	+.003	+.002	+.509‡	1.199	.054	.421
Atchison, Topeka & Santa Fe Ry. Co.	+.205	+.0003	+.001	+.002	+.0001	+.0003	+.589‡	.495		.293
Bethlehem Steel Corp.	+.387	+.0003	+.001	+.002	+.001	+.002	+.600‡	.959		.321
Central & South West Corp.	−.045	−.003	−.005‡	−.007‡	−.009‡	−.006‡	+1.029‡	1.022	.094	.902
Continental Oil Co.	+.349	−.006	−.003	−.001	−.002	−.002	+.713	1.205		.408
Du Pont (E. I.) de Nemours & Co.	+1.081	+.007	−.0001	+.003	+.001	+.003	+.731‡	4.088	.069	.288
Firestone Tire & Rubber Co.	+.621	+.028	+.037‡	+.034‡	+.029	+.010	+.693‡	2.104		.274
General Electric Co.	+.794	+.001	+.001	−.001	−.0001	+.002‡	+.405‡	1.337		.254
General Motors Corp.	+.368	+.001	+.002‡	+.002‡	+.002	+.001	+.593‡	.921	2.76	.555
General Public Utilities Corp.	+.242	−.001	+.003	+.010‡	+.010‡	+.004	+.733‡	.930	.002	.660
Goodrich (B. F.) Co.	+1.026	−.002	+.002	+.002	+.011	+.007	+.275‡	1.411	.135	.195
Goodyear Tire & Rubber Co.	+1.156	+.002	+.002	+.001	+.004	+.003	+.384‡	1.885		.069

*Equation is $\dfrac{M_{it}}{M_t} = a + b_1 P_{it} + b_2 P_{i(t-1)} + b_3 P_{i(t-2)} + b_4 P_{i(t-3)} + b_5 P_{i(t-4)} + b_6 \dfrac{M_{i(t-5)}}{M_{(t-5)}}$

P_i is fund net purchases of security indicated in $100,000.
M_{it} is price per share of security indicated, adjusted for stock splits, etc.
M is Standard and Poor's composite stock index.
†See the following:
$\bar{R}^2_{.123456}$ is based on all 6 independent variables. $\bar{R}^2_{.12345}$ excludes market price as an independent variable.
‡Regression coefficient greater than twice standard error.

APPENDIX TABLE 3.   *Daily relationships between market price and net purchases for individual common stocks,* constants of regression equations and adjusted coefficients of determination (Continued)*

Security	Constants							Mean of dependent variable	Adjusted coefficients of determination†	
	a	b_1	b_2	b_3	b_4	b_5	b_6		$\bar{R}^2_{.12345}$	$\bar{R}^2_{.123456}$
Gulf Oil Corp.	+.843	+.002	−.001	−.0002	+.001	+.003	+.634‡	2.343		.705
International Business Machines Corp.	+3.156	−.106	−.011	−.004	−.006	−.012	+.610‡	7.928	.008	.383
International Paper Co.	+.983	+.005	+.006	+.003	−.003	−.008	+.561‡	2.233		.260
Kennecott Copper Corp.	+1.094	+.003	+.001	+.006	+.002	+.001	+.445‡	1.968		.134
National Lead Co.	+.955	+.0002	−.003	+.002	+.001	+.006	+.550‡	2.128		.261
Phillips Petroleum Co.	+.147	+.003	+.010	+.017‡	+.010	+.016‡	+.850‡	.974	.230	.700
Shell Oil Co.	+.830	−.0004	+.003	+.004	+.005	+.003	+.513‡	1.716	.023	.248
Socony Mobil Oil Co.	+.332	+.002	+.0002	+.001	+.0002	−.002	+.663‡	1.011	.044	.763
Standard Oil Co. (California)	+.672	+.008‡	+.006‡	+.006‡	+.004	+.006‡	+.363‡	1.086	.463	.674
Standard Oil Co. (Indiana)	+.190	+.004‡	−.003	+.002	+.001	+.0004	+.797‡	1.011	.464	.787
Standard Oil Co. (New Jersey)	+.863	+.002	−.001	−.001	−.0002	−.002	+.258‡	1.165	.021	.166
The Texas Co.	+1.041	−.001	−.001	+.001	−.001	−.0003	+.303‡	1.500		.083
Union Carbide Corp.	+.692	+.003	+.006	+.006	+.006	+.005	+.681‡	2.214	.134	.748
United States Steel Corp.	+.102	+.003	+.002	+.003	+.002	−.003	+.938‡	1.529	.054	.662
Westinghouse Electric Corp.	+.606	+.003	−.006	−.007	−.008	+.001	+.543‡	1.303		.194

*Equation is $\dfrac{M_{it}}{M_t} = a + b_1 P_{it} + b_2 P_{i(t-1)} + b_3 P_{i(t-2)} + b_4 P_{i(t-3)} + b_5 P_{i(t-4)} + b_6 \dfrac{M_{i(t-5)}}{M_{(t-5)}}$

P_i is fund net purchases of security indicated in $100,000.
M_i is price per share of security indicated, adjusted for stock splits, etc.
M is Standard and Poor's composite stock index.
†See the following:
$\bar{R}^2_{.123456}$ is based on all 6 independent variables. $\bar{R}^2_{.12345}$ excludes market price as an independent variable.
‡Regression coefficient greater than twice standard error.

APPENDIX TABLE 4. *Daily relationships between net purchases and market prices for individual common stocks,* * constants of regression equations and adjusted coefficients of determination*

Security	a	b_1	b_2	b_3	b_4	b_5	b_6	Adjusted coefficients of determination †	
								$\bar{R}^2_{.12345}$	$\bar{R}^2_{.123456}$
Aluminium Ltd.	+0.510	−1.235	+0.812	−0.206	−1.056	+0.848	+0.041		
Amerada Petroleum Corp.	+.560	−.076	+.026	+.112	−.133	−.171	+.024		
American Telephone & Telegraph Co.	−1.431	+1.812‡	−2.664‡	+.865	−1.110	+1.469	+.091	.090	.080
Armco Steel Corp.	+.178	+.094	−.207	+.591‡	−.261	−.373	+.417	.187	.173
Atchison, Topeka & Santa Fe Ry. Co.	−.200	+1.082	−.196	−.622	−.442	+.574	−.062		
Bethlehem Steel Corp.	−.206	+1.581	−.637	−.830	−.716	+.792	−.015		
Central & South West Corp.	+.011	−.575	+.030	+.375	+.159	−.003	−.055		
Continental Oil Co.	−.221	+.095	−.204	−.592	+.586	+.308	−.082		
Du Pont (E. I.) de Nemours & Co.	−.263	+.048	+.080	−.172	+.142	−.030	+.161		
Firestone Tire & Rubber Co.	+.810	−.958‡	+.801	+.737	−.932	−.035	−.009	.142	.126
General Electric Co.	+2.607	+6.186‡	−10.056‡	+3.132	−1.306	+.085	−.110	.180	.176
General Motors Corp.	−.288	−.115	+1.237	+1.366	−2.602‡	+.449	−.146	.162	.165
General Public Utilities Corp.	+.011	+.505	−.675	+.510	−.327	−.023	−.003	.009	
Goodrich (B. F.) Co.	−.168	+.412	−.671	+.338	−.584	+.616	+.077	.009	
Goodyear Tire & Rubber Co.	+.432	−.038	+.004	−.061	−.038	−.092	+.017	.003	

*Equation is

$$\frac{P_{it}}{P_t} = a + b_1 \frac{M_{i(t-1)}}{M_{(t-1)}} + b_2 \frac{M_{i(t-2)}}{M_{(t-2)}} + b_3 \frac{M_{i(t-3)}}{M_{(t-3)}} + b_4 \frac{M_{i(t-4)}}{M_{(t-4)}} + b_5 \frac{M_{i(t-5)}}{M_{(t-5)}} + b_6 \frac{P_{(t-6)}}{P_{(t-6)}}$$

P is fund net purchases in \$100,000; P_i is fund net purchases of security indicated.
M_i is price per share of security indicated, adjusted for stock splits, etc.
M is Standard and Poor's composite stock index.

†See the following:
$\bar{R}^2_{.123456}$ is based on all 6 independent variables. $\bar{R}^2_{.12345}$ excludes fund net purchases as an independent variable.
‡Regression coefficient greater than twice standard error.
§This large coefficient for United States Steel is attributable principally to one very extreme observation.

APPENDIX TABLE 4. *Daily relationships between net purchases and market prices for individual common stocks,* constants of regression equations and adjusted coefficients of determination (Continued)*

Security	a	b_1	b_2	b_3	b_4	b_5	b_6	$\bar{R}^2_{.12345}$	$\bar{R}^2_{.123456}$
Gulf Oil Corp.	+.601	−.932	+.594	+.895	−1.002	+.249	+.028		
International Business Machines Corp.	+.307	−.024	+.021	−.083	−.108	+.159	−.208	.001	.033
International Paper Co.	+.055	+.561‡	−.576‡	+.390‡	−.403‡	+.006	+.056	.293	.283
Kennecott Copper Corp.	−.109	+.142	−.038	−.403	+.312	+.041	+.089		
National Lead Co.	+.277	+.342	−.280	−.179	+.109	−.127	−.019		
Phillips Petroleum Co.	−.255	−.262	+.654	+.124	−.398	+.136	+.009		
Shell Oil Co.	−.243	−.058	+.268	+.097	−.442	+.279	−.034		
Socony Mobil Oil Co.	−.197	+.214	−.223	+.594	−.424	+.021	−.093		
Standard Oil Co. (California)	−.284	+.644	+.460	−.964	+.438	−.307	−.013	.039	.021
Standard Oil Co. (Indiana)	−.045	+.610	−.968	+1.211	−.736	−.051	−.062		
Standard Oil Co. (New Jersey)	−1.631	+3.191	−2.268	−.619	+1.349	−.244	−.019		
The Texas Co.	−1.102	+1.526	−1.197	+.252	+.125	+.040	−.147		
Union Carbide Corp.	−.098	−.325	+.355	−.320	+.548	−.203	−.163		
United States Steel Corp.	+1.385	−3020.960†§	−9.159‡	+9.347‡	+.342	−1.358	−.039	.142	.128
Westinghouse Electric Corp.	−.018	−17.190	+.525	+.062	+.171	−.751	+.052	.059	.042

*Equation is $\dfrac{P_{it}}{P_i} = a + b_1 \dfrac{M_{i(t-1)}}{M_{(t-1)}} + b_2 \dfrac{M_{i(t-2)}}{M_{(t-2)}} + b_3 \dfrac{M_{i(t-3)}}{M_{(t-3)}} + b_4 \dfrac{M_{i(t-4)}}{M_{(t-4)}} + b_5 \dfrac{M_{i(t-5)}}{M_{(t-5)}} + b_6 \dfrac{P_{(t-5)}}{P_{(t-5)}}$

P is fund net purchases in $100,000; P_i is fund net purchases of security indicated.
M_i is price per share of security indicated, adjusted for stock splits, etc.
M is Standard and Poor's composite stock index.
†See the following:
$\bar{R}^2_{.123456}$ is based on all 6 independent variables. $\bar{R}^2_{.12345}$ excludes fund net purchases as an independent variable.
‡Regression coefficient greater than twice standard error.
§This large coefficient for United States Steel is attributable principally to one very extreme observation.

PART 2. Bonds and Common Stocks
as Long-Term Investments

A Reconsideration
of the Common-Stock Theory*

Gilbert Harold[1]

According to the common-stock theory, common stocks are better long-term investments than bonds with respect to the three major considerations of absentee investment: safety, income, and market value. There are, of course, several necessary assumptions in the tenability of the theory. It assumes the corporate form of ownership, the freedom of choice, and diversification.

Even a brief statement of the theory requires at least one definition, namely the meaning of "long term." As used by some investigators, a long term is a period of one year or more.[2] As used by others, and sometimes by the same analysts, a long-term point of view is one which envisions a period of years, a period which varies with the situation and with the attitude of the individual.[3]

The earliest reference to the desirability of common stocks for long-term investment was a statement by Mr. William Hughes at a convention of the Institute of Actuaries (London) in 1902:

It would be most interesting and valuable if we could ascertain or estimate with any degree of accuracy what would be the effect of investing a large number of

---

*Reprinted from the *Journal of Business*, 7, no. 1, January 1934, pp. 42–59 by Gilbert Harold by permission of The University of Chicago Press.

[1]Instructor in Finance, The Ohio State University.

[2]As in Laurence H. Sloan, *Everyman and His Common Stocks* (McGraw-Hill, 1931), p. 8.

[3]*Ibid.*, pp. 280–81. But "There are three main reasons why one would reverse one's viewpoint and sell:

a. "Development of evidence that a mistake had been made in the investor's original analysis;

b. "Development of outside and previously incalculable and unpredictable forces tending to change the direction of the established or estimated trend line;

c. "Development of evidence of an impending major cyclical change, either in business in the aggregate, or in a particular industrial division of business."

These reverses, of course, could not be entertained in a statistical test because they would involve the factor of hindsight.

the small amounts in what may be called speculative securities, and of carrying the amount of interest realized, in excess of a certain minimum to a guarantee or insurance fund, itself to be invested in first-class securities to be used to make good losses of capital or deficiencies of revenue as they occur. I by no means advocate a trial of the experiment in actual practice, but it might be useful if anybody possessed of the necessary patience and perseverance would make the experiment on paper by selecting a number of such securities, and following their fortunes to see what the result would be.[4]

Nothing of importance was done in the matter until 1912 when Professor Fisher and others suggested the theory, at least in part.[5] The Fisher publication was based almost entirely on the principle that when prices of commodities in general are rising, the purchasing power of the dollar is declining and that, in consequence, the income from bond investments is worth less in its ability to meet the cost of living for the investor. Professor Fisher and colleagues recommended that investments be allotted either to common stocks (which, presumably, adjusted themselves to the rising price level) or to commitments in which common stocks were involved, such as in bonds with a common-stock bonus. In fact, Dr. Norton[6] went so far as to make several tests wherein his hypothetical investor's commitments in common stocks showed, in one case, total increments over a period of nine years of about 100 per cent or an average return of about 11 per cent per annum as against less than 3 per cent per annum for bonds of the same companies. It is obvious to any scientific investigator that there are certain weaknesses in these tests, such as the choice of companies, but research in the social sciences had not progressed, in 1912, to the more scientific bases upon which it stands today.

The next important work along these lines came with the Smith treatise in 1923.[7] Smith sets out to determine, by statistical tests, whether bonds of common stocks are preferable as permanent investments.

Smith offers no formal definition of "long term." Rather he implies one: that a long-term investment, at least for purposes of research, is one to which the investor remains committed irrespective of cyclical changes, though he does allow for the investor's retirement from a commitment if and when a stock in the investor's portfolio should definitely arrive in a state of difficulty, such as a receivership. The periods of the Smith tests range from 17 to 22 years.

In setting up his tests Smith makes several assumptions, all favorable

[4]Quoted by H. E. Raynes in *Journal of the Institute of Actuaries* (London [March, 1928], p. 48.
[5]*How to Invest When Prices Are Rising*, ed. Irving Fisher, with chapters by Irving Fisher, Edwin W. Kemmerer, Harry G. Brown, Walter E. Clark, J. Pease Norton, Montgomery Rollins, G. Lynn Summer (G. Lynn Summer & Co., 1912).
[6]*Ibid.*
[7]Edgar Lawrence Smith, *Common Stocks as Long Term Investments* (Macmillan, 1923). In the same year a hint of the theory was given in a book entitled *Stock Investments* by Robert W. Pomeroy (Buffalo: Author, 1923).

to bonds. He assumes that the investor had no funds with which to take advantage of subscription rights and that in consequence he sold all rights and all fractional shares from stock dividends, although he retained all whole shares. Proceeds from such sales were credited to current income. Whole shares from stock dividends, however, were not so credited. He assumes that because the hypothetical investor had no funds available he was unable to meet assessments and that assessed stock and the stock of companies in receivership were sold at current market prices. The proceeds were deposited in savings accounts at 4 per cent interest. He apparently assumes that in cases of combination the investor followed the recommendations of the corporate directors when no contribution of money was required. Finally, he assumes in some cases that the investments in bonds remained intact with no losses or gains, either as to capital or as to income.

Stocks selected constituted, not a random selection, but those stocks which, in Smith's opinion, would have been the issue attracting investors' attention at the time: companies with largest total capitalization, companies with largest common-stock issues, companies whose common stocks had the greatest number of shares traded in during the week of purchase, companies whose common stocks had "fairly consistent" dividend records and companies which gave the highest yield, and large companies whose common stocks had paid no dividends during the year next previous to the year of purchase.

On these bases of arbitrary-random selection, 11 of the Smith tests showed an advantage for common stocks, and one (Test 6, 1866–83) showed a slight advantage for bonds. In connection with Test 6 Smith pointed out that "There has never been since 1873 a period in which the purchase of long-term interest-bearing bonds was more favorable to the investor from the point of view of yield on purchase price (unless perhaps a short period in 1920) than in the period from 1866 to 1873."[8]

But Smith's tests do not stop there. Following the reasoning set forth in the Fisher book of 1912, Smith's study takes into consideration the purchasing power of the dollar. When prices are rising, this treatise claims, common stocks are more satisfactory investments than bonds because common stocks participate in the growth and prosperity of the corporation. Whether the same action would hold good in periods of declining prices is not completely established. Smith's tests, however, take more of a long-range point of view and include periods of both rising and falling prices, and they prove fairly conclusively that over long periods diversified common stocks of leading companies have been better investments than bonds. Even when dollar income and dollar market value are tempered by the application of the purchasing power of the dollar, common stocks are still

[8]See note 7.

far in the lead. These disclosures, startling to the bond investor of the middle nineteen twenties, brought forth an array of discussions in periodicals and books on finance.

One which attracted some attention was an article by Professor Fisher in which he "recast Smith's calculations in a form to give, in terms of purchasing power, the 'rate of return realized' on the bonds and common stocks studied by him."[9]

Unquestionably the most important publication following Smith was a book by Kenneth S. Van Strum embodying the content of some articles of his published in *Barron's Weekly*.[10] Van Strum measured the performances of bonds and common stocks in 18 tests ranging over various periods from 1873 to 1924, and reached substantially the same conclusions as Smith.

Contrary to the general run of investment writing at this time was an article by Herschel in which he took exception to the common stock theory.[11] He asserts that

> It should be stated clearly and emphatically that *all* corporations do not pay larger dividends when commodity prices are increasing. . . . . The investment risk of common stocks is not a subject which lends itself to statistical analysis. . . . . No one knows when the investment is going to end; if it ends in 1919, we have one result; if it ends in 1921, we have an entirely different result. So with every common stock: by changing the date of purchase and the date of sale, we can obtain a great variety of results. . . . . It is evident that those who recommend common stocks have given so much attention to the purchasing power of money that they have failed to appreciate the larger risk of commercial failure. . . . . Is it a benefit to bondholders and trustees to undermine their faith in bonds and mortgages when they are holding securities which are sanctioned by law? . . . . It is significant to find that stocks have been recommended for a business man, but the writer does not know of any instance where common stocks have been recommended for widows and orphans! . . . . It has been said that the friends of common stocks have thrown a bombshell into the investing world; perhaps they have thrown a boomerang.

It is obvious from Herschel's statements that he did not catch the spirit of the common-stock theory at all. Proponents of the theory do not claim that a given stock is a better investment than a given bond nor that any group of stocks are better than any group of bonds. The theory, as expounded by Smith and Van Strum, is that over long periods diversified portfolios of common stocks in leading corporations yield the investor more income, more safety, more market value per portfolio, and also that such common-stock investments, as a group, keep better pace with the cost of living than do bonds as a group.

[9] *Magazine of Wall Street*, April, 1925.
[10] Investing in Purchasing Power (Barron's 1925).
[11] Arthur H. Herschel, "The Investment Risk of Common Stocks," *Commercial and Financial Chronicle* (November 14, 1925).

Another dissenter is Professor Lagerquist, who makes the usual objections and adds that "If the present tendency in government regulation and control continues, it will not be long before it will be necessary to exclude railroad and utility stocks under the present methods of tests which are made of common stocks."[12]

Nothing of importance about the theory then appeared for more than three years. In the summer of 1929 Smith refined the theory somewhat, with the qualifying statement that high current interest rates call for investment chiefly in short maturities, and low current interest rates call for investment chiefly in common stocks. "At no time, however, will all of the fund be either totally invested in equities or totally in maturities."[13] That was in 1929 at the peak of the greatest bull market in history.

Writers on investment began to make brief mention of purchasing power investments. Dwight C. Rose wrote a more or less technical volume based, in large measure, on these developments.[14] Ray Vance, in an elementary book, gave a chapter to this "new school" of investment.[15]

Even into the realm of insurance has the common-stock theory penetrated. At a convention of the Institute of Actuaries (London) in October, 1927, H. E. Raynes presented a paper in which he discussed the problem from a British point of view and in which he offered a test involving only British securities.[16] Raynes' test covers the 15 years from 1912 to 1927, a period "covering the majority of our tribulations." The test includes 54 companies in nine British industries. In explanation of his attempt to avoid the factor of hindsight Raynes explains that he has "selected examples which, while it would shock the susceptibilities of any respectable stock-broker, would meet with the approval of a sound statistician." Although there is some value in the Raynes test, it is hardly comparable with the Smith and Van Strum tests for the reason that it compiles income after taxes, and also because it embraces the reinvestment of all income above that which might be expected from bonds. Substantially, however, the results are in agreement with American tests. The Raynes test serves a purpose in that it tends to confirm the common-stock theory for British securities over the period studied. In apology for whatever shock may have been experienced by British investors as a result of his paper, Raynes adds that he is "aware that much of this paper may sound disconcerting to many . . . but time brings changes, and as the *Economist* said last month . . . 'it is

[12]Walter E. Lagerquist, "When Are Bonds a Better Investment Than Stocks?" in *System* (the *Magazine of Business*) (January, 1926).
[13]Edgar Lawrence Smith, "Protecting Capital Values of Common Stock Investments," *The Annalist* (August 23, 1929).
[14]*A Scientific Approach to Investment Management* (Harper, 1928).
[15]*Investment Policies That Pay* (Forbes, 1929).
[16]H. E. Raynes, "The Place of Ordinary Stocks and Shares (as Distinct from Fixed Interest-bearing Securities) in the Investment of Life Assurance Funds," in *Journal of the Institute of Actuaries* (London [March, 1928]).

the customary fate of new truths to begin as heresies and end as superstitions.' "[17]

Following the Raynes paper, several of the members of the Institute discussed various phases of the subject. Mr. D. S. Savory contended, in explanation of the remarkable showing for ordinary (common) shares, that the depreciation in the value of bonds was due almost entirely to the differences in the taxation of bonds and of stock for income tax. "Increase in taxation had tended to a decrease in the demand for gilt-edged securities and to a corresponding increase in the demand for ordinary stocks."[18] It is doubtful, however, that differences in the taxation of bonds and of stock could account entirely for the vast difference in results.

In further discussion Sir Joseph Burn expressed disagreement with the Smith (and Raynes) method of testing issues of heterogeneous companies. He thought that some of Smith's conclusions were a bit fanciful, especially when they were expressed as economic laws. He had in mind such conclusions as the idea that common stocks show a natural growth equivalent to $2\frac{1}{2}$ per cent compounded annually. "Had Mr. Smith analyzed several *groups* of companies, he would probably have found nothing like a general increase of $2\frac{1}{2}$ per cent. It might be much more in some cases and much less in others. Generalizations expressed as laws should only be reached after examinations of homogeneous material."[19]

The fact that this discussion took place in a national convention of British insurance executives is indicative of the grip which the common-stock theory has obtained on investment opinion. At American insurance conventions likewise the subject has been debated with some vehemence.

It is not in the field of insurance alone that the common-stock theory has come to be of great concern. Investment trusts have been built up to gigantic proportions partly through the operation of the common-stock principle. Consequently most of the holdings of investment trusts are in common stocks.

Naturally after the break of the market in the fall of 1929 great concern was felt by investment trust managers for the future of their organizations. It was before such a group that Mr. Smith defended the theory "now that the precipitous fall in stock prices is over."[20] Mr. Smith had no fear for the validity of the theory provided that three very important practices remain intact. In a carefully worded statement he assured the members of the Association that

[17] *Ibid.*
[18] *Ibid.*
[19] *Ibid.*
[20] "The Cult of the Common Stock — Now," *Commerce and Finance* (February 19, 1930), quotes Edgar Lawrence Smith in an address before the Corporate Fiduciaries Association.

Even for those who were fully invested in common stocks at the time of the break, there is no great reason for concern, for it remains true that the long term trend in the value of a diversified list of common stocks is gradually upward, and there is every reason to believe that this trend will continue upward:

(1) So long as a majority of the better-managed corporations in the country operate at a profit.

(2) So long as these corporations do not declare in dividends as much as they make annually in profits; and

(3) So long as these corporations are able to invest their growing surplus accounts in a manner to expand their operations and their profits.

And all these things are likely to continue so long as the country continues to make industrial progress. Thus the hazard to asset values in a well-diversified holding of common stocks appears to be one of time alone.[21]

It is not to be inferred, however, that the break in the stock market completely annihilated the favor of the public at large for the common stock idea. By 1931 two schools of thought in this respect had grown up. One held, with Smith, that the principles of the common-stock theory were still in force and still in favor.

The other group, which includes millions of investors, declares that the common-stock theory has fallen into disrepute, that the persistent declines in earnings, in dividends, and in market value have obliterated all claims of the common-stock contenders. They point out as well that political and economic conditions have never been as they are today and that the ability to produce is far greater than the economic ability to consume. It therefore behooves all holders of equity securities to right-about-face and proceed to intrench themselves in good, fortified, high-grade maturities.

An unbiased and more far-sighted observer would probably take a more qualified stand. As Sloan points out,[22] it is obvious from the tenets of the theory that if the long-term trend of business is to be upward, the average good common stock should be a good long-term investment. If the trend is to be downward, it is a very exceptional common stock which will prove to be a good long-term investment. If the trend of business is to be sidewise, then only a minority of common stocks will succeed as good long-term investments.

Sloan is obviously a believer in the upwardness of the long-term trend and of the validity of the common-stock theory over long periods of time. "The truth of the matter is," he states, "that if the time has now arrived to 'liquidate the common stock idea,' it has arrived coincidentally with the time to liquidate the idea of being in business in any way."[23]

[21]*Ibid.*
[22]*Ibid.*, p. 304; *see also* note 2.
[23]*Ibid.*, p. 305.

None of these observers, however, has made public any attempt to investigate the questions of whether the computations of earlier writers (Smith, Van Strum, and others) hold good in the light of 1932 developments. Dividends have been pared almost indiscriminately. Earnings, in many cases, are nil. Market value, it seems, has almost disappeared. With these facts in mind, would the Smith or Van Strum tests still show favorably for common stocks in 1932? Is there any good reason why these tests should not be continued to the present? Some observers feel that, owing to the unusual conditions surrounding present markets, it would be unfair to the tests. In this writer's opinion there is no more justification for postponing such a project than there was for postponing Smith's computations of the market value of bonds in 1925.[24] In the latter instance Smith apprised us of the fact that two strong bonds purchased in April, 1902, for $2,125 sold in July, 1920, for $1,330, a loss of $795. It is not inconceivable that an investor might have been forced to liquidate at these prices, and inasmuch as he had held these bonds for 18 years it could not be argued that the term was not long enough to be considered.

In view of these circumstances a study was made to determine whether the advantages claimed for common stocks still held good at the end of 1932.

Accepting the Smith tests as reasonably valid, the writer selected three of them for further investigation. These were Smith Tests 2, 3, and 11. In making an abridged study, these three tests were selected because they allowed better comparison than the others. All three tests start with January, 1901. Smith brings them to a close in December, 1922. A decade has passed since. Each test contemplates a commitment of approximately $10,000.

Test 3 was selected for continuation because it showed the greatest total advantage of any test during the period studied. Test 2 was selected because it showed the least total advantage during the same period. Test 11 was included because it produced the greatest total advantage among the tests devoted exclusively to railroad stocks.

Tests 2, 3, and 11, as continued through 1932, are hereinafter called Tests A, B, and C respectively.

Each stock, with its accruals, if any, was continued from 1922, to the end of which year Smith had brought it from 1901. The assumptions made by Smith as to subscription rights, stock dividends, assessments, and receiverships, were continued intact.

Test A, which, as Smith Test 2, had shown the poorest results to the end of 1922, consisted of the following common stocks in approximately equal amounts:

[24]Edgar Lawrence Smith, "Speculation and Investment," *Atlantic Monthly* (October, 1925).

Diamond Match
Swift
Erie Telephone and Telegraph
America District Telegraph
Proctor & Gamble
Standard Oil (N.J.)
Central & South American Telegraph
American Sugar Refining
Westinghouse Electric & Manufacturing
American Tobacco

These stocks had been selected on the following arbitrary basis. Poor's *Manual* for 1901 gives a list of miscellaneous industrial stocks with their dividend records for seven years previous. Those companies which had maintained the "most consistent" dividend records were listed, and from this list were selected those companies which, during the week ending January 12, 1901, showed the highest yield on 1900 dividends—a reasonably random basis.

By the end of 1932, shares had been acquired in Diamond Match preferred, in North American Match, and in Anglo-American Oil. Central and South American Telegraph had become All American Cables and finally International Telephone and Telegraph. Erie Telephone and Telegraph stock had been sold according to the assumptions specified above, and so had Westinghouse, and American District Telegraph.

In no year between 1901 and 1932 had income fallen below that of the first year: $607.50, or $207.50 in excess of the hypothetical income from bonds at 4 per cent (which assumes no losses in bond investments). The yield of 4 per cent is justified on the ground that high-grade bonds were quoted in January, 1901, at 3.95 per cent.[25]

Greatest income in this test to the end of 1922 was $1,097.57 in 1916. But, by 1930, this income had mounted to $5,555.72, although it shrank in the two years following.

The original capital investment in this test in 1901 was $9,877.00. By 1922 it had mounted to only $10,830.00. By 1929, however, it had risen to the astounding market value of $90,436.50, and three years later was about half that figure.

It is noteworthy that until 1922 this test had been the least satisfactory of any of the 1901 tests. By 1932 it had proved to be the best.

Test B was based upon the original Smith Test 3. This test was chosen for continuation because it had proved to be the most satisfactory, in point of total return, of the Smith tests. The constituent stocks of this test were the following:

[25]Standard Daily Trade Service, *Bulletin No.* 10 (October 20, 1923).

United States Express
Tennessee Coal, Iron and Railroad
American Car and Foundry
Federal Steel
American Sugar Refining
Western Union Telegraph
Brooklyn Rapid Transit
People's Gas Light and Coke
American Tobacco
United States Rubber

These companies had been selected on the basis of type of industry. In the January 12, 1901, issue of *The Commercial and Financial Chronicle* companies listed on the New York Stock Exchange in 1900 are classified according to type of industry. That company in each industry which had the greatest number of common-stock transactions in the Exchange during the preceding week was arbitrarily selected. As in Test A, this was a reasonably scientific selection. As Smith points out, "It is important to repeat that these methods of selecting stocks are strictly laboratory methods, enabling us to eliminate present-day judgment from our tests."[26]

By the end of 1932 Brooklyn Rapid Transit had been sold, United States Express had been dissolved. Tennessee Coal, Iron and Railroad, and Federal Steel had been consolidated into United States Steel, and part of the securities received in exchange had been called for redemption.

In only one year from 1901 through 1932 had income fallen below that of the hypothetical income from bonds. That was in 1904, and the deficiency was only $6.00. The greatest income came in 1928 when it reached $1,746.33. By 1932 it had declined to about one-fourth that amount to a point only $27.01 in excess of the hypothetical bond income.

The original investment in 1901 in Test B amounted to $10,012.00. By the end of 1922 market value was $20,602.00. In 1929 it reached $35,446.55, and by the end of 1932 it had declined to $9,036.55—less than the amount of the original investment in 1901.

It is interesting that Test B, which showed the best record to 1922, was in a relatively poor position in 1932. Test A, which had shown relatively poor results to 1922, was several times better than Test B in 1932.

Test C was based upon Smith Test 11, which, among the exclusively railroad stocks tests, had enjoyed the most prosperous experience. Test C consisted of approximately equal amounts, in terms of dollars invested, of the stocks of the following companies:

[26]See Note 7.

Atchison, Topeka & Santa Fe
Southern Pacific
Southern Railway
Erie
Reading
Norfolk & Western
Colorado & Southern
Missouri, Kansas & Texas
Denver & Rio Grande
Kansas City Southern

Smith selected these companies because, "Having tested the ten largest rails which were paying dividends in 1900 it . . . seemed fitting, in the spirit of research, to test the ten largest which were not paying dividends in 1900."[27]

By the end of 1932 two of these companies had been sold: Missouri, Kansas & Texas and Denver & Rio Grande.

This group of stocks, as might be guessed, had a very slow start. Lowest annual income was $114.00, in the first year, 1901. There were six years in which annual income was lower than the 4 per cent hypothetical income from bonds. These were 1901, 1902, 1903, 1904, 1905, and 1932. In 1932, however, the deficiency was only $12.86.

In market value the results of Test C are equally interesting. The original investment in 1901 was $10,002.00. By 1922 market value had climbed to $21,992.00, and by 1929 to $60,957.62, a remarkable figure, but by 1932 market value was only $8,403.74—substantially below the original investment in 1901.

It may be of interest to compare the three tests as to total and average income. Total income for the 32 years was $41,596.39 in Test A, $33,230.57 in Test B, $27,608.90 in Test C, and $12,800.00 for bonds. *Average* income per year was $1,299.89 in Test A, $1,038.45 in Test B, $862.75 in Test C, and $400.00 in the case of bonds. Or it may be stated that average income per year for Tests A and B (mostly industrial stocks; Test C was comprised of railroad stocks exclusively) combined was $1,169.17 as compared with $400.00 for bonds, a ratio of almost three to one in favor of common stocks.

The figures for each test and each year are shown in Table 1.

It is important, in pointing out that 1932 brought a slight deficiency of income below that of the hypothetical bond income, in Test C, to bear in mind that the bond income (4 per cent on $10,000, or $400) assumes neither defaults in income nor in payments of principal.

It is important, in pointing out that 1932 brought deficiencies in market values below that of the hypothetical bond investment, in Tests B and C, to

[27] *Ibid.*

TABLE 1. *Income tests**

Year	Test A (Industrials and Utilities)	Test B (Industrials and Utilities)	Test C (Railroads)	Bonds (Hypothetically)
1901	607.25	616.60	114.00	400.00
1902	741.81	515.00	135.00	400.00
1903	678.87	595.50	146.00	400.00
1904	732.80	394.00	146.00	400.00
1905	752.80	481.00	297.00	400.00
1906	1,072.05	732.00	406.50	400.00
1907	798.80	673.21	510.75	400.00
1908	727.80	763.85	754.00	400.00
1909	864.50	824.75	775.00	400.00
1910	763.30	962.75	876.00	400.00
1911	690.30	813.00	881.50	400.00
1912	665.42	985.15	764.00	400.00
1913	827.51	1,049.00	710.00	400.00
1914	657.24	1,008.75	710.00	400.00
1915	657.74	805.00	710.00	400.00
1916	1,097.57	809.00	748.50	400.00
1917	963.51	1,230.25	756.00	400.00
1918	849.26	1,168.50	736.80	400.00
1919	737.66	1,663.04	736.80	400.00
1920	816.66	1,640.54	736.80	400.00
1921	712.91	1,319.79	1,138.80	400.00
1922	673.43	1,114.04	1,160.80	400.00
1923	1,702.42	1,141.42	720.14	400.00
1924	1,800.87	1,247.65	938.87	400.00
1925	1,894.67	1,281.65	1,015.14	400.00
1926	2,249.17	1,347.15	1,593.14	400.00
1927	1,878.18	1,397.87	1,691.14	400.00
1928	2,423.96	1,746.33	1,753.14	400.00
1929	2,732.43	1,576.75	2,061.64	400.00
1930	5,555.72	1,707.26	2,074.14	400.00
1931	2,734.72	1,192.76	1,424.14	400.00
1932	1,534.99	427.01	387.14	400.00
Total income	41,596.39	33,230.57	27,608.90	12,800.00
Average income per year	1,299.89	1,038.45	862.75	400.00

*Data from 1901–22 from Edgar Lawrence Smith, *Common Stocks as Long Term Investments*, by permission of the Macmillan Company, publishers.

bear in mind that the market value of the bonds assumes no decline in quoted prices, and it is obvious even to the casual observer that this is an impractical assumption.

One criticism which may be leveled at the extension of the Smith tests through 1932 is that 32 years is too long a period to be considered. It may be argued that rarely is an investment maintained in any equity security for three decades. Smith's tests from 1901 through 1922 ran for only 22 years. It may be suggested that if a test is made as of the end of 1932 it should include no longer a period than Smith's tests, or 22 years. Acceptance of this suggestion would cause the tests to start in January, 1911. An examination of the data as of 1911, however, reveals the fact that, although the exact figures would be different, the general conclusions would be substantially the same. Furthermore, the criticism that 32 years is too long a test period would be attacked by many students of investment. One writer in a study of common and preferred stocks used the 39-year period from 1866 to 1925 because "for the results to be of greatest possible value the study should begin at as early a date as possible and extend up to the present time."[28]

Another view of these tests is obtained when the factor of purchasing power is added. In tempering the dollar income and the dollar market value of the various tests, the modifier used by the present writer was the Index of General Prices as published by the Federal Reserve Bank of New York. The results invite comment. Expressed in terms of 1913 dollars, the stupendous return of $5,555.72 in 1930 in Test A is reduced to $3,306.98. In the same year the hypothetical bond income of $400.00 is reduced to $238.10. In 1920 this real income from bonds was only $207.25. The comparable figures for other years are equisonant. During the period from the War to 1931 a wide gap is found between dollar income and real income. Prior to the War the scissure was small. But, overlooking one insignificant exception (Test C, 1932), at no time has the hypothetical purchasing power income from bonds exceeded the actual comparable income from common stocks.

It should be borne in mind also that in dealing with present conditions the tax advantage of dividends as compared with interest is quite substantial. No account is taken of this advantage in the tests referred to.

It is obvious that if one accepts the assumptions made originally by Smith and the bases of arbitrary-random selection of stocks set up by him, that if one accepts the adequacy of the Smith tests to 1922 and the continuation of three of them as Tests A, B, and C through 1932, one is forced to accept the validity of the common-stock theory as applied to the period over which the tests were made.

One question which may well be raised at this point is: Of what value are these findings to the average investor? If the small investor is convinced of the validity of the theory, how should he be guided in his selection of investments? To which a triangular reply may be made. First, the small

[28]James Roy Jackson, "Common and Preferred Stocks as Investments," *Journal of Business of the University of Chicago* (July, 1928).

TABLE 2. *Market value tests**

	Test A (*Industrials and Utilities*)	Test B (*Industrials and Utilities*)	Test C (*Railroads*)	Bonds (*Hypothetically*)
January, 1901	9,877.00	10,012.00	10,002.00	10,000.00
December, 1922	10,830.00	20,602.00	21,992.00	10,000.00
August, 1929	90,436.50	35,446.55	60,957.62	10,000.00
December, 1932	44,240.75	9,036.55	8,403.74	10,000.00

*Data from 1901–22 from Edgar Lawrence Smith, *Common Stocks as Long Term Investments*, by permission of the Macmillan Company, publishers.

investor may select common-stock issues in which he has confidence (his method of selection is a matter of analysis outside the scope of this paper). Second, and especially if his total sum is small, he may select the issues of investment trusts which are based upon common-stock portfolios. Third, he may take a middle course and include both bonds and stocks in his holdings.

There are two general objections which a scientific investor might make to the theory as applied to long periods, periods inclusive of both rising and falling prices.

One objection is that the period of the tests (1901–32) was, in general, a period of expansion and that the future may or may not repeat or continue the process.

The second objection has to do with the manner in which the companies were selected by Smith. In two of the Smith tests stocks of leading companies were selected and from these were chosen those issues which gave the highest yield on purchase price. Why Smith stipulated highest yield his book does not reveal. There appears to be here a fundamental weakness. Certainly the careful investor does not ordinarily espouse stocks rendering the highest yields. Is it not more in keeping with conservative practice that he would choose stocks with *lowest* yields? The fact that a stock offers a low yield is *prima facie* evidence that it is held in high esteem. But, whether a selection of ten stocks bearing lowest yields would have brought substantially different results is not known. There is reason to believe that it would not. Had Smith in his Test 2 (later Test A) chosen his stocks on a low-yield basis rather than a high-yield basis, he would have included issues of prime position, issues which later proved to be among the leaders in American industry. Confirmation of this strength of the low-yield common stocks is found in several studies of this phase of the problem. Badger conducted tests on 40 issues from 1913 to 1924, and found the low-yield group to have the advantage both in income and in market appreciation.[29] Another study, by Cox, carried tests over the decade of 1919–29 with 12 industrial and 8 utility issues, and reached the same conclusion.[30] And Stugard, in a more recent study, traced the income from and market value of three groups of common stocks.[31] Of his three groups one was designated high grade, one medium grade, one speculative. Throughout the entire period of the study the high-grade stocks, which were presumably those of low yields, rendered the highest total return on the investment.

Certainly the point may be made that many more tests could be projected on this subject, tests which might reveal interesting figures. Of the truth of such a proposal no doubt is entertained. Many angles present themselves as statistical possibilities. It appears unnecessary, however, to enter into so expansive a task when the truth of the general thesis is so evident. Different figures would be obtained, but it is apparent from the data that the conclusions would stand unmolested.

It is the opinion of the present writer that if one accepts the Smith tests, the Van Strum experiment, and the above-described abridged extension of the Smith tests, the common-stock theory stands upon a firm base, shaken by the developments of 1932, but not destroyed.

2·2

For Long-Term Investment:
Stocks or Bonds*

Donald L. Kemmerer

Most of us try to put aside some savings for a "rainy day." What is the best way to invest any amount from several hundred dollars to a few tens of thousands of dollars for a period of years? That question concerns us especially now because we anticipate that the general price level

[29]Ralph E. Badger, *Investment Principles and Practices* (Prentice-Hall, 1928).

[30]George Clarke Cox, "Buying Low-Yield Stocks for Income," *Barron's Weekly* (February 10, 1930).

[31]Erwin Stugard, "Have the 'Blue Chip' Stocks Stood the Test?" *Barron's Weekly* (September 12, 1932).

*From the *Commercial and Financial Chronicle*, Feb. 1, 1951. Reprinted by permission of the *Commercial and Financial Chronicle*, New York, N. Y.

will creep steadily higher in the years ahead. We face a future of costly armaments, cold wars, and perhaps the devastating effects of a hot war. Under these circumstances how can we best safeguard the principal of our savings?

INFLATION HURTS CREDITORS

One of the chief dangers to savings is loss of purchasing power of the principal. Investors should be more aware of this danger than they generally are. It is an elementary economic fact that creditors lose in a period of rising prices. Nearly all of us are creditors in some respect. This is especially true of people who save. Bondholders, lenders on mortgages, people with savings accounts, people with insurance, and even hoarders of paper money or of silver money are all creditors. Creditors lose during an inflation because they loan dollars whose purchasing power is greater than the dollars that they get back. Government savings bonds are a familiar example. In the 1940s our government urged us to invest in them and thus combine our instinct to save with our desire to be patriotic. The savings bonds, known as E bonds, paid the holder 2.9% interest if the buyer held them to the end of their ten-year maturity. These bonds paid a higher rate of interest than any other type of United States government bonds. In the next few years many such bonds will mature. Thousands of persons will learn first hand how creditors lose in an inflationary period. A person investing $75 in 1940 got back $100 (principal and accumulated interest) in 1950. But the 1950 dollars that he got back buy only 60% of what the 1940 dollars did. In terms of purchasing power, he invested $75 (principal) and got back $60 (principal plus interest). He actually paid the government for borrowing from him. True, World War II had to be financed somehow. We are not concerned here with that, however, but rather with the effect of rising prices on investable funds whose purchasing power we would like to protect as much as possible.

INFLATION IS LESS LIKELY TO HURT PROPERTY OWNERS

There is another way of investing savings so as to avoid or at least minimize this danger of loss of purchasing power in a period of rising prices. It is another elementary economic fact that owners of physical property generally suffer less from inflation than creditors do. The most obvious property owners are those who own land, buildings, equipment, stores and merchandise inventories. But you can also be a property owner by being a stockholder in one or more corporations. It is the stockholders who own the corporations that have title to the various physical properties. Other property owners are all kinds of debtors who have borrowed money to buy property, such as people who have borrowed on a mortgage or corporations that have borrowed by selling bonds. These property owners and debtors fare better because the value of the property that they own or hold title to tends to rise with the general price level. Debtors sometimes do better than break even. For example, if a company sold bonds (borrowed) to get some of its property, the bondholders (lenders) will lose, for they will get back dollars of less purchasing power. Who will gain what the bondholders lost? Chiefly the stockholders will.

It would be a mistake, however, to assume from this that stockholders often gain from an inflation or that they generally break even. Heavier taxes, weaker security markets, the uncertainties of changing demand usually tend to prevent that. Still after taking these factors into account, stocks are a better investment than bonds in a period of inflation. In such times the investor must face the fact that he will probably lose, whatever he does; he must simply strive for the least loss.

THERE IS A LONG RUN TENDENCY FOR PRICES TO RISE

Thus far we have talked as though inflation were a relatively short-run condition, lasting at most a few years. Most persons would admit that stocks are a better investment than bonds under those conditions. But are stocks a better investment than bonds for a longer run period? There is good reason for believing that they are. After all, prices tend to rise more than they tend to fall. Keynesian economists notwithstanding, inflation has been a greater menace in this world of ours than deflation. A quick glance at the history of any of the world's monetary units will demonstrate that. The pound sterling was once worth $4.86; it is now worth $2.80. The franc was once worth 19 cents; it is now worth a third of a cent. The original dollar of 1792 contained 24.75 grains of pure gold; the present dollar contains 13.71 grains of pure gold. In the United States during the past half century prices have risen in 31 years and they have fallen in 17. The cost of living index is triple today what it was in 1900 and is 40% higher than it was 25 years ago.

THE 50-YEAR EXPERIMENT

In light of the generally upward tendency of prices, which is the same as the falling purchasing power of the dollar or gradual inflation, how would investments in stocks compare to those in bonds over the past half century? Let us make a reasonably practical experiment. How would the changing purchasing power have affected ten-year investments, of the E bond type, between 1900 and 1950. Also see how it would have affected investments in a widely diversified list of stocks. That 51-year period contains

41 10-year intervals of the E bond type. To typify bonds we shall use Standard and Poor's index of best grade municipal bonds between 1900 and 1929 and United States government bonds between 1919 and the present. The individual bond buyer of the earlier period would more likely have invested in good municipals or railroads than in governments. Dealings in government bonds were on a relatively small scale then and the records are not easily accessible today. The price behavior of the two types, municipals and governments, where the series overlap in the 1900's and in the 1920's, is reasonably similar (see Columns 5 and 6 in table 1). For stocks we shall use Standard and Poor's index of 416 common stocks and the series spliced to them before 1937 in the Department of Commerce's "Historical Statistics." Finally, we shall divide both indexes by the cost of living index of the Bureau of Labor Statistics, 1913 to the present. Before 1913 the New York Federal Reserve Bank's index has been adjusted for use. In summary, we have a series of broadly representative stock prices and also a series of top-flight bond prices, and both have been reduced to dollars of a common value. These are 1935–39 dollars.

The table is reasonably self-explanatory although we should warn the reader against one possible misinterpretation. The stock index column and the bond price column do not have a common base and accordingly are not comparable. Do not, therefore, draw any conclusions from comparing Column 2 with Columns 5 or 6, or Column 3 with Column 7. The only comparable columns are 4 and 8. These measure the percentage of rise or fall in real value over a 10-year period. The percentage figures in these are obtained by comparing the real value index of, say, stocks in 1900 with stocks in 1910, i.e. 84.8 with 109.1. The 1900 investor got a 28% gain. In contrast notice the real value index of bonds which stood at 196.1 in 1900 and at 142.5 in 1910; the 1900 bond buyer suffered a loss of 27% on his principal. Stocks were therefore the better investment for a 10-year period in 1900. The percentage figure opposite each year represents the gain or loss realized ten years later. Therefore these columns end in 1940. We shall not know the results of 1941 investments until 1951 is over, of 1942 investments until 1952 is past, etc. The figures in Columns 3 and 7 clearly suggest, however, that unless we experience a sizable deflation, which is most unlikely, or a serious stock market crash, the years ahead will favor the investor who chose stocks.

With this table before us, let us now ask several pertinent questions.

SIGNIFICANCE OF THE EXPERIMENT

In how many of the 41 10-year periods between 1900 and 1950 would the investor have been able to gain if he had been a perfect guesser? In only 20 years. In the other 21 he was bound to lose.

In how many of the gainful periods would he have gained by investing in bonds and in how many would he have gained by investing in stocks? At the end of 13 of the periods he would have been ahead had he invested in bonds. At the end of 15 he would have been ahead had he invested in stocks. Eight of the gainful years for bonds coincided with eight of the gainful years for stocks. In eight instances, therefore, the investor could not go wrong; he would have been ahead whether invested in stocks or bonds.

In how many of these 8 periods were stocks better than bonds and in how many were bonds better than stocks? In 6 of the good periods stocks outperformed bonds and in 2 bonds outdid stocks.

In how many of the other 12 periods of the gainful 20 would stocks have been clearly the better investment and in how many would bonds have been clearly better? Stocks were clearly better in 7 instances and bonds were clearly better in 5.

Now let us turn to the 21 periods in which the investor lost something whether he chose stocks or bonds. In how many periods were stocks the lesser evil and in how many were bonds the lesser evil? It is here that the superiority of stocks is most marked. In 18 of the 21 losing periods stocks were the better choice and in only three were bonds the better choice.

Thus far we have reached two conclusions that should be emphasized. The 10-year investor won in 20 years and lost in 21, providing, of course, he chose correctly whether to invest in stocks or bonds. If he chose incorrectly every time, he lost unnecessarily or unduly in 33 of the 41 periods. If he did not know what to do, and most of us do not generally, he would have been safer investing in stocks, for stocks were the better choice in 31 years and bonds were better in only 10 years. Notice also that if anyone had invested for the entire 51 years, he would have lost slightly on his stocks and lost very heavily on his bonds.

Let us proceed now with our 10-year period analysis. In how many instances was the margin of superiority of stocks over bonds, or of bonds over stocks, very small, say 10% or less? In 14 years there was 10% difference or less, usually less, whether it was comparative gain or comparative loss. Making adjustments for this fact, we find that stocks were the better investment in 21 periods, bonds were better in 6, and the difference was not very marked in 14.

But another modification is in order. How much discrepancy was there in yield between the stocks and the bonds? This is significant. A yield margin of 1% per year for 10 years in favor of stocks would make stocks somewhat preferable in all the 14 periods we just considered, virtually, even because the difference in real value was 10% or less. It was generally less in fact. A yield margin favoring stocks of 1% on a compounded interest basis over 10 years is about 14%. A margin of 2% is 27%. This would favor the

TABLE 1. Comparison of stocks and bonds for 10-year investment, 1900–1950

Date	(1) Cost of living index	(2) Common stock index	(3) Stocks real value index	(4) % 10-year gain or loss (stocks)	(5) Standard & Poor 15 Municipals	(6) U.S. govt. bonds	(7) Bonds real value index	(8) % 10-year gain or loss	(9) Better choice for 10 years
1900	56.6	48.6	84.8	28%	110	(104.0)	196.1	−27%	Stocks
1901	58.0	62.0	106.9	1	109.8	(107.3)	189.3	−25	Stocks
1902	56.4	66.2	117.3	−10	108.7	(108.8)	192.7	−31	Stocks
1903	62.2	57.0	91.6	−2	105.7	(107.1)	169.9	−22	Stocks
1904	61.5	55.7	90.6	−2	104.7	(105.0)	170.2	−23	Stocks
1905	61.5	71.1	115.6	−22	105.4	(104.2)	171.4	−23	Stocks
1906	63.6	76.3	119.9	−18	102.8	(104.0)	161.6	−23	Stocks
1907	67.2	62.1	92.4	−19	98.5	(105.2)	146.6	−30	Stocks
1908	64.3	61.6	95.8	−41	97.4	(103.9)	151.3	−44	Stocks
1909	64.3	76.9	119.6	−52	99.6	(101.5)	154.9	−53	Stocks
1910	67.9	74.1	109.1	−58	96.8		142.5	−60	Stocks
1911	67.9	73.2	107.8	−62	96.6		142.3	−54	Bonds
1912	72.1	75.5	104.5	−45	96.0		133.1	−42	Bonds
1913	70.7	67.3	90.1	−37	93.3		131.9	−41	Stocks
1914	71.8	63.8	88.9	−33	94.7		131.9	−27	Bonds
1915	72.5	66.2	91.3	−22	94.1		129.9	−42	Stocks
1916	77.9	76.2	97.5	−18	97.2		124.5	−39	Stocks
1917	91.6	68.3	74.5	26	93.6		102.2	−24	Stocks
1918	107.5	60.7	56.5	116	89.6		83.3	− 7	Stocks
1919	123.8	70.7	57.1	171	90.1	91.9	74.2	17	Stocks
1920	143.3	64.2	44.8	180	83.7	85.9	59.9	27	Stocks

Year	Column 1	Column 2	Column 3	Column 4	Column 5	Column 6	Column 7	Column 8	Column 9
1921	127.7	52.2	40.8	113	82.5	88.2	69.0	22	Stocks
1922	119.7	67.7	56.5	−12	93.2	96.6	80.7	13	Bonds
1923	121.9	69.0	56.6	19	92.9	95.9	78.6	28	Bonds
1924	122.2	72.8	59.6	27	93.7	99.3	81.2	23	Stocks
1925	125.4	89.7	71.5	12	95.2	101.7	81.1	25	Bonds
1926	126.4	100.0	79.1	41	95.3	103.8	82.1	25	Stocks
1927	124.0	118.3	95.4	14	96.7	108.1	87.2	13	Stocks
1928	122.1	149.9	122.3	−32	95.6	108.3	88.3	15	Bonds
1929	122.5	190.3	154.5	−42	93.3	104.8	85.5	24	Bonds
1930	119.4	119.8	125.4	−34		108.8	91.1	17	Bonds
1931	108.7	94.7	87.1	−18		92.8	85.4	24	Bonds
1932	97.6	48.6	49.8	12		88.9	91.1	−5	Stocks

Column 1. The cost of living figures are those of the Bureau of Labor Statistics with a 1935–1939 base. The 1950 figure is that of September. For the years before 1913 the cost of living figures of the New York Federal Reserve Bank have been adjusted for use. Sources are the 1949 *Statistical Abstract*, p. 308 and *Historical Statistics*, p. 235.

Column 2. The common stock index was taken from *Historical Statistics*, p. 281 for as far as 1937. From then until the present the figures were drawn from the *Statistical Abstract* for 1949, p. 482 and the *Survey of Current Business*. The figures since 1937, representing 416 common stocks, had to be adjusted to fit the earlier series.

Column 3. The real value index is simply an attempt to reduce stock values to a common dollar value, the dollar of 1935–1939. It was obtained by dividing the common stock index by the cost of living index, i.e., Column 2 by Column 1.

Column 4. The per cent of gain or loss after 10 years is obtained by comparing the real value of stocks in each year with their real value 10 years later. For example, stocks had a real value of 84.8 in 1900 and of 109.1 in 1910. That meant that the person who invested in 1900 and held until 1910 realized a 28% gain. The 1901 investor, however, realized only a 1% gain, etc.

Column 5. The 15 top grade municipals of Standard and Poor were chosen to represent bond values, 1900 to 1929, because the data on government bonds were so fragmentary before 1919. Investors would more likely have invested in municipals or railroads then, anyway. Source: *Historical Statistics*, p. 281.

Column 6. The U. S. government bonds are 2 per cent of 1930 for the years 1900–1909 and are included purely for purposes of comparison with the municipals. For the years 1919 to the present they are the average of a number of issues, partially tax-exempt. The early figures are quoted in A. P. Andrew, *Statistics for the United States*, 1867–1909, p. 279. The later figures, 1919 on, come from *Historical Statistics*, p. 281 and the 1949 *Statistical Abstract*, p. 482 and the *Survey of Current Business*.

Column 7. The real value index for bonds is derived in the same manner as that for stocks. The bond figure was divided by the cost of living index, i.e., Column 5 or 6 by Column 1. Government bond figures were used from 1919 on.

Column 8. This is like Column 4. The real value of bonds is also compared over a 10-year period. Notice that both Columns 4 and 8 end in 1940, for 1941 cannot yet be compared with 1951.

Column 9. This tells which choice the investor should have made. It is derived by comparing Columns 4 and 8. In a few cases, the decision was close indeed, viz. 1905, 1909, 1936 and 1937.

TABLE 1. *Comparison of stocks and bonds for 10-year investment, 1900–1950 (Continued)*

Date	(1) Cost of living index	(2) Common stock index	(3) Stocks real value index	(4) % 10-year gain or loss (stocks)	(5) Standard & Poor 15 Municipals	(6) U.S. govt. bonds	(7) Bonds real value index	(8) % 10-year gain or loss	(9) Better choice for 10 years
1933	92.4	63.0	68.2	3		93.1	100.7	−19	Stocks
1934	95.7	72.4	75.7	−1		95.4	99.7	−20	Stocks
1935	98.1	78.3	79.8	12		99.5	101.4	−19	Stocks
1936	99.1	111.0	112.0	−15		101.3	102.2	−16	Stocks
1937	102.7	111.8	108.6	−33		100.9	98.2	−33.1	Stocks
1938	100.8	83.5	82.8	−15		102.5	101.7	−42	Stocks
1939	99.4	89.2	89.7	−13		105.2	105.8	−42	Stocks
1940	100.2	83.4	83.2	−3		107.2	106.9	−54	Stocks
1941	105.2	75.7	71.9			111.0	105.5		
1942	116.5	65.7	56.5			100.7	86.4		
1943	123.6	87.0	70.4			100.5	81.3		
1944	125.5	94.5	75.3			100.3	79.9		
1945	128.4	115.0	89.6			102.0	79.4		
1946	139.3	132.5	95.1			104.8	75.2		
1947	159.2	116.5	73.2			103.8	65.2		
1948	171.2	117.8	68.8			100.8	58.8		
1949	169.1	114.9	67.9			103.3	61.8		
1950	173.0	139.4	80.7			102.8	59.4		

See preceding page for explanation of column head numbers.

stock investment even more. Standard and Poor's records and Historical Statistics show that the discrepancy in yields between stocks and bonds, on a 10-year running average basis, ranged from 0.8% to about 3% recently in favor of stocks. In all but two or three years there was at least a 1% yield discrepancy, usually more. Thus we may assume that whenever the difference in the value of the principal between stocks and bonds was not over 10%, actually the stock investment was preferable.

What definite conclusions may we draw from all these calculations? Which investment was the better, on the whole? In 35 years of the 41 an investment in stocks was preferable. In only 6 of the 41 years were bonds preferable. These all fall between 1922 and 1931: bonds paid off in the depression decade. As mentioned above, table 1 strongly indicates that the next few years will also prove stocks were the better choice in 1941, 1942, 1943, etc., because we have had considerable inflation in the last decade and may anticipate more. From all this it might be gathered that if the next half century is at all like the past half century, the long-time investor, say the 10-year investor, would be well advised to put most of his savings in common stocks rather than in bonds. If he is a formula investor, he should choose a formula in which the proportion invested in stocks is considerably greater than that invested in bonds. He should, of course, always keep some funds in bonds or cash because stocks are more volatile than bonds and more time is needed to sell them to best advantage on the market. Also if the investor is in a high income bracket, he may lean more strongly toward tax-exempt bonds. But every investor, whether small or large, formula or non-formula, should be primarily concerned with protecting his principal.

The cynic may remark that this experiment proves chiefly that 10-year investments are dangerous. Perhaps so. Will the amateur investor do better over a shorter period of time in a market that is generally rigged against him from the viewpoint of the purchasing power of the dollar? Let us examine Columns 3 and 7. If he sold out and re-invested every five years over this 51 years he would have gained in 22 five-year periods and lost in 24. On bonds he would have gained in 18 and lost in 28. And in 13 of the 18 periods that he gained in bonds, he could have gained in stocks too and more handsomely. If he did the same thing every year, instead of every 10 or 5 years, he would have gained in 27 years by investing in stocks and lost in 23. With bonds he would have gained in only 20 and lost in 29. Stocks appear to be the better long run investment. Bonds show up to less advantage over shorter periods. This is what we should expect, theoretically, in a rising price level economy. But it is contrary to popular belief or at least to popular behavior. People are more inclined to lay away their bonds and to buy stocks when they have extra funds and sell them when they need extra funds. They would be wiser to do just the opposite.

WHAT ARE THE TRENDS OF THE FUTURE?

Will the future half century be reasonably similar to the past half century? What do recent business experiences and economic trends suggest? With mounting armament costs and possible war ahead, taxes are bound to rise. Total taxes now take about 30% of the national income as compared to 6% in 1900. In view of the immediate prospects and of the long-term trends, corporate profits after taxes may well decline. That may reduce stock yields and retard the rise of stock prices. We must remember, however, that rising taxes and inflation have generally gone hand-in-hand in our financial history because when we face major national emergencies, both taxation and inflation have always been used to pay the government's bills. It is reasonable to conclude, therefore, that if there are sharply rising taxes ahead, there is also inflation ahead. Bonds will then still be a poorer investment than stocks.

Perhaps in the future the yield of stocks will fall to a level nearer that of bonds, especially if more people decide to buy stocks. That seems quite possible. Industrial stocks were barely on the threshold of respectability in 1900. Many are now quite respectable and if they seem safer as well, they may be sought after in increasing quantities. In that event stocks may be the better buy most of the time as they were in the last half century.

The future also is likely to see more and more regulation of business. The past half-century has witnessed fairly close regulation of the public utility industries and closer regulation of railroads. In only 6 of the 29 years since 1921 has the net operating railroad income of the best railroads (Class I) amounted to 5% of their net property investments, and in only one year has it reached 6%, which was assumed in 1920 to be a fair return. This suggests that regulatory bodies are inclined to be strict in setting rates, and that regulated industries as a rule cannot expect very generous profits. The years ahead may well see other heavy industries, like steel, aluminum, copper, cement, autos, electric appliances and some chemicals, subjected to regulation. It may be alleged that these industries are "monopolistic" or are "affected with a public interest" or are "necessary to the national defense." Such a trend would probably affect the profitability of these industries just as it has limited the profits of most railroads.

Industries likewise are faced more and more with labor problems. About 1900 the unions were strongest in industries that were competitive like cigar-making. They tended to be weakest in industries that were monopolistic like iron and steel manufacturing. But the strength of the unions grew steadily and since the mid-1930's (if not before) there have been repeated clashes of giant unions and giant industries and the unions have generally triumphed. The strength of unions is likely to grow in a democracy because of the voting power of their membership. Union demands can reduce profits or threaten to price goods out of the market. Strong unions have virtually driven the textile industry out of New England. For fear of unions some investors have tried to select stocks of companies whose labor costs are only a small part of the total cost. Such companies are likely to be found in the tobacco, drug, food, beverage, chemical, utility and oil industries.

Finally, even if we do not have a war, we seem to be committed for some time to a "low interest rate" policy because of our immense national debt. In everyday language that means that the Treasury will use its influence to make credit plentiful to keep interest rates low in order to keep down the service on the government debt. They may also follow that policy in order to stimulate prosperity. Making credit cheap, however, stimulates borrowing, creates money, and produces creeping inflation. As more persons realize that under such conditions there is greater safety in stocks and choose to invest in them, their price is likely to rise. But as yet the real value of stocks is not high, as a glance at Column 4 of the table will show. Stocks' real value was higher during most of the depressed 1930's than it is today.

HOW TO GET DIVERSIFICATION IN STOCKS

The careful investor has by this time framed at least one important query. "If I want to buy a bond and be sure to get my money back, I can buy a government bond, but how can I get such long-time safety in stocks? It is impractical for me to buy all the 416 stocks on the list that you have used in your experiment for the 1900–1950 period." That is not difficult at all, and is certainly less so than it would have been in 1900. If you have a fairly large sum to invest, you can get adequate diversification yourself. You would do well, of course, to consult an investment counselor. If your funds are modest, diversification can be achieved by buying the shares of good investment trusts or of duPont or of leading fire insurance companies. The holdings of all these are widely diversified.

CONCLUSION

In summary, for long-time investment, say 10 years, a diversified list of stocks has proven better than government bonds during the past half century if the main concern is to preserve the purchasing power of the principal. In 35 of the 41 10-year periods, 1900–1950, stocks would have been better. Stocks will probably be better for the next few years. We cannot be sure that this will be as true for the next half century because industries probably face higher taxes, labor troubles, and more regulation as well as further inflation. Still, as long as rising prices seem likely, and they do, diversified stocks appear the better long-term investment.

Price-Level Variations and the Tenets of High-Grade Investment*

John C. Clendenin

The topic assigned to us for discussion at this meeting clearly implies that there may be price-level variations in this country in the future and that they may be of sufficient moment to require appropriate investment policies. It would therefore be reasonable to debate either the outlook for price levels over the longer term or the nature of conservative investment policies which would best meet the probable situation. However, it has been officially suggested to me that we might focus attention on the suitability of common stocks, especially the variety known as "growth stocks," as high-grade investment vehicles in a period of price-level instability. This is my purpose; and in discussing stocks I shall mean those of competitive industrial and commercial companies only.

Although it is not my intention to involve this meeting in attempts to predict the long-range economic future of the country, it seems idle to discuss investment dispositions without noting the general nature of the situations for which we must be prepared. Obviously, we would not all agree on the details of the economic road ahead, but I suspect that most of us expect a continuation of welfare-minded monetary and public budget interventionism, major emphasis on full-employment objectives, a secondary hope for price stability and a balanced budget, large-scale public expenditures, and extensive research and development efforts by both public and private agencies. Conceding that all quantitative estimates must be liberally sprinkled with plus-and-minus signs, it would appear that a middle of-the-road investment planner might reasonably visualize the coming decade as follows:

1. General characteristics of high-level and growing output, moderate cycles of buoyancy and recession greatly influenced by monetary and public budget

*From the *Journal of Finance*, **14**, no. 2, May 1959, pp. 245–262. Back numbers obtainable from the Kraus Reprint Corporation. The Bureau of Business and Economic Research, University of California, Los Angeles, assisted . . . [John C. Clendenin] in data collection, computations, and in other ways.

manipulation, long-term money rates swinging widely in and about the 1958 range, and an intermittent price-level inflation averaging about 1 per cent per annum, firmly underwritten by habitual cost-push pressures.

2. *Possibility* of occasional short booms or depressions which may make sharp temporary impression on the stock market but relatively little permanent impression on either commodity or stock-market price trends.

3. Rapid technological and competitive change, in which products and enterprises are capable of great development or obsolescence in short time.

4. Continuation of heavy taxes.

5. Possibility of war, which would surely distort profit results and dividend rates temporarily and the price level permanently.

The foregoing propositions definitely do not imply that conventional fixed-dollar-amount investments are about to become obsolete or unproductive. On the contrary, they assume that high-grade bond yields of $3\frac{1}{2}$–5 per cent will clearly exceed an inflation-born loss of 1 per cent per year on the principal, even after allowing for the attrition of taxes. The 1 per cent per year inflationary trend is a guess based on evidences of increasing financial sobriety in Washington and relatively greater desire to couple price stability with full employment. If this hopeful projection works out, tax-paying investors may continue to use taxable senior securities and obtain at least a small amount of real net income from them.

Yet the fact remains that inflationary trends impair the real-income productivity of fixed-income investment, while presumably not adversely affecting typically diversified equity positions. Furthermore, public intervention to prevent recession or depression would appear to be a potent insurer of the safety and stability of a diversified equity position. If these things be true, then there may be occasion to indorse the principle of common-stock investment for conservative funds and even to advocate adapting some of our traditional institutions to make better use of common stocks.

At this point we begin to encounter some arguable questions of fact. The first of these is: After a quarter-century of mounting taxes, labor law, and government intervention in business, do the common stocks of leading corporations retain their profitableness and sturdiness and general good prospects?

EVIDENCE ON QUALITY

Since evidence on the trend of stock quality provides only relative data, it is desirable to recall at the outset some of the well-known absolute findings of prior decades. Most famous of these is Edgar L. Smith's *Common Stocks as Long-Term Investments*, which compares the performances of hypothetical good-quality common-stock and bond portfolios over 17- to 22-year spans in the period 1866–1922. The results, you will recall, strongly favored the stock portfolios. Many subsequent studies point, on balance, to the same conclusion, especially in periods when the general trend of commodity prices is level or upward.[1] The first concern of the present inquiry is, therefore, to ascertain whether the corporate strength which made these records

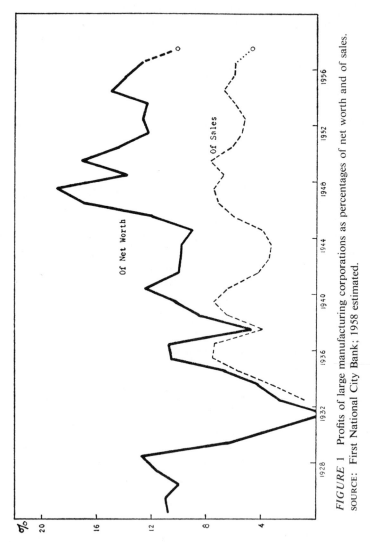

FIGURE 1 Profits of large manufacturing corporations as percentages of net worth and of sales.

SOURCE: First National City Bank; 1958 estimated.

[1]E. L. Smith, *Common Stocks as Long Term Investments* (New York: Macmillan Co., 1924); C. C. Bosland, *Common Stock Investment* (New York: Ronald Press Co., 1937); K. S. van Strum, *Investing in Purchasing Power* (New York: Barron's, 1926); D. C. Rose, *A Scientific Approach to Investment Management* (New York: Harper & Bros., 1928); W. J. Eiteman and F. P. Smith, *Common Stock Values and Yields* (Ann Arbor: University of Michigan Press, 1953); W. C. Greenough, *A New Approach to Retirement Income* (T.I.A.A., 1951); P. L. Howell, "Common Stocks and Pension Fund Investing," *Harvard Business Review*, November–December, 1958.

possible is still with us. Pertinent evidence is afforded in the accompanying Figures 1–3.

Figure 1 reports in line-graph form the net-profit results of leading manufacturing corporations since 1926. The upper line shows profits as a percentage of net worth, the lower one profits as a percentage of sales. These figures are collected by the First National City Bank of New York, mostly by adding figures available in published annual reports. Only large and fairly large concerns are included, and the list of corporations is obviously not uniform through the years, though the large number included— about 1,800 in recent years—gives the series impressive validity. The significant facts to be drawn from Figure 1 are these: First, the percentages earned on net worth in 1953–57 are as good as, or a little better than, those earned in profitable periods in the past—for example, 1940–41, 1936–37, and 1926–29. Labor costs and the corporate income tax have not eroded earning capacity here. Second, there appears to have been a slight decline in the percentage of net profit to the sales of these companies; 1953–57 is a

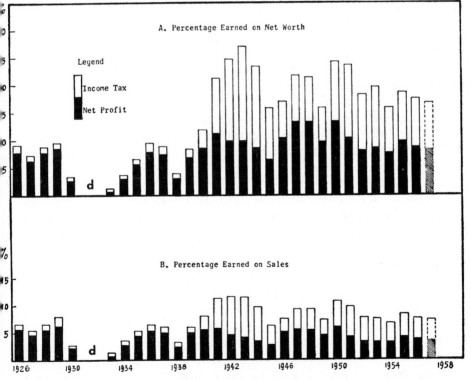

FIGURE 2 Profits of all American manufacturing corporations as percentages of net worth and of sales. SOURCE: Statistics of Income; 1957 estimated.

little below 1940–41, and the latter is, in turn, a little below 1936–37. The disparity between the two trends shown on the chart obviously reflects an increase in the ratio of sales to net worth. Economic logic suggests that the earnings rate on net worth has been a dominant criterion in competitive pricing decisions and that the profit percentage on sales has been cut because a lower percentage would still permit a generous return on invested capital.

Figure 2 presents data drawn from *Statistics of Income*, as compiled by the Internal Revenue Service. The year 1957 is estimated. The bars represent the percentages earned by all manufacturing corporations in the country on their book net worths and sales, before and after income taxes. The pretax earnings are shown by the total heights of the bars, the posttax net by the solid portions. It will be noted that the net profit margins earned by manufacturing corporations in the aggregate are not nearly so large as those earned by the large corporations canvassed in the First National City series but that the trends over time are similar. The earnings rates on net worth are firmly maintained, while those on sales have declined since the war. However, this chart has two more significant messages. First, it is clear that the heavy corporate income taxes imposed during the last 25 years—as represented on the chart by the unshaded segments at the tops of the bars—have been paid by widening the pretax profit margin, presumably at the expense of the consumer, and not by impairing the stockholders' profit margins on net worth. Second, it appears that the pretax profit margins on sales—as shown by the total height of the sales percentage bars —are actually a little larger in recent years than they were in the 1920's and 1930's. There is thus a little wider margin of safety between normal operations and red-ink deficits than we had before income taxes climbed to their present levels.

Figure 3 is similar to Figure 2, except that it presents the combined record of all American trade corporations instead of manufacturing concerns. The trends are very similar, though it is apparent that the profit margins of trade corporations are not so high as those of manufacturers. It will also be noted that economic conditions plus inventory and depreciation accounting methods produced almost fantastic profit records for trade corporations in the years 1946–50. These are clearly abnormal and are as little descriptive of earnings trends as are the war years or the years 1931–34.

But reference to depreciation accounting and inventory accounting methods suggests that other accounting devices may be distorting Figures 2 and 3. What of the undervaluation of prewar fixed assets and the consequent understatement of net worth? What of accelerated amortization? Time does not permit an extended review here, but it is possible to cite a study by the Machinery and Allied Products Institute in which a careful

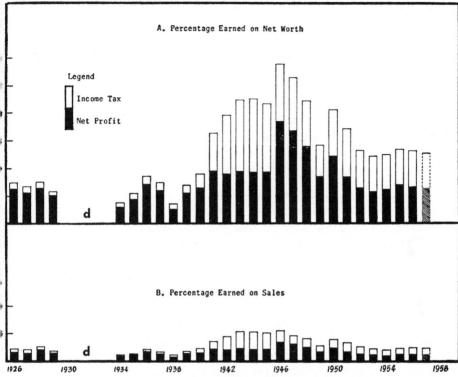

FIGURE 3   Profits of all American retail and wholesale trade corporations as percentages of net worth and of sales. SOURCE: Statistics of Income; 1957 estimated.

attempt is made to measure the ratio of corrected earnings to corrected net worth, the corrections being designed to state both earnings and net worth on an economic replacement-cost basis for each year. The MAPI results indicate that, on a corrected basis, the net profits of all American corporations in 1923–29 and in 1947–56 averaged almost the same percentage on net worth, about 5⅔ per cent.[2] The profit level thus defined is appreciably lower than that shown in Figures 1, 2, and 3; this appears to result both from the revision of profit and net worth figures and from the inclusion of all corporations, especially financial and transportation, in the data—but the absence of any downward trend in the ratio of net earnings to net worth is notable here also.

The data on profit margins thus support the proposition that corporations are retaining their financial strength rather well. Most other aspects of corporate finance corroborate this finding. For example, operating

[2]George Terborgh, *Corporate Profit in the Decade* 1947–56 (New York: Machinery & Allied Products Institute, 1957).

losses seem to be less frequent; in the years 1926–29 corporations operating at a loss had 18 per cent of the gross sales of all corporations in the nation, and their losses amounted to 17 per cent of the pretax earnings of the profitable corporations; but in 1952–56 the losers' sales were less than 10 per cent of the total and their losses less than 6 per cent of the others' profits. Other measures show manufacturers' net worth to be about 65 per cent of total assets in 1956 as compared to 75 per cent in 1928, but the working capital position is about the same and times interest earned coverage and cash flow are substantially improved.

STOCKS AS A PRICE-LEVEL HEDGE

A second issue of fact which must be noted is the matter of the effectiveness of common stocks as price-level hedges or counterweights. This has been so interminably discussed that one must apologize for raising it—yet this problem is the real reason for the topic we are discussing.

It must be conceded at the outset that public policy, expressed in such media as price controls, excess-profits taxes, credit controls, or public competition with private enterprise, could be the definitive answer to the question at hand. Such public policy has been the answer in certain foreign countries and was partly so in this country during our periods of price controls and excess-profits taxes. However, it seems reasonable to assume that the political hazards to capital in the United States are no greater now than they were in the 1930's. It is therefore pertinent to look at the historical data of the period 1926–57 for generalized indications of the impact of the price level on common-stock investment performance.

Figure 4 presents a 32-year study of the earnings per share and the dividends per share applicable to the Standard and Poor's 50-Stock Industrial Stock Price Index. This index is used because its component stocks are those of large companies, mostly good-quality issues of the type considered for long-term investment. The earnings and dividend figures on the chart have been divided through by the GNP deflator index in order to show the data in terms of the prices which presumably affect them.

Inspection of Figure 4 brings out clearly four significant points: (1) Over a span of 32 years the earnings and dividends available on a portfolio of good-grade big-company stocks have risen more than the price level. Their net upward trend has averaged between $1\frac{1}{2}$ and 2 per cent per year, compounded. (2) In periods of price-level gain, the earnings may lag behind the price-level upswings, and the dividends will definitely lag behind the earnings. This observation is not too clear on the chart because of the complications of depression, war, controls, and taxes, but financial common sense adds credence to the rough indications. (3) Depressions, wars, price

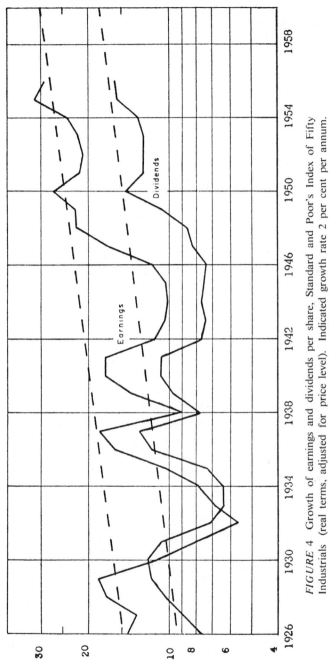

FIGURE 4 Growth of earnings and dividends per share, Standard and Poor's Index of Fifty Industrials (real terms, adjusted for price level). Indicated growth rate 2 per cent per annum.

controls, and excess-profits taxes are contingencies which may depress per share earnings and dividends for considerable periods, at least in terms of purchasing power; and the chart does not show compensating long periods of very large earnings. (4) The data on this chart are of dubious quality in certain years, notably 1947–50, when strong earnings data are in part the product of non-economic inventory and depreciation accounting methods.

The major indication of Figure 4 is, obviously, the finding that the earnings and dividends on this group of industrials over a generation have outclimbed price-level growth and gained an average of nearly 2 per cent per year in real purchasing power. This, of course, means a substantial capital gain in addition to the mounting tide of dividend income. However, it should be noted that the dividend income itself fell by half during the great depression, and, after recovering in part, declined again during the war. It was not until 1947 that the dollar level of dividend payments permanently surpassed the 1927–29 payments. During the interim, the stockholders got less than a fixed-income investment purchased in the 1920's would have brought them and, in addition, had to bear a painful, if temporary, shrinkage in stock prices. This could happen again.

Figure 5 is in all respects similar to Figure 4, except that it shows only dividend records, not earnings, and compares the performances of a list of 9 growth stocks and 10 non-growth stocks. Data for certain abnormal depression and war years are not shown. This chart has been constructed with the advantage of hindsight; it was prepared in order to compare *ex post facto* the performance of typical high-grade growth stocks with that of high-grade non-growth stocks. The upper line shows the record of the non-growth stocks; their dividends declined less than the price level during the depression years but failed by far to keep pace during the war and early postwar years. By 1948, the buying-power level of the 1920's had been regained, and these stocks have since increased their dividends enough to compensate for further increases in the price level, though they have not made up the deficiencies of 1940–48. *They have at no time shown net real-income growth, despite the fact that undistributed profits have been reinvested in the businesses in most years over more than three decades!*

The lower line on Figure 5 shows the record of 9 major growth stocks. Over a 32-year term, these stocks have increased their earnings and dividends *in real terms* by an average of about 3 per cent per annum. Their depression-time payments declined below the 1920's in dollars but not in purchasing power, but at no time since has a significant shrinkage occurred. Obviously, the capital appreciation on these stocks has been very great. Whether their growth can continue or whether investors seeking to enjoy such growth in the future can select stocks capable of this performance are open questions.

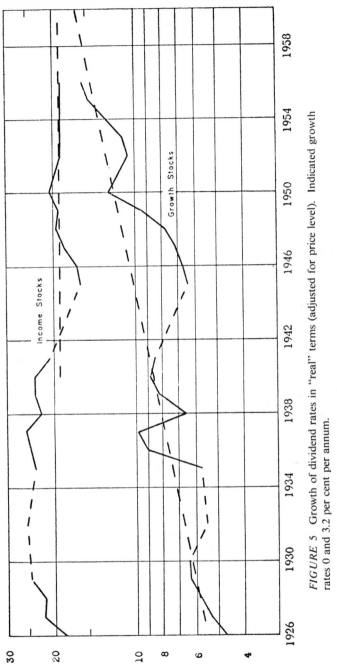

FIGURE 5 Growth of dividend rates in "real" terms (adjusted for price level). Indicated growth rates 0 and 3.2 per cent per annum.

However, one thing is pretty obvious; the average rise of $1\frac{1}{2}$–2 per cent per year *in real terms* shown by the dividends on the Standard and Poor's 50-stock average must be ascribed to the fact that the average contains an assortment of growth and non-growth stocks. The growth stocks have supplied the vital thrust which makes industrial stocks per se appear to outpace an advancing price level. The ten high-grade non-growth stocks depicted on Figure 5 have caught up, on the average, but the laggards among them have not; and we all know that there are many lesser stocks and lagging industries which were once vigorous leaders.[3]

Generalizations at this point are perhaps gratuitous, but the facts suggest that a strong and smartly selected industrial stock portfolio might reasonably be expected to advance its dividend production, earnings, and capital values a little faster than the price level advances, even though earnings and dividend production may be somewhat irregular and prone to gaps. Capital appreciation accompanying earnings and dividend growth will in a sense compensate for inadequate dividends during inclement economic periods. However, our economy is subject to political, technological, and economic change. These are forces which can interrupt income and reverse trends, at least so far as individual corporations and industries are concerned. It is therefore reasonable to inquire whether, over a period of diverse economic trends, reasonably competent investment managements have been able to avail themselves in full measure of the opportunities which seem to be available.

SOME PERFORMANCE RECORDS

For a hasty test of the results of actual common-stock portfolios, the records of major open-end investment companies are most readily available. Accordingly, Table 1 presents some investment company performance data, with performance conventionally measured as the percentage excess of this year's closing asset value plus this year's dividend over last year's closing asset value.

For present purposes, the lessons of Table 1 are two in number. First, the common-stock investment companies do not usually surpass the performance of the market averages. True, they bear a measurable handicap in the form of operating expenses, an unproductive cash position, and a compulsion to diversify, but the fact is that their net performance often does not quite equal that of the averages, despite an enviable opportunity. The only reasonable conclusion is that the imponderables in individual stock situations are so great that good work in times like these parallels the averages, assures against falling far below them, but does not

---

[3] Cf. E. S. Mead and Julius Grodinsky, *The Ebb and Flow of Investment Values* (New York: Appleton-Century, 1939).

TABLE 1. *Performance records of common-stock funds and certain indexes**

	1948	1949	1953	1954	1956	1957	Average 1948– 1957	Average 1940– 1957
S & P 50 Industrial	6	17	− 2	56	7	−11	18	14
S & P 20 Utilities	6	31	8	24	5	6	8	12
S & P 20 Rails	4	8	−12	57	− 3	−28	11	13
S & P 90 Stocks	6	18	− 1	51	7	−10	17	14
General-Purpose Fund No. 1	0	22	2	31	5	0	12	14
General-Purpose Fund No. 2	−1	17	2	43	9	− 4	15	14
General-Purpose Fund No. 3	1	18	0	37	7	− 5	13	11
General-Purpose Fund No. 4	2	19	− 3	52	13	−14	15	14
General-Purpose Fund No. 5	−2	19	− 5	58	12	−22	16	15
General-Purpose Fund No. 6	1	20	0	51	11	−11	16	13
Growth Fund No. 1	−1	16	− 1	48	10	−12	13	NA
Growth Fund No. 2	1	18	− 3	55	19	−12	17	14
Growth Fund No. 3	4	22	− 1	34	8	−12	13	12
Growth Fund No. 4	−3	16	1	63	14	−15	16	NA
Consumer Price Index per cent increase plus 5 per cent	8	3	5	4	7	7	7	10

*Performance = (Asset value end of year + dividend during year) ÷ asset value end of prior year, minus 100 per cent.

far exceed them. The great similarity in the performance of different funds lends credence to this view. The second lesson from Table 1 has to do with investment objectives. Six of the funds in the table announce as objectives the obtaining of income and appreciation. The other four announce that appreciation is their primary objective, with income incidental. The total performance of the two groups is almost identical. Granted that each group is compelled to diversification and that the income-and-appreciation group will seek appreciation avidly when they see a chance to get it, the record still says that stock-market forecasting is an imperfect art and that a competent and conservative analyst will not dependably improve his total score by stressing a search for market gains.

As a further test of the thesis that foresight is a scarce commodity,

Table 2 lists the performance records of 22 stocks which constituted the largest stockholdings of one of our major investment companies in 1946 and 1947. These stocks were not all held throughout both years, but most of them were. Unquestionably the poorer performers among these stocks were bought and held in the expectation of good results in each individual case, and beyond doubt a larger quantity of the more successful holdings could have been carried had their success been anticipated. The table looks at first glance as though the selections were made by guess. However, this is a successful fund, whose total performance ranks high and whose management is deemed astute. Table 2 does not record good and bad luck; it records the process by which good results are achieved with reasonable certainty in a very unstable area.

These last two exhibits seem to justify the conclusion that secure and dependable results with common stocks require both selection and diversification. The very high probability of successful workout which characterizes individual good bonds apparently does not exist to the same extent in stocks, and a diversified position which balances fortuitous gains against unforeseeable losses is an indispensable procedure in a conservative stock account.[4]

SOME OBSERVATIONS ON PRICE

The final point of statistical inquiry before us has to do with price. Stocks are non-reproducible goods; they provide a somewhat irregular income and have no maturity date; the eagerness with which the community desires them varies with popular thought and with the political and economic climate; and the demand for them is also affected by the incomes of stock-buying individuals and institutions and the other uses such buyers have for their money. Even in the absence of emergency conditions, stock prices are stubbornly variable; during the middle 1920's stock yields were very close to those of high-grade bonds; in the late 1940's stocks yielded almost twice as much as bonds; and now they yield considerably less than bonds. There is thus no stable and enduring yield basis for stock valuation, yet the absence of maturity places extreme emphasis on capitalization rate in arriving at a value estimate. It is probably inherent in the nature of things that stock prices and price-earnings ratios and yields should move through wide ranges both at short term and over long but irregular cycles.

The quantitative extent of these price cycles is normally not great enough to do unbearable damage to well-diversified common-stock positions which can be held for long periods, particularly if accumulation

---

[4]For bond performance see W. B. Hickman, *Corporate Bond Quality and Investor Experience* (New York: NBER, 1958).

TABLE 2. *Performance records of leading stocks held by fund portfolio in 1946–47**

Stock	1946	1947	1948	Average 1948–1952	Average 1953–1957
Allied Chemical	10	9	6	15	8
Atchison T. & S.F.	12	− 11	37	26	12
Amerada	17	19	21	40	7
Chrysler	− 4	6	13	20	5
du Pont	16	− 1	1	21	22
Eastman Kodak	19	2	− 6	10	25
General Electric	1	− 12	8	17	32
General Motors	− 5	0	5	27	24
Gulf Oil	25	4	8	15	31
Int'l Harvester	− 2	3	15	11	6
Loew's	11	− 27	− 18	1	9
Montgomery Ward	33	− 18	4	7	9
J. C. Penney	20	− 8	7	15	8
Sears, Roebuck	20	− 15	19	17	12
Standard Oil, N. J.	17	8	18	28	24
Southern Pacific	15	− 14	36	25	4
Texas Company	13	7	4	22	25
20th Century-Fox	43	− 30	− 25	− 2	22
American Telephone	6	5	0	6	7
Commonwealth Edison	8	43	− 3	8	12
Swift & Company	8	1	2	6	9
Liggett & Myers	8	2	5	1	6
Consumer Price Index per cent increase + 5 per cent	25	14	8	7	6

*Performance = (Median price in stated year + dividend of stated year) ÷ median price of prior year, minus 100 per cent.

and liquidation can be advantageously timed or spread over a span of years. This is demonstrated by the studies previously cited. However, we must admit that a wide potential range of stock prices makes an accurate projection of medium-term investment performance almost impossible. Five or even ten years' income plus growth could be heavily impaired by adverse stock-price trends or by adverse liquidating prices. This is not a contingency to be lightly regarded, even in an inflationary era, by any portfolio which must make large distributions or stand ready to do so.[5]

The problem of price may be illustrated by current figures. The immediate dividend yields on the Standard and Poor's 50 stock index, my growth stock index, and my non-growth stock index approximate 3.5 per

[5]W. A. Berridge, "Economic Facts Bearing on Some Variable Annuity Arguments," *Journal of Insurance*, November, 1957.

cent, 2.9 per cent, and 4.5 per cent, respectively. If we make allowance for continued growth and 1 per cent per year of inflation over the next 20 years and assume indefinite retention of holdings, the dividends on each of these groups should over 70 or 80 years amortize today's dollar cost and provide an average income yield of about 5 per cent. But 5 per cent is not an attractive long-term total return by past standards, and principal invested at this level is clearly subject to drastic impairment if the markets revert to a more conservative yield basis.

It is difficult to escape the conclusion that industrial stocks are suitable for conservative investment when the object is the purchase of a very long-term annuity which needs to compensate for price level changes, but that stocks may be troublesome if the portfolio is subject to market-value solvency tests or liquidation.

TENETS OF INVESTMENT IN STOCKS

This cursory review of fact and fancy has been intended to serve as justification for a statement of "The Tenets of High-Grade Investment" in a period of buoyant price levels. A tenet is a principle or a doctrine and, as such, may state either a fact or a way of life. This review has not covered all phases of investment activity, hence will not attempt to phrase a whole creed of investment, but the following tenets certainly would seem to belong in the creed:

1. The corporate institution is as sturdy and vigorous as it was 30 years ago, and a managed cross-section of the better common-stock equities may be regarded as productive and safe for the very long term.

2. Diversification is indispensable.

3. Both stable-income and growth industrial company stocks seem to earn and pay more dollars after an inflation takes place, but decadent industries or companies may not do so.

4. Price-level protection in an era in which the cost of living may rise drastically justifies the investment of relatively large amounts in stocks, by individuals and by institutions whose liabilities may have to be discharged in future years in large amounts of depreciated dollars.

5. Common-stock dividends, earnings, and prices may decline or lag during depressions, wars, periods of price control, and periods of rapid inflation.

6. Extensive common-stock price fluctuations appear likely in the foreseeable future. This seems to require that accounts subject to continuous dollar-value solvency tests or demand withdrawals use stocks only in modest degree and that those partially obligated make provision for liquid payment-reserve funds, deferred payments, or other ameliorative devices.

7. Finally, it is necessary to admit that we are without any effective capacity to estimate "normal" future prices for stocks or stock groups, even if we believe that we can "guesstimate" their probable future earnings and dividends. We have the price-earnings and yield data of the past, but these are not good benchmarks

for judging stock prices in an era when both individuals and institutions fear the value of the dollar and are becoming increasingly uninhibited in their investment policies.

A CONCLUDING DIGRESSION

The foregoing are conventional and unsurprising conclusions. They assume mainly a continuation of existing economic trends and no major institutional changes. However, we are not exempt from rather significant institutional changes which may come about as much because of popular beliefs and fears as because of solid economic fact.

There is abroad among us the conviction that the cost of living will continue to trend upward, probably slowly but possibly rapidly. This has seemingly fostered a "flight into stocks" which has already developed stock-price repercussions and stock-price logic reminiscent of the unlamented New Era. Our new New Era has powerful institutional support in the investment company and the pension trust, among trusts and endowments generally, and may soon have the appealing variable annuity on a substantial scale. It is not unlikely that the entire situation may create a more or less permanent shift in the relative prices and immediate yields of stocks and bonds, with equal or lesser immediate yields on the stocks expected to be compensated by increases due to inflation and growth. This kind of stock-bond price relationship, with the stocks yielding less than bonds, already exists in the case of growth stocks.

No real business damage would of necessity result from this stock-bond pricing situation; financial practices could adjust to a case in which bond and mortgage rates remained above high-grade stock yields. Yet it would be unfortunate if, in hedging against an alleged inflationary drift, individuals and institutions were compelled to abandon too completely the security and liquidity of a senior and guaranteed position. It would be safer public policy to induce debtors and creditors to make some of their bond contracts on a purchasing-power basis, with the bond maturity sums and possibly the coupons adjusted up or down in proportion to changes in the price level. In fact, I am confident that several billions of long-term federal purchasing-power bonds could be sold over a few months' time to people and institutions who are now reluctantly turning to stocks, at an interest rate well below the market rate for straight bonds. Quite possibly the savings on interest rate would finance the excess payments required by our slow inflation. In any event, a successful step in this direction might help to solve several pressing economic needs,[6] including that of holding our second New Era stock market somewhere near the bounds of common sense.

[6]Nearly a third of the 11 million employees now covered by trusteed pension plans enjoy protective clauses which to some extent adjust pension expectations to final pay rates or similar measures. Many of the others obtain revisions of plan as economic elements change (see New York State Banking Department, *Pension and Other Employee Welfare Plans* [1955]).

Economic Growth
and Common-Stock Value*

Ezra Solomon

The rapid rise in industrial stock prices to their present level has intensified discussion, both public and private, regarding objective "norms" against which this rise can be evaluated. This study is an attempt to explore two questions that are relevant to this discussion. (1) What relation has there been, over the long-run, between the course of industrial stock prices and the underlying growth of the economy as measured by gross national production? (2) What guidance do these observed relations provide for an evaluation of the current level of the market?

No attempt to set "intrinsic" or "warranted" values for stock prices can avoid having predictive implications. It is necessary both to recognize these implications and also to recognize that they are valid only in an extremely limited sense. Results obtained from an analysis of relationships over many decades can provide a clue only regarding what *should* happen in the *long-run*. It is generally accepted that what *can* happen in *short-run* is a very different matter. The reason for the often violent deviations of market prices from "warranted" levels lies, of course, in the fact that a majority of traders do not use "warranted" values as a basis for buying and selling common stock. J. M. Keynes has a cynical, but useful, description of these market forces.[1]

... Professional investment may be likened to those newspaper competitions in which the competitors have to pick out the six prettiest faces from a hundred photographs, the prize being awarded to the competitor whose choice most nearly corresponds to the average preferences of the competitors as a whole; so that each competitor has to pick, not those faces which he himself finds prettiest, but those

*Reprinted from the *Journal of Business*, **28**, no. 3, July 1955, pp. 213–221 by Ezra Solomon by permission of the University of Chicago Press.

[1]J. M. Keynes, *The General Theory of Employment, Interest and Money* (London: Macmillan & Co., 1936), p. 156.

which he thinks likeliest to catch the fancy of the other competitors, all of whom are looking at the problem from the same point of view. It is not a case of choosing those which, to the best of one's judgment, are really the prettiest, nor even those which average opinion genuinely thinks the prettiest. We have reached the third degree where we devote our intelligences to anticipating what average opinion expects the average opinion to be. And there are some, I believe, who practice the fourth, fifth, and higher degrees.

However, in spite of this serious limitation on the short-run usefulness of objective analysis, both individual investment managers and national policy seem to require that some answer be assayed to the question, "Are common stock prices too high?" The only real alternative to finding objective criteria, no matter how limited their validity in the short-run, is to deny that the question makes any sense at all.[2]

THE USE OF GROWTH-TREND ANALYSIS

There are two broad approaches to the problem of setting warranted values. One approach is to reason in terms of factors which appear to be the immediate determinants of stock prices, like corporate sales and earnings, dividends and bond-yields. The second approach, and the one used in the present study, is concerned with longer-run behavior. Since trends in earnings, dividends, etc., are themselves a reflection of the trend in economic growth and national prosperity, it is feasible to use these underlying trends as a long-run guide to warranted values in the stock market.

This argument for the use of growth trends as a guide is a justifiable one.[3] However, the trend lines in actual use for this purpose have generally tended to ignore the fact that their validity depends upon their having a reasonable link with economic growth itself. In most cases, these trend lines have been established simply by fitting an appropriate curve to the long-term record of average market prices. One very popular example of these mechanistically fitted trends is a single geometric trend line based on a constant 3 per cent per annum growth rate since 1897. Arithmetic trend lines (equal annual changes) and trends based upon moving averages of stock prices have also been tried. Many of these have been used quite explicitly as a guide to investment timing decisions and as a basis for formula timing plans.[4]

These mechanistic approaches suffer from a number of serious shortcomings.

[2]See, for example, the testimony given by Mr. Bernard Baruch during the recent hearings on the stock market conducted by the Senate Banking and Currency Committee.

[3]For a general discussion of this point, see Hargraves Parkinson, *Ordinary Shares* (3d ed.; London: Eyre & Spottiswoode, 1949), chap. v.

[4]C. S. Cottle and W. T. Whitman, *Investment Timing—The Formula Plan Approach* (New York: McGraw-Hill Book Co., 1953); and Lucile Tomlinson, *Successful Investing Formulas* (New York: Barron's Publishing Co., Inc., 1947).

1. *The effect of two separate and easily separable factors are treated jointly.* The long-term rising trend in the price level of common stock is a result of two elements—a secular change in the purchasing power of the dollar, and a real growth in the underlying economic values which corporate stock represents. These two elements have different rates of change, and this fact should be recognized. Since it is reasonable to expect that over the long-run, changes in the purchasing power of the dollar will tend to be accompanied by a reciprocal change in the dollar value of industrial stocks, the impact of this factor can (and should) be isolated by means of a general price index.

2. *A single trend line is used.* The use of a single trend line for very long periods of time involves an implicit assumption that the pace of economic growth is a constant or that the rate of change in the general price level is constant or that the combined effect of these two changes is a constant. None of these assumptions is justifiable. In addition, the value of the single rate of growth selected will depend to an important extent on the particular time span chosen.[5] A more logical approach would be to use different growth trends for different periods on the basis of observable changes in the pace of underlying economic growth.

3. *The measures which are used for stock prices are not appropriate for long-term analysis.* The general concensus of statistical opinion is that the Standard & Poor's monthly index of 365 industrial stocks is the most suitable measure for the purpose of establishing stock price trends that are supposed to reflect the growth of the economy.[6] This index incorporates several features that the more popular "averages" do not have but which are essential for a good long-run measure. It contains a broad coverage of listed stocks; it is constructed on an index basis and thus allows for additions to be made to the number of stocks covered without affecting the continuity of the series; and it is weighted so as to reflect changes in the total market value of the stocks included. In spite of these facts, many of the trend lines in use are based upon the Dow-Jones and other "averages" of stock-prices.

ECONOMIC GROWTH AND STOCK PRICES

The empirical study below is an attempt to avoid these basic defects. Further refinements are no doubt possible, but these have not been explored. The basic data employed are (1) gross national product, (2) Standard & Poor's industrial stock price index, and (3) a general price index (first quarter, 1955 = 100). The study covers a seventy-five year period from the decade 1874–83 to the first quarter of 1955.

[5]Average annual growth rates of the Standard & Poor's stock price index for some of the typical periods used are:

1889–1919:	3.37 per cent
1889–1949:	3.12 per cent
1899–1949:	3.00 per cent
1909–49:	2.69 per cent
1919–49:	2.11 per cent

Cf. Cottle and Whitman, *op. cit.*, p. 103.

[6]Alfred Cowles and Associates, *Common Stock Indexes* (2d ed.; Bloomington, Ill.: Principia Press, Inc., 1939), pp. 1–40.

In order to isolate the effect of general changes in the purchasing power of the dollar, both the stock price series and the gross national product series have been converted to their constant dollar equivalents by means of the same price index.

GROWTH RATES

The converted series for gross national product (in constant 1955 dollars) is the most comprehensive measure we have for the real growth of the American economy. The pace of economic growth has clearly been subject to fairly large changes over the past seventy-five years. Between 1879 and 1939, there is a steady decline in the growth rate. This decline has been the subject of considerable discussion but has not been fully explained. One of the causal factors involved is the decline in the rate of population growth.[7] Since 1939, we have seen a return to more rapid growth rates. One obvious reason for the rapid increase since 1939 is the war time absorption of the large volume of unemployed resources in existence at that time. But at least two factors of a more fundamental nature have also been operative. One factor is the marked reversal in the rate of population increase. The other is the rapid postwar pace of technological development.

While it is easy enough to recognize these changes in the rate of economic growth, it is extremely difficult to make any exact division of the total period into sub-periods on the basis of changes in the growth rate. If the sub-periods are made too short, the underlying pattern of change in growth rates tends to become obscured by cyclical and random influences. On the other hand, a single-valued growth trend for the entire period ignores changes that clearly exist. Any solution to the problem has to involve the exercise of judgment as well as some recognition of the discontinuities that exist in the data themselves.

For the purpose of this study, two alternative classifications were made, both of which are defensible. One classification contains four sub-periods as follows: 1879–83 to 1909–13—4 per cent per annum; 1909–13 to 1929—3 per cent per annum; 1929 to 1939—0 per cent per annum; 1934–39 to 1955—4.8 per cent per annum. This approach treats the stagnation of the thirties as an underlying change that took place in the growth rate of the economy. An alternative approach is to treat this decade as a broad cyclical interruption of a basic growth trend that did not itself undergo any change. Using this approach, a second type of classification is possible as follows: 1879–83 to 1909–13—4 per cent per annum; 1909–13 to 1955—3 per cent per annum.

[7]See Simon Kuznets, "Long Term Changes in the National Income of the United States," International Association for Research in Income and Wealth, *Income and Wealth: Series II* (Cambridge: Bowes & Bowes, 1952), pp. 29–241.

TABLE 1.   Gross national product*

	Col. 1	Col. 2	Col. 3	Col. 4	Col. 5
Period	Current prices	Price index	In constant (1955) prices	Indicated rate of real growth	Indicated trend of real growth
1874–83	$ 9.0	$ 35.25	$ 25.6 ⎫		$25.6
1879–88	10.7	32.31	33.1 ⎪		31.1
1884–93	11.8	29.96	39.4 ⎪		37.7
1889–98	12.7	27.61	46.0 ⎪	4 per cent	45.9
1894–1903	15.9	28.20	56.4 ⎬	per annum	55.9
1899–1908	21.7	31.14	69.7 ⎪		68.0
1904–13	28.6	34.08	83.9 ⎪		82.7
1909–13	32.2	35.80	89.9 ⎭		89.9
1909–13	$ 35.8	$ 35.80	$100.0 ⎫		$100.0
1914–18	55.6	46.41	119.8 ⎪		115.9
1919–23	85.1	63.59	133.8 ⎪		134.4
1924	85.6	58.57	146.3 ⎪		146.9
1925	90.3	60.08	150.3 ⎪		151.3
1926	96.4	60.63	159.0 ⎪		155.8
1927	94.9	59.46	159.6 ⎪		160.5
1928	97.9	58.75	166.6 ⎬	3 per cent	165.3
1929	103.8	58.75	176.6 ⎪	per annum	170.2
1930–34	69.2	49.20	140.7 ⎪		186.0
1935–39	84.2	48.62	173.2 ⎪		215.6
1940–44	159.5	59.90	266.2 ⎪		250.0
1945–49	235.3	79.72	295.1 ⎪		289.8
1950–54	337.3	96.55	349.3 ⎪		336.0
1955	369.0†	100.00	369.0 ⎭		367.1

*Annual rates in billions of dollars.
†First quarter average.

SOURCES: Col. 1: 1929–55—Department of Commerce, *National Income Supplement: Survey of Current Business* (1953). 1909–29—J. Frederick Dewhurst and Associates, *America's Needs and Resources* (New York: Twentieth Century Fund, 1955), Appendix 4–2, pp. 958–60, based on data by Simon Kuznets. The basic series for 1909–29 differs statistically and conceptually from the 1929–55 series. These data have been spliced to the later data at 1929 in order to provide a continuous series. 1874–83 to 1909–13—Kuznets, *op. cit.*, pp. 30–32.

Col. 2: 1929–55—Department of Commerce, *Implicit Price Deflators for Gross National Product.* 1914–18 to 1929—Dewhurst, *op. cit.*, p. 959, based on U.S. Bureau of Labor Statistics, *Consumer Price Index.* 1874–83 to 1909–13—Kuznets, *op. cit.*, pp. 30–32.

As far as the conclusions of this particular study are concerned, both approaches yield almost identical results.[8] The tables and charts given

[8]The only significant difference in inferences based on these alternatives are for the period 1935–40.

in this paper report the data only on the basis of the second, and simple, classification.

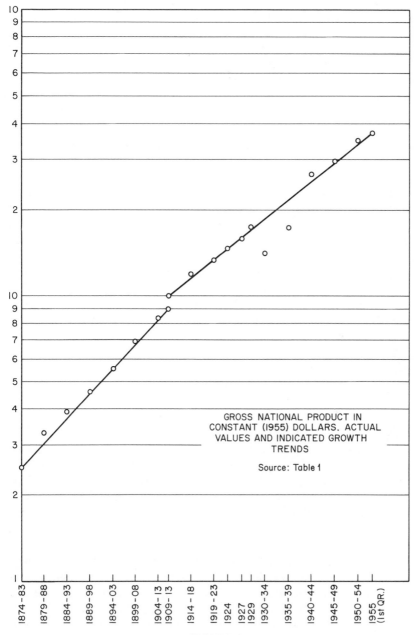

GROSS NATIONAL PRODUCT IN CONSTANT (1955) DOLLARS. ACTUAL VALUES AND INDICATED GROWTH TRENDS

Source: Table 1

FIGURE 1

Gross National Product and Stock Prices

It is reasonable to expect that changes in the real value of stocks (the stock index in constant dollars) would tend to reflect changes in real economic growth. However, the relation between the two rates of change is not a simple one. Rather, it is the overall result of many factors, none of which is easily measurable. Several of these factors operate in conflicting directions, and many of them are likely to have changed over time. These factors can be summarized in terms of two broad influences—one of which tends to alter the share of corporations in the national product and another which tends to alter the share of stockholders (as against other factors of production and the government) in corporate product.

The hypothesis used in this paper is that the joint result of these influences has tended to maintain rather than to change the long-run relationship between the rate of economic growth and the rate of increase in real stock values. The ratio between the rate of economic growth from 1879–83 to 1909–13 (4 per cent) and the rate of change in real stock values (2.667 per cent) is assumed to be a "normal" one that holds over the entire period to 1955. On this basis, it has been assumed that for any given period, the warranted rate of growth in the real value of stocks is equal to two-thirds of the indicated rate of growth in real gross national product. The data in column 2, Table 2, show warranted stock values computed on this basis alongside actual values.

FINDINGS

General

Over the seventy-five year period, the dollar-price of stocks has increased about 1200 per cent and the dollar-value of national product about 4000 per cent. A common cause of both of these increases is the approximate tripling of the general price level. Even if this price factor is removed, the increases are still phenomenal. Due to real growth alone, national product has increased about 1300 per cent and the real value of stocks about 400–500 per cent. Over the period as a whole, the real growth in stock values has proceeded at about two-thirds of the rate of the real growth in gross national product.

In general, stock prices respond only slowly to changes in the general price level and with a considerable lag. During periods of falling general prices, the sluggish response tends to keep real stock values higher relative to warranted values than they might otherwise be. During periods of rising general prices, the real value of stocks tends to fall behind warranted values and to keep lagging for fairly long stretches of time.

TABLE 2. *Industrial stock prices: Standard and Poor's index* (1935-39 = 100) *converted to constant* (1955) *dollars*

	Col. 1	Col. 2	Col. 3
Period	Actual	Warranted	Growth rates used in deriving (2)
1874–83	$ 56.3	$ 56.3	
1879–88	65.6	64.2	
1884–93	82.8	73.3	2.667 per cent per annum
1889–98	90.2	83.6	
1894–1903	98.9	95.4	
1899–1908	111.0	108.8	
1904–13	118.7	124.1	
1909–13	125.9	130.8	
1914–18	129.7	144.4	
1919–23	95.6	159.4	
1924	107.5	169.2	
1925	132.8	172.6	
1926	148.9	176.0	
1927	179.9	179.5	2 per cent per annum
1928	237.0	183.1	
1929	291.1	186.8	
1930–34	152.6	198.2	
1935–39	205.5	218.8	
1940–44	149.0	241.6	
1945–49	164.9	266.7	
1950–54	208.2	294.5	
1955	308.3*	312.5	

*First quarter average.

THE NINETEEN-TWENTIES

During the boom of the nineteen-twenties, stock prices (in constant dollars) climbed far above their warranted levels. During the early postwar period, stocks were far below their warranted level, due in part to their tendency to lag during a period of rising general prices. After 1923, there began a return toward warranted levels. By 1927, stocks were almost exactly in line with warranted levels. The subsequent boom carried stock prices far above these levels, and by the peak of the boom in 1929, stocks were almost twice as high as they should have been.

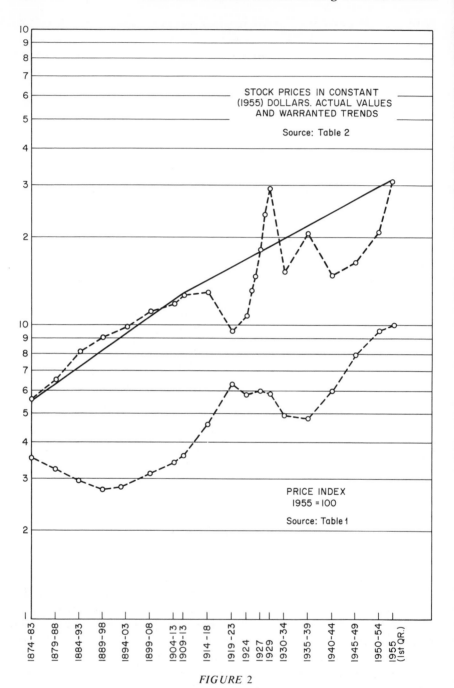

FIGURE 2

THE PRESENT

After 1939, the economy experienced a rapid increase in the rate of real economic growth and a rapid increase in the general price level. Stock values lagged far behind warranted values. After 1949, stock prices began a rise toward warranted values. With the rapid rise that occurred during 1954, stock prices are again at warranted levels. For 1955, the indicated level (in 1955 prices) of the Standard & Poor's index is 312.5. The actual average first quarter level of this index was 308.3.[9]

THE POSTWAR MARKET

According to the analysis above, and on the basis of economic growth alone, stock prices are just about "right." The market in early 1955 is closer to its warranted level than at any time since 1927.

In terms of long-term economic change, what we have experienced since 1939 is a rapid increase in the money supply followed by an upsweep both of the general price level and of real output. The level of corporate earnings, dividends, and current assets also increased to corresponding levels. However, until 1954, the stock market continued to reflect a basic disbelief in the permanence of these new levels; and common stock prices, though rising, lagged behind the level achieved by the rest of the economy. What we have witnessed in 1954 is a late but extremely rapid process of stock prices catching up with other factors in the economy.

The exact reasons for the change in investment attitudes in 1954 cannot of course be measured. But there are several factors worth noticing.

1. The seemingly long period for which stocks lagged does not appear to be unusual when examined either against past history or in the light of events and attitudes since 1946. After World War I, it took stock prices nine years to return to their warranted level. According to the present analysis, it has again taken this long.

2. The refusal of the stock market to recognize the permanence of the post-war level of growth and activity is also understandable. By and large, this refusal simply reflected a considerable body of expert opinion in this matter. Long-run economic expectations have in general been dampened since 1946 by the fear that the stagnancy experienced in the thirties would reassert itself, as well as by the fear of war. Although the performance of the economy in its recovery from the 1949–50 downturn did provide a fairly clear indication that demand factors were basically strong, the outbreak of the war in Korea, coming as it did during the early phase of the recovery, did tend to cast some doubt on the economy's ability to resume and to sustain a high level of growth and activity on its own. It was not until the recent

---

[9]Using the alternative set of growth rates mentioned earlier, the results for 1955 are virtually identical.

recession of 1953–54 that this ability has been more properly vindicated. This recession, in fact, has had the seemingly contradictory effect of increasing the level of confidence with which business views the future.

Several elements of significance for the stock market emerged from the recession and the way in which government policy was directed during 1954. (1) The mildness of the downturn was itself an important factor, especially when viewed against the widely held opinion, in early 1954, that the long-awaited test had come. (2) The shrinkage, especially in durable goods' manufacturing, had a much smaller effect on earnings before taxes than had been anticipated. Industry break-even points were apparently not as high as had been assumed. (3) The revision of the internal revenue code and the tax relief which it gave to corporations and to dividend recipients was unquestionably important. (4) The revival of monetary policy as a prime instrument of control and the very sharp fall in long-term interest rates that it brought were also demand-creating factors in the stock market.

Whether the present confidence in the sustainability of economic growth will prove to be justified by the actual performance of the economy over the next decade is impossible to predict. In any case, it is largely because of different opinions that are held about the future of economic growth that there is today a division of opinion regarding the current level of the stock market. It is not surprising that Professor Galbraith, for example, who has expressed some concern with the present level of stock prices has also expressed concern that, in the absence of aggressive government policy, the economy might find itself "launched on a plateau of rather high level stagnation."[10] If economic growth does not continue at a rate that is sufficient to absorb our growing capacity to produce goods and services, the level of the market, although fully warranted on the evidence thus far, is vulnerable to a serious downturn in the future.

On the other hand, if the economy does achieve its potential growth rate over the coming decade, without increasing assistance from federal expenditures, the projected levels for gross national product and corporate earnings and dividends provide an important clue to future levels in the stock market. On the basis of the generally projected level of gross national product,[11] the warranted level for the industrial stock price index (in 1955 dollars) would be around 375 compared with a present level of 308.

[10]Kenneth J. Galbraith, "The American Prospect." Symposium on "What Business Expects in 1955," *Business Quarterly*, XIX, 185.

[11]For a summary of economic projections that have been made, see Joint Committee on the Economic Report, *Potential Economic Growth of the United States during the Next Decade* (Washington, D.C.: U.S. Government Printing Office, 1954).

The Stock Market in Perspective*

J. Fred Weston

In view of the great need for equity capital, it is unfortunate that investors have no criteria for judging the level of common stock prices and so are uncertain and fearful of a market collapse.

However, an equation can be constructed that relates common stock prices to the gross national product, and it confirms the soundness of the current market level.

Cyclical and random downturns are likely to take place, but new secular highs are also to be expected in line with the long-run growth pattern.

Other implications point to the attractiveness of common stocks despite the narrow differential relative to bonds, and to the wisdom of restraining the flow of credit into the market.

APPREHENSION AND UNCERTAINTY

During 1955 the stock market reached new highs and broke into some sharp declines, both of which were dramatically headlined by the press and news commentators. As the stock market emerged into higher levels, disquieting references to 1929 were made, and each decline was labeled by many observers as the beginning of a major readjustment.

The market was subject to the most critical kind of scrutiny in recent Senate Committee hearings.[1] Particularly significant was the testimony of economist John Kenneth Galbraith, who had just completed a rigorous study of *The Great Crash, 1929*[2]; he asserted that the market was too high, that stock prices were once again at levels which might result in declines of 1929–1932 magnitude.

*From *Harvard Business Review*, **34**, no. 2, March–April, 1956, pp. 71–80. [J. Fred Weston is indebted to William F. Sharpe for aid in the statistical compilations and for critical readings of early drafts of this article.]

[1]Hearings before the Senate Committee on Banking and Currency on "Factors Affecting the Buying and Selling of Equity Securities," March 3–23, 1955, *Stock Market Study*, 84th Congress, Ist Session; p. 1022.

[2]Boston, Houghton Mifflin Company, 1955.

Comparisons of this kind are certain to cause apprehension and uncertainty. Continued warnings of imminent market collapse deter many investors from making equity investments. The fact is that so far the high level of common stock prices has not stimulated any substantial volume of external financing; and if fear and uncertainty continue, the equity markets will not be adequate for the need.

It has been estimated that by 1965 United States corporations will require an additional $375 billion of investment, and that more than 40% of this amount—or some $160 billion—will be financed from outside sources. If at least half of external needs is raised from equity securities, an additional $80 billion of equity financing would have to be realized by 1965—an average of about $8 billion a year, almost four times the recent annual rate.[3]

Need for Criteria

Clearly, it is imperative to have criteria for judging the level of common stock prices. If there is real reason for fear, then knowing about it will help to bring proper safeguards. On the other hand, if the current level, or an even higher stock price level in the future, is shown to be sound, then investors and business firms alike can plan ahead constructively.

It is the purpose of this article to help fill the gap created by the lack of such criteria. I have developed a method of relationship which will serve to measure the secular trend of the market relative to economic growth—in other words, where the market should be in the light of basic, long-run factors. This in turn should serve to identify cyclical or random swings for what they are—temporary movements that should in time correct themselves.

ECONOMIC GROWTH

The most important determinants of stock prices are:

1. The profit and dividend outlook.
2. The size of the residual income of the public after necessary and customary expenses have been met.
3. The state of confidence.
4. Money market conditions, particularly as they influence the availability of funds.
5. The flow of savings into the stock market.
6. The tax outlook for both individuals and corporations.

These influences reflect the pace of general economic activity, and therefore provide a logical basis for investigating the relationship between

[3]G. Keith Funston, "Broader Share Ownership," speech of June 23, 1955 (New York Stock Exchange), pp. 7–9.

stock prices and the level of gross national product—one of the best single measures of the level of business.

INTERRELATED FACTORS

To establish the relationship between stock prices and long-run economic growth requires the development of some link between these two kinds of economic forces—a link provided, in fact, by a *series* of economic interrelationships:

1. There is a close relationship between gross national product and sales in the aggregate (roughly equivalent to the national income produced). As a matter of fact, even individual firms often find that their sales can be forecast against gross national product.

2. A remarkably good correlation also exists between sales (national income) and profits before taxes, as shown in Figure 1. The fit is of course less close with profits after taxes, over any extended period of time, because of changing tax rates.

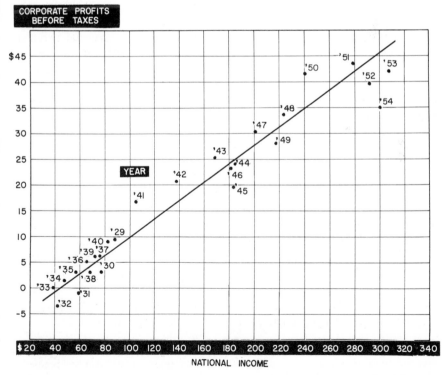

FIGURE 1 Relationship between corporate profits before taxes and national income, 1929–1954 (in billions of dollars).

3. There is, next, a demonstrable relation between profits and dividends. Preliminary research findings indicate that current and recent profits are the single most important influence on dividends. Needless to say, this will vary from company to company, and industry to industry, but the differences should more or less wash out.

4. Finally, there is an obviously close relationship between dividends and stock prices. Again there will be individual differences arising from the age of the company, practices in retaining earnings, and so on, but over time current dividends should be reasonably representative of past, current, and prospective earnings, which determine what investors are willing to pay for stocks.

Thus, since there is a close relationship between gross national product and sales, between sales and profits, between profits and dividends, and between stock prices and dividends, stock prices can be linked directly to gross national product, leaving out the intermediate steps. Therefore, as gross national product grows over the years, we would expect that the *total* value of stock prices will grow in the same proportion.

Of course, the prices of *individual* shares of stock might show a serious distortion if there were any sizable increase in number of shares outstanding. The fact that from 1874 on stock prices have increased at a rate equal to about two-thirds the rate of increase in gross national product *when both are measured in real terms* suggests that the total number of shares has increased only moderately, and that therefore we should expect a straight-line relationship between gross national product and the level of stock prices.[4] (Remember we are talking about the general level of stock prices; particular companies may have sharply different capitalization rates, may or may not correspond to the growth pattern of the economy as a whole, and so on.)

Test of Experience

Now let us test this reasoning by empirical analysis, comparing gross national product with Standard & Poor's Industrial Index of stock prices. As Figure 2 shows, there is a significant straight-line relationship.

More specifically, before 1927 stock prices clustered about the straight line. In 1927, 1928, and 1929 stock prices disengaged somewhat from this close fit and moved above the straight-line relationship (except for 1932) until around 1940. Thereafter they moved below. But in 1954 and 1955 they began again to approach it. This suggests a hypothesis:

By computing the relationship between gross national product and stock prices over long periods of time, a test of the level of stock prices in 1955 can be obtained.

[4]Ezra Solomon, "Economic Growth and Common Stock Values," *Journal of Business*, July 1955, pp. 216–217.

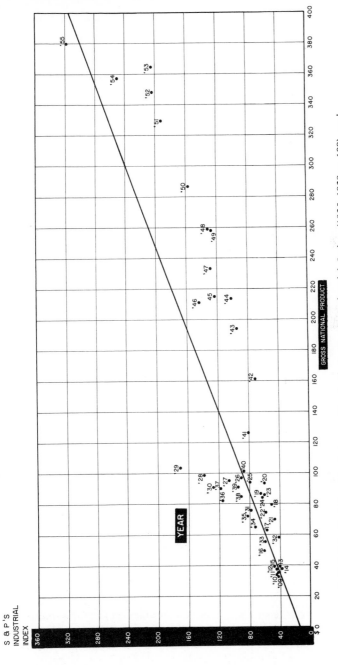

FIGURE 2 Relationship between Standard & Poor's Industrial Index (1935-1939 = 100) and gross national product (in billions of dollars).

Thus the data shown in Figure 2 for the years 1909 through 1927 and for 1933 through 1940 have been used to calculate the relationship between gross national product and Standard & Poor's Industrial Index. The resulting equation is $SP = 15.58 + .7468GNP$, which suggests that the level of stock prices as measured by Standard & Poor's Industrial Index is approximately 0.75 times the current level of gross national product plus a constant of approximately 15 index points.

For a more extended test, the relationship between decade data of gross national product and Standard & Poor's Industrial Index from 1868 through 1928 has been computed (see Table 1). This analysis gives the equation $SP = 14.23$

TABLE 1. *Gross national product and Standard & Poor's Industrial Index, by decades, 1869–1955*

Decade	Gross national product (in billions)	Standard & Poor's Industrial Index (1935–1939 = 100)
1869–1878	$ 7.1	18.5*
1874–1883	9.0	18.7
1879–1888	10.7	20.2
1884–1893	11.8	23.7
1889–1898	12.7	23.8
1894–1903	15.9	26.7
1899–1908	21.7	33.6
1904–1913	28.6	38.6
1909–1918	40.1	47.0
1914–1923	61.9	54.5
1919–1928	81.2	77.0
1924–1933	79.1	95.8
1929–1938	78.3†	95.7
1934–1943	106.5	90.8
1939–1948	179.3	105.6
1944–1953	270.5	151.1
1949–1958	323.1‡	207.4‡

*Includes only 1871–1878.
†Beginning of revised series.
‡Includes only 1949 through the first half of 1955.
SOURCES: Figures for gross national product come from: first column, first 12 decades, Simon Kuznets, "Long-Term Changes in the National Income of the United States of America Since 1870," International Association for Research in Income and Wealth, *Income and Wealth: Series II* (Cambridge, England, Bowes & Bowes, Publishers, Ltd., 1952), p. 30; last 5 decades, *Economic Report of the President*, January 1955; second column, U.S. Department of Commerce, *Historical Statistics of the United States* and *Survey of Current Business*.

$+ .7488GNP$, which is remarkably close to that obtained from the annual data for 1909–1927 and 1933–1940.

It seems reasonable therefore to utilize this type of regression equation in appraising current and prospective levels of stock prices. Averaging the two equations and doing a little rounding we get the simplified equation $SP = 15 + .75GNP$.

1955 Level

If we put into this equation the dollar value of *GNP* for 1955, the resulting stock price index comes out around 300. Actually, Standard & Poor's Industrial Index averaged 341 for 1955. Hence, the stock price index predicted by the equation is approximately 90% of Standard & Poor's actual value; or, to put it the other way, the actual value of Standard & Poor's Industrial Index is somewhat above what would have been expected if the long-run normal relationship between gross national product and stock prices had obtained. This difference of approximately 10 percentage points is not very great.

We conclude, therefore, that stock prices in 1955 are roughly in line with what one would have expected them to be on the basis of historical relationships. In short, they are in line with the growth of gross national product, which represents long-term economic growth.

Projections 1960, 1965, 1975

Projections of gross national product for the years 1960, 1965, 1975 have been brought together in a recent publication of the Joint Committee on the Economic Report.[5] By putting these dollar values into our equation $SP = 15 + .75GNP$, we should be able to obtain estimates of future stock price levels. If the indicated relationship between gross national product and stock prices obtains, stock prices for the years 1960 through 1975 would reach the levels shown in Table 2.

TABLE 2. *Projections of gross national product and stock prices, 1960, 1965, 1975, related to bench-mark years*

Year		Gross national product— 1953 dollars* (in billions)	Standard & Poor's Industrial Index— 420 stocks†	Dow-Jones Industrial Average— 30 stocks‡
1929	Actual	$177.7	171.1	311.2
1955	Actual	385.0	340.7	442.7
1960	Projected	436.0	342.0	450.0
1965	Projected	535.0	416.2	545.8
1975	Projected	634.0	490.5	641.6

*Projected figures from Joint Committee on the Economic Report, *Potential Economic Growth of the United States*, 1954, p. 35.

†Projected figures derived by formula $SP = 15 + .75GNP$ (described in text).

‡Projected figures derived by formula $DJ = 28.20 + .9675GNP$ (method similar to that described in text).

NOTE: The correlation coefficients for the above relationships are all statistically significant. The standard errors of estimate are small.

[5] *Potential Economic Growth in the United States*, Joint Committee on the Economic Report, 1954, p. 35.

The data indicate that stock prices have *already* reached the height they would have been expected to attain in 1960 on the basis of long-term economic growth. This means that investors purchasing stocks in 1955 have discounted all the growth that is likely to take place through 1960. However, if the projections of gross national product are dependable, they suggest that stock prices will go on to new heights in 1965 and 1975.

FURTHER INTERPRETATION

Some other inferences may be drawn from our data:

1. It is *not* remarkable that in 1955 the market rose above the level reached by the Dow-Jones Industrial Average in 1929. The amazing thing is that almost a quarter of a century was required to achieve this. But there is an explanation, and it is a combination of two factors: (a) in the late 1920's the stock market was exces-

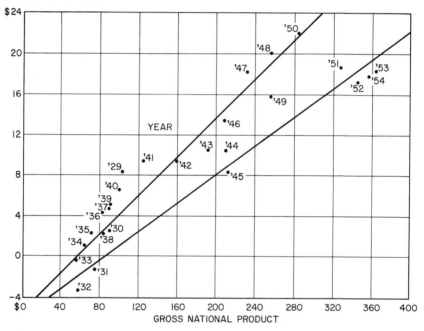

FIGURE 3   Total corporate profits after taxes related to gross national product, 1929–1954 (in billions of dollars). NOTE: The two lines on the chart are intended to show that any attempt to fit a straight-line relationship, even with two lines (one for one period of time, one for another period), fails; and especially that no clean break occurred in the relationship in 1940 or in 1954 to account for the movements in the relationship between GNP and Standard & Poor's Industrial Index in those years, as shown in Figure 2. SOURCE: *Economic Report of the President*, January 1955, pp. 137, 189.

sively high by normal relationships between gross national product and stock prices, and (b) from 1940 on stock prices were abnormally low by the same criteria.

2. Some have suggested that the abnormally low stock prices during the 1940's should be accounted for by the shift to higher tax rates in 1940. This view, however, is not supported by the facts. As Figure 3 shows, the behavior of gross national product and profits after taxes is not sufficiently consistent to explain the distinct pattern in the relationship between gross national product and stock prices after 1940. In other words, this relationship of ours is basic.

3. It would appear that stock prices at the present time are rising in a manner which partakes of both cyclical and secular influences. The cyclical component of current stock market prices is subject to reversal. The secular component, however, promises further growth—a possibility to be recognized by newspaper writers and others dramatizing the stock market whenever it reaches higher levels.

RELATED PHENOMENA

The linkages on which the above observations have been based are anything but precise. A certain amount of skepticism is justified. But when the specific points which might seem to cast doubt are examined, they are not inconsistent with our hypothesis; as a matter of fact, our interpretation in terms of long-run growth helps to explain them.

As the stock market has moved into higher levels, commentators have observed that differentials between the yields of common stocks and of high-grade fixed-income investments are relatively small, and they have suggested that investors are likely to find it more advantageous to buy bonds than common stocks. But such current yield comparisons are fundamentally misleading since they do not take into account the growth potentials of common stocks.

Professor John C. Clendenin has made a searching analysis of this aspect of the subject.[6] He cautions that some common stock price levels at the time of his study were implying growth patterns of large magnitude over a relatively long period of time. He indicates that some growth assumptions appeared reasonable, but that others were overoptimistic. His factual data reveal some relationships not generally recognized. Table 3 sets forth the indicated prices to which a stock might rise under various postulates of growth patterns. For example:

A stock paying $1 per annum, with an expected annual rate of 5% for a 60-year period of time, could support a price of $60. This represents a yield basis of 1.67%.

A more moderate assumption of a 5% rate of growth for only a 30-year period would support an indicated price of $45, or an indicated yield of some 2.2%.

Similarly, an annual rate of growth of 3% for 50 years would support a price of approximately $35, or a yield of some 2.86%.

[6]John C. Clendenin and Maurice Van Cleave, "Growth and Common Stock Values," *Journal of Finance*, December 1954, p. 365.

TABLE 3. *Present value of all future dividends on a stock now paying $1.00 per annum**

Growth period (years)	Stable dividend period	Annual rate of growth in dividends expected					
		5%	4%	3%	2%	1%	0%
0	60	$18.93	$18.93	$18.93	$18.93	$18.93	$18.93
10	50	28.25	26.00	24.00	22.25	20.50	18.93
20	40	37.00	32.25	28.25	24.50	21.50	18.93
30	30	45.25	37.50	31.25	26.25	22.25	18.93
40	20	52.50	41.50	33.50	27.25	22.50	18.93
50	10	57.75	44.25	34.75	27.75	22.50	18.93
60	0	69.00	45.50	35.75	28.00	22.75	18.93

*Computed values to nearest quarter dollar.
NOTE: Calculations are based on these assumptions: (a) that each year's dividend is received at the end of the year and includes in full any augmentation of rate due to growth during the year; (b) that the dividend is expected to increase at the indicated compound rate for the indicated period of years and then stabilize until 60 years from today, at which time it will cease; and (c) that a 5% return is required. See source for full details.
SOURCE: John C. Clendenin and Maurice Van Cleave, "Growth and Common Stock Values," *Journal of Finance*, December 1954, p. 371.

These data illustrate that when the growth in dividends per annum is taken into account, this income potential, which is not present in government bonds or high-grade corporate bonds, makes it entirely reasonable for common stocks to be selling on a yield basis even below the yield of long-term bonds. But actually common stocks are still yielding more than corporate bonds. On this basis common stock yields during 1955 are well in line with our criteria.

Another conceivable danger is the risk that the stock market, when it is at its 1955 levels, may be approaching an *absolute* peak, like 1929, which may not again be attained for another quarter of a century. This problem has also been dealt with at considerable length by other writers. For example, Richard W. Lambourne has made a detailed comparison between 1929 and February 1955 market relationships.[7] His data, which are reproduced in Table 4 indicate that prices as a multiple of latest annual earnings are relatively moderate for 1955. Dividend yields are higher than in 1929, both absolutely and relatively to corporate bonds (they were below corporate bonds in 1929). Table 4 also shows that stock market credit is used to a much smaller extent in 1955 than in 1929.

[7]See Source, Table 4; see also *Is the Market High?* (pamphlet, New York, National Securities and Research Corporation, 1955).

TABLE 4. *Comparison between 1929 and 1955 market relationships*

	1955 (February)	1929 (high)
Price as multiple of latest annual earnings		
Dow-Jones Industrial Average	14.8 times	19.1 times
Standard & Poor's Industrial Index	13.0 times	20.0 times
Barron's 50-Stock Composite	14.8 times	20.8 times
Price as multiple of latest 5-year average earnings,		
Barron's 50-Stock Composite	13.4 times	24.8 times
Dividend yields		
Dow-Jones Industrial Average	4.4%	3.3%
Standard & Poor's Industrial Index	4.3%	2.9%
Barron's 50-Stock Composite	4.4%	2.8%
High-grade corporate bond yields		
Short-term, 5-year	2.75%	6.00%
Long-term, 30-year	3.25%	5.00%
Federal Reserve discount rate	1.50%	6.00%
Margin requirements	60.00%*	5.25%†
Total stock market credit		
In billions of dollars	$5‡	$16§
As percentage of total value of listed stocks¶	3%‡	19%§
Annual rate of trading	12%#	132%**
Annual rate of turnover¶	28%††	119%‡‡
Dow-Jones Industrial Average		
Estimated earnings	$30.00§§	$20.00††
Estimated dividends	$18.00	$12.75
Dividend payout	60%	64%

*Private.
†Federal Reserve Board.
‡December 1954.
§September 1929.
¶New York Stock Exchange.
#1954.
**1928.
††January–February 1955.
‡‡1929.
§§1955.
SOURCE: Richard W. Lambourne, "Is It Another 1929 in the Market?" *Analysts Journal*, May 1955, p. 3.

CYCLICAL SWINGS

While it is not likely that this is another 1929 in the stock market, a considerable cyclical component of course exists in the movement of stock prices.

Figures 4 and 5 present data on stock prices in the United States and Great Britain, respectively. Note that the patterns of price movements in

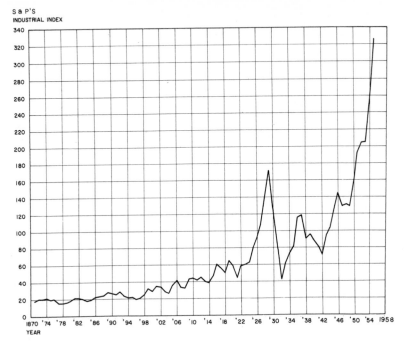

FIGURE 4   Standard & Poor's Industrial Index, 1870–1955 (1935–1939 = 100).
SOURCE: U. S. Department of Commerce, *Survey of Current Business.*

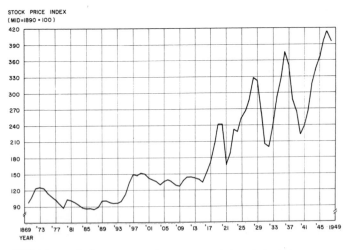

FIGURE 5   Ordinary share prices, Great Britain, 1870–1948. SOURCE:
Hargreaves Parkinson, *Ordinary Shares* (London, Eyre and Spottiswoode, 1949), p. 275.

the two countries exhibit many similarities, the one big difference being that the 1928 high in Great Britain was exceeded in eight years in comparison with the almost quarter-century it took to exceed the 1929 high in the United States. The outstanding characteristics of both charts are (a) that a strong cyclical pattern is exhibited, and (b) that stock prices have attained most of their growth during relatively short periods of time.

There seems to be a clear pattern. A strong cyclical upward movement pulls stocks up to new highs. This peak is followed by a cyclical downturn. But in the next upswing the new peak typically carries stock prices above their previous high.

These charts caution the observer that stock prices can experience cyclical downturns of relatively large magnitude. Three factors may cause prices to move in a downward direction:

1. *A decline in profit and dividend prospects.* The downturn which began in the early part of August 1955 was not surprising in view of the trend of economic events. Forecasts of business activity for 1956 indicated that the very sharp rise in business activity taking place in the first and second quarters of 1955 was going to slow down during the last two quarters and then peak in the first quarter of 1956. Hence, since the stock market discounts the future, the prospective flattening of the rise in general business in early 1956 would be a depressant on stock prices in late summer of 1955.

2. *The supply of money.* This was an aggravating force in the downturn of early August 1955. The concern of the monetary and fiscal authorities, as well as of the economic advisers of the President, that the boom was proceeding at a too rapid rate, led to tightening the money supply. The many actions taken reduced the supply of funds which ordinarily would have flowed into the stock market.

3. *Psychological sensitivity of the market.* The influence on the stock market of the President's illness was a dramatic illustration of the fact that a large blow to confidence can trigger a sharp decline. The present stock market is still relatively thin; any factor which makes for uncertainty will cause stock prices to fall, at least for a limited period of time. Regardless of the nature of the uncertainty, the market will decline until the uncertainty has been reduced or digested, as the behavior of stock prices since September 26, 1955, clearly demonstrates.

While the long-term growth of the economy points to movements of the Dow-Jones Industrial Average to 546 by 1965 and to 642 by 1975, intermediate downturns may take place. At the same time, the very fact that we can differentiate these swings from the secular trend and identify them as temporary makes it easier to give investment recognition to the long-term growth potential.

THE NEW MARKET

Other more sophisticated considerations support the results suggested by our relatively simple mathematical relationships. In many ways we have indeed a "new stock market" with more probability of stability and therefore closer relationship with the long-term growth pattern:

1. Institutional investors are coming to play a larger part in the market. For example, according to the Fulbright Staff Committee Report, in 1951 institutions accounted for some 43% of net purchases of common and preferred stocks, while by 1954 they accounted for some 77%. (See Table 5.) The point is that the investment

TABLE 5. *Estimated net purchases of common and preferred stocks* *

Net purchases	1951		1952		1953		1954	
Institutions	$1.15	42.6%	$1.69	56.5%	$1.61	68.2%	$1.83	76.6%
Foreign interests	0.12	4.4			0.06	2.5	0.13	5.4
Individuals	1.43	53.0	1.30	43.5	0.69	29.3	0.43	18.0
Total	$2.70	100.0%	$2.99	100.0%	$2.36	100.0%	$2.39	100.0 %

*In billions of dollars and as a percentage of total.
SOURCE: Report of the Committee on Banking and Currency, *Factors Affecting the Stock Market* (1955), p. 92.

behavior of institutions is not likely to be subject to the wide swings in psychological moods to which the small investor is subject or to be panicked by moderate market changes like the September-October 1955 experience.[8]

The increased role of professionals is especially important in view of new patterns in the money market. It is now clear that the goal of economic stability will override the goal of fixity in government bond prices. In pursuing the goal of economic stability, government bond prices and interest rates are likely to fluctuate. Variations in the supply of money will influence stock prices and subject the market to appreciable swings. But professional investors will be better able to understand and see beyond such temporary fluctuations, knowing that in a rising secular trend the common stocks of companies in a net debtor position will afford protection to them.

2. The increased stability in the pattern of business equipment expenditures, as corporate financiers take the long view of company needs and opportunities rather than react to temporary fluctuations in company and industry sales, provides the market with an element of long-range strength. This trend is shown, for example, by the fact that between the fourth quarter of 1948 and the fourth quarter of 1949, when gross national product declined by $8\frac{1}{2}\%$, gross investment declined by 12% of gross national product of 1948; but between the third quarter of 1953 and the fourth quarter of 1954, when total gross national product declined by 12%, the decline in gross investment was only 2% of gross national product in 1953.

[8]*The Exchange*, November 1955, p. 2, Table 1.

3. Another favorable influence is the systematic purchase of common stocks by the growing monthly investment plans. These plans represent a method of dollar averaging which will accomplish gains if the secular trend of stock prices is positive.[9] From the standpoint of the behavior of the market as a whole, these plans develop an appreciable flow of funds into the market, providing a sustaining influence.

Thus in the structure and composition of the market, in terms of the kinds of investors whose influence now dominates stock market prices, we have a stock market which is not likely to be subject to the excesses or wide gyrations that have occurred in the past. These factors too should dispel the fear which may seize investors when new market levels are overdramatized.

CONCLUSION

In view of the financing needs of corporations in the next decade and the appreciable portion of such external financing that must come from equity sources if balance in the financial structure is to be attained, equity prices must be attractive. While equity financing has increased during the past year relative to previous years, it still has not attained the volume necessary relative to the total financial stability needs of corporations. It is reassuring, therefore, to observe that the data presented on the relationship between gross national product and stock prices indicate that current stock prices are not excessively high in terms of long-run secular growth patterns.

Much comment has attended the movement of the stock market to new high levels. The usual comparisons with 1929 levels suggest that a cyclical downturn of the magnitude which took place from 1929 to 1932 is a real danger. However, these implications confuse cyclical and secular movements in stock prices. They imply that a rise above the 1929 level inevitably means a subsequent fall. It is true, as the data presented in Table 2 and Figure 4 indicate, that recurring cyclical movements in common stock prices take place. But a strong secular trend is also observable. And while stock prices may be expected to move in cyclical swings, over a period of time, they may also be expected to reach new secular highs. Projections of stock prices to 1960, 1965, and 1975 suggest that temporary cyclical downturns in stock prices will be offset by strong and persistent upward growth trends.

Growth stocks selling on a yield basis below that of fixed value investments may still represent an attractive investment opportunity. The growth factor makes it possible for common stocks to sell on a lower yield basis

[9] J. F. Weston, "Some Theoretical Aspects of the Construction of Formula Timing Plans," *Journal of Business*, October 1949, p. 249.

because of the potential increases in income and possibilities for capital gains not available from fixed investments such as government bonds. Hence a narrowing of yield differentials between common stocks and bonds is not evidence that common stock prices have reached unsupportably high levels.

The findings do not suggest that an investor may blindly buy securities, depending on growth patterns to rescue him from bad judgments. Prudent standards of security analysis and portfolio selection will always be prime requisites of successful investment. Particular care must be taken that the companies selected will experience as much growth as the economy as a whole. Indeed, the portfolio will perform even better if it contains companies whose growth is greater than the average for the economy as a whole.[10]

When the market has risen above its long-term secular trend, even though not excessively, the risks of an intermediate downward movement are that much greater. To protect himself against such risks, the investor should maintain a reserve of cash assets which will enable him to weather adverse market movements. Excessive use of credit in the stock market can pull security prices loose from moorings based on prospective profits and dividends. From a social standpoint, therefore, the flow of credit into a market which has risen to levels as high as in 1955 may properly be restrained.

[10]Robert W. Anderson, "Unrealized Potentials in Growth Stocks," HBR March–April 1955, p. 51.

PART **3.** Factors Affecting Stock
and Bond Prices

Evaluation of the Rule
of Present Worth*

John Burr Williams

1. FUTURE DIVIDENDS, COUPONS, AND PRINCIPAL

Now that we have disposed of the troublesome misconception that stock prices are somehow determined in accordance with a
quantity theory of money, we are at last ready to take up the main thesis of
this book.

Let us define the investment value of a stock as the present worth of all
the dividends[1] to be paid upon it. Likewise let us define the investment
value of a bond as the present worth of its future coupons and principal. In
both cases, dividends, or coupons and principal, must be adjusted for expected changes in the purchasing power of money. The purchase of a stock
or bond, like other transactions which give rise to the phenomenon of
interest, represents the exchange of present goods for future goods—
dividends, or coupons and principal, in this case being the claim on future
goods. To appraise the investment value, then, it is necessary to estimate
the future payments. The annuity of payments, adjusted for changes in the
value of money itself, may then be discounted at the pure interest rate demanded by the investor. This definition of investment value can be expressed by the following equations:[2]

*Reprinted by permission of the publishers from John Burr Williams, *The Theory of Investment
Value*, Cambridge, Mass.: Harvard University Press, Copyright 1938, chap. 5, pp. 55–75, by the
President and Fellows of Harvard College.

[1]Cf. Robert F. Wiese, "Investing for True Values," *Barron's*, September 8, 1930, p. 5: "*The
proper price of any security, whether a stock or bond, is the sum of all future income payments
discounted at the current rate of interest in order to arrive at the present value.*"

[2]*Note for the non-technical reader:* It is not necessary to master all of the algebra in the
following chapters to understand the rest of this book, for the text between the equations has
been so written as to summarize the argument and make it possible to take the derivation of the
formulas for granted. The symbols used in the formulas are defined one by one when first introduced, but for easy reference they are reprinted with explanations in a systematic "Table of
Symbols" at the end of the book.

For stocks—

$$V_o = \sum_{t=1}^{t=\infty} \pi_t v^t = \pi_1 v + \pi_2 v^2 + \pi_3 v^3 + \cdots \qquad (1a)$$

where

V_o = investment value at start

π_t = dividend in year t

$v = \dfrac{1}{1+i}$, by definition

i = interest rate sought by the investor

For bonds—

$$V_o = \sum_{t=1}^{t=n} \pi_t v^t + C v^n \qquad (1b)$$

where

π_t = coupon in year t

C = face value, or principal, of bond

n = number of years to maturity

The way in which dividends, or coupons and principal, should be adjusted for changes in the value of money in future years will be discussed later.

The subscripts 1, 2, 3, etc., attached to the Greek letter π in the equations below signify the first, second, third, etc., value of the variable π. Thus π_1 is the amount of the dividend in the first year, π_2 in the second year, π_3 in the third, etc., and π_t in the tth year, where t means time.

The series of terms $\pi_1 v + \pi_2 v^2 + \pi_3 v^3 + \cdots$ is called an infinite series because there is no end to the number of terms. In this particular series each term is constructed according to the rule that the exponent of the factor v shall be the same as the subscript of the factor π, thus $\pi_3 v^3$, $\pi_t v^t$, etc. In certain special cases the sum of all the terms in an infinite series is a finite number, and not infinity, even though the number of terms is infinite; under these circumstances, the series is said to be convergent. Suffice it to say that a series will often be convergent if each additional term is smaller than the preceding one; any further discussion of convergency would take us too far into higher mathematics.

Two ways of denoting an infinite series are as follows:

$$\pi_1 v + \pi_2 v^2 + \pi_3 v^3 + \cdots\cdots$$

and

$$\sum_{t=1}^{t=\infty} \pi_t v^t$$

The second notation, using the Greek letter Σ, means exactly the same as the first, but is briefer. This notation is read "Summation from t equals one, to t equals infinity, of pi sub t, times v to the tth power." It should be noted that

$\sum_{t=1}^{t=\infty}$ is not a factor to be multiplied by the other factors π_t and v^t, but is an operational sign applied to these two factors taken together.

If the series runs from $t = 1$ to $t = n$, as in formula (1b) applying to bonds, the series is a finite series instead of an infinite series, because the number of terms is limited and is given in this case by the number of coupons payable during the life of the bond.

A series of the kind under discussion here, whether finite or infinite, is known as a geometric progression if π_t is constant.

2. FUTURE EARNINGS OF STOCKS

Most people will object at once to the foregoing formula for stocks by saying that it should use the present worth of future *earnings*, not future *dividends*. But should not earnings and dividends both give the same answer under the implicit assumptions of our critics? If earnings not paid out in dividends are all successfully reinvested at compound interest for the benefit of the stockholder, as the critics imply, then these earnings should produce dividends later; if not, then they are money lost. Furthermore, if these reinvested earnings will produce dividends, then our formula will take account of them when it takes account of all future dividends; but if they will not, then our formula will rightly refrain from including them in any discounted annuity of benefits.

Earnings are only a means to an end, and the means should not be mistaken for the end. Therefore we must say that a stock derives its value from its dividends, not its earnings. In short, a stock is worth only *what you can get out of it.* Even so spoke the old farmer to his son:

A cow for her milk,
A hen for her eggs,
And a stock, by heck,
For her dividends.

An orchard for fruit
Bees for their honey,
And stocks, besides,
For their dividends.

The old man knew where milk and honey came from, but he made no such mistake as to tell his son to buy a cow for her cud or bees for their buzz.

In saying that dividends, not earnings, determine value, we seem to be reversing the usual rule that is drilled into every beginner's head when he starts to trade in the market; namely, that earnings, not dividends, make prices. The apparent contradiction is easily explained, however, for we are discussing permanent investment, not speculative trading, and dividends for years to come, not income for the moment only. Of course it is true that low earnings together with a high dividend for the time being should be looked at askance, but likewise it is true that these low earnings mean low dividends *in the long run.* On analysis, therefore, it will be seen that no contradiction really exists between our formula using dividends and the common precept regarding earnings.

How to estimate the future dividends for use in our formula is, of course, the difficulty. In later chapters ways of making an estimate will be given for such stocks as we now know how to deal with. In so doing, this book seeks to make its most important contribution to Investment Analysis.

3. PERSONAL VERSUS MARKET RATE OF INTEREST

In applying the foregoing formulas, each investor should use his own personal rate of interest. If one investor demands 10 per cent and another 2 per cent as minimum wages of abstinence, then the same stock or bond will be accorded a lower value by the one than by the other.

The only case in which the market rate of interest should be applied is when the analyst is speaking not for himself personally but for investors in general. Then he should use the pure interest rate as it is expected to be found in the open market in the years to come.

4. COMPOUND INTEREST AT A CHANGING RATE

In the usual discussion of compound interest, it is always assumed that the rate of interest stays the same throughout the period in question. The assumption of a changing rate is never met with, and apparently the possibility of such a thing is not even considered.[3] Yet in theory a changing rate is easily conceivable, and so provision for it, when it occurs, should be made in our formula, thus:

$$V_o = \sum_{t=1}^{t=\infty} \pi_t v_1 v_2 \cdots v_t \tag{1c}$$

where

$$v_1 = \frac{1}{1 + i_1}; \ v_2 = \frac{1}{1 + i_2}; \ \text{etc.} \tag{2}$$

and

$$i_1 = \text{interest rate in first year}$$
$$i_2 = \text{interest rate in second year}$$
$$i_t = \text{interest rate in } t\text{th year}$$

The interest rate i_t in every case is that for one-year loans made at the beginning of the year t, and paid at the end of it.

The meaning of the equation can be shown by an example. Suppose that investors think that the interest rate for one-year loans, as determined by the equilibrium of the demand and supply for new savings, will be

$$i_1 = \tfrac{1}{2}\% \text{ in 1937}$$
$$i_2 = 1\% \text{ in 1938}$$
$$i_3 = 1\tfrac{1}{2}\% \text{ in 1939}$$
$$i_4 = 2\% \text{ in 1940}$$
$$i_5 = 2\tfrac{1}{2}\% \text{ in 1941}$$
$$i_6 = 3\% \text{ in 1942}$$

---

[3]An exceptional case in which the possibility of changing interest rates is in fact considered occurs in life insurance, where actuaries of non-participating companies occasionally use a split rate in computing premiums and making other calculations.

Then the present worth of π dollars payable

at the end of 1937 will be $\dfrac{\pi}{(100\frac{1}{2}\%)}$

at the end of 1938 will be $\dfrac{\pi}{(100\frac{1}{2}\%)(101\%)}$

at the end of 1939 will be $\dfrac{\pi}{(100\frac{1}{2}\%)(101\%)(101\frac{1}{2}\%)}$

and at the end of t years will be $\pi v_1 v_2 \cdots v_t$

Long-term interest rates are not a genus wholly distinct from short-term interest rates, and they are not determined separately from short-term rates by independent considerations. Rather, long-term rates are only a thing derived, an average of a special kind, a mere figure of substitution that can be used in place of the series of short-term rates for the years covered. This average is not an ordinary arithmetic average, nor even a geometric average, but is a more complicated average whose formula is given implicitly by the formula for the value of the bond or stock under consideration.

5. RIGHTS AND ASSESSMENTS

In the case of growing companies,[4] rights to subscribe to additional shares may be offered from time to time, and this will affect the annuity of payments received by the stockholder. Such an issue of rights is equivalent to a stock dividend paid to the stockholder together with an assessment levied on him. Since it is well recognized that a stock dividend, like a split-up, does not change the values behind a given percentage of a company's stock, it follows that an offering of "rights," in so far as it increases the number of shares outstanding but leaves unchanged the percentage owned by each stockholder, adds nothing to the value of the stockholder's equity. And in so far as the offering brings new money into the company's treasury, it is like any other assessment in building up the stockholder's equity. But in so far as the offering draws this money out of the stockholder's pocket, it increases the total cost of his commitment. This latter fact is clearly reflected by the change in the market worth of an issue of stock when it goes

[4]Cf. Gabriel A. D. Preinreich, *The Nature of Dividends* (New York: Lancaster Press, Inc., 1935), p. 9: "There are various kinds of corporations. Some are unable to reinvest their earnings, others can do so only in part, still others can use every cent they earn and there are cases where the retention of the entire earnings is insufficient to provide for expansion. It is an important duty of the corporate management to formulate dividend policies which conform to these conditions. A company which can not reinvest its earnings must distribute them; slowly expanding companies will distribute the difference between the total earnings and that portion which can be reinvested, while rapidly expanding companies will not only endeavor to retain all earnings but must in addition attract new capital."

ex-rights. Then the new value of the entire issue becomes greater than that of the old by exactly the amount of new money paid in, and the stock-holders' bank accounts become less by the same amount. The operation is thus exactly the opposite of the payment of a cash dividend, in that the payment of dividends reduces the value of the stockholders' investment and increases the value of their bank accounts, while the exercise of rights does the reverse.

But, it may be asked, will not the new money collected by the company be invested at a good profit, and so will not the stock rise as the profits accrue in the future? No, it may be answered, the rise will not occur in the future, because it has already occurred in the past. The price does not ordinarily wait for the profits to accrue, or even for the funds to be collected, but responds as soon as the investment opportunity appears, because usually there is no question as to the power of a company to secure such new money as may be needed to enable it to exploit any new opportunities that may arise. For established companies, the mechanism of issuing rights to take advantage of recognized opportunities for profit is known to be so sure that when the feat is successfully accomplished each time, the market sees no cause for surprised elation. The assessment is viewed as merely a routine operation in the company's growth.

That the word "assessment" used above carries an invidious connotation is true. The word "contribution" could have been used instead, but such a choice of terms would have been less challenging to old views. Just because my opponents call the contribution a "right," I shall retort by calling it an "assessment."[5] In either case, however, innuendo obscures the real facts. Assessments and dividends are opposite aspects of the same thing, differing only with respect to the direction in which the money flows. A company which pays liberal cash dividends and offers frequent rights should not be considered doubly generous—the usual interpretation of such a policy—but rather as taking back with one hand what it doles out with the other. Its *gross* dividend is offset by an assessment which often makes its *net* dividend very small, or even negative. Nevertheless, such a course does not affect the intrinsic, long-run value of the stock, for, be it remembered, the investment value of a common stock is the present worth of its *net* dividends to perpetuity.

"Rights" should not be treated as income. Methods of evaluation based on such a treatment involve endless difficulties and often certain bad errors. A method which assumes, for instance, that the investor is to sell some of his rights to provide cash for subscribing with the rest makes it

---

[5]Cf. Stephen Heard, in *Stock Growth and Discount Tables*, by S. E. Guild (Boston: Financial Publishing Company, 1931). Heard says on page 293, in an appendix written by him for that book, "If, therefore, a stockholder wishes to maintain his position, rights are in reality an assessment."

necessary to know the price at which these rights can be sold, and thus also the price of the stock at intervals during the period treated. If the past is drawn upon, as is sometimes done, to provide a figure for the worth of rights, then the answer becomes dependent on the general level of stock prices prevailing in the past, with the result that this method of evaluation becomes of no use in estimating the price which should prevail in the future. Not what has been but what should be the price of a given stock is our problem; and we must not use the widely fluctuating and hence mostly incorrect prices of the past as data in our calculations.[6]

The relation which exists between gross dividends, subscriptions, and net dividends may be expressed by the following equation:

$$\pi = \kappa - \sigma \tag{3a}$$

where

π = pure, or net, dividend in any given year $\quad$ per share
κ = actual, or gross, dividend in any given year $\quad$ of original
σ = subscription, or assessment in any given year $\quad$ stock

If no rights are issued in a particular year, then the assessment, or subscription, in that year will be nil, and $\sigma = 0$. It usually happens that assessments are large but infrequent, hence in the years when they do occur, σ exceeds κ and π becomes temporarily negative. Even though the assessments do not come every year, however, and even though they are spaced at irregular intervals, we may still treat them as items in an annuity (a negative one this time), and then find their present worth, and deduct this sum from the present worth of the gross dividends, to get a figure for the fair value of a stock, thus:

$$V_o = \sum_{t=1}^{t=\infty} \kappa_t v^t - \sum_{t=1}^{t=\infty} \sigma_t v^t \tag{1d}$$

From the foregoing discussion of the place of rights in the evaluation of common stocks, it should be clear that nothing but *cash* dividends ought to be included in the formulas for appraisal, and that neither rights nor stock dividends nor option warrants nor any other form of distribution should be considered except in terms of the cash payments to which it may later give rise.

6. THE FORMATION POINT FOR INCOME

If, as argued above, assessments add to the value of one's stockholdings only so much as they subtract from one's bank account, and if dividends do only the opposite, how can either operation add to one's wealth, and how can anyone get rich from his stockholdings? Surely income accrues sometime, somewhere. The behavior of stock prices indicates, and reason con-

[6]Heard's method of adjusting for rights (Guild, *Stock Growth and Discount Tables*, pp. 296–297) would seem to be open to this objection.

firms, the conclusion that a man's income arises and his wealth increases at that point in the chain between customer and stockholder where a company's earnings reach its cash account. When a corporation, after making and paying for its wares and selling them at a profit, finally collects the cash due on them, then at last it realizes its profit. From that moment on, shareholders may take their money at will.[7] The date of distribution does not matter. But when the dividend is once allotted, on that day the stock goes ex-dividend by the amount of the payment, and then what a man gains in cash assets he loses in invested assets.

The reason for drawing the line at the time when profits reach the cash account instead of earlier in their development is because at the cash stage they are no longer among the earning assets of a business. Plant, inventories, receivables, all in their proper proportions, make up a going concern, and are expected to earn a higher return than cash assets. Cash assets, however, if loaned in the money market, yield the same return to all companies, just as they would to their individual stockholders; but invested assets yield varying returns to different companies. A stockholder does not give his cash to a corporation to be lent for him, but to be invested in bricks and mortar, or in current assets. He can do his own lending. When profits are still in the form of invested assets, their final cash equivalent is uncertain, but when they reach the cash account, their exact amount is known, and no variation results from the mere processes of distribution or contribution. Hence the place to draw the line is between cash and other assets.

Of course if cash piles up in a company's treasury, and is then spent again, unwisely this time, that is another story, and the stockholders' wealth decreases when the unwise expenditure is made. It still remains true, nevertheless, that the stockholders' wealth had previously increased when operations succeeded in yielding a cash profit.

7. THE VALUE OF A RIGHT

After each assessment, or offering of new stock, the old shares go ex-rights, and change their value because the number of shares and the cash assets of the company have increased. The value of a right is derived as follows:

Let

M = market price rights-on
$\hat{M}$ = market price ex-rights[8]
M_w = market price of right, or subscription warrant
S = subscription price of new stock offered
N = number of rights required for subscription to one new share

[7]Cf. Schabacker, *Stock Market*, p. 348, section entitled "Dividends not a Fundamental Benefit."

[8]The symbol $\hat{M}$ is read "M-cap," and may be thought of as meaning "M after recapitalization in the manner specified."

Since

N = total number of shares held before subscription to one new share

NM = total value of shares held before subscription to one new share

and

$N + 1$ = total number of shares held after subscription

$NM + S$ = total value of holdings after subscription

and

$\hat{M}(N + 1)$ = total value of shares held after subscription

therefore

$$\hat{M}(N + 1) = NM + S \tag{4a}$$

and

$$\hat{M} = \frac{NM + S}{N + 1}, \text{ the price of the stock ex-rights} \tag{4b}$$

and

$$M_w = M - \hat{M}, \text{ the price of a right} \tag{5}$$

8. UNCERTAINTY AND THE PREMIUM FOR RISK

If the investor is uncertain about the future, he cannot tell for sure just what is the present worth of the dividends or of the interest and principal he will receive. He can only say that under one set of possible circumstances it will have one value and under another, another. Each of these possible values will have a different probability, however, and so the investor may draw a probability curve to express the likelihood that any given value, V, will prove to be the true value. Thus, if he is appraising a risky twenty-year bond bearing a 4 per cent coupon and selling at 40 to yield 12 per cent to

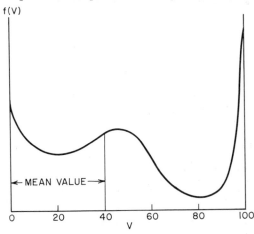

FIGURE 1 Probability curve for true value.

maturity, even though the pure interest seems to be only 4 per cent, he may conclude that the probabilities are as shown in Figure 1.

The various possible values, V, of the bond, from zero to par, are shown by the abscissae of the curve, while the likelihood, $f(V)$, that any given value will prove to be the true value, is shown by the ordinates. A unimodal curve, of the form usual for probability curves, could not be used in this case, because it would fail to show the relatively high chances of receiving all or none of the interest and principal.

Whenever the value of a security is uncertain and has to be expressed in terms of probability, the correct value to choose is the mean value,[9]

$$\bar{V} = \frac{\int_0^\infty V \, f(V) dV}{\int_0^\infty f(V) dV} \qquad (6)$$

The customary way to find the value of a risky security has always been to add a "premium for risk" to the pure interest rate, and then use the sum as the interest rate for discounting future receipts. In the case of the bond under discussion, which at 40 would yield 12 per cent to maturity,[10] the "premium for risk" is 8 per cent when the pure interest rate is 4 per cent.

Strictly speaking, however, there is no risk in buying the bond in question if its price is right. Given adequate diversification, gains on such purchases will offset losses, and a return at the pure interest rate will be obtained. Thus the *net risk* turns out to be nil. To say that a "premium for risk" is needed is really an elliptical way of saying that payment of the full face value of interest and principal is not to be expected on the average. This leads to the mathematical definition of the "premium for risk" as the value of x that will satisfy the following two equations:

$$x = i - \imath \qquad (7)$$

$$V = \sum_{t=1}^{t=n} \frac{\pi_t}{(1 + i)^t} + \frac{C}{(1 + i)^n} \qquad (1e)$$

where

  x = premium for risk
  i = yield, at face value of interest and principal
  $\imath$ = pure interest rate[11]

---

[9]The value of the denominator is always unity because the sum of all the separate probabilities is necessarily one. For values of V above the maximum, $f(V) = 0$.

[10]See, for instance, *High Yield Tables of Bond Values* (Boston: Financial Publishing Co., and London: George Rutledge and Sons, Ltd., 1919), p. 83.

[11]Although it would make a more consistent notation to use $\bar{\imath}$ instead of i for the risk-inclusive rate, so as to correspond with $\bar{V}$ for the risk-inclusive value, the more common symbol was made the simpler, and i was used for the risk-inclusive, $\imath$ for the riskless, rate of interest.

The economic "premium for risk" is not to be confused with the accounting "premium" on a bond bought above par.

V = mean of all possible values of bond, as defined in equation (6)
π = face value of coupons
C = face value of principal
n = number of years to maturity of bond

If the mean value, $\overline{V}$, is known, equation (1e) can be solved for i, the proper yield. Or, if i is known, the same equation can be solved for $\overline{V}$. The problem can be approached in either way. Most people are used to going about it in the latter way, however, and find it easier to think in terms of interest and principal at face value heavily discounted than in terms of interest and principal at reduced value lightly discounted. They think they can make a better estimate of the proper rate of discount in any given situation than of the various possibilities of partial or complete default. If they can, their method has the advantage of being quicker and easier, because it requires the calculation of the present worth of one simple, instead of many varied, annuities. The final choice depends on whether the element of uncertainty in forecasts can be handled by the mind more easily in the one way or the other. Usually the method of using an enlarged discount rate will prove to be the simpler to think of, and so we shall generally employ it in the pages to follow.

9. SENIOR AND JUNIOR ISSUES OF THE SAME CONCERN

As everyone knows, the risk factor varies between the several securities of the same company. Usually the bonds are considered safer than the shares, with the underlying bonds having a better rating than the junior bonds, and the preferred stock than the common stock. Sometimes, however, this rule appears to be refuted by actual market prices, especially in the case of overcapitalized enterprises that nevertheless enjoy good speculative prospects. With such enterprises, the senior securities usually sell to give a high yield, the common stock a low yield. Yet the market is quite right in thus reversing the usual rule, for if the venture should fail, the bondholders would lose much; but if it should succeed, they would gain little, since all the profits in excess of stipulated interest would go to the common stockholders, who have but little to lose and much to gain. A notable instance of the foregoing was the United States Steel Corporation at the beginning of its career. . . . . , its senior securities sold to yield 6.5 per cent on the average soon after it was formed, while its stock sold at a high price-earnings ratio, because the success of the new trust was then still in doubt, although the company was thought to have great speculative possibilities.

The proper yield on the *common* stock of such an enterprise is fixed and determined, after the manner of a dependent variable, once the proper yield on the *senior* secuirites and on the enterprise as a whole are agreed upon, as the following algebraic analysis shows   (For simplicity a horizontal trend to earnings is assumed.)

Let

$$V_b = \text{investment value of bonds, per share of common}$$
$$V_c = \text{investment value of stock, per share of common}$$
$$V_a = \text{investment value of entire enterprise, per share of}$$
$$\text{common}$$

Then

$$V_a = V_b + V_c \tag{8a}$$

Likewise let

$$\beta = \text{bond interest, per share of common}$$
$$\pi = \text{pure dividend, per share of common}$$
$$i_b = \text{fair interest rate for bonds}$$
$$i_c = \text{fair interest rate for common stock}$$
$$i_a = \text{fair interest rate for entire enterprise}$$

Then

$$V_b = \frac{\beta}{i_b} \quad \text{(For simplicity, the bonds are assumed to be perpetual bonds.)} \tag{8c}$$

$$V_c = \frac{\pi}{i_c} \tag{8a}$$

$$V_a = \frac{\beta + \pi}{i_a} \tag{8b}$$

Combining (18a) and (8b), we get

$$V_b + V_c = \frac{\beta + \pi}{i_a} \tag{8d}$$

and combining (8c) and (8a) with (8d), we get

$$\frac{\beta}{i_b} + \frac{\pi}{i_c} = \frac{\beta + \pi}{i_a}$$

$$\frac{\pi}{i_c} = \frac{\beta + \pi}{i_a} - \frac{\beta}{i_b}$$

whence

$$i_c = \frac{\pi}{\dfrac{\beta + \pi}{i_a} - \dfrac{\beta}{i_b}} \tag{8e}$$

Q. E. F.

The foregoing formula shows the proper yield for a common stock once the fair yield for the senior securities and the enterprise as a whole have been decided upon.

10. THE LAW OF THE CONSERVATION OF INVESTMENT VALUE

If the investment value of an enterprise as a whole is by definition the present worth of all its future distributions to security holders, whether on interest or dividend account, then this value in no wise depends on what the company's capitalization is. Clearly if a single individual or a single institutional investor owned all the bonds, stocks, and warrants issued by a corporation, it would not matter to this investor what the company's capitalization was.[12] Any earnings collected as interest could not be collected as dividends. To such an individual it would be perfectly obvious that total interest- and dividend-paying power was in no wise dependent on the kind of securities issued to the company's owner. Furthermore, no *change* in the investment value of the enterprise as a whole would result from a *change* in its capitalization. Bonds could be retired with stock issues, or two classes of junior securities (i.e., common stock and warrants) could be combined into one, without changing the investment value of the company as a whole. Such constancy of investment value is analogous to the indestructibility of matter or energy; it leads us to speak of the Law of the Conservation of Investment Value, just as physicists speak of the Law of the Conservation of Matter, or the Law of the Conservation of Energy.

Since market value does not usually conform exactly to investment value, no "conservation of market value" is to be found in general. Only to a rough extent do total market values remain the same regardless of capitalization. The exceptions in practice are important enough to afford many opportunities for profit by promoters and investment bankers.

11. REFUNDING OPERATIONS

If a bond issue matures, or if general interest rates decline enough to allow the replacement of a callable issue with another bearing a lower interest rate, a refunding operation may be undertaken that will alter the corporation's interest charges and change the investment value of its common stock. Since the distributable fraction of a company's quasi-rents is independent of its capital structure and is entirely available for taxes, interest, and dividends, any saving in interest can be used for dividends, and any increase in interest must come out of dividends. Hence the resulting increment or decrement in earnings per share must be capitalized at a different rate from the original earnings per share. If by refunding its bonds at a lower rate and replacing its preferred stock with low-coupon notes, for instance, a company saves a dollar a share in senior charges, then—assuming that dividends are capitalized at 5 per cent, and earnings at 10 per cent

---

[12]Except for details concerning the income tax.

(the usual rule of thumb)—it adds twenty dollars a share, and not ten, to the value of its common stock. If, on the other hand, a company is forced to refund a maturing issue at a higher rate, as might happen if its bonds came due during a banking crisis, then the decrease in earnings per share, resulting from the higher interest charges, would have to be capitalized at twenty times, and not at ten as would an ordinary change in earnings.

12. MARKETABILITY

Marketability, or salability, or liquidity, is an attribute of an investment to which many buyers of necessity attach great importance. Yet it would not be helpful to amend our definition of investment value in such a way as to make it take cognizance of marketability. Risk, to be sure, should be covered by the definition, as done above, but not marketability, for the inclusion of marketability would only lead to confusion. Better to treat intrinsic value as one thing, salability as another. Then we can say, for instance, that a given investment is both cheap and liquid, not that it is cheap partly because it is liquid; the latter phraseology would only raise the question of how much of the cheapness was due to liquidity and how much to other factors. To divorce liquidity, or salability, or marketability, from the concept of investment value is in conformity, moreover, with accepted usage outside the field of investment. In speaking of goods and services, for instance, one does not say that a pound of sugar is cheap at six cents because it is so "salable." Nothing of the sort; for the sugar is bought for consumption and not for resale. By the same token, why should one say that a bond is cheap because it is so salable? For if the bond is bought for investment, as by a life insurance company, it is not intended for resale at all, but for holding to maturity. Of course, if the buyer is a speculator, that is another matter, since investment value is only one of several things considered by a speculator. But even a speculator should not confuse salability with cheapness, any more than he should confuse popularity with cheapness. Just as market price determined by marginal opinion is one thing, and investment value determined by future dividends is another, so also salability is one thing and cheapness another.

Likewise *stability* is a thing distinct from investment value, and from marketability as well. While the expected stability of the price of a security in future years is a consideration of great importance to some investors, particularly banks, yet it is not a component of investment value as the latter term ought to be defined. Many individual investors who buy and hold for income do not need to concern themselves with stability any more than with liquidity; hence to include the concept of stability in the definition of investment value would only make investment value mean something different for each and every investor, according to his own personal need for stability as compared with other things.

In conclusion, therefore, it may be said that neither marketability nor stability should be permitted to enter into the meaning of the term *investment value*.

3·2

Dividend Growth as Determinant of Common-Stock Values*

John C. Clendenin

Although the selection of stocks for long-term holding must always involve a number of criteria, the heart of the problem is usually productivity—how much over a period of time can be expected from Stock A, and how does this compare with Stock B or other available alternatives? Some high-quality stocks are stable dividend producers, promising immediate and continuing good yields. Others are "growth stocks" promising small yields now but better ones later. If the portfolio can use either, which will be the more productive over the longer term, a stable producer priced to yield $5\frac{1}{2}$ per cent or a growth stock currently yielding 3 per cent? As of now there is no standard approach to an answer. The securities business has neither an accepted theory of growth stock values nor a device for measuring them.

It is the purpose of this article to advance a simple and familiar theory of stock values—a theory based entirely on future dividend productivity—and to suggest some easy rule-of-thumb methods for comparing the values of nongrowth, slow-growth, and fast-growth stocks. We shall show, for example, that a nongrowth stock at 17 times dividends, a medium-growth stock at 26 times dividends, and a fast-growth stock at 36 times dividends may all be equally attractive in price—and we shall show how to find out if they are.

Our methods are not intended to predict the course of the stock market or even to predict the prices which a trading market will assign to individual stocks. Rather, they are intended to indicate, for the stocks and groups of

*From *Trusts And Estates Magazine*, February, 1957. This is an abridgement of a longer study published under the title *Theory and Technique of Growth Stock Valuation* by the Bureau of Business and Economic Research, University of California, Los Angeles (1957).

stocks to which they are applicable, the long-term average yield to be expected on stock investments made at existing prices, or, conversely, the stock prices upon which desired average yields may be expected.

We shall not neglect the capital gains aspect of earnings and dividend growth. Our stock value theory will indicate the causes of the great gains of the past decade and provide a basis upon which future possibilities may be judged.

THEORY OF STOCK VALUE

The most satisfactory theory for our purpose is the old and familiar concept upon which bond tables are based—namely, that the investment value of any security is the total of the mathematical present values of all future distributions to be obtained from it, with present values computed at interest rates (yields) commensurate with the risk and other features of the security.[1] This theory implies that in the last analysis stockholders will obtain nothing from a stock investment except such cash dividends (plus possibly a few rights, spin-offs, and other fringe benefits) as the corporation may pay before its ultimate oblivion. The dividends represent both income *and recovery of principal* to the stockholders, and the value of a share at any given time is simply the present value of the probable future dividends as foreseen at that time. Since a future sale of a share will merely transfer subsequent dividends to the purchaser, a share held for sale has the same value as one for permanent investment.

It is sometimes urged that a theory of stock value based upon the dividends of future years is impractical because long-term dividend forecasts cannot be exact. It is true that long-term dividend projections are not likely to be perfect, but it is also essential to remember that future dividends are in the long run the sole source of value, and the long-term investor who fails to anticipate them is ignoring the basic reason for his investment—the payments which will return his principal and the earned income. Investors who arrive at stock appraisals by multiplying past or current earnings and dividends by capitalization factors, or who rely on book values or market price histories, are simply obtaining substitutes for the dividend values which they need to evaluate. Whether these vaguely related substitute figures come any closer to sensible appraisals than an "inexact" estimate of the essential future dividends is somewhat doubtful.

Table 1 illustrates the ideas involved in this present-value-of-dividends approach. The table is purely mathematical; the figures in it are the current

[1]This approach is not confined to securities. It is also basic to the valuation of installment notes, mortgages, buildings, farms, and most other property. Nor is its application to stocks a new idea. It was utilized 20 years ago by J. B. Williams in his *Theory of Investment Value*, and has recently been discussed by Parker in the *Analysts Journal*, by Bing in the *Commercial and Financial Chronicle*, and by Clendenin and Van Cleave in the *Journal of Finance*.

price-dividend ratios applicable to any stocks which fit into the table. For example, the stock of a company whose business, earnings record, balance sheet, and other factors imply an indefinite continuation of the existing dividend rate is worth 17.01 times dividends, assuming a stock quality to which the table's 4–5–6–7 per cent yield schedule properly applies. However, the existence of an average 3 per cent per year dividend growth trend which gave promise of continuing for the next 30 years would permit a current price-dividend ratio of 26.08, and still (under the conditions of the table) afford the investor the yields contemplated by the table. Similarly, a 5 per cent growth trend expected to continue for 20 years would justify a current price-dividend ratio of 31.21, and one expected to continue for 30 years would justify a ratio of 35.97.

Table 1 can also be used to check the rationality of quoted prices. For example, a $200 price for du Pont would be 30.8 times the 1956 dividend of $6.50; a projection of du Pont's long-term growth rate plus an allowance for future inflation suggests a possible dividend growth approximating 5 per cent per year. The table indicates that a price of 30.8 times current dividends would meet its yield standards (4-5-6-7 per cent) if a 5 per cent dividend growth rate continued for about 20 more years, or 4 per cent rate for 30 years.

Table 2 is included in our presentation to console the skeptics who hesitate to base stock valuations upon uncertain estimates of the dividends of far distant years. (These skeptics base their valuations upon past earnings and dividends which have no bearing at all on value recoveries in the future.) Table 2 shows the present values of dividends under assumed conditions for each of the next three decades and for the ensuing 70 years, and a total

TABLE 1. *Approximate present values of all future dividends on a stock now paying $1.00 per annum, if the dividend is expected to increase at the indicated compound rate for the indicated period of years and then remain stable until 100 years from today, and if the dividends of the first decade are discounted at 4%, those of the second at 5%, those of the third at 6%, and those of the remaining 70 years at 7%.*

| Growth period | Annual growth rates | | | | |
	5%	4%	3%	1%	0%
None	$17.01	$17.01	$17.01	$17.01	$17.01
10 years	24.85	23.04	21.37	18.37	17.01
20 years	31.21	27.51	24.27	19.12	17.01
30 years	35.97	30.55	26.08	19.51	17.01
40 years	39.65	32.67	27.22	19.69	17.01
50 years	42.63	34.23	27.99	19.80	17.01

TABLE 2. *Approximate present values of the future dividends on a stock now paying $1.00 per annum, if the dividends are expected to grow at the indicated rates for 20 years and then remain stable for the next 80 years, and if the dividends of the first decade are discounted at 4%, those of the second at 5%, those of the third at 6%, and those of the remaining 70 years at 7%.*

% Growth rate per year	Present dollar values				
	First decade	Second decade	Third decade	Next 70 years	Total
6	10.85	11.36	7.36	5.96	35.53
5	10.35	9.84	6.09	4.93	31.21
4	9.87	8.53	5.03	4.08	27.51
3	9.40	7.37	4.14	3.36	24.27
2	8.96	6.39	3.41	2.76	21.52
1	8.53	5.52	2.80	2.27	19.12
0	8.11	4.74	2.30	1.86	17.01

which in each case is the theoretical proper current price-dividend ratio for the stock.

It will be observed that on a nongrowth stock the theoretical value is 70 per cent recovered in the first two decades, and only about 11 per cent of the value arises in periods more than 30 years hence. On a stock promising a rapid 5 per cent growth the first two decades account for about 65 per cent of the value, and the period beyond the third decade about 16 per cent. These figures clearly indicate that the bulk of the value attaching to any stock tends to originate in the dividends of the first two decades, which are not beyond the scope of reasonable estimate.

DIVIDEND GROWTH TRENDS

In the process of studying dividend growth we have examined the long-term per-share earnings and dividend records of many stocks and a number of market averages. Three salient facts emerge. First, it appears that most major stocks other than the rate-regulated utilities have ultimately earned and paid more—perhaps about proportionately more—as a result of the 1940–1953 price-level inflation. Inflationary tendencies still persist, and therefore must be allowed for both in judging the past and in estimating future earnings and dividends. Second, when we remove the effects of price-level change from the historical figures, average dividend growth rates on major stocks during the past 30 years have not been very fast—for example, about 4 per cent per year for du Pont, 3 per cent for General Electric, an average of 3 per cent for 8 major growth stocks, 2 per cent for Standard and

Poor's index of 50 industrials, 0 for a group of 10 good quality nongrowth industrials which we compiled ourselves. Third, the growth rates and growth patterns are diverse, and except for the very large companies, are more predictable when combined into groups.

Despite stout resistance by the Federal Reserve System and an anti-inflationary attitude by the administration, the general price level in the United States has risen nearly 5 per cent in the past four years. These have been good years, it is true, but it is also evident that public policy is basically inflationary, and for the long pull it seems reasonable to count on an average of one per cent per year of price-level inflation. The one per cent per year figure is only a guess, and it will accrue intermittently rather than steadily, but almost certainly something of the sort can be expected to influence future earnings and dividends, and must therefore be included as a factor in any estimates.

Thus far we have repeatedly referred to a need for estimates on future earnings and dividends, without suggesting any methods. There are many statistical approaches to this type of estimation, including projections based on GNP, on industry growth trends, on sales and profit margin trends, and on product and resource development. We have been charting past earnings and dividend trends deflated for prices to obtain an idea of current and historic growth rates, and projecting these into the future with arbitrary allowances for industry and company outlook and our ideas of future price levels. Admittedly we are guessing, but we are guessing at indispensable data, and we feel that our guesses are good enough to be worth while on the stocks of large established concerns and on groups of stocks combined.

A word of caution is in order on the subject of earnings and dividend growth trends. We think that the rapid growth rate in the years 1946–1956 is in many cases abnormal, since the period is one of recovery from wartime price controls and excess profits taxes, of unusual technological progress and of almost uninterrupted prosperity. A long-term "trend" continuing the profits progress of 1946–1956 would be almost too good to be true.

YIELDS ON STOCKS

Although "yields" of 4 to 5 per cent are commonplace on the market averages and considerably lower ones are accepted on leading growth stocks, these are not generally regarded as the measure of long-range performance on stock investment. Most dividends are expected to grow and long-range performance thus will exceed the current yield.

An inspection of the yields (based on cash dividends plus nondiluting rights if any) on high-grade nongrowth or slow-growth stocks since 1950 leaves the impression that the market has usually offered between 5 and 6 per cent on good quality nongrowth industrial equities. Since it seemed only reasonable that near-term dividends of fairly certain amounts should be evaluated at lower rates of yield than were applied to the rather conjectural dividend estimates of distant years, we decided that our valuation tables (Tables 1 and 2, previously discussed) should evaluate the dividends of the first decade at 4 per cent yield, the second decade at 5 per cent, the third decade at 6 per cent, and the balance of significant time at 7 per cent. Other tables of various sorts were constructed, but this one seems to fit market experience and common sense better than most. In our opinion, the table is applicable only to quality stocks with established dividend and earnings records.

It would be possible, using Table 1 and a few others based on different growth and yield assumptions, to make very practical comparisons of the prices of stocks being considered for long-term investment. However, Table 1 calls for certain specific estimates which may be bypassed if one of two rule-of-thumb methods is used.

TWO PRACTICAL RULES OF THUMB

A rule of thumb is a convenient calculation process which obtains approximate results by short-cut methods. Because of the compensating tendencies of certain mathematical factors, two such short cuts seem feasible. These short cuts are specifically designed to give results consistent with the 20-year growth values presented in Table 1.

METHOD NO. 1

Estimate the probable annual payment rate (*dividends plus rights*) *twelve years hence, and divide by current prices.* This process will provide comparable estimates of weighted average future yields on the current prices of fast-growth, slow-growth, and nongrowth stocks. Its chief weakness, if it be a weakness, is its inherent assumption that the growth trend embodied in the 12-year dividend estimate will continue for a total of about 20 years and then level out. For a strong growth stock this is probably conservative—but, on the other hand, it may not be conservative to pay cash money for any growth trend beyond its 20th year.

An illustration of Method No. 1 may be in order. The 1956 du Pont dividend was $6.50 per share, a figure which seems quite in line with the company's earning power and policies. Rights do not appear to be a significant factor. Next, a study of the company's long-term past growth on a *constant-dollar basis* indicates a growth rate of about 4 per cent per annum compounded. If this growth rate is accepted as continuing (and here we are illustrating, not predicting), our expectation of a future average annual price-level inflation of 1 per cent will lead us to place our dividend growth estimate at 5 per cent compounded. It therefore appears reasonable to estimate du Pont's dividend 12 years hence at $6.50 $\times$ 1.05^{12}, or $11.65 per share. On du Pont's recent price of 190 this would "yield" 6.13 per cent—and we think that this yield provides an arithmetic comparison with yields similarly calculated on other stocks and by conventional methods on preferred stocks or bonds. Quality factors other than growth tendencies could obviously justify differences in yields, and optimism regarding the duration of a growth trend would lead to a belief that the computed yield was understated or overstated.

METHOD No. 2

Estimate the annual distribution rate twelve years hence, and appraise the stock by multiplying by 15 to 19 depending on stock quality. In this context the word quality does not include growth capacity, but does include capital structure, trade position, management and other strength aspects of the firm. Most of the inherent assumptions of Method No. 1 and its conservative handling of strong growth trends are inherent in Method No. 2 also.

Obviously, stock appraisals, made by this method will be out of line with both high and low markets. They are chiefly useful as devices for comparing the values of different stocks, and to a less degree in establishing intrinsic values for comparison with market quotations.

CAPITAL GAINS

Thus far our discussion has stressed dividends and prospective dividends and has largely disregarded future stock prices. Two observations on the subject of capital gains are now in order.

First, a growth stock which is correctly appraised at the present time will show a higher appraisal a decade or two hence, for when the predicted larger dividends have become current or imminent their present values (hence, presumably, the market value of the stock) become substantially greater. This is not an advantage over nongrowth stocks; the nongrowth stocks pay more in the earlier years, and the value gains in the growth issues merely represent the compensating deferred income as it becomes more imminent. If taken by sale as a low-taxed capital gain, this is of course an advantageous form of income.

Second, a growth stock which is bought at a price which contemplates 15 to 20 years' growth, but which retains its growth tendencies for a longer period, will obviously show a great profit. There would be an equal or greater profit in a nongrowth stock which began to grow, or in a growth stock which grew faster than anticipated—and disappointments could occur, too. But we make a particular point of years of growth because conservative appraisals must needs estimate strong growth trends at 15 to 20 years' duration, whereas history shows the clear possibility of longer periods. These longer periods may be recognized by the market in higher prices almost year by year, if time passes without any evidence of slackening growth capacity.

A WORD OF CAUTION

Before concluding this article it seems desirable to emphasize the need for common sense in the appraisal of growth stocks. As our tables indicate, it is easy to "prove" that a fast-growth stock is worth 40 to 50 times current dividends, simply by assuming an impending 40 or 50 years of rapid growth and a 6 per cent or less yield basis. But we feel that growth rates projected beyond 20 or 30 years should be evaluated at rather high yield rates—at least 7 per cent—and if this is done, our tables indicate that 30 or 35 times current dividends (and this would usually mean 20 to 27 times current earning power) is high enough for all but the most promising stocks and too high for most.

It is perhaps necessary to defend any counsel of conservatism in growth stocks, for since the war almost any indiscriminate purchase of a growth issue has seemed to result in a large profit. There have been a number of factors behind this, and in our opinion most of them are nonrecurring. Among these factors are the following:

1. *General market rise.* The post-1950 popularity of stock investments has resulted in increased price-earnings and price-dividend ratios for all high-grade stocks, including growth stocks.

2. *The general price-level inflation.* Corporate earnings and dividends since 1945 have been "catching up" to the general inflation of 1940–1953. During this period many growth stocks doubled their earnings and dividends in real terms and the price-level inflation doubled them again, resulting in multiplication by four.

3. *Commencement of growth.* When a stock enters a promising long-term growth phase its value may rise rapidly from 15 or 20 times dividends to 30 or 35 times dividends. Thereafter, even as the expected growth takes place, the present value of future dividends (and presumably the price of the stock) may rise relatively slowly.

4. *Irregular growth.* Long-range earnings and dividend progress is often made in irregular spurts and market recognition occurs similarly. In consequence, short-term gains of sizable amounts give an impression of high-average speed.

5. *Improved quality.* Many spectacular stock price gains since the war have

reflected the "growing up" of a company or its industry, with a consequent shift from a speculative 7 per cent yield basis to an investment-grade low-yield rating for the stock. This gain will of course occur but once.

When all of the nonrecurring elements in these five factors are given due weight, the postwar record can hardly be held to prove that any growth stock at any indiscriminate price is certain to provide capital gains in the future.

3·3

The New Speculation in Common Stocks*

Benjamin Graham

What I shall have to say will reflect the spending of many years in Wall Street, with their attendant varieties of experience. This has included the recurrent advent of new conditions, or a new atmosphere, which challenge the value of experience itself. It is true that one of the elements that distinguish economics, finance, and security analysis from other practical disciplines is the uncertain validity of past phenomena as a guide to the present and future. Yet we have no right to reject the lessons of the past until we have at least studied and understood them. My address today is an effort toward such understanding in a limited field—in particular, an endeavor to point out some contrasting relationships between the present and the past in our underlying attitudes towards investment and speculation in common stocks.

Let me start with a summary of my thesis. In the past the speculative elements of a common stock resided almost exclusively in the company itself; they were due to uncertainties, or fluctuating elements, or downright weaknesses in the industry, or the corporation's individual set-up. These elements of speculation still exist, of course; but it may be said that they have been sensibly diminished by a number of long-term developments to which I shall refer. But in revenge a new and major element of speculation has been introduced into the common-stock arena from *outside* the com-

*From Benjamin Graham, *The Intelligent Investor*, Second Revised Edition, Copyright © 1959 by Harper & Brothers, pp. 273–284. Reprinted with permission of Harper & Row, Publishers, Incorporated. An address of Benjamin Graham before the Annual Convention of the National Federation of Financial Analysts Societies, May 1958.

panies. It comes from the attitude and viewpoint of the stock-buying public and their advisers—chiefly us security analysts. This attitude may be described in a phrase: primary emphasis upon future expectations.

Nothing will appear more logical and natural to this audience than the idea that a common stock should be valued and priced primarily on the basis of the company's expected future performance. Yet this simple-appearing concept carries with it a number of paradoxes and pitfalls. For one thing, it obliterates a good part of the older, well-established distinctions between investment and speculation. The dictionary says that "speculate" comes from the Latin "specula," a look-out or watch-tower. Thus it was the speculator who looked out from his elevated watch-tower and saw future developments coming before other people did. But today, if the investor is shrewd or well-advised, he too must have his watch-tower looking out on the future, or rather he mounts into a common watch-tower where he rubs elbows with the speculator.

Secondly, we find that, for the most part, companies with the best investment characteristics—i.e., the best credit rating—are the ones which are likely to attract the largest speculative interest in their common stocks, since everyone assumes they are guaranteed a brilliant future. Thirdly, the concept of future prospects, and particularly of continued growth in the future, invites the application of formulae out of higher mathematics to establish the present value of the favored issues. But the combination of precise formulae with highly imprecise assumptions can be used to establish, or rather to justify, practically any value one wishes, however high, for a really outstanding issue. But, paradoxically, that very fact on close examination will be seen to imply that no one value, or reasonably narrow range of values, can be counted on to establish and maintain itself for a given growth company; hence at times the market may conceivably value the growth component at a strikingly *low* figure.

Returning to my distinction between the older and newer speculative elements in common stock, we might characterize them by two outlandish but convenient words, viz.: endogenous and exogenous. Let me illustrate briefly the old-time speculative common stock, as distinguished from an investment stock, by some data relating to American Can and Pennsylvania Railroad in 1911–13. (These appear in *Security Analysis*, 1940 Edition, pp. 2–3.)

In those three years the price range of "Pennsy" moved only between 53 and 65, or between 12.2 and 15 times its average earnings for the period. It showed steady profits, was paying a reliable $3 dividend, and investors were sure that it was backed by well over its par of $50 in tangible assets. By contrast, the price of American Can ranged between 9 and 47; its earnings between 7¢ and $8.86; the ratio of price to the average earnings moved between 1.9 times and 10 times; it paid no dividend at all; and sophisticated investors were well aware that the $100 par value of the common represented nothing but undisclosed "water," since the preferred issue exceeded the tangible assets available for it. Thus American Can common was a representative speculative issue, because American Can Company was then a speculative-capitalized enterprise in a fluctuating and uncertain industry. Actually, American Can had a far more brilliant long-term future than Pennsylvania Railroad; but not only was this fact not suspected by investors or speculators in those days, but even if it had been it would probably have been put aside by the investors as basically irrelevant to investment policies and programs in the years 1911–13.

Now, to expose you to the development through time of the importance of long-term prospects for investments, I should like to use as my example our most spectacular giant industrial enterprise—none other than International Business Machines, which last year entered the small group of companies with $1 billion of sales. May I introduce one or two auto-biographical notes here, in order to inject a little of the personal touch into what otherwise would be an excursion into cold figures? In 1912 I had left college for a term to take charge of a research project for U. S. Express Company. We set out to find the effect on revenues of a proposed revolutionary new system of computing express rates. For this purpose we used the so-called Hollerith machines, leased out by the then Computing-Tabulating-Recording Company. They comprised card-punches, card-sorters, and tabulators—tools almost unknown to businessmen, then, and having their chief application in the Census Bureau. I entered Wall Street in 1914, and the next year the bonds and common stock of C.-T.-R. Company were listed on the New York Stock Exchange. Well, I had a kind of sentimental interest in that enterprise, and besides I considered myself a sort of technological expert on their products, being one of the few financial people who had seen and used them. So early in 1916 I went to the head of my firm, known as Mr. A. N., and pointed out to him that C.-T.-R. stock was selling in the middle 40s (for 105,000 shares); that it had earned $6.50 in 1915; that its book value—including, to be sure, some non-segregated intangibles—was $130; that it had started a $3 dividend; and that I thought rather highly of the company's products and prospects. Mr. A. N. looked at me pityingly. "Ben," said he, "do not mention that company to me again. I would not touch it with a ten-foot pole. [His favorite expression.] Its 6 per cent bonds are selling in the low 80s and they are no good. So how can the stock be any good? Everybody knows there is nothing behind it but water." (Glossary: In those days that was the ultimate of condemnation. It meant that the asset-account on the balance-sheet was fictitious. Many industrial companies—notably U. S. Steel —despite their $100 par, represented nothing but water, concealed in a written-up plant account. Since they had "nothing" to back them but earning power and future prospects, no self-respecting investor would give them a second thought.)

I returned to my statistician's cubbyhole, a chastened young man. Mr. A. N. was not only experienced and successful, but extremely shrewd as well. So much was I impressed by his sweeping condemnation of Computing-Tabulating-Recording that I never bought a share of it in my life, not even after its name was changed to IBM in 1926.

Now let us take a look at the same company with its new name in 1926, a year of pretty high stock markets. At that time it first revealed the good-will item in its balance-sheet, in the rather large sum of $13.6 millions. A. N. had been right. Practically every dollar of the so-called equity behind the common in 1915 had been nothing but water. However, since that time the company had made an impressive record under the direction of T. L. Watson, Sr. Its net had risen from $691,000 to $3.7 million—over five-fold—a greater percentage gain than it was to make in any subsequent 11-year period. It had built up a nice tangible equity for the common, and had split it 3.6 for one. It had established a $3 dividend rate for the new stock, while earnings were $6.39 thereon. You might have expected the 1926 stock market to have been pretty enthusiastic about a company with such a growth history and so strong a trade position.· Let us see. The price range for that year was 31 low, 59 high. At the average of 45 it was selling at the same 7-times multiplier of earnings and the same 6.7 per cent dividend yield as it had done in 1915. At its low of 31 it was not far in excess of its tangible book value, and in that respect was far more conservatively priced than 11 years earlier.

These data illustrate, as well as any can, the persistence of the old-time investment viewpoint until the culminating years of the bull market of the 1920's. What has happened since then can be summarized by using 10-year intervals in the history of IBM. In 1936 net expanded to twice the 1926 figures, and the average multiplier rose from 7 to 17½. From 1936 to 1946 the gain was 2½ times, but the average multiplier in 1946 remained at 17½. Then the pace accelerated. The 1956 net was nearly 4 times that of 1946, and the average multiplier rose to 32½. Last year, with a further gain in net, the multiplier rose again to an average of 42, if we do not count the unconsolidated equity in the foreign subsidiary.

When we examine these recent price figures with care we see some interesting analogies and contrasts with those of 40 years earlier. The one-time scandalous water, so prevalent in the balance-sheets of industrial companies, has all been squeezed out—first by disclosure and then by write-offs. But a different kind of water has been put back into the valuation by the stock market—by investors and speculators themselves. When IBM now sells at 7 times its book value, instead of 7 times earnings, the effect is practically the same as if it had no book value at all. Or the small book-value portion can be considered as a sort of minor preferred-stock component of the price, the rest representing exactly the same sort of commitment as the old-time speculator made when he bought Woolworth or U. S. Steel common entirely for their earning power and future prospects.

It is worth remarking, in passing, that in the 30 years which saw IBM transformed from a 7-times earnings to a 40-times earnings enterprise, many of what I have called the endogenous speculative aspects of our large industrial companies have tended to disappear, or at least to diminish greatly. Their financial positions are firm, their capital structures conservative; they are managed far more expertly, and even more honestly, than before. Furthermore, the requirements of complete disclosure have removed one of the important speculative elements of years ago—that derived from ignorance and mystery.

Another personal digression here. In my early years in the Street one of the favorite mystery stocks was Consolidated Gas of New York, now Consolidated Edison. It owned as a subsidiary the profitable New York Edison Company, but it reported only dividends received from this source, not its full earnings. The unreported Edison earnings supplied the mystery and the "hidden value." To my surprise I discovered that these hush-hush figures were actually on file each year with the Public Service Commission of the state. It was a simple matter to consult the records and to present the true earnings of Consolidated Gas in a magazine article. (Incidentally, the addition to profits was not spectacular.) One of my older friends said to me then: "Ben, you may think you are a great guy to supply those missing figures, but Wall Street is going to thank you for nothing. Consolidated Gas with the mystery is both more interesting and more valuable than ex-mystery. You youngsters who want to stick your noses into everything are going to ruin Wall Street."

It is true that the three M's which then supplied so much fuel to the speculative fires have now all but disappeared. These were Mystery, Manipulation, and (thin) Margins. But we security analysts have ourselves been creating valuation approaches which are so speculative in themselves as to pretty well take the place of those older speculative factors. Do we not have our own "3 M's" now—none other than Minnesota Mining and Manufacturing Company—and does not this common stock illustrate perfectly the new speculation as contrasted with the old? Consider a few figures. When M.M. & M. common sold at 101 last year the market was valuing it at 44 times 1956 earnings, which happened to show no increase to speak of in 1957. The enterprise itself was valued at $1.7 billion, of which $200 million was covered by net assets, and a cool $1½ billion represented the market's appraisal of "good-will." We do not know the process of calculation by which that valuation of good-will was arrived at; we do know that a few months later the market revised this appraisal downward by some $450 million, or about 30 per cent. Obviously it is impossible to calculate accurately the intangible component of a splendid company such as this. It follows as a kind of mathematical law that the more important the good-will or future earning-power factor the more uncertain becomes the true value of the enterprise, and therefore the more speculative inherently the common stock.

It may be well to recognize a vital difference that has developed in the valuation of these intangible factors, when we compare earlier times with today. A generation or more ago it was the standard rule, recognized both in average stock prices and in formal or legal valuations, that intangibles were to be appraised on a more conservative basis than tangibles. A good industrial company might be required to earn between 6 per cent and 8 per cent on its tangible assets, represented typically by bonds and preferred stock; but its excess earnings, or the intangible assets they gave rise to, would be valued on, say, a 15 per cent basis. (You will find approximately these ratios in the initial offering of Woolworth Preferred and Common stock in 1911, and in numerous others.) But what has happened since the 1920's? Essentially the exact reverse of these relationships may now be seen. A company must now typically earn about 10 per cent on its common equity to have it sell in the average market at full book value. But its excess earnings, above 10 per cent on capital, are usually valued more liberally, or at a higher multiplier, than the base earnings required to support the book value in the market. Thus a company earning 15 per cent on the equity may well sell at $13\frac{1}{2}$ times earnings, or twice its net assets. This would mean that the first 10 per cent earned on capital is valued at only 10 times, but the next 5 per cent—what used to be called the excess—is actually valued at 20 times.

Now there is a logical reason for this reversal in valuation procedure, which is related to the newer emphasis on growth expectations. Companies that earn a high return on capital are given these liberal appraisals not only because of the good profitability itself, and the relative stability associated with it, but perhaps even more cogently because high earnings on capital generally go hand in hand with a good growth record and prospects. Thus what is really paying for nowadays in the case of highly profitable companies is not the good-will in the old and restricted sense of an established name and a profitable business, but rather for their assumed superior expectations of increased profits in the future.

This brings me to one or two additional mathematical aspects of the new attitude toward common-stock valuations, which I shall touch on merely in the form of brief suggestions. If, as many tests show, the earnings multiplier tends to increase with profitability—i.e., as the rate of return on book value increases—then the arithmetical consequence of this feature is that value tends to increase directly as the square of the earnings, but *inversely* with book value. Thus in an important and very real sense tangible assets have become a drag on average market value rather than a source thereof. Take a far from extreme illustration. If Company A earns $4 a share on a $20 book value, and Company B also $4 a share on $100 of book value, Company A is almost certain to sell at a higher multiplier, and hence at higher price than Company B—say $60 for Company A shares and $35 for Company B shares. Thus it would not be inexact to declare that the $80 per share of greater assets for Company B are responsible for the $25 per share lower market price, since the earnings per share are assumed to be equal.

But more important than the foregoing is the general relationship between mathematics and the new approach to stock values. Given the three ingredients of (a) optimistic assumptions as to the rate of earnings growth, (b) a sufficiently long projection of this growth into the future, and (c) the miraculous workings of compound interest—and the security analyst is supplied with a new kind of Philosopher's Stone which can produce or justify any desired valuation for a really "good stock." I have commented in a recent article in the *Analysts Journal* on the vogue of higher mathematics in bull markets, and quoted David Durand's exposition of the striking analogy between value calculations of growth stocks and the famous Petersburg Paradox, which has challenged and confused mathematicians for more than 200 years. The point I want to make here is that there is a special paradox in the relationship between mathematics and investment attitudes on common stocks, which is this: Mathematics is ordinarily considered as producing precise and dependable results; but in the stock market the more elaborate and abstruse the mathematics the more uncertain and speculative are the conclusions we draw therefrom. In 44 years of Wall Street experience and study I have never seen dependable calculations made about common-stock values, or related investment policies, that went beyond simple arithmetic or the most elementary algebra. Whenever calculus is brought in, or higher algebra, you could take it as a warning signal that the operator was trying to substitute theory for experience, and usually also to give to speculation the deceptive guise of investment.

The older ideas of common-stock investment may seem quite naive to the sophisticated security analyst of today. The great emphasis was always on what we now call the defensive aspects of the company or issue— mainly the assurance that it would continue its dividend unreduced in bad times. Thus the strong railroads, which constituted the standard investment commons of 50 years ago, were actually regarded in very much the same way as the public-utility commons in recent years. If the past record indicated stability, the chief requirement was met; not too much effort was made to anticipate adverse changes of an underlying character in the future. But, conversely, especially favorable future prospects were regarded by shrewd investors as something to look for but not to pay for.

In effect this meant that the investor did not have to pay anything substantial for superior long-term prospects. He got these, virtually without extra cost, as a reward for his own superior intelligence and judgment in picking the best rather than the merely good companies. For common stocks with the same financial strength, past earnings record, and dividend stability, all sold at about the same dividend yield.

This was indeed a short-sighted point of view, but it had the great advantage of making common-stock investment in the old days not only simple but also basically sound and highly profitable. Let me return for the last time to a personal note. Somewhere around 1920 our firm distributed a series of little pamphlets entitled *Lessons for Investors*. Of course it took a brash analyst in his middle twenties like myself to hit on so smug and presumptuous a title. But in one of the papers I made the casual statement that "If a common stock is a good investment it is also a good speculation." For, reasoned I, if a common stock was so sound that it carried very little risk of loss it must ordinarily be so good as to possess excellent chances for future gains. Now this was a perfectly true and even valuable discovery, but it was true only because nobody paid any attention to it. Some years later, when the public woke up to the historical merits of common stocks as long-term investments, they soon ceased to have any such merit, because the public's enthusiasm created price levels which deprived them of their built-in margin of safety, and thus drove them out of the investment class. Then, of course, the pendulum swung to the other extreme, and we soon saw one of the most respected authorities declaring (in 1931) that no common stock could *ever* be an investment.

When we view this long-range experience in perspective we find another set of paradoxes in the investor's changing attitude towards capital gains as contrasted with income. It seems a truism to say that the old-time common-stock investor was not much interested in capital gains. He bought almost entirely for safety and income, and let the speculator concern himself with price appreciation. Today we are likely to say that the more experienced and shrewd the investor, the less attention he pays to dividend returns, and the more heavily his interest centers on long-term appreciation. Yet one might argue, perversely, that precisely because the old-time investor did not concentrate on future capital appreciation he was virtually guaranteeing to himself that he would have it, at least in the field of industrial stocks. And, conversely, today's investor is so concerned with anticipating the future that he is already paying handsomely for it in advance. Thus what he has projected with so much study and care may actually happen and still not bring him any profit.

If it should fail to materialize to the degree expected he may in fact be faced with a serious temporary and perhaps even permanent loss.

What *lessons*—again using the pretentious title of my 1920 pamphlets—can the analyst of 1958 learn from this linking of past with current attitudes? Not much of value, one is inclined to say. We can look back nostalgically to the good old days when we paid only for the present and could get the future for nothing—an "all this and Heaven too" combination. Shaking our heads sadly we mutter, "Those days are gone forever." Have not investors and security analysts eaten of the tree of knowledge of good and evil prospects? By so doing have they not permanently expelled themselves from that Eden where promising common stocks at reasonable prices could be plucked off the bushes? Are we not doomed always to run the risk either of paying unreasonably high prices for good quality and prospects, or of getting poor quality and prospects when we pay what seems a reasonable price?

It certainly looks that way. Yet one cannot be sure even of that pessimistic dilemma. Recently, I did a little research in the long-term history of that towering enterprise, General Electric—stimulated by the arresting chart of 59 years of earnings and dividends appearing in their recently published 1957 Report. These figures are not without their surprises for the knowledgeable analyst. For one thing they show that prior to 1947 the growth of G.E. was fairly modest and quite irregular. The 1946 earnings, per share adjusted, were only 30% higher than in 1902—52¢ vs. 40¢—and in no year of this period were the 1902 earnings as much as doubled. Yet the price-earnings ratio rose from 9 times in 1910 and 1916 to 29 times in 1936 and again in 1946. One might say, of course, that the 1946 multiplier at least showed the well-known prescience of shrewd investors. We analysts were able to foresee then the really brilliant period of growth that was looming ahead in the next decade. Maybe so. But some of you remember that the next year, 1947, which established an impressive new high for G.E.'s per share earnings, was marked also by an extraordinary fall in the price-earnings ratio. At its low of 32 (before the 3-for-1 split) G.E. actually sold again at only 9 times its current earnings, and its average price for the year was only about 10 times earnings. Our crystal ball certainly clouded over in the short space of twelve months.

This striking reversal took place only eleven years ago. It casts some little doubt in my mind as to the complete dependability of the popular belief among analysts that prominent and promising companies will now always sell at high price-earnings ratios; that this is a fundamental fact of life for investors and they may as well accept and like it. I have no desire at all to be dogmatic on this point. All I can say is that it is not settled in my mind, and each of you must seek to settle it for yourself.

But in my concluding remarks I can say something definite about the structure of the market for various types of common stocks, in terms of their investment and speculative characteristics. In the old days the investment character of a common stock was more or less the same as, or proportionate with, that of the enterprise itself, as measured quite well by its credit rating. The lower the yield on its bonds or preferred, the more likely was the common to meet all the criteria for a satisfactory investment, and the smaller the element of speculation involved in its purchase. This relationship, between the speculative ranking of the common and the investment rating of the company, could be graphically expressed pretty much as a straight line descending from left to right. But nowadays I would describe the graph as U-shaped. At the left, where the company itself is speculative and its credit low, the common stock is of course highly speculative, just as it has always been in the past. At the right extremity, however, where the company has the highest credit rating because both its past record and future prospects are most impressive, we find that the stock market tends more or less continuously to introduce a highly speculative element into the common shares through the simple means of a price so high as to carry a fair degree of risk.

At this point I cannot forbear introducing a surprisingly relevant, if quite exaggerated, quotation on the subject which I found recently in one of Shakespeare's sonnets. It reads:

> Have I not seen dwellers on form and favor
> Lose all and more by paying too much rent?

Returning to my imaginary graph, it would be the center area where the speculative element in common-stock purchases would tend to reach its minimum. In this area we could find many well-established and strong companies, with a record of past growth corresponding to that of the national economy and with future prospects apparently of the same character. Such common stocks could be bought at most times, except in the upper ranges of a bull market, at moderate prices in relation to their indicated intrinsic values. As a matter of fact, because of the present tendency of investors and speculators alike to concentrate on more glamorous issues, I should hazard the statements that these middle-ground stocks tend to sell on the whole rather below their independently determinable values. They thus have a margin-of-safety factor supplied by the same market preferences and prejudices which tend to destroy the margin of safety in the more promising issues. Furthermore, in this wide array of companies there is plenty of room for penetrating analysis of the past record and for discriminating choice in the area of future prospects, to which can be added the higher assurance of safety conferred by diversification.

When Phaëthon insisted on driving the chariot of the Sun, his father, the experienced operator, gave the neophyte some advice which the latter failed to follow—to his cost. Ovid summed up Phoebus Apollo's counsel in three words:

> Medius tutissimus ibis
> You will go safest in the middle course

I think this principle holds good for investors and their security-analyst advisers.

3·4

Growth Stocks and the Petersburg Paradox*

David Durand

At a time like the present, when investors are avidly seeking opportunities for appreciation, it is appropriate to consider the difficulties of appraising growth stocks. There is little doubt that when other things are equal the forward-looking investor will prefer stocks with growth potential to those without. But other things rarely are equal—particularly in a sophisticated market that is extremely sensitive to growth. When the growth potential of a stock becomes widely recognized, its price is expected to react favorably and to advance far ahead of stocks lacking growth appeal, so that its price-earnings ratio and dividend yield fall out of line according to conventional standards. Then the choice between growth and lack of growth is no longer obvious, and the astute investor must ask whether the market price correctly discounts the growth potential. Is it possible that the market may, at times, pay too much for growth?

*From the *Journal of Finance*, **12,** no. 3, September 1957, pp. 348–363. Back numbers obtainable from the Kraus Reprint Corporation, New York. Financial assistance was received from a grant by the Sloan Research Fund of the School of Industrial Management at Massachusetts Institute of Technology. Intellectual assistance, in the form of ideas, helpful suggestions, and critical comment was received from William Beranek, Joseph N. Froomkin, Myron J. Gordon, J. Arthur Greenwood, Avram Kisselgoff, Paul A. Samuelson, Eli Shapiro, Volkert S. Whitbeck, and from various persons interviewed by the author while touring Wall Street as a guest of the Joint Committee on Education representing the American Securities Business. All this assistance is gratefully acknowledged, but the author [David Durand] must assume full responsibility, since some of the views expressed here are controversial.

Most problems encountered in appraising growth stocks seem to fall into two categories. First there are the practical difficulties of forecasting sales, earnings, and dividends. Then come the theoretical difficulties of reducing these forecasts to present values. For a long time it seems to have been assumed, altogether too casually, that the present value of a forecasted dividend stream could be represented simply as the sum of all expected future payments discounted at a uniform rate. Doubts, however, are beginning to manifest themselves. As early as 1938, J. B. Williams suggested non-uniform discount rates, varying from payment to payment.[1] More recently, Clendenin and Van Cleave have shown that discounting forecasted dividends at a uniform rate in perpetuity may lead to absurdities or paradoxes, since implied present values of infinity sometimes result. "We have not yet seen any growth stocks marketed at the price of infinity dollars per share," they remark, "but we shall hereafter be watching. Of course, many investors are skeptical and would probably wish to discount the very large and remote dividends in this perpetually growing series at a high discount rate, thus reducing our computed value per share to a figure somewhat below the intriguing value of infinity."[2] Clendenin and Van Cleave might have made a good point even better had they noticed a remarkable analogy between the appraisal of growth stocks and the famous Petersburg Paradox, which commanded the attention of most of the important writers on probability during the eighteenth and nineteenth centuries.

THE PETERSBURG PARADOX

In 1738 Daniel Bernoulli presented before the Imperial Academy of Sciences in Petersburg a classic paper on probability, in which he discussed the following problem, attributed to his cousin Nicholas: "Peter tosses a

TABLE 1

Sequence of tosses	Probability	Payment
H	$\frac{1}{2}$	1
TH	$\frac{1}{4}$	2
TTH	$\frac{1}{8}$	4
TTTH	$\frac{1}{16}$	8
TTTTH	$\frac{1}{32}$	16

[1]John B. Williams, *The Theory of Investment Value* (Cambridge, Mass.: Harvard University Press, 1938), pp. 50–60.
[2]John C. Clendenin and Maurice Van Cleave, "Growth and Common Stock Values," *Journal of Finance*, IX (1954), 365–76. Quotation appears on p. 369.

coin and continues to do so until it should land 'heads' when it comes to the ground. He agrees to give Paul one ducat if he gets 'heads' on the very first throw, two ducats if he gets it on the second, four if on the third, eight if on the fourth, and so on, so that with each additional throw the number of ducats he must pay is doubled. Suppose we seek to determine the value of Paul's expectation."[3]

One may easily obtain a solution according to the principles of mathematical expectation by noting the sequence of payments and probabilities in Table 1: Paul's expectation is the sum of the products of probability by payment or

$$\tfrac{1}{2} + \tfrac{2}{4} + \tfrac{4}{8} + \tfrac{8}{16} + \tfrac{16}{32} + \dots$$

If the players agree to terminate the game after n tosses, whether a head shows or not, the series will contain n terms and its sum will be $n/2$; but if they agree to continue without fail until a head shows, as the rules of the game stipulate, then n is infinite and the sum $n/2$ is infinite as well. Thus the principles of mathematical expectation imply that Paul should pay an infinite price to enter this game, but this is a conclusion that virtually no one will accept. A variety of explanations have been given to show that the value of the game to Paul is, in fact, only a finite amount—usually a small finite amount; and all of these explanations are relevant to growth stock appraisal. But before considering them, we shall do well to examine an important modification of the original Petersburg problem.

One modification, which is obvious enough, consists in stipulating some figure other than $\tfrac{1}{2}$, say $1/(1 + i)$, for the probability of tossing a tail and some figure other than 2, say $1 + g$, for the rate of growth; but this has no particular interest for security appraisal. A more extensive modification, which is of interest, provides for a series of increasing payments, instead of a single lump sum. In effect, Peter agrees to pay D ducats if the first toss is a tail, $D(1 + g)$ if the second is a tail, $D(1 + g)^2$ if the third is a tail, $D(1 + g)^3$ if the fourth is a tail, and so on until a head shows—at which point the game ceases. Then, if the probability of a tail is $1/(1 + i)$, the mathematical expectation is (see Appendix)

$$\frac{D}{1 + i} + \frac{D(1 + g)}{(1 + i)^2} + \frac{D(1 + g)^2}{(1 + i)^3} + \dots \quad (1)$$

This series is arithmetically equivalent to a discounted series of dividend payments, starting at D ducats, growing at a constant rate g, and discounted

[3]Daniel Bernoulli, "Exposition of a New Theory on the Measurement of Risk," *Econometrica*, XXII (1954), 23–36, which is a translation by Dr. Louis Sommer of Bernoulli's paper "Specimen Theoriae Novae de Mensura Sortis," *Commentarii Academiae Scientiarum Imperialis Petropolitanae*, V (1738), 175–92.

at rate i.[4] The summation of the series is a simple exercise in actuarial mathematics. The sum of the first n terms is[5]

$$D\frac{1 - (1 + g)^n/(1 + i)^n}{i - g},$$ (2)

provided i is different from g; and the sum of an infinite or very large number of terms approaches the very simply formulated quantity

$$\frac{D}{(i - g)}$$ (3)

provided that i exceeds g. If, however, $g \geqslant i$, the sum of an infinite number of terms would again be infinite—as in the original Petersburg problem— and a reasonable Paul might again object to paying the price.

The applicability of formulas (2) and (3) to growth stock appraisal is not new. In 1938, for example, J. B. Williams[6] derived (3), or its equivalent, in order to appraise the retained portion of common-stock earnings. He made the derivation, using quite different notation, on essentially the following assumptions: first, that in any year j, earnings per share E_j bear a constant ratio, r, to book value, B_j; second, that dividends, D_j, bear a constant ratio, p, to E_j. Then,

$$B_{j+1} = B_j + E_j(1 - p) = B_j[1 + r(1 - p)].$$

Hence, book value, dividends, and earnings are all growing at the same constant rate $g = r(1 - p)$ and formula (3) can be rewritten

$$\frac{D_1}{i - g} = \frac{E_1 p}{i - g} = \frac{B_1 p r}{i - g}.$$ (3a)

Williams realized, of course, that these formulas are valid only when i exceeds g, and he mentioned certain other limitations that are best discussed with some of the proposed solutions for the Petersburg Paradox.

[4]Possibly the objection may be raised that series (1) is conceptually quite different from a discounted series of dividends on the grounds that the discount rate ordinarily represents the price paid for waiting in addition to the price paid for assuming risk. To meet this objection, it suffices to discount the dividend series twice, first, by an amount just sufficient to cover the price of waiting, and second, by the amount required to cover the risk of dividend termination when Peter finally tosses a head. Then, the growth rate g in (1) would represent the real growth rate less an adjustment for waiting, and i would represent only the risk of termination.

[5]See, for example, Ralph Todhunter, *The Institute of Actuaries' Text-Book on Compound Interest and Annuities-Certain*, 4th ed., revised by R. C. Simmonds and T. P. Thompson (Cambridge, England: University Press, 1937), pp. 48–49.

[6]*Op. cit.*, pp. 87–89, 128–135.

ATTEMPTS TO RESOLVE THE PETERSBURG PARADOX[7]

The many attempts to resolve the paradox, summarized very briefly below, fall mostly into two broad groups: those denying the basic assumptions of the game as unrealistic, and those arguing from additional assumptions that the value of the game to Paul is less than its mathematical expectation.

The basic assumptions of the game are open to all sorts of objections from the practically minded. How, in real life, can the game continue indefinitely? For example, Peter and Paul are mortal; so, after a misspent youth, a dissipated middle age, and a dissolute dotage, one of them will die, and the game will cease—heads or no heads. Or again, Peter's solvency is open to question, for the stakes advance at an alarming rate. With an initial payment of one dollar, Peter's liability after only 35 tails exceeds the gold reserve in Fort Knox, and after only three more, it exceeds the volume of bank deposits in the United States and approximately equals the national debt. With this progression, the sky is, quite literally, the limit. Even if Peter and Paul agree to cease after 100 tosses, the stakes, though finite, stagger the imagination.

Despite these serious practical objections, a number of writers chose to accept the assumption of an indefinitely prolonged game at face value, and to direct their attention toward ascertaining the value of such a game to Paul. First among these was the Swiss mathematician Gabriel Cramer, who early in the eighteenth century proposed two arbitrary devices for resolving the Petersburg Paradox by assuming that the utility of money is less than proportional to the amount held.[8] First, if the utility of money is proportional to the amount up to $2^{24} = 166,777,216$ ducats and constant for amounts exceeding 2^{24}, so that the utility of the payments ceases to increase after the 24th toss, Paul's so-called moral expectation is about 13 ducats. Second, if the utility of money is assumed equal to the square root of the amount held, Paul's moral expectation is only about 2.9 ducats. Cramer believed that 2.9 was a more reasonable entrance fee than 13.

A little later and apparently independently, Daniel Bernoulli devised a solution only slightly different from Cramer's. Assuming that the marginal utility of money is inversely proportional to the amount held, he derived a formula that evaluates Paul's expectation in terms of his resources at the beginning of the game. From this formula, which does not lend itself to lightning computation, Bernoulli estimated roughly that the expectation is

[7]For a general history of the paradox, see Isaac Todhunter, *A History of the Mathematical Theory of Probability from the Time of Pascal to that of Laplace* (reprint, New York: G. E. Stechert & Co., 1931), pp. 134, 220–222, 259–262, 275, 280, 286–289, 332, 345, 393, 470. For a briefer treatment, see John Maynard Keynes, *A Treatise on Probability* (London: Macmillan and Co., 1921), pp. 316 ff.

[8]Cf. Bernoulli, *op. cit.*, pp. 33 ff.

worth about 3 ducats to Paul when his resources are 10 ducats, about 4 ducats when his resources are 100, and about 6 when his resources are 1000.[9] At this rate, Paul must have infinite resources before he can value his expectation at infinity; but then, even his infinite valuation will constitute only an infinitesimally small fraction of his resources.

An interesting variant of Bernoulli's approach was proposed about a century later by W. A. Whitworth[10]—at least some of us would consider it a variant, though its author considered it an entirely different argument. Whitworth was, in fact, seeking a solution to the Petersburg Problem that would be free of arbitrary assumptions concerning the utility of money; and he derived a solution by considering the risk of gamblers' ruin, which is always present when players have limited resources. Thus, for example, if A with one dollar matches pennies indefinitely against B with $10, it is virtually certain that one of them will eventually be cleaned out; furthermore, A has 10 chances out of 11 of being the victim. Accordingly, a prudent A might demand some concession in the odds as the price of playing against B. But how much concession? Whitworth attacked this and other problems by assuming a prudent gambler will risk a constant proportion of his resources, rather than a constant amount, on each venture; and he devised a system for evaluating ventures that entail risk of ruin. Applied to the Petersburg Game, this system indicates that Paul's entrance fee should depend upon his resources. Thus Whitworth's solution is reminiscent of Bernoulli's—particularly when one realizes that Whitworth's basic assumption implies an equivalence between a dime bet for A with $1 and a dollar bet for B with $10. Bernoulli, of course, would have argued that the utility of a dime to A was equal to the utility of a dollar to B. Finally, the notion of a prudent gambler seeking to avoid ruin has strong utilitarian undertones, for it implies that the marginal utility of money is high when resources are running out.

But Whitworth's approach—regardless of its utilitarian subtleties—is interesting because it emphasizes the need for diversification. The evaluation of a hazardous venture—be it dice game, business promotion, or risky security—depends not only on the inherent odds, but also on the proportion of the risk-taker's resources that must be committed. And just as the prudent gambler may demand odds stacked in his favor as the price for betting more than an infinitesimal proportion of his resources, so may the prudent portfolio manager demand a greater than normal rate of return (after allowing for the inherent probability of default) as the price of investing more than an infinitesimal proportion of his assets in a risky issue.[11]

---

[9] *Ibid.*, pp. 32 ff.

[10] W. A. Whitworth, *Choice and Chance* (Cambridge, England: Deighton, Bell & Co., 4th edition, enlarged, 1886), chap. 9.

[11] Section 87 of the New York Insurance Law states: "Except as more specifically provided in this chapter, no domestic insurer shall have more than ten per cent of its total admitted assets invested in, or loaned upon, the securities of any one institution; . . . " Section 81, subsection 13, places additional restrictions on common stock investment.

Although the preceding historical account of the Petersburg Paradox has been of the sketchiest, it should serve to illustrate an important point. The various proposed solutions, of which there are many, all involve changing the problem in one way or another. Thus some proposals evaluate the cash value of a finite game, even when the problem specifies an infinite game; others evaluate the utility receipts, instead of the cash receipts, of an infinite game; and still others foresake evaluation for gamesmanship and consider what Paul as a prudent man should pay to enter. But although none of these proposals satisfy the theoretical requirements of the problem, they all help to explain why a real live Paul might be loath to pay highly for his infinite mathematical expectation. As Keynes aptly summed it up, "We are unwilling to be Paul, partly because we do not believe Peter will pay us if we have good fortune in the tossing, partly because we do not know what we should do with so much money . . . if we won it, partly because we do not believe we should ever win it, and partly because we do not think it would be a rational act to risk an infinite sum or even a very large sum for an infinitely larger one, whose attainment is infinitely unlikely."[12]

IMPLICATIONS OF PETERSBURG SOLUTIONS FOR GROWTH-STOCK APPRAISAL

If instead of tossing coins, Peter organizes a corporation in a growth industry and offers Paul stock, the latter might be deterred from paying the full discounted value by any of the considerations that would deter him from paying the full mathematical expectation to enter the Petersburg game. And again, these considerations fall into two categories: first, those denying the basic assumptions concerning the rate of indefinitely prolonged growth; and, second, those arguing that the value of the stock to Paul is less than its theoretical discounted value.

Underlying J. B. Williams' derivation of formula (3) is the assumption that Peter, Inc., will pay dividends at an increasing rate g for the rest of time. Underlying the derivation in the Appendix is a slightly different assumption: namely, that Peter will pay steadily increasing dividends until the game terminates with the toss of a head, and that the probability of a head will remain forever constant at $i/(1 + i)$. Under neither assumption is there any provision for the rate of growth ever to cease or even decline. But astronomers now predict the end of the world within a finite number of years —somewhere in the order of 10,000,000,000—and realistic security analysts may question Peter, Inc.'s ability to maintain a steadily increasing dividend rate for anywhere near that long. Williams, in fact, regarded indefinitely increasing dividends as strictly hypothetical, and he worked up formulas for evaluating growth stocks on the assumption that dividends will follow a growth curve (called a logistic by Williams) that increases exponentially for

[12]Keynes, *op. cit.*, p. 318.

a time and then levels off to an asymptote.[13] This device guarantees that the present value of any dividend stream will be finite, no matter how high the current, and temporary, rate of growth. Clendenin and Van Cleave, though not insisting on a definite ceiling, argued that continued rapid growth is possible only under long-run price inflation.

The assumption of indefinitely increasing dividends is most obviously objectionable when the growth rate equals or exceeds the discount rate ($g \geqslant i$) and the growth series (1) sums to infinity; then formula (3) does not even apply. If Peter, Inc., is to pay a dividend that increases at a constant rate $g \geqslant i$ per year, it is absolutely necessary, though not sufficient, that he earn a rate on capital, $r = E/B$, that is greater than the rate of discount— more exactly, $r \geqslant i/(1 - p)$. But this situation poses an anomaly, at least for the equilibrium theorist, who argues that the marginal rate of return on capital must equal the rate of interest in the long run. How, then, can Peter, Inc., continually pour increasing quantities of capital into his business and continue to earn on these accretions a rate higher than the standard rate of discount? This argument points toward the conclusion that growth stocks characterize business situations in which limited, meaning finite though not necessarily small, amounts of capital can be invested at rates higher than the equilibrium rate. If this is so, then the primary problem of the growth-stock appraiser is to estimate how long the departure from equilibrium will continue perhaps by some device like Williams' growth curve.

If, for the sake of argument, Paul wishes to assume that dividend growth will continue indefinitely at a constant rate, he can still find reasons for evaluating Peter's stock at somewhat less than its theoretical value just as he found reasons for evaluating his chances in the Petersburg Game at less than the mathematical expectation. The decreasing-marginal-utility approach of Cramer and Bernoulli implies that the present utility value of a growing dividend stream is less than the discounted monetary value, because the monetary value of the large dividends expected in the remote future must be substantially scaled down in making a utility appraisal. Or again, Whitworth's diversification approach implies that a prudent Paul with finite resources can invest only a fraction of his portfolio in Peter's stock; otherwise he risks ruinous loss. And either argument is sufficient to deter Paul from offering an infinite price, unless, of course, his resources should be infinite.

THE PROBLEM OF REMOTE DIVIDENDS

There is, moreover, another important limitation on Paul's evaluation of a growth stock that has not arisen in the discussion of the Petersburg Paradox, namely, the remoteness of the large dividend payments. Con-

[13]Williams, *op. cit.*, pp. 89–94.

ventional theory argues that a dividend n years hence is adequately evaluated by the discount factor $1/(1 + i)^n$, but this is open to question when n is very large. The question is, of course, academic for ordinary instruments like long-term bonds or preferred stock, since discounted coupons or preferred dividends many years hence are negligible when discounted in the conventional manner. Thus, for example, if $5.00 a year in perpetuity is worth exactly $100.00 (assuming 5 per cent compounded annually), then $99.24 is attributable to the first 100 payments. But for a stock growing according to series (1) and with $g \geqslant i$, the discounted value of remote dividends, say 10,000 years hence, is anything but negligible; in fact, it may be astronomic. But how should Paul evaluate such remote growth dividends?

If Paul is a real live person without heirs or other incentives for founding an estate, his problem is fairly clearcut. Dividends payable beyond his reasonable life span are useless to him as income, although claims on them may be convertible into useful income through the medium of the market place. At retirement, for example, he might easily be able to increase his income for the remainder of his life by selling long-term securities and buying an annuity. If, however, Paul has heirs, he may look forward several generations and place a very real value on dividends that will be payable to his grandchildren and great-grandchildren. But even here his investment horizon may be limited by the uncertainty of planning for offspring not yet born.

If Paul is a life insurance company, he has a special interest in evaluating remote dividends; for the shades of obligations currently contracted may extend far into the future as the following fanciful though not impossible sketch will indicate. In 1956 John Doe, aged 21, buys for his own benefit a whole life policy containing the customary guaranty of a rate of interest if the insured elects to settle the proceeds in instalments. In 2025, aged 90, John Doe decides to settle this policy on his newborn great-grandson Baby Doe and directs the insurance company to accumulate the proceeds at the guaranteed rate of interest until Baby Doe shall reach the age of 21 and thereupon pay them out to him as a life income, according to the table of guaranteed rates in the policy. Encouraged by his monthly checks, Baby Doe now lives to the ripe old age of 105, so that only in 2130 does the insurance company finally succeed in discharging its obligation of 1956, based on the then current forecasts of long-term interest rates.

Even though the case of John Doe may be a bit out of the ordinary, it illustrates forcefully why life insurance companies must concern themselves with dividend income up to perhaps 200 years hence and how a future decline in the earning rate on assets may threaten the solvency of an insurance fund. Although the purchase of long-term bonds is an obvious form of protection against falling interest rates, it is not entirely effective when the liabilities extend too far into the future. To illustrate the difficulty of long-term protection, it will be convenient at this point to introduce a concept called "duration" by Macaulay,[14] which may apply to an individual security, a portfolio of securities, or even to a block of liabilities. Duration, incidentally, must not be confused with a related concept known as "equated time."

The duration of an individual security or a portfolio is the arithmetic mean of the several coupon or maturity dates, each date weighted by the present value at the valuation rate of interest of the expected income on that date. The duration of an E bond or noninterest-bearing note is simply the term to maturity; and the duration of a portfolio consisting, for example, of two $100 E bonds due two years hence and a $500 E bond due five years hence would be

$$\left[\frac{2 \times 200}{(1.03)^2} + \frac{5 \times 500}{(1.03)^5}\right] \div \left[\frac{200}{(1.03)^2} + \frac{500}{(1.03)^5}\right],$$

if evaluated at 3 per cent compounded annually. The duration of an interest-bearing bond is less than the term to maturity, because the long-term of the principal payment at maturity must be averaged against the shorter terms of the various coupons. Macaulay's formula for the duration of interest-paying bonds is somewhat complex; but for perpetuities, such as Canadian Pacific debenture 4's, it simplifies to $(1 + i)/i$.[15] At $i = .03$, the duration of a perpetuity is therefore about 34 years.

In seeking suitable methods for matching the assets of a fund to its liabilities so as to minimize risk of loss from fluctuations in the interest rate, British actuaries have shown that the possible loss is very small when both present value and duration of the assets equal present value and duration of the liabilities; and, indeed, they have given examples where the "loss" is a small gain for fluctuations either up or down.[16] But although the portfolio manager can ordinarily achieve satisfactory matching by merely selecting long- and short-term bonds in such proportions that their average duration equals that of the liabilities, he runs into difficulty when the duration of the

[14]F. R. Macaulay, *Some Theoretical Problems Suggested by the Movement of Interest Rates, Bond Yields and Stock Prices in the United States since* 1856 (New York: National Bureau of Economic Research, 1938), pp. 44–51.

[15]Macaulay, *op. cit.*, pp. 49–50. In Macaulay's formula for perpetuities (p. 50) let $R = 1 + i$.

[16]See, for example, J. B. H. Pegler, "The Actuarial Principles of Investment," *Journal of the Institute of Actuaries* (England), Vol. 74 (1948), pp. 179–211; F. M. Redington, "Review of the Principles of Life-Office Valuations," *ibid.*, Vol. 78 (1952), pp. 286–340; G. V. Bayley and W. Perks, "A Consistent System of Investment and Bonus Distribution for a Life Office," *ibid.*, Vol. 79 (1953), pp. 14–73; A. T. Haynes and R. J. Kirton, "The Financial Structure of a Life Office," *Transactions of the Faculty of Actuaries* (Scotland), Vol. 21 (1953), pp. 141–218; D. J. Robertson and I. L. B. Sturrock, "Active Investment Policy Related to the Holding of Matched Assets," *ibid.*, Vol. 22 (1954), pp. 36–96. Also see Paul A. Samuelson, "The Effect of Interest Rate Increases on the Banking System," *American Economic Review*, XXXV (1945), 16–27, especially p. 19.

Interest of the British in this subject, which seems to be greater than that of the Americans, may be due to their relative freedom from liability for policy loans. Although the British companies are prepared to make such loans, they are not forced to do so.

liabilities is exceptionally long. Thus, for example, the duration of the liability of a pension fund with many young workers and only a few pensioners can easily exceed 40 years: and this is too long to be matched by a portfolio consisting wholly of perpetuities, whose duration at current interest rates is only about 30 years. In such a difficulty, however, growth stocks offer a possible solution; for when dividends are growing according to series (1), the duration is longer than a perpetuity. In fact, if we define

$$1 + b = \frac{1 + i}{1 + g}$$

then $(1 + b)b$ is the duration of the series.[17] Thus growth stocks provide a possible means of increasing the average duration of a portfolio when the composition of the liabilities requires this. W. Perks has, in fact, hinted as much.[18]

There is, in fact, no theoretical limit to the duration of a stock with dividends growing as in (1). When $g = .05$ and $i = .06$, say, the duration is approximately 100 years; and as the difference between g and i decreases, durations of 1,000 years, 10,000 years, or even 1,000,000 years might result. Moreover, when $g \geqslant i$, $b \leqslant 0$ and formula $(1 + b)/b$ is no longer valid; then the duration is infinite as well as the present value. But although securities with a duration of 100 years might be useful to British life companies for increasing average duration of pension fund assets, or for providing protection against contingencies illustrated by the case of John Doe above, securities with much greater duration would begin to lose appeal. The essential characteristic of a very long duration is that the security holder or his legatees must expect to wait a long time before the security begins to pay a substantial return; and with those hypothetical securities having infinite duration, the legatees must literally expect to wait forever. Even the most forward looking of investors, who are probably those who leave bequests to such institutions as universities and religious organizations, cannot afford to look that far into the future; for, to paraphrase Keynes, it would not be a rational act to risk an infinite sum or even a very large sum for an infinitely larger one, whose attainment is infinitely remote. In effect, the very remote dividends in series (1) cannot be worth their actuarially discounted value when g is large; whether they are worth it when g is small is probably academic, for then the discounted value will be negligible.

To allow for various uncertainties in evaluating dividends in the very remote future, Clendenin and Van Cleave made a significant suggestion, namely, to increase the discount rate applicable to the more remote dividends. The difficulty, of course, is to find some reasonable, objective basis

[17]This can be proved by using Macaulay's method of finding the duration of a perpetuity and making the substitution $b = i$.

[18]See his remarks following the paper by Redington, *op. cit.*, p. 327.

for setting up an appropriate schedule of rates. To illustrate their suggestion, Clendenin and Van Cleave worked out valuations for hypothetical
securities by discounting the first twenty years of dividends at 4 per cent, the
second twenty at 6 per cent, the third twenty at 8 per cent, and considering
all subsequent dividends as worthless. But although such a schedule,
totally disregarding all dividends after 60 years, might appeal to a man aged
40 without heirs, it would not appeal to insurance companies and pension
managers, who have to look forward 150 to 200 years; and it would certainly not appeal to the loyal alumnus, who wishes to leave a bequest to
alma mater. But the essential point is that by setting up a schedule of discount rates that increase fast enough to render very remote dividends
negligible, one can assure himself that the present value of any increasing
stream of dividends will be finite. And although many investors would
object to neglecting dividends after 60 years, few would object to neglecting
them after 600.

SUMMARY AND IMPLICATIONS
FOR SECURITY APPRAISAL IN GENERAL

There are, to sum up, a number of potent reasons any one of which
suffices to dissuade Paul from paying an infinite price for a growth stock
under even the most favorable circumstances, namely when $g \geqslant i$ and the
sum of series (1) is infinite. Moreover, these reasons do not lose all their
force when $g < i$ and the sum of (1) is finite. In appraising any growing
stream of dividends, Paul might wish to make provision for eventual decline and perhaps cessation of the growth rate, as suggested by J. B. Williams; he might adjust large dividends to allow for the decreasing marginal
utility of money, somewhat in the manner of Cramer and Bernoulli; or
again he might apply Whitworth's reasoning and scale down his valuation
to a sum he can afford to risk, given his resources; or finally he might,
following Clendenin and Van Cleave, apply a very high discount rate to
remote dividends that have no significance to him. And he might, of course,
apply a combination of such approaches.

But, oddly enough, the very fact that Paul has so many good reasons
for scaling down the sum of series (1) when g is high, and so many ways to
accomplish this end, leaves him with no clear basis for arriving at any
precise valuation. Thus, the possible adjustments for the decreasing
marginal utility of money are many and varied. Cramer's two proposals
yielded very different solutions for the Petersburg Problem and would yield
very different appraisals if applied to rapidly growing growth stocks; and
Daniel Bernoulli's proposal would yield yet another result. Or again, there
are many ways by which Paul can allow for an eventual decline in the

current rate of growth, all of which entail major forecasting problems. Williams' formula, for example, which is stated here in the form[19]

$$V = D\left[\frac{(1 + g)^n - (1 + i)^n}{(g - i)(1 + i)^n} + \frac{(2g + i + 2gi)(1 + g)^n}{i(g + i + gi)(1 + i)^n}\right]$$

after the substitution $D = \Pi_0(1 + g)$ and some rearrangement, rests on the somewhat restrictive assumption that dividends grow annually at a constant rate g for n years and then taper off exponentially to a level equal to exactly twice the dividend in the nth year. Even when the assumptions are acceptable in principle, practical application of the formula may require more accurate information on g, i, and n than one could possibly expect to obtain. This is particularly true when n is large and g is only slightly larger than i; then $g - i$ in the denominator of the first fraction is small and tremendously sensitive to errors in either g or i. Nor is this difficulty peculiar to Williams' formula. Table 2, abridged from Clendenin and Van Cleave,[20] gives the present value of 60 dividend payments discounted at 5 per cent. It is assumed that the initial dividend rate of $1.00 grows at either 4 per cent or 5 per cent for a period of years and then remains constant for the remainder of the 60-year period, after which dividends either cease or are considered worthless. This table again illustrates the difficulty of mak-

TABLE 2

	Rate of growth	
Growth period	5 per cent	4 per cent
0	$18.93	$18.93
10	$28\frac{1}{4}$	26
20	37	$32\frac{1}{4}$
30	$45\frac{1}{4}$	$37\frac{1}{2}$
40	$52\frac{1}{4}$	$41\frac{1}{2}$
50	$57\frac{3}{4}$	$44\frac{1}{4}$
60	60	$45\frac{1}{2}$

ing appraisals without an accurate forecast of the growth rate and the length of the growth period.

More conventional securities such as bonds and preferred stocks, though much less troublesome than growth stocks, still present some of the same difficulties of evaluation, and a single example should make this clear. In evaluating bonds—even bonds of supposedly uniform quality—one must

[19]Williams, *op. cit.*, formula (27a), p. 94.
[20]*Op. cit.*, Table 4, p. 371.

make some adjustment for term to maturity. Ordinarily one does this by summing a discounted series of coupons and principal

$$\frac{C}{1 + i_n} + \frac{C}{(1 + i_n)^2} + \cdots + \frac{C}{(1 + i_n)^n} + \frac{P}{(1 + i_n)^n}$$

in which the uniform discount factor depends on the number of years to maturity. Alternatively, however, one could follow the suggestion of Clendenin and Van Cleave, which would entail summing the series

$$\frac{C}{1 + i_1} + \frac{C}{(1 + i_2)^2} + \frac{C}{(1 + i_3)^3} + \cdots + \frac{C}{(1 + i_n)^n} + \frac{P}{(1 + i_n)^n}$$

in which each discount factor i_1, i_2, etc. depends on the date of the coupon or principal payment discounted. But whether one prefers the conventional method or the alternative, the issue is clear: one cannot apply a standard discount factor i uniformly to all bonds; some adjustment for the length, or duration, of the payment stream is essential.

The moral of all this is that conventional discount formulas do not provide completely reliable evaluations. Presumably they provide very satisfactory approximations for high-grade, short-term bonds and notes. But as quality deteriorates or duration lengthens, the approximations become rougher and rougher. With growth stocks, the uncritical use of conventional discount formulas is particularly likely to be hazardous; for, as we have seen, growth stocks represent the ultimate in investments of long duration. Likewise, they seem to represent the ultimate in difficulty of evaluation. The very fact that the Petersburg Problem has not yielded a unique and generally acceptable solution to more than 200 years of attack by some of the world's great intellects suggests, indeed, that the growth-stock problem offers no great hope of a satisfactory solution.

APPENDIX

Proof of Formula (1) for Paul's Expectation in the Modified Petersburg Game

The table below lists a few possible outcomes, with associated probabilities, for the modified Petersburg Game, in which Peter pays Paul a series of dividends according to the number of tails that occur before a head finally shows. There is,

Sequence of tosses	Probability	Dividend	Total pay (Cumulated dividends)
H	$i/(1 + i)$	0	0
TH	$i/(1 + i)^2$	D	D
TTH	$i/(1 + i)^3$	$D(1 + g)$	$D + D(1 + g)$
TTTH	$i/(1 + i)^4$	$D(1 + g)^2$	$D + D(1 + g) + D(1 + g)^2$

of course, an infinite number of such possible outcomes, because every finite sequence of tails, no matter how long, has a finite, though possibly very small, probability of occurring. It is assumed, moreover, that throughout even the longest sequence, the probability of a tail remains constant at $1/(1 + i)$, leaving $i/(1 + i)$ as the probability of a head.

Paul's mathematical expectation is obtained by summing the products of probability in the second column by payout in the fourth. Thus, the sequence TTH, for example, has probability $i/(1 + i)^3$ and results in the payout of two dividends, D and $D(1 + g)$. The product appears in the table below along with similar products for the sequences H, TH, and TTTH.

Sequence	Product
H	0
TH	$Di/(1 + i)^2$
TTH	$[D + D(1 + g)]\, i/(1 + i)^3$
TTTH	$[D + D(1 + g) + D(1 + g)^2]\, i/(1 + i)^4$

To sum these products, it is convenient to break them up and to rearrange the parts in powers of $1 + g$. Thus, for example, all elements containing $(1 + g)^2$ form an infinite series

$$\frac{Di(1 + g)^2}{(1 + i)^4}\left[1 + \frac{1}{1 + i} + \frac{1}{(1 + i)^2} + \cdots\right],$$

where the factor in the bracket is a well-known actuarial form having the sum to infinity $(1 + i)/i$. Thus, the sum of all elements in $(1 + g)^2$ is $D(1 + g)^2/(1 + i)^3$, which is one of the terms in series (1). The other terms are obtained in an analogous manner.

The Influence of Growth Duration
on Share Prices*

Charles C. Holt

INTRODUCTION

The spectacular investment performance of "growth stocks" in recent years has focused attention on the problem of evaluating the securities of fast-growing companies. Unfortunately, methods for placing valuations on such securities are not yet adequately developed, and investors make their buy-and-sell decisions as best they can.

That a company's high rate of "growth" may come to an end is an important, but little-emphasized, investment consideration in the evaluation of growth stocks. To call attention to this point, we present in this paper an exploratory analysis of the relationship between price-earnings ratio, rate of growth, and the duration of growth. In omitting risk from the present analysis, we are explicitly neglecting the fact that investments in growth stocks are often riskier than in non-growth stocks. Consistent with this, the capitalization rates for both kinds of securities are assumed to be the same, and hence any differences in their price-earnings ratios are attributable to differences in their growth of earnings.

The obvious investment success of growth stocks has led investors to seek out these securities for purchase, with the result that their prices have been driven up so that growth stocks now generally carry high price-earnings ratios. But just how high it is wise for investors to drive price-earnings ratios is not clear. If a growth stock is evaluated by discounting future growing dividends back to the present, the paradoxical result is obtained that an infinite price-earnings ratio is justified for a stock whose dividends per share are expected to grow at a (per cent per annum) rate that is higher than the discount rate. This clearly untenable result comes from the implicit assumption of an *indefinite* continuation of exponential growth and

*From the *Journal of Finance*, **17**, no. 3, September 1962, pp. 465–475. Back numbers obtainable from the Kraus Reprint Corporation, New York. Conversations with M. H. Miller and F. Modigliani supplied much of the stimulation for writing this paper.

may be avoided by limiting the assumed growth period.[1] Another method[2] has received considerable attention in investors' literature and seems to have had considerable influence. The growth in earnings per share of a company is extrapolated, say five years into the future, at the growth rate indicated from the recent past. The current price of the stock is divided by this forecast of earnings five years hence, to obtain a price-earnings ratio. In this way, more normal, i.e., lower price-earnings ratios are obtained for growth stocks and some useful indication is given on whether the existing price of the security is justified or not. However, this method is rather crude in ignoring any dividends that might be received during the five-year period or growth that might occur after this arbitrarily selected period.[3]

DURATION OF GROWTH

If investments in the common stocks of growth companies were expected to continue growing indefinitely at a constant exponential rate, then the investor's problem would be largely one of selecting the companies with the highest forecasted growth rates.[4] But before anyone chose to follow such an investment policy, he would be well advised to question seriously the assumption of indefinitely continued growth. Studies of the past growth in the applications of inventions and in the sales of companies and industries show growth curves in which very high rates of growth are achieved initially, but ultimately the growth rates tend to slow down or stop as maturity is reached. This logistic type of growth curve is rather complicated, and the forecasting of its leveling-off is quite difficult from both the statistical and the forecasting points of view. Although we shall not attempt this degree of refinement, it does seem desirable to assume that the growth opportunities of a "growth" company are likely at some point in time to slow down to the rate that is normally achieved by companies generally. Presumably, this more modest growth rate can be maintained indefinitely. As the period of high growth passes, the price-earnings ratio of a company will drop back to

[1]O. K. Burrell, "A Mathematical Approach to Growth Stock Valuation," *Financial Analysts Journal*, XVI (May–June, 1960), 69–76; John C. Clendenin and Maurice Van Cleave, "Growth and Common Stock Values," *Journal of Finance*, IX (1954), 365–76.

[2]Julian G. Buckley, "A Method of Evaluating Growth Stocks," *Financial Analysts Journal*, XVI (March–April, 1960), 19–21.

[3]The more subtle point that the dividend returns from a growth stock are farther in the future than those from non-growth stocks and hence that forecasts of the dividends are riskier has not been adequately treated as yet, nor will it be considered here. See David Durand, "Growth Stocks and the Petersburg Paradox," *Journal of Finance*, XII (September, 1957), 348–63; and Henry Allen Latané, "Individual Risk Preference in Portfolio Selection," *Journal of Finance*, IV (March, 1960), 45–52.

[4]For a more refined analysis of growth see M. H. Miller and F. Modigliani, "Dividend Policy, Growth, and the Valuation of Shares," *Journal of Business*, XXXIV (October, 1961), 22. Growth in earnings of itself does not necessarily justify a high price-earnings ratio, if dividends are correspondingly low—i.e., the growth requires some form of expanding opportunities for profit. The present paper will not analyze the source of "growth" but only the problem of determining its value.

the normal level characteristic of "non-growth stocks." This perhaps distant, but almost inevitable, decline in price-earnings ratio constitutes one of the important risks of investing in a growth stock, especially since the termination of rapid growth is so difficult to forecast.

To simplify matters, we shall make the assumption that the growth in earnings per share (adjusted for stock dividends and splits) of a company will continue at a high constant exponential rate until some point in time when the rate drops abruptly to the average rate for non-growth companies. Under this assumption, the *duration of growth* for a company becomes a simple concept, i.e., the time duration of the high growth rate. Clearly, companies with long durations of growth should be valued more highly than those with short durations of growth, other things being equal. Also companies with high growth rates of earnings should be valued higher than companies with low growth rates, other things being equal.

Both the duration and the rate of growth need to be taken into account in valuing a growth stock. One way to do this is to consider the following question. How long, at a minimum, will the present high rate of earnings growth of a company have to continue in order to attain the same level of earnings that can be achieved by an alternative investment in non-growth stocks of comparable risk? Assume that beyond this time the high growth rate drops to the normal rate, the low dividend pay-out rises, and the high price-earnings ratio falls so that the two investments become virtually equivalent. In saying this, we have, of course, roughed over the uncertainty problem by assuming comparable risk for both investments. This time is the *minimum* required growth duration for the growth stock to justify its high price-earnings ratio. Of course, in both cases we need to take into account the dividend yields.

If we can formulate an analysis for determining the duration of growth estimate that is implicit in the market price of a growth stock, this may be useful to investors in making judgments as to whether the high price-earnings ratio of the growth stock is justified or not. We can obtain the market's estimate of duration of growth as follows: If we let $E'(t)$ be the earnings per share (adjusted for stock splits and stock dividends) of a common stock in the year t (measured from the present, when $t = 0$) and let ΔE be the per cent per annum growth rate of earnings per share, then an estimate of future earnings per share as long as this growth rate continues is given by the following expression:

$$E'(t) = E'(0)(1 + \Delta E)^t. \tag{1}$$

It is convenient for analysis to assume the reinvestment of dividend income to obtain additional "growth" so that it can be combined simply with the above expression.[5] This is done by pretending that the dividends are used to buy more (perhaps fractional) shares of the same stock. This assumption is purely for analytical purposes, to put all securities on a common "no dividend payment" basis.

Thus if D is the constant per cent per annum dividend yield (i.e., ratio of dividends to market price), the number of shares $N(t)$ at the end of year t is

$$N(t) = (1 + D)^t, \tag{2}$$

assuming that one share was bought originally when $t = 0$. The total earnings $E(t)$ at the end of year t on the original and purchased shares combined are

$$E(t) = E'(t)N(t) = E'(0)[(1 + \Delta E)(1 + D)]^t. \tag{3}$$

Since D and ΔE are "small" and for the one original share $E'(0) = E(0)$, we obtain

$$E(t) \approx E(0)(1 + \Delta E + D)^t. \tag{4}$$

This growth measurement of investment return is equally applicable to growth and non-growth stocks. We apply it to both and introduce the subscript g to indicate a growth stock and the subscript a to indicate an alternative non-growth stock of comparable risk.

After the *duration of growth*, which we designate as τ, we have assumed that the growth stock has the *same* general characteristics as the non-growth stock. Hence in the year τ their market values will be in direct proportion to their earnings of that year.[6] Since uncertainty has been left out of our analysis and since no dividends are withdrawn, we would expect that the market would tend to value the shares of the two stocks for current purchase in direct proportion to their value in year τ and hence in direct proportion to the forecasted earnings in the year τ. If this proportionality condition were not satisfied, investors would tend to buy the relatively underpriced stock, in order to be in a better position in the year τ, thereby driving up the low price. Thus the market will tend to satisfy this relation between the current share prices of the growth and the non-growth stocks, $P_g(0)$ and $P_a(0)$, respectively:

$$\frac{P_g(0)}{P_a(0)} \approx \frac{E_g(0)(1 + \Delta E_g + D_g)^\tau}{E_a(0)(1 + \Delta E_a + D_a)^\tau}, \tag{5}$$

or, equivalently,

$$\left(\frac{P_g(0)/E_g(0)}{P_a(0)/E_a(0)}\right) \approx \left(\frac{1 + \Delta E_g + D_g}{1 + \Delta E_a + D_a}\right)^\tau. \tag{6}$$

[5]There is little meaningful distinction between dividend income and capital gains aside from factors that we are not considering now, namely, risk, taxes, brokerage commissions for odd-lot transactions, and administrative convenience.
[6]$E(t)$ is given by substituting τ for t in expression (4).

Here we see that the ratio between the price-earnings ratios of the two stocks is equal to the ratio of their composite growth rates raised to the τth power. The compounded growth offsets the high price-earnings ratio of the growth stock.

We may solve for τ by taking logarithms. For simplicity, we have

$$\left(\frac{1+\Delta E_g+D_g}{1+\Delta E_g+D_a}\right) \text{ Relative Growth Rate}$$

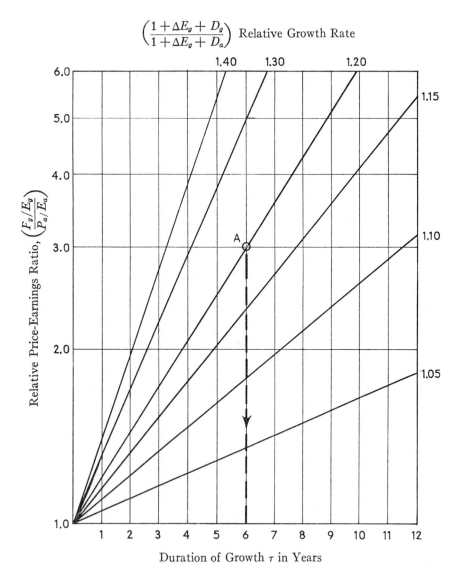

FIGURE 1   Growth versus non-growth companies.

dropped the time parentheses indicating current prices and earnings but without changing the meaning:

$$\ln\left(\frac{P_g/E_g}{P_a/E_a}\right) \approx \tau \ln\left(\frac{1 + \Delta E_g + D_g}{1 + \Delta E_a + D_a}\right) \tag{7}$$

Since this equation is linear in the logarithms, we may graph it on semilog paper to obtain the simple relation shown in Figure 1. Fortunately, the log scales on the graph avoid any necessity of dealing with logarithms. The intersection of a horizontal line representing the relative price-earnings ratio with a sloping line representing the relative growth rate determines a point. Dropping vertically, we can read the market estimate of growth duration τ. In this way, by plotting the point of intersection, we can obtain τ for a security. An example will clarify the results of the analysis. Suppose that the current price-earnings ratio for a growth stock is 45 and for a non-growth stock of comparable risk is 15. Then the relative price-earnings ratio is $(P_g/E_g) \div (P_a/E_a) = 45/15 = 3$, as shown by the heavy horizontal line on Figure 1. Suppose, further, that the growth in earnings per share of the growth stock is expected to continue at the rate of 30 per cent per year but the dividend yield is only 1 per cent per year. The non-growth stock, on the other hand, is expected to have only a 5 per cent growth in earnings but has a 5 per cent dividend yield. Thus the relative growth rate is $(1 + \Delta E_g + D_g) \div (1 + \Delta E_a + D_a) = (1 + 0.30 + 0.01) \div (1 + 0.05 + 0.05) = 1.31/1.10 = 1.2$, as shown by the heavy sloping line through the origin of Figure 1. The intersection of these two lines determines a point labeled A. Dropping vertically, we can read from the horizontal scale that the market estimate of duration of growth is evidently 6 years. That is to say, the market is valuing the growth stock *as if* its present high rate of growth would continue for 6 years and then decline sharply to the normal level. The graph has made it easy to find that $\tau = 6$. This value, of course, satisfies equation (6) for this example:

$$\frac{45}{15} \approx \left(\frac{1 + 0.30 + 0.01}{1 + 0.05 + 0.05}\right)^6.$$

Another way to interpret the six-year growth duration is in terms of total growth potential. A 30 per cent growth rate is, say, 25 per cent above the normal growth rate, taking the non-growth stock as the standard. If this rate continues for 6 years, we would have a total growth potential of $(1.25)^6 = 3.82$ or 382 per cent. This amounts to forecasting that the ratio of earnings per share of the growth stock to the non-growth stock will ultimately improve by almost a factor of 4.

AN ILLUSTRATION USING MARKET DATA

The use of this analysis may be illustrated by selecting the Dow-Jones index as a representative alternative non-growth investment, and selecting the following growth common stocks: Ampex, International Business Machines, Litton, Polaroid, and Texas Instruments. The dividend yields and price-earnings ratios for May, 1960, were used.

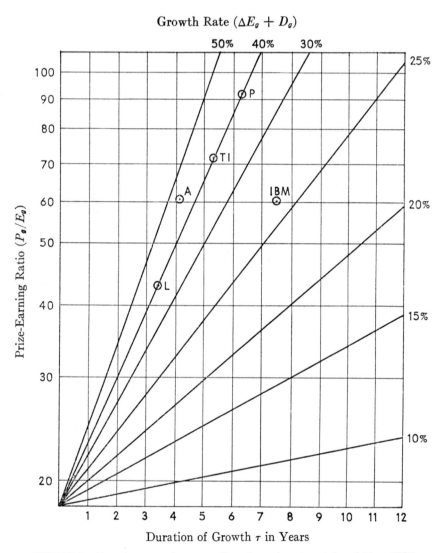

FIGURE 2   Growth companies versus Dow-Jones investment (as of May, 1960).

For the Dow-Jones index, the price earnings ratio P_a/E_a was 18, D_a was 3 per cent per year, and ΔE_a was 5 per cent per year. These forecasts were extrapolations of the previous 5 years' history. We have obtained ΔE_g for each of the growth companies by plotting on semilog paper the earnings per share, adjusted for stock splits and stock dividends, for 1956 through 1959 and estimated the slope.

Before plotting points for each growth company, Figure 1 was modified by changing its scales to incorporate the Dow-Jones index as the standard non-growth alternative[7] (see Figure 2). Plotting these data on Figure 2 indicates the growth duration periods shown in the second column of Table 1. In interpreting these results, one is tempted, at first blush, to say that Litton is the better buy because it will justify its high price-earnings ratio relative to a Dow-Jones investment in a shorter period of time than the other companies. However, valid conclusions require a comparison for each company between the market estimate of duration of growth and the investor's own estimate. The investor can compare his judgments with those of the market and act accordingly where he feels the market is in error. Clearly, if growth duration actually proves to be longer than the market's estimate, the stock will have proved to be a bargain purchase. A stock with growth duration shorter than the market estimate will prove to have been a poor investment. As always, the investor must bet that his forecast is better than that of the market. If he can forecast growth durations successfully, growth stocks may offer important investment opportunities.

This analysis may be used in another way. An estimate of the growth duration for a company may be made by the investor and the corresponding line drawn vertically on Figure 1 or Figure 2 until it intersects the sloping growth-rate line and then move left horizontally to read the price-earnings ratio. This is the price-earnings ratio that would be warranted by this duration of growth. This could be compared with the price-earnings ratio existing in the market and purchase-sell decisions made accordingly.

ADJUSTMENT FOR TAXES

An extension of the analysis might well take into account the fact that long-term capital gains are taxed at an advantageously low rate, so that income through price appreciation is more desirable than dividend income. An exact adjustment for taxes would greatly complicate the analysis, but, by ignoring the fact that capital gains taxes are postponable, we may make an approximate adjustment. By making the simplifying assumption that capital gains are taxes in the year in which they occur, we can modify formula (7) to reflect growth after taxes.

---

[7]The growth-rate scale on Fig. 2 plus 1 equals the relative growth-rate scale of Fig. 1 multiplied by $(1 + 0.30 + 0.01)$.

TABLE 1

Company	Market estimate of duration of growth (Years)	Adjusted for taxes (Years)
Ampex	4.1	4.2
International Business Machines	7.5	7.5
Litton	3.4	3.4
Polaroid	6.3	6.8
Texas Instruments	5.3	5.7

The growth from dividend reinvestment is reduced by taxes to $(1 - K_D)D$, where K_D is the marginal tax rate applicable to dividend income. Similarly, the growth of earnings is reduced to $(1 - K_C)\Delta E$, where K_C is the marginal tax rate applicable to capital gains income. A person whose marginal income tax rate was 30 per cent would be taxed at half that rate on capital gains, i.e., $K_D = 0.3$ and $K_C = 0.15$. The maximum K_C is, of course, 0.25.

Recalling that the price-earnings ratio of the growth stock falls as the termination of the high growth rate approaches, we need to recognize that all the gain in earnings is not reflected in gain in market price of the shares. Since we have applied the capital gains tax to the full earnings appreciation, we need to make an offsetting adjustment by applying the capital gains tax to the decline in price-earnings ratio. If we rewrite the left parentheses of formula (7),

$$\frac{P_g/E_g}{P_a/E_a} \approx \frac{P_a/E_a + (P_g/E_g - P_a/E_a)}{P_a/E_a} \tag{8}$$

we can interpret the right parentheses in formula (8) as the capital "loss" component for the growth stock as the result of the reduction in price-earnings ratio to that of the non-growth stock. We apply the capital gains tax to this "loss" adjustment by multiplying the "loss" term by $(1 - K_C)$:

$$\frac{P_a/E_a + (P_g/E_g - P_a/E_a)(1 - K_C)}{P_a/E_a} \approx 1 + \left(\frac{P_g/E_g}{P_a/E_a} - 1\right)(1 - K_C). \tag{9}$$

Incorporating the above adjustments in formula (7), we obtain

$$\ln\left[1 + \left(\frac{P_g/E_g}{P_a/E_a} - 1\right)(1 - K_C)\right]$$
$$\approx \tau \ln\left[\frac{1 + (1 - K_C)\Delta E_g + (1 - K_D)D_g}{1 + (1 - K_C)\Delta E_a + (1 - K_D)D_a}\right]. \tag{10}$$

The inclusion of the tax adjustment does not complicate the graphs, but it does complicate somewhat the computation step before entering the graphs. The effect of the adjustment will be to reflect the preference of the high-income person for companies that do not pay out their growth in the form of dividends. Applying this adjustment to the companies that we have already considered and assuming an investor whose tax rates are $K_D = 0.5$ and $K_C = 0.25$, we obtain the overtake periods shown in the third column of Table 1. In this case, the overtake periods were not greatly affected by the adjustment for taxes.

CONCLUSION

Four limitations of this analysis need to be noted. First—and most important—the uncertainty of forecasting earnings in the distant future is a much more important consideration for growth stocks than for non-growth stocks. Hence, ignoring the risk inherent in probabilistic forecast errors is an important omission which will tend to make growth stocks appear more attractive than they really are. Second, the analysis rests on forecasts of constant earnings-per-share growth rates and constant dividend-per-share yields. Such forecasts on a per share basis need to be made critically because past data may reflect purely financial transactions, such as increasing leverage, etc., which may reflect increasing risk rather than growth. Third, the relative tax advantage of capital gains income, which is the principal return from growth stocks, is somewhat understated by neglecting the deferred collection of the capital gains tax, so that growth stocks appear less attractive than they really are—especially for high-income investors. Fourth, we hardly expect the growth of earnings to terminate sharply but, rather, would expect the growth rate to decline gradually as the special advantages enjoyed by the growth company are whittled away by increasing competition, expiration of patents, appearance of substitute products, etc. Thus the high growth rate would tend to last longer than the above analysis would indicate, but the rate of growth would be reduced.

The need for a really adequate theory of investment under certainty is emphasized by the gross approximations that were used in this exploratory analysis. Granting these limitations, the analysis does offer a systematic framework for evaluating growth stocks that includes many of the relevant variables with a minimum of complexity and computation. Hopefully, the analysis is simple enough—even using the adjustment for taxes—to be useful to investors.[8]

[8]An independent, but equivalent, analysis by Robert Ferguson has recently yielded a nomograph which reduces the computations to a simple mechanical procedure ("A Nomograph for Valuing Growth Stocks," *Financial Analysts Journal*, XVII [May–June, 1961], 29–34). Unfortunately, the underlying assumptions of his analysis are not fully explicit.

Dividend Policies
and Common-Stock Prices*

James E. Walter

1

In ... [one] issue of this journal, Professor Harkavy pre-
sented a statistical analysis of the relationship between retained earnings and
common stock prices.[1] His principal conclusion is that, while common stock
prices vary directly with dividend payout ratios at any given time, their
degree of appreciation over a period of time is associated with the proportion of earnings which are retained. Only brief reference is made to the
fact that the crucial consideration is the profitable utilization of investors'
funds. Empirical studies of this type should be encouraged and are of
definite value provided careful consideration is given, both before and after
their preparation, to the underlying theoretical propositions.

Based upon the belief that stock-market behavior is susceptible of
rationalization, an attempt is made in this paper to fabricate a theoretical
model which depicts the relationship between dividend policies and common
stock prices. Attention is of necessity restricted to the common stocks of
large public corporations because of the imperfect market for the securities
of small companies and of the close identification of small firms with their
principal shareholders. The fundamental premise upon which the formulation rests is that, over longer periods, stock prices reflect the present values
of expected dividends.[2] The phrase "over long periods" is inserted to
permit abstraction from the distortions caused by short-run speculative
considerations.

Granted this premise, retained earnings influence stock prices principally through their effect upon future dividends. The fact that some stocks

*From the *Journal of Finance*, 11, no. 1, March 1956, pp. 29–41. Back numbers obtainable
from the Kraus Reprint Corporation, New York.

[1]Oscar Harkavy, "The Relation between Retained Earnings and Common Stock Prices
for Large, Listed Corporation," *Journal of Finance*, VIII, No. 3 (Sept., 1953), 283–97.

[2]See J. B. Williams, *The Theory of Investment Value* (Cambridge: Harvard University Press,
1938), p. 6, for a similar position.

may have substantial market value even though little or no dividends are anticipated in the foreseeable future need not contradict this proposition. Undistributed earnings are immediately realizable to the shareholder, at least in part, provided prospective investors can be found who are willing to wait and to assume the required risk.

In analyzing the present worth of future dividends, the concept of capitalization rate is utilized in preference to that of multiplier, which is customarily employed by security analysts. The capitalization rate for any stock is simply the reciprocal of the multiplier. Since capitalization rates are expressed in percentage terms, their use simplifies the presentation and facilitates direct comparisons with rates of return on additional investment.

Capitalization rates are determined by the underlying yield on safe securities and by the required risk premiums. The yield on safe securities is conditioned by such factors as monetary and debt policy, income distribution, the intensity of present as opposed to future wants, and productivity. The basic risk premium, as measured by the difference between the yield on safe securities and the capitalization rate on high-grade common stocks, is dependent upon the economic climate and government policy. Inter-industry differences in size, capital structure, efficiency, and diversification occasion substantial variations in capitalization rates among corporations.

The level and diversity of capitalization rates influence the succeeding analysis in at least two respects. The higher the level of capitalization rates, both individually and generally, the fewer are the companies whose stocks qualify as growth stocks. The greater the diversity of capitalization rates and the more numerous their determinants, the less feasible it becomes to talk in terms of average or normal capitalization rates. The concept of market capitalization rate must therefore be defined arbitrarily in order to exclude irrelevant heterogeneity.

The proposition that all common stocks behave in a reasonably uniform manner does not appear to be warranted by the observed variations in stock prices. As a result, three groups, referred to respectively as growth stock, intermediate and creditor stock categories, are isolated for consideration. A fourth possibility, the declining stock category, is ignored because of its presumed unimportance in a growing economy.

Diversity of dividend policy is often regarded as one of the principal features which differentiate among these groups. Growth stocks are customarily characterized by low dividend payout ratios; intermediate stocks, by medium to high ratios; and creditor stocks, by fixed dividend rates irrespective of short-run earnings. With the possible exception of creditor stocks, however, the dividend-earnings relationship is neither a necessary nor a sufficient condition for assigning stocks to any given category. The crucial consideration is the rate of return on additional investment. The greater the profitability, the more likely is management—in the interests of rapid expansion—to retain a substantial percentage of earnings.

2

The concept "growth stock" is familiar to investors and is understood to refer, in general terms, to common stocks which possess superior prospects for long-term appreciation. Surface characteristics of growth stocks include low dividend payout ratios, high market multipliers (i.e., low capitalization rates), and prices which increase through time with relative rapidity. Low dividend payout ratios constitute an accepted feature of growth stocks, since shareholders are presumed to benefit more from the retention of earnings than from their employment elsewhere at the going rates.

In qualifying for membership in the growth stock category, marginal profitability is the basic criterion. The rate of return on additional investment determines the magnitude of future dividends obtainable from given amounts of retained earnings or external financing. The anticipated level of future dividends, when discounted at the appropriate capitalization rate, in turn yields the present value for a given stock. If the rate of return on added investment is sufficiently great, it follows that low dividend payout ratios may add to, rather than subtract from, stock values.

For the purpose of demonstrating the potential influence of retained earnings uoon stock prices, let us assume that earnings retention is the sole source of additional funds; that both the rate of return on added investment and the market capitalization rate are constants; and that all increments to earnings are immediately distributed to shareholders. The market capitalization rate for any given corporation is defined as the reciprocal of the multiplier which would prevail in the market if the dividend payout ratio were 100 per cent.[3] Treating the stream of future earnings as perpetual (or at least of indefinite duration), the present value of any common stock can then be expressed in mathematical terms as

$$V_c = \frac{D + \frac{R_a}{R_c}(E - D)}{R_c} = \frac{E}{R_c} + \frac{R_a - R_c}{R_c^2}(E - D), \tag{1}$$

[3]This definition is introduced simply to preclude the possibility that capitalization rates will be interpreted to reflect the effect of varying dividend policies. To illustrate, let us assume that companies A and B have identical earnings per share ($10), R_a (20 per cent), and R_c (10 per cent), but have payout ratios of 75 per cent and 50 per cent respectively. Substituting in equation (1), we find that A has a V_c of $125 and B, of $150. The ratio of E to V_c, which might be called the unadjusted or composite capitalization rate, is thus 8 per cent for A and $6\frac{2}{3}$ per cent for B. The difference is attributable to divergent dividend policies.

where D is cash dividends, E is earnings, R_a is the rate of return on additional investment, and R_c is the market capitalization rate.[4]

Equation (1) reveals the importance of both the dividend payout ratio and the relationship between R_a and R_c. Whenever R_a exceeds R_c, the present worth of future dividends resulting from the retention of earnings is greater than the dollar magnitude of retained earnings. The lower the dividend payout ratio, under such circumstances, the higher is the value of the growth stock.

A currently high rate of return on additional investment for a given corporation need not automatically transform its stock into a growth stock. In the first place, the high rate must persist over a reasonable period of time. The market's judgment of a common stock is of necessity based primarily upon past experience. The corporation's willingness to invest is also influenced by the anticipated permanence of R_a to the extent that increments to earnings lag behind the retention of earnings. In the second place, high rates of return on added investment must not be offset by correspondingly high market capitalization rates. In so far as new industries are characterized by small, insufficiently capitalized firms and mature industries by large, conservatively financed companies, R_a and R_c may well be directly associated.

As observed in footnote 4, modifications in equation (1), which provide added realism at the expense of simplicity, do not alter the results in any fundamental respect. Anticipated declines in the return on additional investment (R_a) affect stock values and raise serious doubts as to the propriety of permanently low dividend payout ratios. As long as R_a continues to exceed R_c, however, the substantial retention of earnings appears beneficial to shareholders.

The recognition of external sources of new financing enables growth stocks to possess low "composite" capitalization rates even in the presence of high dividend payout ratios.[5] The market in effect endeavors to forecast the willingness and ability to use external sources and discounts

---

[4]The second version of equation (1) is presented to show the extent to which V_c will exceed (or fall short of) the ratio of E to R_c. As in the case of most gross simplifications, equation (1) presents difficulties if used without modification. To illustrate the point and to indicate the type of modification which might be made, let us consider time as an endless succession of periods. Based upon equation (1) and its underlying assumptions, the value of the stock in question will rise in each period (without cessation) by an amount equal to $R_a(E-D)/R_c$. Since diminishing returns are an almost inevitable consequence, R_a must be viewed—for practical purposes—as a weighted average of $r_1, r_2, \ldots, r_{n-1}$, where r represents the rate of return on added investment at any given point (period) in time and $r_n = 0$. By weighted is simply meant that r_1, r_2, etc., must, because of the proximity to the present, be assigned greater importance than r_{n-1}, r_{n-2}, etc.

[5]The prevailing ratio of earnings to stock prices for a given company at any time can be thought of as a composite rate. The basic component is the market capitalization rate (R_c), as interpreted above. From R_c is deducted (if a growth stock) a percentage equivalent to the relative increase in the present worth of future dividends which is attributable to earnings retention or, as the case may be, to external financing.

future dividends attributable thereto. Despite this consideration, stock prices can still be expected to vary inversely with dividend payout ratios, provided R_a exceeds R_c.

Even without reference to capital gains taxation, the market appears justified in according special treatment to growth stocks in the sense of low "composite" capitalization rates. The all pervasiveness of uncertainty may of course occasion conservative interpretations of future earnings and may restrict recognized membership in the growth stock category to a relatively few outstanding corporations. For doubtful cases, retained earnings and dividends may simply be regarded as equivalents. Alternatively, the prices of marginal growth stocks may be adversely affected, provided dividend payout ratios are below what the market believes to be a reasonable compromise.

At least one further factor functions to lessen the present worth of retained earnings relative to current dividends. This consideration concerns the emphasis placed upon balanced portfolios, i.e., diversification by investors. To the extent that the market values of growth stocks appreciate through time more rapidly than those of their asset holdings, investors may be induced to redistribute the increment among all components of their portfolios.[6]

Whenever portfolio readjustment must be achieved through the sale of shares, as opposed to the utilization of cash dividends, certain costs and risks are incurred.[7] Transfer costs, comprising commissions and taxes, have to be met. Market prices are conditioned by short-run influences and need not reflect longer-run capitalized values at any given time. In addition, the augmented supply of growth shares on the market—resulting from efforts to diversify—may depress their prices below what they otherwise would have been.

The consequence is that the appropriate test for growth stocks from the viewpoint of shareholders may not be simply R_a exceeds R_c, but rather R_a exceeds R_c by an amount sufficient to cover the cost of added diversification. That is to say,

$$V_c = \frac{D + \dfrac{R_a}{R_c + p}(E - D)}{R_c}, \tag{1a}$$

where p is the premium associated with the cost of diversification.

Except for outstanding cases, the isolation of growth stocks for empirical study does not appear to be a simple task. As suggested pre-

[6]The line of reasoning is quite similar to that underlying the "substitution effect" in the theory of consumer choice. For the sake of simplicity, however, it is assumed that the problem of present versus future consumption does not arise.

[7]As indicated subsequently, these considerations may be partially offset by the preferential tax treatment of capital gains.

viously, changes in earnings from period to period are likely to be discontinuous and to be associated with past, rather than current, sources of funds. The reason is simply that the expansion of both facilities and markets takes time. The reported levels of historical earnings, which is the principal basis for estimating future earnings, are dependent upon arbitrary accounting techniques. In addition, price-level changes often provide a misleading illusion of growth. In some instances, these and other factors lead the market astray; in other cases, they lead the analyst to believe that the market's evaluation is incorrect when in actual fact it is not.

3

Preferential tax treatment of capital gains, as opposed to dividend income, affects growth stocks in at least two respects. It augments the value of retained earnings and hence increases growth stock prices, provided personal income taxes levied upon marginal shareholders exceed zero. It also gives certain superior non-growth stocks the status of growth stocks.

Wherever rates of return on additional investment are positive, the retention of earnings by corporations raises both the anticipated level and the present worth of future dividends. As the present values of future dividends change through time and are reflected in stock prices, shareholders are able to realize these gains by selling portions of their holdings. Shareholders benefit from this form of income realization to the extent that the preferential tax treatment of capital gains reduces their total tax. In addition, the realization criterion for the capital gains tax enables shareholders to time security sales so as to minimize further their total tax burden.

The presence of organized security exchanges limits rather substantially the observed impact of capital gains taxation. The more perfect the market in which common stocks are traded, the less is the ability to distinguish among buyers or sellers unless legal or institutional barriers are erected. In the absence of discrimination and of individual bargaining, only the tax savings derived by marginal shareholders from capital gains taxation will be reflected in security prices.

Equation (1) indicates that, given certain simplifying assumptions which do not distort the underlying relationships, a dollar of retained earnings is the equivalent of a dollar of dividends multiplied by the ratio of R_a to R_c. If this equivalence is adjusted for the special tax treatment of captial gains, the equation becomes

$$s\frac{R_a}{R_c} = t; \quad \text{or} \quad R_a = \frac{t}{s}R_c, \tag{2}$$

where s is one *minus* the tax rate on capital gains and t is one *minus* the marginal tax rate on personal income, both as related to marginal shareholders. If allowance is also made for the existence of dividend tax credits, as provided in the recently passed technical tax relief bill (1954), form (2) is transformed into

$$R_a = \frac{t + c}{s} R_c, \qquad (2a)$$

where c is the dividend tax credit, expressed in percentage terms.

Equations (2) and (2a) demonstrate that superior non-growth stocks may be raised to the status of growth stocks as a result of preferred tax treatment for capital gains. That is to say, the retention of earnings need not be disadvantageous to shareholders even though R_a is somewhat less than R_c.

For illustrative purposes, let us assume that the marginal tax rate on the personal income of marginal shareholders is 50 per cent; that the tax rate on capital gain is 25 per cent; that the dividend tax credit is 4 per cent; and that the market capitalization rate (R_c) is 10 per cent. Substituting these figures into equation (2a), R_a is found to be 7.2 per cent. At this point it is immaterial to marginal shareholders whether earnings are retained or distributed. In the event that R_a exceeds 7.2 per cent, under these conditions the stock in question takes on the characteristics of a growth stock.

Alternative assumptions may produce significantly different results. If, for example, the marginal tax rate on personal income is 20 per cent and the rate on capital gains is 10 per cent, R_a becomes 9.3 per cent. The basic propositions nonetheless continue to hold.

4

A substantial majority of all "listed" industrial common stocks undoubtedly belong to the intermediate stock group. Surface characteristics of this category are dividend payout ratios in excess of 50 per cent, multipliers which range in the neighborhood of the average multiplier for all "listed" corporations, and prices which increase slowly through time. Shareholder pressure is exerted for substantial payout ratios, since stock prices tend to vary directly with the level of dividend payout ratios. Although the retention of earnings leads to appreciation in stock values, shareholders benefit from the receipt of dividends and their investment elsewhere at the going market rate.

In assigning stocks to this category, the underlying consideration is whether the present value of future dividends attributable to retained earnings at the margin is greater or less than the corresponding dollar amount of earnings retention. This question is essentially the same as that raised in connection with growth stocks. Its resolution hinges, in similar fashion, upon the relationship between R_a, adjusted for the preferred tax treatment of capital gains, and R_c. As shown by equation (1) and as modified by equation (2), if "adjusted" R_a exceeds R_c, the common stock in question is a growth stock; if "adjusted" R_a is less than R_c but greater than zero, it is an intermediate stock.

The preponderance of the intermediate stock group, particularly where large and mature public corporations are concerned, apparently leads many investment analysts to recommend high dividend payout ratios as a general rule. The best-known advocates, Graham and Dodd, state that the investment value of any industrial common stock equals

$$M(D + \tfrac{1}{3}E),\tag{3}$$

where M, the multiplier, is the reciprocal of the "assumed" appropriate capitalization rate, D is expected dividends, and E is expected earnings.[8] Essentially theirs must be regarded as a conservative approach which presumably emphasizes both the uncertainness of future earnings and the inevitable decline, at some point in time, in the rate of return on additional investment even for expanding enterprises.

Since equation (3) stresses the dividend factor, it is reasonably well adapted to the intermediate stock category. In the equation proper, a dollar of dividends is presumed to be the equivalent of four dollars of retained earnings. In terms of equation (1), the ratio of "adjusted" R_a to R_c is thus fixed at one-fourth. Inasmuch as the numerous other possible relationships between R_a and R_c are ignored, the multiplier must be adjusted for differences between the assumed normal relationship and the actual relationship in any given circumstance. For growth stocks, the magnitudes of the adjustments required in M assume such significance that the general application of equation (3) does not appear to be feasible.

Whatever the approach employed to evaluate intermediate stocks, the presumed level of current dividends is important, but not all important. Expansion may still be beneficial to shareholders even though R_a is less than R_c, provided the added investment is financed at least in part by borrowed funds.[9] The essential requirements are that the corporation in question be conservatively financed and that the excess of R_a over the interest rate be sufficient to offset the excess of R_c over R_a. If conserv-

[8]B. Graham and D. L. Dodd, *Security Analysis* (New York: McGraw-Hill Book Co., 1951; 3d ed.), p. 410.
[9]Unlike the case of capital gains taxation, benefits derived from the use of borrowed funds do not accrue automatically to shareholders. Their existence depends upon management policy. For this reason, the possibility of utilizing borrowed funds is introduced simply as a qualification to the intermediate stock category.

atively financed, the augmented use of borrowed funds need not appreciably affect either the multiplier or its reciprocal.

For illustrative purposes, let us assume that the conventional debt-equity ratio is one-half; that the market capitalization rate is unaffected as long as this relationship holds; and that added investment is financed by the same proportions of debt and retained earnings as the conventional ratio. If, under such conditions, R_a is 6 per cent and the interest rate is 3 per cent, the rate of return on retained earnings becomes 7.5 per cent. The retention of earnings is thus beneficial to shareholders, provided R_c is less than 7.5 per cent.

Even if the use of borrowed funds is ignored, the maximum feasible dividend payout ratio is likely to be something less than 100 per cent for intermediate stocks. In some instances, maintenance of relative position within the industry may be essential for profit maintenance. Whatever the relation of R_a to R_c, the affected corporation must then keep pace with the industry and with other firms. Otherwise, the company loses out, and its over-all profit rate declines. In other instances, a substantial portion of reported earnings may be attributable to price-level changes. If the real position of a given company is to be maintained, a portion of reported earnings will then have to be retained. In still other instances, cash may simply be unavailable for dividends.

5

A third group, the creditor stock category, may now be isolated for examination. Creditor stocks are so named because they possess many of the attributes of debt instruments. The most important of the similarities is that, in determining the present worth of creditor stocks, almost exclusive emphasis is placed upon the prevailing level of dividends. Average yields on creditor stocks are somewhat higher than those on bonds, for shareholders lack legal protection and have no equity cushion upon which to rest. The limited ability of institutional investors to hold any type of equity share, due principally to legislative restrictions and to the nature of their obligations, also contributes to the yield differential between bonds and creditor stocks.[10]

As contrasted with the growth and intermediate stock categories, the retention of earnings occasions little or no appreciation in creditor stock prices over time. The low present value of retained earnings may be attributable to the fact that the rate of return on additional investment approximates zero. It may be attributable to management which elects to retain earnings during prosperous periods and to hold them in liquid

[10]As the pressure to obtain satisfactory yields on investments increases, however, the gradual relaxation of legislative restrictions is likely to occur.

form for distribution during depressed periods. It may be attributable to public regulatory commissions which pass the benefits derived from earnings retention on to the public.

In a relevant sense the inclusion of this category modifies, as well as extends beyond, the preceding analysis. Stocks can no longer be said to qualify automatically for membership in the growth and intermediate stock groups depending upon whether "adjusted" R_a is greater or less than R_c. The ultimate distribution of additional earnings is not a foregone conclusion; retained earnings need not be employed in the most profitable fashion; and economic considerations are not the sole criterion.

The ability of shareholders to influence the policies of either management or regulatory commissions is frequently circumscribed. As a result, stock prices are of necessity conditioned by the expected behavior of management and government in the light of their past actions. If management and/or regulatory commissions regard shareholders as creditors and if the underlying economic conditions permit their treatment as such, it follows that the stocks which are thus affected will assume many of the characteristics of credit instruments.

Common stocks of large, well-established public utilities offer excellent possibilities for inclusion in the creditor stock category.[11] Public utilities in general are characterized by an underlying element of stability and by close regulation. Rates tend to be adjusted so as to provide reasonable and stable returns to shareholders. Dividend payout ratios normally range in the neighborhood of 75 per cent, and sources of additional funds are largely external.[12]

The acceptance of the idea that shareholders are creditors is reflected in the dividend policy of the largest of all public utilities. For more than three decades American Telephone and Telegraph has annually declared a nine-dollar dividend.

Common stocks of large, mature industrial corporations whose earnings possess a reasonable degree of stability are likely to exhibit at least some features of creditor stocks. Management often elects to stabilize the dollar amount of dividends declared annually, thereby reducing dividend payout ratios during prosperous periods and raising them during depressed periods. To the extent that retained earnings are then held in liquid form, "cash" cushions are created which bear marked similarities to the equity or earning-power cushions provided for senior securities.

Needless to say, the point of delineation between intermediate stocks

---

[11]It is not meant to imply that all, or even the great majority, of utility stocks are creditor stocks. Some may actually be growth stocks. The crucial considerations appear to be whether regulatory commissions permit retained earnings to augment the invested capital base and whether the allowable rate of return exceeds or falls short of R_c.

[12]Postwar payout ratios are noticeably below those for the immediate prewar period, perhaps reflecting the impact of substantial price-level changes.

and creditor stocks is difficult to ascertain.[13] Given the separation of ownership from control for large, public corporations, it may well be that shareholders are generally viewed by the managements of these companies as a form of creditor. In numerous instances, however, the nature of the corporation may be such that this attitude cannot readily be translated into policy.

A further consideration relates to the willingness of the market to recognize and accept creditor stocks. Unless the corporation in question is extremely well known and has a long and stable dividend record, it is doubtful whether the market will accord its stock special treatment. Special treatment, in this instance, refers to lower capitalization rates and to more stable stock prices than would otherwise be the case. If market acceptance is not forthcoming, the stock remains simply an inferior member of the intermediate stock category.

As a final point, the behavior of creditor stock prices can still be expected to resemble in many respects that of common stock prices in general. First, even where common stocks are creditor oriented, dividends ordinarily exhibit some relation to earnings and vary accordingly. This proposition follows from the absence of contractual agreements between management and shareholders. Second, since common stocks have no maturity dates, creditor stock prices are not conditioned by maturity values. This situation is, however, little different from that of bonds possessing remote maturities and no different from that of Consols.

Third, wherever regulatory commissions exist, rate revisions customarily operate with a lag. During the interim, higher earnings attributable to the retention of earnings may permit higher dividends. The converse is, of course, also true. Finally, the possibility is always present that, as management and commissions change, policies may also change.

6

The basic premise that stock prices, over longer periods, reflect the present values of anticipated future dividends permits derivation of a model which possesses substantial plausibility. In distinguishing between growth and intermediate stocks, the crucial question becomes whether or not the capitalized values of future dividends attributable to the retention of earnings are greater than the dollar magnitudes of retained earnings. Wherever greater, i.e., wherever rates of return on additional investment exceed market capitalization rates, the common stocks in question belong to the growth stock category. In the case of growth stocks, low dividend payout ratios can be expected to enhance stock values.

In certain instances, common stocks may assume the characteris-

---

[13]In other words, R_a—in the sense of most profitable uses of funds—may be less than R_c, but greater than zero, for creditor stocks as well as intermediate stocks.

tics of growth stocks despite the fact that rates of return on added invest-ment are less than market capitalization rates. The preferred tax treat-ment of capital gains augments the worth of retained earnings and enables more stocks to qualify as growth stocks. In addition, the combined use of borrowed funds and retained earnings makes it beneficial to retain earnings under special circumstances.

For most large industrials, rates of return on additional investment are presumed to exceed zero, but to be less than the corresponding market capitalization rates. This condition leads to the commonly observed, direct relationship between dividend payout ratios and common stock prices. Although earnings retention occasions appreciation in stock prices over time, shareholders benefit from the distribution of the maximum feasible amount of earnings.

Acceptance of the fact that the control over large public corpora-tions is often vested in management and regulatory commissions gives rise to the creditor stock category. For this group, the principal deter-minant of common stock prices is the prevailing level of dividends, capital-ized at appropriate rates. Although retained earnings may augment dividend stability and thereby reduce capitalization rates, they contribute little to the prospects for higher dividends in the future.

Granted the inadequacies and diversity of statistical data, a model of this type has considerable utility as a foundation for empirical analysis. Most important of all, it provides a tentative basis for classifying common stocks. Even in the event that the model is not entirely valid, the heter-ogeneity of the statistical sample may still be reduced. Secondly, it specifies the necessary information and establishes interesting relationships for empirical verification. Finally, if—as is more than likely—the statistical data are inadequate for thoroughgoing analyses, they may nonetheless be sufficient to confirm or deny the model.

3·7

Dividends, Earnings, and Stock Prices*

M. J. Gordon

The three possible hypotheses with respect to what an investor pays for when he acquires a share of common stock are that he is buying (1) both the dividends and the earnings, (2) the dividends, and (3)

*See footnote on next page.

the earnings. It may be argued that most commonly he is buying the price at some future date, but if the future price will be related to the expected dividends and/or earnings on that date, we need not go beyond the three hypotheses stated. This paper will critically evaluate the hypotheses by deriving the relation among the variables that follows from each hypothesis and then testing the theories with cross-section sample data. That is, price, dividend, and earnings data for a sample of corporations as of a point in time will be used to test the relation among the variables predicted by each hypothesis.

The variation in price among common stocks is of considerable interest for the discovery of profitable investment opportunities, for the guidance of corporate financial policy, and for the understanding of the psychology of investment behavior.[1] Although one would expect that this interest would find expression in cross-section statistical studies, a search of the literature is unrewarding.

Cross-section studies of a sort are used extensively by security analysts to arrive at buy and sell recommendations. The values of certain attributes such as the dividend yield, growth in sales, and management ability are obtained and compared for two or more stocks. Then, by some weighting process, a conclusion is reached from this information that a stock is or is not an attractive buy at its current price.[2] Graham and Dodd go so far as to state that stock prices should bear a specified relation to earnings and dividends, but they neither present nor cite data to support the generalization.[3] The distinguished theoretical book on investment value by J. B. Williams contains several chapters devoted to the application of the theory, but his empirical work is in the tradition of the investment analyst's approach.[4] The only study along the lines suggested here that is known to the writer is a recent one on bank stocks by David Durand.[5]

*Reprinted by permission of the publishers from *The Review of Economics and Statistics*, 41, no. 2, May 1959, pp. 99–105, Cambridge, Mass.: Harvard University Press, Copyright, 1959, the President and Fellows of Harvard College. For further development of the ideas raised in this article see M. J. Gordon, *The Investment Financing and Valuation of the Corporation*, Homewood, Ill.: R. D. Irwin, 1962. The research for this paper was supported by the Sloan Research Fund of the School of Industrial Management at Massachusetts Institute of Technology. The author has benefited from the advice of Professors Edwin Kuh, Eli Shapiro, and Gregory Chow. The computations were done in part at the M.I.T. Computation Center.

[1]Assume that the hypothesis stock price, $P = f(x_1, x_2, \ldots)$, is stated so that it can be tested, and it is found to do a good job of explaining the variation in price among stocks. The model and its coefficients thereby shed light on what investors consider and the weight they give these variables in buying common stocks. This information is valuable to corporations insofar as the prices of their stocks influence their financial plans. It is also true that a stock selling at a price above or below that predicted by the model deserves special consideration by investors.

[2]Illustrations of this method of analysis may be found in texts on investment analysis such as: Graham and Dodd, *Security Analysis*, 3rd ed. (New York, 1951); and Dowrie and Fuller, *Investments* (New York, 1941).

[3]Graham and Dodd, op. cit., 454 ff.

[4]*The Theory of Investment Value* (Cambridge, 1938).

[5]*Bank Stock Prices and the Bank Capital Problem*, Occasional Paper 54, National Bureau of Economic Research (New York, 1957).

In contrast with the dearth of published studies the writer has encountered a number of unpublished cross-section regressions of stock prices on dividends, earnings, and sometimes other variables. In these the correlations were high, but the values of the regression coefficients and their variation among samples (different industries or different years) made the economic significance of the results so questionable that the investigators were persuaded to abandon their studies. There is reason to believe that the unsatisfactory nature of the findings is due in large measure to the inadequacy of the theory employed in interpreting the model, and it is hoped that this paper will contribute to a more effective use of cross-section stock price studies by presenting what might be called the elementary theory of the variation in stock prices with dividends and earnings.

Before proceeding, it may be noted that there have been some time series studies of the variation in stock prices with dividends and other variables. The focus of these studies has been the relation between the stock market and the business cycle[6] and the discovery of profitable investment opportunities.[7] They have not been concerned with explaining the variation in price among stocks, and it is questionable whether such data can be effectively used for this purpose. Auto-correlation in the time series would impair the significance of the regression coefficients for many of the variables. Possibly even more important, the use of time series assumes that the coefficient of a variable is constant over time but different among stocks. The exact opposite is assumed in any attempt to explain preference among investment opportunities.

THE SAMPLE

To test each of the theories, price, dividend, and earnings data were obtained for four industries and two years, so that there are eight samples in all. The years chosen were 1951 and 1954, and the industries and number of corporations for each industry are Chemicals, 32; Foods, 52; Steel, 34; and Machine Tools, 46.

Including only those corporations which conformed to a narrow definition of the industries mentioned did not provide samples of adequate size. Therefore, certain fringe classifications were included in each category. For instance, Chemicals includes pharmaceutical manufacturers, and Steel includes forging manufacturers and certain other fabricators of

[6]J. Tinbergen, "The Dynamics of Share-Price Formation," this Review, XXI (November 1939), 153–60; and Paul G. Darling, "A Surrogative Measure of Business Confidence and Its Relation to Stock Prices," Journal of Finance, X (December 1955), 442–58.
[7]The outstanding example of this is The Value Line Investment Survey. In addition, numerous articles in the Analysts Journal and the Journal of Finance analyze the change over time of price with other variables. A paper of some interest is D. Harkavy, "The Relation Between Retained Earnings and Common Stock Prices for Large, Listed Corporations," Journal of Finance, VIII (September 1953), 183–97.

steel as well as the basic steel producers. In general, while the corporations included in each sample can be considered to come under the label, there is considerable variation among them in such attributes as size, profitability, structure of the markets in which they buy and sell, and investor status.[8]

The use of eight samples rather than one provides a more rigorous test of the hypotheses. The industry and year selection of the data has the further advantage of allowing the use of *a priori* economic knowledge in evaluating the regression statistics. For instance, if the dividend coefficient is considered an estimate of the rate of profit, we want to know whether the estimate is reasonable on grounds broader than statistical significance. Good preferred stocks sold in these years at dividend yields of four to five per cent, and companies acquired in mergers were purchased for about five times their earnings before income taxes. Therefore, we would expect the rate of profit on common stocks to fall between four and ten per cent and the coefficient in question to fall between ten and twenty-five. Further, we would expect a particular rank in the coefficients. Corporations in the chemical industry are considered to have the advantages of size, growth, and stability; foods represent an industry that is considered stable; steels represent an industry with large corporations which are considered vulnerable to cyclical fluctuations; and machine tools represent an industry of comparatively small corporations which are also vulnerable to the business cycle. Accordingly, one might expect the rate of profit to vary among the industries in the order just given. Further, 1951 was a year of war profits with the outlook for the future somewhat uncertain. By contrast, while there was some talk of recession in 1954, there was little evidence that the high level of income extending back a number of years would fall sharply in the near future. Accordingly, one might expect that the coefficients would differ in a predictable manner between the two years.

DIVIDENDS AND EARNINGS

Given the task of explaining the variation in price among common stocks, the investigator may observe that stockholders are interested in both dividend and income per share and derive immediately from this observation the model:

$$P = a_0 + a_1 D + a_2 Y \tag{1}$$

where P = the year-end price, D = the year's dividend, and Y = the year's income. The equation may be considered of interest solely for the

[8]A list of the corporations and a description of how they were selected may be obtained from the writer on request.

multiple correlation between the actual and predicted price, in which case no meaning can be given to the regression coefficients. Alternatively, the equation may be read to mean that the coefficients a_1 and a_2 represent the value the market places on dividends and earnings respectively, a possible objective being the measurement of the relative importance of the two variables. However, a share of stock like any other asset is purchased for the expected future income it provides. This income may be the dividend or it may be the earnings per share, but it cannot be both. The model is therefore conceptually weak.

The unfortunate consequence of this pragmatic approach to the measurement of the variation in stock prices with dividend and earnings is illustrated by the data of Table I. The dividend coefficient for chemicals in 1951 is negative and machine tools has the highest coefficient. Between 1951 and 1954 the chemicals coefficient changes from approximately zero to 25. Many of the dividend coefficients are materially below ten, and in 1954 the highest coefficient is five times the lowest. The income coefficients, with the exception of chemicals in 1951, are extraordinarily low as measures of the price the market is willing to pay for earnings.

TABLE 1. *Model I, regression of price on dividend and income*

| | | Coefficient and standard error of | | |
Sample	Constant term	D	Y	Multiple correlation
1951 — Chemicals	−7.0	−.8	16.7	.93
		(5.2)	(3.1)	
Foods	.1	7.0	5.5	.90
		(1.5)	(.9)	
Steels	5.5	6.6	2.0	.86
		(1.8)	(.6)	
Machine tools	2.4	12.0	.8	.90
		(1.2)	(.5)	
1954 — Chemicals	−3.0	25.7	.3	.92
		(5.2)	(3.3)	
Food	− .4	10.4	5.6	.91
		(2.2)	(1.0)	
Steels	8.7	8.4	2.0	.94
		(1.7)	(.8)	
Machine tools	6.3	5.5	4.1	.89
		(1.4)	(.6)	

Machine tools in 1951 and chemicals in 1954 have income coefficients that are not significantly different from zero, and three of the other coefficients are materially below five. Armed only with the theory just stated, it would be most difficult to infer from the data the existence of a logical structure in the pricing of common stocks.

THE DIVIDEND HYPOTHESIS

The hypothesis that the investor buys the dividend when he acquires a share of stock seems intuitively plausible because the dividend is literally the payment stream that he expects to receive. In implementing the hypothesis it must be recognized that the stockholder is interested in the entire sequence of dividend payments that he may expect and not merely the current value. For the purpose of arriving at an operational model we may represent this infinite sequence by two quantities, one the current dividend and the other a measure of the expected growth in the dividend.

Among the events which will lead to an increase in a corporation's dividend are: successful trading on its equity, an increase in its return on investment, and selling additional common stock when the rate of profit the corporation can earn is above the rate at which its stock is selling. However, there is no doubt that the most important and predictable cause of growth in a corporation's dividend is retained earnings. For those interested in a more rigorous argument it has been shown that if a corporation is expected to earn a return r on investment and retain a fraction b of its income, the corporation's dividend can be expected to grow at the rate br.[9] If the investment or book value per share of common stock is B, then

$$br = \left(\frac{Y - D}{Y}\right)\left(\frac{Y}{B}\right) = \frac{Y - D}{B}. \tag{2}$$

Investors are interested in growth and not rate of growth, since a high rate of growth starting with a low initial value will pay off in the heavily discounted distant future, and it will not be as attractive as a lower rate of growth starting from a higher initial value. Therefore, in a model where price and dividend are absolute quantities, it is likely that retained earnings per share without deflation by book value is a better measure of growth than the rate of growth.

The previous discussion has provided the economic rationale for using the equation

$$P = a_0 + a_1 D + a_2(Y - D) \tag{3}$$

to represent the hypothesis that the investor buys the dividend when he acquires a share of stock. The reciprocal of the dividend coefficient

[9]The argument is developed more fully in M. J. Gordon and Eli Shapiro, "Capital Equipment Analysis: The Required Rate of Profit," *Management Science*, III (October 1956), 102–10.

may be looked on as an estimate of the rate of profit the market requires on common stocks without growth, and the retained earnings coefficient is the estimate of what the market is willing to pay for growth.

Table 2 presents the eight sample estimates of the model's coefficients. The 1951 dividend coefficients are considerably superior to those of Model I under the criteria stated earlier for their absolute and relative values. Only the machine tools coefficient appears comparatively high. The 1954 coefficients vary among the industries as expected and they fall within the expected range. The spread in the coefficients is only one-half the range of those in Model I, but it still seems quite large. In particular one might wonder at the high chemicals-1954 coefficient, the low steels-1951 and machine tools-1954 values, and the strong inverse correlation between the coefficients and the constant terms.

Turning now to the retained earnings coefficients, what would we expect of them? Since they represent the price the market is willing to pay for growth in the dividend, with retained earnings serving as an index of growth, the only statement with respect to their values that follows from the theory is that they should be positive. It may be thought none-theless that their values seem low, and the absence of statistical signifi-cance at the five per cent level for two coefficients, machine tools-1951 and chemicals-1954, is particularly disturbing. The really surprising result is the negative chemicals coefficients for 1954. On the other hand there is some *a priori* credibility in the findings. Growth is most uncertain and it becomes quantitatively important by comparison with the current dividend in the distant future. Also, apart from the 1954 chemicals there is a rough correspondence between the rank of the coefficients and notions as to the comparative stability of earnings among the industries.

The reader may have noted (1) the multiple correlation coefficients in Tables 1 and 2 are the same for each industry year, (2) the earnings and retained earnings coefficients, a_2 and a_2 are the same, and (3) the dividend coefficient $a_1 = a_1 + a_2$. On the first point, in both equations price is a linear function of the same variables, so that they both yield the same correlation coefficients. The earnings and retained earnings coefficients are the same, since the change in earnings is the same as the change in retained earnings when the dividend is held constant. The difference in the dividend coefficients is due to the fact that in equation (1) the increase in dividend involves a corresponding reduction in retained earnings, whereas in equation (3) retained earnings is held constant.

The dividend hypothesis provides a more reasonable interpretation of equation (1) than the interpretation given in the previous section. If growth is valued highly, an increase in the dividend with a corresponding reduction in retained earnings will not increase the value of a share as much as when a low value is placed on growth. There is some tendency

TABLE 2. *Model II, regression of price on dividend and retained earnings*

	Sample	Constant term	Coefficient and standard error of		Multiple correlation
			D	Y − D	
1951	Chemicals	−7.0	15.9 (2.7)	16.7 (3.1)	.93
	Foods	.1	12.5 (1.1)	5.5 (.9)	.90
	Steels	5.5	8.6 (1.5)	2.0 (.6)	.86
	Machine tools	2.4	12.8 (1.0)	.8 (.5)	.90
1954	Chemicals	−3.0	30.0 (2.6)	.3 (3.3)	.92
	Foods	− .4	15.9 (1.5)	5.6 (1.0)	.91
	Steels	8.7	10.4 (1.4)	2.0 (.8)	.94
	Machine tools	6.3	9.6 (1.2)	4.1 (.6)	.89

for the a_1 coefficients to vary among industries accordingly. Another point to be noted is that the standard error of a_1 is below that for a_1. This combined with the higher values of the former coefficients means that the change in price with the dividend can be predicted with much greater accuracy when retained earnings are held constant than when the increase comes out of retained earnings.

THE EARNINGS HYPOTHESIS

The third hypothesis is that the investor buys the income per share when he acquires a share of stock. The rationale is that regardless of whether they are distributed to him the stockholder has an ownership right in the earnings per share. He receives the dividend in cash and the retained earnings in a rise in the share's value, and if he wants additional cash he can always sell a fraction of his equity. In short, the corporate entity is a legal fiction that is not material with respect to his rights in the corporation or the value he places on them.[10] One can argue further that the different tax treatment of dividends and capital gains creates a stockholder preference for retained earnings.

[10]This appears to be a widely held point of view in the economics literature. See for example Lutz and Lutz, *The Theory of Investment of the Firm* (Princeton, 1951). The question is nowhere considered explicitly, but it is implicit in the material treated on pages 155 ff.

The hypothesis may be tested by reference to the data of Table 2. If the investor is indifferent to the fraction of earnings distributed, the dividend and retained earnings coefficients of Model II should be the same. However, with the exception of chemicals-1951 the difference between the coefficients is statistically significant. Durand's bank stock study presents the same picture on this question.[11]

Since the proposition that the rate of profit at which a common stock sells is independent of the dividend rate has some intuitive merit, a theoretical explanation of the statistical findings presented above is of interest. The first point to be noted is that the dividend hypothesis is correct regardless of whether the earnings hypothesis is correct. The only point at issue is whether the dividend hypothesis is unnecessary. Can one study the pricing of common stocks and related questions without considering the fraction of income paid in dividends? It is therefore possible to investigate the problem by using a more rigorous formulation of the dividend hypothesis to establish the condition for the validity of the earnings hypothesis.

Let k be the rate of profit at which a stock is selling, Y_t the income expected in year t, b the fraction of income the corporation is expected to retain, and r the rate of profit it is expected to earn on investment. The corporation's dividend is expected to grow at the rate br, and the price of the stock at $t = 0$ is:

$$P_0 = \int_0^\infty (1 - b)Y_t e^{-kt} dt$$

$$= \int_0^\infty (1 - b)Y_0 e^{brt} e^{-kt} dt. \tag{4}$$

The price of the share is finite and the integration may be carried out if $k > br$, in which case

$$P_0 = \frac{(1 - b)}{k - br} Y_0. \tag{5}$$

It may be noted that if $k = r$, equation (5) reduces to

$$P_0 = \frac{1}{k} Y_0, \tag{6}$$

but this is not relevant to the question at issue. For the earnings hypothesis to be valid, it is necessary that k be independent of b. That is, the rate of profit required by the market should be independent of the fraction of income retained.

We could reason as follows. A necessary condition for the price of a stock to be finite is $k > br$. This condition is most easily satisfied if k is an

[11]Durand, op. cit., 10–11.

increasing function of br, and if this is true we would also expect that k will vary with b. Other things equal, the rate of profit required on a common stock will vary for a corporation and among corporations inversely with the dividend rate.

An argument with considerably more theoretical content can be derived from the two following assumptions, both of which appear reasonable. (1) The rate at which a future payment is discounted increases with its uncertainty; and (2) the uncertainty of a future payment increases with the time in the future at which it will be received. It follows that *the* rate of profit at which a stream of expected payments is discounted is really an average of rates, each weighted by the size of the payment. The larger the distant payments relative to the near payments, the higher the average rate that equates the stream of payments with the price, the latter obtained by discounting each future payment at its appropriate rate. The relative size of the distant payments will of course vary with the rate of growth. Therefore, given the current earnings, the rate of profit required on a share increases with the fraction of income retained. The same reasoning provides an explanation for the tendency of interest rates on bonds to increase, other things being the same, with the maturity of the bond.

REFINEMENTS IN THE MODEL

Equation (3) is an extremely simple and crude expression of the dividend hypothesis, and insofar as the values of the coefficients are suspect, it may be due to limitations of the model. In this section we shall discuss the more important limitations, suggest how they may be dealt with, and then present data for a model that attempts to overcome some of these limitations.

1. Correlation between the variables and variation in the coefficients among industries is due in part to the scale factor. The problem may be stated as follows. Assume a sample of n corporations for all of which the dividend is the same, the price differs among the shares, and the average of the prices is higher than the dividend. There is no correlation between dividend and price. However, if n numbers are selected at random and the price and dividend of each share is multiplied by one of these numbers, correlation between the variables will be created. Further, if each of the n random numbers is first multiplied by a constant greater than one, the correlation and the regression coefficient will be larger the larger the value of this constant. The presence of so-called high-priced and low-priced stocks in a sample reflects in some part this scale factor. It is possible that by deflating the data, say by book value, and/or using logs we will moderate the influence of scale on the coefficients.

2. The independent variables in equation (3) are the current values of dividends and retained earnings. These quantities are of interest, however, only because they represent the latest available information for the prediction of future dividends.

Insofar as these current values depart from averages over some prior period for extraordinary reasons, investment analysts maintain that the changes should be discounted to arrive at what might be considered normal values. This suggests that some combination of current values and averages over a prior period for dividends and retained earnings would provide a superior explanation of the variation in price among shares.

3. The value the market places on a dividend expectation derived from past dividends and retained earnings may be expected to vary among corporations with the confidence in the dividend stream. This would suggest that the price of a share varies with other variables such as the size of the corporation, the relation of debt to equity, and the stability of its earning record. Insofar as the values of these variables vary among industries, failure to include them introduces variation and error in the dividend and retained earnings coefficients.

4. In the present model the variation in price with growth in the dividend is estimated by using an index of growth, retained earnings, as the independent variable. A model in which it is possible to use the rate of growth itself might yield better results. More important, the definition of the rate of growth has considerable theoretical merit—to date nothing superior has been proposed—but there are empirical problems involved in using it. Variation in accounting practice among firms makes the use of book value as a measure of return on investment questionable. Also, the instability of corporate retained earnings and the possibility that they vary over time differently among industries may make the use of past values to predict the future an heroic assumption. This is particularly true if investors give considerable weight, rationally or otherwise, to other variables in predicting future earnings.

Table 3 presents the regression statistics for the following model

$$P = \beta_0 + \beta_1 \bar{d} + \beta_2(d - \bar{d}) + \beta_3 \bar{g} + \beta_4(g - \bar{g}). \tag{7}$$

In this equation:

P = year-end price divided by book value,

$\bar{d}$ = average dividend for the prior five years divided by book value,

d = current year's dividend divided by book value,

$\bar{g}$ = average retained earnings for the prior five years divided by book value,

g = current year's retained earnings divided by book value.

The deflation by book value was undertaken to eliminate the scale effect discussed previously.[12] The objective was only partially accomplished, since correlation exists between the deflated and undeflated variables. For instance, correlation between P and p for the eight samples ranged from zero to .65 and was more than .4 for six of the samples.

[12]The use of deflated variables in regression analysis is a debatable question. See David Durand, op. cit., 56; and Edwin Kuh and John R. Meyer, "Correlation and Regression Estimates when the Data are Ratios," *Econometrica*, XXIII (October 1955), 400–16.

The use of $\bar{d}$ and $(d - \bar{d})$ assumes that the investor values a stock on the basis of the average dividend during the prior five years and the amount by which the current value differs from this average. The same reasoning applies to $\bar{g}$ and $(g - \bar{g})$, which by the way should be interpreted as deflated retained earnings and not as growth rates in the context of this model. The coefficients β_i may be interpreted as follows: $\beta_1 = \beta_2$ (or $\beta_3 = \beta_4$) implies that the investors ignore the average dividend for the prior five years and consider only the current dividend; $\beta_2 = 0$ implies that the current dividend is ignored; $\beta_1 > \beta_2$ implies that investors adjust to a change in the dividend with a lag,[13] i.e., the elasticity of expectations is less than one. The opposite is true if $\beta_1 < \beta_2$.

TABLE 3. *Regression of price on dividend, retained earnings, change in dividend, change in retained earnings, all deflated by book value*

Sample	Constant term	Coefficient and standard error of				Multiple correlation
		$\bar{d}$	$d - \bar{d}$	$\bar{g}$	$g - \bar{g}$	
1951 Chemicals	−.23	12.42	9.79	18.74	14.36	.80
		(2.63)	(5.98)	(5.96)	(5.60)	
Foods	.04	14.04	8.06	3.16	4.57	.90
		(1.04)	(2.49)	(1.39)	(1.58)	
Steels	.15	9.88	6.38	1.45	.41	.88
		(1.05)	(1.87)	(1.09)	(1.06)	
Machine tools	.12	12.62	5.93	.12	1.11	.91
		(1.17)	(2.75)	(.99)	(.80)	
1954 Chemicals	.54	17.38	12.71	.12	3.44	.79
		(2.92)	(8.93)	(6.39)	(4.78)	
Foods	−.03	15.51	8.74	5.15	5.96	.92
		(1.04)	(2.82)	(1.66)	(1.67)	
Steels	.18	9.69	3.85	2.02	2.85	.91
		(.99)	(1.13)	(.68)	(.67)	
Machine tools	.05	11.65	6.06	3.70	1.92	.87
		(1.16)	(1.74)	(1.12)	(1.04)	

Turning to the data of Table 3 we see that five of the eight multiple correlation coefficients are lower than in Table 2, and for some the difference is large. This is due to the deflation by book value. For dividends, deflation and/or the use of both the average value and the departure from average appears to have done some good. The range of the dividend coefficient has been reduced by comparison with Table 2, and the change in dividend co-

[13]We are talking about an unexpected change in the dividend, since d is the percentage that the dividend bears to book value. A rise in the dividend proportional to the rise in book value counts as no change in the dividend.

efficient is interesting. All but the chemicals coefficients are significant at the five per cent level, and they all are less than the $\bar{d}$ coefficients. Therefore, as expected, a rise in the dividend is discounted until the average has risen to the new level.

The growth coefficients, however, are disappointing. First, the values for $\bar{g}$ are if anything poorer than the values for $Y - D$ in Table 2. Second, three of the eight coefficients are not statistically significant at the five per cent level. Third, for some of the samples $\beta_4 \geqq \beta_3$, which means that investors are either indifferent to past performance or prefer a share for which retained earnings has increased to one for which it has fallen.

The performance of the model just discussed in explaining the variation in price among stocks is far superior to the simple empirical approach presented earlier. However, considerable room for improvement remains. The lines along which it will be realized appear to be a more effective representation of growth and the recognition of variables which influence the valuation of a dividend expectation. Solution of the scale problem through a different structural relation among the variables may also be of value.

3·8

Dividend Policy, Growth, and the Valuation of Shares[*]

Merton H. Miller and Franco Modigliani

The effect of a firm's dividend policy on the current price of its shares is a matter of considerable importance, not only to the corporate officials who must set the policy, but to investors planning portfolios and to economists seeking to understand and appraise the functioning of the capital markets. Do companies with generous distribution policies consistently sell at a premium over those with niggardly payouts? Is the reverse ever true? If so, under what conditions? Is there an optimum payout ratio or range of ratios that maximizes the current worth of the shares?

Although these questions of fact have been the subject of many empirical

*Reprinted from the *Journal of Business*, **34**, no. 4, October 1961, pp. 411–433, by permission of The University of Chicago Press. [Merton Miller and Franco Modigliani] . . . wish to express their thanks to all who read and commented on earlier versions of this paper and especially to Charles C. Holt, now of the University of Wisconsin, whose suggestions led to considerable simplification of a number of the proofs.

studies in recent years no consensus has yet been achieved. One reason appears to be the absence in the literature of a complete and reasonably rigorous statement of those parts of the economic theory of valuation bearing directly on the matter of dividend policy. Lacking such a statement, investigators have not yet been able to frame their tests with sufficient precision to distinguish adequately between the various contending hypotheses. Nor have they been able to give a convincing explanation of what their test results do imply about the underlying process of valuation.

In the hope that it may help to overcome these obstacles to effective empirical testing, this paper will attempt to fill the existing gap in the theoretical literature on valuation. We shall begin, in Section 1, by examining the effects of differences in dividend policy on the current price of shares in an ideal economy characterized by perfect capital markets, rational behavior, and perfect certainty. Still within this convenient analytical framework we shall go on in Sections 2 and 3 to consider certain closely related issues that appear to have been responsible for considerable misunderstanding of the role of dividend policy. In particular, Section 2 will focus on the long-standing debate about what investors "really" capitalize when they buy shares; and Section 3 on the much mooted relations between price, the rate of growth of profits, and the rate of growth of dividends per share. Once these fundamentals have been established, we shall proceed in Section 4 to drop the assumption of certainty and to see the extent to which the earlier conclusions about dividend policy must be modified. Finally, in Section 5, we shall briefly examine the implications for the dividend policy problem of certain kinds of market imperfections.

1. EFFECT OF DIVIDEND POLICY WITH PERFECT MARKETS, RATIONAL BEHAVIOR, AND PERFECT CERTAINTY

THE MEANING OF THE BASIC ASSUMPTIONS

Although the terms "perfect markets," "rational behavior," and "perfect certainty" are widely used throughout economic theory, it may be helpful to start by spelling out the precise meaning of these assumptions in the present context.

1. In "perfect capital markets," no buyer or seller (or issuer) of securities is large enough for his transactions to have an appreciable impact on the then ruling price. All traders have equal and costless access to information about the ruling price and about all other relevant characteristics of shares (to be detailed specifically later). No brokerage fees, transfer taxes, or other transaction costs are incurred when securities are bought, sold, or issued, and there are no tax differentials either between distributed and undistributed profits or between dividends and capital gains.

2. "Rational behavior" means that investors always prefer more wealth to less and are indifferent as to whether a given increment to their wealth takes the form of cash payments or an increase in the market value of their holdings of shares.

3. "Perfect certainty" implies complete assurance on the part of every investor as to the future investment program and the future profits of every corporation. Because of this assurance, there is, among other things, no need to distinguish between stocks and bonds as sources of funds at this stage of the analysis. We can, therefore, proceed as if there were only a single type of financial instrument which, for convenience, we shall refer to as shares of stock.

THE FUNDAMENTAL PRINCIPLE OF VALUATION

Under these assumptions the valuation of all shares would be governed by the following fundamental principle: the price of each share must be such that the rate of return (dividends plus capital gains per dollar invested) on every share will be the same throughout the market over any given interval of time. That is, if we let

$d_j(t)$ = dividends per share paid by firm j during period t
$p_j(t)$ = the price (ex any dividend in $t - 1$) of a share in firm j at the start of period t,

we must have

$$\frac{d_j(t) + p_j(t + 1) - p_j(t)}{p_j(t)} = \rho(t) \text{ independent of } j; \tag{1}$$

or, equivalently,

$$p_j(t) = \frac{1}{1 + \rho(t)}[d_j(t) + p_j(t + 1)] \tag{2}$$

for each j and for all t. Otherwise, holders of low-return (high-priced) shares could increase their terminal wealth by selling these shares and investing the proceeds in shares offering a higher rate of return. This process would tend to drive down the prices of the low-return shares and drive up the prices of high-return shares until the differential in rates of return had been eliminated.

THE EFFECT OF DIVIDEND POLICY

The implications of this principle for our problem of dividend policy can be seen somewhat more easily if equation (2) is restated in terms of the value of the enterprise as a whole rather than in terms of the value of an individual share. Dropping the firm subscript j since this will lead to no ambiguity in the present context and letting

$n(t)$ = the number of shares of record at the start of t

$m(t + 1)$ = the number of new shares (if any) sold during t at the ex dividend closing price $p(t + 1)$, so that

$n(t + 1) = n(t) + m(t + 1)$

$V(t) = n(t)p(t)$ = the total value of the enterprise and

$D(t) = n(t)d(t)$ = the total dividends paid during t to holders of record at the start of t,

we can rewrite (2)

$$V(t) = \frac{1}{1 + \rho(t)}[D(t) + n(t)p(t + 1)]$$

$$= \frac{1}{1 + \rho(t)}[D(t) + V(t + 1) - m(t + 1)p(t + 1)]. \tag{3}$$

The advantage of restating the fundamental rule in this form is that it brings into sharper focus the three possible routes by which current dividends might affect the current market value of the firm $V(t)$, or equivalently the price of its individual shares, $p(t)$. Current dividends will clearly affect $V(t)$ via the first term in the bracket, $D(t)$. In principle, current dividends might also affect $V(t)$ indirectly via the second term, $V(t + 1)$, the new ex dividend market value. Since $V(t + 1)$ must depend only on future and not on past events, such could be the case, however, only if both (a) $V(t + 1)$ were a function of future dividend policy and (b) the current distribution $D(t)$ served to convey some otherwise unavailable information as to what that future dividend policy would be. The first possibility being the relevant one from the standpoint of assessing the effects of dividend policy, it will clarify matters to assume, provisionally, that the future dividend policy of the firm is known and given for $t + 1$ and all subsequent periods and is independent of the actual dividend decision in t. Then $V(t + 1)$ will also be independent of the current dividend decision, though it may very well be affected by $D(t + 1)$ and all subsequent distributions. Finally, current dividends can influence $V(t)$ through the third term, $-m(t + 1)\ p(t + 1)$, the value of new shares sold to outsiders during the period. For the higher the dividend payout in any period the more the new capital that must be raised from external sources to maintain any desired level of investment.

The fact that the dividend decision affects price not in one but in these two conflicting ways—directly via $D(t)$ and inversely via $-m(t)\ p(t + 1)$—is, of course, precisely why one speaks of there being a dividend policy *problem*. If the firm raises its dividend in t, given its investment decision, will the increase in the cash payments to the current holders be more or less than enough to offset their lower share of the terminal value? Which is the better strategy for the firm in financing the investment: to reduce dividends and rely on retained earnings or to raise dividends but float more new shares?

In our ideal world at least these and related questions can be simply and immediately answered: the two dividend effects must always exactly cancel out so that the payout policy to be followed in t will have *no* effect on the price at t.

We need only express $m(t + 1) \cdot p(t + 1)$ in terms of $D(t)$ to show that such must indeed be the case. Specifically, if $I(t)$ is the given level of the firm's investment or increase in its holding of physical assets in t and if $X(t)$ is the firm's total net profit for the period, we know that the amount of outside capital required will be

$$m(t + 1)p(t + 1) = I(t) - [X(t) - D(t)]. \tag{4}$$

Substituting expression (4) into (3), the $D(t)$ cancel and we obtain for the value of the firm as of the start of t

$$V(t) \equiv n(t)p(t) = \frac{1}{1 + \rho(t)}[X(t) - I(t) + V(t + 1)]. \tag{5}$$

Since $D(t)$ does not appear directly among the arguments and since $X(t)$, $I(t)$, $V(t + 1)$ and $\rho(t)$ are all independent of $D(t)$ (either by their nature or by assumption) it follows that the current value of the firm must be independent of the current dividend decision.

Having established that $V(t)$ is unaffected by the current dividend decision it is easy to go on to show that $V(t)$ must also be unaffected by any future dividend decisions as well. Such future decisions can influence $V(t)$ only via their effect on $V(t + 1)$. But we can repeat the reasoning above and show that $V(t + 1)$—and hence $V(t)$—is unaffected by dividend policy in $t + 1$; that $V(t + 2)$—and hence $V(t + 1)$ and $V(t)$—is unaffected by dividend policy in $t + 2$; and so on for as far into the future as we care to look. Thus, we may conclude that given a firm's investment policy, the dividend payout policy it chooses to follow will affect neither the current price of its shares nor the total return to its shareholders.

Like many other propositions in economics, the irrelevance of dividend policy, given investment policy, is "obvious, once you think of it." It is, after all, merely one more instance of the general principle that there are no "financial illusions" in a rational and perfect economic invironment. Values there are determined solely by "real" considerations—in this case the earning power of the firm's assets and its investment policy—and not by how the fruits of the earning power are "packaged" for distribution.

Obvious as the proposition may be, however, one finds few references to it in the extensive literature on the problem.[1] It is true that the literature abounds with statements that in some "theoretical" sense, dividend policy

[1]Apart from the references to it in our earlier papers, especially [16], the closest approximation seems to be that in Bodenborn [1], but even his treatment of the role of dividend policy is not completely explicit. (The numbers in brackets refer to references listed . . . [at the end of this reading].

ought not to count; but either that sense is not clearly specified or, more frequently and especially among economists, it is (wrongly) identified with a situation in which the firm's internal rate of return is the same as the external or market rate of return.[2]

A major source of these and related misunderstandings of the role of the dividend policy has been the fruitless concern and controversy over what investors "really" capitalize when they buy shares. We say fruitless because as we shall now proceed to show, it is actually possible to derive from the basic principle of valuation (1) not merely one, but several valuation formulas each starting from one of the "classical" views of what is being capitalized by investors. Though differing somewhat in outward appearance, the various formulas can be shown to be equivalent in all essential respects including, of course, their implication that dividend policy is irrelevant. While the controversy itself thus turns out to be an empty one, the different expressions do have some intrinsic interest since, by highlighting different combinations of variables they provide additional insights into the process of valuation and they open alternative lines of attack on some of the problems of empirical testing.

2. WHAT DOES THE MARKET "REALLY" CAPITALIZE?

In the literature on valuation one can find at least the following four more or less distinct approaches to the valuation of shares: (1) the discounted cash flow approach; (2) the current earnings plus future investment opportunities approach; (3) the stream of dividends approach; and (4) the stream of earnings approach. To demonstrate that these approaches are, in fact, equivalent it will be helpful to begin by first going back to equation (5) and developing from it a valuation formula to serve as a point of reference and comparison. Specifically, if we assume, for simplicity, that the market rate of yield $\rho(t) = \rho$ for all t,[3] then, setting $t = 0$, we can rewrite (5) as

$$V(0) = \frac{1}{1 + \rho}[X(0) - I(0)] + \frac{1}{1 + \rho}V(1). \qquad (6)$$

Since (5) holds for all t, setting $t = 1$ permits us to express $V(1)$ in terms of $V(2)$ which in turn can be expressed in terms of $V(3)$ and so on up to any arbitrary terminal period T. Carrying out these substitutions, we obtain

$$V(0) = \sum_{t=0}^{T-1} \frac{1}{(1 + \rho)^{t+1}}[X(t) - I(t)] + \frac{1}{(1 + \rho)^{T}}V(T). \qquad (7)$$

[2] See below page 243.

[3] More general formulas in which $\rho(t)$ is allowed to vary with time can always be derived from those presented here merely by substituting the cumbersome product

$$\prod_{\tau=0}^{t} [1 + \rho(\tau)] \qquad \text{for} \qquad (1 + \rho)^{t+1}.$$

In general, the remainder term $(1 + \rho)^{-T}$. $V(T)$ can be expected to approach zero as T approaches infinity[4] so that (7) can be expressed as

$$V(0) = \lim_{T \to \infty} \sum_{t=0}^{T-1} \frac{1}{(1 + \rho)^{t+1}} \times [X(t) - I(t)], \tag{8}$$

which we shall further abbreviate to

$$V(0) = \sum_{t=0}^{\infty} \frac{1}{(1 + \rho)^{t+1}} [X(t) - I(t)]. \tag{9}$$

THE DISCOUNTED CASH FLOW APPROACH

Consider now the so-called discounted cash flow approach familiar in discussions of capital budgeting. There, in valuing any specific machine we discount at the market rate of interest the stream of cash receipts generated by the machine; plus any scrap or terminal value of the machine; and minus the stream of cash outlays for direct labor, materials, repairs, and capital additions. The same approach, of course, can also be applied to the firm as a whole which may be thought of in this context as simply a large, composite machine.[5] This approach amounts to defining the value of the firm as

$$V(0) = \sum_{t=0}^{T-1} \frac{1}{(1 + \rho)^{t+1}} \times [\Re(t) - \mathcal{O}(t)] + \frac{1}{(1 + \rho)^{T}} V(T), \tag{10}$$

where $\Re(t)$ represents the stream of cash receipts and $\mathcal{O}(t)$ of cash outlays, or, abbreviating, as above, to

$$V(0) = \sum_{t=0}^{\infty} \frac{1}{(1 + \rho)^{t+1}} [\Re(t) - \mathcal{O}(t)]. \tag{11}$$

But we also know, by definition, that $[X(t) - I(t)] = [\Re(t) - \mathcal{O}(t)]$ since, $X(t)$ differs from $\Re(t)$ and $I(t)$ differs from $\mathcal{O}(t)$ merely by the "cost of goods sold" (and also by the depreciation expense if we wish to interpret $X(t)$ and $I(t)$ as net rather than gross profits and investment). Hence (11) is formally equivalent to (9), and the discounted cash flow approach is thus seen to be an implication of the valuation principle for perfect markets given by equation (1).

THE INVESTMENT OPPORTUNITIES APPROACH

Consider next the approach to valuation which would seem most natural from the standpoint of an investor proposing to buy out and operate some

[4]The assumption that the remainder vanishes is introduced for the sake of simplicity of exposition only and is in no way essential to the argument. What is essential, of course, is that $V(0)$, i.e., the sum of the two terms in (7), be finite, but this can always be safely assumed in economic analysis. See below, n. 14.

[5]This is, in fact, the approach to valuation normally taken in economic theory when discussing the value of the *assets* of an enterprise, but much more rarely applied, unfortunately, to the value of the liability side. One of the few to apply the approach to the shares as well as the assets is Bodenhorn in [1], who uses it to derive a formula closely similar to (9) above.

already-going concern. In estimating how much it would be worthwhile to pay for the privilege of operating the firm, the amount of dividends to be paid is clearly not relevant, since the new owner can, within wide limits, make the future dividend stream whatever he pleases. For him the worth of the enterprise, as such, will depend only on: (a) the "normal" rate of return he can earn by investing his capital in securities (i.e., the market rate of return); (b) the earning power of the physical assets currently held by the firm; and (c) the opportunities, if any, that the firm offers for making additional investments in real assets that will yield more than the "normal" (market) rate of return. The latter opportunities, frequently termed the "good will" of the business, may arise, in practice, from any of a number of circumstances (ranging all the way from special locational advantages to patents or other monopolistic advantages).

To see how these opportunities affect the value of the business assume that in some future period t the firm invests $I(t)$ dollars. Suppose, further, for simplicity, that starting in the period immediately following the investment of the funds, the projects produce net profits at a constant rate of $\rho^*(t)$ per cent of $I(t)$ in each period thereafter.[6] Then the present worth as of t of the (perpetual) stream of profits generated will be $I(t) \rho^*(t)/\rho$, and the "good will" of the projects (i.e., the difference between worth and cost) will be

$$I(t)\frac{\rho^*(t)}{\rho} - I(t) = I(t)\left[\frac{\rho^*(t) - \rho}{\rho}\right].$$

The present worth as of now of this future "good will" is

$$I(t)\left[\frac{\rho^*(t) - \rho}{\rho}\right](1 + \rho)^{-t+1},$$

and the present value of all such future opportunities is simply the sum

$$\sum_{t=0}^{\infty} I(t)\frac{\rho^*(t) - \rho}{\rho}(1 + \rho)^{-t+1}.$$

Adding in the present value of the (uniform perpetual) earnings, $X(0)$, on the assets currently held, we get as an expression for the value of the firm

$$V(0) = \frac{X(0)}{\rho} + \sum_{t=0}^{\infty} I(t) \times \frac{\rho^*(t) - \rho}{\rho}(1 + \rho)^{-t+1}. \tag{12}$$

[6]The assumption that $I(t)$ yields a uniform perpetuity is not restrictive in the present certainty context since it is always possible by means of simple, present-value calculations to find an equivalent uniform perpetuity for any project, whatever the time shape of its actual returns. Note also that $\rho^*(t)$ is the *average* rate of return. If the managers of the firm are behaving rationally, they will, of course, use ρ as their cut-off criterion. In this event we would have $\rho^*(t) \geq \rho$. The formulas remain valid, however, even where $\rho^*(t) < \rho$.

To show that the same formula can be derived from (9) note first that our definition of $\rho^*(t)$ implies the following relation between the $X(t)$:

$$X(1) = X(0) + \rho^*(0)I(0),$$

$$X(t) = X(t-1) + \rho^*(t-1)I(t-1)$$

and by successive substitution

$$X(t) = X(0) + \sum_{\tau=0}^{t-1} \rho^*(\tau)I(\tau),$$

$$t = 1, 2 \ldots \infty.$$

Substituting the last expression for $X(t)$ in (9) yields

$$V(0) = [X(0) - I(0)](1+\rho)^{-1} + \sum_{t=1}^{\infty} \left[X(0) + \sum_{\tau=0}^{t-1} \rho^*(\tau)I(\tau) - I(t) \right](1+\rho)^{-t(+1)}$$

$$= X(0) \sum_{t=1}^{\infty} (1+\rho)^{-t} - I(0)(1+\rho)^{-1} + \sum_{t=1}^{\infty} \left[\sum_{\tau=0}^{t-1} \rho^*(\tau)I(\tau) - I(t) \right]$$

$$\times (1+\rho)^{-t(+1)}$$

$$= X(0) \sum_{t=1}^{\infty} (1+\rho)^{-t} + \sum_{t=1}^{\infty} \left[\sum_{\tau=0}^{t-1} \rho^*(\tau)I(\tau) - I(t-1) \times (1+\rho) \right](1+\rho)^{-(t+1)}.$$

The first expression is, of course, simply a geometric progression summing to $X(0)/\rho$, which is the first term of (12). To simplify the second expression note that it can be rewritten as

$$\sum_{t=0}^{\infty} I(t) \left[\rho^*(t) \sum_{\tau=t+2}^{\infty} (1+\rho)^{-\tau} - (1+\rho)^{-t(+1)} \right].$$

Evaluating the summation within the brackets gives

$$\sum_{t=0}^{\infty} I(t) \left[\rho^*(t)\frac{(1+\rho)^{-(t+1)}}{\rho} - (1+\rho)^{-(t+1)} \right] = \sum_{t=0}^{\infty} I(t) \left[\frac{\rho^*(t) - \rho}{\rho} \right](1+\rho)^{-(t+1)},$$

which is precisely the second term of (12).

Formula (12) has a number of revealing features and deserves to be more widely used in discussions of valuation.[7] For one thing, it throws considerable light on the meaning of those much abused terms "growth" and "growth stocks." As can readily be seen from (12), a corporation does not become a "growth stock" with a high price-earnings ratio merely because its assets and earnings are growing over time. To enter the glamor category, it is also necessary that $\rho^*(t) > \rho$. For if $\rho^*(t) = \rho$, then however large the growth

---

[7]A valuation formula analogous to (12) though derived and interpreted in a slightly different way is found in Bodenhorn [1]. Variants of (12) for certain special cases are discussed in Walter [20].

in assets may be, the second term in (12) will be zero and the firm's price-earnings ratio would not rise above a humdrum $1/\rho$. The essence of "growth," in short, is not expansion, but the existence of opportunities to invest significant quantities of funds at higher than "normal" rates of return.

Notice also that if $\rho^*(t) < \rho$, investment in real assets by the firm will actually reduce the current price of the shares. This should help to make clear among other things, why the "cost of capital" to the firm is the same regardless of how the investments are financed or how fast the firm is growing. The function of the cost of capital in capital budgeting is to provide the "cut-off rate" in the sense of the minimum yield that investment projects must promise to be worth undertaking from the point of view of the current owners. Clearly, no proposed project would be in the interest of the current owners if its yield were expected to be less than ρ since investing in such projects would reduce the value of their shares. In the other direction, every project yielding more than ρ is just as clearly worth undertaking since it will necessarily enhance the value of the enterprise. Hence, the cost of capital or cut-off criterion for investment decisions is simply ρ.[8]

Finally, formula (12) serves to emphasize an important deficiency in many recent statistical studies of the effects of dividend policy (such as Walter [19] or Durand [4, 5]). These studies typically involve fitting regression equations in which price is expressed as some function of current earnings and dividends. A finding that the dividend coefficient is significant—as is usually the case—is then interpreted as a rejection of the hypothesis that dividend policy does not affect valuation.

Even without raising questions of bias in the coefficients,[9] it should be apparent that such a conclusion is unwarranted since formula (12) and the analysis underlying it imply only that dividends will not count given current earnings *and growth potential*. No general prediction is made (or can be made) by the theory about what will happen to the dividend coefficient if the crucial growth term is omitted.[10]

[8]The same conclusion could also have been reached, of course, by "costing" each particular source of capital funds. That is, since ρ is the going market rate of return on equity any new shares floated to finance investment must be priced to yield ρ; and withholding funds from the stockholders to finance investment would deprive the holders of the chance to earn ρ on these funds by investing their dividends in other shares. The advantage of thinking in terms of the cost of capital as the cut-off criterion is that it minimizes the danger of confusing "costs" with mere "outlays."

[9]The serious bias problem in tests using current reported earnings as a measure of $X(0)$ was discussed briefly by us in [16].

[10]In suggesting that recent statistical studies have not controlled adequately for growth we do not mean to exempt Gordon in [8] or [9]. It is true that his tests contain an explicit "growth" variable, but it is essentially nothing more than the ratio of retained earnings to book value. This ratio would not in general provide an acceptable approximation to the "growth" variable of (12) in any sample in which firms resorted to external financing. Furthermore, even if by some chance a sample was found in which all firms relied entirely on retained earnings, his tests then could not settle the question of dividend policy. For if all firms financed investment internally (or used external financing only in strict proportion to internal financing as Gordon assumes in [8]) then there would be no way to distinguish between the effects of dividend policy and investment policy .

THE STREAM OF DIVIDENDS APPROACH

From the earnings and earnings opportunities approach we turn next to the dividend approach, which has, for some reason, been by far the most popular one in the literature of valuation. This approach too, properly formulated, is an entirely valid one though, of course, not the only valid approach as its more enthusiastic proponents frequently suggest.[11] It does, however, have the disadvantage in contrast with previous approaches of obscuring the role of dividend policy. In particular, uncritical use of the dividend approach has often led to the unwarranted inference that, since the investor is buying dividends and since dividend policy affects the amount of dividends, then dividend policy must also affect the current price.

Properly formulated, the dividend approach defines the current worth of a share as the discounted value of the stream of dividends to be paid on the share in perpetuity. That is

$$p(t) = \sum_{\tau=0}^{\infty} \frac{d(t+\tau)}{(1+\rho)^{\tau+1}}. \tag{13}$$

To see the equivalence between this approach and previous ones, let us first restate (13) in terms of total market value as

$$V(t) = \sum_{\tau=0}^{\infty} \frac{D_t(t+\tau)}{(1+\rho)^{\tau+1}}, \tag{14}$$

where $D_t(t+\tau)$ denotes that portion of the total dividends $D(t+\tau)$ paid during period $t+\tau$, that accrues to the shares of record as of the start of period t (indicated by the subscript). That equation (14) is equivalent to (9) and hence also to (12) is immediately apparent for the special case in which no outside financing is undertaken after period t, for in that case

$$D_t(t+\tau) = D(t+\tau) = X(t+\tau) - I(t+\tau).$$

To allow for outside financing, note that we can rewrite (14) as

$$V(t) = \frac{1}{1+\rho} \left[D_t(t) + \sum_{\tau=1}^{\infty} \frac{D_t(t+\tau)}{(1+\rho)^{\tau}} \right] \tag{15}$$

$$= \frac{1}{1+\rho} \left[D(t) + \sum_{\tau=0}^{\infty} \frac{D_t(t+\tau+1)}{(1+\rho)^{\tau+1}} \right].$$

The summation term in the last expression can be written as the difference between the stream of dividends accruing to all the shares of record as of

---

[11]See, e.g., the classic statement of the position in J. B. Williams [21]. The equivalence of the dividend approach to many of the other standard approaches is noted to our knowledge only in our [16] and, by implication, in Bodenhorn [1].

$t + 1$ and that portion of the stream that will accrue to the shares newly issued in t, that is,

$$\sum_{\tau=0}^{\infty} \frac{D_t(t + \tau + 1)}{(1 + \rho)^{\tau+1}} = \left(1 - \frac{m(t + 1)}{n(t + 1)}\right) \times \sum_{\tau=0}^{\infty} \frac{D_{t+1}(t + \tau + 1)}{(1 + \rho)^{\tau+1}}. \tag{16}$$

But from (14) we know that the second summation in (16) is precisely $V(t + 1)$ so that (15) can be reduced to

$$V(t) = \frac{1}{1 + \rho}\left[D(t) + \left(1 - \frac{m(t + 1)p(t + 1)}{n(t + 1)p(t + 1)}\right) \times V(t + 1)\right] \tag{17}$$

$$= \frac{1}{1 + \rho}[D(t) + V(t + 1) - m(t + 1)p(t + 1)],$$

which is (3) and which has already been shown to imply both (9) and (12).[12]

There are, of course, other ways in which the equivalence of the dividend approach to the other approaches might have been established, but the method presented has the advantage perhaps of providing some further insight into the reason for the irrelevance of dividend policy. An increase in current dividends, given the firm's investment policy, must necessarily reduce the terminal value of existing shares because part of the future dividend stream that would otherwise have accrued to the existing shares must be diverted to attract the outside capital from which, in effect, the higher current dividends are paid. Under our basic assumptions, however, ρ must be the same for all investors, new as well as old. Consequently the market value of the dividends diverted to the outsiders, which is both the value of their contribution and the reduction in terminal value of the existing shares, must always be precisely the same as the increase in current dividends.

THE STREAM OF EARNINGS APPROACH

Contrary to widely held views, it is also possible to develop a meaningful and consistent approach to valuation running in terms of the stream of earnings generated by the corporation rather than of the dividend distributions actually made to the shareholders. Unfortunately, it is also extremely easy to misstate or misinterpret the earnings approach as would be the case if the value of the firm were to be defined as simply the discounted sum of

---

[12]The statement that equations (9), (12), and (14) are equivalent must be qualified to allow for certain pathological extreme cases, fortunately of no real economic significance. An obvious example of such a case is the legendary company that is expected *never* to pay a dividend. If this were literally true then the value of the firm by (14) would be zero; by (9) it would be zero (or possibly negative since zero dividends rule out $X(t) > I(t)$ but not $X(t) < I(t)$); while by (12) the value might still be positive. What is involved here, of course, is nothing more than a discontinuity at zero since the value under (14) and (9) would be positive and the equivalence of both with (12) would hold if that value were also positive as long as there was some period T, however far in the future, beyond which the firm would pay out $\epsilon > 0$ per cent of its earnings, however small the value of ϵ.

future total earnings.[13] The trouble with such a definition is not, as is often suggested, that it overlooks the fact that the corporation is a separate entity and that these profits cannot freely be withdrawn by the shareholders; but rather that it neglects the fact that additional capital must be acquired at some cost to maintain the future earnings stream at its specified level. The capital to be raised in any future period is, of course, $I(t)$ and its opportunity cost, no matter how financed, is ρ per cent per period thereafter. Hence, the current value of the firm under the earnings approach must be stated as

$$V(0) = \sum_{t=0}^{\infty} \frac{1}{(1+\rho)^{t+1}} \times \left[X(t) - \sum_{\tau=0}^{t} \rho I(\tau) \right]. \tag{18}$$

That this version of the earnings approach is indeed consistent with our basic assumptions and equivalent to the previous approaches can be seen by regrouping terms and rewriting equation (18) as

$$V(0) = \sum_{t=0}^{\infty} \frac{1}{(1+\rho)^{t+1}} X(t) - \sum_{t=0}^{\infty} \left(\sum_{\tau=t}^{\infty} \frac{\rho I(t)}{(1+\rho)^{\tau+1}} \right)$$

$$= \sum_{t=0}^{\infty} \frac{1}{(1+\rho)^{t+1}} X(t) - \sum_{t=0}^{\infty} \frac{1}{(1+\rho)^{t+1}} \times \left(\sum_{\tau=0}^{\infty} \frac{\rho I(t)}{(1+\rho)^{\tau+1}} \right). \tag{19}$$

Since the last inclosed summation reduces simply to $I(t)$, the expression (19) in turn reduces to simply

$$V(0) = \sum_{t=0}^{\infty} \frac{1}{(1+\rho)^{t+1}} [X(t) - I(t)], \tag{20}$$

which is precisely our earlier equation (9).

Note that the version of the earnings approach presented here does not depend for its validity upon any special assumptions about the time shape of the stream of total profits or the stream of dividends per share. Clearly, however, the time paths of the two streams are closely related to each other (via financial policy) and to the stream of returns derived by holders of the shares. Since these relations are of some interest in their own right and since misunderstandings about them have contributed to the confusion over the role of dividend policy, it may be worthwhile to examine them briefly before moving on to relax the basic assumptions.

[13]In fairness, we should point out that there is no one, to our knowledge, who has seriously advanced this view. It is a view whose main function seems to be to serve as a "straw man" to be demolished by those supporting the dividend view. See, e.g., Gordon [9, esp. pp. 102–3]. Other writers take as the supposed earnings counter-view to the dividend approach not a relation running in terms of the *stream* of earnings but simply the proposition that price is proportional to current earnings, i.e., $V(0) = X(0)/\rho$. The probable origins of this widespread misconception about the earnings approach are discussed further below.

3. EARNINGS, DIVIDENDS, AND GROWTH RATES

THE CONVENIENT CASE OF CONSTANT GROWTH RATES

The relation between the stream of earnings of the firm and the stream of dividends and of returns to the stockholders can be brought out most clearly by specializing (12) to the case in which investment opportunities are such as to generate a constant rate of growth of profits in perpetuity. Admittedly, this case has little empirical significance, but it is convenient for illustrative purposes and has received much attention in the literature.

Specifically, suppose that in each period t the firm has the opportunity to invest in real assets a sum $I(t)$ that is k per cent as large as its total earnings for the period; and that this investment produces a perpetual yield of ρ^* beginning with the next period. Then, by definition

$$
\begin{aligned}
X(t) &= X(t-1) + \rho^* I(t-1) \\
&= X(t-1)[1 + k\rho^*] \\
&= X(0)[1 + k\rho^*]^t
\end{aligned}
\tag{21}
$$

and $k\rho^*$ is the (constant) rate of growth of total earnings. Substituting from (21) into (12) for $I(t)$ we obtain

$$
\begin{aligned}
V(0) &= \frac{X(0)}{\rho} + \sum_{t=0}^{\infty} \left(\frac{\rho^* - \rho}{\rho} \right) \times kX(0)[1 + k\rho^*]^t \times (1 + \rho)^{-(t+1)} \\
&= \frac{X(0)}{\rho} \left[1 + \frac{k(\rho^* - \rho)}{1 + \rho} \times \sum_{t=0}^{\infty} \left(\frac{1 + k\rho^*}{1 + \rho} \right)^t \right].
\end{aligned}
\tag{22}
$$

Evaluating the infinite sum and simplifying, we finally obtain[14]

$$
\begin{aligned}
V(0) &= \frac{X(0)}{\rho} \left[1 + \frac{k(\rho^* - \rho)}{\rho - k\rho^*} \right] \\
&= \frac{X(0)(1 - k)}{\rho - k\rho^*},
\end{aligned}
\tag{23}
$$

[14]One advantage of the specialization (23) is that it makes it easy to see what is really involved in the assumption here and throughout the paper that the $V(0)$ given by any of our summation formulas is necessarily finite. In terms of (23) the condition is clearly $k\rho^* < \rho$, i.e., that the rate of growth of the firm be less than market rate of discount. Although the case of (perpetual) growth rates greater than the discount factor is the much-discussed "growth stock paradox" (e.g. [6]), it has no real economic significance as we pointed out in [16, esp. n. 17, p. 664]. This will be apparent when one recalls that the discount rate ρ, though treated as a constant in partial equilibrium (relative price) analysis of the kind presented here, is actually a variable from the standpoint of the system as a whole. That is, if the assumption of finite value for all shares did not hold, because for some shares $k\rho^*$ was (perpetually) greater than ρ, then ρ would necessarily rise until an over-all equilibrium in the capital markets had been restored.

which expresses the value of the firm as a function of its current earnings, the rate of growth of earnings, the internal rate of return, and the market rate of return.[15]

Note that (23) holds not just for period 0, but for every t. Hence if $X(t)$ is growing at the rate $k\rho^*$, it follows that the value of the enterprise, $V(t)$, also grows at that rate.

THE GROWTH OF DIVIDENDS AND THE GROWTH OF TOTAL PROFITS

Given that total earnings (and the total value of the firm) are growing at the rate $k\rho^*$ what is the rate of growth of dividends per share and of the price per share? Clearly, the answer will vary depending on whether or not the firm is paying out a high percentage of its earnings and thus relying heavily on outside financing. We can show the nature of this dependence explicitly by making use of the fact that whatever the rate of growth of dividends per share the present value of the firm by the dividend approach must be the same as by the earnings approach. Thus let

g = the rate of growth of dividends per share, or, what amounts to the same thing, the rate of growth of dividends accruing to the shares of the current holders (i.e., $D_0(t) = D_0(0)[1 + g]^t$);

k_r = the fraction of total profits retained in each period (so that $D(t) = X(0)[1 - k_r]$);

$k_e = k - k_r$ = the amount of external capital raised per period, expressed as a fraction of profits in the period.

[15]An interesting and more realistic variant of (22), which also has a number of convenient features from the standpoint of developing empirical tests, can be obtained by assuming that the special investment opportunities are available not in perpetuity but only over some finite interval of T periods. To exhibit the value of the firm for this case, we need only replace the infinite summation in (22) with a summation running from $t = 0$ to $t = T - 1$. Evaluating the resulting expression, we obtain

$$V(0) = \frac{X(0)}{\rho}\left\{1 + \frac{k(\rho^* - \rho)}{\rho - k\rho^*} \times \left[1 - \left(\frac{1 + k\rho^*}{1 + \rho}\right)^T\right]\right\}. \tag{22a}$$

Note that (22a) holds even if $k\rho^* > \rho$, so that the so-called growth paradox disappears altogether. If, as we should generally expect, $(1 + k\rho^*)/(1 + \rho)$ is close to one, and if T is not too large, the right hand side of (22a) admits of a very convenient approximation. In this case in fact we can write

$$\left[\frac{1 + k\rho^*}{1 + \rho}\right]^T \cong 1 + T(k\rho^* - \rho)$$

the approximation holding, if, as we should expect, $(1 + k\rho^*)$ and $(1 + \rho)$ are both close to unity. Substituting this approximation into (22a) and simplifying, finally yields

$$V(0) \cong \frac{X(0)}{\rho}\left[1 + \frac{k(\rho^* - \rho)}{\rho - k\rho^*} \times T(\rho - k\rho^*)\right] = \left[\frac{X(0)}{\rho} + kX(0) \times \left(\frac{\rho^* - \rho}{\rho}\right)T\right]. \tag{22b}$$

The common sense of (22b) is easy to see. The current value of a firm is given by the value of the earning power of the currently held assets plus the market value of the special earning opportunity multiplied by the number of years for which it is expected to last.

Then the present value of the stream of dividends to the original owners will be

$$D_0(0) \sum_{t=0}^{\infty} \frac{(1+g)^t}{(1+\rho)^{t+1}} = \frac{D(0)}{\rho - g} = \frac{X(0)[1 - k_r]}{\rho - g}. \tag{24}$$

By virtue of the dividend approach we know that (24) must be equal to $V(0)$. If, therefore, we equate it to the righthand side of (23), we obtain

$$\frac{X(0)[1 - k_r]}{\rho - g} = \frac{X(0)[1 - (k_r + k_e)]}{\rho - k\rho^*}$$

from which it follows that the rate of growth of dividends per share and the rate of growth of the price of a share must be[16]

$$g = k\rho^* \frac{1 - k_r}{1 - k} - k_e \rho \frac{1}{1 - k}. \tag{25}$$

Notice that in the extreme case in which all financing is internal ($k_e = 0$ and $k = k_r$), the second term drops out and the first becomes simply $k\rho^*$. Hence

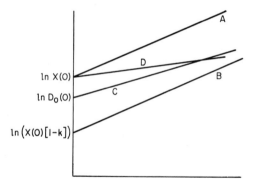

FIGURE 1   Growth of dividends per share in relation to growth in total earnings:

A. Total earnings: $\ln X(t) = \ln X(0) + k\rho^* t$;

B. Total earnings minus capital invested: $\ln [X(t) - I(t)] = \ln X(0) [1 - k] + k\rho^* t$; Dividends per share (all financing internal): $\ln D_0(t) = \ln D(0) + gt = \ln X(0) [1 - k] \pm k\rho^* t$;

C. Dividends per share (some financing external): $\ln D_0(t) = \ln D(0) + gt$;

D. Dividends per share (all financing external); $\ln D_0(t) = \ln X(0) + [(k/1 - k) (\rho^* - \rho)] t$.

[16]That g is the rate of price increase per share as well as the rate of growth of dividends per share follows from the fact that by (13) and the definition of g

$$p(t) = \sum_{\tau=0}^{\infty} \frac{d(t + \tau)}{(1 + \rho)^{\tau+1}} = \sum_{\tau=0}^{\infty} \frac{d(0) [1 + g]^{t+\tau}}{(1 + \rho)^{\tau+1}} = (1 + g)^t \sum_{\tau=0}^{\infty} \frac{d(\tau)}{(1 + \rho)^{\tau+1}} = p(0) [1 + g]^t.$$

the growth rate of dividends in that special case is exactly the same as that of total profits and total value and is proportional to the rate of retention k_r. In all other cases, g is necessarily less than $k\rho^*$ and may even be negative, despite a positive $k\rho^*$, if $\rho^* < \rho$ and if the firm pays out a large fraction of its income in dividends. In the other direction, we see from (25) that even if a firm is a "growth" corporation ($\rho^* > \rho$) then the stream of dividends and price per share must grow over time even though $k_r = 0$, that is, even though it pays out *all* its earnings in dividends.

The relation between the growth rate of the firm and the growth rate of dividends under various dividend policies is illustrated graphically in Figure 1 in which for maximum clarity the natural logarithm of profits and dividends have been plotted against time.[17]

Line A shows the total earnings of the firm growing through time at the constant rate $k\rho^*$, the slope of A. Line B shows the growth of (1) the stream of total earnings minus capital outlays and (2) the stream of dividends to the original owners (or dividends per share) in the special case in which all financing is internal. The slope of B is, of course, the same as that of A and the (constant) difference between the curves is simply $\ln(1 - k)$, the ratio of dividends to profits. Line C shows the growth of dividends per share when the firm uses both internal and external financing. As compared with the pure retention case, the line starts higher but grows more slowly at the rate g given by (25). The higher the payout policy, the higher the starting position and the slower the growth up to the other limiting case of complete external financing, Line D, which starts at $\ln X(0)$ and grows at a rate of $(k/1 - k)$ $\cdot (\rho^* - \rho)$.

THE SPECIAL CASE OF EXCLUSIVELY INTERNAL FINANCING

As noted above the growth rate of dividends per share is not the same as the growth rate of the firm except in the special case in which all financing is internal. This is merely one of a number of peculiarities of this special case on which, unfortunately, many writers have based their entire analysis. The reason for the preoccupation with this special case is far from clear to us. Certainly no one would suggest that it is the only empirically relevant case. Even if the case were in fact the most common, the theorist would still be under an obligation to consider alternative assumptions. We suspect that in the last analysis, the popularity of the internal financing model will be found to reflect little more than its ease of manipulation combined with the failure to push the analysis far enough to disclose how special and how treacherous a case it really is.

[17]That is, we replace each discrete compounding expression such as $X(t) = X(0) [1 + k\rho^*]^t$ with its counterpart under continuous discounting $X(t) = X(0)e^{k\rho^*t}$ which, of course, yields the convenient linear relation $\ln X(t) = \ln X(0) + k\rho^*t$.

In particular, concentration on this special case appears to be largely responsible for the widely held view that, even under perfect capital markets, there is an optimum dividend policy for the firm that depends on the internal rate of return. Such a conclusion is almost inevitable if one works exclusively with the assumption, explicit or implicit, that funds for investment come *only* from retained earnings. For in that case *dividend policy* is indistinguishable from *investment policy;* and there *is* an optimal investment policy which does in general depend on the rate of return.

Notice also from (23) that if $\rho^* = \rho$ and $k = k_r$, the term $[1 - k_r]$ can be canceled from both the numerator and the denominator. The value of the firm becomes simply $X(0)/\rho$, the capitalized value of current earnings. Lacking a standard model for valuation more general than the retained earnings case it has been all too easy for many to conclude that this dropping out of the payout ratio $[1 - k_r]$ when $\rho^* = \rho$ must be what is meant by the irrelevance of dividend policy and that $V(0) = X(0)/\rho$ must constitute the "earnings" approach.

Still another example of the pitfalls in basing arguments on this special case is provided by the recent and extensive work on valuation by M. Gordon.[18]   Gordon argues, in essence, that because of increasing uncertainty the discount rate $\tilde{\rho}(t)$ applied by an investor to a future dividend payment will rise with t, where t denotes not a specific date but rather the distance from the period in which the investor performs the discounting.[19]   Hence, when we use a single uniform discount rate ρ as in (22) or (23), this rate should be thought of as really an average of the "true" rates $\tilde{\rho}(t)$ each weighted by the size of the expected dividend payment at time t. If the dividend stream is growing exponentially then such a weighted average ρ would, of course, be higher the greater the rate of growth of dividends g since the greater will then be the portion of the dividend stream arising in the distant as opposed to the near future. But if all financing is assumed to be internal, then $g = k_r\rho^*$ so that given ρ^*, the weighted average discount factor ρ will be an increasing function of the rate of retention k_r which would run counter to our conclusion that dividend policy has no effect on the current value of the firm or its cost of capital.

For all its ingenuity, however, and its seeming foundation in uncertainty, the argument clearly suffers fundamentally from the typical confounding of dividend policy with investment policy that so frequently accompanies use

---

[18]See esp. [8]. Gordon's views represent the most explicit and sophisticated formulation of what might be called the "bird-in-the-hand" fallacy. For other, less elaborate, statements of essentially the same position see, among others, Graham and Dodd [11, p. 433] and Clendenin and Van Cleave [3].

[19]We use the notation $\tilde{\rho}(t)$ to avoid any confusion between Gordon's purely subjective discount rate and the objective, market-given yields $\rho(t)$ in Sec. I above. To attempt to derive valuation formulas under uncertainty from these purely subjective discount factors involves, of course, an error essentially analogous to that of attempting to develop the certainty formulas from "marginal rates of time preference" rather than objective market opportunities.

of the internal financing model. Had Gordon not confined his attention to this special case (or its equivalent variants), he would have seen that while a change in dividend policy will necessarily affect the size of the expected dividend payment on the share in any future period, it need not, in the general case, affect either the size of the *total* return that the investor expects during that period or the degree of uncertainty attaching to that total return. As should be abundantly clear by now, a change in dividend policy, given investment policy, implies a change only in the distribution of the total return in any period as between dividends and capital gains. If investors behave rationally, such a change cannot affect market valuations. Indeed, if they valued shares according to the Gordon approach and thus paid a premium for higher payout ratios, then holders of the low payout shares would actually realize consistently higher returns on their investment over any stated interval of time.[20]

CORPORATE EARNINGS AND INVESTOR RETURNS

Knowing the relation of g to $k\rho^*$ we can answer a question of considerable interest to economic theorists, namely: What is the precise relation between the earnings of the corporation in any period $X(t)$ and the total return to the owners of the stock during that period?[21] If we let $G_t(t)$ be the capital gains to the owners during t, we know that

$$D_t(t) + G_t(t) = X(t) \times (1 - k_r) + gV(t) \qquad (26)$$

[20]This is not to deny that growth stocks (in our sense) may well be "riskier" than non-growth stocks. But to the extent that this is true, it will be due to the possibly greater uncertainty attaching to the size and duration of future growth opportunities and hence to the size of the future stream of total returns quite apart from any questions of dividend policy.
[21]Note also that the above analysis enables us to deal very easily with the familiar issue of whether a firm's cost of equity capital is measured by its earnings/price ratio or by its dividend/price ratio. Clearly, the answer is that it is measured by neither, except under very special circumstances. For from (23) we have for the earnings/price ratio

$$\frac{X(0)}{V(0)} = \frac{\rho - k\rho^*}{1 - k},$$

which is equal to the cost of capital ρ, only if the firm has no growth potential (i.e., $\rho^* = \rho$). And from (24) we have for the dividend/price ratio

$$\frac{D(0)}{V(0)} = \rho - g,$$

which is equal to ρ only when $g = 0$; i.e., from (25), either when $k = 0$; or, if $k > 0$, when $\rho^* < \rho$ and the amount of external financing is precisely

$$k_e = \frac{\rho^*}{\rho} k [1 - k_r],$$

so that the gain from the retention of earnings exactly offsets the loss that would otherwise be occasioned by the unprofitable investment.

since the rate of growth of price is the same as that of dividends per share. Using (25) and (26) to substitute for g and $V(t)$ and simplifying, we find that

$$D_t(t) + G_t(t) = X(t)\left[\frac{\rho(1 - k)}{\rho - k\rho^*}\right].$$ (27)

The relation between the investors' return and the corporation's profits is thus seen to depend entirely on the relation between ρ^* and ρ. If $\rho^* = \rho$ (i.e., the firm has no special "growth" opportunities), then the expression in brackets becomes 1 and the investor returns are precisely the same as the corporate profits. If $\rho^* < \rho$, however, the investors' return will be less than the corporate earnings; and, in the case of growth corporations the investors' return will actually be greater than the flow of corporate profits over the interval.[22]

SOME IMPLICATIONS FOR CONSTRUCTING EMPIRICAL TESTS

Finally the fact that we have two different (though not independent) measures of growth in $k\rho^*$ and g and two corresponding families of valuation formulas means, among other things, that we can proceed by either of two routes in empirical studies of valuation. We can follow the standard practice of the security analyst and think in terms of price per share, dividends per share, and the rate of growth of dividends per share; or we can think in terms of the total value of the enterprise, total earnings, and the rate of growth of total earnings. Our own preference happens to be for the second approach primarily because certain additional variables of interest—such as dividend

[22]The above relation between earnings per share and dividends plus capital gains also means that there will be a systematic relation between retained earnings and capital gains. The "marginal" relation is easy to see and is always precisely one for one regardless of growth or financial policy. That is, taking a dollar away from dividends and adding it to retained earnings (all other things equal) means an increase in capital gains of one dollar (or a reduction in capital loss of one dollar). The "average" relation is somewhat more complex. From (26) and (27) we can see that

$$G_t(t) = k_r X(t) + kX(t)\,\frac{\rho^* - \rho}{\rho - k\rho^*}.$$

Hence, if $\rho^* = \rho$ the total capital gain received will be exactly the same as the total retained earnings per share. For growth corporations, however, the capital gain will always be greater than the retained earnings (and there will be a capital gain of

$$kX(t)\left[\frac{\rho^* - \rho}{\rho - k\rho^*}\right]$$

even when all earnings are paid out). For non-growth corporations the relation between gain and retentions is reversed. Note also that the absolute difference between the total capital gain and the total retained earnings is a constant (given, ρ, k and ρ^*) unaffected by dividend policy. Hence the *ratio* of capital gain to retained earnings will vary directly with the payout ratio for growth corporations (and vice versa for non-growth corporations). This means, among other things, that it is dangerous to attempt to draw inferences about the relative growth potential or relative managerial efficiency of corporations solely on the basis of the ratio of capital gains to retained earnings (cf. Harkavy [12, esp. pp. 289–94]).

policy, leverage, and size of firm—can be incorporated more easily and meaningfully into test equations in which the growth term is the growth of total earnings. But this can wait. For present purposes, the thing to be stressed is simply that two approaches, properly carried through, are in no sense *opposing* views of the valuation process; but rather equivalent views, with the choice between them largely a matter of taste and convenience.

4. THE EFFECTS OF DIVIDEND POLICY UNDER UNCERTAINTY

UNCERTAINTY AND THE GENERAL THEORY OF VALUATION

In turning now from the ideal world of certainty to one of uncertainty our first step, alas, must be to jettison the fundamental valuation principle as given, say, in our equation (3)

$$V(t) = \frac{1}{1 + \rho(t)}[D(t) + n(t)p(t + 1)]$$

and from which the irrelevance proposition as well as all the subsequent valuation formulas in Sections 2 and 3 were derived. For the terms in the bracket can no longer be regarded as given numbers, but must be recognized as "random variables" from the point of view of the investor as of the start of period t. Nor is it at all clear what meaning can be attached to the discount factor $1/[1 + \rho(t)]$ since what is being discounted is not a given return, but at best only a probability distribution of possible returns. We can, of course, delude ourselves into thinking that we are preserving equation (3) by the simple and popular expedient of drawing a bar over each term and referring to it thereafter as the mathematical expectation of the random variable. But except for the trival case of universal linear utility functions we know that $V(t)$ would also be affected, and materially so, by the higher order moments of the distribution of returns. Hence there is no reason to believe that the discount factor for expected values, $1/[1 + \rho(t)]$, would in fact be the same for any two firms chosen arbitrarily, not to mention that the expected values themselves may well be different for different investors.

All this is not to say, of course, that there are insuperable difficulties in the way of developing a testable theory of rational market valuation under uncertainty.[23] On the contrary, our investigations of the problem to date have convinced us that it is indeed possible to construct such a theory— though the construction, as can well be imagined, is a fairly complex and

[23]Nor does it mean that all the previous certainty analysis has no relevance whatever in the presence of uncertainty. There are many issues, such as those discussed in Sec. 1 and 2, that really relate only to what has been called the pure "futurity" component in valuation. Here, the valuation formulas can still be extremely useful in maintaining the internal consistency of the reasoning and in suggesting (or criticizing) empirical tests of certain classes of hypotheses about valuation, even though the formulas themselves cannot be used to grind out precise numerical values for specific real-world shares.

space-consuming task. Fortunately, however, this task need not be undertaken in this paper which is concerned primarily with the effects of dividend policy on market valuation. For even without a full-fledged theory of what *does* determine market value under uncertainty we can show that dividend policy at least is *not* one of the determinants. To establish this particular generalization of the previous certainty results we need only invoke a corresponding generalization of the original postulate of rational behavior to allow for the fact that, under uncertainty, choices depend on expectations as well as tastes.

"IMPUTED RATIONALITY" AND "SYMMETRIC MARKET RATIONALITY"

This generalization can be formulated in two steps as follows. First, we shall say that an individual trader "imputes rationality to the market" or satisfies the postulate of "imputed rationality" if, in forming expectations, he assumes that every other trader in the market is (*a*) rational in the previous sense of preferring more wealth to less regardless of the form an increment in wealth may take, and (*b*) imputes rationality to all other traders. Second, we shall say that a market as a whole satisfies the postulate of "symmetric market rationality" if every trader both behaves rationally and imputes rationality to the market.[24]

Notice that this postulate of symmetric market rationality differs from the usual postulate of rational behavior in several important respects. In the first place, the new postulate covers not only the choice behavior of individuals but also their expectations of the choice behavior of others. Second, the postulate is a statement about the market as a whole and not just about individual behavior. Finally, though by no means least, symmetric market rationality cannot be deduced from individual rational behavior in the usual sense since that sense does not imply imputing rationality to others. It may, in fact, imply a choice behavior inconsistent with imputed rationality unless the individual actually believes the market to be symmetrically rational. For if an ordinarily rational investor had good reason to believe that other investors would not behave rationally, then it might well be rational for him to adopt a strategy he would otherwise have rejected as irrational. Our postulate thus rules out, among other things, the possibility of speculative "bubbles" wherein an individually rational investor buys a

---

[24]We offer the term "symmetric market rationality" with considerable diffidence and only after having been assured by game theorists that there is no accepted term for this concept in the literature of that subject even though the postulate itself (or close parallels to it) does appear frequently. In the literature of economics a closely related, but not exact counterpart is Muth's "hypothesis of rational expectations" [18]. Among the more euphonic, though we feel somewhat less revealing, alternatives that have been suggested to us are "putative rationality" (by T. J. Koopmans), "bi-rationality" (by G. L. Thompson), "empathetic rationality" (by Andrea Modigliani), and "panrationality" (by A. Ando).

security he knows to be overpriced (i.e., too expensive in relation to its expected *long-run* return to be attractive as a permanent addition to his portfolio) in the expectation that he can resell it at a still more inflated price before the bubble bursts.[25]

THE IRRELEVANCE OF DIVIDEND POLICY DESPITE UNCERTAINTY

In Section 1 we were able to show that, given a firm's investment policy, its dividend policy was irrelevant to its current market valuation. We shall now show that this fundamental conclusion need not be modified merely because of the presence of uncertainty about the future course of profits, investment, or dividends (assuming again, as we have throughout, that investment policy can be regarded as separable from dividend policy). To see that uncertainty about these elements changes nothing essential, consider a case in which current investors believe that the future streams of total earnings and total investment whatever actual values they may assume at different points in time will be identical for two firms, 1 and 2.[26] Suppose further, provisionally, that the same is believed to be true of future total dividend payments from period one on so that the only way in which the two firms differ is possibly with respect to the prospective dividend in the current period, period 0. In terms of previous notation we are thus assuming that

$$\tilde{X}_1(t) = \tilde{X}_2(t) \qquad t = 0 \ldots \infty$$

$$\tilde{I}_1(t) = \tilde{I}_2(t) \qquad t = 0 \ldots \infty$$

$$\tilde{D}_1(t) = \tilde{D}_2(t) \qquad t = 1 \ldots \infty$$

the subscripts indicating the firms and the tildes being added to the variables to indicate that these are to be regarded from the standpoint of current period, not as known numbers but as numbers that will be drawn in the future from the appropriate probability distributions. We may now ask: "What will be

[25]We recognize, of course, that such speculative bubbles have actually arisen in the past (and will probably continue to do so in the future), so that our postulate can certainly not be taken to be of universal applicability. We feel, however, that it is also not of universal inapplicability since from our observation, speculative bubbles, though well publicized when they occur, do not seem to us to be a dominant, or even a fundamental, feature of actual market behavior under uncertainty. That is, we would be prepared to argue that, as a rule and on the average, markets do not behave in ways which do not obviously contradict the postulate so that the postulate may still be useful, at least as a first approximation, for the analysis of long-run tendencies in organized capital markets. Needless to say, whether our confidence in the postulate is justified is something that will have to be determined by empirical tests of its implications (such as, of course, the irrelevance of dividend policy).

[26]The assumption of two identical firms is introduced for convenience of exposition only, since it usually is easier to see the implications of rationality when there is an explicit arbitrage mechanism, in this case, switches between the shares of the two firms. The assumption, however, is not necessary and we can, if we like, think of the two firms as really corresponding to two states of the same firm for an investor performing a series of "mental experiments" on the subject of dividend policy.

the return, $\tilde{R}_1(0)$ to the current shareholders in firm 1 during the current period?" Clearly, it will be

$$\tilde{R}_1(0) = \bar{D}_1(0) + \tilde{V}_1(1) - \tilde{m}_1(1)\bar{p}_1(1). \tag{28}$$

But the relation between $\bar{D}_1(0)$ and $\tilde{m}_1(1)$ $\bar{p}_1(1)$ is necessarily still given by equation (4) which is merely an accounting identity so that we can write

$$\tilde{m}_1(1)\bar{p}_1(1) = \tilde{I}_1(0) - [\tilde{X}_1(0) - \bar{D}_1(0)], \tag{29}$$

and, on substituting in (28), we obtain

$$\tilde{R}_1(0) = \tilde{X}_1(0) - \tilde{I}_1(0) + \tilde{V}_1(1) \tag{30}$$

for firm 1. By an exactly parallel process we can obtain an equivalent expression for $\tilde{R}_2(0)$.

Let us now compare $\tilde{R}_1(0)$ with $\tilde{R}_2(0)$. Note first that, by assumption, $\tilde{X}_1(0) = \tilde{X}_2(0)$ and $\tilde{I}_1(0) = \tilde{I}_2(0)$. Furthermore, with symmetric market rationality, the terminal values $\tilde{V}_i(1)$ can depend only on prospective future earnings, investment and dividends from period 1 on and these too, by assumption, are identical for the two companies. Thus symmetric rationality implies that every investor must expect $\tilde{V}_1(1) = \tilde{V}_2(1)$ and hence finally $\tilde{R}_1(0) = \tilde{R}_2(0)$. But if the return to the investors is the same in the two cases, rationality requires that the two firms command the same current value so that $V_1(0)$ must equal $V_2(0)$ regardless of any difference in dividend payments during period 0. Suppose now that we allow dividends to differ not just in period 0 but in period 1 as well, but still retain the assumption of equal $\tilde{X}_i(t)$ and $\tilde{I}_i(t)$ in all periods and of equal $\bar{D}_i(t)$ in period 2 and beyond. Clearly, the only way differences in dividends in period 1 can affect $\tilde{R}_i(0)$ and hence $V_i(0)$ is via $\tilde{V}_i(1)$. But, by the assumption of symmetric market rationality, current investors know that as of the start of period 1 the then investors will value the two firms rationally and we have already shown that differences in the current dividend do not affect current value. Thus we must have $\tilde{V}_1(1) = \tilde{V}_2(1)$—and hence $V_1(0) = V_2(0)$—regardless of any possible difference in dividend payments during period 1. By an obvious extension of the reasoning to $\tilde{V}_i(2)$, $\tilde{V}_i(3)$, and so on, it must follow that the current valuation is unaffected by differences in dividend payments in *any* future period and thus that dividend policy is irrelevant for the determination of market prices, given investment policy.[27]

[27]We might note that the assumption of symmetric market rationality is sufficient to derive this conclusion but not strictly necessary if we are willing to weaken the irrelevance proposition to one running in terms of long-run, average tendencies in the market. Individual rationality alone could conceivably bring about the latter, for over the long pull rational investors could enforce this result by buying and holding "undervalued" securities because this would insure them higher long-run returns when eventually the prices became the same. They might, however, have a long, long wait.

Dividend Policy and Leverage

A study of the above line of proof will show it to be essentially analogous to the proof for the certainty world, in which as we know, firms can have, in effect, only two alternative sources of investment funds: retained earnings or stock issues. In an uncertain world, however, there is the additional financing possibility of debt issues. The question naturally arises, therefore, as to whether the conclusion about irrelevance remains valid even in the presence of debt financing, particularly since there may very well be interactions between debt policy and dividend policy. The answer is that it does, and while a complete demonstration would perhaps be too tedious and repetitive at this point, we can at least readily sketch out the main outlines of how the proof proceeds. We begin, as above, by establishing the conditions from period 1 on that lead to a situation in which $\bar{V}_1(1)$ must be brought into equality with $\bar{V}_2(1)$ where the V, following the approach in our earlier paper [17], is now to be interpreted as the total market value of the firm, debt plus equity, not merely equity alone. The return to the original investors taken as a whole—and remember that any individual always has the option of buying a proportional share of both the equity and the debt—must correspondingly be broadened to allow for the interest on the debt. There will also be a corresponding broadening of the accounting identity (4) to allow, on the one hand, for the interest return and, on the other, for any debt funds used to finance the investment in whole or in part. The net result is that both the dividend component and the interest component of total earnings will cancel out making the relevant (total) return, as before, $[\bar{X}_i(0) - \bar{I}_i(0) + \bar{V}_i(1)]$ which is clearly independent of the current dividend. It follows, then, that the value of the firm must also therefore be independent of dividend policy given investment policy.[28]

The Informational Content of Dividends

To conclude our discussion of dividend policy under uncertainty, we might take note briefly of a common confusion about the meaning of the irrelevance proposition occasioned by the fact that in the real world a change in the dividend rate is often followed by a change in the market price (sometimes spectacularly so). Such a phenomenon would not be incompatible with irrelevance to the extent that it was merely a reflection of what might be called the "informational content" of dividends, an attribute of particular dividend payments hitherto excluded by assumption from the discussion and proofs. That is, where a firm has adopted a policy of dividend stabilization

---

[28]This same conclusion must also hold for the current market value of all the shares (and hence for the current price per share), which is equal to the total market value minus the given initially outstanding debt. Needless to say, however, the price per share and the value of the equity at *future* points in time will not be independent of dividend and debt policies in the interim.

with a long-established and generally appreciated "target payout ratio," investors are likely to (and have good reason to) interpret a change in the dividend rate as a change in management's views of future profit prospects for the firm.[29] The dividend change, in other words, provides the occasion for the price change though not its cause, the price still being solely a reflection of future earnings and growth opportunities. In any particular instance, of course, the investors might well be mistaken in placing this interpretation on the dividend change, since the management might really only be changing its payout target or possibly even attempting to "manipulate" the price. But this would involve no particular conflict with the irrelevance proposition, unless, of course, the price changes in such cases were not reversed when the unfolding of events had made clear the true nature of the situation.[30]

5. DIVIDEND POLICY AND MARKET IMPERFECTIONS

To complete the analysis of dividend policy, the logical next step would presumably be to abandon the assumption of perfect capital markets. This is, however, a good deal easier to say than to do principally because there is no unique set of circumstances that constitutes "imperfection." We can describe not one but a multitude of possible departures from strict perfection, singly and in combinations. Clearly, to attempt to pursue the implications of each of these would only serve to add inordinately to an already overlong discussion. We shall instead, therefore, limit ourselves in this concluding section to a few brief and general observations about imperfect markets that we hope may prove helpful to those taking up the task of extending the theory of valuation in this direction.

First, it is important to keep in mind that from the standpoint of dividend policy, what counts is not imperfection per se but only imperfection that might lead an investor to have a systematic preference as between a dollar of current dividends and a dollar of current capital gains. Where no such systematic preference is produced, we can subsume the imperfection in the (random) error term always carried along when applying propositions derived from ideal models to real-world events.

Second, even where we do find imperfections that bias individual preferences—such as the existence of brokerage fees which tend to make young "accumulators" prefer low-payout shares and retired persons lean toward "income stocks"—such imperfections are at best only necessary but not sufficient conditions for certain payout policies to command a permanent premium in the market. If, for example, the frequency distribution of corpo-

---

[29]For evidence on the prevalence of dividend stabilization and target ratios see Lintner [15].
[30]For a further discussion of the subject of the informational content of dividends, including its implications for empirical tests of the irrelevance proposition, see Modigliani and Miller [16, pp. 666–68].

rate payout ratios happened to correspond exactly with the distribution of investor preferences for payout ratios, then the existence of these preferences would clearly lead ultimately to a situation whose implications were different in no fundamental respect from the perfect market case. Each corporation would tend to attract to itself a "clientele" consisting of those preferring its particular payout ratio, but one clientele would be entirely as good as another in terms of the valuation it would imply for the firm. Nor, of course, is it necessary for the distributions to match exactly for this result to occur. Even if there were a "shortage" of some particular payout ratio, investors would still normally have the option of achieving their particular saving objectives without paying a premium for the stocks in short supply simply by buying appropriately weighted combinations of the more plentiful payout ratios. In fact, given the great range of corporate payout ratios known to be available, this process would fail to eliminate permanent premiums and discounts only if the distribution of investor preferences were heavily concentrated at either of the extreme ends of the payout scale.[31]

Of all the many market imperfections that might be detailed, the only one that would seem to be even remotely capable of producing such a concentration is the substantial advantage accorded to capital gains as compared with dividends under the personal income tax. Strong as this tax push toward capital gains may be for high-income individuals, however, it should be remembered that a substantial (and growing) fraction of total shares outstanding is currently held by investors for whom there is either no tax differential (charitable and educational institutions, foundations, pension trusts, and low-income retired individuals) or where the tax advantage is, if anything, in favor of dividends (casualty insurance companies and taxable corporations generally). Hence, again, the "clientele effect" will be at work. Furthermore, except for taxable individuals in the very top brackets, the required difference in before-tax yields to produce equal after-tax yields is not particularly striking, at least for moderate variations in the composition of returns.[32] All this is not to say, of course, that differences in yields (market values) caused by differences in payout policies should be ignored by managements or investors merely because they may be relatively small. But it may help to

---

[31]The above discussion should explain why, among other reasons, it would not be possible to draw any valid inference about the relative preponderance of "accumulators" as opposed to "income" buyers or the strength of their preferences merely from the weight attaching to dividends in a simple cross-sectional regression between value and payouts (as is attempted in Clendenin [2, p. 50] or Durand [5, p. 651]).

[32]For example, if a taxpayer is subject to a marginal rate of 40 per cent on dividends and half that or 20 per cent on long-term capital gains, then a before-tax yield of 6 per cent consisting of 40 per cent dividends and 60 per cent capital gains produces an after-tax yield of 4.32 per cent. To net the same after-tax yield on a stock with 60 per cent of the return in dividends and only 40 per cent in capital gains would require a before-tax yield of 6.37 per cent. The difference would be somewhat smaller if we allowed for the present dividend credit, though it should also be kept in mind that the tax on capital gains may be avoided entirely under present arrangements if the gains are not realized during the holder's lifetime.

keep investigators from being too surprised if it turns out to be hard to measure or even to detect any premium for low-payout shares on the basis of standard statistical techniques.

Finally, we may note that since the tax differential in favor of capital gains is undoubtedly the major *systematic* imperfection in the market, one clearly cannot invoke "imperfections" to account for the difference between our irrelevance proposition and the standard view as to the role of dividend policy found in the literature of finance. For the standard view is not that low-payout companies command a premium; but that, in general, they will sell at a discount![33] If such indeed were the case—and we, at least, are not prepared to concede that this has been established—then the analysis presented in this paper suggests there would be only one way to account for it; namely, as the result of systematic irrationality on the part of the investing public.[34]

To say that an observed positive premium on high payouts was due to irrationality would not, of course, make the phenomenon any less real. But it would at least suggest the need for a certain measure of caution by long-range policy-makers. For investors, however naïve they may be when they enter the market, do sometimes learn from experience; and perhaps, occasionally, even from reading articles such as this.

REFERENCES

1. BODENHORN, DIRAN. "On the Problem of Capital Budgeting," *Journal of Finance*, XIV (December, 1959), 473–92.
2. CLENDENIN, JOHN. "What Do Stockholders Like?" *California Management Review*, I (Fall, 1958), 47–55.
3. CLENDENIN, JOHN, and VAN CLEAVE, M. "Growth and Common Stock Values," *Journal of Finance*, IX (September, 1954), 365–76.
4. DURAND, DAVID. *Bank Stock Prices and the Bank Capital Problem.* ("Occasional Paper," No. 54.) New York: National Bureau of Economic Research, 1957.
5. ———. "The Cost of Capital and the Theory of Investment: Comment," *American Economic Review*, XLIX (September, 1959), 639–54.
6. ———. "Growth Stocks and the Petersburg Paradox," *Journal of Finance*, XII (September, 1957), 348–63.
7. FISHER, G. R. "Some Factors Influencing Share Prices," *Economic Journal*, LXXI, No. 281 (March, 1961), 121–41.
8. GORDON, MYRON. "Corporate Saving, Investment and Share Prices," *Review of Economics and Statistics* (forthcoming).
9. ———. "Dividends, Earnings and Stock Prices," *ibid.*, XLI, No. 2, Part I (May, 1959), 99–105.

[33]See, among many, many others, Gordon [8, 9], Graham and Dodd [11, esp. chaps. xxxiv and xxxvi], Durand[4, 5], Hunt, Williams, and Donaldson [13, pp. 647–49], Fisher [7], Gordon and Shapiro [10], Harkavy [12], Clendenin [2], Johnson, Shapiro, and O'Meara [14], and Walter [19].

[34]Or, less plausibly, that there is a systematic tendency for external funds to be used more productively than internal funds.

10. GORDON, MYRON, and SHAPIRO, ELI. "Capital Equipment Analysis: The Required Rate of Profit," *Management Science*, III, 1956, 102–10.
11. GRAHAM, BENJAMIN, and DODD, DAVID. *Security Analysis.* 3d ed. New York: McGraw-Hill Book Co., 1951.
12. HARKAVY, OSCAR, "The Relation between Retained Earnings and Common Stock Prices for Large Listed Corporations," *Journal of Finance*, VIII (September, 1953), 283–97.
13. HUNT, PEARSON, WILLIAMS, CHARLES, and DONALDSON, GORDON. *Basic Business Finance.* Homewood, Ill.: Richard D. Irwin, 1958.
14. JOHNSON, L. R., SHAPIRO, ELI, and O'MEARA, J. "Valuation of Closely Held Stock for Federal Tax Purposes: Approach to an Objective Method," *University of Pennsylvania Law Review*, C, 166–95.
15. LINTNER, JOHN. "Distribution of Incomes of Corporations among Dividends, Retained Earnings and Taxes," *American Economic Review*, XLVI (May, 1956), 97–113.
16. MODIGLIANI, FRANCO, and MILLER, MERTON. " 'The Cost of Capital, Corporation Finance and the Theory of Investment': Reply," *American Economic Review*, XLIX (September, 1959), 655–69.
17. ———. "The Cost of Capital, Corporation Finance and the Theory of Investment," *ibid.*, XLVIII (1958), 261–97.
18. MUTH, JOHN F. "Rational Expectations and the Theory of Price Movements," *Econometrica* (forthcoming).
19. WALTER, JAMES E. "A Discriminant Function for Earnings-Price Ratios of Large Industrial Corporations," *Review of Economics and Statistics*, XLI (February, 1959), 44–52.
20. ———. "Dividend Policies and Common Stock Prices," *Journal of Finance*, XI (March, 1956), 29–41.
21. WILLIAMS, JOHN B. *The Theory of Investment Value.* Cambridge, Mass.: Harvard University Press, 1938.

3·9

The Ex-Dividend Behavior of American Telephone and Telegraph Stock*

David Durand and Alan M. May

This paper results from an experiment in using modern times-series methods to analyze the daily movements of a single security— American Telephone and Telegraph capital stock (hereafter abbreviated

*See footnote on next page.

"AT&T"). The experiment itself considered a variety of questions, which included the possible presence of a weekly cycle in the daily movements, the correlation between the daily movements of the stock and those of the market averages, the possible presence of trends or waves that might offer opportunities for short-term forecasting, and the effect of going ex-dividend on the daily movements. The present discussion deals only with the ex-dividend effect or with closely related questions.

The financial community believes that the price of a stock will drop off on the ex-dividend data by an amount approximately equal to the dividend, other things being equal. Explicit acceptance is to be found in the papers of financial writers;[1] implicit acceptance is found in certain stock-exchange rulings.[2] Campbell and Beranek,[3] however, have challenged this belief. First, they argue, if stocks really dropped by the full amount of the dividend, tax-conscious individuals would have a tremendous incentive to sell with dividend and buy ex-dividend; and such buying and selling would exert great market pressure to reduce the amount of the dropoff. Second, they present statistical evidence on 399 dividend payments that seems to show a tendency for stocks to drop off by less than the amount of their dividends. Further statistical work by Readett, covering 2,335 common dividend payments and 409 preferred dividend payments, confirms this tendency.[4] But, although these researches have established the presence of a tendency for stocks to drop off by less than the dividend, they have not shown that the discrepancy between dropoff and dividend is particularly pronounced. In fact, stocks seem to drop off, on the average, by about 90 per cent of the dividend.

I. ANALYSIS OF AT&T DROPOFFS

AT&T is a good medium for studying the ex-dividend effect. It is widely held and of general interest to individual and institutional investors. It enjoys a broad, active, and orderly market. Its regular quarterly dividend

*From the *Journal of Finance*, 15, no. 1, March 1960, pp. 19–31. Back numbers can be obtained from the Kraus Reprint Corporation, New York. Financial assistance for this project was provided by a grant from the Sloan Research Fund of the School of Industrial Management at the Massachusetts Institute of Technology. The computations, of which only a small fraction appear in this article, were performed partly on IBM equipment at the Division of Statistical Services at M.I.T. and partly on the IBM 704 calculator at the M.I.T. Computation Center. The authors extend personal thanks to Dr. Enders A. Robinson for aid and advice in some of the technical problems of time-series analysis.

[1]See, for example, C. A. Kulp, *The Discounting of Dividends by the Stock Market* (Philadelphia: University of Pennsylvania, 1924), p. 12; George L. Leffler, *The Stock Market* (New York: Ronald Press, 1951), p. 37; or Lester V. Plum and Joseph H. Humphrey, *Investment Analysis and Management* (Homewood, Ill.: Richard D. Irwin, Inc., 1953), p. 119.

[2]An example is the rule requiring all open orders to be reduced on the ex-dividend date by the amount of the dividend rounded off to the nearest eighth of a point.

[3]James A. Campbell and William Beranek, "Stock Price Behavior on Ex-Dividend Dates," *Journal of Finance*, X (1955), 425–29.

[4]Paul B. Readett, Jr., "The Price Behavior of Stocks on their Ex-Dividend Dates" (unpublished Master's thesis, Massachusetts Institute of Technology, Cambridge, Mass., 1956).

of $2.25 over the years studied is large in relation to the one-eighth-point minimum price differential, and this, coupled with the orderly market, makes the ex-dividend effect easily observable.

Table 1 summarizes the ex-dividend behavior of AT&T for a series of 45 consecutive dividends, beginning with the first quarter of 1948 and ending

TABLE 1. *Distribution of dropoffs in AT&T common on ex-dividend dates, March 11, 1948, to March 6, 1959*

*Dropoff**		*Period I,†*	*Period II,‡*	*Period III,*	
Actual	Per cent of dividend	Mar 11, 1948 to Sept. 10, 1952	Dec. 10, 1952 to Mar. 6, 1957	June 5, 1957 to Mar. 5, 1959	*Periods I, II, and III combined*
$1\frac{1}{4}$	56		1		1
$1\frac{5}{8}$	72		2		2
$1\frac{3}{4}$	78	2	1	1	4
$1\frac{7}{8}$	83	3	2		5
2	89	5	2	1	8
$2\frac{1}{8}$	94	3	3	1	6
$2\frac{1}{4}$	100	2	1	2	5
$2\frac{3}{8}$	106		3	1	4
$2\frac{5}{8}$	117	1	1	1	3
$2\frac{3}{4}$	122	1			1
$2\frac{7}{8}$	127		1		1
$3\frac{3}{8}$	150	1		1	2
Total		18	17	8	43
Average dropoff in dollars		2.15	2.07	2.34	2.16
in per cent of the $2.25 dividend		96	92	104	96

*Net difference between the closing price with dividend and the closing price ex-dividend (see Sec. I).
†Omits June 11, 1952, when AT&T went ex-rights, in addition to ex-dividend, and dropped $3\frac{7}{8}$.
‡Omits September 11, 1956, when AT&T went ex-rights, in addition to ex-dividend, and dropped $10\frac{3}{4}$.

with the first quarter of 1959, thus including the last dividend before the stock split. Omitting two maverick quarters when AT&T went ex-rights and ex-dividend simultaneously—dropping off $10\frac{3}{4}$ in one quarter and $3\frac{7}{8}$ in the other—the table gives a frequency distribution of 43 ex-dividend dropoffs, measured from the closing price with dividend to the closing price ex-dividend. Normally, one would prefer to measure ex-dividend dropoffs from the closing price with dividend to the opening price ex-dividend; and certainly this has been the procedure adopted by Campbell and Beranek, by Readett, and by others.[5] But in a study primarily con-

[5]For example, C. Austin Barker, "Price Changes of Stock-Dividend Shares at Ex-Dividend Dates," *Journal of Finance*, XIV (1959), 373–78.

cerned with a time series of daily movements, measured from closing to closing,[6] consistency demanded that ex-dividend dropoffs also be measured from closing to closing.

The average dropoff on 43 ex-dividend dates was $2.16, or about 4 per cent less than the $2.25 dividend. But the question immediately arises whether such a small difference is significant or not; and the question becomes particularly pertinent in view of the substantial amount of variation exhibited by individual dropoffs, ranging from $1\frac{1}{4}$ to $3\frac{3}{8}$ even after the elimination of the mavericks, and also in view of the appreciable amount of variation in the averages for the three periods into which the total series is divided.[7] Such variation is a serious obstacle to the understanding of ex-dividend behavior in general; it plagued the earlier efforts of Campbell and Beranek and of Readett, and it complicates the AT&T analysis. To highlight the uncertainty due to variability of experience, we present, in Table 2, 95 per cent symmetrical confidence limits calculated for the three periods individually as well as for the entire series. From these, the best one can say is that AT&T tended to fall off, on the average, by an amount lying somewhere between 90 per cent and 102 per cent of the $2.25 dividend. This evidence alone would certainly not justify the conclusion that stocks drop off by less than the amount of the dividend; but, coming as it does on the heels of considerable other evidence, it adds a little collateral support.

II. IMPLICATIONS FOR TAX-CONSCIOUS INVESTORS

Although the variability exposed in Table 1 is sufficient to prevent us from concluding with certainty that the average dropoff in AT&T is less than the dividend, it does permit some conclusions about the proper strategy for individual taxpayers who want to buy or sell AT&T approximately on the ex-dividend day. The advantage of capital gains to taxpayers in high brackets, or even in medium brackets, is great enough to compensate

[6]We chose to measure daily movements from closing to closing rather than from opening to opening because the Standard and Poor's averages are more readily available at the close. The relevance of these averages is brought out in the Appendix.

[7]Perhaps a word of explanation for the three periods is required. Alan May made an exploratory analysis of Period II and wrote up the results in "The Ex-Dividend Behavior of A.T. and T.: An Examination for Profit Maximization" (unpublished Bachelor's thesis at the Massachusetts Institute of Technology, June, 1957). The beginning date of this period, the last quarter of 1952, roughly coincides with the abolition of Saturday trading on the New York Stock Exchange. Hence this period contains only five-day weeks (holidays were interpolated) and appeared to provide a suitable hunting ground for a weekly (5-day) cycle, if one should exist. Actually, no appreciable weekly cycle was found.

Since May's exploratory analysis showed that Period II was not long enough to provide the desired precision, Period I was added and a new set of computations was run off. In the process, however, the division between the two periods was maintained on the chance that it might show a significant shift over time

Period III is more or less of an afterthought. Once the main computations were finished, it was difficult to bring most of the charts and tables up to date. Table 1, however, was easy to bring up to date—hence the appearance of Period III in this table only.

TABLE 2

	Limits	
	In dollars	In per cent of dividend
Period I	1.95–2.35	87–104
Period II	1.87–2.28	83–101
Period III	1.93–2.75	86–122
Entire series	2.03–2.29	90–102

for a good deal of uncertainty. Consider, for example, the individual tax-payer in the X per cent bracket who has decided to sell long-term holdings of AT&T, or any other stock, on which he has a profit. The question is whether to sell it with dividend or ex-dividend. If he waits to sell ex-dividend, he will increase his income by D per share, the amount of the dividend, and he will reduce his long-term capital gain by C per share, the amount of the dropoff. Thus his net gain attributable to waiting will be $D - C$ before taxes. After taxes, however, his increase in dividend income will amount to only $D(1 - X/100)$ in the X per cent bracket, and his lost capital gains will amount to either $C(1 - X/200)$ or $3C/4$—the first figure being appropriate for tax brackets up to and including 50 per cent, and the second for brackets of 50 per cent and up. The net gain or loss attributable to waiting is, therefore,

$$D\left(1 - \frac{X}{100}\right) - C\left(1 - \frac{X}{200}\right) \qquad (X \leq 50)$$

$$D\left(1 - \frac{X}{100}\right) - \frac{3C}{4} \qquad (X \geq 50).$$

The two equations formed by equating each of the above quantities to zero determine either the break-even dropoff, given the tax bracket, or the break-even tax bracket, given the dropoff. When the dividend D is $2.25, these two equations produce the graph in Figure 1, which is drawn as a solid line in spite of the fact that the current tax laws provide only a discrete set of tax brackets—that is, X values. For combinations of C and X above the graph, selling with dividend is the proper procedure; for combinations below, selling ex-dividend is better.

For a dropoff of $2\frac{1}{8}$, which is the value nearest to the $2.16 average that can actually occur, the break-even tax bracket would be $10\frac{1}{2}$ per cent. But $10\frac{1}{2}$ per cent is an almost non-existent tax bracket.[8] Most individuals and

[8] A widow with an income of about $1,300, all from AT&T, might consider herself in the $10\frac{1}{2}$ per cent bracket on the grounds that $10\frac{1}{2}$ per cent was an average of the untaxed portion of her income and the portion taxed at 20 per cent.

profit-making corporations will be above it, whereas insurance companies and eleemosynary institutions will be below. Thus, if AT&T had invariably dropped off by $2\frac{1}{8}$, virtually all the individuals would have been well advised

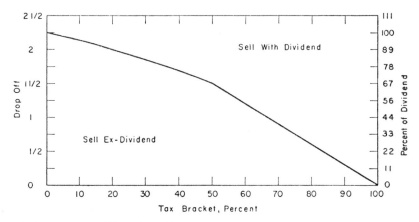

FIGURE 1   Conditions for selling AT&T with dividend or ex-dividend at the $2.25 dividend rate: dropoff versus tax bracket.

to sell on the eve of the ex-dividend date, and the institutions, on the other hand, would have been well advised to wait. But dropoff experience varied considerably, and action based on the average would sometimes have seemed ill advised after the event. Thus, with a dropoff of $1\frac{7}{8}$ or less, which occurred 7 times out of 43, individual taxpayers in the 26 per cent bracket would have done better to wait; and with a dropoff of only $1\frac{1}{4}$, which occurred once out of 43, even an individual in the 50 per cent tax bracket should have waited. Or again, with a dropoff of $2\frac{3}{8}$ or more, which occurred 11 times, tax-exempt institutions would have done better to sell with dividend. But the exceptions to the average do not seem either common enough or extreme enough to warrant extraordinary behavior—unless extraordinary dropoffs can be accurately forecast; and the evidence gathered to date (see appendix) affords little hope that they can.

The above analysis, leading to the conclusion that individual investors should ordinarily sell AT&T with dividend rather than ex-dividend, applies to those who intend to sell the stock for a long-term profit on or about the ex-dividend date and also to those who intend to sell for a long-term loss against offsetting long-term gains in other securities. It obviously does not apply to the very few investors who may be able to sell at a loss and deduct this directly from income; these latter are in much the same position as a tax-exempt institution and might gain slightly by selling ex-dividend.

Modification of the above analysis to meet the needs of investors who intend to buy rather than sell AT&T on or about the ex-dividend date is complicated by the fact that few investors know exactly what their tax position will be when they finally sell their holdings. Hence the graph of Figure 1 does not mark the exact dividing line between the area for purchase with dividend (below the graph) and the area for purchase ex-dividend (above the graph). Nevertheless, it is hard to see how a high-tax-bracket individual can lose by deferring his purchase until the ex-dividend date. By so doing, he avoids an immediate and certain high tax liability for dividend income, and he incurs only a remote and probably small potential liability for capital gains; and if he should die holding the stock, he and his heirs would, under the present tax law, escape the latter liability altogether.

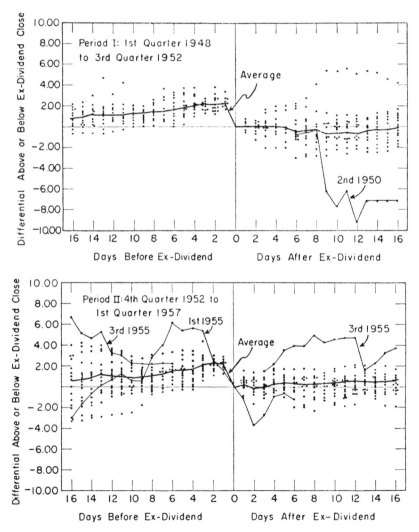

FIGURE 2 Comparative behavior of AT&T before and after ex-dividend dates.

III. BEHAVIOR OF AT&T NEAR THE EX-DIVIDEND DATE

Clearly, it is unduly restrictive to limit attention to just 2 days out of each quarter. Must the individual who holds AT&T at a profit and wants to sell it wait until the eve of the ex-dividend date, or can he just as well sell it any time within, say, the 2-week period just prior to the ex-dividend date? Or again, might he not, perhaps, be able to have his cake and eat it by holding a few days past the ex-dividend date, which would assure him of the dividend and might give the stock a chance to recover from its ex-dividend dropoff? Table 3 shows AT&T's average differential price above or below the ex-dividend closing for a period of about 3 weeks before and after the ex-dividend date.[9] These same averages appear as heavy lines in Figure 2, accompanied by a scatter of points to indicate the observations from which these averages were derived.

In spite of the scatter evident in Figure 2, the averages seem to show a tendency to rise steadily during the last 2 or 3 weeks before ex-dividend—at a rate of roughly one-half point per week—and to show no appreciable

TABLE 3. *Price movements of AT&T in relation to ex-dividend closing*

Days before ex-dividend	Av. price above or below ex-dividend close		Days after ex-dividend	Av. price above or below ex-dividend close	
	Period I	Period II		Period I	Period II
16	0.82	0.53	1	0.01	+0.23
15	0.89	0.65	2	− .01	− .07
14	1.10	0.90	3	− .02	− .02
13	1.08	1.15	4	.03	+ .29
12	1.07	0.98	5	− .15	+ .35
11	1.10	0.94	6	− .47	+ .26
10	1.24	0.83	7	− .40	+ .23
9	1.28	0.89	8	− .33	+ .25
8	1.40	1.01	9	− .63	+ .28
7	1.43	1.18	10	− .66	+ .36
6	1.59	1.55	11	− .58	+ .47
5	1.77	1.59	12	− .72	+ .48
4	1.96	1.74	13	− .42	+ .41
3	2.08	3.06	14	− .37	+ .40
2	2.10	2.21	15	− .28	+ .49
1	2.15	2.07	16	−0.21	+0.58

[9]The question of what constitutes a week on these charts may call for comment. In Period II the normal week was 5 market days with holidays filled in by interpolation; therefore, 16 days on the chart represent 3 weeks and 1 day. In Period I, however, the normal week was 6 days in winter and 5 days in summer, so that 16 days may represent more or less than 3 weeks.

tendency to recover from the dropoff during the 2 or 3 weeks immediately following. From this evidence one is tempted to conclude that the last 2 or 3 days before the ex-dividend date are a good time for a taxpaying individual to sell AT&T and a poor time for almost anyone to buy; a taxpaying individual should wait to buy until ex-dividend, and a tax-exempt institution should have anticipated the price rise by buying a week or so earlier. But this conclusion needs critical review, for the ex-dividend behavior of AT&T is subject to a number of disturbing influences that might distort the averages.

Of all these disturbing influences, one of the easiest to dispose of is the long-term trend. During the period covered by Figure 2, which coincided roughly with one of the great bull markets of history, AT&T rose from 149¾ on February 2, 1948, to 178 on March 28, 1957 (making a low of 138 and a high of 187⅜ between the end dates). The difference of 28¼ points over the period averages only about 0.06 point per week, which constitutes only a very small fraction of the one-half-point-per-week pre-dividend price rise. But note that if the same technique were applied to a stock with a much faster rate of appreciation, the long-term effect might have to be reckoned with; it could create the appearance of a pre-dividend rise or post-dividend recovery.

Much more disturbing than the long-term trend is the fact that AT&T's movements about the ex-dividend date sometimes follow patterns very different from the average. Four such patterns are indicated in Figure 2, and two of them seem to be traceable directly to events peculiar to AT&T itself. Thus, in the third quarter of 1955, shortly before the ex-dividend data, AT&T went ex-rights (on August 22)—dropping 2¼ points on the ex-rights date but showing weakness both before and after.

Another movement associated with rights appears in the first quarter of 1955: on February 16, AT&T's directors voted to authorize a new preemptive issue of convertible bonds, and the stock promptly rose from 177⅜ to 186½ (closing prices), then reacted sharply; but since there were rumors of a stock split at this time,[10] it is not clear how much of this movement was due to the proposed financing. In any event, the movement is clearly disturbing and illustrates one difficulty in studying ex-dividend behavior. Although we felt impelled, as indicated, to expunge from our records two quarters when AT&T went ex-rights and ex-dividend simultaneously, we did not consider such drastic treatment appropriate for all quarters in which a disturbing event occurred somewhere in the proximity of the ex-dividend date.

Sometimes a conspicuous pattern in AT&T will be associated with a major event affecting the entire market. Figure 2 (*top*) shows the big drop

[10]See the *Wall Street Journal*, March 15, 1955, "Abreast of the Market," p. 23.

following the outbreak of the Korean War in the second quarter of 1950, shortly after AT&T's ex-dividend date. A similar, if not so precipitous, drop followed President Eisenhower's heart attack, shortly after the third ex-dividend date in 1955 (see Fig. 2, *bottom*). Reactions of this magnitude and even those of lesser magnitude may considerably upset the normal ex-dividend behavior of any stock. Previous workers have recognized this problem and have attempted to meet it in one way or another. Campbell and Beranek, for example, analyzed two samples of ex-dividend dropoffs— one limited to days on which the market was quiet, the other unrestricted. They obtained essentially the same results from each sample. Readett analyzed several samples, two of which constituted a pair especially designed to explore the relation between ex-dividend behavior and general market movements. One sample of the pair covered 139 common dividends and 20 preferred dividends occurring in a period of 50 market days (September 18–November 18, 1941) when stock prices were falling; the other covered 146 common and 43 preferred dividends occurring in a period of 50 market days (December 8–February 5, 1943) when prices were rising. As might be expected, the average dropoff was appreciably greater during the first period, when prices were falling, than during the second.

Although Readett made an important first step in providing evidence that dropoffs are related to general market movements, he did not attempt the next step of isolating the ex-dividend effect from that of the general market. This step we have attempted as part of the time-series analysis of AT&T, and we discuss the results in the appendix.

IV. CONCLUSION

As we see it, the AT&T experience provides only meager support for the proposition that stocks tend to drop off by less than the amount of the dividend. Over the period studied, AT&T tended to drop off by *approximately* the amount of the dividend; and the discrepancy, if any, was not very great. But if one is inclined to grant the existence of a small discrepancy, then one must conclude that the stock tends to drop off less, not more, than its dividend. This conclusion is not inconsistent with previous results. Neither Campbell and Beranek nor Readett found any evidence of a large discrepancy between typical market dropoffs and dividends, and only by analyzing very large numbers of dropoffs could they show that a small discrepancy was in fact a reality.

On the evidence that AT&T's typical dropoff is not very different from its dividend, the last 2 or 3 days with dividend would seem to be a good time for the tax-conscious individual to sell AT&T and a poor time for almost anyone to buy. There is some evidence that the pre-dividend anticipatory price rise tends to be concentrated in the last 2 or 3 weeks before the ex-dividend date, instead of being spread evenly over the entire quarter. If this is true, the ideal time to buy, especially for a tax-exempt institution, would be some 3–4 weeks prior to the ex-dividend date; for this procedure would enable the buyer to enjoy the dividend while paying little, if any, additional price for the stock.

But these briefly sketched recommendations on the timing of trans-actions should be taken with a large grain of salt, and we trust they will be. The maximum benefit that could be attributed to good timing in respect to dividends would be in the order of 1 per cent of the total transaction, and this is not sufficient to induce a buyer or seller to undergo any particular inconvenience, to take any uncalled-for risks, or to overlook other and more important timing considerations. We should not expect a prospective buyer of AT&T who acquired funds on, say, July 1 to postpone buying until August 15, which would be our estimate of the beginning of the price rise preceding the September dividend; the delay could be inconvenient, and the market might rise several points for reasons having nothing to do with divi-dend anticipation. As we see it, the only positive recommendation is against the purchase of AT&T, especially by high-tax-bracket individuals, during the last 3 days before the ex-dividend date; and even this may turn out to be wrong if many buyers take our advice, for this could have the effect of squeezing the ex-dividend dropoff to much less than its present normal amount of about 95 per cent of the dividend.

APPENDIX

AN EXPERIMENT IN TIME-SERIES ANALYSIS

The time-series experiment was concerned with the possibility of forecasting the daily price movements of AT&T, given the daily movements of one or two market averages. If a reliable system of forecasting could be found, it would provide the means of adjusting ex-dividend dropoffs on days when the market was appreciably up or down. If, say, AT&T were to drop off $2\frac{5}{8}$ on a day when the market was down 2 points, how much of this dropoff would be due to the stock's going ex-dividend and how much to the market decline? The question implies an estimate, or forecast, of the amount by which AT&T would have moved if it had not, in fact, been ex-dividend.

But the time-series experiment failed to produce an effective forecasting system. An example of what it did produce is afforded by the following two regression equations, of which the first refers to Period I and the second to Period II:

$$Y_j = -0.0462 + 27.4\Delta U_j + 13.6\Delta I_j + 8.34\Delta P_{j-1} + 0.037 U_{j-1} - 1.91 I_{j-1}, \quad (1)$$

$$Y_j = -0.0602 + 34.81\Delta U_j + 5.80\Delta I_j + 13.1\Delta P_{j-1} - 2.43\Delta U_{j-1} - 0.26 I_{j-1}. \quad (2)$$

In both these equations, the symbols have the following meanings:

Y_j is the forecasted price change in AT&T,

ΔU_j is the change in the Standard and Poor's utility index on j day,[11]

ΔI_j is the change in the Standard and Poor's industrial index on j day,

ΔP_{j-1} is the change in AT&T on $(j-1)$ day,

ΔU_{j-1} is the change in the utility index on $(j-1)$ day,

ΔI_{j-1} is the change in the industrial index on $(j-1)$ day.

Thus the forecast of AT&T's current movements is based partly on the current movements of the two Standard and Poor's indexes and partly on the most recent past movements of these indexes as well as on the most recent past movement of AT&T itself.

The effectiveness of these two formulas as forecasting devices can be judged roughly by either of the following two measures:

	Period I	Period II
Coefficient of determinaion, R^2	0.33	0.30
Coefficient of alienation, k	0.82	0.84

The coefficient of determination is a familiar statistical measure to be interpreted as indicating the fraction of the total variation in Y associated with, or explained by, variations in the five independent variables. By this measure, only about one-third of the total variation in AT&T's daily movements is explained. The coefficient of alienation, k, is not nearly so familiar as R^2, but it has an important interpretation—measuring the standard error of Y about the regression equation as a fraction of the original standard error.[12] By this measure, which is essentially more pessimistic than R^2, at least 80 per cent of the variation in AT&T's daily movements is unexplained. Thus, by either measure, the major part of the variation in AT&T's daily movements is unexplained by, or unrelated to, the five independent variables and therefore unpredictable in terms of them.

Since equations (1) and (2) represent a sort of average experience over 18 quarters (Period I) or 17 quarters (Period II), it is appropriate to ask whether or not the ineffectiveness of these formulas might not be due to seasonal variation of secular drift during the period covered. To investigate this possibility, we calculated an individual formula for each quarter, having exactly the same five variables

[11]This study was undertaken before the big revision (March, 1957) in the Standard and Poor's averages. Hence our forecasting formulas apply to the old index rather than the new.

[12]For further discussion see Truman L. Kelley, *Statistical Methods* (New York: Macmillan Co., 1924), pp. 173–74.

as equations (1) and (2); we found that some individual formulas were appreciably more effective than the average formulas, and some were appreciably less effective. Coefficients of determination ranged from $R^2 = 0.11$ to $R^2 = 0.78$.

The immediate conclusion to be drawn from all these results is that, although forecasts of AT&T's daily movements derived from formulas like (1) and (2) are a little better than no forecast at all, they are not very much better. In particular, when these forecasts are used to adjust AT&T's ex-dividend dropoffs for market movements, the adjusted dropoffs showed just about as much variability as did the unadjusted. The standard deviations for the adjusted and unadjusted dropoffs were as follows:

		Adjusted by	
	Unadjusted	Average formula (1) or (2)	Individual formula for each quarter
Period I	0.39	0.32	0.29
Period II	0.39	0.39	0.41

But, although the time-series experiment provided no aid in the analysis of AT&T's ex-dividend behavior, it provided some confirmation of previous analyses of the behavior of successive movements in speculative price series—both of stocks and of commodities. Successive differences in such series—at daily, weekly, bi-weekly, or monthly intervals—tend to behave very much like random numbers.[13] According to Roberts, "If, for example, weekly *changes* of the Dow Jones Index are examined statistically, it is apparent that these changes behave very much as if they had been generated by an extremely simple chance model."[14] In our time-series experiment, we found that the successive daily movements of AT&T were almost completely independent of earlier movements in either AT&T or the Standard and Poor's averages. Although the regression formulas (1) and (2) contain three variables representing these past movements—ΔP_{j-1}, ΔU_{j-1}, and ΔI_{j-1}—these three did not carry much weight; if they had been left out entirely, the effectiveness of the formulas (such as it was) would have suffered hardly at all. Judged by the coefficients of determination, R^2, the five-variable formula shows only a very small improvement over a two-variable formula based on the movements of the two indexes, ΔU_j and ΔI_j:

	Period I	*Period II*
R^2 for two variables	0.32	0.28
R^2 for five variables	0.33	0.30

[13]See, for example, M. G. Kendall, "The Analysis of Economic Time-Series. I. Prices," *Journal of the Royal Statistical Society*, Ser. A, CXVI (1953), 11–25.

[14]Harry V. Roberts, "Stock Market 'Patterns' and Financial Analysis," *Journal of Finance*, XIV (1959), 1–10.

Determinants of Risk Premiums on Corporate Bonds*

Lawrence Fisher[1]

I. INTRODUCTION

Economists have long agreed that the rate of interest on a loan depends on the risks the lender incurs. But how lenders estimate these risks has been left largely to conjecture. This paper presents and tests a hypothesis about the determinants of risk premiums on corporate bonds. By risk premium is meant the difference between the market yield on a bond and the corresponding pure rate of interest.

My hypothesis is as follows: (1) The average risk premium on a firm's bonds depends first on the risk that the firm will default on its bonds and second on their marketability. (2) The "risk of default" can be estimated by a function of three variables: the coefficient of variation of the firm's net income over the last nine years (after all charges and taxes), the length of time the firm has been operating without forcing its creditors to take a loss, and the ratio of the market value of the equity in the firm to the par value of the firm's debt. (3) The marketability of a firm's bonds can be estimated by a single variable, the market value of all the publicly traded bonds the firm has outstanding. (4) The logarithm of the average risk premium on a firm's bonds can be estimated by a linear function of the logarithms of the four variables just listed.

For convenience, these variables will usually be designated as follows: earnings variability, x_1; period of solvency, x_2; equity/debt ratio, x_3; and

*From the *Journal of Political Economy*, **67**, no. 3, June 1959, pp. 217–237. Reprinted by permission of The University of Chicago Press.

[1]I am greatly indebted to Professor Arnold C. Harberger, who suggested that I undertake this research and guided me throughout the study. Professors Carl Christ and Phillip D. Cagan made valuable comments and criticisms, as did other members of the Research Group in Public Finance of the University of Chicago. An Earhart Foundation Fellowship facilitated the completion of this study.

This paper was read at the September, 1956, meeting of the Econometric Society in Detroit. An abstract was printed in *Econometrica*, XXV (1957), 366–67.

bonds outstanding, x_4. Risk premium will be called x_0. Capital letters will indicate common logarithms of the variables. Earnings variability and the equity/debt ratio are pure numbers. Risk premium will be expressed in per cent per annum, compounded semiannually; bonds outstanding, in millions of dollars; and the period of solvency, in years.[2]

Security analysts generally regard some form of each of these variables to be of value in appraising the "quality" of bonds. But, to the best of my knowledge, this is the first time they have been used together in an attempt to discover how much investors are influenced by various aspects of bond quality.[3]

More precise definitions of the variables will be given later, and the derivation of the hypothesis, alternative hypotheses, and statistical procedures will be explained. But first let us look at some of the main results.

II. THE MAIN RESULTS

The hypothesis was tested by least-squares regressions for cross-sections of domestic industrial corporations for five dates: December 31 of the years 1927, 1932, 1937, 1949, and 1953. The cross-sections included all firms for which I had meaningful data.[4] The cross-sections were for 71 firms in 1927, 45 firms in 1932, 89 firms in 1937, 73 firms in 1949, and 88 firms in 1953.

For each of these cross-sections the logarithms of the four variables accounted for approximately three-fourths of the variance in the logarithm of risk premium. Furthermore, I found that the elasticity[5] of risk premium with respect to each of the four variables is relatively stable over time. In view of this stability, it was possible to pool the observed variances and covariances and obtain a single set of "best" estimates of the elasticities. Figure 1 is the scatter of the 366 measured risk premiums against the risk premiums calculated by using this single set of elasticities. The regression equation from which these risk premiums were estimated is

$$X_0 = 0.262X_1 - 0.223X_2 - 0.469X_3 - 0.290X_4 + \text{a constant}, \qquad (1)$$

where the constant is equal to 0.966 in 1927; 1.235 in 1932; 0.918 in 1937; 0.847 in 1949; and 0.829 in 1953. This equation accounts for 81 per cent of the total variance in the logarithm of risk premium. Part of this variance,

---

[2]Some alternative variables will be introduced below. They will be expressed in the following units: equity, x_5 and debt, x_6—millions of dollars; annual volume of trading, x_7—millions of dollars a year; an alternative index of variability of earnings, x_8—the reciprocal of years.

[3]The study by Herbert Arkin, discussed in note 41, bears a superficial resemblance to this one.

[4]For the sources of data and the criteria used in selecting the firms see Section VI.

[5]Logarithmic regression coefficients are estimates of elasticities.

however, can be accounted for by differences in the mean of X_0 among the cross-sections. When that part of the variance is eliminated, equation (1) accounts for 74 per cent of the remaining or intra-cross-section variance. To

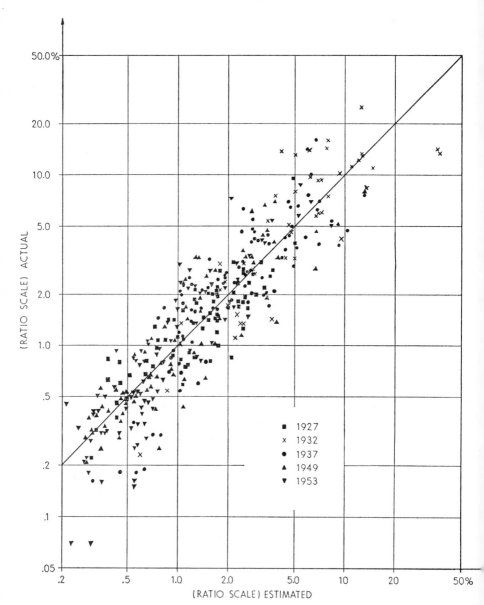

FIGURE 1 Scatter of actual risk premiums against risk premiums estimated from equation (1).

make the data strictly comparable among the cross-sections, it would have been necessary to make adjustments for such things as changes in tax rates. But, since we do not know whether the determinants of stock prices are stable and since the market value of equity was used in computing one of the variables, these adjustments were not made. Hence there was no reason to expect the constant term of this regression equation to be the same for each date, even if investors' behavior in the bond market were perfectly stable over time.[6]

Figure 2 permits us to compare the fraction of the intra-cross-section variance in the logarithm of risk premium, X_0, that is accounted for by the

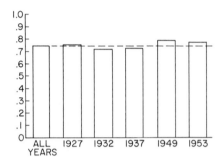

FIGURE 2 Proportion of intra-cross-section variance in the logarithms of risk premiums accounted for by the logarithms of earnings variability, period of solvency, equity/debt ratio, and bonds outstanding.

pooled-variance regression, equation (1), with the squares of the multiple correlation coefficients (R^2) obtained by fitting regression equations to each cross-section separately.

Figure 3 shows the estimates of elasticities and their standard errors obtained from the pooled-variance regression, equation (1), and from the regressions for the separate cross-sections. The larger bars show the estimated elasticities, η. The right ends of the small bars are at points one standard error, s, greater than the estimated elasticity; the left ends are at $\eta - s$. The estimates from equation (1) may be compared with the estimates from the separate regressions with the aid of the dashed lines. These results are summarized in Table 1, which shows the elasticities, standard errors of estimate, constant terms, and squares of the coefficients of multiple correlation.

[6]The regression equation found by keeping the constant term (as well as the elasticities) the same for all cross-sections is

$$X_0 = 0.307 X_1 - 0.253 X_2 - 0.537 X_3 - 0.275 X_4 + 0.987 \ (R^2 = 0.75). \tag{2}$$

For a complete description of equation (2) see Table 1.

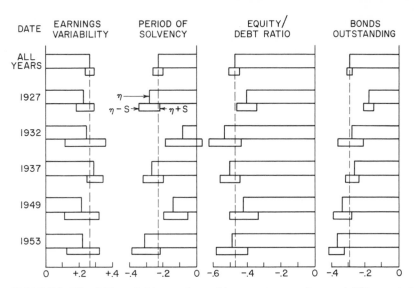

FIGURE 3   Elasticities of risk premium with respect to earnings variability, period of solvency, equity/debt ratio, and bonds outstanding estimated from cross-sections (together with standard errors of estimate).

All the coefficients shown in Table 1 have the expected sign.[7]   All estimated values of the elasticities are significantly different from zero at the 5 per cent level or lower except the estimates for period of solvency, x_2, for 1932 and 1949.[8]

III.   THEORETICAL FRAMEWORK

The apparent cost of borrowed capital to a firm with publicly traded bonds outstanding is the market rate of return on those bonds (which generally will be the pure rate of interest plus a risk premium) plus the cost of floating the issue.[9]   The determinants of the pure rate of interest have long been the subject of extensive study, both theoretical and empirical. Costs of flotation have also been studied.[10]   But the matter of what determines risk premiums has been left almost entirely to conjecture.

[7]See Section IV.

[8]This variable, however, was not measured with any great accuracy (see Section VI). Errors in the measurement of x_2 probably had only a negligible effect on the coefficients of equation (1) (see Section VII).

[9]This is only the apparent cost because the cost of equity capital probably depends on the firm's capital structure.

[10]For examples see Securities and Exchange Commission, *Costs of Flotation, 1945–1949* (Washington, 1951), and Arthur Stone Dewing, *Financial Policy of Corporations* (5th ed.; New York, 1953), II, 1131–32.

TABLE 1. Regression equations for estimating logarithm of average risk premium on a firm's bonds as a linear function of logarithms of earnings variability, period of solvency, equity–debt ratio, and bonds outstanding*

Equation	Date	No. of observations	Degrees of freedom	R^2	a_0	a_1 (s_1)	a_2 (s_2)	a_3 (s_3)	a_4 (s_4)
1	All	366	357	0.811†	‡	+0.262 (.032)	−0.223 (.033)	−0.469 (.029)	−0.290 (.019)
2	All	366	361	.750	0.987	+.307 (.032)	−.253 (.036)	−.537 (.031)	−.275 (.021)
3	1927	71	66	.756	0.874	+.233 (.048)	−.269 (.062)	−.404 (.039)	−.169 (.031)
4	1932	45	40	.726	1.014	+.248 (.128)	−.067 (.114)	−.531 (.092)	−.286 (.071)
5	1937	89	84	.731	0.949	+.286 (.051)	−.254 (.061)	−.491 (.060)	−.271 (.038)
6	1949	73	68	.786	0.711	+.228 (.100)	−.124 (.076)	−.426 (.084)	−.329 (.046)
7	1953	88	83	0.773	1.012	+.228 (0.091)	−.300 (0.089)	−.474 (0.085)	−.363 (0.043)

*Hypothesis that $X_0 = a_0 + a_1 X_1 + a_2 X_2 + a_3 X_3 + a_4 X_4$
†0.741 after the effects of differences in a_0 are eliminated.
‡1927: 0.966; 1932: 1.235; 1937: 0.918; 1949: 0.847; 1953: 0.829.

The basic theory of risk premiums on loans was stated by J. R. McCullough, who wrote:

There are comparatively few species of security to be obtained in which there is no risk, either as to the repayment of the loans themselves, or the regular payment of the interest. . . . Other things being equal, the rate of interest must of course vary according to the supposed risk incurred by the lender of either not recovering payment at all, or not receiving it at the stipulated term. No person of sound mind would lend on the personal security of an individual of doubtful character and solvency, and on mortgage over a valuable estate, at the same rate of interest. Wherever there is risk, it must be compensated to the lender by a higher premium or interest.[11]

Mercantile bills of unquestionable credit and having two or three months to run, are generally discounted at a lower rate of interest than may be obtained for sums lent upon mortgage, *on account of the facility they afford of repossessing the principal*, and applying it in some more profitable manner.[12]

In other words, the yields on almost all securities include compensation for risk. These risk premiums depend on lenders' estimates of the risk of default and on the ease of turning the securities into cash. Let us consider the risk of default first.

The risk premium on a bond has been defined as the difference between its market yield to maturity and the corresponding pure rate of interest. Market yield is defined as the rate of interest at which the principal and interest payments specified in the bond contract must be discounted if their present value is to equal the current market price of the bond. The corresponding pure rate of interest is defined as the market yield on a riskless bond maturing on the same day as the bond under consideration.

Risk premiums defined in this way must in general be either zero or positive if, other things being equal, bondholders prefer high incomes to low incomes. A bondholder has no expectation of receiving more than the payments called for by his bond and, since corporations have limited liability, he may receive less.[13] Hence, regardless of whether he likes or tries to avoid being in situations of uncertain income and wealth, a bond-

---

[11]*The Principles of Political Economy: With a Sketch of the Rise and Progress of the Science* (2d ed.; Edinburgh, London, and Dublin, 1830), pp. 508–9.

[12]*Ibid.*, p. 508 (italics mine).

[13]There have been cases in which creditors have received equity interests in firms through reorganizations in bankruptcy, and the firms subsequently made such large profits that the bondholders ultimately received payments larger than those called for by their bonds (but it is doubtful whether, at the time of the reorganizations, the new securities received had a market value as great as the accumulated value of the bonds). But bondholders receive such payments only after expenses of the receivership have been paid and only if the earning power of the firm is underestimated at the time of reorganization. So long as bondholders do not become stockholders, they cannot receive more than the amounts called for by their contracts. (Sinking fund and call provisions in bond indentures complicate this argument slightly, but they limit the bondholders' opportunity for capital gains; hence considering them would probably strengthen these conclusions.) We can conclude that the expectation of a bondholder's receiving more than contractual payments is negligible.

holder will demand a risk premium as compensation for holding any bond that is not certain to be paid.[14]

A lender's estimate of the "risk of default" must depend on his estimates of the probability that a default will occur[15] and of the magnitude of his loss in the event of a default.[16] Let us assume that lenders do not behave capriciously. Then our problem is to find how a rational investor can most readily estimate the probability that a bond will be defaulted. Investors' estimates must be based on information available to them. In general, if a corporation defaults on its bonds, it is because the market value of its assets is less than its liabilities. The value of its assets—that is, the value of its total capital—depends on the earning power of those assets. Hence the "risk of default" is given by the probability that the firm's earnings will not be large enough to meet the payments on its debts.

Recall that risk premium also depends on marketability. The theory of the determinants of risk premiums may then be restated: If investors are rational, the risk premium on any bond will depend on the probability that the issuing firm's earnings will be too small to permit it to pay its debts and on the ease with which the bondholder can turn the bond into cash before it matures.

Let us now turn to the problem of finding ways to measure these variables.

IV. AN OPERATIONAL HYPOTHESIS

Risk of Default

There are three sorts of variables that it is plausible to use together in estimating risk of default: measures of the variability of the firm's earnings; measures showing how reliable the firm has been in meeting its obligations; and measures depending on the firm's capital structure.

Variability of earnings In 1903, J. Pease Norton suggested the probability that a firm will fail to pay interest on its bonds in any particular year could be found by computing the coefficient of variation of the firm's income in past years, over and above the amount required for fixed charges,

---

[14]That is, if a bondholder's utility is a function of his income and the first derivative of the function is positive, a dollar a year with certainty must have a greater utility than a dollar a year with probability $p < 1$ plus an amount less than one dollar a year with probability $1 - p$. This proposition is, of course, independent of the sign of the second derivative of the utility function.

[15]More precisely, the probabilities of default at each moment in time.

[16]It can easily be shown that the expected loss in the event of a default is likely to depend on two of the determinants of the probability of default—earnings variability and the equity/debt ratio. My procedure enables one to find an index of the probability of default but not to estimate the probability itself. Hence, to simplify the analysis, the magnitude of loss in the event of a default will not be discussed explicitly. Those who demand rigor may read the phrase "probability of a default" as "expected loss."

and by looking up the probability in a table of the normal distribution.[17] This naïve procedure may be correct for non-cumulative income bonds (which are rare), but it is not correct for other types of bonds because corporations often continue to meet fixed charges during periods of losses. Nevertheless, it provides a useful point of departure.

Let us make an assumption which is implicit in Norton's procedure— that a series of observations of a firm's annual net income may be treated as a random sample from a normally distributed population of potential annual net incomes. The coefficient of variation of this series is an estimate of the coefficient of variation of the underlying population.[18] Other things being equal, a firm with a small coefficient of variation of earnings is less likely to default on its bonds than a firm with a large coefficient. Hence the variable suggested by Norton appears to be a promising one, even in analyses of bonds for which his complete procedure is invalid.

In practice, data on the earnings of a firm for its entire history are usually not available. To test the partial hypothesis that investors believe that a bond issued by a firm whose earnings have varied little is a better risk than a bond issued by a firm whose earnings have varied much, one must have comparable earnings data for the two firms. Because my tests covered a large number of firms, it was necessary to place an arbitrary limit on the number of years' earnings used in computing the coefficient of variation. Nine years was the limit selected. During the period considered, nine years was long enough for the earnings of most firms to fluctuate substantially.

In the abstract, one could take as "net earnings" either income after the payment of fixed charges or income after the payment of both charges and corporation income taxes. If taxes were proportional to income and tax rates did not vary during the nine-year period and if one year's losses could not be deducted from another year's profits in computing taxes, the two methods would give the same computed coefficient of variation. But tax rates do vary from year to year, and there are loss carryback and carry-forward provisions in our tax laws; neither measure is ideal. I did not use both measures together because, if I found that risk premium varied with the coefficient of variation in earnings, I wanted to measure the elasticity of risk premium with respect to this measure of the risk of default. And, since the two coefficients of variation were expected to be highly correlated with each other, a precise estimate of either elasticity could not be expected with both variables in the regression.

My choice was made on practical grounds. The appropriate measure of marketability, bonds outstanding, is highly correlated with size of firm.

[17]"The Theory of Loan Credit in Relation to Corporation Economics," *Publications of the American Economic Association*, 3d ser., V (1904), 298. Cf. Irving Fisher, *The Nature of Capital and Income* (New York, 1906), p. 409.

[18]The coefficient of variation is the ratio of the standard deviation of a sample (adjusted for degrees of freedom) to the arithmetic mean of the sample.

If both coefficients of variation in earnings are equally reliable, the measure that allows the use of the larger range of firms gives the more precise estimate of the elasticity of risk premium with respect to marketability. Issues of *Moody's Manual*, an important secondary source, give data on earnings after taxes for more firms than on earnings before taxes, particularly for very large and for small firms. Therefore, earnings after taxes ("net income") were taken as "earnings" and used in computing x_1, earnings variability.

In many studies it is necessary to adjust data for changes in the general price level. Since bond obligations are in "money" rather than "real" units, no such adjustment was necessary here.

Reliability in meeting obligations The coefficient of variation in earnings computed from a "sample" is only an estimate of the coefficient of variation in the underlying population. This estimate may be either larger or smaller than the actual coefficient. But, other things being equal, the longer a firm has conducted its business without requiring its creditors to take a loss, the less likely it is that its estimated coefficient of variation in earnings is much less than the coefficient in the hypothetical underlying population of annual net incomes. Hence, a measure of the length of time a firm has met all its obligations—the length of time the firm has been solvent—provides a correction for the estimate of risk of default derived from earnings variability. This measure has been designated as x_2. In estimating a firm's period of solvency, I took the length of time since the latest of the following events had occurred: The firm was founded; the firm emerged from bankruptcy; a compromise was made in which creditors settled for less than 100 per cent of their claims.

Capital structure Thus far, variations in a firm's earnings have been treated as though they were purely random fluctuations about some mean. Now let us modify this assumption and allow not only for these "random" fluctuations but also for shifts in the underlying mean income (or permanent earning power) of the firm, because we know that industries and firms do rise and fall over the years.

Capital assets have value only because they earn income. If investors believe that the earning power of a particular collection of assets has changed, the market value of those assets will change. When earnings variability is observed, it is impossible to distinguish between "random" fluctuations about the mean and fluctuations due to shifts in the mean itself. It is reasonable to believe that investors attribute variations in earnings to both causes. Earnings variability, then, is no longer a pure measure of random fluctuations. It also gives some information about the likelihood of future shifts in the earning power of the firm—about shifts in the value of the firm's assets. The investor will then be interested in how much the firm's assets can decline in value before they become less than its liabilities and the firm becomes insolvent. A measure of this factor is the ratio of the market value of the firm's equity to the par value of its debts. When this ratio is, say, nineteen, the firm's assets may fall 95 per cent in value before it becomes insolvent. But when the equity/debt ratio is one-fourth, a default can be expected if the assets lose only 20 per cent of their value. The equity/debt ratio has been designated as x_3.

MARKETABILITY

I have developed the hypothesis that investors believe that the risk that a firm's bonds will be defaulted depends on the firm's earnings variability, its period of solvency, and its equity debt ratio. Now let us consider the measurement of the other type of risk an investor incurs by holding a corporate bond, the risk associated with the difficulty of turning the bond into cash before it matures.

If securities markets were "perfect" (in the sense that the actions of a single individual could have only an infinitesimal effect on the price of a security), it would not be necessary to take up this topic at all; turning a bond into cash would be no problem. It is true that an investor who disposes of any interest-bearing security before maturity may have to take a loss because of changes in the pure interest rate between the time he buys his bond and the time he sells it. But such losses are allowed for by defining risk premium as the difference between the yield on the bond under consideration and the yield on a bond of the same maturity which is sure to be paid, so that compensation for possible changes in the pure rate of interest is present even in the yields on riskless bonds. Thus marketability can influence the risk premium only if it measures the degree of imperfection—the effect of a single individual's action on price—in the market for a particular security.[19]

How can an investor estimate the degree of imperfection of the market for a particular security? There are several possible ways. Imperfection of the market for bonds can be expected to result in bondholders' demanding compensation for risk because it makes the price and yield of a bond at any particular moment uncertain. Ideally, one might measure this uncertainty by finding the "random" fluctuations in the price of a bond over a short period. However, the bond market is often rather inactive.[20] Bond prices are subject both to random fluctuations and to changes caused by changes in the prospects of the firm and in the pure rate of interest. If the period of observation is made so short that the non-random changes in bond prices are negligible, it will also be too short to permit much random fluctuation.

[19]The holder of a risky bond may demand compensation simply because expectations about his bond may be subject to frequent change. But this type of "risk" is, I believe, merely an aspect of the risk of default itself.

[20]Total sales on the New York Stock Exchange of some of the listed issues included in the cross-sections were less than $50,000—50 bonds—a year. An issue may be quoted almost every day but not traded for six months or more.

The volume of trading and the "spread" between "bid" and "ask" prices are variables sometimes suggested as measures of marketability.[21] The volume of trading can be used only for bonds listed on some securities exchange.[22] In the abstract, "spread" could be applied to both listed and unlisted securities. But published quotations for listed bonds are "inside" (actual) prices, and quotations for over-the-counter securities are generally "outside" (nominal) prices. Hence neither of these measures can be used in this study, which includes both listed and unlisted securities.

The third variable that can be used as a measure of marketability is x_4, the total market value of the publicly traded bonds the firm has outstanding. This variable was used because it is applicable to both listed and over-the-counter securities. One of the reasons for believing that it is a good measure of marketability may be summarized as follows: Other things being equal, the smaller the amount of bonds a firm has outstanding, the less frequently we should expect its bonds to change hands. The less often its bonds change hands, the thinner the market; and the thinner the market, the more uncertain is the market price. Hence, other things being equal, the larger the market value of publicly traded bonds a firm has outstanding, the smaller is the expected risk premium on those bonds.

Thus we have the proposition that risk premium depends on estimated risk of default and on marketability. Risk of default depends on earnings variability, x_1; period of solvency, x_2; and equity/debt ratio, x_3. Marketability depends on bonds outstanding, x_4.[23]

---

[21]Cf. Graham and Dodd, *Security Analysis* (3d ed.; New York, 1951), p. 31.

[22]For a comparison of "volume of trading" with "bonds outstanding," the measure of marketability used in this study, see Section VII.

[23]This hypothesis might, perhaps, have been derived directly from Alfred Marshall's statements on the considerations involved in determining risk premiums on loans to entrepreneurs: "It is then necessary to analyse a little more carefully the extra risks which are introduced into business when much of the capital used in it has been borrowed. Let us suppose that two men are carrying on similar businesses, the one working with his own, the other chiefly with borrowed capital.

"There is one set of risks which is common to both; which may be described as the *trade risks* [A] of the particular business in which they are engaged. ... But there is another set of risks, the burden of which has to be borne by the man working with borrowed capital, and not by the other; and we may call them *personal risks*. For he who lends capital to be used by another for trade purposes, has to charge a high interest as insurance against the chances of some flaw or deficiency in the borrower's personal character or ability.

"The borrower may be less able than he appears [B], less energetic, or less honest. He has not the same inducements [C], as a man working with his own capital has, to look failure straight in the face, and withdraw from a speculative enterprise as soon as it shows signs of going against him ..." (*Principles of Economics* [4th ed.; London, 1898], p. 674; [8th ed.; New York, 1952], pp. 589–90 [italics his]).

My coefficient of variation of earnings can be identified with Marshall's "trade risks" [A] on the ground that the greater is the coefficient of variation, the greater are the trade risks; my period of solvency with Marshall's "the borrower may be less able than he appears" [B] on the ground that the longer a firm has operated successfully, the less likely it is that its success has been due to a run of good luck; and my equity/debt ratio directly with Marshall's "inducements" [C]. Marshall also notes the possible value of marketability (4th ed., p. 673 n.; 8th ed., p. 589 n.) and points out that investors may demand more than actuarial risk premiums (4th ed., p. 196 n.; 8th ed., p. 122 n.).

FORM OF THE FUNCTION

My hypothesis may now be stated as

$$x_0 = f(x_1, x_2, x_3, x_4).$$

To test the hypothesis, it was necessary to assume some form of the function.

If the influence of one independent variable on risk premium is independent of the magnitudes of the other independent variables, a linear function may be appropriate. If, however, the influence of one variable depends on the magnitudes of the other variables, then some other form is required.

It would appear that the latter is the case here. Let us again consider the two firms, one with an equity/debt ratio of 19, the other with an equity/debt ratio of one-fourth.[24] The risk of default on bonds of the first firm will probably be very small no matter how unstable its earnings may be; for in order for bondholders to suffer much of a loss if the firm's business should become unprofitable, the resale value of its assets would have to be less than 5 per cent of their present value to the business as a going concern. But holders of the bonds of the second firm will be very much interested in how likely it is that the firm will continue to earn enough to meet its obligations; for if its current business should become unprofitable, its assets would probably not be worth enough to pay off the bonds in full. Hence, we should expect the influence of one variable on risk of default to depend on the magnitudes of the other variables. If the risk of default is small, an investor can be quite certain of what the equilibrium price of his bonds is. For when the risk of default is small, estimates of that risk are unlikely to change much over time.[25] Hence if an investor wants to liquidate his holdings, he exposes himself to little uncertainty by borrowing temporarily on the security of his bonds. But when the risk of default is large, his collateral does not enable the bondholder to obtain so large a loan at any given rate of interest. Thus the holder of a risky bond will have more incentive to sell quickly, at less than equilibrium price. Marketability, then, also becomes more important as the other variables indicate more risk of default.

A function which behaves in the manner implied by the preceding paragraph is given in equation (8)[26]

$$x_0 = a_0' x_{11}^a x_{22}^a x_{33}^a x_{44}^a. \tag{8}$$

[24]These numbers are well within the range of the equity/debt ratios of firms included in the cross-sections.

[25]See any recent *Moody's Manual*, p. v.

[26]Eqs. (1) = (7) are described in Table 1.

This form is particularly convenient for multiple regression analysis because the method of least squares may be applied when equation (8) is transformed to

$$X_0 = a_0 + a_1 X_1 + a_2 X_2 + a_3 X_3 + a_4 X_4,$$

which is the hypothesis described in the introduction.[27]

This hypothesis was tested for cross-sections of domestic industrial corporations. The results it gave will be compared with the results given by alternative hypotheses and with the results of some other studies not directly related to this one.

V. SOME ALTERNATIVE MEASURES

The independent variables used in my hypothesis are plausible, but they were selected rather arbitrarily. Some alternatives are also plausible. The use of x_1, the coefficient of variation in earnings for the last nine years, requires the implicit assumption that investors expect the firm's average annual earnings in the future to equal the average for the last nine years. We do not know that this is true. But we do know that the market value of a firm's expected future earnings is given by the market value of the firm's equity and that this market value is highly correlated with expected future earnings. Thus an alternative to x_1, earnings variability, for measuring expected variability of earnings is the ratio of the standard deviation in earnings for the last nine years to the market value of the equity in a firm. Let us call this measure x_8.

When the equity/debt ratio is included in the function (eq. 8), the measure of marketability, x_4, becomes an inefficient measure of the size of a firm, for total debt and bonds outstanding are highly correlated. Is it not possible that investors merely prefer to invest their funds in securities issued by large firms? If the answer to this question is in the affirmative, it would be better to use a more efficient measure of firm size. When the equity/debt ratio is included, such a measure is the market value of the equity in a firm. Let us call this measure x_5.[28]

The results obtained by substituting x_8 for x_1 and x_5 for x_4 will be reported in Section VII.

---

[27]Recall that $X_i = \log_{10} x_i$.

[28]Equity is the more efficient measure because, when the equity/debt ratio is held constant, total capital of a firm and equity are perfectly correlated. In this context, total debt is an equally efficient measure of firm size.

VI. SUMMARY OF STATISTICAL PROCEDURES

SELECTION OF THE CROSS-SECTIONS

The hypotheses presented in Sections I and V were tested on cross-sections of domestic industrial companies. The tests were restricted to firms domiciled in the United States because a lender to a foreign corporation may incur risks of a kind not present in lending to domestic corporations. Only "industrial" corporations[29] were included because public utilities and transportation companies are subject to forms of regulation which prevent their maximizing profits.[30] In the event of a decline in earnings, the regulatory bodies are presumably required to relax their restrictions enough to allow earnings to return to a "fair" level. Hence there are grounds for believing that, other things being equal, if a public utility and a manufacturing or retailing firm have the same earnings variability, the public utility is less likely to default on its bonds. If this is true, public utilities and industrial firms should not be analyzed in the same cross-section.

All domestic industrial corporations were included if meaningful data for testing the hypothesis described in Section I could be obtained for them from the sources consulted. The *Commercial and Financial Chronicle* and the *Bank and Quotation Record* were the main sources for security prices; *Moody's Industrial Manual* was the chief source of other data. In general, "meaningful data" were not available for companies with any of the following characteristics:

1. The firm's risk premium could not be estimated if
   a. Price quotations were not available for at least one bond issue at each significant level of seniority
   b. The only price quotations available for a class of bonds were for issues quoted at substantially above the call price or for issues whose quotations had obviously been affected by convertibility privileges or by the issue's having been called
   c. Substantial bond issues were those of subsidiaries or affiliates and the parent firm was not responsible for their debts
   d. The firm was in or about to go into receivership
   e. The firm had defaulted or was about to default on at least one of its bond issues

---

[29]For the purposes of this study, industrial firms are defined as firms which would have been included in recent issues of *Moody's Industrial Manual*. This definition includes all types of corporations except public utilities, transportation companies, financial institutions, governments, or corporations not incorporated for profit.
[30]Inclusion of financial institutions would probably require analyzing the structure of their assets.

2. Earnings variability could not be estimated if
   a. Substantially complete and comparable consolidated income statements were not available for either the firm's period of solvency or for nine years
   b. The firm's period of solvency was less than two years
3. The market value of the firm's equity could not be estimated if quotations were lacking for substantial stock issues

December 31, 1953, was chosen for the initial test because it was the most recent date for which data were available in *Moody's Industrial Manual* when this study was begun (May, 1955). The other dates were chosen in order to get the cross-sections spaced over time and from periods of widely differing business and financial conditions.

MEASUREMENT OF THE VARIABLES

Risk premium, x_0 I have defined the risk premium on a bond as the difference between its market yield to maturity and the yield on a riskless bond having the same maturity date. When the coupon rate and maturity date of a bond are known, its yield may be found by finding its price and looking up the yield in a book of bond tables. In general, price was found by taking the last sale price on December 31 or the mean of the closing "bid" and "ask" quotations on December 31.[31] In computing yields, this price was adjusted by adding a quarter of a point (for 1927 and 1932) or half a point[32] (for 1937, 1949, and 1953) to allow for a buyer's transactions cost. Thus the yields I computed were estimates of yields facing potential buyers.

Hypothetical pure rates for 1949 and 1953 were obtained from yields on fully taxable United States treasury bonds. On the earlier dates, interest on government bonds was wholly or partially exempt from income taxes. Hence, yields on governments were not directly comparable with yields on industrials. For 1927, 1932, and 1937, estimates of pure rates were based on "basic yield" series compiled by the National Bureau of Economic Research for the first quarter of the year following.[33]

The average risk premium on a firm's bonds, x_0, was taken as a weighted average of the risk premiums on its individual issues.

Earnings variability, x_1 The coefficient of variation in earnings, x_1, was generally computed from statements of consolidated net income

---

[31]Bond prices are in per cent of par value. Stock prices are usually in dollars a share.
[32]For bonds, a point is 1 per cent of par value; for stocks, usually one dollar a share.
[33]For a description of these series see David Durand, *Basic Yields on Corporate Bonds,* 1900–1942 (National Bureau of Economic Research, technical paper No. 3) (New York, 1942).

for nine consecutive years.[34] If a firm engaged in unusual accounting practices—for example, if it had set up surplus reserves out of income or was using last-in–first-out inventory valuation—it was necessary to exclude the firm from the cross-section unless its statements could be adjusted.

Period of solvency, x_2 The methods used to estimate this variable have been described in Section IV. It should be pointed out, however, that for many firms the information in *Moody's* permits only a very rough estimate to be made of x_2, the period of solvency.

Equity/debt ratio, x_3 In computing the equity/debt ratio, it was first necessary to estimate equity, x_5, and debt, x_6. Equity was taken as the total market value of all shares of stock (both preferred and common) and all warrants for the purchase of stock outstanding and in the hands of the public. In general, total debt, x_6, was taken as total par value outstanding of bonds, notes, debentures, conditional sales contracts, mortgages, and judgments for which the firm was obligor or guarantor. Any current liabilities other than these were not counted because they often vary a great deal during the course of a firm's fiscal year. The equity/debt ratio, x_3, was then obtained by dividing x_5 by x_6.

Bonds outstanding, x_4 Bonds outstanding, the market value of publicly traded debt, was found by multiplying the par value of each publicly traded issue included in a firm's total debt by its unadjusted price. I assumed that an issue was publicly traded if I had price quotations for it or if *Moody's* stated that the issue was listed or traded on an organized securities exchange or quoted in some financial center.

Volume of trading, x_7 To find the volume of trading, total sales of each issue on each securities exchange were multiplied by the mean of the high and low sales price of the bond for the year preceding the date of the cross-section. The estimates of the volume of trading in each issue for the year were then added to get x_7, the volume of trading in a firm's publicly traded bonds. This variable was computed for firms which had all their bonds outstanding listed or traded on the New York Stock Exchange or the American Stock Exchange, provided that no issue had been offered or retired during the year and there was no issue whose price had obviously been affected by convertibility privileges.

Ratio of standard deviation in earnings to equity, x_8 This alternative

[34]If the firm's period of solvency was less than nine years, years before the beginning of the period of solvency were excluded. Except for 1949, the nine-year period ended approximately on the date for which the cross-section was taken. For 1949 the period ended near December 31, 1953. The latter date had been used for the initial cross-section; 1949 was used for the first recheck. By using the same period for the computation of x_1 for both cross-sections, much labor was saved. The partial regression coefficients of X_1 computed in this manner were identical for both cross-sections. In view of this result, it was decided not to make the effort necessary to have the data for 1949 strictly comparable with the data for the other dates.

index of the variability of earnings was computed by dividing the standard deviation of earnings, which had been used in computing x_1, by equity, x_5.

SEQUENCE IN WHICH THE TESTS WERE CARRIED OUT

Before any data were gathered for 1953, I had tentatively concluded that risk premium was a function of earnings variability, x_1, and equity/ debt ratio, x_3. While these data were being collected, it became apparent to me that period of solvency, x_2, would probably be an empirically significant variable. The first test of this hypothesis was performed by finding the multiple regression of X_0 on $X_1, X_2, X_5,$ and X_6 for December 31, 1953. All these variables were found to be significant, but it was also found that the simple correlation between X_0 and X_6 was negative and almost as great as the multiple correlation.[35] The necessity for finding a plausible explanation for this phenomenon led to the use of the hypothesis summarized in Section I and developed in Sections III and IV. No further change was made in this hypothesis. When data for the third cross-section (1937) were obtained, it was noted that twenty firms had to be excluded only because they had negative values of x_1, and no X_1 could be defined for them. The alternative index of variability of earnings, x_8, was thought of as a means of avoiding this restriction on the scope of the hypothesis.

VII. FURTHER RESULTS

The data from the five cross-sections are summarized in Table 2. This table and some simple calculations[36] reveal that, although the simple regression coefficients all have the signs which would be expected on the basis of the analysis in Section IV, these simple regression coefficients and the coefficients of simple correlation between the logarithm of risk premium, X_0, and the logarithms of the independent variables vary widely between dates.

But, as shown in Section II, both the multiple correlation coefficients and the partial regression coefficients which result from testing the hypothesis stated in the introduction are remarkably stable from cross-section

[35]For 1953, $r_{06} = -0.76$; $R_{0.1256} = 0.89$. However, r_{06} was unstable. It was not significantly different from zero for 1932.
[36]The simple regression coefficients and simple correlation coefficients may be obtained from Table 2 by applying the formulas

$$b_i = \sigma_0^2 i / \sigma_i^2,$$

$$r_0^2 i = b_i \sigma_0^2 i / \sigma_0^2.$$

TABLE 2. Means, variances, and covariances of the common logarithms of the variables*

Variable	Date	Mean				Variance or covariance				
			X_0	X_1	X_2	X_3	X_4	X_5	X_6	
X_0	1927	0.1251	0.0740	0.0554	-0.0098	-0.0368	-0.0322	-0.1132	0.1565
	1932	0.6997	.2008	.0871	-.0441	-.1757	-.0976	-.2130	.0853
	1937	0.3385	.1706	.0913	-.0562	-.0936	-.1397	-.2261	
	1949	0.0261	.1752	.0770	-.0970	-.0861	-.2168	-.2837	
	1953	-0.0811	.2058	.0907	-.0717	-.0623	-.2405	-.3071	
	Average	0.1783	.1650	.0808	-.0576	-.0933	.1533		
	Over-all	0.1783	0.2260	.1176	-.0768	-.1257	.1684		
X_1	1927	-0.0873		.1404	.0141	-.0578	-.0186	-.0739	.1426
	1932	-0.0134		.1238	-.0108	-.1023	-.0044	-.0774	.1384
	1937	0.1650		.2430	.0417	-.0289	-.0669	-.0929	
	1949	-0.3240		.0882	-.0603	-.0378	-.1010	-.1260	
	1953	-0.3276		.1045	-.0375	-.0250	-.1208	-.1415	
	Average	-0.1219		.1443	-.0095	-.0443	-.0696		
	Over-all	-0.1219		0.1843	-.0303	-.0554	-.0855		
X_2	1927	1.3646			.0759	-.0232	.0118	-.0102	-.0324
	1932	1.3692			.1163	.0487	.0271	.0642	.0285
	1937	1.2620			.1680	.0300	.0389	.0628	
	1949	1.4495			.1529	.0464	.1349	.1694	
	1953	1.5717			.0896	.0116	.0849	.0995	
	Average	1.4070			.1219	.0208	.0624		
	Over-all	1.4070			0.1344	.0257	.0716		

X_3

1927	0.4688	.2270	—.0735	.1419	—.1919
1932	—0.0522	.2628	.0263	.2348	—.0594
1937	0.2942	.1639	—.0101	.1454	
1949	0.3510	.1011	.0869	.1705	
1953	0.4010	.0896	.0360	.1126	
Average	0.3225	.1567	.0125		
Over-all	0.3225	0.1799	.0201		

X_4

1927	1.0117		.3218	.2473	—.0287
1932	0.8624		.2819	.2703	.0594
1937	0.7000		.4217	.3876	
1949	0.8541		.4249	.4858	
1953	0.9830		.4692	.4967	
Average	0.8792		.3972		
Over-all	0.8792		0.4112		

X_5

1927	1.5265			.3800	—.1732
1932	0.9984			.4418	.1399
1937	1.1259			.5566	
1949	1.3035			.6366	
1953	1.5691			0.6360	

X_6

1932	0.6484				.2274
1937	1.0368				0.1483

*For definitions of variables see text.

to cross-section.[37] Thus we have concluded that the partial elasticities of risk premium with respect to coefficient of variation in earnings, period of solvency, equity/debt ratio, and market value of publicly traded bonds outstanding are significantly different from zero and are relatively stable over time for domestic industrial corporations.

COMPARISONS WITH ALTERNATE HYPOTHESES

Equity, x_5, was substituted for bonds outstanding, x_4, in order to use a better measure of the size of firms in the regression for each of the five cross-sections. The resulting coefficient of multiple correlation, $R_{0.1235}$,

[37]An approximate test of the significance of the differences of the partial regression coefficients among the cross-sections is provided by the following:

Suppose that the estimated partial regression coefficients, b_{it}, from the separate samples $t = 1 \ldots T$ are all estimates from the same population. Let s_{it} be the standard error of estimate of b_{it} and let

$$b_{t^*} = \frac{\sum\limits_{t=1}^{T} b_{it}/s_i^2{}_t}{\sum\limits_{t=1}^{T} 1/s_i^2{}_t}.$$

Then the statistic

$$y = \sum_{t=1}^{T} \frac{(b_{it} - b_i{}^*)^2}{s{t}^2{}_i}$$

has approximately the χ^2 distribution with $T - 1$ degrees of freedom. Hence an improbably high value of y is cause for rejecting the hypothesis that the partial regression coefficients are estimates from the same population. (This test was suggested by David L. Wallace.)

When the test was applied to the partial regression coefficients shown in Table 1 for $t = 1927, 1932, 1937, 1949, 1953$, the results shown in the following table were obtained.

Coef- ficient	y	Probability of obtaining as large a χ^2	Accept hypoth- esis that all samples have the same coefficient?
(1)	(2)	(3)	(4)
a_1	0.72	0.95	Yes
a_2	5.13	.275	Yes
a_3	2.72	.61	Yes
a_4	16.86	0.0022	No

The partial regression coefficient is shown in column 1. The value of y actually obtained is shown in column 2. The probability of obtaining a value of χ^2 as large as that actually found, if the regression coefficients are independent and the differences in a_i among the cross-sections are due entirely to random errors of sampling, is shown in column 3. The decision concerning the hypothesis is indicated in column 4.

Although a_4, the coefficient of bonds outstanding, appears to vary significantly, the effects of this variation are small. The root mean-square standard error of estimate X_0 from the regressions for the separate cross-sections is 0.2076. For the pooled-moments regression (eq. [1]) it is only 0.2094—less than 1 per cent greater.

was slightly smaller than $R_{0.1234}$ for all but the 1953 cross-section, for which it was slightly larger.[38] The largest difference between corresponding values of a_1 and $b_{01.235}$, a_2 and $b_{02.135}$, and a_4 and $b_{05.123}$ was 0.035. However, the range of values for $b_{03.125}$ was -0.149 to -0.324, while the range for a_3 was only -0.404 to -0.531. Thus bonds outstanding, x_4, appears to be the better variable. It seems to lead to better prediction of risk premiums and, when it is used, the elasticity estimates are more nearly stable. This result was confirmed when it was found that when both variables are used, although the estimates of $b_{03.1245}$, $b_{04.1235}$, and $b_{05.1234}$ are all rather poor because of the multicollinearity among X_3, X_4, and X_5; the minimum ratio of $b_{04.1235}$ to its standard error is 0.86, a value exceeded by the ratio of $b_{05.1234}$ to its standard error in only two of the five cross-sections. However, we must distinguish between the two hypotheses chiefly on economic, rather than statistical, grounds. Both risk premium, x_0, and bonds outstanding, x_4, depend on market price. While the correlation between X_0 and X_4 from this source is undoubtedly very small, the multicollinearity among X_3, X_4, and X_5 is so great that the influence of the autocorrelation on $b_{04.1235}$ may not be negligible. On economic grounds, X_4 is clearly superior to X_5. Large corporations, we find, are able to borrow at lower cost than small corporations, other things being equal. Variable X_4 offers an explantion; X_5 merely repeats the statement.

My tests of the ratio of the standard deviation of earnings to equity, x_8, as an alternative to the coefficient of variation of past earnings, x_1, are also somewhat inconclusive.[39] For 1932, X_8 appears to be a slightly better variable. For 1937, X_1 appears to be a considerably better variable. Of the two, X_8 has meaning for the larger number of firms; but X_8 is more highly correlated with X_2, X_3, and X_4 than is X_1.[40] It would appear that the market value of the equity in a firm depends not only on the expectation of the firm's earnings but also on the other factors which determine the risk premiums on the firm's bonds. Since the use of X_1 is based on the arbitrary assumption that investors expect the future average annual earnings of a firm to equal the arithmetic mean of the last nine years' earnings and since neither X_1 nor X_8 is clearly superior to the other, I am sure that an index of expected future earnings can be found that is better than that used in computing either X_1 or X_8. Such a variable could probably best be found in a study of the determinants of market value of equity organized along lines similar to those followed in this study.

[38]The difference between the R's for this sample was the third largest of five.

[39]Compare equations (9) and (10) (Table 3) with equations (4) and (5) (Table 1).

[40]Other things being equal, the standard errors of partial regression coefficients increase as certain elements of the inverse of the variance-covariance matrix of the independent variables increase. These elements depend in part on the collinearities among the independent variables. For 1932 and 1937, five out of six such elements were greater when X_8 was used than the corresponding elements when X_1 was used.

TABLE 3. *Regression equation under the hypothesis that*
$$X_0 = d_0 + d_8X_8 + d_2X_2 + d_3X_3 + d_4X_4$$

Equation	Date	No. of firms	Degrees of freedom	R^2	d_0	d_8 (s_8)	d_2 (s_2)	d_3 (s_3)	d_4 (s_4)
9	1932	45	40	0.738	1.186	+0.295 (.123)	−0.060 (.112)	−0.415 (.117)	−0.272 (.069)
10	1937	89	84	0.693	1.304	+.326 (0.080)	−.254 (0.067)	−.423 (0.072)	−.261 (0.042)

TABLE 4. *Comparison of Moody's daily indexes of yields on industrial bonds with similar indexes implied by this study*

Dec. 31 (1)	Moody's Daily Indexes (Per Cent)			Indexes implied by this study (Per Cent)		
	Aaa (2)	Baa (3)	Difference (4)	High grade (5)	Medium grade (6)	Difference (7)
1927	4.60*	5.50*	0.90*	4.59	5.71	1.12
1932	4.53	7.22	2.69	4.27	6.81	2.54
1937	2.95	4.64	1.69	2.60	4.20	1.60
1949	2.51	2.87	0.39	2.48	3.68	1.20
1953	3.07	3.64	0.57	3.03	4.42	1.39

*Read from a graph, not strictly comparable with other dates.
SOURCES: Moody's Indexes: *Moody's Investment Survey* and *Moody's Bond Survey* Implied Indexes. Yields on bonds of firms with risk premiums implied by equation (1) (1953 constant term) of less than 0.40 per cent for high grade and between 1.00 per cent and 1.50 per cent for medium grade.

The major reason for using X_8, however, was to test the applicability of the general hypothesis to firms whose net earnings have been negative. Figure 4 shows the scatter of 1937 risk premiums for the 89 firms included in regression equation (10), Table 3, and for 20 firms with negative mean earnings not included in that regression, plotted against values of x_0 estimated from that regression equation. It is obvious from Figure 4

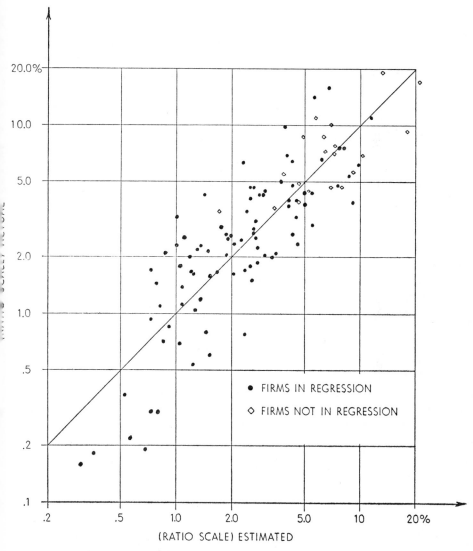

FIGURE 4 Scatter of December 31, 1937, risk premiums against risk premiums estimated from equation (10).

that these 20 risk premiums are predicted with about as much precision as the 89.

Thus it appears that, where applicable, the variables of the main hypothesis, specified in Section I, are superior to the alternative variables suggested in Section V for the purpose of estimating the elasticities of risk premium with respect to factors indicating risks incurred by lenders.

Possible Sources of Error

When X_0, the logarithm of risk premium, is estimated from equation (1), its standard error of estimate is 0.2094, which indicates that approximately two thirds of the estimates of x_0, risk premium, are between 62 per cent and 162 per cent of the measured values. Let us consider the possible reasons for the errors in these estimates. If the variables I have used are proper ones and the form of the function I have used is correct, these errors must be due to four causes: errors in the measurement of risk premium; errors in the measurement of the independent variables; omission of relevant variables from the hypothesis; and randomness of bond prices or imperfect adjustment of the market prices of securities to their "equilibrium" values.

Errors in risk premiums   Errors in the measurement of risk premium exist for two reasons. There are errors in the yields of bonds, and there are errors in the "pure rate of interest." Errors in the yields of the bonds arose because for many firms I had to rely on the mean of "bid" and "ask" prices. Since these two prices are not the same, one can observe only a range within which the true yield of a bond must lie. Given the "spread" (difference between the bid and ask prices), this uncertainty in the bond yield becomes more serious (since the logarithm of risk premium is used in the regression equations) the nearer the yield is to the pure rate and the shorter the time until the bond matures.

I believe that the errors in X_0, the logarithm of risk premium, introduced by the "random" errors in price are, in general, uniformly distributed over the range of risk premiums. For the spread in price quotations generally narrows as a bond approaches maturity and as its market yield approaches the pure rate. That part of the standard error of estimate of X_0 which is due to the uncertainty of bond prices is perhaps 0.05 (or about 11 per cent of the value of x_0). Elimination of random errors of this magnitude would raise the squares of the coefficients of multiple correlation by only about 0.02. Not much of the error in estimating risk premium can be due to this cause.

Errors in the pure rate of interest introduce both random and systematic errors in the values of X_0. Errors in the "pattern" of rates may introduce random errors in X_0. But errors in the general level of the pattern can produce nonlinearities in the function, for an error of given magnitude in the pure rate will cause a larger error in the logarithm of a small risk premium than it will cause in the logarithm of a large risk premium. Overestimating the level of pure interest rates may be the cause of the slight nonlinearities of the scatter in Figure 1 for 1937 and 1953. Since I do not know the errors in the pure rates, I cannot estimate the effects of such errors on the correlation coefficients. It is interesting to note, however, that the multiple correlation coefficients for the dates before World War II are less than the multiple correlation coefficients for the postwar dates. For the former dates basic yield series of the National Bureau of Economic Research were used in estimating pure rates—these series are hypothetical; for the latter dates yields on United States government bonds were used—these series were actually observed.

Errors in independent variables The errors in the measurement of all independent variables except X_2 are believed to be negligible. Random errors in X_2 resulting in a standard error of estimate of X_2 of 0.0791 (20 per cent of the period of solvency, x_2) would have a negligible effect on equation (1). A standard error of 0.176 (two-thirds of observed values of x_2 between $\frac{2}{8}$ and $\frac{3}{2}$ times the actual values) would have decreased R^2 by about 0.02, a_1 by 0.005, and a_2 by 0.088 and increased a_3 by 0.012 and a_4 by 0.014 (all in absolute magnitude) from their "true" values.[41] I believe that 0.176 is larger than the actual standard error of estimate of X_2. Furthermore, it would appear that the errors in X_2 are negatively correlated with the actual values. Such errors would tend to increase the absolute magnitude of a_2. Hence it appears that the estimates of elasticities in equation (1) can be taken at their face value.

Omission of variables The problem of the omission of relevant variables is a difficult one. Possible omitted variables are of two kinds: those which would indicate the probability of default and expected loss in the event of a default, and those which take account of the differences in the ways in which interest income and capital gains are taxed.

The latter is a less serious problem. If a bond is bought for par or above, all income from the bond is taxed as ordinary income if the investor holds the bond until maturity. If, however, the investor buys the bond below par, only the interest payments on the bonds are taxed as ordinary income. The difference between the purchase price and the amount for which the bond is redeemed is a capital gain. This difference in tax is difficult to take into account. One would expect the market yield on a bond with a high coupon rate to be higher than the yield on a bond with a low coupon rate because the former is more likely to sell above par if other

[41]For a method of finding biases in partial regression coefficients when one independent variable is subject to (known) random error, see Gregory C. Chow, "Demand for Automobiles in the United States" (Doctoral dissertation in the University of Chicago Library), Appendix I.

things are equal. But bonds with the highest coupon rates will tend to be issued by the firms most likely to default. Hence one would expect to find the coupon rate correlated with other independent variables. Another effect also tends to obscure any effect of a high coupon rate. The investor in such a bond will get his income somewhat sooner than the investor in an equivalent bond with a low coupon rate—the high-coupon-rate bond has a shorter "duration." If the term-structure of interest rates is higher for long-term securities than for short-term securities, the high-coupon-rate bond will tend to have the lower yield—the tax and duration effects will largely offset each other. Long-term rates were substantially higher than short-term rates for all dates in this study except December 31, 1927.

Other variables that might have been taken into account are various terms contained in the bond indenture. These terms relate to the type of lien the bondholders have; the conditions, if any, under which the firm may issue additional bonds having the same or a higher lien; restrictions on dividends and sale of assets; conditions under which the indenture may be modified; sinking-fund and call provisions; the ratio of current assets to liabilities which the firm must maintain; and possibly other provisions.

One would expect that, if these provisions were included in the regressions, much of their effect on risk premiums would be obscured; for the companies least likely to default usually borrow without incurring many restrictions on their future operations. Even where this is not the case, it is difficult to appraise the effects of many indenture provisions on risk premium. Perhaps an indenture can be modified if holders of two-thirds of the issue consent, or perhaps there is not provision for modification. If the company must extend its bonds to avoid receivership, some bondholders will be better off if the indenture can be modified; others may consider themselves worse off. Hence, it is difficult to say whether a provision permitting modification will tend to raise or lower risk premium. This is an illustration of the difficulties of taking indenture provisions into account. I am not a professional security analyst and was forced to neglect these provisions largely because of my lack of knowledge.[42]

RELATIONSHIP BETWEEN x_4 AND x_7

Some attempt was made to compare bonds outstanding, x_4, with volume of bonds traded, x_7. For each of the prewar cross-sections a

[42]Herbert Arkin, in "A Statistical Analysis of the Internal Factors Affecting the Yields on Domestic Corporate Bonds" (Doctoral dissertation, Columbia University [Hewlett, N.Y., 1940]), attempted to measure the influence on bond yields of factors that are almost all specified by the bond contract. He could account for only 23 per cent and 13 per cent of the variance in yields of industrials at year-end 1927 and mid-year 1932, respectively. Since Arkin did not take the chief determinants of risk premiums into account (only coupon rate was significant in both of his industrial samples), it is difficult to say what the real importance of indenture provisions is. Arkin's is the only previous study I have found in which multiple regression analysis was used in attempting to discover how market prices of bonds are determined.

correlation coefficient of about 0.8 was found between the logarithms of these variables; for the postwar cross-sections a correlation coefficient of about 0.7 was found. The annual volume of trading was about 10 per cent of bonds outstanding for the prewar years, but only about 1 per cent for the postwar years. Furthermore, the data for x_7 appear to be poor. For many issues different publications showed rather different volumes of trading. Moreover, there appears to be no relationship between residual risk premiums estimated from equation (1) and residual volume of trading estimated from bonds outstanding. These results, which show lower correlations in years of inactive markets, are consistent with the argument advanced in Section IV for bonds outstanding, x_4, as a measure of marketability.

STABILITY OF THE LEVEL OF RISK PREMIUMS

This study was not designed to measure whether the level of the regression equation is constant between cross-sections, since to do so we would have to know whether the determinants of stock prices are stable. Nevertheless, it appears that investors' behavior in the bond market is more stable than one would infer merely from inspecting the spreads between Moody's Aaa and Baa indexes of corporate bond yields. These spreads are shown in Table 4 [see page 290].

The coefficient of variation of the differences between Moody's Baa and Aaa indexes is 0.76. The similar coefficient for the implied indexes is only 0.365. If these spreads are assumed to be normally distributed over time, one must reject the hypothesis that the spreads between Moody's indexes are at least as stable as the spreads between the implied indexes if one uses the 10 per cent level of significance, even though each series shown in Table 4 has only four degrees of freedom. The spreads, however, are highly correlated. The coefficient of correlation between the values in columns 4 and 7 of Table 4 is 0.924, which is significantly different from zero at the 2.5 per cent level, even though this regression has only three degrees of freedom. However, if the values of x_1 and x_3 were adjusted to take changes in corporation income tax rates into account, the spread in the implied indexes for 1932 would almost certainly be reduced.

The problem of whether or not the level of risk premiums, given the factors showing risks incurred by investors, is stable over time cannot be answered conclusively on the basis of this study. If the variables I have used should prove to give the most nearly stable level of risk premiums over time, then it is clear that investors' behavior could not be deemed stable over time. For the improvement of the estimates of risk premium which occurs when one goes from equation (2), which assumes both a stable level and stable elasticities, to equation (1), which does not assume a stable level, is clearly significant.

CONCLUSION

This study shows that economic and statistical methods are applicable to security analysis. Although by its design it could not show whether investor behavior is rational or even stable, we now know that, at least in the bond market, elasticities are reasonably stable over time.

PART 4. Portfolio Selection,
Common Stocks,
and Institutional Portfolios

Portfolio Selection*

Harry Markowitz

The process of selecting a portfolio may be divided into two stages. The first stage starts with observation and experience and ends with beliefs about the future performances of available securities. The second stage starts with the relevant beliefs about future performances and ends with the choice of portfolio. This paper is concerned with the second stage. We first consider the rule that the investor does (or should) maximize discounted expected, or anticipated, returns. This rule is rejected both as a hypothesis to explain, and as a maxim to guide investment behavior. We next consider the rule that the investor does (or should) consider expected return a desirable thing *and* variance of return an undesirable thing. This rule has many sound points, both as a maxim for, and hypothesis about, investment behavior. We illustrate geometrically relations between beliefs and choice of portfolio according to the "expected returns—variance of returns" rule.

One type of rule concerning choice of portfolio is that the investor does (or should) maximize the discounted (or capitalized) value of future returns.[1] Since the future is not known with certainty, it must be "expected" or "anticipated" returns which we discount. Variations of this type of rule can be suggested. Following Hicks, we could let "anticipated" returns include an allowance for risk.[2] Or, we could let the rate at which we capitalize the returns from particular securities vary with risk.

The hypothesis (or maxim) that the investor does (or should) maximize discounted return must be rejected. If we ignore market imperfections the foregoing rule never implies that there is a diversified portfolio which

*From the *Journal of Finance*, 7, no. 1, March 1952, pp. 77–91. Back numbers can be obtained from the Kraus Reprint Corporation, New York. This paper is based on work done by the author while at the Cowles Commission for Research in Economics and with the financial assistance of the Social Science Research Council. It will be reprinted as Cowles Commission Paper, New Series, No. 60.

[1]See, for example, J. B. Williams, *The Theory of Investment Value* (Cambridge, Mass.: Harvard University Press, 1938), pp. 55–75.

[2]J. R. Hicks, *Value and Capital* (New York: Oxford University Press, 1939), p. 126. Hicks applies the rule to a firm rather than a portfolio.

is preferable to all non-diversified portfolios. Diversification is both observed and sensible; a rule of behavior which does not imply the superiority of diversification must be rejected both as a hypothesis and as a maxim.

The foregoing rule fails to imply diversification no matter how the anticipated returns are formed; whether the same or different discount rates are used for different securities; no matter how these discount rates are decided upon or how they vary over time.[3] The hypothesis implies that the investor places all his funds in the security with the greatest discounted value. If two or more securities have the same value, then any of these or any combination of these is as good as any other.

We can see this analytically: suppose there are N securities; let r_{it} be the anticipated return (however decided upon) at time t per dollar invested in security i; let d_{it} be the rate at which the return on the ith security at time t is discounted back to the present; let X_i be the relative amount invested in security i. We exclude short sales, thus $X_i \geq 0$ for all i. Then the discounted anticipated return of the portfolio is

$$R = \sum_{t=1}^{\infty} \sum_{i=1}^{N} d_{it} r_{it} X$$

$$= \sum_{i=1}^{N} X_i \left(\sum_{t=1}^{\infty} d_{it} r_{it} \right)$$

$R_i = \sum_{t=1}^{\infty} d_{it} r_{it}$ is the discounted return of the ith security, therefore

$R = \Sigma X_i R_i$ where R_i is independent of X_i. Since $X_i \geq 0$ for all i and $\Sigma X_i = 1$, R is a weighted average of R_i with the X_i as non-negative weights. To maximize R, we let $X_i = 1$ for i with maximum R_i. If several Ra_a, $a = 1, \ldots, K$ are maximum then any allocation with

$$\sum_{a=1}^{K} Xa_a = 1$$

maximizes R. In no case is a diversified portfolio preferred to all non-diversified portfolios.[4]

It will be convenient at this point to consider a static model. Instead of speaking of the time series of returns from the ith security (r_{i1}, $r_{i2}, \ldots, r_{it}, \ldots$) we will speak of "the flow of returns" (r_i) from the ith

[3]The results depend on the assumption that the anticipated returns and discount rates are independent of the particular investor's portfolio.

[4]If short sales were allowed, an infinite amount of money would be placed in the security with highest r.

security. The flow of returns from the portfolio as a whole is $R = \Sigma X_i r_i$. As in the dynamic case if the investor wished to maximize "anticipated" return from the portfolio he would place all his funds in that security with maximum anticipated returns.

There is a rule which implies both that the investor should diversify and that he should maximize expected return. The rule states that the investor does (or should) diversify his funds among all those securities which give maximum expected return. The law of large numbers will insure that the actual yield of the portfolio will be almost the same as the expected yield.[5] This rule is a special case of the expected returns— variance of returns rule (to be presented below). It assumes that there is a portfolio which gives both maximum expected return and minimum variance, and it commends this portfolio to the investor.

This presumption, that the law of large numbers applies to a portfolio of securities, cannot be accepted. The returns from securities are too intercorrelated. Diversification cannot eliminate all variance.

The portfolio with maximum expected return is not necessarily the one with minimum variance. There is a rate at which the investor can gain expected return by taking on variance, or reduce variance by giving up expected return.

We saw that the expected returns or anticipated returns rule is inadequate. Let us now consider the expected returns—variance of returns $(E\text{-}V)$ rule. It will be necessary to first present a few elementary concepts and results of mathematical statistics. We will then show some implications of the $E\text{-}V$ rule. After this we will discuss its plausibility.

In our presentation we try to avoid complicated mathematical statements and proofs. As a consequence a price is paid in terms of rigor and generality. The chief limitations from this source are (1) we do not derive our results analytically for the n-security case; instead, we present them geometrically for the 3 and 4 security cases; (2) we assume static probability beliefs. In a general presentation we must recognize that the probability distribution of yields of the various securities is a function of time. The writer intends to present, in the future, the general, mathematical treatment which removes these limitations.

We will need the following elementary concepts and results of mathematical statistics:

Let Y be a random variable, i.e., a variable whose value is decided by chance. Suppose, for simplicity of exposition, that Y can take on a finite number of values $y_1, y_2, \ldots, y_N$. Let the probability that $Y = y_1$, be p_1; that $Y = y_2$ be p_2 etc. The expected value (or mean) of Y is defined to be

$$E = p_1 y_1 + p_2 y_2 + \ldots + p_N y_N$$

[5]Williams, *op. cit.*, pp. 68, 69.

The variance of Y is defined to be

$$V = p_1(y_1 - E)^2 + p_2(y_2 - E)^2 + \ldots + p_N(y_N - E)^2$$

V is the average squared deviation of Y from its expected value. V is a commonly used measure of dispersion. Other measures of dispersion, closely related to V are the standard deviation, $\sigma = \sqrt{V}$ and the coefficient of variation, σ/E.

Suppose we have a number of random variables: $R_1, \ldots, R_n$. If R is a weighted sum (linear combination) of the R_i

$$R = a_1R_1 + a_2R_2 + \ldots + a_nR_n$$

then R is also a random variable. (For example, R_1 may be the number which turns up on one die; R_2, that of another die, and R the sum of these numbers. In this case $n = 2$, $a_1 = a_2 = 1$).

It will be important for us to know how the expected value and variance of the weighted sum (R) are related to the probability distribution of the $R_1, \ldots, R_n$. We state these relations below; we refer the reader to any standard text for proof.[6]

The expected value of a weighted sum is the weighted sum of the expected values. I.e., $E(R) = a_1E(R_1) + a_2E(R_2) + \ldots + a_nE(R_n)$. The variance of a weighted sum is not as simple. To express it we must define "covariance." The covariance of R_1 and R_2 is

$$\sigma_{12} = E\{[R_1 - E(R_1)][R_2 - E(R_2)]\}$$

i.e., the expected value of [(the deviation of R_1 from its mean) times (the deviation of R_2 from its mean)]. In general we defined the covariance between R_i and R_j as

$$\sigma_{ij} = E\{[R_i - E(R_i)][R_i - E(R_j)]\}$$

σ_{ij} may be expressed in terms of the familiar correlation coefficient (p_{ij}). The covariance between R_i and R_j is equal to [(their correlation) times (the standard deviation of R_i) times (the standard deviation of R_j)]:

$$\sigma_{ij} = p_{ij}\sigma_i\sigma_j$$

The variance of a weighted sum is

$$V(R) = \sum_{i=1}^{N} a_i^2 V(X_i) + 2\sum_{i=1}^{N}\sum_{i>1}^{N} a_i a_j \sigma_{ij}$$

If we use the fact that the variance of R_i is σ_{ii} then

$$V(R) = \sum_{i=1}^{N}\sum_{j=1}^{N} a_i a_j \sigma_{ij}$$

[6]E.g., J. V. Uspensky, *Introduction to Mathematical Probability* (New York: McGraw-Hill, 1937), chapter 9, pp. 161–81.

Let R_i be the return on the ith security. Let μ_i be the expected value of R_i; σ_{ij}, be the covariance between R_i and R_j (thus σ_{ii} is the variance of R_i). Let X_i be the percentage of the investor's assets which are allocated to the ith security. The yield (R) on the portfolio as a whole is

$$R = \sum R_i X_i$$

The R_i (and consequently R) are considered to be random variables.[7] The X_i are not random variables, but are fixed by the investor. Since the X_i are percentages we have $\Sigma X_i = 1$. In our analysis we will exclude negative values of the X_i (i.e., short sales); therefore $X_i \geq 0$ for all i.

The return (R) on the portfolio as a whole is a weighted sum of random variables (where the investor can choose the weights). From our discussion of such weighted sums we see that the expected return E from the portfolio as a whole is

$$E = \sum_{i=1}^{N} X_i \mu_i$$

and the variance is

$$V = \sum_{i=1}^{N} \sum_{j=1}^{N} \sigma_{ij} X_i X$$

For fixed probability beliefs (μ_i, σ_{ij}) the investor has a choice of various combinations of E and V depending on his choice of portfolio $X_1, \ldots, X_N$. Suppose that the set of all obtainable (E, V) combinations were as in Figure 1. The E-V rule states that the investor would (or should) want to select one of those portfolios which give rise to the (E, V) combinations indicated as efficient in the figure; i.e., those with minimum V for given E or more and maximum E for given V or less.

There are techniques by which we can compute the set of efficient portfolios and efficient (E, V) combinations associated with given μ_i and σ_{ij}. We will not present these techniques here. We will, however, illustrate geometrically the nature of the efficient surfaces for cases in which N (the number of available securities) is small.

The calculation of efficient surfaces might possibly be of practical use. Perhaps there are ways, by combining statistical techniques and the judgment of experts, to form reasonable probability beliefs (μ_i, σ_{ij}).

[7] I.e., we assume that the investor does (and should) act as if he had probability beliefs concerning these variables. In general we would expect that the investor could tell us, for any two events (A and B), whether he personally considered A more likely than B, B more likely than A, or both equally likely. If the investor were consistent in his opinions on such matters, he would possess a system of probability beliefs. We cannot expect the investor to be consistent in every detail. We can, however, expect his probability beliefs to be roughly consistent on important matters that have been carefully considered. We should also expect that he will base his actions upon these probability beliefs—even though they be in part subjective.

This paper does not consider the difficult question of how investors do (or should) form their probability beliefs.

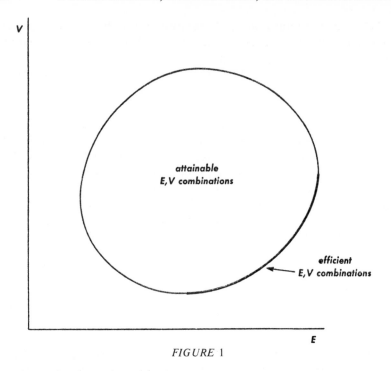

FIGURE 1

We could use these beliefs to compute the attainable efficient combinations of (E, V). The investor, being informed of what (E, V) combinations were attainable, could state which he desired. We could then find the portfolio which gave this desired combination.

Two conditions—at least—must be satisfied before it would be practical to use efficient surfaces in the manner described above. First, the investor must desire to act according to the E-V maxim. Second, we must be able to arrive at reasonable μ_i and σ_{ij}. We will return to these matters later.

Let us consider the case of three securities. In the three security case our model reduces to

$$1) \qquad E = \sum_{i=1}^{3} X_i \mu_i$$

$$2) \qquad V = \sum_{i=1}^{3} \sum_{j=1}^{3} X_i X_j \sigma_{ij}$$

$$3) \qquad \sum_{i=1}^{3} X_i = 1$$

$$4) \qquad X_i \geq 0 \qquad \text{for} \qquad i = 1, 2, 3$$

From (3) we get

$$3') \qquad X_3 = 1 - X_1 - X_2$$

If we substitute (3') in equations (1) and (2) we get E and V as functions of X_1 and X_2. For example we find

$$1') \qquad E = \mu_3 + X_1(\mu_1 - \mu_3) + X_2(\mu_2 - \mu_3)$$

The exact formulas are not too important here (that of V is given below).[8] We can simply write

$$a) \qquad E = E(X_1, X_2)$$

$$b) \qquad V = V(X_1, X_2)$$

$$c) \qquad X_1 \geq 0, X_2 \geq 0, 1 - X_1 - X_2 \geq 0$$

By using relations (a), (b), (c), we can work with two dimensional geometry.

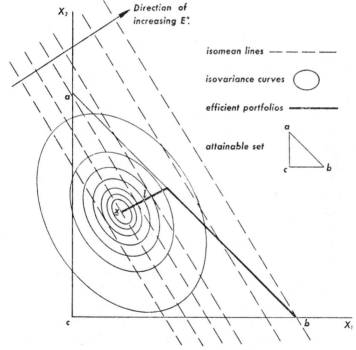

FIGURE 2

$$^8V = X_1^2(\sigma_{11} - 2\sigma_{13} + \sigma_{33}) + X_2^2(\sigma_{22} - 2\sigma_{23} + \sigma_{33}) + 2X_1X_2(\sigma_{12} - \sigma_{13} - \sigma_{23} + \sigma_{33})$$
$$+ 2X_1(\sigma_{13} - \sigma_{33}) + 2X_2(\sigma_{23} - \sigma_{33}) + \sigma_{33}.$$

The attainable set of portfolios consists of all portfolios which satisfy constraints (c) and $(3')$ (or equivalently (3) and (4)). The attainable combinations of X_1, X_2 are represented by the triangle abc in Figure 2. Any point to the left of the X_2 axis is not attainable because it violates the condition that $X_1 \geq 0$. Any point below the X_1 axis is not attainable because it violates the condition that $X_2 \geq 0$. Any point above the line $(1 - X_1 - X_2 = 0)$ is not attainable because it violates the condition that $X_3 = 1 - X_1 - X_2 \geq 0$.

We define an *isomean* curve to be the set of all points (portfolios) with a given expected return. Similarly an *isovariance* line is defined to be the set of all points (portfolios) with a given variance of return.

An examination of the formulae for E and V tells us the shapes of the isomean and isovariance curves. Specifically they tell us that typically[9] the isomean curves are a system of parallel straight lines; the isovariance curves are a system of concentric ellipses (see Fig. 2). For example, if $\mu_2 \neq \mu_3$ equation $1'$ can be written in the familiar form $X_2 = a + bX_1$; specifically (1)

$$X_2 = \frac{E - \mu_3}{\mu_2 - \mu_3} - \frac{\mu_1 - \mu_3}{\mu_2 - \mu_3}X_1$$

Thus the slope of the isomean line associated with $E = E_0$ is $-(\mu_1 - \mu_3)/(\mu_2 - \mu_3)$ its intercept is $(E_0 - \mu_3)/(\mu_2 - \mu_3)$. If we change E we change the intercept but not the slope of the isomean line. This confirms the contention that the isomean lines form a system of parallel lines.

Similarly, by a somewhat less simple application of analytic geometry, we can confirm the contention that the isovariance lines form a family of concentric ellipses. The "center" of the system is the point which minimizes V. We will label this point X. Its expected return and variance we will label E and V. Variance increases as you move away from X. More precisely, if one isovariance curve, C_1, lies closer to X than another, C_2, then C_1 is associated with a smaller variance than C_2.

With the aid of the foregoing geometric apparatus let us seek the efficient sets.

X, the center of the system of isovariance ellipses, may fall either inside or outside the attainable set. Figure 2 illustrates a case in which X falls inside the attainable set. In this case: X is efficient. For no other portfolio has a V as low as X; therefore no portfolio can have either smaller V (with the same or greater E) or greater E with the same or smaller V. No point (portfolio) with expected return E less than E is efficient. For we have $E > E$ and $V < V$.

---

[9]The isomean "curves" are as described above except when $\mu_1 = \mu_2 = \mu_3$. In the latter case all portfolios have the same expected return and the investor chooses the one with minimum variance.

As to the assumptions implicit in our description of the isovariance curves see footnote 12.

Consider all points with a given expected return E; i.e., all points on the isomean line associated with E. The point of the isomean line at which V takes on its least value is the point at which the isomean line

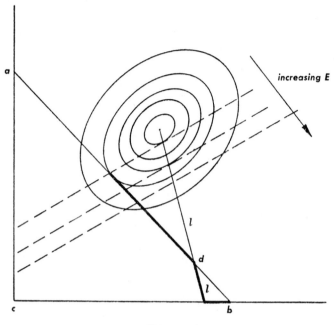

FIGURE 3

is tangent to an isovariance curve. We call this point $\hat{X}(E)$. If we let E vary, $\hat{X}(E)$ traces out a curve.

Algebraic considerations (which we omit here) show us that this curve is a straight line. We will call it the critical line l. The critical line passes through X for this point minimizes V for all points with $E(X_1, X_2) = E$. As we go along l in either direction from X, V increases. The segment of the critical line from X to the point where the critical line crosses the boundary of the attainable set is part of the efficient set. The rest of the efficient set is (in the case illustrated) the segment of the ab line from d to b. b is the point of maximum attainable E. In Figure 3, X lies outside the admissible area but the critical line cuts the admissible area. The efficient line begins at the attainable point with minimum variance (in this case on the ab line). It moves toward b until it intersects the critical line, moves along the critical line until it intersects a boundary and finally moves along the boundary to b. The reader may wish to construct and examine the following other cases: (1) X lies outside the attainable set and the critical line does not cut the attainable set. In this case there is a security which does not enter into any efficient portfolio. (2) Two securities have the same μ_i. In this case the isomean lines are parallel to a boundary line. It may happen that the efficient portfolio with maximum E is a diversified portfolio. (3) A case wherein only one portfolio is efficient.

The efficient set in the 4 security case is, as in the 3 security and also the N security case, a series of connected line segments. At one end of the efficient set is the point of minimum variance; at the other end is a point of maximum expected return[10] (see Fig. 4).

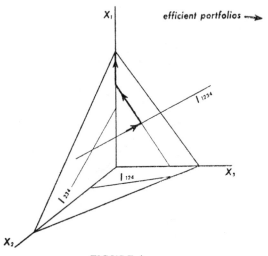

FIGURE 4

Now that we have seen the nature of the set of efficient portfolios, it is not difficult to see the nature of the set of efficient (E, V) combinations. In the three security case $E = a_0 + a_1X_1 + a_2X_2$ is a plane; $V = b_0 + b_1X_1 + b_2X_2 + b_{12}X_1X_2 + b_{11}X_1^2 + b_{22}X_1^2$ is a paraboloid.[11] As

[10]Just as we used the equation $\sum\limits_{i=1}^{4} X_i = 1$ to reduce the dimensionality in the three security case, we can use it to represent the four security case in 3 dimensional space. Eliminating X_4 we get $E = E(X_1, X_2, X_3)$, $V = V(X_1, X_2, X_3)$. The attainable set is represented, in three-space, by the tetrahedron with vertices $(0, 0, 0)$, $(0, 0, 1)$, $(0, 1, 0)$, $(1, 0, 0)$, representing portfolios with, respectively, $X_4 = 1$, $X_3 = 1$, $X_2 = 1$, $X_1 = 1$.

Let s_{123} be the subspace consisting of all points with $X_4 = 0$. Similarly we can define $s_{a1}, \ldots, aa$ to be the subspace consisting of all points with $X_i = 0$, $i \neq a_1, \ldots, aa$. For each subspace $s_{a1}, \ldots, aa$ we can define a *critical line* $la_1, \ldots aa$. This line is the locus of points P where P minimizes V for all points in $s_{a1}, \ldots, aa$ with the same E as P. If a point is in $s_{a1}, \ldots, aa$ and is efficient it must be on $la_1, \ldots, aa$. The efficient set may be traced out by starting at the point of minimum available variance, moving continuously along various $la_1, \ldots, aa$ according to definite rules, ending in a point which gives maximum E. As in the two dimensional case the point with minimum available variance may be in the interior of the available set or on one of its boundaries. Typically we proceed along a given critical line until either this line intersects one of a larger subspace or meets a boundary (and simultaneously the critical line of a lower dimensional subspace). In either of these cases the efficient line turns and continues along the new line. The efficient line terminates when a point with maximum E is reached.

[11]See footnote 8.

shown in Figure 5, the section of the E-plane over the efficient portfolio set is a series of connected line segments. The section of the V-paraboloid over the efficient portfolio set is a series of connected parabola

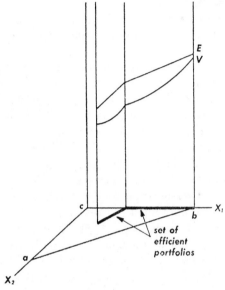

FIGURE 5

segments. If we plotted V against E for efficient portfolios we would again get a series of connected parabola segments (see Fig. 6). This result obtains for any number of securities.

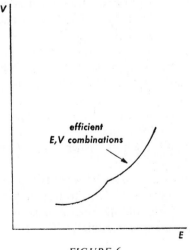

FIGURE 6

Various reasons recommend the use of the expected return-variance of return rule, both as a hypothesis to explain well-established investment behavior and as a maxim to guide one's own action. The rule serves better, we will see, as an explanation of, and guide to, "investment" as distinguished from "speculative" behavior.

Earlier we rejected the expected returns rule on the grounds that it never implied the superiority of diversification. The expected return-variance of return rule, on the other hand, implies diversification for a wide range of μ_i, σ_{ij}. This does not mean that the E-V rule never implies the superiority of an undiversified portfolio. It is conceivable that one security might have an extremely higher yield and lower variance than all other securities; so much so that one particular undiversified portfolio would give maximum E and minimum V. But for a large, presumably representative range of μ_i, σ_{ij} the E-V rule leads to efficient portfolios almost all of which are diversified.

Not only does the E-V hypothesis imply diversification, it implies the "right kind" of diversification for the "right reason." The adequacy of diversification is not thought by investors to depend solely on the number of different securities held. A portfolio with sixty different railway securities, for example, would not be as well diversified as the same size portfolio with some railroad, some public utility, mining, various sort of manufacturing, etc. The reason is that it is generally more likely for firms within the same industry to do poorly at the same time than for firms in dissimilar industries.

Similarly in trying to make variance small it is not enough to invest in many securities. It is necessary to avoid investing in securities with high covariances among themselves. We should diversify across industries because firms in different industries, especially industries with different economic characteristics, have lower covariances than firms within an industry.

The concepts "yield" and "risk" appear frequently in financial writings. Usually if the term "yield" were replaced by "expected yield" or "expected return," and "risk" by "variance of return," little change of apparent meaning would result.

Variance is a well-known measure of dispersion about the expected. If instead of variance the investor was concerned with standard error, $\sigma = \sqrt{V}$, or with the coefficient of dispersion, σ/E, his choice would still lie in the set of efficient portfolios.

Suppose an investor diversifies between two portfolios (i.e., if he puts some of his money in one portfolio, the rest of his money in the other. An example of diversifying among portfolios is the buying of the shares of two different investment companies). If the two original portfolios have *equal* variance then typically[12] the variance of the resulting (compound) portfolio will be less than the variance of either original portfolio. This is illustrated by Figure 7. To interpret Figure 7 we note that

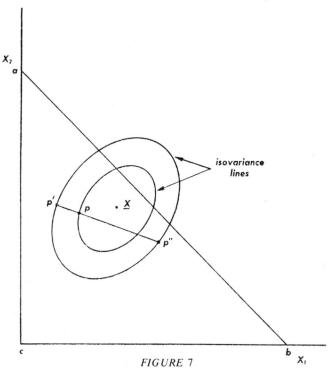

FIGURE 7

a portfolio (P) which is built out of two portfolios $P' = (X_1', X_2')$ and $P'' = (X_1'', X_2'')$ is of the form $P = \lambda P' + (1 - \lambda)P'' = (\lambda X_1' + (1 - \lambda)X_1'', \lambda X_2' + (1 - \lambda)X_2'')$. P is on the straight line connecting P' and P''.

The *E-V* principle is more plausible as a rule for investment behavior as distinguished from speculative behavior. The third moment[13] M_3 of the probability distribution of returns from the portfolio may be connected with a propensity to gamble. For example if the investor maxi-

---

[12]In no case will variance be increased. The only case in which variance will not be decreased is if the returns from both portfolios are perfectly correlated. To draw the isovariance curves as ellipses it is both necessary and sufficient to assume that no two distinct portfolios have perfectly correlated returns.

[13]If R is a random variable that takes on a finite number of values $r_1, \ldots, r_n$ with probabilities $p_1, \ldots, p_n$ respectively, and expected value E, then $M_3 = \sum\limits_{i=1}^{n} p_i(r_i - E)^3$.

mizes utility (U) which depends on E and $V(U = U(E, V), \partial U/\partial E > 0$, $\partial U/\partial E < 0)$ he will never accept an actuarially fair[14] bet. But if $U = U(E, V, M_3)$ and if $\partial U/\partial M_3 \neq 0$ then there are some fair bets which would be accepted.

Perhaps—for a great variety of investing institutions which consider yield to be a good thing; risk, a bad thing; gambling, to be avoided— E, V efficiency is reasonable as a working hypothesis and a working maxim.

Two uses of the E-V principle suggest themselves. We might use it in theoretical analyses or we might use it in the actual selection of portfolios.

In theoretical analyses we might inquire, for example, about the various effects of a change in the beliefs generally held about a firm, or a general change in preference as to expected return versus variance of return, or a change in the supply of a security. In our analyses the X_i might represent individual securities or they might represent aggregates such as, say, bonds, stocks and real estate.[15]

To use the E-V rule in the selection of securities we must have procedures for finding reasonable μ_i and σ_{ij}. These procedures, I believe, should combine statistical techniques and the judgment of practical men. My feeling is that the statistical computations should be used to arrive at a tentative set of μ_i and σ_{ij}. Judgment should then be used in increasing or decreasing some of these μ_i and σ_{ij} on the basis of factors or nuances not taken into account by the formal computations. Using this revised set of μ_i and σ_{ij}, the set of efficient E, V combinations could be computed, the investor could select the combination he preferred, and the portfolio which gave rise to this E, V combination could be found.

One suggestion as to tentative μ_i, σ_{ij} is to use the observed μ_i, σ_{ij} for some period of the past. I believe that better methods, which take into account more information, can be found. I believe that what is needed is essentially a "probabilistic" reformulation of security analysis. I will not pursue this subject here, for this is "another story." It is a story of which I have read only the first page of the first chapter.

In this paper we have considered the second stage in the process of selecting a portfolio. This stage starts with the relevant beliefs about the securities involved and ends with the selection of a portfolio. We have not considered the first stage: the formation of the relevant beliefs on the basis of observation.

---

[14]One in which the amount gained by winning the bet times the probability of winning is equal to the amount lost by losing the bet, times the probability of losing.

[15]Care must be used in using and interpreting relations among aggregates. We cannot deal here with the problems and pitfalls of aggregation.

Portfolio Selection:
A Heuristic Approach*

Geoffrey P. Clarkson and Allan H. Meltzer

I. INTRODUCTION

The problem of selecting a portfolio can be divided into two components: (1) the analysis of individual securities and (2) the selection of a portfolio or group of securities based on the previous analysis. Up to now, the majority of writers have focused on the first part of the problem and have developed several, well-accepted methods of analysis.[1] Little attention has been paid to the second phase of the problem. It is to this second part of the portfolio selection process that this paper is principally devoted.

Recently a normative approach to portfolio selection for a particular kind of investor has been proposed by Markowitz.[2] He defines a decision problem (in this case the selection of a set of securities), assumes a decision function, and observes the behavior which the system generates when inputs are varied. In his analysis, Markowitz shows that, for given securities, a rational investor can determine the "efficient" set.[3] To obtain an optimal portfolio from the efficient set, additional assumptions are required: namely, a Markowitz investor must choose that combination of mean and variance which provides maximum utility. But, whatever form the decision function

*From the *Journal of Finance*, **15**, no. 4, December 1960, pp. 465–480. Back numbers can be obtained from the Kraus Reprint Corporation, New York. The research was supported by grants of the Graduate School of Industrial Administration, from the school's research funds and from funds provided by the Ford Foundation for the study of organizational behavior.

The authors gratefully acknowledge assistance furnished by the trust department of a local bank. Without the kind co-operation of the investment officer and other officials of that department, this research would have been impossible. Their comments on an earlier draft of this paper were most helpful in eliminating ambiguities.

[1]B. Graham and D. Dodd, *Security Analysis* (3d ed.; New York: McGraw-Hill Book Co., Inc., 1951), is an example of one of the more comprehensive works in this area.

[2]H. Markowitz, *Portfolio Selection* (New York: John Wiley & Sons, 1959).

[3]*Ibid.* Portfolios which provide the maximum return for a given variance are "efficient."

takes, it must be such as to make its mathematical representation tractable and soluble.

A positive theory of portfolio selection does not yet exist. Such a theory must describe and predict the investment behavior of individuals under uncertainty. Whether one constructs a positive theory or compares the results of a normative theory with existing procedures, knowledge of actual behavior is a prerequisite. Since neither a theory nor an adequate description of the selection process is available, the aim of this paper is partially to fill both gaps.

The focus of our study is the investment of trust funds held by banks. We view this process as a problem in decision-making. A heuristic[4] model, written as a computer program, simulates the procedures used to assign accounts to a common trust fund or to select particular portfolios. The analysis is based on the operations at a medium-sized national bank (with trust assets approximately equal to the average for all national banks). The decision-maker of our problem is the trust investment officer;[5] our simulation asks the computer program to select a portfolio based on information available to the investment officer at the time his decision is made.

This approach is related to the traditional literature of financial analysis and portfolio selection. Like the traditional approach, it is based on rules of thumb (heuristics) which guide the decision-maker from the original input of information about the client, the securities markets, and the economy to the choice of particular portfolios. But, unlike that approach, the rules must be completely specified, unambiguous, and capable of being refuted by empirical tests. When the rules for processing information (or heuristics) yield results consistent with those obtained by human subjects, the model is said to have "simulated" the decision process; the set of heuristics (or simulation model) has "predicted" the behavior of the subject.[6]

Even if the model fails to predict, simulation provides valuable information about the decision process in the form of a step-by-step record of the procedures used. Sources of error can frequently be identified and eliminated. In this way, the model, through a series of successive tests, can be designed to approximate the behavior of the subject or subjects.

Simulation accommodates both the inductive and the deductive approach. One may simulate the processes used by a number of individuals

---

[4]Heuristics are important, as they often lead us quickly to solutions which we would otherwise reach much more expensively by analytic techniques. For a more extensive discussion of heuristic programs see—H. A. Simon and A. Newell, "What Have Computers To Do with Management?" (RAND Publication P-1708 [May 21, 1959]).

[5]It should be noted carefully that our results reflect the behavior of one investor and hence may not describe the general case.

[6]For a more complete discussion of the theory and technique of simulation see the forthcoming symposium on simulation in the December, 1960, *American Economic Review*.

and attempt to generalize the results. Alternatively, one can construct a model and test it against a wide variety of observed behavior. The latter approach has been used in this paper.

Simulation need not involve a computer, just as addition does not require an adding machine. The advantage of the computer is its ability to solve complex problems more accurately. Moreover, the computer permits the addition to the simulation program of as many mechanisms as are interesting and important, subject only to the speed and storage capacity of the computer. Thus, by using the computer, one can move farther away from an assumed decision function and focus on the actual operations performed by a decision-maker.

The next section briefly describes some recent developments in the theory of human problem-solving. Section III discusses the application of problem-solving to the trust investment decision. We then describe the computer model which selects the assets to be held in particular accounts. The results of some of the tests of the model are shown in the appendix.

II. COMPUTERS AND THE THEORY OF HUMAN PROBLEM-SOLVING

Recent interest in the theory of human problem-solving[7] has focused on the computer programing of mental processes. Most of this work has been directed toward developing an understanding of the operations performed in thinking; some recent work has focused on the application of these techniques to industrial or business problems.[8]

Basic to these studies is the assumption that thinking processes can be isolated as well as identified and that they can be represented by a series of straightforward mechanical operations. This is not to say that thought processes are simple and easy to represent but rather that they can be broken down into their elemental parts, which, in turn, consist of collections of simple mechanisms. These operations are written as a set of statements and rules which, when coded in computer language, become a computer program. The program is tested by running it on a digital

---

[7]This section is largely based on A. Newell and H. A. Simon, *The Simulation of Human Thought* (RAND Corporation, June, 1959).

[8]For examples, see the following: L. A. Hiller, Jr., and L. M. Isaacson, *Experimental Music* (New York: McGraw-Hill Book Co., Inc., 1959); A. Newell, J. C. Shaw, and H. A. Simon, "Empirical Explorations of the Logic Theory Machine," *Proceedings of the Western Joint Computer Conference*, February 26–28, 1957, pp. 218–30; A. Newell, J. C. Shaw, and H. A. Simon, "Chess-playing Programs and the Problem of Complexity," *IBM Journal of Research and Development*, No. 2 (October, 1958), pp. 320–35; E. A. Feigenbaum, "An Information Processing Theory of Verbal Learning" (unpublished Ph.D. thesis, Carnegie Institute of Technology, 1959); J. Feldman, "An Analysis of Predictive Behavior in a Two-Choice Situation" (unpublished Ph.D. thesis, Carnegie Institute of Technology, 1959); and F. M. Tonge, "A Heuristic Program for Assembly Line Balancing" (unpublished Ph.D. thesis, Carnegie Institute of Technology, 1959).

computer, and, as in the more familiar case of mathematical theory, the logical consequences of the initial conditions are derived by performing the operations according to the specified rules.

In an actual simulation the derived computer statements are compared with the output of human subjects who have verbally reported (in detail) their thought processes and decisions. If the humans and the computer use similar processes, the computer is said to have successfully simulated the behavior of the humans. Moreover, if this occurs, the computer program is sufficient to account for the "observed" behavior.

It must be remembered, however, that computers are neither necessary nor sufficient devices for building heuristic models. A human can replace the computer and perform each operation as directed by the program. But humans are inefficient at this task and are usually replaced by digital computers.

One particular characteristic of computers, called "transfer" or "branching," is essential to the study of problem-solving and information-processing. Conditional transfer operations permit a program to choose between alternatives and/or follow strategies.

As a hypothetical example, in a problem-solving contest, consider the following translation problem:[9] The computer is supplied with a Russian-language dictionary, a program, and a Russian story. The program specifies that symbols representing Russian words be read and that the corresponding English words be printed out. The program finds a word in the Russian story. It is instructed to *search* through a list of commonly used words (or dictionary), until it finds symbols identical with the symbols it is using to represent the Russian word. The conditional transfer operation specifies that (1) if the symbols are identical, replace the Russian symbols with the corresponding English symbols and transfer to the next word (set of symbols) in the story, then repeat the process for the next Russian word in the *story*, but (2) if the symbols are not identical, transfer to the next Russian word in the *dictionary*.

Three points are worth emphasizing. First, the program is iterative, i.e., it uses its operations repetitively to process different pieces of information or to solve quite separate problems. During the processing, it sorts information, retaining those parts which are useful, discarding the irrelevant. Second, the program is capable of modifying the "dictionary" or lists. Frequently used "words" may be separated, to narrow future search activity in the interests of economizing time. Third, the hypothetical program described above is general. Any type of list could replace the Russian dictionary as an input without necessitating modification of the search-compare-transfer operations.

[9]While this is not the process followed by most translation programs, it is illustrative of the economies inherent in conditional transfer operations.

While the general processes which the computer follows remain unchanged, each successful simulation must recognize the constraints which arise within the context of the particular problem. These constraints restrict the program to those processes that are consistent with the operations performed by humans engaged in similar tasks. In the translation example, a constraint might call for initiating search by looking at the first letter of the word; in searching a list of Treasury notes, the computer might first consider their yields or maturities.

In our work, a list of common stocks becomes the basic list of the problem—i.e., the dictionary. The goals of the client and the amount of money to be invested represent the Russian story of our example. And conditional transfer operations allow the program to follow the strategies of portfolio selection.

When the constraints which arise in the choice of portfolios are imposed on the general theory of human problem-solving, a theory of portfolio selection emerges. The following section describes the constraints and the resulting theory.

III. SIMULATION OF THE TRUST INVESTMENT PROCESS

An investor is confronted with a large assortment of information which he may use in making decisions. There is a wide variety of data, past and current, on the operation of firms and the market valuation of their stocks. There are many published predictions about the present and future state of the general economy, the stock market, and particular industries and firms. There are legal restrictions and the desires of clients to be considered when an investor acts in an agency of fiduciary capacity. These factors, when evaluated and combined with an investment policy, ultimately result in a decision to buy specific quantities of particular stocks and bonds.

An investor choosing a portfolio is processing information: he sorts the useful from the irrelevant and decides which parts of the total information flow are most important. As we have seen, the theory of human problem-solving was built to handle problems of this type. The postulates of the theory particularly relevant for our purposes are that the following exist:

1. A control system consisting of a number of *memories*, which contain symbolized information and are interconnected by various ordering relations. . . .

2. A number of *primitive information processes*, which operate on the information in the memories. . . .

3. A perfectly definite set of rules for combining these processes into whole

programs of processing. From a program it is possible to deduce unequivocally what externally observable behavior will be generated.[10]

In the portfolio selection problem, these postulates consist of (1) The memory, i.e., lists of industries each of which has associated a sublist of companies. The memory also contains lists of information associated with the individual companies.[11] (2) Search procedures for selecting a portfolio from the information stored in the memory. These function in a manner similar to the traditional clerk who prepares lists of stocks suitable for current investment by scanning a master list. (3) A set of rules or criteria which guide the decision-making processes by stipulating when and how each primitive process is to be used. The set of rules constitutes the processing program for an individual investor. It might be compared with the heuristics of the traditional "expert," but, as noted, there is an important difference—the program must be unambiguous.

Like any problem-solving program, the simulation of the portfolio selection process relies principally on this set of basic operating rules. The rules are specified in advance and may be modified by the outcome of specific decisions. In particular, the record of past successes, failures, and the processes involved in each are stored in memory. The program modifies its behavior by eliminating such unsuccessful procedures. In this sense it learns from its past experience.[12]

In common with other heuristic programs, the process is iterative. Lists of industries and companies are searched for particular attributes; sublists are created, searched, and again divided. For example, to obtain a high-growth portfolio, the list of companies stored in memory is searched to obtain shares with the desired characteristics. Additional criteria are employed to narrow (or expand) this list. Further search and matching against desired criteria yield the specific selection of stocks to buy.

Like the investor it simulates, the computer stores the final result (list) for future use. When the same problem recurs, the entire search process need not be repeated. The list may be judged by present criteria, accepted, adapted to new conditions, or completely rejected. In the latter event, the computer would use a conditional transfer operation to renew search activity until a new list had been formed.

Within this general framework, the problem of constructing a model

[10]A. Newell, J. C. Shaw, and H. A. Simon, "Elements of a Theory of Human Problem Solving," *Psychological Review*, LXV (1958), 151 ff.

[11]Investors categorize companies by industry. Not all investors may associate identical companies with a given industry, but the process of classification by industry remains invariant as the primary basis for listing companies in the memory. The information associated with each company also varies among investors, but each has a list of attributes and values stored in memory (e.g., growth rate, dividend rate, price, price/earnings ratio, expected earnings, expected yields, etc.).

[12]For a complete discussion see G. P. E. Clarkson and H. A. Simon, "Micro-Simulation: The Simulation of Individual and Group Behavior," *American Economic Review*, December, 1960.

of investment behavior becomes a problem of uncovering the basic rules (operations) which lead to a decision to purchase particular securities. The following procedure was used to obtain these data: First, the trust department of a local bank was observed by attending committee meetings called to review past and future decisions. Interviews were then conducted with departmental officers to obtain a better understanding of the lines of authority. From these procedures it became apparent that the investment officer was the primary locus of all decisions relevant to the choice of portfolios.

Interviewing as a technique provided helpful background information. However, as portfolio selection has a well-developed lore, this technique failed to separate the relevant from the irrelevant criteria.

Second, the history of several accounts was examined. Naïve behavioral models were constructed to approximate the recorded behavior and to help uncover those processes which appeared to be invariant between accounts.

Third, and most important, the investment officer was asked to permit "protocols" to be made of his decision processes.[13] To accustom the subject to verbalizing his procedures, the first case was based on an account with which he had dealt before. Artificiality was introduced into the description of the beneficiary and the past history of the account. Successive protocols recorded the investment officer's decision processes for accounts which arose in the course of his work. The decisions made during these problem sessions determined the particular securities which were purchased for these accounts.

From these protocols a program of the investment decision process was built. As yet, the number of protocols is insufficient to answer all the problems that are raised in writing such a program. But our experience has shown that programing focuses our attention on precisely those details for which our specific knowledge is weakest. To date, there are still large gaps in our understanding of the decision-making process, especially in the areas of goal formation[14] and the association of particular industries with particular goals. Also the selection process which determines the particular company and the number of shares to be purchased has not been completely determined. However, an adequate amount of information has been gathered to program a substantial part of the portfolio selection process.

[13]A "protocol" is a transcript of the verbalized thought and actions of a subject when the subject has been instructed to think or problem-solve aloud. Thus the transcript is a record of the subject's thought processes while engaged in making a decision. Since a protocol is a detailed description of what a person does, it avoids some of the problems inherent in interview and questionnaire techniques, which ask the subject to state his reasons for behaving as he does. For further discussion see Newell, Shaw, and Simon, "Elements of a Theory of Human Problem Solving," *op. cit.*

[14]E.g., the precise way in which a "growth account" differs from an "income account."

IV. THE PORTFOLIO SELECTION PROCESS

This section describes the step-by-step simulation of the trust investment process in a medium-sized bank. At present we are directly concerned with the way in which common stocks are chosen for individual portfolios. The selection of bonds and preferred stocks has not yet been explicitly considered.

The investment officer's behavior can be described by a flow chart (Fig. 1) detailing the sequential pattern followed in the decision-making

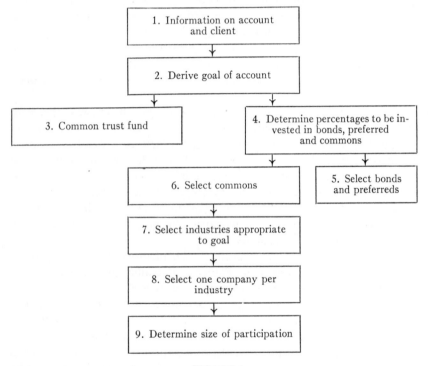

FIGURE 1

process. Each of the elements in the flow chart requires a specific decision by the investment officer. Although the model operated with a basic list of eighty stocks, specification of the goal of the account (step 2) eliminates securities inconsistent with the goal and reduces the list to approximately thirty stocks.

The model was required to predict the portfolios for two accounts with different goals. That is, operations 6–9 were performed as directed by the program. The output was compared with the investment officer's recorded decisions. The results are shown in the appendix.

The descriptions which follow detail the processes used. Translated into symbolic form, they become the computer program.[15]

Information on account and client There are two basic sources of information on each account: the administrative officer's interviews with the client and the written record, containing a copy of the legal instrument (often a will) setting up the trust.[16] From the accumulated data and the subjective impressions of the administrative officer, the investment officer proceeds to step 2: formulating a concept of what the client wants the trust to do, i.e., the goal of the account. Before transforming this concept into a goal (or investment policy) for the account, the investment officer must choose between two courses of action. Conditional transfer operations direct the program to (1) invest the assets in the common trust fund (C.T.F.),[17] (2) set up an individual portfolio for the account.

The bank prides itself on the "individual" investment service which it offers to its customers. Thus there are clear preferences for setting up individual accounts whenever the size of the account permits. The following rules (or procedures) guide the decision to invest the assets in the common trust fund:

a. All "legal"[18] trusts are eligible for investment in C.T.F. The funds of beneficiaries who have waived legal requirements are not so invested.

b. All legal trusts which have less than $K[19] in assets are automatically placed in the C.T.F.

c. Legal trusts greater than $K may or may not be placed in C.T.F., depending on the goals of the beneficiary. However, as noted, no account may participate

[15]The program was written in an information-processing language IPL-V (Newell and Simon).

[16]In most cases, this contains information about the beneficiaries, the investment powers of the bank, what is to happen to the principal, what should be done with the income, etc. From these sources he also gets information on what the beneficiaries' age, marital status, number and age of dependents, place of legal residence, income tax bracket, and status and age of future beneficiaries, if any.

[17]The common trust fund was established to provide a medium for the collective investment of trust funds held by the bank in a fiduciary capacity. Investments are restricted to those considered legal for investment in Pennsylvania. Under Federal Reserve Board regulations, no account may participate for more than $100,000. Under Orphan's Court rulings, not more than 10 per cent of the fund may be invested in securities of any one corporation, with the exception of direct and guaranteed obligations of the United States government. In addition, the fund may not own more than 5 per cent of any one class of stock of any corporation or have the amount invested in common stocks exceed one-third of the total investment in the fund.

[18]" 'Legal investment' statutes fall into two general categories: (1) those that restrict all or part of the investments to specific investments or specific classes of investments, and (2) those that limit investment in non-legal securities to a given percentage of the account or fund. The statutory limitations on investment in non-legal securities range from 30 per cent to 50 per cent of the market value (in one state, inventory value) of the fund" ("Survey of Common Trust Funds, 1958" *Federal Reserve Bulletin*, May, 1959, p. 477). Many people, when setting up the trust relation, specifically waive these investment restrictions. Thus "legal" refers to situations in which the investment officer must comply with these investment restrictions.

[19]To protect the bank's anonymity, the precise dollar values are not revealed. Nationally, the average C.T.F. participation is approximately $22,000 (*Federal Reserve Bulletin*, May, 1958, p. 537).

for more than $100,000. Thus, in the range between K and $100,000 the decision will be determined by the goal of the account. If the client has goals consistent with expected C.T.F. results and does not have assets which permit the purchase of five common stocks in round lots, C.T.F. is indicated, and the process ends.[20]
The investment of assets in the C.T.F. is an all-or-none decision. But all legal accounts greater than $100,000[21] and all accounts which are not of a fiduciary nature have their own portfolios. The minimum size for these accounts depends on the asset composition. For accounts with participation in bonds, as well as common stocks, a minimum of $\frac{1}{2}K$ is required; if the account participates only in common stocks, a minimum of $0.4K$ is required. Smaller accounts are refused or placed in C.T.F. The funds of very small accounts are deposited in a savings bank.

Derive the goal For all portfolios not invested in C.T.F., the investment officer must formulate a goal. Data previously collected are transformed into an investment policy that approximates his perception of what the client wants. The number of possible combinations is very large. But the goal he decides on must lie somewhere along a continuum between the extremes of growth and income. The bank's records indicate that accounts are categorized into four or five classes: pure growth, growth with some income, income with some growth, and income alone.[22]

Determine percentages to be invested in bonds, preferreds and commons The main function of the program is to select the particular common stocks to be held in any given account.

In legal trusts, the maximum amount that can be invested in common stocks is $33\frac{1}{3}$ per cent.[23] In trusts where the legal requirements are waived or do not exist, this decision is left to the investment officer. Except under unusual circumstances, such as a statement that the entire fund be placed

[20]This problem and many of those which follow clearly lend themselves to "conditional transfer" operations in computer terminology.

[21]As yet, we have not programed the heuristics underlying the choice of the C.T.F. portfolio. As noted above, we are concerned here only with explaining the mechanisms underlying the decisions on common stocks for individual accounts.

[22]A growth account is roughly defined as one in which the monetary value of the assets appreciates at an average rate of 10 per cent per year for a five-year period. In an account seeking current dividend and interest income, a minimum yield of 4–4½ per cent is expected. In a mixed growth and income account, a capital appreciation of 5 per cent combined with a dividend of 3–4 per cent is customary.

The goal of an account is determined from the initial data in the following manner. Data on the client: lawyer, high current income, high tax bracket, no pension on retirement, married with no children, desires security after retirement, earnings to be reinvested. The goal of growth with current income as a secondary goal is indicated for the present. Income will be emphasized after the client has retired and is in a lower income tax bracket.

[23]This figure is determined by Pennsylvania state law (Act. No. 340 of 1951) and is the amount designated by the state as constituting a "prudent investment." The prudent-investment criterion limits banks, in practice, to choosing securities which, if preferred stocks, have paid dividends for 16 years and which, if commons, have had positive earnings and have paid dividends in 12 out of 16 years. A list of securities meeting these requirements is prepared by the Pennsylvania Bankers Association.

in commons, the amount invested in commons ranges between 40 and 65 per cent.[24]

Select industries appropriate to goal Despite the large overlap between industries, the investment officer associates a set of industries with each goal. These are chosen from a previously selected "preference list."[25] A one-to-one correspondence between goal and industry does not exist. But each goal invokes a search of the preference list (memory), which leads to the selection of a particular list of industries. The length of the list depends on the size of the account, since each industry is represented only once in any given account. Thus the association of industries with goals narrows the search for appropriate securities to a much shorter list.[26]

Select companies Once an industry has been selected, the company to be chosen for participation is picked by the following series of conditional transfer operations. Companies are examined on the following criteria: (i) subject to tax in Pennsylvania, (ii) legal in Pennsylvania, (iii) current uncertainty, (iv) growth, (v) yield, (vi) expected earnings, (vii) past earnings, (viii) expected dividends, (ix) expected price-earnings ratio, (x) past price-earnings ratio, (xi) amount spent on expansion and/or research and development.[27] The first three criteria are used in an absolute manner to reduce the lists further:

Rule a: If the beneficiary is a resident of Pennsylvania, reject all stocks which are subject to personal property tax in Pennsylvania.

Rule b: If the trust is a legal trust, reject all stocks which do not have legal status in Pennsylvania.

Rule c: Reject further purchases of stocks in which there are "current uncertainties." The investment officer would not buy du Pont stock pending the

---

[24]It is abundantly clear from the protocols that the process involved in choosing government bonds is similar to the one described for common stocks. Under present market conditions, it appears to consist of selecting the highest yield from a table listing short-term governments. Hence it is a search procedure using established processes within a given memory.

[25]The preference list is the investment officer's working list of stocks. This list of approximately 80 stocks is categorized by industry. The investment officer refers to it on every selection that he makes. The preference list is designed to cover various economic situations. Although it is re-examined every three months, few changes are made. We take the list as given.

[26]The investment officer's rule of thumb seeks to spread risk by diversification. But, as Markowitz (*op. cit.*, p. 109) has shown, when the returns on securities are correlated, this may not be accomplished if the amount which the client deposited is relatively small.

Further recording of protocols is expected to specify the selection process that associates particular industries and particular goals. However, it is clear that this association depends on the characteristics of the goal and the general characteristics of the companies within each industry. Some industries contain companies which vary only slightly in their individual characteristics, e.g., banks or utilities. Others, like oils, are more heterogeneous, i.e., appear on several lists.

[27]Large current expenditures on plant expansion and/or research and development will lower current dividends while raising expectations of future earning power. For companies heavily dependent on the discovery of new products, e.g., chemicals, drugs, and office equipment, the amount spent on research and development is used as an indicator of the company's intention to continue developing new and profitable products.

court's decision on what they are to do with their holdings in General Motors. During the Middle East crisis of 1958, international oil companies were labeled "current uncertainties."

The next two criteria (iv and v) are used in a somewhat similar manner. If the goal is growth, all stocks which do not meet minimum growth criteria are rejected. Similarly, if income is desired, low-yielding stocks are rejected.

The rest of the criteria are used in a relative manner. A rough simulation has been achieved by matching the remaining companies on these criteria and seeing which has the most points in its favor. To do this, the program sets up a three-valued scale for each criterion (low = 1, medium = 2, high = 3) and makes binary choices by subtracting the value of a particular criterion of one company from the value of the same criterion for the other company. The result of any one comparison will be a positive, negative, or zero number. All the remaining criteria are matched in this manner, and the resulting scores are added algebraically to yield a unique value for the particular comparison. Since one company's criteria are always subtracted from the other's, a positive sign on the summation will denote that the first company is chosen; a negative sign, the second company. In the case where the sum is zero, no choice has been indicated.[28]

An example will clarify this process. Assume that a portfolio of high-yield stocks is required and that the selection process has reached the point where it is starting to select stocks on the basis of attributes vi through xi. At this point the choice lies between Company A and Company B. Since we are considering only attributes vi through xi, let their values for Company A be given by the vector (3, 3, 1, 3, 3, 2) and for Company B by the vector (2, 3, 1, 3, 2, 2). As mentioned above, the selection process consists of subtracting the values of the attributes of Company B from the values of the similar attributes of Company A. In this case the result of this subtraction yields a vector whose values are given by the following six numbers: 1, 0, 0, 0, 1, 0. Since the algebraic sum of these numbers is positive, Company A is selected. If more alternatives are available, a transfer operation directs the program to match Company A against the next alternative.

Determine the size of participation   The investment officer divides the accounts into two classes. For accounts with less than $\$\frac{5}{8}K$ to invest in commons, his rules are as follows:

---

[28]More recent protocols suggest an alternative selection routine, which lists all the companies in a preference order on the two basic criteria of growth and income. For the goal of growth or income the program would take the first company on the growth or income list and check through each of the remaining criteria to see whether it met a specified standard or not. If it did, the company would be accepted, and search in that industry would terminate. If it did not, the first company would be interchanged with the second company on the list, and the test would be repeated. Changes in suitability occur because the stored data on price, income, earnings, dividends, etc., are kept up to date.

a. Given the amount to be invested and the number of participations, determine the average amount which can be invested in each company.

b. Divide this average amount by the current price of the stock to obtain the number of shares which can be purchased.[29]

c. Since each purchase may be slightly over or under the average dollar amount to be spent, maintain a continuous count of "funds remaining" figure and not the average number.

In accounts with more than $\$\frac{5}{8}K$ to invest in commons, a different procedure is used. Once the amount to be invested and the number of participations are determined as above, the minimum round lot is purchased for each company that is selected. Again a "funds remaining" account is kept to determine the size of the last participation.

V. CONCLUSIONS

In recent years new techniques for the study of human problem-solving have been developed. Of these, the simulation of individual behavior is most apposite to the study of problems of choice under uncertainty. Application of this technique has been facilitated by the use of digital computers capable of storing and processing large blocks of information.

This paper proposes the use of simulation as a basis for studying portfolio selection. Clearly, the choice of securities by individuals or their agents is an application of the theory of decision-making under uncertainty. We contend that focusing on the decision-making process per se is a more appropriate technique for dealing with this problem than those which, though mathematically more elegant, either (1) lead to non-testable implications or (2) rest on probabilistic assumptions.

Building computer programs focuses attention on areas of least knowledge. Moreover, since computer statements must be operational, hypotheses advanced must clearly specify assumptions about the mechanisms at work.

Using information recorded from "protocols," we programed portions of the decision rules employed by a trust investment officer. The program was tested by two simulations, and, although such small samples are never conclusive, we believe that the results strongly indicate the potential power of the theory as a predictor. (A crude test for "goodness of fit" is shown in the appendix.)

---

[29]If this number of shares is 90 or greater, 100 shares (a round lot) are purchased; if less than 90, but greater than 10, the number is reduced to its nearest multiple of 5, and that number of shares is purchased; if less than 10 but greater than 5, 10 shares are purchased; if less than 5, 5 shares are purchased. Note, however, that, in general, this process will not lead to selection of a portfolio which is "Markowitz-efficient."

Future work will be directed at discovering the rules that are used in the formation of goals, in the association of industries with goals, and on parts of the present program that are not yet fully defined. As programs are added, we expect to generate more of the recorded behavior. We suggest that in this way a descriptive theory of portfolio selection can be developed to serve either (1) as a predictor of investor behavior or (2) as the basis for a theory of optimal portfolio selection.

APPENDIX

RESULTS OF SIMULATION OF ABC ACCOUNT, 7/7/58

Description of Account:

1. Agency account
2. Revocable
3. Goal of account: high growth with little or no concern for income; fluctuations in principal not a problem
4. Investment restrictions: not a legal trust, hence not restricted to legal list; donor stated that all assets were to be invested in common stocks
5. Amount available for investment in common stocks: assumed to be given

The *program* selected the following portfolio for the ABC Account:

85 shs. Monsanto Chem. comm.
10 shs. I.B.M. comm.
50 shs. Continental Oil comm.
45 shs. Owens Corning comm.

The portfolio selected by the investment officer on 7/7/58 was:

80 shs. Monsanto Chem. comm.
10 shs. I.B.M. comm.
45 shs. Continental Oil comm.
50 shs. Owens Corning comm.

The funds-remaining figure was too small to generate new activity.

RESULTS OF SIMULATION OF XYZ ACCOUNT, 3/28/58

Description of Account:

1. Agency account
2. Revocable
3. Goal of account: high income and stability of income
4. Investment restrictions: not a legal trust, hence not restricted to legals
5. Amount available for investment in common stocks: assumed to be given

The *program* selected the following portfolio for the XYZ Account:

100 shs. Philadelphia Elec. comm.
100 shs. Equitable Gas comm.
 60 shs. Socony Mobil Oil comm.

The portfolio selected by the investment officer on 3/28/58 was:

100 shs. Philadelphia Elec. comm.
100 shs. Equitable Gas comm.
 50 shs. Socony Mobil Oil comm.

Managing Our Trusts as Prudent Men Would Do*

Charles W. Buek

The subject of my paper was announced in the advance program for the Trust Conference as "Investment Diversification in Personal Trust Portfolios." That was my assignment, and I did some preliminary work on that topic. However, one by one I ran up against the big questions which trustees have never answered. How could I discuss equity ratios or growth stocks when we have not yet agreed what trustees should do about inflation—if anything. It is not easy to recommend taking profits today when the courts so often frown on our taking losses.

So, with the approval but not the endorsement of the Trust Division, I am going to talk instead about the peculiar form of halfhearted prudence dispensed by trustees today. As you will see, it is my opinion that we cannot go on much longer deciding what is prudent on the one hand, and then what is proper for trusts on the other.

Sometime this year, if all goes well, trustees in New York State will finally be allowed the privilege of the Prudent-Man Rule. This will be a long-awaited day, for we have been disappointed more than once in our efforts to free ourselves of so-called legal investments. We look forward happily to the day when we shall be free—free to manage our trusts as prudent men would do.

If we have been carried away by this exhilarating thought, this vision of freedom, we have a sobering disappointment ahead of us. We shall be far from free to act as prudent men do today in the conduct of their own affairs. As trustees, we shall still be tightly controlled by a strong legal network, some of which dates back more than a hundred years. We will be more like prisoners who have finally sawed through the bars of their cells, only to find themselves still within the high outer walls of the prison.

*From the *Commercial and Financial Chronicle*, March 3, 1960. Reprinted by permission of the *Commercial and Financial Chronicle*, New York.

However, we won't be alone in our continuing confinement, for we will find the trustees of other Prudent-Man states strolling contentedly in the prison yard outwardly unmindful of the fact that they really are not free.

There is surprisingly little discussion of the limitations and handicaps imposed upon trustees by more than a hundred years of court decisions and rulings. Perhaps this is because we were all born in captivity, and have never known real freedom in the conduct of trust affairs.

INVESTMENT DECISIONS BECOME OBSOLETE

The legal framework within which trustees are confined delineates far more than the responsibilities of trustees and the rights of beneficiaries and remaindermen, and that is where the trouble lies. An attempt has been made by the courts over the years to pronounce what investment media and what types of investment procedures are prudent and proper. These decisions have not always reflected expert investment judgment, and have always been influenced by conditions prevailing at the time. Right or wrong, they have invariably been subject to rapid obsolescence in an ever changing economy.

Yet it is the way of our legal system that these decisions must stand, sometimes for many years, limiting the investment activities of trustees, and sometimes precluding investment procedures which have become widely accepted by prudent men dealing with a new set of financial conditions and problems. If we were to observe faithfully every rule in the book, the investment activities of trustees would very nearly grind to a stop. If that were to happen, the situation would be similar to a phenomenon peculiar to the New York City subway system. Sometimes the platforms are jammed with people, and it seems at first glance that the subways have broken down. However, we find that what is going on is a "Rule Book Strike," when the motormen, to enforce their demands, have merely undertaken to obey every rule in the book. On that basis, the trains don't run.

We are in an unsound situation when trustees must break rules, cut corners, and risk surcharge to do what they believe is prudent for their trusts. Please do not misunderstand my purpose in saying this. I have not merely grown restive under the yoke of regulation and accountability. Trustees will always be accountable, of course. What worries me is that experienced and capable trustees are unnecessarily deterred from doing the best investment job they know how to do.

I say "unnecessarily deterred" advisedly. Under the rules of the trust game as we all now play it, these legal safeguards—these legal handicaps, if you will—are wisely imposed by the courts. But it is within our power, collectively, to change the way we play the game, and to make it unnecessary for the courts to limit our investment activities to a few elementary steps.

We should give more thought than we do to the handicaps under which we function as trustees, and to the obsolescence which creeps into all decisions which concern investment activities. If this problem has never seemed urgent before, it is urgent now. There are three reasons for taking this matter seriously:

1. Trust investment procedures which conform to every rule in the book prove to be out-of-date and inadequate in the light of prevailing conditions.
2. Our competitive position as managers of wealth has been weakened; and others are entering our field, prepared to do a more effective job.
3. This unsatisfactory situation need not continue if we are willing to face up to the underlying fallacy which causes it.

First let us think for a moment about the shortcomings of a trustee, even when he has been blessed with the Prudent-Man Rule. Prudent men today are obsessed by two problems—the avoidance of taxes and the protection of their assets against inflation. Trustees deal effectively with neither of them.

HANDICAP 1 THE AVOIDANCE OF TAXES

It is now one of the facts of life that taxes can erode a fortune more certainly and more rapidly than any other factor. Yet, to this day it is not the duty of a trustee to avoid the payment of taxes, and many of the prudent steps he should take for this very purpose are not acceptable to the courts.

To be sure, many of us in a gingerly manner have been switching tax-exempt bonds at a loss to offset capital gains. Of course, like good trustmen, we have been meticulously careful to match coupons, yields, price, and maturity as well as quality. But the steps taken by expert investment managers, such as the writing up of blocks of stocks, the writing down of other holdings, switching from one corporate bond to another, the offsetting of losses in a bond portfolio by profits in the stock list—these things we generally believe we cannot do.

The simple reason is that the avoidance of taxes is not an acceptable reason for establishing losses. We are not allowed to argue in court that a loss taken in stock A was made up by a subsequent profit in stock B. Undoubtedly, this blind spot in the law traces back to the fact that case law relative to the investment conduct of a trustee began to accumulate long before income taxes were invented.

HANDICAP 2   THE PRESERVATION OF PURCHASING POWER

Trustees who try to offset inflation and the declining purchasing power of the dollar must give some other reason for what they are doing. The law is clear—it is not the duty of a trustee to increase the market value of a trust. It is not acceptable to explain that you bought a common stock because you hoped and believed that it would increase in market value. The court held in 1869 that trustees must not undertake the "hazard of adventures" in the hope of growing rich. How could the court have foreseen the time when the preservation of principal would be equivalent to growing poor!

There is nothing in the law—yet—about inflation. Perhaps by 1980, when we account for the investments we are making today, it will be recognized that inflation was a new hazard, justifying investment action which had not previously been considered proper.

Two years ago, at the American Bankers Association's Mid-Winter Trust Conference, Bascom Torrance demonstrated that growth stocks are not always satisfactory investments and inflation hedges. Today may well be one of those times when such stocks should be sold and high-yielding bonds bought in their stead, thereby bringing the purchasing power of the beneficiary up-to-date. However there have been many opportunities in the past 15 years, and there will be again in the future, to increase the principal amount of a trust. It is regrettable that so many trustees, lacking a clear precedent and legal encouragement, have debated their way clear through this period when decisive action would have afforded a really effective hedge.

HANDICAP 3   DIVERSIFICATION

One of the greatest handicaps to prudent investment procedure in trusts is the inability of trustees to present both sides of a transaction in justifying a sale or purchase. The insistence by the courts that each individual transaction stand on its own feet is inconsistent with good investment principles and practices. It penalizes diversification, the basic principal of which is that gains will offset an occasional inevitable loss.

If a trustee diversifies thoroughly in 20 stocks, and at the end shows 19 profits and one loss, he may be surcharged. This doesn't make sense! If he were really cynical about it, he might decide to buy only 4 or 5 stocks, keep a voluminous record on them, and run 5 chances of being surcharged instead of 20.

You may think that this is not a vitally important point. But the law is unfair and unbusinesslike in this respect, and trustees do a poorer job because of it.

HANDICAP 4   SELECTIVITY

When a prudent man finds that he has made a poor investment in a common stock, he is quick to change it. These are times in which great selectivity is necessary in the purchase of equities. A portfolio should consist only of the best situated issues under rapidly changing conditions. Stocks which have lost their attractiveness should be weeded out.

Trustees are very poor weeders. When a stock goes down, they are prone to grit their teeth and hang on, for the loss cannot legally be made up in any other issue. A trustee cannot explain to the court that he sold one stock at a loss because he thought that another one offered better prospects of recovery. Yet that is routine procedure for the expert investment manager.

HANDICAP 5   BUYING STOCKS FOR INCOME

Many, many years ago the courts held that a trustee must buy common stocks for income and not for appreciation. To meet this requirement, we at the United States Trust Company first had a rule-of-thumb that a common stock had to yield more than a high grade corporate bond in order to qualify as an income-producing trust investment. Then of necessity we shifted to measuring a stock against government bond yields, because that gave us a little better selection. But finally we realized that in buying common stocks for income we were sifting through the dregs of the market.

Market conditions had changed, and investment requirements had changed, since the time when a liberal dividend had been the criterion in appraising a common stock.

HANDICAP 6   REDEMPTION OF SERIES G BONDS

It was disappointing and frustrating to discover, in New York State at least, that trustees could not redeem Series G Bonds prior to maturity, without recovering the discount from the beneficiary. We sacrificed market-ability to obtain a guaranteed redemption price. Yet, when the high grade bond market dropped far below that redemption scale, we were not allowed to cash in on our prudence. As a result, we and our Series G Bonds both were unpopular with our customers from start to finish.

All these difficulties besetting a trustee emphasize how impossible it has proven to be to reduce to writing these matters of investment policy and prudence, without doing more harm than good. No one has ever written an entirely adequate book on the subject of investments, and all of them have been somewhat out-of-date before they came off the press. The same is true of legislation and judicial decisions on this subject. Laws regarding human rights may be imperishable, but there is a fatal obsolescence factor in legislation regarding investments.

We beg our customers to leave restrictive provisions out of their wills—not to specify railroad bonds, or tax-exempt bonds, or equity ratios. We know that the best thinking of today will be out-of-date and probably costly within a decade. Yet, the entire trust industry is so accustomed to these legal procedures that we accept our handicaps as a part of life. Somehow we must make it unnecessary for the courts to attempt the impossible, as they have for the last century and a half, which is to specify what is right and wrong in investments in an ever changing economy.

NOT ALL TRUSTEES ARE SKILLFUL

Talk to a legislator or your surrogate about these difficulties, and you will find that he is deeply concerned about them. But his point of view will be very different from yours. Surrogates will be quick to explain that their findings concern all trustees, not only banks and trust companies. They will remind you that not all trustees are capable investors. They will explain, as they have many times to all of us, that legislation and the courts must guide the unqualified trustee, and protect life tenants and remaindermen from his incompetence. They will make the point, and quite properly, that resourceful and aggressive management conducted by an expert becomes wild speculation in the hands of the novice trustee.

If a profit on one stock were allowed to offset a loss on another, they point out that an irresponsible trustee might count on one lucky speculation to bail him out of a succession of negligent losses. Nor can they accept from such a man the glib explanation that his losses were all incurred for tax purposes. Wherever fully qualified trustees turn in their campaign for businesslike freedom, the shadow of the novice trustee follows them.

Think what this means! Because a simple little housewife may be a trustee, the entire trust industry must walk slowly at her side, at her pace. We must walk because she does not know how to run.

Because a young garage mechanic may be trustee for his mother, we must wait while he reads chapter one of "An Introduction to Investments." There are trustees, I am sure, who will tell you that a profit margin is found in the annual report, at the bottom of the page, and that it is usually about two inches wide.

"TRUST INVESTMENTS MADE EASY"

Ours is the original "do it yourself" business. We have never persuaded the public, nor any one for that matter, that investment management is something for experts, requiring training and experience and full-time attention. You will see advertised at times a book on "How to Make Money at Home in Your Spare Time." This may concern dressmaking, but I suspect it is a handbook for the novice trustee.

I said novice trustee advisedly, for I mean no criticism of the many highly skillful individual trustees. There are many individuals to whom I would entrust my own family with complete confidence, but the point which I want to make today with great care is this: that there are in this country an unknown number of trustees, many individual and some corporate, who are completely unskilled, inexperienced, and unqualified for the responsibilities they have assumed. It makes no difference whether they are many or few. So long as the possibility exists that a financially uneducated housewife may be a trustee, the lawmakers and the courts have no choice but to be mindful of this possibility. There is no law against incompetence among trustees, and we must all be limited in our discretion because some trustees might abuse the privilege of complete freedom.

There is our problem. Under the rules of the game as we play it now, our pace must be that of the slowest trustee on the field. We might live forever, submissively, in this situation, if we were not losing ground constantly as a result of it. Our investment privileges and practices as trustee are more out-of-date and less adequate than they ever were before. Much of our trust law was written before the Federal Reserve System was established, before income taxes were devised, before the government debt soared into the billions.

TRUSTEES LOSING GROUND COMPETITIVELY

In a study of all financial institutions made by the Federal Reserve Bank of Philadelphia, it was revealed that the share of the nation's assets held by personal trust departments, expressed as a percentage of the whole, has been declining for 20 years. At the same time, other institutions, including the insurance companies and mutual funds, have been increasing their percentage. Now insurance companies are beginning to offer variable annuities, which have the avowed purpose of combatting the effects of inflation. Mutual funds have been established for growth, and some have even been designed to avoid the production of current income. Neither of these media offers the advantages of trust investments, but both of our competitors are alert to prevailing problems.

We should never forget that we have to sell our trust services. We have no monopoly on the management of wealth, and our product may become uncompetitive and some day unsalable. If we do not do something to rid ourselves of our hobbies and our handicaps, others may offer something better than our kind of underprivileged prudence.

Our problem cannot be solved by attempting to obtain special privileges for corporate trustees. This would be grossly unfair to the many highly qualified individuals of all kinds. Many law firms, for example, are staffed and equipped to do an excellent job in investments. It is, of course, not feasible for banks and trust companies to have a law to themselves.

UNLIMITED DISCRETION FOR QUALIFIED TRUSTEES

What we must do is separate the beginners from the experts, the incompetent from the competent, the unqualified from the qualified trustees. It would be entirely logical to insist that a man, or a bank, be capable of assuming responsibility for a trust before being granted unlimited discretion in the conduct of its affairs.

The requirement that trustees be qualified would not be unprecedented, but actually in keeping with what we have always done in this country whenever the public welfare was involved. Doctors must attend medical school and serve a period of internship. Lawyers must attend law school and pass bar examinations. Certified public accountants have been thoroughly tested before gaining the coveted title of CPA. Even a plumber must be qualified to work on the sanitary system in your home. Surely trustees have as much influence over the well-being of their customers, and as much opportunity for good or terrible harm, as these other men who have been so wisely qualified for their work.

If a trustee were to qualify for the responsibilities he assumes, he would have to have a basic understanding of investments, a working knowledge of taxes, and some continuing source of information on these subjects. To meet these standards, he would not have to be an expert by any means, but have only a basic knowledge and a minimum flow of information. This is not a novel suggestion, for it is far less than we demand of others who are responsible for the health and welfare of the public.

I have no thought that a testator should be prevented from naming an unqualified trustee. He would have a way of knowing whether or not his trustee was qualified, however; and he would know that the discretion allowed an unqualified trustee was limited.

NO MONOPOLY FOR BANKS AND TRUST COMPANIES

I know that it will be charged that this is merely a way to obtain the whole trust field for banks and trust companies to the exclusion of individuals. That is by no means the true intent of my proposal. This proposal would be unattainable, and politically unthinkable, if it appeared to be an effort by banks and trust companies to monopolize the trust field.

To assure the authorities of our good intentions, we must add this provision: that trust powers should be withheld from any bank which was unable to qualify at least one of its trustmen.

How this would affect the banks in the trust field I do not know, for it would depend upon the standards which were agreed upon for qualification. However, I do believe, in the light of studies made in New York State in anticipation of Bank Fiduciary Fund, that there is a minimum level of ability below which a bank should not exercise trust powers. Only if we qualify ourselves, while others must be qualified, will this long-awaited freedom be attainable.

Let me summarize briefly the points I have made. Even the Prudent-Man law leaves trustees in most jurisdictions exercising only a substandard form of underprivileged prudence. We are hesitant to take businesslike action to avoid the payment of taxes, and we question our duty to offset the effects of inflation. Even in such matters as diversification and the selection of equities, we offer our trusts something less than our best.

The reason why legislators and surrogates permit us only limited discretion in these matters is that they are mindful of the fact that trustees are a heterogeneous group, some veterans and some beginners, some competent and some incompetent, some qualified and some unqualified. The pace we are required to set is that of the slowest trustee in the group.

I suggest that we must have a means by which trustees, whether they be corporate or individual, may be required to establish their right to full discretion. We have long since crossed this bridge in other professions concerned with the public welfare, such as doctors, lawyers, and certified public accountants.

I propose that we should establish the title of "Qualified Trustee." This would be a joint undertaking by legislators, bar associations, and corporate fiduciaries. I do not underestimate the size of the task. However, anything which is fundamentally sound and urgently needed will inevitably be done, and there is an element of inevitability in this change in the rules of the game.

Having accomplished this, it would at last be feasible to ask for legislation giving greater freedom to Qualified Trustees and relief from the legal handicaps which have accumulated in the past. I believe that in future accountings, the courts would allow greater latitude to Qualified Trustees, for they would know that they were not setting dangerous precedents for the unqualified and the incompetent. Until we achieve this goal, the financial management we give our trusts will be something less than the best of which we are capable.

As matters now stand, our investment product is condemned to mediocrity, because our best effort calls for more skill and more experience than a novice trustee can muster. This fundamental weakness in the trust field will persist, until trustees are required to prepare themselves and qualify themselves for the responsibilities they assume.

In the meanwhile, we shall gain little by amending the law, and by attaining over the years a bit more latitude in the narrow area of discretion allowed us. There is a better course available. We need not be content to play the game forever under a set of rules whereby uninhibited prudence, modern prudence, farsighted prudence will still be prosecuted.

4·4

The Trustee's Dilemma in Growth Stock Investing*

Robert R. Duncan

I propose to re-examine an old familiar subject in the light of modern conditions. I refer to the relationship between life tenant and remainderman in a trust with successive beneficiaries and its effect upon the portfolio of such a trust operated under the Prudent-Man Rule.

The trust relationship can be described as a splitting up of the incidents of property ownership. The legal title to the property and all that usually goes along with legal title is put in one corporation or individual while the equitable interest is vested in others who really have the beneficial enjoyment of the property. The bulk of our business as corporate fiduciaries is built around this device, ancient of origin, and firmly established not only in the law of English-speaking peoples but in the Roman law as well. At a very early time in England, the basic relative rights and duties of the persons holding the legal title, or the trustee, and the owners of the equitable title, the beneficiaries, were established. Thus, for many years the incidents of this split ownership have in general been quite clearly defined. But where there are successive equitable interests, in time, there has always been a problem of fairness in treatment between the two; and the very nature of the problem indicates that there always will be differences of opinion between the successive beneficiaries as to whether or not they have been equally well treated. The basic law on the subject is simple and has for

*From the *Commercial and Financial Chronicle*, June 29, 1961. Reprinted by permission of the *Commercial and Financial Chronicle*, New York.

many decades been firmly established. Professor Scott states it plainly in his work on Trusts as follows (Par. 232):

"Where there are two or more beneficiaries of a trust, the trustee is under a duty to deal impartially with them. This principle has its commonest application where there are successive beneficiaries. Where the trustee is directed to pay the income to a beneficiary during his life and on his death to pay the principal to another beneficiary, the interests of the two beneficiaries are to a certain extent antagonistic and the trustee is under a duty so to administer the trust as to preserve a fair balance between them."

Later on in the same paragraph:

"Thus (the trustee) is under a duty to the beneficiary entitled to the income not to purchase unproductive property or property which yields an income substantially lower than that which is normally earned by trust investments although it may be probable that the property will appreciate in value."

The rule seems fair and reasonable. But as every lawyer knows, the application of the most simple legal rules becomes complicated when varying facts are introduced. The problem was once much simpler because the avenues of investment were so much more limited. In the early days of trusts, when the law was in the process of development, investment by trustees in equities, so-called, was practically unknown. The few common stocks that were in existence were uniformly regarded as improper for the investment of trust funds, and risk-taking of any sort was quite definitely frowned upon. The rate of return to be achieved by a good trustee was the rate which top-grade fixed obligations produced. If the remainderman received, in dollar value, what the trustee had inventoried at the time the trust was created, he was content. The word "growth" as associated with investments had not yet achieved the almost compulsive emphasis it sometimes now seems to have. Nor had inflation come to be accepted by so many as more or less a necessary companion to "economic growth."

SHIFT FROM SAFETY IN PRINCIPAL

Under these conditions, the law of strict impartiality between successive equitable interests was reasonably easy to follow. The trustee who was bound not to give the life tenant more income at the expense of the principal nor skimp the life tenant in order to build up the value of the interest of the remainderman had only to keep the trust funds invested in top-grade fixed obligations to stay within the rule. There was no real incentive for the trustee to consider appreciation in principal value. Safety of principal became the overriding consideration—the standard by which many trustees governed their entire investment policy.

Gradually over the years the emphasis changed. The appearance of many new kinds of investment, the tremendous growth in the number of business corporations, and the corresponding increase in the common stocks available for purchase gave trustees new avenues of investment which could not be ignored. In 1831, the Supreme Judicial Court of Massachusetts laid down the Prudent-Man Rule in Harvard College vs. Amory, and trustees began to see the wisdom of acquiring a stake in the country's future through the purchase of common stocks.

About the same time there began to appear more and more evidence of an especial tenderness for the life tenant. One court held that a trustee was under no duty to realize profits on certain tax-exempt bonds held in the trust although that course would have been most beneficial to the remainderman. In 1941, a Massachusetts judge, speaking before the Mid-Winter Trust Conference in New York, went so far as to say: "I declare with emphasis the trustee should vary investments to meet the needs of the life beneficiary."

This tendency to favor the life tenant is also frequently observed in the language of trust instruments. Perhaps the most common provision is permission to the trustee to invade principal for the benefit of the life tenant. I think it may be generally said that while the rule of impartiality remained, the trustee was justified in resolving any doubtful questions in favor of the life tenant. As one authority put it, the trustee is under no duty to starve the life tenant so that the remainderman may feast. This development seems to me to be only natural. I suggest that it came about because in normal human relationships successive generations of lawyers and trustees have wrestled with the legal requirements of impartiality between successive beneficiaries and their own desire to see the life tenant get the breaks. This feeling is entirely understandable because trustees have all seen at first-hand the real immediate object of the testator's bounty struggle to eke out an existence because the principal must be kept sacredly intact for the benefit of the remainderman. These remainder-men may never even have been known to the creator of the trust. This is more true now than it was in the past because of the desire to escape death duties by stretching the existence of the trust over another generation. Thus, grandchildren and even great-grandchildren of the testator are apt these days to be the ultimate remaindermen as often as children.

The parallel developments of more and more investment in common stocks and particular care for the life tenant went along together quite happily for many years. Common stocks usually produced substantially more income for the life tenant than did fixed obligations and at the same time carried within themselves the possibility of capital improvement that was good for the remainderman. But changes in the economic picture and the technological and scientific revolution since the last war have put additional pressures upon trustees to cope with new problems which have greatly complicated their task. I refer to the decline in the value of the dollar and the related problems of inflation and to the use of the so-called growth stocks.

PROBLEMS OF INFLATION

During the last generation we have seen the value of the dollar in terms of purchasing power more than cut in half as the economy and the money supply have endeavored to sustain the changes which our social revolution has brought about. "Buy now—pay later" has become a governmental as well as an individual slogan. Even apart from the more or less specific policies which have been responsible for the bulk of our inflation, many of our best known economists speak glibly in terms of "creeping inflation" of the order of 3% per year as if that is something to be borne in silence and ignored in prosperity. Under these circumstances, remaindermen cannot be blamed if they take a dim view of receiving, in dollar value, only the appraised value of the estate a generation earlier. These remaindermen demand, and it seems to me with considerable justice, that trust funds should be invested so that there will be an appreciation in their value to offset the lessening in the worth of the dollar over the period of the operation of the trust.

When the performance of a trustee or investment manager today is examined as to the success of his operation, he can no longer point proudly to the fact that the principal of the trust is intact. Rather will he be asked when he established his original book value, what the averages were at that time; and his success will be measured by how much more than that is the current market of the trust portfolio. It is difficult to quarrel with this approach under our present economic system, and certainly it is an appropriate criterion when the demands of the contract do not require any particular segregation of principal and income. But at times it puts a conscientious trustee who is under the necessity of impartial treatment between successive beneficiaries, and who really wishes to be especially sure that the life tenant gets the benefit of the doubt, in an almost intolerable position.

RULE AGAINST SPECULATION

The trustee also has another important consideration which he must watch. Regardless of the treatment of successive beneficiaries, it has always been plain that a trustee is not permitted to speculate. Webster defines this word as "to enter into a transaction or venture, the profits of which are conjectural or subject to chance." He also gives another meaning to the word, which he characterizes as "how rare"—namely, "to theorize from conjectures without sufficient evidence." Sometimes I think I might differ from him as to how "rare" that course of procedure is today. In any event, we are all familiar with the prohibition against speculation. That great fountainhead of all wisdom on the subject, Harvard College vs. Amory, specifically limited the wide discretions which it laid down by saying that investments should not be made by a trustee "with regard to speculation."

With all these considerations in mind, let us try to analyze further the problem which faces the trustee under a trust with successive beneficiaries which must be operated under the Prudent-Man Rule. Let us particularly consider the nature of some of these investments which eager remaindermen seem so anxious to include in the trust portfolio. I refer, of course, to the so-called growth stocks. How are we to reconcile the duty of the trustee not to speculate, to produce a reasonable income for the life tenant, and to protect the remainderman from the erosion caused by the forces of inflation. I am sure it is necessary only to state the proposition to become aware of the seriousness of the trustees' dilemma. I think it is also plain that no one rule can be laid down which will point the way out of the dilemma in all cases.

DEFINING AN ACCEPTABLE GROWTH STOCK

How shall we define a growth stock? Very obviously, it is one which the investor believes will increase in value in the market. But the reasons which may be responsible for that increase are varied. It is in the difference between these reasons for listing a stock as a growth stock that most of the difficulty lies. There is also involved the degree of growth which is hoped for. Over the last decade, I would think that good utility stocks have been an excellent example of what I might call "conservative" growth stocks. Their financial position has been good, the increase in their business has rested upon the sound expansion of business in their territories, and there has been a reasonable return in the process.

The difficulty with growth stocks arises over the preoccupation of so many people with making capital gains. When a "glamor" stock first begins to show signs of promise, it is likely to partake too much of speculation to justify its inclusion in a Prudent-Man-portfolio. At that time, individual investors, frankly looking for capital gains only, step into the picture. Their effort to "get in on the ground floor" sends the stock skyrocketing and by the time when in ordinary course the stock might have escaped from the category of speculation, its price earnings ratio has gone so high that the Prudent-Man trustee finds himself on the other horn of the dilemma—i.e., there is no longer sufficient income available to satisfy the trustee's obligations to the life tenant. Yet, under these circumstances many remaindermen continue to press for the inclusion of such stocks in the portfolio.

Trustees would all agree, I'm sure, that in any trust portfolio we do want a reasonable portion of stocks that have the possibility of growth. The difficulty is that we have become, as Bascom Torrance said in 1958, "by growth obsessed." Insufficient attention has been paid to a definition of the term and to attempting to determine what kind of growth stocks is appropriate for inclusion in a Prudent-Man portfolio. The general public has become obsessed with the idea that a growth stock must be one operating in a relatively new field with particular attention to the rapid changes in technology and science. Attention has been focused almost entirely upon the thing which is being produced and the possibilities of profit in the competitive field which accrue from the marketing of such a product when it is "new."

It seems to me time for us trustees to do a little defining of growth stocks. It seems to me time for us to recognize that we need to find new measures against which we can evaluate growth stocks with a view to including them in our portfolio. There are many qualifications which should be considered in the nature of any stock before it can qualify as a trust investment, and the hope and belief that it will advance in price in the market is only one of them. The specific product and the demand for it from the public, the use of new scientific and technological processes, is another part of the definition. We must realize that in addition we must find that management has the know-how to convert the exploitation of a product or a process into net income. Managerial skills for our purposes are not to be confined to the ability to create new and shiny products. So far as trustee investors operating under the Prudent-Man Rule are concerned, they must include in addition a facility to convert that ability into income dollars.

We should admit at the outset that a rationalization of our approach to this problem is almost surely going to bar us from acquiring these fantastic growth or "glamor" stocks in the early stages of their development. Hence, we are going to be barred from the tremendous price appreciation which may accrue to the benefit of speculatively minded individuals; and we must recognize that even the most astute individual investors, on the record, have found the only way to accomplish a successful participation in this field is to divide the risk. Such an investor will almost invariably make a number of investments in such promising corporations, realizing that he need pick only one or two winners out of a dozen in order to make his program pay off. But this is no program for a Prudent-Man trustee. He is constantly under the necessity of staying within the law, which does not permit a portfolio to be considered as a whole nor to offset a loss in one stock against a gain in another. This alone would be enough to bar him from following a program such as I have suggested.

Now, I want to make it plain that my remarks are confined solely to a trustee who is bound to follow a rule no broader than the Prudent-Man Rule. We all understand, I am sure, that in the governing instrument there may be appropriate words giving authority to the fiduciary to proceed beyond the bounds of the Prudent-Man Rule. Typical of such a situation is the agency account where the difference between income and principal is of no importance so far as our present situation is concerned. Here the fiduciary can feel free to make recommendations which concern themselves entirely with anticipated improvements in market value. But in a true trust situation, where there are no special investment powers and the trustee must rely on the trust law of his own state (which will certainly be no broader than the Prudent-Man Rule), how should he make his choice?

ADVOCATES DUAL APPROACH

I suggest that the trustee, in such circumstances, should make a dual approach: first, he should look very carefully at the circumstances of the beneficiaries in the particular trust; secondly, he should divide growth stocks into categories.

As to the first point, the need of the specific life tenant is of the utmost importance. If we assume a case of an elderly widow who needs the income for tomorrow morning's breakfast, it seems to me wrong to speak in terms of substantial sacrifice of income for possible later capital gains. It does not follow that the entire fund must be invested in interest-bearing securities. There are many stocks which produce a reasonable income and yet have growth possibilities.

Take another case. Suppose a substantial trust held for the benefit of a widow with remainder to her children. There is ample income for the widow's needs, and her main interest is that her children shall inherit substantial property. A prudent trustee in this situation might well go a little further down the road of lower-income growth stocks than in the case earlier mentioned. At least in the matter of treating successive beneficiaries fairly he would not be subject to criticism. I submit that the solution of this question of fairness as between successive beneficiaries requires a close analysis of the facts in each trust and a tailor-made investment portfolio to fit the situation.

What about the second point—the separation of growth stocks into groups? Now, there is almost an infinite number of stocks which to some degree might be called growth issues. I hope none of us buys any stocks unless we think that for one reason or another the company whose stock we acquire has the possibility of growing. The issue lies in the degree of growth. Unfortunately, in recent years there has been some tendency to confuse growth with glamor, to import into the meaning of the word "growth" some content of "mushroom" growth, of new and violently active exploitation of the new technological and scientific breakthroughs that have come so rapidly in the years since the war. But that is not the only kind of growth that we should think about. I have already pointed out the dilemma that the trust faces here.

UTILITY STOCKS

There is an extensive middle ground in which vigorous elements of growth may be found and yet where management has already found the skills to conduct a reasonably profitable enterprise while the growth is occurring. Many utility stocks, unglamorous though they may be, are a shining example of this group. They have grown because their product—energy—has been more and more needed, and because the users of that product have multiplied. I doubt that any trustee, upon reviewing common stocks list over the last decade, will find another group of common stocks, eligible for Prudent-Man Rule investment, which has grown more in market value than the utilities. Some may have seen the quip of the chap who said he'd stuck by A. T. & T. because it seemed to him that come depression—come boom—the amount of yackety-yak seemed constantly on the increase.

Then there are the stocks of companies which have become firmly established on a profitable basis but whose managements have been constantly venturing in the new fields that our scientists and technologists are pulling out of the hat every day. I'm not talking only about the old-line blue-chip stocks, although I certainly wouldn't sell them short in this connection. There are other and smaller companies which have been able to do pretty well for themselves dollar-wise and at the same time found funds to conduct their own R&D program.

In summary, I would say that the Prudent-Man trustee must view the whole spectrum of common stocks through glasses which have no rosy tint of speculation. He must know the needs of his beneficiaries, and in the light of those needs he must decide upon an investment program which will stand the test of impartiality if it be questioned. He must nevertheless acquire in his common stock portfolio stocks which have the reasonable expectation of increasing in value while they continue to provide a living for the income beneficiaries.

4·5

Common Stocks
and Pension Fund Investing*

Paul L. Howell

Rising wages, higher living costs, and lower bond yields demand a more dynamic and productive investment policy for the huge pension reserves which are now being accumulated for the protection of the aged. With the development of collective bargaining for "fringe benefits," the responsibility for supplying a major portion of this old-age security is being transferred from the individual to the enterprise that employed him during his working life. Consider these facts and problems of the existing pension fund situation:

Inflation has already doubled and may soon triple the expense of providing this deferred wage benefit for the retired worker. The impact on pension costs of the rising price level is only beginning to be felt by industry as the demand mounts for increased benefits based on higher future terminal wages, together with fuller funding, earlier vesting, and earlier retirement. This impact on costs is forcefully illustrated by the fact that even at the present time one-third of the current pension contributions of the Bell Telephone System are required to make up the inadequacies of past contributions caused by subsequently rising wage levels and liberalization of benefits which could not have been forecast when the original accrual rates were established. The pension expense now constitutes over 6% of the Bell payroll, exclusive of OASI taxes.

The percentage of the wage bill attributable to pensions will increase. Walter Reuther, in the pattern-setting negotiations with the Big Three in the automobile industry, has already demanded a "cost of living" adjustment in pensions for auto workers. Moreover, further inflation seems indicated, what with increased defense spending, the Federal Reserve's easy-money policy, Treasury deficits, and recession spending for schools, roads, and so forth. Forward-looking actuaries are suggesting the inclusion of a factor in their cost estimates for secular inflation.

In the implementation of these retirement programs, pension funds have become a new financial giant. These funds are growing at a rate of $4.3 billion a year

*From *Harvard Business Review*, **36**, no. 6, November–December 1958, pp. 92–106.

and currently aggregate $1.4 billion and $19 billion for insured and corporate-trusteed plans, respectively. The public interest in these industrial pension funds centers around their earning power, since this is fundamental in minimizing the cost of the increased retirement benefits. Current easy-credit policies and the resulting lower interest rates are of special significance, for they reduce the earning power of these funds at a most crucial time.

Of similar importance are the amounts and quality of the fund assets "guaranteeing" the ability of the employer corporation to perform its promise of a deferred wage payment. These accumulating funds may be considered as collateral or a pledge for the specific performance of the employer's promise to pay pension benefits years or even several decades later. Currently, 11 million workers, plus a substantial number of dependents, rely on private noninsured retirement plans as a major portion of their old-age security. To them, the employers' contributions are, in effect, a form of involuntary savings.

With situations such as these in existence, it is appropriate now, after 15 years of mushroom growth, to review the principles and accomplishments of pension fund management. It is the purpose of this article to question the validity of certain customarily accepted institutional thinking and the resultant "orthodox" practices. In essence, one might call this article a study of the more efficient use of a major business resource.

PROPOSED APPROACH

Careful analysis of retirement programs brings to light the following factors that are of significance in the current formulation of fund investment policy:

There is an extremely long period of accumulation and distribution of funds. In fact, although employees come and go, there is no prospect that accumulating pension funds will ever be liquidated.

Inflow of money (contributions and earnings) will exceed outgo by a substantial margin for the foreseeable future. Sustained growth of pension funds is to be expected for the next generation.

A qualified pension fund is completely exempt from income and capital gains taxation as a "charitable" trust.

Retirement plans are not subject to catastrophic hazards; retirements and payouts can be forecast years in advance.

There are virtually no legislative investment restrictions.

There is no need to distinguish between principal and income in recording capital appreciation and cash receipts as is required for life tenant or remainderman interests.

Investment-portfolio managers are generally concerned with a few basic specifications. Safety of principal and liquidity are major items of interest. Others include: certainty and adequacy of return, capital appreciation, marketability, collateral value and maturity, and, finally, the tax aspects of the portfolio. The attainment of some of these objectives necessarily conflicts with or limits the achievement of other objectives.

In the light of the framework outlined above, I submit that these five criteria should govern the formulation and execution of pension fund investment policy:

1. In the management of pension funds, their productivity (dividend yield and capital appreciation) should be the primary objective, completely overshadowing all others.

2. As a corollary of this, inflation should not play a part in determining pension fund investment policy. Investment management should get as large a return as is feasible, regardless of stable or rising prices. The only situation in which inflation becomes a factor is the selection of industries and companies which will be benefited or impeded by changing price levels.

3. There is almost complete absence of any need for liquidity.

4. Pension funds should be invested as received, i.e., full investment all the time. This amounts to "dollar-cost averaging."

5. Because of full investment, growth, the absence of catastrophic hazards, and dollar-cost averaging (instead of formula programing), there is little need to take a defensive position with the resultant lowering of over-all portfolio yield.

INCREASING THE RETURN

Most retirement plans are set up on an actuarial expectation of earning 2.5% to 3.0%. Because of the long period of accumulation and subsequent distribution, the rate of return on invested funds is the dominant factor in determining pension costs to employers or benefits to retired workers.

An increase of pension fund yield of 1% (e.g., from 2.5% to 3.5%) will increase benefits approximately 25% or decrease costs about 20%. Needless to say, an increase of benefits to retired employees is of no small significance, whether there are stable prices or inflationary losses of purchasing power, for in many cases industrial pensions are not far above the subsistence level for most workers.

Because of the time period over which compound interest has an opportunity to work its miracle, an increase in the effective return from 2.5% to 6% will increase the accumulations so that benefits can be nearly doubled or costs correspondingly reduced. Is the achievement of a 6% return so difficult or revolutionary? Or is it reasonably attainable in actual conservative practice? I believe that it is attainable, and that a systematic program of periodic purchases of diversified, professionally selected common stocks is the soundest way to achieve the lowest cost or the greatest retirement benefits.

I recognize that a program of 100% investment in common stock is quite contrary to orthodox institutional investment thinking. At the same time, I want to emphasize that my quarrel is not with accepted pension fund objectives—who can dispute the soundness of such goals as liquidity and safety of the principal? Rather, I challenge the appropriateness, under modern conditions, of conventional assumptions as to how these objectives can best be attained. It is time to break out of the strait jacket of past thinking, which, in my opinion, is most inept and extremely costly.

RECORD OVER TIME

What does the record reveal? The monumental investigation of the performance of common stocks by the Cowles Commission[1] shows that the achievement of a 6% return over a sustained period is not impossible. On the contrary, the mediocre results of the market averages do *better* than 6%. In fact, when the Cowles Commission made its intensive analysis of the market and income results of a broad list of industrial, rail, and utility common stocks, covering the period from just after the Civil War to the middle of the 1930's depression, it found that these stocks averaged a net return (dividends and market appreciation) over this 68-year period of nearly 7%. In detail:

	Dividends	Gains	Total
Industrials	5.3%	2.8%	8.1%
Rails	4.8	0.0	4.8
Utilities	5.5	0.6	6.1
Composite	5.0%	1.8%	6.8%

If this study were extended through 1957 it would be found that the average return (dividends and appreciation) would exceed 7.5%.[2]

Similarly, the Dow-Jones industrial average of market prices has increased nearly 3% per year during the past 50 years, with an annual dividend yield exceeding 5% and an earnings payout of less than 60%. As Edgar Lawrence Smith pointed out many years ago, the compound effect of retained earnings upon market performance is enormous.[3] If $100 had been invested in the Dow-Jones industrial average securities each year beginning with 1929, results at the end of 1957 would be as follows:

[1]Alfred Cowles et al., *Common-Stock Indexes*, 1871–1937, Cowles Commission for Research in Economics, Monograph No. 3 (Bloomington, Principia Press, 1938); see also R. Minturn Sedgwick, "A New Pension Plan," HBR January–February 1953, p. 70.
[2]See performance of *Standard & Poor's Common Stock Index* during the past two decades.
[3]*Common Stocks as Long Term Investments* (New York, The Macmillan Company, 1924).

Total investment	$2,900
Market value (at 1957 average prices)	$8,551
Compound annual increase in market value	6.60%
Total dividends received (29 years); not reinvested	$3,903
Average dividend yield on cumulative investment	7.20%
Over-all effective rate of ncrease	13.80%

That the attainment of a 6% yield is a reasonable pension fund objective is corroborated by the actual accomplishment by conservatively minded life insurance companies during 1929–1955, a period which included one of the most disastrous depressions in our economic history.

While life insurance investment has been predominately in bonds, there has been sufficient common stock investment to provide a reliable guide to what these institutions have been able to earn in the crucible of actual performance. Combined common stock holdings of 18 representative life insurance companies have grown from $57 million in 1929 to over $700 million today. For the 27-year period, 1929–1955, the over-all rate of total return was 6.49%; this exceeded the bond return by 100%. The earnings experience of these life insurance companies is summarized in Table 1. (Many other studies have been made which also confirm this long-run productivity of common stocks.[4])

It is indeed true that if an *entire* fund had been invested in 1928 or 1929, history would show that it would take nearly 15 years to recoup itself. But pension funds do not invest huge amounts *en masse* at the top of a bull market. Regular periodic investment or dollar averaging, during the subsequent depression, would have more than compensated for the losses sustained on the small proportion of funds invested at the height of the stock market boom.

PROFESSIONAL COUNSELING

Who should oversee the handling of pension fund investment policy? Investment management is a complex technical job which requires ex-

[4]See, for instance, Chelcie C. Bosland, *The Common Stock Theory of Investment* (New York, The Ronald Press Company, 1937); Wilford J. Eiteman, "Yield on Common Stock Investment," *The Analysts Journal*, February 1957, p. 13; Wilford J. Eiteman and Frank P. Smith, "Common Stock Values and Yields," Michigan Business Studies (Ann Arbor, University of Michigan Press, June 1953); Benjamin Graham, "Long Term Outlook for Equities," *The Commercial and Financial Chronicle*, November 27, 1952, p. 4; August Ihlefeld, *Equity Investing by Mutual Savings Banks* (New York, Savings Bank Trust Company, 1953); *A Report in Support of the Proposed Amendments to Article 5, Section 81 of the New York Insurance Law* (New York, Life Insurance Association of America, January 30, 1951); Dwight C. Rose, *A Scientific Approach to Investment Management* (New York, Harper & Brothers, 1928); Winthrop B. Walker, *A Reexamination of Common Stocks as Long Term Investments* (Portland, Maine, Anthoesen Press, 1954); and James J. Jehring, *The Investment and Administration of Profit Sharing Trust Funds* (Evanston, Profit Sharing Research Foundation, 1957).

TABLE 1. *Comparison of rates of return secured on bonds and on preferred and common stocks by 18 life insurance companies, 1929–1955*

	Over-all rate of return*	Rate of interest or dividend return†
Bonds	3.26%	3.15%
Preferred	4.71	4.52
Common	6.49	5.55

*Includes interest earnings (dividend earnings) plus net profits or losses on the disposal of securities.
†Includes interest earnings (dividend earnings) only.
NOTE: Base is the average cost of the portfolios as of beginning and end of year. The bond portfolios include accrued interest.
SOURCE: James J. O'Leary, 1957 *Record of Life Insurance Investments* (New York, Life Insurance Association of America, December 1957), Table 7, p. 22.

perienced managerial skill supported by extensive staff research. Such specialized management should show earnings results substantially above unsupervised averages. A professionally managed common stock fund should earn at least 25% more than does the average unmanaged stock fund. Thus, a professionally managed pension fund should earn, over an extended period, a net return, including allowances for capital losses, in excess of 7.5%.

If such returns are to be realized, the pension fund should have the services of an investment counselor upon whose competence, personal attention, research staff, and continuity of advice the fund can depend. Too often lawyers or accountants are asked to advise when they do not have either the specialized training, a research staff, or the time to devote to this activity. Trust officers, through long adherence to fiduciary principles of protecting the principal of the estate, may not have the proper mental attitude for equity investment.

The professional investment analyst, with his training and staff, can provide the type of direction a fund must have to earn its fullest potential. Moreover, such counseling should be retained on a fee basis (as opposed to the way stockbrokers are compensated) to avoid conflicts of interest where a commission is at stake.

NEED FOR BALANCE?

It is frequently urged that portfolios should contain a "proper" balance. Although this is of the utmost importance in certain types of portfolios, a pension fund has the characteristics of being large, diversified, dollar-averaged, fully invested, long-term, and growing—with almost no need for liquidity. For such a fund there is virtually no need for a bond defense.

There may be times—as in the summer of 1957, when interest rates were high, stock yields low, and stock prices beginning to soften—when it would seem appropriate for an alert management to switch to bonds. This, however, would probably be a short-run operation which might obscure or even defeat the long-run dollar-averaging objective. As a matter of fact, most of such switch investors remained in bonds too long and thus missed out on the market rise in early 1958. Consequently, their over-all investment performance was inferior to those who consistently dollar-averaged in equities. Fixed-dollar obligations, since they are no protection against inflation, may be just as speculative as common stocks. It should be remembered that investment in bonds is not all a bed of roses. Bonds can default, too!

The memory of 1929 and 1932 is still strong. Actually, the stock market fall from 1929 to 1932 offset the previous unwarranted rise. A person who was in equities *before* 1928 would have found his book losses of 1932–1933 soon converted back into profits. Persons who practiced dollar-cost averaging by systematic stock purchases month by month through this period came out much better than those who kept their funds in fixed-income obligations.

In speaking of balance, it should be recalled that balance refers to the *over-all* situation. Most pension recipients will be receiving Social Security which, of course, is backed up by government bonds. Also, many will have savings accounts and insurance programs, with perhaps an interest in real estate. These all help provide "balance." Cash reserves in the pension fund do not do the retired worker any good.

Higher Standards

Great institutional changes have taken place which make common stock investment increasingly appropriate. And substantial progress has been made in developing financial responsibility and adherence to high fiduciary standards since the Armstrong Insurance Investigation of 1906. Moreover, improved accounting and auditing standards, together with full disclosure and Securities and Exchange Commission (SEC) supervision, have made company reports a sturdy foundation on which to analyze common stock earning prospects.

Administrative controls of common stock trading, by the stock exchanges and the SEC, likewise provide a much steadier foundation for common stock purchases and subsequent valuations. In addition, current controls by the Federal Reserve Board on margins, credit, and interest rates are far more effective.

Recent legislative events point to a liberalizing of investment thinking. In 1950–1957 New York State amended its laws to allow up to 35% investment in common stocks for nondiscretionary trusts, and for insurance companies, up to 50% of surplus or 5% of assets, whichever is smaller. Commercial banks' commingled trust funds, developed pursuant to Regulation F of the Federal Reserve Board, now hold substantial amounts of common stock.

In brief, the country has matured substantially. Cannot we expect a diversified list of common stocks, professionally selected, to provide, over a long period of time and on a reliable basis, substantially greater net results than a bond fund?

SOME ACCOMPLISHMENTS

In evaluating investment management it is of utmost importance to look at the record and see what has been accomplished. There are, however, several difficulties in comparing the performance of various pension funds:

Many pension funds, for real or fancied reasons, have different managerial objectives. These may be influenced by what is considered to be the best interests of prospective pensioners, by the financial or tax status of the employer, and by the financial status of the pension fund. These varying influences affect management policy and trust-indenture instructions. In fact, it may not be appropriate to compare the operating results of two funds managed by the same trustee. Furthermore, short-term comparisons may be quite inappropriate where one fund is investing for income and another for long-pull capital gains. Nevertheless, market averages *do* provide a rough standard for measurement of performance.

A serious shortcoming in evaluating management performance is the lack of adequate and reliable data on fund earnings. Despite the public interest in pension funds and the fact that they do not belong to the employer corporation, there is at present only a grudging release of fragmentary data with respect to the composition and earnings of funds. The recent passage during the closing days of the 85th Congress of the Welfare and Pension Plans Act of 1958 should go far in providing these desirable data.

Comparison of actual management performance is currently difficult because of lack of homogeneity of the data. For instance, are comparisons being made on a cost, accrual, or market basis? Are realized capital gains taken into account? What considerations should be weighed in evaluating management performance with respect to unrealized appreciation? Does not the decision to sell or hold assets with capital gains change the resulting yield without changing the actual performance?

TABLE 2. *Distribution by types of assets of corporate pension funds, as of December 31, 1957**

	Amount — Value			Per cent of excess market over book
Type of asset	Book	Per cent	Market	
Cash and deposits	$ 368	2.9%	$ 368	
U. S. Government securities	2,032	10.5	1,987	− 2.3%
Corporate bonds	10,392	53.8	9,784	− 5.9
Own company	641		†	
Other companies	9,751		†	
Preferred stock	611	3.1	550	−10.0
Common stock	4,770	24.7	6,024	26.2
Own company	584		860	47.3
Other companies	4,186		5,164	23.2
Mortgages	313	1.6	313	
Other assets	833	4.3	833	
Total assets	$19,319	100.0%	$19,859	2.7%

*In millions of dollars.
†Data not available.
SOURCE: Securities and Exchange Commission, Statistical Release No. 1533 (June 8, 1958), pp. 3–4.

PORTFOLIO STRUCTURE

Table 2 shows the fixed-income component of corporate-trusteed pension funds to be 70%. Common stock holdings on a book value basis amount to 25%, while on a market value basis they represent 30% of the combined funds. The distribution of common stock holdings is shown in Table 3 (derived from the Mooney Report[5]). Common stock holdings of trusteed pension funds are concentrated in the industrial field to the extent of 72%, while bond holdings are concentrated in the utility field. A list of the 20 most popular stocks with pension trustees is set forth in Table 4. On a cost basis, net purchases of common stock aggregating $970 million were made in 1957. This is as much as 37% of net receipts of trusteed funds.

Two other points worthy of note are (a) the small amount of preferred stock holdings and (b) the almost insignificant holdings of real estate mortgages and related assets. It is alleged that administrative details deter

[5]George A. Mooney, *Pension and Other Employee Welfare Plans: A Survey of Funds Held by State and National Banks in New York State* (New York, New York State Banking Department, December 30, 1955).

TABLE 3. *Distribution by industry of common-stock holdings of pension funds trusteed with New York banks, as of September 30, 1954*

Industry	Amount*	Per cent
Railroads	$ 11.7	0.9%
Public utilities	181.3	13.4
Industrials	981.0	72.4
Banks & insurance companies	139.6	10.3
Investment companies	26.0	1.9
Finance companies	7.1	0.5
Miscellaneous	8.0	0.6
Total	$1,354.7	100.0%

*In millions of dollars.
SOURCE: Mooney Report, Table 3.

TABLE 4. *List of 20 most popular common stocks held by pension funds trusteed with New York banks, as of December 31, 1954* *

Company	Number of banks	Market value*
Socony Mobil Oil Co.	30	$50.3
J. C. Penney & Co.	17	49.4
General Electric Co.	24	39.4
International Business Machines	15	38.3
Standard Oil Co. (New Jersey)	37	35.6
Texas Co.	21	35.3
American Tel. & Tel.	45	33.4
Westinghouse Electric Co.	29	29.0
General Motors Corp.	29	27.6
International Paper Co.	15	25.6
Union Carbide & Carbon	13	23.0
E. I. Du Pont de Nemours	36	21.9
Gulf Oil Corp.	25	17.3
Standard Oil Co. of California	16	16.5
B. F. Goodrich Co.	9	16.0
Christiana Securities Co.	8	15.5
National Lead Co.	15	15.3
Dow Chemical Co.	21	15.0
Sears, Roebuck & Co.	17	13.9
American Can Co.	17	13.3

*In millions of dollars.
SOURCE: Mooney Report, Table 4.

entrance into this latter field. Insurance companies, however, have overcome these servicing difficulties, and mortgages are the backbone of their earnings assets. Recent proposals have been made for central servicing and should go far to improve the marketability and attractiveness of such an outlet for funds.

The distribution shown in Table 2 is, of course, not typical of any particular portfolio. There are great individual variations, with some funds invested almost entirely in government bonds while other funds have a

TABLE 5. *Corporate pension funds classified by industry of employer* *

Industry	Amount †	Per cent	Yield‡
Manufacturing	$12,224	63%	3.83%
Electric, gas, & water	928	5	3.94
Transportation	873	5	4.03
Communication	2,769	14	3.24
Trade	1,528	8	4.57
Financial & real estate	734	4	4.41
Other§	263	1	3.86
All industries	$19,319	100%	3.84%

*In millions of dollars.
†Assets listed at book value.
‡Income from dividends, interest, and rent divided by average of assets at book value at beginning and end of year, less one-half investment income; no allowance made for realized or unrealized capital gains.
§Extractive, construction, and services.
SOURCE: Securities and Exchange Commission, op. cit., Tables 2 and 4.

substantial proportion of their assets invested in common stock of the employer corporation. Distribution of pension funds according to industrial groups accumulating them and their relative earnings is set forth in Table 5.

KINDS OF EARNINGS

Table 6 tabulates the reported investment return for 541 pension funds in the fiscal year 1953. From this exhibit it is easily seen that there is substantial variation in the earnings rate of different pension funds. Earnings average about a quarter of a per cent lower when net capital gains are excluded. What is surprising is the number of funds earning less than 3%. (Of course, true comparisons of performance should take into consideration unrealized capital gains, which would make the figures of Table 6 higher. Though not an advocate of "counting chickens before they are hatched," I think that capital gains—or losses—*are* an important aspect of investment proficiency.)

Analysis of the SEC data shows that, except for very small ones, the

TABLE 6. *Distribution of pension funds according to the approximate rate of investment return earned for fiscal 1953*

Reported rates of return (including profits and losses)	Number of funds	Per cent of total	Cumulative per cent of total
0.01%–1.99%	15	2.8%	2.8%
2.00 −2.24	7	1.3	4.1
2.25 −2.49	26	4.8	8.9
2.50 −2.74	41	7.6	16.5
2.75 −2.99	87	16.1	32.6
3.00 −3.24	116	21.4	54.0
3.25 −3.49	97	17.9	71.9
3.50 −3.74	70	12.9	84.8
3.75 −3.99	38	7.0	91.8
4.00 −4.49	23	4.3	96.1
4.50 −4.99	10	1.9	98.0
5.00 and over	11	2.0	100.0
Total number of funds	541	100.0%	

SOURCE: Mooney Report, Table 33.

size of the fund does not seem to be correlated with the rate of return. Small funds, reported as earning much less than other funds, may be new and may not have had a chance to "hit their stride," or they may be funds of small corporations "conservatively" managed with a large holding of governments.

Table 7 classifies pension funds managed by New York bank trustees according to whether the trust indenture restricted trustees to "legals" for

TABLE 7. *Average rate of investment return earned on pension funds trusteed with New York banks*

Type of portfolio	Number of funds	Amount*	Per cent	Rate of return†
Only in "legals" for New York life insurance companies	126	$1,954‡	39.9%	2.93%
No general investment restrictions	627	2,051	41.9	3.49
Others	271	890	18.2	
Total	1,024	$4,895	100.0%	3.18%

*In millions of dollars.
†Covers last available year prior to September 30, 1954. Excluded from "earnings" are all profits or losses on sale or redemption of investments. The common stock funds might well have a "real" return of a much larger amount.
‡Mostly Bell Telephone System.
SOURCE: Mooney Report, Table 27.

New York life insurance companies or whether the trustees were permitted general investment discretion. This exhibit shows that discretionary funds earned 56 basis points (i.e., hundredths of 1%) or 19% more than the restricted accounts. Although the restricted accounts include 126 funds, the dollar amount is dominated by the conservative Bell Telephone pension fund.

This differential, of course, does not represent or express the true differential between bonds and common stocks as investments. A number of the so-called discretionary funds are still heavily weighted with fixed-income assets.

IMPORTANCE OF CAPITAL GAINS

Table 8 shows net income from interest and dividends and realized net profits from capital transactions (principally net capital gains) for each of the last three years.

TABLE 8. *Analysis of receipts of pension funds, 1955–1957*

Source	Amount* 1955	Amount* 1956	Amount* 1957	Per cent 1955	Per cent 1956	Per cent 1957
Employer contributions	$1,802	$2,052	$2,303	69.8	69.7	69.3
Employee contributions	222	267	316	8.6	9.1	9.5
Income (interest & dividends)	463	558	677	17.9	18.8	20.3
Net profits realized from capital transactions	84	49	11	3.3	1.7	0.4
Miscellaneous	12	19	15	0.4	0.7	0.5
Total	2,583	2,945	3,322	100.0	100.0	100.0

*In millions of dollars.
SOURCE: Securities and Exchange Commission, op. cit., Table 3.

Security and Exchange Commission figures, presented in Table 9, show that the over-all rate of earnings, exclusive of capital gains, was 3.58%, 3.68%, and 3.84% for the past three years. Capital gains would, when added, increase the yield rate to 4.22%, 3.92%, and 3.90%, respectively. When compounded over a number of years, such an increment in yield is an important supplement in fund accumulation.

Net capital gains were not large in 1957 according to Table 8, because the gross gains realized were greatly reduced by losses, primarily in the bond account. For example, the net earnings rate on the all-bond portfolio of the New York Telephone Company was reduced from 3.23% to 3.02% by the losses sustained on liquidation of governments.

The importance, however, of common stocks and capital gains for pension funds is greatly understated even in these figures because:

In the first place, the common stock component of pension funds is still relatively small as a per cent of the total fund. Thus, realized capital gains represent a very substantial addition to the dividend income of common stocks.

A large amount of the capital gains realized on common stocks was used to offset losses on the bond account, such as liquidation of governments.

Another factor that does not show in the realized-gains figures is the fact that most of the common stock held by pension funds has been of recent acquisition and that it takes time for capital to appreciate.

Another factor, and one of great importance, is that a large amount of capital gains is below the surface—unrealized and only occasionally recognized. The fact that these gains are unrealized does not make them any less important in achieving the long-run fund objectives. There is not much point in simply selling stocks to record the capital gain. The fact that these gains exist *is* of extreme significance in helping to fund liabilities and to pay future benefits.

It is a conventional, and probably sound, accounting practice in most business situations not to record unrealized capital appreciation—sometimes referred to as "paper profits." Nevertheless, it is absolutely necessary

TABLE 9. *Rate of return earned on corporate pension funds compared with earnings of insurance companies, 1951–1957*

		Insurance companies	
Year	Pension funds*	Before federal income tax	After federal income tax
1951	3.05%	3.18%	2.98%
1952	3.21	3.28	3.07
1953	3.34	3.36	3.15
1954	3.65	3.46	3.24
1955	3.58	3.51	3.23
1956	3.68	3.63	3.33
1957	3.84	3.75	3.44

*No adjustment for capital gains or losses sustained.
NOTE: For 1951–1954, return computed as follows: income from dividends, interest, and rent divided by average of assets at book value at beginning and end of year for universe data. For 1955–1957, return computed as follows: income from dividends, interest, and rent divided by averages of assets at book value at beginning and end of year, less one-half of investment income.
SOURCE: Vito Natrella, *Implications of Pension Fund Accumulations*, Proceedings of the Business and Economic Statistics Section of the American Statistical Association (Washington, 1957), pp. 140 ff; Securities and Exchange Commission, *Survey of Corporate Pension Funds*, 1951–1954 (Washington, 1956), Table 8, p. 32; Securities and Exchange Commission, Statistical Release No. 1533 (June 8, 1958), Table 4; and Institute of Life Insurance, *Life Insurance Fact Book* (New York, 1957), p. 55.

to consider such gains in making valid or appropriate comparisons of fund policy and performance. To leave such gains out of consideration would be to omit an essential element.

APPRECIATION GIVES PROTECTION

Although an increase in earnings of 10% (or 35 basis points) resulting from realized capital gains is not to be dismissed lightly, the magnitude of unrealized capital appreciation is even larger and should become still more important as larger proportions of common stock are held, and held for longer periods of time. For example, Table 2 contrasts the book cost and market values of pension assets as of the end of 1957, after interest rates and stock prices had reached a peak. Government and corporate bonds showed unrealized capital losses of 2.3% and 5.9%, respectively, and fixed-dividend preferred stock showed a decline of 10.0%; but common stock, which probably had an average holding of less than four years, showed an appreciation of 26%.

Thus, the common stock component provided a net over-all portfolio appreciation of 2.7% on funds reporting to the SEC. Instead of bonds being a defensive protection, common stock appreciation provided the protective reserve against fluctuations in the interest rate. The sometimes maligned common stock came to the rescue of the "conservative bonds." Of course, for pension funds these short-term fluctuations are largely irrelevant; my thesis is that only the earnings—current receipts and appreciation *over the long run*—are important.

Although the dividend yield on current market price may be quite modest, when the dividend income is related to invested capital the return is often surprisingly high. A 6% return on a stock which has doubled in market value means a 12% return on book cost. For example, Consolidated Edison Company of New York, Inc., which is not considered a dynamic growth utility, sold for an average price of about $25 in 1949, with a dividend of $1.60 to yield 6.40%. As of the middle of 1958, the stock was paying $2.80 to yield 5.10% on its market price of $55. In terms of 1949 investment cost of $25, the actual dividend yield experienced is 11.40% with a market appreciation of 100% lurking in the background in case of sale at some future date.

The unrealized capital appreciation can also act as a "hidden reserve." Because of market swings and actuaries' desire for continuity and stability, it is appropriate—in fact, almost imperative—that a reserve be set up. Treasury regulations, however, prevent employer corporations from setting up any portfolio reserves out of deductible contributions or even out of realized capital gains on the contention that the pension liabilities would be overfunded. In lieu of such formal reserves, market appreciation can be used as a "hidden reserve."

A CONSERVATIVE CASE

An illustration of a conservatively managed pension portfolio is that of the Bell Telephone System. This is a noncontributory plan which now covers almost a million employees and pensioners in the 33 corporations that make up the Bell System. Pension fund reserves for each corporate entity are kept separate. Founded in 1913, the fund is by far the largest private industrial fund in the country, with its aggregate investment of $2.6 billion. It is growing at the rate of nearly $1 million every working day.

In 1938 the Bell System management completely reversed itself from its previous policy of investing 100% in telephone properties and went to a policy of 100% investment in a diversified bond portfolio with no member company holding its own bonds. In that year the pension fund trustee (Bankers Trust Company of New York) was instructed by the company's board of directors to invest the pension fund assets solely in "legals" for New York insurance companies. Furthermore, investments were restricted to governments, municipals, and obligations of domestic corporations of the highest quality. This has been construed to mean bonds rated "A" or better, and to exclude railroad equipment certificates, sale and leaseback properties, and real estate mortgages.

The wisdom of limiting investments only to high-grade bonds conflicts with the findings of the monumental bond survey undertaken by the National Bureau of Economic Research. This study reveals that, despite their greater loss ratio, the net investment return from lower-grade bonds *exceeds* that of top-rated bonds because of the importance of yield differential.[6] Thus, while there is danger to small funds in low-quality bonds, with diversification there is safety and greater yield. Since 1945, the New York Telephone Company pension fund (which is slightly more than 10% of the Bell System) has earned an average of 2.77%. This is 24 basis points less than the average cost of its "Aaa"-rated mortgage bonds.

COMPARATIVE EARNINGS

It is interesting to note (see Table 10) that during the postwar period gains and losses on the sale of securities have made a considerable difference

---

[6]W. Braddock Hickman, *Corporate Bond Quality and Investor Experience* (New York, National Bureau of Economic Research, 1958).

TABLE 10. *New York Telephone Company pension fund earnings rate compared with earnings rate of United States life insurance companies*

| Year | N. Y. Telephone pension fund | | | N. Y. Telephone debt cost | Life insurance companies' earnings | | Metropolitan Life's earnings before federal income tax‡ |
	Average balance (millions of dollars)	Net rate earned*	Earnings†		Before federal income tax	After federal income tax	
1946	$ 79.8	2.64%	2.53%	3.21%	2.93%	2.89%	3.01%
1947	91.5	2.51	2.53	3.08	2.88	2.88	2.94
1948	105.3	2.58	2.58	2.87	2.96	2.96	3.03
1949	121.0	2.66	2.65	2.85	3.06	2.98	3.07
1950	138.6	2.77	2.67	2.95	3.13	3.00	3.07
1951	157.6	2.65	2.71	2.86	3.18	2.98	3.07
1952	178.2	2.67	2.83	2.90	3.28	3.07	3.21
1953	201.3	2.96	2.93	3.03	3.26	3.15	3.31
1954	226.2	3.05	2.99	3.31	3.46	3.24	3.41
1955	250.8	2.99	2.99	2.95	3.51	3.23	3.48
1956	274.8	2.74	3.06	2.87	3.63	3.23	3.65
1957	299.3	3.02	3.23	3.15	3.75	3.44	3.75
Average		2.77%	2.81%	3.01%	3.25%	3.08%	3.25%

*Determined by dividing the net amount realized for each year, including profit or loss on sale or redemption of fund assets, by the average of beginning and end-of-year balances in the fund, less one-half of the net amount realized. Trustee's fee (ranging from 2 to 4 basis points of yield) deducted to compute the net earnings rate.

†Before adjustment for realized capital gains and losses.

‡After all investment expenses and charges, such as real estate taxes, depreciation, acquisition and servicing fees, mortgage loans, operating cost of housing, and proportionate amount of company overhead at head office (salaries, etc. of investment department).

SOURCES: Institute of Life Insurance, *Life Insurance Fact Book* (New York, 1957); Metropolitan Life Insurance Company, *Annual Reports* (New York, 1946–1957); and American Telephone & Telegraph Company, Treasury Office.

in earnings in particular years, but have been a small factor over the entire period. As with all big funds, the Bell System earnings rate has a substantial inertia from past commitments. On funds invested during 1957 the Bell companies achieved a return in the neighborhood of 3.96%. In 1957 the American Telephone & Telegraph Company's pension fund earned approximately 3.19%, excluding gains or losses on sales of securities, and earned 3.06%, including capital transactions. As of December 31, 1957, the market value of its portfolio was about 7% below the amortized book cost.

Table 10 also presents a comparison of the Bell pension fund earnings with those of leading life insurance companies, most of which are qualified to do business in New York State. The earnings of Metropolitan Life Insurance are also shown separately. It is important to note in comparing investment results that pension funds pay no federal income taxes, while insurance companies do.

It is also instructive to contrast Bell pension fund earnings with those achieved in alternative investment opportunities. As Table 11 shows, the dividend yield on AT&T common stock (which is not noted for its growth characteristics) is 5.53% for the 12 postwar years. If allowance were made for the value of rights received during this period, the yield would have been over 6.50%. AT&T's dividend yield has averaged approximately 6% since the retirement program was installed in 1913. The returns on Moody's utilities and on life insurance company investments, by class of security, are also set forth in Table 11.

From these data, it is seen that the earnings on the Bell System pension fund are substantially less than the yield on its own common stock and less than the average net earnings for life insurance companies, which have to pay taxes.

The Bell pension fund investment policy was drafted in the light of the depressed economic conditions that existed during the early 1930's. Twenty years have passed since the last major change in investment policy. Is not a more dynamic, aggressive, and enterprising investment policy needed—at least, for the typical fund today? Many other funds do earn substantially more with safety—and even at that their averages are mediocre (3.84% in 1957, according to SEC figures). It is time to undertake a review of portfolio policy, considering the comparative record of bonds and stocks from the point of view of stability, capital appreciation, earnings, and purchasing power.[7]

[7]In line with the author's recommendation the American Telephone & Telegraph Company announced on September 11, 1958, a basic change in the investment policy for its pension fund. The trustee is now authorized to purchase listed common stocks in amounts not to exceed 10% of the total fund. No limitation, other than the listing requirement, was placed on the trustee's discretion as to individual selections. It is expected that the common stock component will not reach this modest percentage for several years and will include shares of AT&T. Preferred stocks and mortgages remain in the excluded category.

TABLE 11. *Earnings achieved in alternative investment opportunities, 1946–1957*

Year	AT&T dividend yield*	Moody's utilities		18 LIFE INSURANCE COMPANIES†		
		Yield "Aa"	24 public utility stocks	*Experienced rate of return*		
				Bonds	Preferred	Common
1946	4.85%	2.58%	4.23%	3.09%	4.71%	5.17%
1947	5.58	2.67	5.32	2.78	4.46	4.82
1948	5.91	2.92	5.85	2.84	4.57	5.35
1949	6.22	2.76	5.86	2.96	4.16	5.28
1950	5.91	2.66	5.66	3.07	4.47	6.22
1951	5.77	2.95	5.77	2.94	4.50	8.63
1952	5.81	3.05	5.39	3.05	4.41	7.65
1953	5.77	3.32	5.33	3.11	4.36	7.38
1954	5.35	3.00	4.81	3.35	5.06	8.32
1955	4.98	3.13	4.50	3.29	4.94	10.02
1956	5.03	3.43	4.68	‡	‡	‡
1957	5.19	4.03	4.92	‡	‡	‡
Average	5.53%	3.04%	5.20%	3.04%	4.56%	6.88%

*If the $9 dividend were augmented by the average market value of the rights received for the postwar period, the experienced yield on AT&T common stock would be over 6.50%.
†James J. O'Leary, op. cit. (Table 1); includes realized gains and losses.
‡Data not available.

A DYNAMIC PORTFOLIO

By way of contrast, let us now look at the pension fund of the General Electric Company. Starting in 1912, GE pioneered a liberal retirement program on a "pay as you go" basis. As experience accumulated, the wisdom of voluntary funding became apparent. In 1927 a separate trust fund was set up and administered by the company. GE, unlike most industrials, has had a long investment experience. In fact, Electric Bond & Share Company, formerly a subsidiary, was formed by GE in 1904 to help buyers finance costly electrical equipment.

The investment management of these accumulating funds falls into distinct periods:

When funding was begun in 1927, the assets of the pension trust were invested in notes of the Electrical Securities Corporation, whose common stock was owned by GE. In turn, the Electrical Securities Corporation invested in a diversified portfolio.

Nearly 20 years later, in 1946, Electrical Securities Corporation was dissolved and the pension fund assets invested entirely in government bonds.

In 1947—in response to changing times—a more flexible approach was adopted for these funds, which had by then accumulated to $150 million. Policy was altered to permit investments in "legals" for New York life insurance companies, which at that time included corporate bonds, mortgages, preferred stock—but no common stock.

With further postwar economic changes taking place, management remained flexible and continued to shift its position. In 1950 a decision to go into equities was made after careful consideration and was executed according to a detailed plan worked out in advance. This permitted the purchase of common stocks on a dollar-averaging basis with provision for accelerated purchases on market declines.

The reasons stated for following a stock purchase program were: (a) to secure a higher yield, and (b) to set up a hedge against inflation. A higher yield offered the advantage, of course, of reducing the funding cost of the plan. Prior to 1950 it had sometimes been difficult to obtain a $2\frac{1}{2}\%$ rate to meet the actuarial requirements. The investment managers of the fund felt that if bond quality were to be sacrificed in order to secure a higher yield, there would be few, if any, capital gains to offset the inevitable losses of principal on the lower-grade obligations. Consequently, a partial solution to the problem was the inclusion of a limited amount of carefully selected equities in the portfolio. However, preferred stocks have been left out of the program in favor of common stocks because it was felt that the yield on preferred stocks was not sufficiently above that obtainable on bonds to justify the purchase. Bonds also have the maturity and cash flowback features that preferred stocks lack.

Thus, GE feels that securities which represent ownership can reasonably be expected to grow in both value and income return as the economy grows. Careful consideration has been given to the effect of decreased dividends during a period of recession. With 30% of the fund in common stocks, dividends can be reduced about 40% below the average 5% rate before the fund as a whole will earn less than 3%.

STRUCTURE & SIZE

Table 12 sets forth in detail the changing structure of the GE pension fund during the postwar period. The decline in government bonds and the increase in diversified common stock holding are noteworthy. GE's thinking on the common stock component is not fixed. Currently management is inching above its earlier limit of 30%. In addition, the fund trustees have raised their investment horizon and have included commitments in industrial mortgages, sales and leasebacks, and oil-production participations (an equity-type security).

The GE pension fund has nearly quintupled in the last decade. Currently the fund is increasing at the rate of $88 million a year. This yearly

TABLE 12. *Structure and earnings of the General Electric Company pension fund portfolio*

Year end	U.S. Government bonds	Other fixed income	Miscellaneous	Common stocks	Going rate of return
1947	98%	2%			2.20%
1950	33	63		4%	2.74
1952	17	73		10	3.15
1954	13	70	2%	15	3.40
1957	7	53	9	31	3.80

SOURCE: General Electric Company, Pension Investment Department.

increment, plus maturities and switches to more attractive investments, requires new investment commitments approaching $500,000 each working day. A fund which is growing so rapidly is, of course, constantly faced with broad questions of investment policy, with a tremendous need for flexibility of administration.

RELATIVE EARNINGS

The earnings of the GE fund should be analyzed in relation to the structure of the fund, as set forth in Table 12. With changing interest rates

TABLE 13. *Analysis of market values and capital gains of the General Electric Company pension fund, December 31, 1957**

| | | | Difference | |
Holdings	Book value	Market value	Amount	Per cent
Cash & Receivables	$ 21.4	$ 21.4		
U. S. Government bonds	52.8	49.9	−$ 2.9	−5.5%
Corporation bonds	412.9	380.9	− 32.0	−7.8
Common stocks	242.2	283.7	41.5	17.1
Miscellaneous	74.1	74.1		
Total	$803.4	$810.0	$ 6.6	0.8%

*In millions of dollars.
SOURCE: General Electric Company, Pension Investment Department.

one cannot make too dogmatic a deduction, but it does seem fair to conclude that the increasing common stock proportion has had a definite influence in increasing the over-all yield. This exhibit also sets forth the "going rate of return," as of the year end, on amortized book value. Note that realized capital gains are not included.

A forceful illustration of the extent to which common stocks can provide not only an increase in earning capacity but also a reserve for market fluctuations is set forth in Table 13, which compares the amortized book and market values as of the end of 1957. The $41 million of common stock market appreciation is indeed an important "hidden reserve" or an important adjunct to the formally reported earnings. This appreciation more than offsets the market depreciation in the larger defensive portion.

The importance of the capital appreciation should be related to the average life of the common stock portion of the fund, which, at the end of 1957, was about three years. A $41 million unrealized appreciation in seven years on the common stock component, which has averaged less than $90 million (from zero at the beginning of 1950 to $242 million book value at the end of 1957—see Tables 12 and 13) is very substantial indeed. It would be most interesting if the GE pension fund accountants segregated the equity earnings from the fixed-income earnings return and compared the two yields, both before and after capital gain.

STOCK SELECTION

Although the portfolio is under continuous study and is in a perpetual state of flux, a basic diversification pattern for stocks has been followed. In early 1958, about one-half of the common stock fund was in oils, chemicals, and utilities. Around one-quarter of the common stock portion of the portfolio was in retail trade, foods, automobiles and accessories, and building. The balance was spread over other groups of industries.

No more than 4% of the stock component is put into any one company, and no more than 1% of a corporation's outstanding stock is ever held.

TABLE 14. *College retirement equities fund earnings and capital gains*

Fiscal year ending March 31	*Total market value (millions of dollars)*	*Accumulation unit value**	*Per cent of appreciation*	*CREF dividend rate†*	*TIAA yield‡*
1953	$ 1.8	$10.00		4.43%	3.33
1954	7.6	11.46	14.6%	4.04	3.48
1955	17.9	15.17	32.4	3.34	3.51
1956	33.0	19.84	30.8	2.84	3.58
1957	41.2	18.37	− 7.4	3.23	3.70
1958	55.8	18.45	0.4	3.36	3.78

*Accumulation unit values stated at market price; the most recent figure (September 30, 1958) is $21.76.
†Yield on market value at end of period.
‡Yields computed on the usual life insurance formula and for calendar years; i.e., they should be set back three months.

Depending on the relative attractiveness of current yields, the trustees may go all the way from putting all of the new money in common stock to committing themselves for months in advance for private placements. Though self-administered, the GE treasury department retains outside investment counsel.

While the principle of dollar averaging has been followed in buying common stocks, purchases are not made straight across the board. Furthermore, purchases are not made every day, open orders are not given at the market, and there is no individual stock purchased at regular intervals. Rather, purchases of common stocks are made selectively from an approved list of about 85 stocks on the basis of whichever selected issues seem to be the most attractive. The stock purchase policy also calls for accelerated purchases with a falling market, with emphasis on stocks which have been the hardest hit.

Although the past is no sure guide for the future, the experience of the GE fund to date has been most favorable. A conservatively enterprising investment policy has been followed. A modest portion of common stock has assisted in increasing the net yield and has augmented its value with substantial capital gains. The important thing is that the management has adopted a dynamic and adaptable investment policy for our changing world.

CREF—VARIABLE ANNUITY

Postwar declining purchasing power has resulted in an intense interest in variable annuity retirement plans.[8] Unlike the Bell pension, which has been wholly in bonds, or the GE pension, only partly in equities, these funds are invested *wholly* in equities. The recent court holding that variable annuity contracts could be sold by insurance companies without registration with the SEC has provided further advancement for this new development.[9]

Variable annuity retirement plans have now been adopted by over 30 employer organizations. Among these are the air transport industry, the Wisconsin State Employees Retirement Fund, the Tennessee Valley Authority, and Atlas Corporation.

INVESTMENT LESSON

College Retirement Equities Fund (CREF), set up by the Teachers Insurance and Annuity Association in 1952, led the way. From the start, CREF funds have been invested in a diversified list of quality common stocks which had a market value, as of the end of the fiscal year March 31, 1958, of $55 million. Already $8 million of unrealized appreciation has been accumulated during its short existence.

The investment performance of the fund is comparatively easy to measure. Monthly joint teacher-university contributions buy "accumulation units," much as periodic purchases might buy shares in an open-end investment company. Dividends received on the fund's holdings are credited to participants in the form of additional accumulation units. Thus, the value of each unit is an exact measure of price changes in the fund's stocks and is directly comparable with stock averages like Dow-Jones and the others. As shown in Table 14, the accumulation unit has grown from $10.00 to $18.45, an increase of 84.5% in five fiscal years. On a compound interest basis, this rate of growth exceeds 13% annually. Supplemented by the reinvestment of the cash dividends in additional units, a participation purchased early in 1953 has more than doubled in total worth five years later. And as of July 31, 1958, the accumulation unit alone has further increased from $18.45 to $20.71.

[8]See William C. Greenough, *A New Approach to Retirement Income* (New York, Teachers Insurance and Annuity Association, 1951); and Leonard E. Morrissey, "Dispute Over the Variable Annuity," HBR January–February 1957, p. 75.

[9]*SEC v. Variable Annuity Life Insurance Co. et al.*, May 22, 1958, Docket No. 14253, U.S. Court of Appeals for the District of Columbia.

Although five years is too short a period to make sweeping, long-run investment generalizations, the contrast between CREF and any fixed-income fund, including the Teachers Insurance Annuity Association, is disconcertingly sharp. It should be emphasized that this is an actual and not a theoretical performance. Whatever the future may bring, there has already been created a substantial amount of capital appreciation to cushion any future market declines and still to maintain a substantial earnings differential over bond fund performance. The investment lesson of the competitive advantage of common stock is most evident.

UNION FUNDS

The investment policies of the GE fund and certain other corporate-trusteed funds contrast sharply with the policies of funds administered by unions for the benefit of their members. The latter are noteworthy for their extreme conservatism and poor investment performance. For example:

The Amalgamated Clothing Workers union has a sizable retirement fund invested, as of the end of 1957, as follows:

U.S. Government bonds	$44,500,000
Cash	8,400,000
Other assets	400,000
Total	$53,300,000

There is almost a complete absence of any investment management, and there is no diversification. The fund also shows a lack of alert management in that 15% of it is in idle cash. In 1957 earnings of $1,200,000 provided a return of only 2.35% on the average fund, and there still appears to be little attempt to obtain better yields. In fact, at the end of 1957, the market value of the portfolio had declined as much as $1,800,000 below purchase price.

Again, International Ladies' Garment Workers' Union has a pension fund which was invested as follows at the end of 1957:

Cash accounts	$ 3,000,000
Savings	3,600,000
U.S. Government bonds	93,400,000
East River Housing bonds	4,700,000
VA and FHA mortgages	6,000,000
Other	800,000
Total resources	$111,500,000

Like the Amalgamated Clothing Workers fund, the Garment Workers fund is heavily committed to government securities. However, it has broadened its investment horizon. A controller with financial experience has been appointed to administer the fund. Recently, it was announced by David Dubinsky that the fund was going into the corporate-bond market. This is a slight improvement, but at this rate it will take years to reconstitute the fund on a more economic basis.

The high-minded officials who set up the Amalgamated Clothing Workers and Garment Workers pension funds in the pioneer days leaned over backwards to prevent any possible mismanagement. These funds were surrounded with safeguards for the prevention of "loss" either through individual crookedness or managerial incompetence, and were put into cash, savings accounts, and government securities because they represented the most conservative type of investments.[10]

Unions still are reluctant to invest in corporate securities, not only because of their unfamiliarity with investment finance, but also because of the belief that such a commitment of funds would constitute an unholy alliance with the employer group, with whom they like to deal at arm's length. Here a basic and, as yet, unresolved conflict arises. If the union wants a high return on its investment, must it support management in its effort to make more profits and thus to keep costs, including wages, low? Should picket lines be observed or products boycotted when that means a lower return on the union fund?

AN EXCEPTIONAL CASE

In striking contrast, the enterprising policies adopted by the Amalgamated Lithographers of America are an exception to the union rule. The First National City Bank of New York has been appointed investment advisory agent and custodian for the Lithographers pension fund. The bank has been directed to exercise its discretion in making investments for the fund as long as it does not put more than 15% of the portfolio in preferred stocks and not more than 16% in common stocks. The balance of the portfolio handled by the bank must consist of government and corporate bonds. The results, as of March 31, 1957, are shown in Table 15.

TABLE 15. *The portfolio of Amalgamated Lithographers of America pension fund*

Type of security	Book value	Ratio	Yield on book value
U.S. Government bonds	$ 4,300,000	27%	2.53%
Public utility bonds	5,300,000	34	3.22
Industrial bonds	2,000,000	12	3.42
Railroad bonds	400,000	2	3.58
Preferred stocks	1,900,000	12	4.16
Common stocks	1,400,000	9	3.89
First mortgages	600,000	4	4.18
	$15,900,000	100%	3.27%

[10]Paul L. Howell, "Investment Management of Union Pension Funds," *The Commercial and Financial Chronicle*, August 1, 1957, p. 11.

A shortcoming of the Amalgamated Lithographers setup is that union members must pay income taxes on all contributions to the fund since the employers make no direct contribution. To avoid Taft-Hartley Act surveillance, when the fund was set up in 1947 an increase in wages and dues was negotiated instead of pension fringe benefits. Furthermore, although currently segregated from other treasury funds, the fund does not appear to be irrevocably dedicated to pensions, but is subject, under certain conditions, to reversion into the general union treasury. The rights of the union members in these funds are only vaguely defined by the general wording of the union constitution. Funding and vesting appear to be insecure.

CONCLUSIONS

To sum up, I believe that six conclusions are justified by a careful examination of past experience in pension fund investment and of developing trends in the economy.

1. Pension costs will continue to rise because of: the demand for more adequate benefits in relation to a given level of wages, rising wage levels that make past contributions inadequate, and the trend toward earlier vesting to give greater coverage and mobility to labor.

2. Pension funds, although not a formal asset of the employer corporation, are nevertheless an important industrial resource which can be utilized to reduce wage costs. Better earnings (yield and appreciation) are the only effective method of holding pension costs to a minimum. Therefore, every effort should be made to invest pension funds so that they will earn the greatest return possible over the long run.

3. Investment is a complex, technical job requiring the highest skill and adherence to fiduciary responsibilities. Corporate management, just as in many other fields, needs expert, independent professional investment counsel, without conflicts of interest. Good advice is worth many times its cost.

4. Earnings and appreciation are jointly of the utmost importance in providing retirement benefits because of the duration of the investment period and the absence of the need for liquidity. History demonstrates that a well-diversified list of professionally selected common stocks will, over the long run—and taking into consideration cash dividends and capital appreciation—earn a substantial differential over fixed-income obligations.

5. Insured pension plans which must operate under severe investment limitations and pay taxes are at a distinct disadvantage compared with nonrestricted trusteed funds that can participate in the growth of the economy through holdings of good common stocks.

6. There is imperative need for a more aggressive and enterprising investment policy in the management of pension funds. Retirement benefits that are based on

low earning power of bonds become an expensive luxury for stockholders and consumers and a source of hardship to the aged. In the long run, pensions will be no sounder than the industrial economy to which they are tied. Everybody concerned—employers, employees, and the financial institutions—should move away from the concept that a pension plan can provide iron-clad financial guarantees into a recognition that it is essentially a cooperative effort to accumulate an old age savings reserve.

The end result may well be a dynamic investment policy which will lie somewhere between the ultraconservatism of many trustees and insurance companies, on the one hand, and the very liberal policies of some of the investment trusts, on the other hand.

4·6

A Study of Mutual Funds: Investment Policy and Investment Company Performance*

Irwin Friend, F. E. Brown, Edward S. Herman and Douglas Vickers

INVESTMENT POLICY

Investment policy, in the present study, encompasses the actions of investment managers as reflected in the structure of portfolios at given dates, and the frequency, timing, and to some extent the methods of portfolio changes.

On September 30, 1958, some 93.5 percent of the $12 billion of assets controlled by the funds was held in corporate securities, and U.S. corporate issues accounted for 88 percent. At each of the four benchmark dates examined in this study, December 31, 1952, 1955, and 1957 and September 30, 1958, approximately 75 percent of the total net assets of the funds was held in U.S. common stocks. The remaining assets were spread fairly

*From "Summary and Conclusions," in *A Study of Mutual Funds*, prepared for the Securities and Exchange Commission by the Wharton School of Finance and Commerce, Report of the Committee on Interstate and Foreign Commerce, 87th Congress, 2d Session, August 28, 1962, chap. 1, pp. 9–21. [All footnotes referring to pages in the rest of the report are omitted.]

evenly among U.S. corporate bonds, U.S. preferreds, foreign securities, and net liquid position. The most significant changes during the period under study were a marked increase in the percentage of assets held in foreign securities and an offsetting decline in U.S. preferred stocks. Between 1952 and 1955 the increase in the percentage of assets held in foreign securities was due to heavier investments in Canadian stocks, but between 1955 and 1958 the expansion of Canadian investment slackened and heavier investments were made in non-Canadian foreign stocks.

During the 1952–58 period the net assets of the funds increased by 213 percent, U.S. common stock investments expanded by the comparable rate of 217 percent, and at the final date the funds holdings of U.S. common stocks represented $3\frac{1}{2}$ percent of the value of all stocks listed on the New York Stock Exchange. During the same period Canadian stock holdings rose by 585 percent, and the rate of increase in non-Canadian foreign stocks (from $1.5 million to $144 million) was many times larger than the 213 percent increase in the funds' total assets.

Throughout the $5\frac{3}{4}$ years studied the smaller funds generally maintained a larger proportionate defensive portfolio position. If a certain minimum size of dollar investment is required in cash, near-cash, bonds, or any other categories of senior securities, it will force the smaller funds to devote a greater percentage of their resources to these items than the larger funds hold in the same forms. The largest funds (those with net assets of $300 million and over at September 30, 1958) had the lowest percentage liquidity at each of the four benchmark dates, and for each of the first three dates (1952, 1955, and 1957), there was a continuous reduction in the percentage liquidity as the size of fund increased. With the passage of time, moreover, the smallest funds have decreased their relative liquidity as they have grown in size. It was found that the tendency for the smallest funds to hold a larger relative liquidity position was not closely related to the age of the fund.

The principal differences in portfolio distributions among the funds are the result of differences of announced investment objectives. Common stock funds held $87\frac{1}{4}$ percent of their assets in U.S. common stocks in September 1958, the percentage having fallen from 91 percent in 1952. Their net liquid position accounted for 7 percent of the portfolio in 1958 and the remaining assets were distributed among foreign securities and domestic bonds and preferred stocks, there security groups accounting for about 3, 2, and 1 percent of the portfolio, respectively.

The balanced funds as a whole held 63 percent of their assets in domestic common stocks in 1958 and 15 and 14 percent, respectively, in domestic bonds and preferred stocks. The most interesting feature of the industry's corporate bond investments was the fact that the bond and preferred stock funds stressed heavily the holding of "other" grade bonds, rather than "investment grade." In 1958 the "other" grade bonds accounted for the rather high proportion of 89 percent of the total U.S. corporate bond holdings of those funds. There had been little change in this figure since 1952. For the balanced funds, on the other hand, investment grade bonds were stressed.

An analysis of portfolios by industrial composition was based on a classification of corporate securities under five principal headings: industrial, utility, transportation, financial, and foreign. In the bond section the transportation share (principally railroads) of the total fell sharply over the period covered and this was offset by a doubling in the relative share of the general industrial bond holdings and by an even larger proportionate expansion of the financial bonds. In the preferred stock section, a similar fall in the transportation securities was offset by an increase in utility preferreds. In the common stock section, transportation and utility securities both declined in relative importance, and the strongest relative increase occurred in the foreign stock investments.

A more detailed division into 33 industrial classes revealed that the funds placed the largest share of their combined corporate portfolio in oils and utilities, each of which accounted for more than 10 percent of the corporate portfolio at every benchmark date. The greatest relative increases during the study period were in steel and drugs. In addition to utilities and oils, the largest industries in 1958 were chemicals and glass, steel, railroads, and machinery, each of which comprised over 5 percent of the total corporate portfolio. Utility holdings were the largest for every size group of funds in 1958, but there were differences in other aspects of the industrial composition of the various size groups. Only four industries had accounted for more than 5 percent in 1952: utilities, oils, rails, and chemicals and glass.

Between 1952 and 1958 there was a decrease in the tendency to concentrate portfolio holdings in particular industries. The top four industries accounted for $49\frac{1}{2}$ percent of the combined corporate portfolio in 1952, and only $39\frac{1}{2}$ percent in 1958. A greater degree of concentration by industry existed in the largest funds' portfolios than in those of the smaller funds, though the industrial concentration for each size group of funds, as well as for all funds combined, declined progressively between 1952 and 1958.

An analysis of the industry distributions of the funds' common stock investments, as distinct from their total corporate investments as referred to in the foregoing, reveals that oils occupied the highest rank in 1958, and utilities and rails each represented smaller relative shares of the common stock portfolio than they did of the total corporation holdings at each of the four benchmark dates. In the total common stock portfolio, also, the degree of concentration by industry declined during the period covered by the study.

Some appreciation of the market significance of the funds' holdings in selected securities can be obtained by viewing the 30 common stocks in which the funds had their largest dollar investment during the years 1951 through 1957. At September 1958, these stocks accounted for 36.4 percent of the total value of all stocks listed on the New York Stock Exchange, but of course, a much smaller percentage of all outstanding stock, and for the smaller figure of 23.5 percent of the funds' common stock portfolio. The largest four stocks listed on the exchange, American Telephone & Telegraph, Du Pont, General Motors, and Standard Oil of New Jersey, represented 19.4 percent of all listed values, though they accounted for only 4.3 percent of the funds' common stock portfolio.

More important from the viewpoint of the capital market significance of the funds' portfolios, however, is the percentage of the total listed issue of each of those 30 stocks hold by the funds. In September 1958, the funds' total holdings of the 30 stocks amounted to 2.6 percent of the stocks' total listed value. In 1952 the corresponding figure had been somewhat lower at 1.5 percent. Wide variations occurred, however, in the individual stocks. In 1958 the percentages of issues held ranged from 0.6 percent of American Telephone & Telegraph stock to 10 percent of Goodyear stock. While the funds had large absolute dollar holdings in large corporations, the percentage of these corporations' voting stock held was not as high as in some of the stocks which occupied lower places by dollar values in the funds' portfolios. The funds held less than 5 percent in 1958 of each of the stocks which comprised the highest five ranks by dollar values in the funds' portfolios: International Business Machines, United States Steel, Texas Co., Standard Oil of New Jersey, and Bethlehem Steel. In the case of the largest four stocks listed on the New York Stock Exchange, the funds held less than 1 percent of American Telephone & Telegraph, Du Pont, and General Motors, and 1.3 percent of Standard Oil of New Jersey.

A further view of the relative importance of this sample of 30 stocks is provided by an analysis of purchase and sale volumes. The total purchases of these stocks on the New York Stock Exchange by all investors was approximately 15 percent of the total of all stock purchases on the exchange throughout the study period. Investment fund purchases of these stocks rose from 6.2 percent of the total market trading in these stocks in 1953 to 8.9 percent in 1958, though a significant portion of the funds' purchases in the latter year (approximately 25 percent) was due to the formation and entry into the stock market of two large funds. Throughout the period

1955–57, investment fund purchases as a percentage of total market trading remained below the 1953 level, although they increased slightly during that interval. Investment fund sales of the same stocks rose throughout the period from 2.4 percent of market trading in the stocks in 1953 to 5.5 percent in 1958 (in this case the two new funds did not contribute significantly to the 1958 figure). During the last 3 years of the study period the importance of these sample 30 stocks in the funds' total stock purchases increased, after having fallen to a lower level in 1955. But the tendency for the relative importance of the sample stocks to increase is subject to modification when data for each of the 30 stocks are examined separately.

The analysis took as a convenient measure of the relative importance of fund trading in each of these stocks the ratio between the sum of the funds' purchases and sales of each stock (including transactions in all securities markets) and the total value, sales only, of the New York Stock Exchange activity in the stock. An analysis was made covering the 13 quarterly periods of fluctuating market conditions between July 1955 and September 1958. It was found that the funds' share of market trading rose above 10 percent in at least one quarter for each of the 30 stocks. Consistently high market shares were attained by the funds in three stocks: Armco, Goodrich, and Goodyear, in which the funds' share was more than 10 percent of market volume in 12 of the 13 quarters.

In five other stocks, Central and South West, Firestone, International Paper, Kennecott Copper, and Shell Oil, the funds accounted for more than 10 percent of the market volume in 10 of the 13 quarters. If these ratios were based on the relation between the funds' purchases only, or sales only where the funds were net sellers of the relevant security, and total stock exchange purchases, or sales, the ratios would be approximately three-fourths their present values. It should be noted also that if the funds' transactions were related to public sales on the stock exchange, or probably even to public sales on all exchanges and over-the-counter markets, the ratios would be higher.

The total impact of the funds' portfolio policies on activity in the capital markets is determined partly by the distribution of their security holdings by market place of listing. This distribution, as well as the facilities available in alternative markets, is influential in determining the extent to which differing market channels are employed to effect portfolio transactions. The size of transaction and the technique of effecting it are determined by the volume of transactions which can be accommodated by existing market structures; and there exists a tendency for institutional activity to affect the structure of capital market usage. Investment funds, as they expand in size, may tend to change the percentage of their portfolios which they hold in securities other than those listed on the New York Stock Exchange; and as the size of individual transactions increases, a larger percentage of their portfolio sales may be effected in the over-the-counter markets, by means of secondary offerings for example, rather than on the established exchanges.

Between 1952 and 1958 the proportion of the funds' stock portfolios held in stocks listed on the New York Stock Exchange fell from 85.3 percent to 81.1 percent; the proportions held in stocks listed on other exchanges and in stocks traded only over-the-counter both increased by 2 percentage points during the same period. This relative movement from New York Stock Exchange stocks occurred in both balanced funds and common stock funds. In the case of the balanced funds the movement was observed in both their common stock and preferred stock sections.

The analysis of the distributions of portfolios by place of listing for each type and size class of funds confirmed the general conclusions based on the aggregate data. Wide dispersions existed; however, between the various types and size classes of funds, with a smaller dispersion appearing among common stock funds owing to their more uniformly high percentage holdings of New York Stock Exchange stocks.

Turning from the distribution of portfolios by market place of listing to the distribution of transactions by market channel employed, the funds effected 75.5 percent of their common stock purchases on the New York Stock Exchange in each of two time periods analyzed, the second quarters of 1953 and 1958. A similar distribution of transactions occurred in both the balanced funds and the common stock funds in each of the periods. About 75–80 percent of total purchases were effected on the New York Stock Exchange, and 15 to 20 percent were made in the over-the-counter markets. In no case did the other exchanges attract a significant share of the total. The most significant departure from this pattern of trading occurred in the specialty funds. In 1958, 45.6 percent of their purchases were effected in the over-the-counter markets, and over half of their total stock portfolio was held in unlisted stocks.

The changes in the market distribution of common stocks sales have been more marked than in the case of purchases. The use of the over-the-counter markets has expanded and sharp increases have occurred in the volume of portfolio sales effected by secondary distributions. For all funds combined the use of the New York Stock Exchange declined from 83.7 percent of sales in 1953 to 74.9 percent in 1958, the over-the-counter share rose from 12.4 percent to 18.9 percent, and other exchanges, slightly more important than for purchases, rose from 3.9 percent to 6.3 percent.

The pattern of change in market usage is not as regular on the sales side of portfolio operations as on the purchases side. The common stock funds offset the reduction in the New York Stock Exchange share by increasing the over-the-counter share from 9.9 percent to 21.2 percent. The balanced funds, on the other hand, increased the relative importance of the other exchanges, whose share of sales rose from 2.8 percent to 9.8 percent, rather than increasing the relative importance of the over-the-counter markets.

An analysis of the sales data by size groups of funds reveals that the expansion in size of each of the classes of funds between 1953 and 1958 was accompanied by a reduction in the relative importance of the New York Stock Exchange, and an increase in the use of the over-the-counter markets. Both these movements were most marked in the case of the largest class of funds.

The increasing use of secondary offerings as a medium for security sales, particularly by the largest funds, is one of the more significant phenomena associated with the growth of investment company size. In 1953 sales of stock by secondary offerings accounted for 4.3 percent of the funds' total sales, and by 1958 the corresponding percentage had risen sharply to 10.2 percent. This increase was due to the heavier activity of the common stock funds whose sales by secondary offerings rose from 4.1 percent to 13.3 percent of total sales. An anaysis of the data by size of fund indicates the preponderant importance of the largest and second largest groups of funds, which used this technique in 1958 for 18.5 percent and 10 percent of their sales, respectively.

A further partial index of the funds' investment policy is provided by an analysis of their rates of portfolio turnover. Between 1953 and 1958 the weighted average rate of turnover of fund portfolios (after adjusting for net money inflow or outflow) increased from 17.6 percent to 23.6 percent.[1] The increase was most marked in the case of the common stock funds, whose turnover rates had been lower than those of the balanced funds at the beginning of the study period, a relationship which was reversed by 1958.

Specialty funds displayed low turnover rates throughout the period studied, their rate exceeding 10 percent in only 2 years and never rising as high as 11 percent. The foreign security funds turned over their portfolios rapidly in 1955 and 1956, though by 1958 they had rates of slightly less than 15 percent, more in line with the rates for the industry as a whole. The combined rates for the bond and preferred stock funds were uniformly high, varying between 20 percent and 30 percent for the entire period.

Throughout the period studied turnover rates were inversely related to investment fund size. The funds in the smallest size group had the

---

[1]The measure of portfolio turnover rates on which the weighted average computations were based was computed as the ratio of one-half of purchases and sales less net inflow or outflow, divided by average net assets.

highest turnover rates throughout the period, never falling below 32 percent and rising as high as 47 percent in 1957. The largest size class of funds, on the other hand, showed the lowest turnover rates for each year, though their rates rose during periods of stock market upswing, for example the first half of 1957 and in 1958.

It is conceivable that a part of the explanation of relatively higher portfolio turnover rates in the smaller funds could depend on the age of the fund, on the expectation that a newly formed fund may record higher turnover rates as it shifted its assets from a temporary liquid position into permanent portfolio securities. An analysis of relevant data does lend some support to such an hypothesis, but the tendency for higher turnover rates in recently formed funds is clearly observable only in the years 1955 through 1957. This, however, does not eliminate the inverse relationship between turnover and size, for the larger funds had generally lower rates than those smaller funds which had been in existence for several years.

Turnover rates within the industry demonstrated wide dispersion throughout the period covered by the study. In 1955 the industry had its lowest combined turnover rate, but 9.2 percent of the funds had rates greater than 50 percent. In every other year more than 10 percent of the funds had rates in excess of 50 percent, and 20.3 percent of the funds were in this category in 1958. At the other extreme, there were many funds with quite low turnover rates. In 1958, when the industry had the highest combined turnover, 15.1 percent of all funds had rates below 10 percent. A more complete analysis of the data suggests, moreover, that the dispersion among the turnover rates of the individual funds has been increasing with the passage of time.

Funds in which the controlling organization and/or individual of the fund were affiliated with a broker exhibited higher turnover rates than did the industry as a whole in every year 1953 through 1958. The disparity in rates diminished between 1953 and 1958, however, and more important, the differences in turnover rate seemed primarily attributable to the differences in size of the funds. One small broker-affiliated fund (assets $1.4 million as of September 1958) had turnover rates in excess of 100 percent in each of the 6 years studied. Another such fund which held assets of $27.7 million reached a high rate of 201 percent in 1957 and exceeded 100 percent in 4 of the 6 years.

The foregoing summary of the funds' turnover experience has referred to the turnover of total portfolios, including securities of all types and maturity dates. It was also necessary to estimate the rate at which the funds were turning over the equity sections of their portfolios in order that a direct comparison might be made with the rate of turnover of stocks in the securities market. For this purpose the turnover rates for all stocks listed on the New York Stock Exchange were taken as appropriate external bases of comparison.

The equity turnover rates, while they are in general lower than the comparable total portfolio turnover rates, exhibit a similar and pronounced negative relation between investment fund size and the rate of turnover of stock portfolios. The equity turnover rates for all funds combined and for each size group of funds increased with the rising market of 1954, fell in 1955 and rose in the strong upward market of 1958, following the price cycles of 1956 and 1957.

More important, in each of the years examined except 1955 the equity turnover rate for all funds combined (adjusted for inflow on the most reasonable assumptions) was higher than the comparable turnover rate on the New York Stock Exchange for all stocks listed in that market. The heightened activity of 1958 widened the gap between the funds' rate and the market rate to 4 percentage points, 16.9 percent compared with 12.9 percent.[2] Much the same relationship held for all size groups of funds except the largest, in which case the equity turnover rates were consistently lower than those of the New York Stock Exchange.

When attention is focused on the sample 30 stocks . . . it is noteworthy that in each of two time periods examined (1956–57, and the first three quarters of 1958) the funds' combined turnover rate in the sample stocks exceeded the comparable rate for activity on the New York Stock Exchange. The turnover rate in these 30 stocks combined was again lower for the largest funds than the industry total in each of the periods.

These relationships did not hold uniformly for each of the 30 stocks considered separately. In 1956–57 the funds' turnover rate exceeded that of the market in only 13 of the 30. In 1958 this relation held for 21 of the 30. In 11 of the 30 stocks the funds' turnover rates were higher than the corresponding market rate in both the time periods: American Telephone & Telegraph, Du Pont, General Electric, General Motors, Gulf Oil, Phillips Petroleum, Shell Oil, Socony Mobil, Standard Oil (New Jersey), Union Carbide, and Westinghouse Electric.

An analysis of the funds' actual transactions in common stocks provided significant comparisons with stock market transactions in general. The funds' gross purchases of common stocks averaged $56 million per month in 1953, rose to a monthly total well in excess of $100 million by the beginning of 1956, and during 1958 the monthly average rose to $195 million, or $3\frac{1}{2}$ times their level in 1953. The average monthly sales of

---

[2]The New York Stock Exchange turnover rate is based on total transactions in that market, and the rates would of course be lower if they had been based only on public transactions and lower still if they had been based only on odd-lot transactions.

common stocks in 1953 were slightly more than $30 million, and an average monthly level of $100 million was not reached till 1958. Monthly net purchases of common stock averaged $23 million in 1953 and $75 million in 1958. Considerable variation in purchases and sales volumes occurred from month to month throughout the study period, but in only one month, January 1958, were the funds net sellers of stocks.

Between 1953 and 1958 the funds' gross purchases of stocks, common plus preferred, increased from 5.3 percent of the total New York Stock Exchange volume to 8.7 percent. Net purchases increased during the same period from 2.3 percent to 3.5 percent of the exchange volume. In the rising market of the third quarter of 1958 the funds' gross purchases rose to 10 percent of the exchange volume and net purchases were also higher.[3] But during the study period as a whole the increase in the funds' share of total market volume was considerably less than the increase in the absolute value of their portfolio operations. Between 1953 and 1957 their net purchases volume rose by 136 percent, but their corresponding share of New York Stock Exchange activity rose by only 23 percent.

INVESTMENT COMPANY PERFORMANCE

The analysis of investment policy summarized above raises questions regarding the success with which the funds have realized their investment and portfolio objectives. The degree to which announced objectives are successfully attained from year to year, or during a longer period of time, is of course important as a measure of the extent to which the performance of the funds either vindicates or disappoints investor expectations. The degree of success of investment fund performance also bears on the basic economic question of the efficiency of allocation of investible funds among alternative economic uses.

From the investor's standpoint the purchase of investment company shares is but one of a number of ways of disposing of personal savings. And one way of assessing the relative merits of holding personal wealth in this rather than in alternative forms is by an examination of comparative performance measures. While the number of potential comparisons available in this connection is as extensive as the bases of investor motivation and their reasons for holding investment company shares, it is convenient for practical purposes to measure investment fund performance in terms of the annual or periodic change in net asset values per share, adjusted for dividend and capital gain distributions, or in terms of the periodic dividends paid on the shares. At the same time, a classification of the funds

[3]As was noted earlier the entry of two new large funds in 1958 contributed to the increase in the funds' stock purchases in that year.

according to differences in their announced portfolio objectives can be made the basis of comparison of performance measures with appropriate external standards, such as stock market price indexes or other weighted or composite security price measures.

A detailed analysis has not been made of the specific motivations leading to the investors' purchases of investment fund shares. However, the frequently quoted reasons for purchase—availability of expert investment advice, diversification of portfolio risks, convenience of security management, economy of bookkeeping activities, as well as differing requirements as to income, capital gains, capital stability, liquidity, or growth—can all be subsumed under the classifications of the funds adopted throughout this study; namely, the division of the funds into the broad types of common stock funds, balanced funds, and other numerically less important types and the subdivision of these into funds announcing investment objectives stressing "income" and "growth" in differing degrees.

It is clear from the variety of investment objectives announced by the funds that a single measure of performance for all funds and for all investors is inadequate. There is no strong reason, for example, why a balanced fund should record, or be expected to record, changes in asset values similar to those of a common stock fund. Similarly it is to be expected that funds which announce an "income" objective will yield different rates of return and will experience different changes in asset values from funds with a "growth" objective. It should be noted, moreover, that reliable data were not available for this study to permit a comparative analysis of the performance of other financial institutions with similar investment objectives.

During the period under study, performance records varied considerably, both within and among types of funds, but on the average conformed rather closely to the behavior of the securities markets as a whole. For the $5\frac{3}{4}$ years covered by the study, the Standard and Poor's Composite Common Stock Index was definitely superior to the average performance of the funds, but the disparity can be explained by the portfolio structure of the funds; i.e., the division of their portfolios among common stocks, preferred stocks, corporate bonds, Government securities, and other assets. When adjustments are made for this composition, the average performance by the funds did not differ appreciably from what would have been achieved by an unmanaged portfolio with the same division among asset types. About half the funds performed better, half worse, than such an unmanaged portfolio. Performance records, unadjusted for portfolio composition, of the smallest funds were somewhat inferior to those of the other funds, but these differences can again be largely explained by differences in portfolio structure.

Since perhaps the major function effectively served by mutual funds is the provision of diversification, a feature particularly important to small investors who can ill afford large risks, it is important to point out that such an investor who attempted to achieve a comparable degree of diversification by direct purchases might incur acquisition costs in excess of the 8 percent sales charge typically imposed by the funds.[4] And this would undoubtedly be so if he turned over his portfolio fairly rapidly. In addition, further costs or at least inconvenience would be incurred due to such an investor's bookkeeping problems. On the other hand, if an individual investor were to hold portfolio securities for long-term investment, or if he bought securities in sizable lots, his costs would be lower. For purchasers of front-end-load contractual plans, only limited returns can usually be realized unless such plans are held for substantial periods of time. When such plans are discontinued during the first 2 years of their life the deductions for sales charges may exceed 30 percent of the total investments made (and much more if discontinued earlier). It may be noted that even if such plans are held to maturity the effective sales charge is greater than the nominal rate, since the sales charge is concentrated in the early years of the plan whereas the shareholder's equity builds up most rapidly in the later years. In comparing the mutual funds' performances with that of composite unmanaged portfolios, it should be noted, finally, that an individual investor would have lessened the degree of risk in his portfolio by giving more weight to fixed interest-bearing obligations, but in such a case he also would have reduced his rate of return.

Every fund recorded an increase in adjusted net asset values during the $5\frac{3}{4}$-year period, and the average cumulative increase (assuming annual reinvestment of all distributions) was about 100 percent. There were, of course, pronounced differences in the performance of funds of different types. The common stock funds and the specialty funds exhibited the greatest amount of volatility, and because of the generally rising stock market of the period covered, they also recorded the largest increases in adjusted net assets. The bond and preferred stock funds, on the other hand, were less variable but recorded the smallest increases. Balanced funds and the foreign security funds occupied intermediate positions with respect to both these characteristics. These differences, particularly those between common stock funds and balanced funds, which, taken together, account for the largest number of funds in the industry, once more were attributable to portfolio composition and each group performed more or less according to the theoretical expectations generated by appropriately weighted indexes.

---

[4]The 8-percent sales charge can, of course, be avoided by investment in a no-load fund.

The more volatile nature of common stocks was apparent in comparisons between the Standard and Poor's Composite Common Stock Index and the average performance measures for all funds or for the various subgroups. Except during the periods of most rapid market advance, the funds' performance approximated that of the index but the greater volatility of the index was constantly present and persisted regardless of the direction of the movement. The cumulative result yielded an increase of approximately 140 percent in the index as contrasted to the fund average of 100 percent, though the relatively poorer performance of the fund average is largely due to the influence of nonequity securities in fund portfolios. Only 13 percent of the funds exceeded the Standard and Poor's figure, and every one of them was either a common stock fund or a specialty fund. However, when the more meaningful comparison of common stock funds with the index is made, the cumulative increase in the funds' performance measure amounted to 124 percent compared with the market increase of 140 percent. In the case of common stock funds, 25 percent exceeded the market average. In 1957 and 1958, there was a suggestion that the common stock funds were beginning to demonstrate at least as much volatility as the index. This phenomenon appeared in both the declining phase of the market and the subsequent recovery. Preliminary data for the period September 1958 to June 1962, including the December 1961 to June 1962 downturn, suggest that the common stock funds continued to show fully as much volatility as the index.

There was considerable variability in performance among funds of the same general type, both for individual years and on a cumulative basis, but no fund recorded below average results annually throughout the $5\frac{3}{4}$ years. Two funds, on the other hand, one common stock fund and one balanced fund, recorded above average results annually; that is, they were in the upper half of the funds of the same type groups in each year. There appeared to be certain funds that performed well during rising markets but rather poorly when the market declined. Other funds withstood the declines well but did not enjoy a great deal of success during the market increases. Both for balanced funds and common stock funds separately, the distribution of funds classified by the number of years in which they demonstrated above-average performance seems completely random or conforming to chance.

The existence of rather substantial differences in portfolio turnover rates within the investment company industry raises the question of the effect of such differences on performance. A high turnover rate that results in superior performance should cause little concern to the shareholder, but a high rate that results in mediocre or inferior performance is another matter. The brokerage commissions generated by high turnovers are expenses to the fund and the shareholder has a right to question management if consistently high expenses of this type are accompanied by relatively poor performance. The analysis revealed no strong relationship between turnover rates and performance, either when the variables were examined for the same time period or when performance lagged 1 year behind turnover. Thus, there has been no consistent evidence to indicate that high portfolio turnover rates have worked either to the advantage or disadvantage of the shareholder. However, it might be argued that a strong justification for high turnover rates would lie only in superior performance, since any tendency toward portfolio churning may be suspect from the viewpoint of the shareholder's interest.

It might be expected that investors would be willing to pay higher prices, in the form of management fees or sales charges, for those funds with the better performance records. There is some variability in the industry with respect to these rates and the investors could weigh costs against performance. Nevertheless, the evidence does not indicate the existence of any relationship between performance and either of these principal rate schedules. The implication is that these rate schedules are not indicative of performance. The fact that the analysis does not reveal a significant relation between management fees and performance indicates, in other words, that investors cannot assume the existence of higher management fees implies that superior management ability is thereby being purchased by the funds. In the same way, the absence of a relation between sales charge and performance means that the investor is not able to conclude that the existence of a higher sales charge is associated with the existence of superior performance.

The previous finding that the rate of new money inflow was positively related to sales charges suggested that the sale of fund shares might be based on selling efforts stimulated by higher sales commissions. The present finding indicates that these sales charges were not in turn related to performance. If performance measures had been based on the total investment made by the shareholders, including sales charges, rather than on the funds' net asset values, it is clear that less favorable results would have been recorded by the funds imposing a higher sales charge. The annual payment of the management fee, on the other hand, has already been taken into account in the performance measures, and from the shareholder's view, therefore, no further adjustment would be necessary.

If investors are conscious of the performance records of the various funds, they might be expected to direct their purchases toward the funds that have been most successful. If this be the case, there should be a positive relationship between performance in one period and net inflow in a later period. Annual figures, with inflow lagged 1 year behind performance, do reveal a weak positive pattern among the common stock funds but no relationship among the balanced funds. Cumulative figures for the entire $5\frac{3}{4}$ years show a stronger positive pattern.

Annual dividend yield would seem most relevant as an index of performance for those funds that announce an "income" objective. Within both the common stock funds and balanced funds, those announcing this objective consistently recorded the highest dividend yields, and their return exceeded that of the Standard and Poor's Stock Index for each of the last 4 years of the study, although they were below the index in 1953 and 1954. Funds announcing a "growth" objective had the lowest yields and the "mixed" funds occupied an intermediate position. Bond and preferred stock funds recorded the highest yields throughout the study. The postwar rise in interest rates together with the decline in common stock yields produced a shift in the relationship between the yields of common stock funds and balanced funds with the latter higher in the second half of the study, whereas the common stock funds had been higher in the first half. The average yield for all funds was lower than that of the Standard and Poor's Index for every year prior to 1958.

PART **5.** Short-Term Price Movements
and Forecasting

Playing the Market with Charts*

Daniel Seligman

The charting of stocks, once a recondite art practiced only by a few Wall Streeters, is becoming the recondite preoccupation of masses of investors. All over the U.S. tens of thousands of chartists are peering at their charts, trying to discern in the patterns and configurations of the past a clue to the future—the future of their stocks, that is, not the future in general. Though not all of them use the same system, the chartists will tell you, to a man, that the system they use works. And they must believe it, since many of them spend hour after hour every night keeping charts and interpreting them. Chartists sometimes speak of their wives as "chart widows."

Charting is also a growing profession. Virtually every substantial brokerage firm uses some charts, either because they are an effective selling device with certain customers or because the research department thinks that charting is an effective aid in stock forecasting. And there is a sizable business done in providing chartists of all types with ready-made charts and interpretations. Chartcraft, Trendline, Graphic Stocks, Trend & Value, Securities Research, Trendex, Marketlines—all these and many other services have attracted thousands of customers. Several of them charge fairly hefty fees: Marketlines offers a custom service for $2,500 a year. Wyckoff Associates in Chicago gives a correspondence course in charting that has attracted some 5,000 students over the years; they pay $500 and, because the lectures arrive on tape, must equip themselves with a tape recorder. The New School for Social Research in New York last fall offered a Monday-night course in charting that outdrew virtually everything else the school had to offer in literature, philosophy, psychology, and the social sciences. A book called *Technical Analysis of Stock Trends* by Robert D. Edwards and John Magee, first published in 1948, has gone through four editions and eleven printings and sold nearly 50,000 copies—at $12 apiece. The book is used as a text in a number of business schools.

*Reprinted from the February 1962 issue of *Fortune* Magazine by Special Permission; © (1962) Time Incorporated.

A chartist is, to begin with, a "technician." And he ordinarily explains what a technician is by contrasting himself with a "fundamentalist." A fundamentalist is a man who tries to estimate the present value and future course of stocks by looking for information about the companies' assets, net worth, past and prospective earnings, etc. A militant technician regards this kind of information as only secondarily useful, if of any use at all. He argues that all such information has been taken into account in the market and so is already reflected in the recent movements of the stock, which he sees on his charts. The man who gets "fundamental" information can never be certain that what he knows is complete, and maybe it isn't even accurate. A chartist, however, feels that *everything* about a stock—not only its earnings prospects, but also the emotions that people bring to it, the influence of tax selling and of other extraneous forces—is subsumed in the chart configurations. His task is to figure out what the configurations mean.

THE WONDERFUL WORLD OF CHARTS

Charting was generally in bad odor during the 1920's and early 1930's. It was associated with stock manipulations—i.e., the manipulators kept charts of price and volume activity, looking for ways to control the prices of stocks on minimal investments; at the same time a few traders tried to use charts in an effort to detect manipulations. Aside from these shady connotations, there was always a widespread suspicion that the chartists were all a little crazy. It is apparent that charting has now become respectable.

Charting appeals to investors at several different levels of sophistication. Securities Research of Boston includes among the subscribers to its charts the First National City Bank, the prestigious investment-counseling firm of Scudder, Stevens & Clark, and the Rockefeller Brothers organization; until he went to Washington Securities Research also had Defense Secretary McNamara on its list. It is, of course, unclear to what extent these sophisticated clients are real chartists; some of them, undoubtedly, use the charts only as handy reference works. Many of the most dedicated and least critical chartists are small investors. They may feel that they do not have access to good information, feel remote from "the insiders," and despair of their ability to understand complex financial information even if they had access to it. Retired business and professional men are also likely to be avid chartists: they have investments to watch over and time on their hands, and besides, living in California or Florida, they may feel a long way from the fundamentals of Wall Street.

It is also fair to conclude that charting has a special appeal for a certain personality type—the collector. Listening to one such chartist describe the satisfaction he derives from sitting down after dinner with his charts for a few hours, one is reminded of the philatelist or lepidopterist. Finding certain patterns on the charts gives chartists satisfaction that transcends the possibilities of turning the patterns into money. In his book, *The General Semantics of Wall Street*, Magee writes rhapsodically about "the wonderful world of the logarithmic spirals [which] contains so much of beauty and so much of the sheer wonder of pattern and rhythm . . . "

Some chartists reject any fundamental information about stocks, on the ground that earnings, book-value figures, and the like only tend to blur the big picture. This group includes Magee, whom many regard as the leading chartist theoretician today; the window in his workroom in Springfield, Massachusetts, is boarded up, symbolizing and reinforcing Magee's unconcern with the outside world—the world in which real, live investors pay money for the securities of companies that sell their products to real, live customers. Recently Magee's charting service recommended Colonial Corp. stock. A visitor to Magee's windowless workroom, looking at the Colonial charts with him, asked what business the company was in. "I haven't the faintest idea," Magee said, agreeably. (Colonial makes low-priced apparel.) Some chartists are opposed even to reading the business news in the daily papers. "It puts poison in the mind," says Robert G. Evans, proprietor of the Wyckoff organization. The more reasonable-sounding of the chartists, among whom is Edmund Tabell, head of institutional research for Walston & Co., the brokerage firm, take the view that charts are mainly useful for spotting interesting stock-market situations, but that investors should not act in these situations until they have gone out and examined the fundamentals.

There are, in general, two main charting techniques, or schools of thought. One school works with bar charts, like the one below, the other with so-called "point and figure" charts. This article will examine the techniques and claims of the bar chartists . . . . Before discussing either one, however, it may be well to gain a perspective on Dow Theory, the first of any "technical approach" to gain a wide following.

Some of the underlying concepts of Dow Theory may be detected in the thinking of chartists today—especially bar chartists. Unfortunately, a certain vagueness enshrouds Dow Theory. The vagueness begins with the question of whether it really *is* a theory. Is Dow Theory a hypothesis tested by events and found useful in predicting the future? Or does it merely supply us with a handy vocabulary for describing the past?

WHERE THE DOW THEORY CAME FROM

Charles H. Dow himself, the editor of the *Wall Street Journal* around the turn of the century, did not seem to believe that he had a method of forecasting. He once wrote that "there is no way of telling when the top of an advance or the bottom of a decline has been reached until some time after such top or bottom has been made." But around 1910 a *Journal* editor named William P. Hamilton began to interpret Dow's ideas somewhat more ambitiously, and to use them in forecasting. Hamilton's interpretations, as set forth and further embellished by another writer, Robert Rhea, in a 1932 volume called *The Dow Theory*, have come to be accepted as the definitive statement of the theory.

Dow theorists draw a vivid analogy between the movements of the stock market and those of the sea: there are tides (the major trends), waves (intermediate corrections), and ripples (minor fluctuations). Dow, Hamilton, and Rhea all believed that investors should ride with the major trend. But how is one to tell the tides from the waves? Hamilton offered several clues. He suggested that major trends are characterized by three distinct phases. A bull market, for example, begins with a reaction against the panic selling at the end of a bear market. The second phase is a long, persistent rise as the news of improved profits begins to come in. The third phase is marked by wildly speculative and emotional buying as the uninformed public begins climbing aboard. A reaction against this buying is the first phase of a bear market, in which the whole process is reversed.

In retrospect, most bull and bear markets can be fitted into this pattern. But at the time it is happening it is ordinarily hard to tell the difference between, say, a "correction" of the trend and the beginning of a major reversal. Hamilton laid down several rules in an effort to help the perplexed investor. The most important rule is that the market can be considered in a major upward trend when—and only when—the Dow-Jones industrial and rail averages both hit important new highs, and in a major downtrend when both hit important new lows. Rhea explained that "the validity of the last primary trend confirmation stands until countermanded by an equally valid countermovement."

How well does the method work? Hamilton himself incorrectly called a bear market in 1926, but later he achieved fame by proclaiming a bear market four days before October 29, 1929. Since then Dow theorists have often had more difficulty, or perhaps less luck, in applying the method. In 1946 the industrial and rail averages both hit new highs just before a setback; in the fall of 1957 the averages signaled a bear trend just before a major advance; and in March, 1960, the averages again signaled a bear market that did not materialize.

At least, the averages signaled these turns to *some* Dow theorists. One of the maddening perplexities about the theory is that it does not say how to tell which highs and lows are truly significant. There is also no agreement as to the exact duration and extent required of an advance or decline before it shall be construed as a major trend rather than an intermediate correction.

For these reasons, practicing Dow theorists often disagree with one another about the present character and future prospects of the market. A majestic simplicity marks their reconstructions of the past, but their formulations about the future are often elaborately woolly—e.g., "In coming years the stock market may be in for a tumble of major proportions, possibly before the year 1962 is out." (This warning was delivered by E. George Schaefer, who publishes "The Dow Theory Trader" out of Indianapolis; he has generally sounded bullish in the past decade.) One of the few Dow theorists whose predictions have been unambiguous is Richard Russell, who publishes the "Dow Theory Letters" out of San Diego. Writing in *Barron's* at the time of the March, 1960, "bear signal," Mr. Russell stated categorically that "the great bull market which began on June 13, 1949, ended on July 8, 1959." In the fall of 1960, just before the market began to rise, Mr. Russell wrote that the bear signal had been "confirmed." For a while he viewed the rise as an intermediate correction of a major downward trend, but as the market kept right on rising he abandoned this line and allowed that he had been wrong.

GET THEM WHILE THEY'RE GOING UP

Dow Theory, of course, has been concerned only with the market as a whole. But in the 1930's, Richard W. Schabacker, a financial editor of *Forbes*, wrote several books that attempted to apply some of the Dow-Hamilton ideas in forecasting the prices of individual stocks. He was helped by his brother-in-law, Robert D. Edwards, a professor of meteorology who later began to write about stocks himself, and in 1948 combined with John Magee to write *Technical Analysis of Stock Trends*. This book is pretty much the bible of modern chartists.

The chartists' indebtedness to Dow and Hamilton is considerable. In *Technical Analysis* one may, for example, rediscover the old Dow doctrine of riding with the trend until it is countermanded. To many nonchartists, this doctrine may sound like an ideal and obvious objective rather than a program for action, but virtually all chartists attach great weight to the doctrine. In practice, it seems to lead them to prefer stocks that *have been rising*, and to frown on stocks that have been falling—stocks that a fundamentalist might regard as "oversold." Bar chartists tend especially to prefer stocks that are at their all-time highs—stocks that a fundamentalist might regard as "overbought." The chartists' view of these stocks has a certain hard logic to it. When a stock is well below its high, they reason, there are always a certain number of investors who have losses and who will try to recoup by selling as the stock gets back to the price at which they originally bought. These sales create "resistance areas" that impede the advance of the stock; and the greater the volume of trading near the high, the greater the resistance is presumed to be on the way back up. A stock at a new high has no such impediment; the chartists would say that it has "clear sailing."

The opposite of a resistance area is a "support area"—i.e., a price level at which a falling stock may expect to be supported by buyers. Ordinarily, a support area exists at a level where a rising stock had earlier been accumulated by investors. As the stock goes up from, say, 25 to 30, the investors feel that their original judgment has been vindicated, but they wish they had bought more—and vow that they *will* buy more if the stock ever comes back down. At the same time, the sellers who had earlier "given up" on the stock now find their interest in it rekindled, and they decide to get back in if they can at around the price they sold at. And so plenty of support for the stock will turn up when it falls back to 25. Again, the extent of the support depends on the volume of trading that took place when the stock was earlier at that level.

Still, when you buy stocks that have been rising, and sell stocks that have been falling, you would appear to face the danger of buying at the top and selling at the bottom. The bar chartists say that this problem is manageable, however. For one thing, they maintain, strong trends are not apt to be reversed suddenly. Says Edwards in *Technical Analysis:* "One does not bring instantly to a stop a heavy car moving at seventy miles an hour and, all within the same split second, turn it around and get it moving back down the road in the opposite direction at seventy miles an hour." Before a stock turns around, its price movements will usually form one of a number of "reversal patterns" on the chart. The basic assumptions of the chartists here are that the big, sophisticated insiders are "distributing" their stock at the top (or "accumulating" at the bottom); that the entire operation is too complex to complete in a day or two; and that, for these reasons, reversal patterns tend to involve a fairly extensive sideways movement.

Unfortunately, no chartists have ever got around to demonstrating statistically that these patterns really do presage reversals in the trend of a stock's price. Edwards and Magee have festooned *Technical Analysis* with examples of reversal patterns being followed by reversals, but a skeptic has no trouble finding reversals without patterns and patterns without reversals. To begin with, it is not hard to find stocks that reversed their major trends suddenly, without slowing down from 70 mph. From the end of 1958 to the summer of 1960, Amerada Petroleum fell steadily, to a low of 55. It then turned around and rose sharply, forming a "V"; recently it has been around 110. An "inverted V" was formed about a year ago by Kerr-McGee Oil, which rose sharply from about 40 to 120, was split two for one, then fell sharply to around 40. To be sure, not all chartists will be discomfited by such examples. There are, indeed, some who regard V's, whether erect or inverted, as significant reversal patterns themselves. William Jiler of the Trendline

Corp. has recently completed a book (*How Charts Can Help in the Stock Market*) in which V formations are said to "spark the most dynamic of all price swings." He notes that because "the V-turn strikes with little warning," it is "among the most difficult to analyze."

PICASSO, MOVE OVER

But Jiler agrees with Magee and Edwards about the reliability of one major reversal pattern, the so-called "head-and-shoulders formation." As this is described in *Technical Analysis*, it has four main elements when it is a "top":

A. A strong rally, climaxing a more or less extensive advance, on which trading volume becomes very heavy, followed by a minor recession on which volume runs considerably less than it did during the days of rise and at the top. This is the "left shoulder."

B. Another high-volume advance which reaches a higher level than the top of the left shoulder and then another reaction on less volume which takes prices down to somewhere near the bottom level of the preceding recession, somewhat lower perhaps or somewhat higher but, in any case, *below the top* of the left shoulder. This is the "head."

C. A third rally, but this time on decidedly less volume than accompanied the formation of either the left shoulder or the head, which fails to reach the height of the head before another decline sets in. This is the "right shoulder."

D. Finally, decline of prices in this third recession down through a line (the "neckline") drawn across the bottoms of the reactions between the left shoulder and head and the head and right shoulder, respectively, and a close below that line by an amount approximately equivalent to 3 per cent of the stock's market price. This is the "confirmation" or "breakout."

This sounds clear enough, but unfortunately stock movements fitting this pattern unambiguously are hard to find. Practicing chartists are sometimes nagged by the question of whether to construe small ripples on their chart lines as "shoulders" or to ignore them. Sometimes a stock whose movement is ambiguous on a daily chart will look like a neat head-and-shoulders on a weekly chart; which one is the perplexed chartist to follow? Chartists are fond of citing the beautiful head-and-shoulders top on Texas Instruments in mid-1960, when the stock hit its high of 256 (see page 396); a lot of chartists sold out of T.I. or went short at that point—or rather, at about 200, where the "downside breakout" was "confirmed." (T.I. later went on down to 95.) But now observe that Litton Industries also formed a nice head-and-shoulders top in 1960. This induced some chartists to sell or go short around 70; and Litton's recent price has been over 150.

The T.I. and Litton patterns were relatively close to the ideal. But a

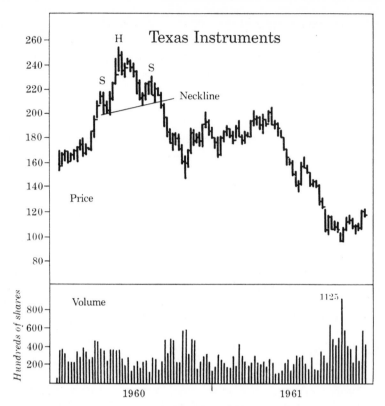

FIGURES 1 AND 2 A "head-and-shoulders formation" coming after a sustained rise is supposed to signal a "top" — i.e., that the rise is over. Bar chartists are always watching out for this formation. When it appeared in Texas Instruments in 1960 many chartists sold out at around 200. The head and shoulders on Litton proved to be a "false signal," however; after a brief decline in September, 1960, that stock resumed its long upward trend. Among those led astray on Litton was the charting advisory service run by John Magee, a leading chart theorist, who had been right on the T.I. downturn. He advised his subscribers to sell Litton if the stock closed below 76; fortunately, he advised them to buy back in at 82. (The weekly charts shown here were supplied by the Mansfield chart service.)

head may have more than two shoulders and still be allowable, and the shoulders may have more than one head between them. Says Jiler: "This need not frighten a public that pays fortunes for paintings by Picasso." *Technical Analysis* reproduces, with evident pride, a chart of Marshall Field & Co. in the spring of 1946. On this chart the authors have drawn *three* heads between the two shoulders, whose neckline slants upward. The price was at 52 when the neckline was broken; the authors remark proudly that M.F. was selling at 23 a year later.

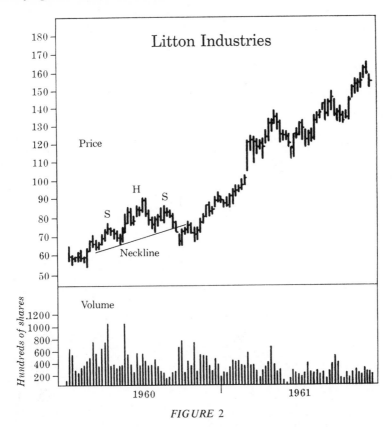

FIGURE 2

THOSE UNTRUSTWORTHY TRIANGLES

Of all the reversal patterns, triangles are among the hardest to cope with. The authors of *Technical Analysis* warn that "a downside breakout from a Symmetrical Triangle which is attended right from the start by conspicuously heavy volume is much more apt to be a false signal rather than the start of a genuine downtrend . . . Here is a very pretty technical pattern and it cannot always be trusted." Worst of all, the triangle may turn out to be a *consolidation pattern*, rather than a *reversal pattern;* in other words, the triangle may represent a breathing spell on the way up rather than the end of a rise.

Magee and Edwards identify many other reversal patterns: rectangles, double and triple tops and bottoms, rounding turns, diamonds, wedge formations, etc. Their book is profusely illustrated with bar charts on which all these patterns have been exemplified by the authors. But the dismaying fact is that many of the patterns could, without doing any great violence to the

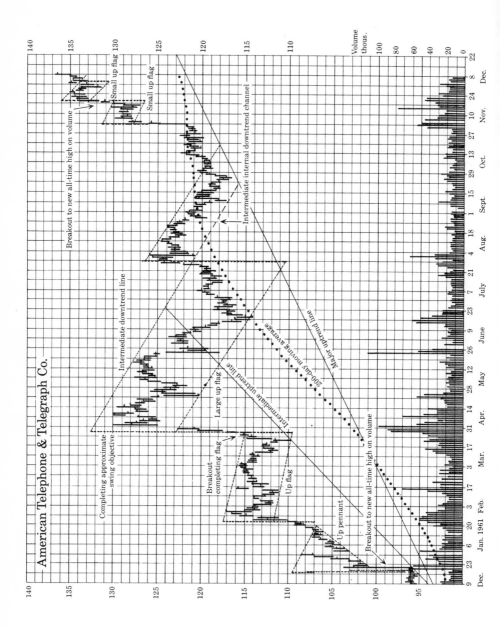

American Telephone & Telegraph Co.

authors' definitions, be construed as other patterns. The same holds true, unhappily, of the "consolidation formations" identified by Magee and Edwards: flags and pennants, ascending and descending triangles, scallops, etc.

It is apparent, then, that in seeking to identify the configurations on their charts investors often find themselves adrift on a sea of ambiguities. But the ambiguities do not end with the configurations formed by price patterns. There is also a problem about the trend lines and channels in which stocks allegedly move. All bar chartists—indeed *all* chartists—pay a great deal of attention to trend lines, which are straight lines drawn along the successive tops and bottoms of stocks' price fluctuations (see the A.T.&T. chart on page 398). Chartists register the delight of discovery whenever they can draw lines showing that a stock has moved between two trend lines—i.e., within a single channel—for a considerable period of time. But just what is it that is discovered by the trend lines? This is not so clear. Says *Technical Analysis:* "[Trend lines] are all always broken ultimately and some very shortly after they are set up. The problem is to decide which breaks (i.e., penetrations by a price movement) are of important technical significance and which are of no practical consequence."

This appears to be a sizable problem indeed, for the book goes on to say that a "break" may be followed by several different patterns. When the price has, for example, broken an "intermediate up trendline," drawn off several recent bottoms, several things may ensue: there may be "a full intermediate recession or a period of consolidation"; in other words, the stock may go down or go sideways. In addition, it may go up: "a more immediate but less important probable consequence" is the so-called "pullback." In any case, what should the investor *do* when his up trend line has been broken? Should he sell? Or sit tight and hope for a pullback? Or draw another trend line, off other bottoms? Which trend lines really count? Magee and Edwards are invincibly vague on these matters.

FIGURE 3   Flags up at A.T.&T. *Fortune* recently asked William Jiler, who publishes the Trendline and Commodity Research Bureau charts, to analyze a daily chart of A.T.&T. Ordinarily, chartists spend a lot of time looking for "reversal patterns," which are presumed to signal a change in direction. But the important configurations on this chart, as Jiler sees it, are the "consolidation patterns" — flags and pennants denoting breathers on the way up. Jiler finds a swing objective by noting the difference between breakout point (A.T.& T. at 97) and the top of the next important consolidation pattern (the highest point in the first "up flag," 117); this distance (twenty points) is then added to the lowest point in the flag (110) to get the objective in the next move. A.T.& T. did indeed make it to 130 on the next move.

Jiler regards A.T.& T.'s pattern as distinctly bullish because the company has not yet broken its major uptrend line. Jiler drew it off some earlier "bottoms" not shown on this chart. Unfortunately, there is no general agreement among chartists as to which trend lines are significant.

IT'S FUN, BUT IS IT TRUE?

Bar charts have certain obvious and indisputable uses. First of all, they give a clear and concise picture of the past, and enable an investor to get a quick sense of the stability or volatility he might expect in a certain stock; they are certainly useful as *records* in the same way that an ordinary sales or profits chart is. And the record of the volume of trading, which ordinarily appears at the bottom of a bar chart, is a handy clue to the extent of public interest in a stock. Moreover, it is often relevant for an investor to know whether a sharp rise or decline on a certain day was on heavy or thin volume; a two-point rise on only 200 shares is presumably just a temporary aberration in the market; but if the rise was on 20,000 shares, the investor might legitimately wonder whether the big "insiders" know something that has not reached the public, and are beginning to accumulate. The chartists' general view that volume fluctuations can be used to identify support areas and resistance levels also seems to be built on fairly sturdy underpinnings. Finally, it might be repeated that bar charting is obviously *fun* for a lot of people, and on this count alone it is apt to continue attracting fans. Indeed, it is possible that the technique will get so many followers that it will itself become an important influence of the market. If everyone were a chartist, Magee observed recently, "it would become self-defeating."

But right now investors interested in bar charting might well have some other concerns about it. The major concern is the fact that the scores of claims made for different chart patterns are simply unproved. They have not been tested and, in fact, are probably untestable—i.e., because they are so vaguely formulated and so thoroughly hedged. Joseph Mindell, a partner in the specialist firm of Marcus & Co., and the author of *The Stock Market*, says that he spent years studying the patterns but finally gave up on them. He asks: "What's the use of a pattern that works except when it doesn't work?"

5·2

The Mystique of Point-and-Figure*

Daniel Seligman

Burton Crane, who writes a daily report on the stock market for the New York *Times*, noted one day last October that chartists were

*Reprinted from the March 1962 issue of *Fortune* Magazine by Special Permission; © (1962) Time Incorporated.

enthusiastic about Brunswick Corp., then selling at 64: "Brokers said that the stock had pushed through the tops attained on the last two rallies . . . and therefore had been attractive to chart readers." Unfortunately for the chart readers, the stock then fell back below 60, and Crane was reporting that "its failure to behave as predicted probably brought selling." He later added that "all the reported company news was good but that the chart readers . . . were exerting a heavy influence on the stock." Toward the end of October, with Brunswick at 57, he said that the chartists felt it was just above "a major support area." But early this year it fell through this support area and then through another one even lower, and Crane reported that the chartists were taking the news hard: "It broke through the 50-51 range that chart readers have described as a support area. This touched off stop orders . . . the stock touched a low of $46\frac{1}{8}$ before making a slight recovery." Later in January, Brunswick was still giving chartists a rough time. "Brokers said that customers were watching the chart action of the stock," Crane reported, "and that the break through the 40-41 level had brought selling." The following day the stock hit a low of $38\frac{5}{8}$, and chart readers were beginning to talk of support in *that* area.

Whatever the foregoing may suggest about the acumen of stock chartists, it is at least clear that they are becoming hard to ignore; by sheer weight of numbers they often seem able, at least temporarily, to affect the market prices of some stocks. The brokerage community itself is obliged to heed the chartists. Although many brokers are skeptical of chart interpretations, investor demand for them is so great that virtually all big brokerage firms today have at least one or two chartists on hand. These days most of them use the so-called "point-and-figure" technique.

Students of stocks, an article in these pages observed last month (see "Playing the Market with Charts"), are of two kinds: There are "fundamentalists," who try to foresee the future of a stock by analyzing financial and operating data about the company; and there are "technicians," who try to foresee the future by analyzing the behavior of the stock itself. Technicians are usually chartists, and chartists, as the article last month also observed, may themselves be divided into two main camps. There are those who draw bars showing the daily (or weekly or monthly) high, low, and closing prices, and attempt to discern in the patterns formed by successive bars a guide to the future. . . .

THE METHOD, WITH A CAPITAL M

At first glance, point-and-figure charts are a mysterious proposition, and indeed they are harder to read than ordinary bar charts. Yet p. and f. is actually the oldest of all charting techniques; it was probably in use as early as 1880. It picked up a lot of followers after 1933, when a man named Victor de Villiers wrote a booklet about it called *The Point and Figure Method of Anticipating Stock Price Movements;* he said he was presenting what he had learned about the Method (he always capitalized it) after twenty years' study of market movements. It was his hope that many investors would start using p. and f., and his expectation that, if they did, "the peaks and valleys of booms and depressions" would be "moderated," because investors would recognize and avoid technically weak markets and, conversely, prop up oversold markets.

What makes p. and f. initially confusing to the beholder is that the time represented on the chart is not divided into regular intervals. P.-and-f. scholars believe that many significant patterns may take months, or even years, to develop, and that their identity is obscured on a bar chart, where a given unit of time takes up a given unit of space, moving from left to right. To make the patterns clearer, p. and f. "compresses" them. So long as a stock is moving in one direction, the record of the price changes is made by marking x's in a line straight up or down. Only when the direction changes— and the change must be at least from one whole number to another—does the chartist move to the right, where in the next vertical column he starts another row of x's. Most p. and f. men keep such "one-point-reversal" charts; however, chartists trying for an especially broad view, or dealing with unusually high-priced stocks, may keep three-point-reversal or even five-point-reversal charts. This may mean that they will not make an entry on their charts for weeks at a time; chartists plotting, say, General Motors on a three-point chart recently would not have made an entry from January 8 to January 25, because the stock, in the mid-50's, scarcely moved at all in either direction. Conversely, charts recording changes of less than one point are ordinarily reserved for low-priced stocks, although some chartists say that to get to really close quarters with *any* stock you should chart it in fractions.

Point-and-figure technicians look for several things in the patterns formed by their columns of x's. To some extent they look for "reversal patterns" similar to those on bar charts; a booklet of *Study Helps in Point and Figure Technique*, published by Morgan, Rogers & Roberts, Inc., a publishing firm catering to p. and f.'ers, suggests, for example, that the following patterns are useful in identifying so-called "tops": Inverse Fulcrum, Inverse Compound Fulcrum, Delayed Ending, Head and Shoulders, Inverted V, Inverted V Extended, Duplex Horizontal, and Inverse Saucer. The booklet, written by Alexander H. Wheelan, also includes questions and answers for students. Question (accompanied by chart data): "Does this look like reaccumulation preparatory to a new upthrust? If so, why? If not, why not?" Answer: "No—because fulcrum characteristics are not present. Furthermore, to be bullish the decline from 42 should have held at 40 or 39 instead of sinking to the bottom of the congestion area . . . "

WHERE DOES THE COMPASS POINT?

But in practice, p. and f.'ers attach less significance to major reversal patterns than to the congestion areas referred to in Wheelan's answer. A congestion area is formed by a lateral movement of columns of x's—i.e., instead of a pronounced vertical trend, there is a series of reversals after only brief advances or declines. The extent of this lateral movement is held by p. and f.'ers to be a clue to the extent of the next major upward or downward move. Their operating equipment often includes a compass like those used by geometry students; the stock's "price target" is ordinarily found by opening the compass to measure the lateral congestion area, then swinging the compass upward (or downward). Disheartening as the fact may appear to "fundamentalists," at least some of the investment recommendations coming out of Wall Street these days are made by men whose principal equipment for the task is a compass.

Thus far, p. and f. doubtless seems terribly arbitrary and mysterious. Why should the width of the congestion area determine the upward or downward prospects of the stock? What proof is there of any such relationship? The mystery deepens when you discover that the leading exponents of p. and f. do not agree on how to answer these questions. Before getting at their answers, it may be advisable to meet some of the men. Among the big names of p. and f. in the brokerage community:

Edmund W. Tabell, fifty-eight, a former actor, is a partner of, and head of institutional research for, Walston & Co. His weekly market letter has a circulation of 30,000, and is a major source of new business for Walston, from which he draws around $100,000 a year.

Kenneth Ward, sixty-two, senior vice president of Hayden, Stone & Co., writes a weekly *General Technical Survey* with a circulation of 60,000. "Charting has been very good to me," Ward remarked recently. "People are always asking why, if I'm such a good chartist, I'm not rich. I always tell them that I *am* rich."

James Dines, thirty, began writing a market letter for A. M. Kidder & Co. less than two years ago, has already got 12,000 circulation, is bringing in a lot of business.

Eugene Peroni, fifty-one, is a partner of Hill, Darlington & Grimm, for which he writes a market letter; it appears to be responsible for a large part of the firm's recent growth. Peroni is a graduate architect and businessman who retired in 1949, then spent seven years trading and studying the market, and working out his own refinements of charting (which he refuses to disclose).

John W. Schulz, forty-three, is a partner and major asset of Wolfe & Co. and the author of a market letter that, unlike those mentioned above, is not free; it comes as part of the service called Trend & Value, published by a corporate affiliate of Wolfe, that sells for $175 a year and goes to "several hundred" subscribers. Schulz gives his readers heavy doses of charting theory, along with logorrheic (some people think) reconstructions of his thinking about individual stocks. Here, for example, is Schulz' writing about Kern County Land some months back, when the stock was at 73 (it has lately been around 80):

Long-term three-point-unit base targets can now be plotted in the 90's, as shown. The major-trend base of 1959–60 yields a "first" one-point target at 85, suggesting an uptrend potential that has now been realized in large part. Secondary major-trend targets projected from the 1960 base structure on the one-point chart stand at 72–75 and have been liquidated. Since March, a mild deceleration of the advance (into channel D) seems to have taken place. A top reversal of any consequence has not so far materialized, but allowing for vulnerability to pressure from profit-taking sales, it may be reasonable to allow for penetration of potential support indicated by the chart in the 68–72 range and thus to hypothesize an intermediate-trend top-reversal structure with H-targets as shown. Allowing for a possible 50 per cent retracement of the 30-point advance to 77, the H-targets in the lower 60's would seem to be a reasonable description of latent reaction risks. Nevertheless, given a favorable general-market climate, the above-mentioned support potential astride the 70 line could remain intact and further major-uptrend development could materialize within either channel C or D.

It is probably fair to say that all of these men have had successful forecasting records. Some of them maintain an updated list of buy and sell recommendations on individual stocks, and the records look pretty good. If, for example, you had put $1,000 on every recommendation Dines made since he began his letter in June, 1960, and sold when Dines told you to, then by January, 1962, you would have realized gains in seventy-two stocks and losses in only twenty-six; your maximum investment at any one time would have been around $40,000; and your over-all profit today would be $12,800. Some p.-and-f. letters put out by independent services have also shown good results. Take, for example, the Marketlines service, founded by Walter Goldberg, forty-three, an ex-lingerie salesman who got fascinated by charts about ten years ago. In 1961 Marketlines closed out 153 positions in the imaginary portfolio it runs for its subscribers; all together, it had a net profit of $323\frac{1}{2}$ points.

But if Dines, Goldberg, and other luminaries of the point-and-figure community are generally successful, it does not exactly follow that the technique itself works. Blurring the picture is the fact that (like many successful bar chartists) they are students of the fundamentals too, and it is often hard to say on which grounds they are basing their recommendations. Ward stresses the primacy of fundamentals and Tabell thinks they are important too, even while insisting that p. and f. is useful for "bird-dogging" interesting stocks. Peroni maintains that p. and f. is the single most important element in his forecasting success, but he is also a close student of the fundamentals. And even Schulz, for all his elaborate exegeses on the charts, turns out in conversation to know a lot about company operations. How, then, is one to ascertain the value of p. and f. by itself? The problem is complicated by the experts' resolute lack of precision in describing the technique; words like "usually" and "perhaps" keep getting into their descriptions of what it is they do, and efforts to pin them down to rigorous definitions that would enable an outsider to test their systems are met with protestations that the systems cannot be applied mechanically—that they require "interpretation." To the outsider, it may seem that what they really require is faith.

WHAT'S MY LINE?

Take, for example, a fairly crucial question about the central operation of p. and f.: measuring the width of the lateral movement, or "congestion area." In theory, a breakout from this congestion area suggests that a significant vertical move is about to take place; whether it is to be a rise or decline is indicated by the direction of the breakout, and its likely extent is suggested by the width of the congestion area. Actually, however, most lateral movements may be measured at several different price levels, and picking one rather than another usually gives you a different target. For example, in analyzing the chart on page 398, John Schulz got a target of 160 for A.T. & T. by measuring the lateral trend along the 120 line and another target of 146 by measuring along the 117 line; in addition, he got two "near-term" targets by measuring shorter segments of the main trend. But how is one to know which measurements are valid? In short, what are the rules of this game? Schulz himself is not very helpful on this point; he has written that "on the question of where, in actual practice, measurements of lateral action should be taken, we are far from doctrinaire . . . we advocate the utmost flexibility because this tends to obviate the dangerous rigidity of preconceived notions." It would also seem to obviate any test.

There is also a maddening problem of definition about the "price target" itself. Does it represent a flat prediction that a certain price will be reached by a certain date—a prediction that can be put to the test? Unfortunately, it doesn't seem to be that specific. Tabell was asked recently how long a target could remain unfulfilled before the chartist should acknowledge that he had gone wrong; the answer was that no time limit could be put on a target's fulfillment. Schulz is especially mysterious on this subject. "Price targets," he has written, "may generally be presumed to imply a degree of probability that the price level they identify will, in due course, be reached." If the targets are not reached, in other words, nothing has really gone wrong with the system. In retrospect, the chartist will say that he should have measured the lateral trend differently; or possibly he will blame things on a "false breakout." According to Dines, "a false breakout is the curse of the chartist."

WAITING FOR FINER MINDS

Beyond these operating difficulties, there is a larger problem. Why *should* p. and f. work? Specifically, why should the width of a lateral movement suggest anything at all about the extent of a subsequent vertical move? Anyone who raises this interesting question with the leading p.-and-f. technicians is apt to arrive at an interesting conclusion: most of them haven't thought much about it. Tabell, for example, said recently that the method "works" 70 per cent of the time, but "I know of no valid rationale for it. The scientific reason it works just is not known." Dines observed that "when people with finer minds than mine come into the market, they will be able to determine the forces at work here." Meanwhile, Dines just doesn't know any good reason for relating the lateral and vertical moves—except that the system works, he says.

The only p.-and-f. technician who seems to have thought seriously about a rationale for the system is Schulz. He has not been completely consistent on the subject, but the drift of his recent thinking is clear. He believes that the lateral movement represents a redistribution of the floating supply of the stock; the longer the lateral trend remains in effect—i.e., the wider the congestion area—the more stock is presumed to change hands. Thus the width of the congestion area is related to a drying up of the floating supply of the stock. This means, Schulz wrote in a *Forbes* column last year, that when the stock begins to move up, "the normal deficit of supply that prevails in any uptrend is temporarily made more acute." And by the same token, "the deficit of demand that characterizes a downtrend is temporarily increased when a lateral trend is concluded."

This sounds plausible, but note several facts about it. Different stocks have different numbers of shares outstanding, of course, and also have floating supplies of widely varying size. A lateral movement that "dries up," say, 10 per cent of the floating supply will obviously have much less effect in a price advance than a movement that dries up 80 per cent of the supply. This suggests that the system, if it has any validity at all, depends on a close analysis of stock turnover. Yet in practice most p. and f.'ers pay no attention to volume; or rather, they insist that it is somehow implied by the number of price reversals—though why there should be a precise relationship between the two is quite unclear. Schulz himself has been paying more attention to volume in his recent analyses.

There is, it happens, one point-and-figure technique that is testable. This is the technique used by Chartcraft, Inc., a service operating out of Larchmont, New York. The Chartcraft service has about 5,000 customers, perhaps 40 per cent of whom are brokers. It is run by A. W. Cohen, fifty-two, a lawyer who formerly owned the William-Frederick Press, and got interested in charting when he published a book called *Stock Market Trading*, by Ernest J. Staby. He and Staby set up Chartcraft in 1948; Staby has since retired.

Like many other p.-and-f. technicians, Cohen has a few wrinkles that are all his own. He keeps three-point-reversal charts, but does not pay as much attention to congestion areas or price targets as other p. and f.'ers do; instead, his emphasis is on short-term trading and modest (but fast) profits. "Being a pig," Cohen has written, "often leads to disaster." His followers are supposed to buy, or go short, on certain "signals" that are clearly defined; there are five buy signals and five sell signals. Most of these signals may be viewed as "breakouts" similar to those that other p. and f.'ers look for, except that Chartcraft's are apt to come fairly soon in a lateral movement. With each new commitment, the Chartcraft follower is advised to place a stop order to limit possible losses; the stop is placed at the point where a change in direction would cancel the previous signal. The fundamentals are ignored entirely. In short, the entire system is defined in unambiguous terms, and anyone who pleases can go off and test it.

Oddly enough, Chartcraft itself has never run a test of the technique. The service claims that "trades established on the Chartcraft formations should yield a 10 per cent profit 85 per cent of the time." Cohen was asked recently for the evidence behind this claim; he replied that the statement was based "on what brokerage firms have told us."

10 PER CENT OR BUST

To test the claim, FORTUNE examined every buy and sell signal given on every one of the more than 700 New York Stock Exchange stocks that Chartcraft routinely covers. (The firm also offers American Stock Exchange, over-the-counter, and commodity services.) The time period covered was the first nine months of 1961; this period was selected instead of the full year because many of the signals given in the last quarter of 1961 were not resolved when this article was being written—i.e., the signals had neither led to a 10 per cent profit (at which point a sale was assumed) nor touched off a stop order. Ninety per cent of the signals given in the nine-month period were resolved.

For the nine months, Chartcraft's record may be called disappointing, to say the least. Of the stocks tested, nearly 300 gave no signal at all. The remaining stocks gave a total of 855 signals. A trader who acted on these signals would have made his 10 per cent profit on 342 trades, or 40 per cent of the time. He would have touched off a stop-loss 426 times (50 per cent), and the average loss would have been 9.98 per cent—i.e., virtually the same as the average profit. One stock, Carter Products, gave Chartcraft fans an especially hard time: it gave off four buy signals and four sell signals; all but one were losers.

On the whole, however, Chartcraft did better on buy signals than on sell signals, perhaps because it was in a rising market. Of the 421 buy recommendations, 220 (52 per cent) made the 10 per cent profit and 180 (43 per cent) were stopped out; of the 434 sell recommendations, only 122 (28 per cent) were profitable, and 246 (57 per cent) were stopped out.

Other p.-and-f. technicians will surely argue that, because of special features of the Chartcraft system, these results suggest nothing about their own systems. Perhaps not. But meanwhile Chartcraft is the only point-and-figure technique available for testing—and the results of one test inspire no special confidence in p. and f.

5·3

Advance-Decline Line: A Clue to the Underlying Strength or Weakness of the Market*

George K. Freeman

One of the most respected of all "technical" indicators—those based on the action of the market itself—is the Advance-Decline Line. The A-D Line not only is logical in construction and application, but also, unlike many indices which require complex calculation and occult interpretation, it possesses the beauty of simplicity. Even investors who have scant interest in the technical approach to the stock market undoubtedly could profit by a study of the A-D Line's behavior patterns.

Most investors find it hard to recognize that the underlying trend of the stock market is not always represented accurately by the well-known "averages." Toward the end of a bull market, for instance, the performance of the

*Reprinted by courtesy of Barron's *National Business and Financial Weekly*, January 21, 1963.

broad list of stocks increasingly lags behind that of the Dow-Jones Industrials. Brokers naturally hear complaints about this discrepancy every day; the typical customer refuses to believe that only his stocks are failing to keep up with the Average. Nevertheless, it is an elemental fact that nearly every bull market ends, for most stocks, long before the averages reach their ultimate peak. The time during which the odds are on the side of the securities' buyer often is less than half the full duration of the bull market.

THREE-PHASE MARKETS

Even the Dow Theory, which is based wholly on the trends of the Dow-Jones Industrial and Railroad Averages, gives a tacit nod to the internal deterioration of a bull market—and the strengthening of a bear market—before the Averages signal any such change. Under Dow Theory, both bull markets and bear markets are divided into three broad phases. Only in the middle phase do the Averages faithfully depict the sub-surface condition of the market. The third and final phase of a bull market is a "distribution" area, wherein farsighted investors obligingly sell stocks to feverish late-comers; the comparable phase in a bear market is an "accumulation" area, in which the more astute element buys stocks from a discouraged public. Clearly, the third phase of one and the first phase of the opposite trend overlap.

Technical analysts devote a large part of their energies—and devise scores of statistical indices—to identifying these periods of disparate movements. The simplicity of the Advance-Decline Line is only one of the qualities which commend it for the task. Most major newspaper accounts of the day's market action include the total number of stocks the price of which gained from the previous day's close (Advances); the number which posted losses (Declines); and the number which closed at the same price as the day before (Unchanged).

While these figures can be grouped, charted, and analyzed in many ways, the Advance-Decline Line is derived simply by subtracting Declines from Advances. These differentials, which naturally will be minus numbers whenever Declines exceed Advances, are added each day to form a continuous, cumulative total. Plotted on a chart as a series of connected daily totals, these cumulative differentials between Advances and Declines form the Advance-Decline Line.

CLEARCUT BAROMETER

What single statistic could describe the underlying condition of the market better than this relationship between the number of stocks advancing and the number declining? The trend of the Advance-Decline Line reveals whether the number of stocks which are rising is growing larger or smaller—a readily intelligible barometer of the strength of bull markets and the weakness of bear markets.

To illustrate the computation of the Advance-Decline Line, let us suppose the index was started on December 24. That day, 472 issues rose and 566 fell. Thus, the first A-D Line entry would be −94 (472 − 566 = −94). On the following trading day, 718 issues advanced and 291 declined, a difference of +427. This figure would be added to the previous A-D Line reading, −94, for a new reading of +333 (−94 + 427 = +333).

The next day, 428 issues advanced, 597 declined: net difference, −169. When this minus number is added to the previous cumulative total, +333, the A-D Line entry becomes +164 (+333 − 169 = +164).

Net day saw 494 advances, 509 declines. Net difference, −15. New index reading, +149 (+164 − 15 = +149). The following day's trading brought 594 advances, 459 declines. Difference, +135. Index reading, +284 (+149 + 135 = +284).

WEEKLY TABULATION

As simple as it is, this daily calculation—and its plotting on a chart—may constitute a more rigid regimen than an investor cares to undertake. Also, in a very short time the cumulative total may run to extreme figures, making the choice of a scale for the chart a difficult problem. A weekly tabulation, based on Friday-through-Friday price changes, appears in Barron's and in many Sunday newspapers. Calculated from these data, the Advance-Decline Line conforms closely, in its general pattern, to a daily index; at the same time, the mathematical work and the chart scale are reduced by four-fifths.

Several services present this as a weekly index, and the accompanying chart, showing the A-D Line from 1960 to the present, is drawn from weekly calculations. (From 1950 through 1955, the weekly average of the daily Advances and Declines was used in the computation; from 1956 to the present, the full week Friday-through-Friday tabulation was employed.)

MOMENTUM PEAKS

As the chart indicates, bull markets generally reach a "momentum peak" well before a final top in the Averages. Only in early 1953, in the span of our graph, did the Average make a significant peak (this one preceding a 9-month, 13% drop in the Industrials) while the A-D Line continued upward. This was one of the rare occasions—not seen since—when the market actually was stronger than the Average around a top area.

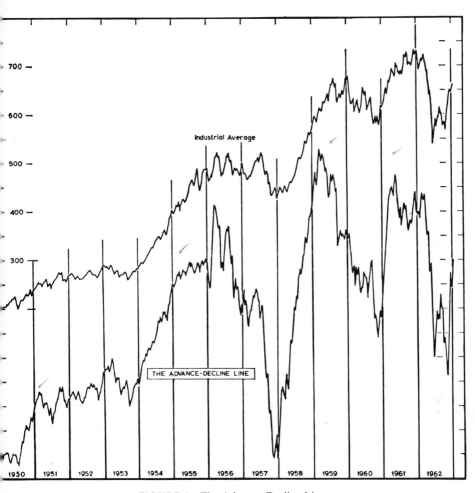

FIGURE 1   The Advance-Decline Line.

In early 1951, early 1955, early 1959 and in mid-1961, the Advance-Decline Line revealed a weakening of the market coincidentally with, or slightly ahead of, minor or intermediate tops, but substantially ahead of far more important peaks in the Average. Indeed, though complete studies are not available, it seems certain that practically every salient market top would have showed up early in this index. Except for reactions caused by unexpected news events—which usually do not alter the underlying trend for very long—bear markets result from the gradual deterioration of investment support. The waning interest is bound to show up in the Advance-Decline Line.

The typical pattern, as revealed in the chart, runs something like this. The absolute peak in the A-D Line ordinarily occurs very shortly before a market peak of intermediate importance. However, the first A-D peak seldom coincides with the final top in the Average. The market rebounds from its correction and goes on to new highs, but the A-D Line, which also has retreated on the correction, fails to reach new highs on the upswing. This disparity means that some stocks already have passed their bull-market peaks.

The sequence may recur for many months, with each subsequent move into new high territory on the part of the Average finding fewer and fewer stocks participating. Eventually, the bull market facade no longer can be maintained. The trend of the Average reverts to down—as the Advance-Decline Line had done long before.

TIME TO SELL

Which top is the final one? Unfortunately, the Advance-Decline Line does not ordinarily furnish this information (though some analysts, by means of refinements of their own, have come up with the answer). However, in practice it is not essential to identify the ultimate top; few investors own all 30 Industrials and no other stocks. In most cases, when waning momentum shows up in the Advance-Decline Line, the proper investment procedure depends on the relative strength of the issues in the investor's own list. If they all should be weak holdings, conceivably they all should be sold at the first sign of ebbing market momentum.

Contrariwise, a portfolio might comprise the relatively few stocks which are destined to rise for many more months, in which case their relative strength (a simple comparison of their action with that of the Average) would show that they all should be held. Sooner or later, of course, when the market plainly is a dying swan—as shown, among other ways, in a long series of lower tops in the A-D Line, against higher tops in the Average—profits should probably be taken. Most commonly, however, the investor will hold some strong stocks and some weak ones, so that the sensible course simply is to weed out the softer issues as the A-D Line signals the onset of general weakness.

WATCHING THE TREND

In other words, it doesn't especially matter what the Average does after the A-D Line makes its peak. The investor who is alert to the Line's signal merely gears his program to the Line's trend, rather than that of the Average, and refuses to be deceived by the apparent strength of the market.

Like many character-of-the-market indicators, the Advance-Decline Line does not "lead" at market bottoms. A low in this index usually will synchronize—to the very day—with a low in the Average. However, in some cases the Line actually will make its absolute low well after the nadir in the Industrials; this happens frequently after a severe break in the market, when popular sentiment is at a low ebb. At such times, with the public largely out of the market, the Average well may be more buoyant than the overall list of stocks.

In 1962, for example, the Average bottomed in late June. However, the A-D Line, after an initial bounce, fell to a deeper trough in October, at which time the Average held above its comparable June level.

Absolute lows in the Average are reasonably easy to recognize, by numerous technical signs; yet, except for trading purposes or the purchase of a few top-grade securities at rock-bottom prices, there is no great premium on identifying those points. In the aftermath of a bear market, there customarily is a long readjustment before most stocks make their final lows. The Advance-Decline Line is an excellent guide in this often tedious period.

DESCRIBES ACTION

In his book, Strategy of Daily Stock Market Timing (Englewood Cliffs, N.J.: Prentice-Hall, 1961), Joseph Granville describes the action of the Advance-Decline Line on the 1958 market upturn (the figures are based on a daily computation begun on January 2, 1958):

"On February 4, 1958, the Dow-Jones Industrial Average reached a minor recovery high of 458.65 and the advance-decline line (cumulative differential) was up to 5,593. This was followed by a decline in the market but on March 24, 1958, the advance-decline line got up to 5,982 (a new recovery high) while the Dow-Jones Industrial Average was still under the February 4th high at 453.75. This was followed by another decline in the market but on April 18, 1958, the advance-decline line rolled through the previous top of 5,982 and reached a new high of 6,270 while the Dow-Jones Industrial Average was simultaneously down to 449.31. That second breakthrough by the advance-decline line above a previous top marked the prime buy point of the massive 1958-59 market upswing."

The Advance-Decline Line is not only a useful key to the market's long-term position, but also a fine-focusser on lesser turning points. In fact, no other technical indicator is quite so consistent in picking market tops, whatever their eventual dimension. From even a very short-term standpoint, disparate movements by the A-D Line and the Average call for trusting the message given by the Line.

Thus, on January 2, 1963, the Industrials fell 5.31 points, while the daily A-D Line rose +108. Next day the Average was up 10.63 points, showing in microcosm how the A-D Line may disclose the underlying trend of the market better than the Average.

Not every disparate movement brings such fast results. From the longer view, the Average and the A-D Line may be out of harmony for years, before the Average gets in tune; observe the patterns of 1955-57 and 1959-60 or, in even broader perspective, 1959-62. This same sort of lag, on a much smaller scale, may appear at shorter-term junctures. In general, the longer the disparity lasts, the more violent is the eventual catching-up.

There are many short-term variations on the Advance-Decline concept. Most are built on moving averages, of such length as the technician finds best suited to his purpose. Since any length might be selected, an almost infinite variety of Advance-Decline indices could be developed; however, seldom does an A-D moving average index cover a period shorter than 10 days or longer than 25 weels. Additional variations arise from the use of two lines —one for Advances and one for Declines—oscillating around a "zero" line between overbought and oversold extremes.

Moreover, whether a one- or two-line index is chosen, the use of percentages rather than raw figures gives further opportunity for variation on the theme. The object of any of these indices is merely to place the Advance-Decline data under a sharper microscope, so that short-term and intermediate-term trend changes may be pinned down more precisely.

If analysts were allowed only one set of statistics from which to draw their market judgments, it seems certain that most would select the Advance-Decline data. It is literally impossible for distribution and accumulation, signifying fundamental changes in investors' sentiments, not to show up in the Advance-Decline indices—particularly in the Advance-Decline Line.

The A-D Line is a simple yet highly sophisticated indicator, which tells more about the condition of the market than any price average possibly could. The less reliance an investor places on outward appearances—on "averages" —the brighter are his chances for stock market success.

5·4

A New Slant on the Stock Market*

Irwin Friend and Sanford Parker

What's the stock market going to do next? This incorrigibly interesting question has led to the construction of a good many gimmicks

*Reprinted from the September 1956 issue of *Fortune* Magazine by Special Permission; © (1956) Time Incorporated. All charts associated with this article are omitted.

and theories and systems. There is one thing, however, that had never been tried (in any systematic way) until FORTUNE tried it for this article. That was simply this: to go to the people who make the market move—the investors themselves—and ask them what they plan to do.

Most formal systems of market forecasting are highly mechanistic: the statistics of past behavior (of key components of the market or the economy) are expected to foretell the future behavior of investors and stocks; a past *result*, in other words, is expected to foretell a future result. What FORTUNE offers here is a survey addressed to the *cause* of short-run market movement— the attitudes and intentions of flesh-and-blood investors.

Specifically, FORTUNE has polled . . . and received answers from:

970 individual investors (their common-stock holdings ranging from under $5,000 to $1 million-plus, the median holdings amounting to somewhat over $25,000). Individual investors account for 65 per cent—or $188.5 billion—of the $290 billion worth of common stocks outstanding.

105 financial institutions—corporate pension funds, life-insurance companies, other insurance companies, and banks administering personal trust accounts. Institutions account for about 25 per cent of common-stock ownership.

Eighty securities dealers, corporate insiders (officers, directors, and principal stockholders), and investment counselors.

These individual, institutional, and professional investors were asked, as of midyear, what they had done in the stock market during the first half of 1956, what they expected to do during the second half of 1956, and what developments might cause them to change their plans. The general drift of their replies was decidedly bullish.

HOW NEW A MARKET?

Broadly speaking, there are only two ways to look at the present stock market, at its levels of around 500 (give or take 5 per cent) on the Dow-Jones industrials. One view is heavily tinged with skepticism; it preserves a very lively respect for the roller-coaster history of the stock market; it draws frequently on principles and rules of thumb laid down long ago ("watch out when the little fellows come in," etc.); and it attributes the tremendous surge of the past three years, in which stock prices have nearly doubled, to essentially cyclical forces—which must inevitably turn and carry prices at least part way back to where they came from. The other view is that the U.S. *does* have a "New Economy," and that one of the results is a new kind of stock market, in which prices (subject to occasional setbacks, of course) are at last adjusting to the enhanced prospects for growth and stability of the economy and its thousands of corporations. The replies to FORTUNE's survey suggest that, for the second half of 1956, more money is being influenced by the "new" school of thought than by the "old." In appraising the replies, however, the reader will note, and by no means laugh off, the fact that many of the skeptics and holdouts are concentrated in Wall Street itself, among the professionals.

In mid-June, when FORTUNE sent out its questionnaires, a pall of uncertainty hung over the stock market. President Eisenhower had just had his emergency operation for ileitis. The Dow-Jones industrials were wobbling around in the neighborhood of 480, up some from the low of May (464), but still far below the high of 524 in April. The April-to-May decline, which knocked sixty points off the average in less than eight weeks, had been the most severe deflation of market values since 1953. Contradictory signals were coming from some of the best-known forecasting mechanisms—the Dow Theory, the "breadth" (of trading) indexes, the tempo of odd-lot transactions, the indexes of new factory orders, the ratio of gross national product (or of bank debits) to business loans, the pattern of money rates, etc. Many professional traders were convinced that a bear market was long overdue and was finally arriving.

Where the bears were wrong (or at least premature) was in their appraisal of investor sentiment, and it is this factor that FORTUNE has tried to measure directly in the present survey. Sentiment, or confidence, as FORTUNE pointed out in "The Future for Stocks" (March, 1955), is one of the three major forces playing on the market.[1] Sentiment, money rates, and earnings and dividends —these largely determine the long-run demand for stocks. (On the supply side of the price equation, the only significant changes come from new issues, and the volume of new issues usually doesn't vary much from one year to the next.) Sentiment seems to be decisive in the short-run fluctuations that occur so often without any changes in earnings, dividends, or interest rates, and it is sentiment that all short-term forecasts try to measure, but by indirect and mechanistic devices.

As for the tangible forces at work in the market at mid-June, the spread of dividend yields (Moody's 125 industrials) over AAA bond yields was only .7 per cent, about as low as it has been during the postwar period. (Stock and bond yields were even closer together through the 1920's, and in 1928 and 1929 stocks actually yielded much less than bonds.) With common stocks yielding barely more than high-grade bonds, it might seem a priori that the mid-June market was "too high." But in return for the risks of common-stock ownership, vis-à-vis bonds, the investor can buy reinvested earnings nearly as large as dividends. And who but investors themselves can say whether that is enough reward or too little?

[1]In its article of eighteen months ago, *Fortune* projected large 1955–59 increases in earnings and dividends, and only a partly offsetting rise in interest rates, and concluded that Dow-Jones might rise from a level of 420 then to 500 "or a little more" in 1957.

A BUYING MOOD

All of which leads back to the factor of sentiment. Amidst all the confusing crosscurrents and uncertainties of mid-June, investor sentiment was in fact strongly optimistic.

Investors responding to FORTUNE's survey were planning to buy almost as much common stock in the second half as they did in the first. And they were expecting prices to rise. Four of every ten investors thought they would enlarge their buying plans if business activity improved. (Four out of ten would buy less—or sell more—if business worsened.) And three out of ten would buy more if the Republicans win in November (as many would buy less—or sell more—if the Democrats win). If investors fulfill their plans, therefore, and if business activity holds up as expected, stock prices should continue strong up to Election Day, and, in the event of a Republican victory, throughout the rest of the year. The strength of the market would be dampened, however, if interest rates rose appreciably or if there were an unexpected increase in new stock offerings.

To some extent, of course, investors have already fulfilled their second-half intentions. The 8 per cent rise of the Dow-Jones industrials from 480 in mid-June to 520 in early August confirms what the survey shows: i.e., investors found stocks undervalued at 480 to 485. The survey also suggests that this was no mere technical rebound in a "basically bear" market that set in with the April-to-May decline and has much deeper to go. The inference from the survey is that no such bear market has begun. In mid-July, moreover, when the D-J was already up to 510, a small follow-up sampling showed investors to be still virtually as optimistic as in mid-June. This second survey was promptly confirmed, in turn, by the rising market of late July and early August. The FORTUNE survey does not say, of course, how many more points on the D-J it would take to turn investor sentiment toward a general belief that stocks are "too high." Nor do the survey results rule out dips in prices below the early August highs, or even below the mid-July levels.

WHAT THEY SAY

Here are further highlights of the survey:

Investors' planned net purchases in the second half, at a $3-billion annual rate, will be close to the postwar record of the first half. Their planned net purchases will also match or exceed the prospective flow of new corporate issues. Demand for stock, in other words, will at least equal supply.

Individual investors not only planned to buy as much stock on balance in the second half as in the first but, also, as much in the fourth quarter as in the third. Their optimism about prices was more pronounced for the fourth quarter than for the third.

Institutions plan to buy as heavily in the second half of 1956 as in the first, even though the proportion of institutional investors expecting a rise in stock prices is not so high as among individual investors.

Wall Street brokers were nearly as optimistic as the general public about a rise in stock prices, but they plan to take advantage of the higher prices—i.e., to sell more stock in the second half than they did in the first half (when they were net sellers).

Half the public said they would buy more than planned if corporate earnings and dividends advanced. Only one in four, by contrast, will buy less if earnings or dividends dip. And most investors reported that changes in net earnings would influence their plans more than dividend changes.

Buying plans would be raised by 42 per cent of the individual investors if there were a pickup in business; by 31 per cent if there were a Republican victory; by 23 per cent if interest rates declined; and by 15 per cent if margin requirements were cut. On the bearish side of each of these ifs, similar proportions of investors would cut their buying plans.

Aside from the common assumption that Ike is the only Republican who could win, a surprising number of individual investors say that *Ike* as President is a more bullish factor than "a Republican President." One Texas investor ventured these reactions to the November election: To a Republican victory: "Ike—increase buying; other than Ike—sit tight." To a Democratic victory: "Lyndon Johnson— continue buying, not increase. Anyone other than Johnson—seriously consider moving to the Antarctic."

"Copper the trend"—i.e., the professional practice of betting against the prevailing market trend—is now the fashion among "amateurs," too. Two-thirds of the individual investors say that if stock prices rise, without accompanying gains in net earnings or dividends, they will sell more than they planned as of midyear. One in three would ride the trend—buy on a rise, sell on a decline. The institutional investors almost unanimously say they will sell on advances that do not reflect increases in earnings, and buy on declines that do not reflect dips in earnings.

Some investors are watching for a bearish development as an occasion to buy: "If Dems win, look out—sell out—hold cash and prepare to buy cheap after crash" is the strategy of one investor in Washington, D.C. (party affiliation unspecified). A good many respondents suggest the same strategy if business slows down and the market breaks.

Investment counselors, the pros who administer large personal accounts, reported much the same optimism, plans, and price expectations as did individual investors. Those in New York City were an exception; they were pessimistic about the market outlook—"but this may be purely wishful thinking," said one, who presumably meant that he would like to buy more if stocks were to go down.

Thirty per cent of the individual investors say they would buy more stock if income taxes were cut (5 per cent would buy less). But 30 per cent would *sell* more stock if capital-gains taxes were cut (15 per cent would buy more).

Industries that individual investors liked best: oils and chemicals. Least: autos and textiles.

Investors usually switch their funds between stocks and cash balances, rather than between stocks and other investments. But an Oklahoman who sold on balance in the first half says: "Working-capital needs increased in my own business." A Californian: "Market too high—bought luxuries like Continental Mark II."[2]

On inflation, a Maryland investor said: "If a new effort is made by the government to pump more money into circulation, bringing on a new spiral of inflation, I would most likely buy stocks for the ride, but fearfully." A New Yorker: "The only answer to the trend of inflation is investment in equities."

All groups of institutional investors expect to increase the proportion of their assets invested in stocks in the long run.

BEHIND THE SCHEDULE

All this information—on investors' plans, price expectations, and other attitudes—constitutes what economists call a demand schedule. Such a schedule, whether for soybeans, or soap, or securities, can shed light on the future course of prices. And when investors plan—as they did at midyear—net purchases of stock in excess of prospective new issues, the situation normally points to higher prices. For investors cannot, on balance, buy more than the available supply of new stock, and when they attempt to do so, prices rise until demand and supply are again in balance. Both the demand for common stocks and the supply, of course, are influenced by the total supply of money, the public's willingness to save, business's desire to raise new capital, the level of national income, and investors' and businessmen's current preferences as between stocks and bonds.

Simply relating planned purchases of stock to the known supply, moreover, is not enough. It is also necessary to know the key assumptions behind investors' plans. Suppose, for example, that investors planned to buy more stock—net—than was likely to be issued; stock prices could be expected to rise, but only on the assumption that investors were willing to pay higher prices for shares. Some investors in FORTUNE's survey, however, reported that they expected stock prices to decline and that they planned to buy only after prices declined. Obviously, if all investors planned high purchases on the assumption of declining prices, the situation would not necessarily imply market strength. Nor, conversely, could one anticipate market weakness if the majority of investors planned to sell—but solely on the assumption that prices were going higher.

Finally, to appraise the probable market trend it is also necessary to know how investors' plans are likely to be affected by such *external* developments as a business recession, tax changes, etc.

[2]Not a very good switch. The Dow-Jones average, which stood at 486 at the beginning of 1956, was 519 on August 1. A new Continental Mark II, which sold for near list price ($10,000) in January, sold for as little as $8,000 on August 1.

HUNGRY BUYERS

One striking point about the bullishness of the current survey is the internal consistency of the replies. Investors, taken collectively, plan to buy more than the prospective supply of new stock. Moreover, they also expect stock prices to go up. Presumably this means their buying intentions will hold good even if there is some rise in stock prices from the mid-June level. It is this consistency of plans, expectations, and assumptions that adds up to a bullish prospect.

As previously stated, investors plan net purchases of stock during the second half of 1956 almost as large as during the first half. During the first half, net purchases reached a record postwar rate of $3.3 billion a year. And since purchases and sales must balance, this means that net new issues of common stock (including conversions of debentures and preferred stock, but excluding sales of mutual-fund shares) also hit an annual rate of $3.3 billion in the first half.

The first-half issues, however, included the $643-million sale of Ford Motor Co. stock, the largest common-stock offering in history (equivalent to $1.3 billion on an annual rate basis). Excluding Ford, therefore, first-half stock issues were at the rate of $2 billion, which is about the rate at which the volume of outstanding common stock has been increasing annually since 1951.

This month A.T. & T. stockholders will vote on a $575-million stock issue, most of which probably will be marketed before the end of 1956. Partly as a result of this second abnormally large stock flotation, the total supply of new issues in the second half of 1956 may run at a rate of about $2.8 billion.

Thus the present prospect is for a slightly smaller supply of new stock in the second half of 1956 than in the first. This is important because plans for large net purchases can be swamped by a flood of new common-stock issues. A generation ago, new issues (excluding those of investment companies) soared from less than $1 billion in 1927 to $4 billion in 1929. The present record high level of stock prices might conceivably cause corporations to increase their new issues substantially. But this has not happened to date, despite a doubling of prices since 1951.

Turning to purchase plans, there are several reasons for thinking investors may attempt to buy at an even faster clip than the $3-billion rate now reported for the second half. First, the FORTUNE survey tends to understate the total buying by small new investors who are intering the market for the first time. Second, most other surveys of expected purchases that FORTUNE has conducted—whether of inventories, capital goods, consumer durables—have tended to understate the actual amounts subsequently bought. This may prove true for stock investment plans too. Third, investors in FORTUNE's survey were asked about their purchase plans before the A.T. & T. issue was announced; this offering may create additional demand for stock just as the Ford issue did.

FORTUNE's survey shows that the most important groups of net buyers in the first half of 1956—the individual round-lot and odd-lot investors— plan to buy as much stock on balance in the second half of 1956 as in the first. So do corporate pension funds. Life-insurance companies, other insurance companies, and mutual funds will probably buy more. The only groups of investors who do not plan to buy as much in the second half are the corporate insiders, the securities brokers and dealers, and the personal trusts and estates. (Banks administering personal trusts plan small net sales in the second half, and estate liquidations to pay taxes will as usual result in large net sales.) All in all, the demand for stocks in the second half should exceed the net new supply available.

THE LITTLE BULLS

The survey turned up some interesting discrepancies between the plans of big investors and those of little investors. Ninety per cent of the smallest traders, for example (those whose first-half transactions totaled less than $2,500), had net purchase balances in the first half. Three-fourths of the next group ($2,500–$10,000) had purchase balances as did 59 per cent of the next group ($10,000–$50,000) and 54 per cent of the traders whose transactions totaled more than $50,000.

The attitude of many small traders is typified by a Michigan investor who started buying stocks two years ago. "I use a systematic plan of purchasing stocks . . . and hold them for long-term development. Therefore my purchases are constant and sales are very low. I am *not* trying to make a million in the market." Or as a small New York investor put it: "All common stocks I purchase are held. Industry and people will go on and on. U.S.A. will always go forward."

The smallest traders intend to expand their purchases a little in the second half of 1956. Since a great many small investors are buyers of mutual funds, sales of mutual shares by the open-end funds should go higher in the second half of 1956. And so, in turn, should the mutual funds' purchases of corporate securities. (Because mutual funds' net purchases of stock are tied to the sale of their own shares, the funds were not asked about their investment plans.)

FORTUNE's survey also included a special sample of odd-lot traders, and, as might be expected, the answers from this group were very similar to those received from the two smallest trader groups (transactions up to $10,000). Since roughly 60 per cent of the purchasing by odd-lot traders is done by investors with incomes under $10,000, the odd-lot traders by and large *are* the small traders. As a group they are increasingly important. Net purchases by odd-lot traders have expanded sharply in the last few years, to a new peak rate of $1.6 billion in 1956.

Individuals who traded more than $10,000 of stock in the first half of 1956 did so mostly in round lots. But surprisingly, their total net purchases were smaller than those of the two smallest trading groups. Round-lot purchases reached a rate of just over $1 billion a year in the first half of 1956 as against $2.5 billion for odd-lot and mutual-fund purchases, most of which were made by the smallest trading groups.

One-third of the over-$10,000 traders, moreover, were net sellers of stock in the first half. And the survey indicates that in the second half an even larger proportion of the big traders (over $50,000) will cut their buying or increase their selling. But since the optimists among the big traders plan substantial increases in their net purchases, the top trading group, as a whole, plans about as much net buying in the second half of 1956 as in the first.

HIGHER PRICES

Forty-five per cent of the institutional investors expect no change in prices in the second half of 1956 and almost as many (25 per cent) anticipate lower prices as look for higher prices. Yet the institutions, except for the personal trusts and estates, plan to maintain or increase their buying. What is more surprising is that there is greater optimism about prices among the big individual traders than among the small ones (under $2,500). Two-thirds of the big traders expect prices to rise; yet they do not plan to buy more stocks in the second half of 1956 than in the first, whereas the small traders do.

When asked why their investment plans for the second half of 1956 were different from their plans for the first half, many large traders said they were feeling cautious until the election is over. Some said they planned to realize capital gains; others that they lacked additional investment funds; and a small group said that they had made unusually large purchases in the first half of the year because of the Ford issue. But another and more interesting motive often mentioned for paring purchase plans was the intention of many large traders to sell (or buy less) *after* an expected rise in stock prices.

HOW FIRM ARE THE PLANS?

The major uncertainty in this whole approach to the stock market, of course, is whether investors will in fact act as they said they would in the survey. And if they should revise their plans, will they do so in the ways and for the reasons they said they would? Some Wall Street observers feel that most investors simply veer with the changing winds of the market, and that even men in top investment posts usually pretend to more of a market "policy" than they actually practice.

There are some reasons, however, for thinking that people will behave, in economic matters, the way they say they will. Surveys of businessmen's plans and expectations, for instance, have been used with considerable success in forecasts of the business outlook by FORTUNE's Business Roundup. The most accurate forecasts have been those dealing with business plans for the purchase or production of capital goods. Somewhat less accurate, but still of considerable value, have been the surveys of business inventory plans, home builders' expectations, and consumers' intentions to buy major durable goods.

In reply to a specific query in FORTUNE's survey, most investors said either that they had adhered to their first-half investment plans fairly closely, or that they had changed them in ways that could have been predicted beforehand. For example, among those who did alter their plans, Ike's health was frequently cited as a reason for the change. Another reason for shifting was the business readjustment. "Market reaction" was the third reason most often cited for changing plans; some investors bought more, some less than they had planned as a result of the market's movements.

As to this last reason, whether investors reacted the way they could have predicted beforehand is the big question. If they did, the prospect for high and stable stock prices for the rest of this year is exceedingly good. For two out of three individual investors say they would sell on a market rise not related to earnings, buy on a decline. But on this point, old Wall Street hands are skeptical; they think most investors move like sheep—into the market on a rise, and out on a decline.

The investors themselves think they know how they would react to economic developments. Among individual investors, big traders would be far more sensitive to economic, political, and other developments than small investors; institutions, as a group, would be influenced least of all. Not surprisingly, the tempo of economic activity was mentioned by more than 50 per cent of all individual investors as a possible reason for changing their investment plans. About half the round-lot investors intend to buy more than planned if business improves, and as many would sell on a decline in activity. But almost one-half of *all* investors said that a change in business, either way, would *not* affect their stock-buying plans.

INVESTOR REFLEXES

The survey also sheds light on how various financial developments, such as changes in interest rates, margin requirements, income taxes, and capital-gains taxes, would affect investors' stock-buying plans:

Few small investors, it appears, would be influenced much by changes in interest rates. But interest rates are very important to large institutions, particularly to bank-administered personal trusts. Says one pension-fund manager: "[It] would depend on degree of rise or decline; presently anticipated change in interest rates probably would not significantly affect our plans." Almost as many big traders (41 per cent) would change their stock-buying plans in response to a turn in bond yields as would be influenced by the election outcome or economic trends.

Big traders also would be importantly influenced by a cut in margin requirements (41 per cent would buy more if margins were cut, but a rise in margins would have less tendency to increase selling). Only 5 per cent of the small traders would react to a margin cut.

Fewer than one-third of the large traders would be influenced in their market policies by a cut in income taxes.

One of the most interesting points turned up by the survey was that a cut in the capital-gains tax rate might have an immediate bearish effect on the market. Apparently many investors who now feel they are "locked in" by the gains tax would take their capital gains if the tax were cut; nearly 30 per cent of all individual investors (and 35 per cent of the big traders) would sell more stock on balance if capital gains rates were cut (only 15 per cent would buy more).[3]

Investors who say a change in corporate earnings would influence their investment plans outnumber by three to one those who would be influenced by a change in dividends. Until recently, by contrast, dividends were rated much more important than retained earnings. But today earnings retained by a company are an untaxed asset so long as the shareholder holds his stock, and if he sells the tax may be only one-third as high as the tax he pays on dividend income.

COMMON PREFERRED

Institutional investors plan to increase their holdings of common stock substantially in the future.

Since FORTUNE last surveyed the long-range investment plans of institutional investors three years ago (see "New Influences in the Stock Market," March, 1953), pension funds have increased their comon-stock holdings from 15 per cent to 25 per cent of total assets, as they planned to do. Life-insurance companies have not quite achieved their common-stock goals, but personal trusts have gone beyond their old objectives. Now all these institutions have raised their common-stock goals despite a dramatic narrowing of

---

[3]In the long run, of course, a cut in the capital-gains tax would probably have a bullish effect on the stock market, for it would tend to raise the net return on stocks as compared with other investments.

the gap between stock and bond yields since 1952 (interest rates have risen while dividend yields have fallen).

Seventy per cent of the corporate pension funds reported that they plan to increase the proportion of their assets in common stock (30 per cent plan no change). So did 78 per cent of the life-insurance companies (13 per cent plan a decrease), 67 per cent of the non-life-insurance companies (4 per cent planned to buy less, 29 per cent planned no change), and half the banks administering personal trust accounts (40 per cent plan no change). Thus the common-stock portion of the portfolios of institutional investors is expected eventually to rise (on the basis of market value) as follows:

	Current proportion of assets	Long-run expectation
Self-insured pension funds	27%	33%
Life insurance companies	2	4
Other insurance companies	27	29
Personal trust funds	54	59

These future percentages would involve a switch from other assets into common shares on the order of $1 billion for pension funds, $2 billion for life-insurance companies, close to $500 million for non-life-insurance companies, and over $3.5 billion for personal trusts. These long-run objectives, moreover, are higher than the proportion of new assets currently being put into common stocks by institutional investors—which means there should be a somewhat higher rate of investment in equities in the future by these groups.

Nor is this all. More than one life-insurance-company official would like to invest "more than the law allows in common stocks." Another says, "After we reach $1\frac{1}{2}$ per cent at the end of 1958, we anticipate extending our program . . . to approximately 3 per cent." A pension fund that presently has 16 per cent of its assets in common stocks says its program "will be reappraised upon reaching 20 per cent."

On balance, it seems clear that investors were still definitely bullish about the market's future when FORTUNE took its survey at mid-year. And there were persuasive reasons for a favorable long-term evaluation of stocks. The economy has expanded at an average rate of 4 per cent a year in the postwar decade. The rise was interrupted only twice by minor business readjustments in 1949 and 1954. That is the best business performance in U.S. history. If this economic growth can be projected into future dollar sales and earnings, and if interest rates do not rise too much, there will be an economic basis for further advances in stock prices.

VISIBILITY: LIMITED

This is not to say that the bears have been routed—or as yet proved wrong. Reasons for their uneasiness are put this way by a Virginia investor: "The odd-lot indexes, volume, new highs and lows, amount of short selling, and banking figures all paint a deteriorating picture. . . . There would have to be a complete reversal of odd-lot data, banking figures, and stock-market technical indications before any change in plans would be effected. These reversals would need more time than the six months remaining in the present calendar year." Sophisticated bears would still argue that the current surge in capital and expenditures must eventually bring about increased stock and bond flotations that will tighten up interest rates and expand the supply of new stock offerings. The supply of stock, they say, will eventually swamp a market that is becoming more and more dependent on an inflow of funds from small investors—which, say the bears, cannot last.

FORTUNE's survey would seem to challenge this view. The survey, of course, has yet to withstand the test of time as a forecasting device. And apart from the possibility that prices may fluctuate considerably even in a "strong" market, or that there may be unforeseen developments which investors will regard as bearish—e.g., a major rise in interest rates—the survey has a limited horizon. At best it is good only for the six-month period for which investors were asked their plans and expectations. Nevertheless the experiment should provide a clearer view of the short-run direction of the market, and if it throws light on the general market *approach* of major investor groups, it could contribute something to a long-run appraisal of the future for stocks.

FORTUNE'S INVESTMENT SURVEY

The survey findings discussed in this article are based on over 5,000 detailed questionnaires that FORTUNE sent out in mid-June to a selected cross sample of investors in common stocks. There were 1,155 replies. A small follow-up survey (fifty responses from 250 questionnaires) was run and showed essentially the same results as the original survey. A supplementary questionnaire also was sent to investment counselors.

Included in the survey were all of the largest institutional investors in the U.S.—the biggest trusts, insurance companies, etc.—as well as a sampling of the smaller institutional investors. The institutions that replied account for two-thirds of total life-insurance holdings of common stock, one-fourth of the holdings of other insurance companies and pension funds, and 8 per cent of the stock held in bank-administered personal trust accounts.

Two samples of individual investors were used—one a sample of people believed to hold stock and one derived from lists of customers of brokerage firms. All together nearly 5,000 individuals were queried and almost 1,000 replies were received from small, medium, and large investors. Since the questions applied only to people who own common stock, or had common-stock transactions in the first half of 1956, some of the failures to reply simply meant that the individual was not an investor. Of those who were traders, about one-third replied. One-third of the investment counselors queried replied, and 15 per cent of the corporate insiders and broker-dealers.

Not everyone in the survey received precisely the same questionnaire. Some of the queries included more detailed and complex questions than others in order to test the feasibility of obtaining replies to such questions. All included the same basic questions, however.

While there is always the danger of statistical bias in a survey that does not achieve a 100 per cent response, it is noteworthy that the different question-naires used in FORTUNE's survey all showed similar results. However, the survey did suggest average transactions and a ratio of purchases to sales somewhat higher than those that actually occurred in the first half of 1956. The effect of this error was minimized by the use of actual purchase figures for the first half of 1956; the sample data were used only to extend these to the second half.

Aside from questions of bias, it should finally be noted that in a sample of roughly 1,000 the mathematical probability is that the error will be small— at least on questions of investor attitude. Where dollar figures are involved, of course (for example, an estimate of probable dollar spending for stocks in the second half), there is a larger margin for error. But if a survey of inves-tors' plans proves to be a useful guide to short-term market trends, FORTUNE expects to repeat the experiment and refine its survey technique.

All data for the first half of 1956 are based on statistics from the N.Y.S.E. and the SEC, supplemented by results of the FORTUNE survey.

Irwin Friend, co-author of this article (with Sanford Parker, FORTUNE's chief economist), is professor of finance at the Wharton School of Finance, University of Pennsylvania. Dr. Friend, a past contributor to FORTUNE, was formerly chief of the Business Structure Division of the Department of Commerce.

"Can Speculators Forecast Prices?"*

Hendrik S. Houthakker

The role of speculation in the economic system is still a matter of controversy. In popular parlance the word has acquired an unfavorable connotation; most economists would probably say speculation is at best a necessary evil, though some would regard it as an unnecessary source of instability. One of the main issues in evaluating speculation is no doubt the degree of skill with which speculators can forecast prices: the more accurately prices are forecast, the less they will fluctuate, and the easier therefore the adjustments which interested parties have to make. Thus formulated the question leaves open to what extent the prices that actually emerge are in some sense optimal, for steadiness is only a minor characteristic of optimality. The very difficulty of defining optimality in a dynamic context, however, is a sufficient reason for separately considering speculators' success in predicting prices as they are. For this purpose we shall consider data concerning three important American commodity markets.[1]

In commodity futures markets a measure of the forecasting ability of speculators is not hard to find, for it is immediately reflected in their profits and losses. Except for hedgers, whose futures commitments are offset by commitments in the cash market, the buying and selling of futures contracts has no purpose other than to profit from changes in futures prices. The problem, then, consists in estimating and analyzing speculators' profits.

The best source of information on this subject would be the actual trading records of speculators, but these are rarely available. An important study based on data of this type was presented by Blair Stewart,[2] who made a

*Reprinted by permission of the publishers from *The Review of Economics and Statistics*, **39**, no. 2, May 1957, pp. 143–151. Cambridge, Mass.: Harvard University Press, Copyright, 1957, by the President and Fellows of Harvard College.

[1]These results are part of an investigation of commodity futures undertaken at the Cowles Commission for Research in Economics with the valuable assistance of Lester G. Telser and supported by the Rockefeller Foundation. Further acknowledgments and details will be given in a forthcoming Cowles Foundation monograph.

[2]Blair Stewart, "An Analysis of Speculative Trading in Grain Futures," U.S. Department of Agriculture Technical Bulletin No. 1001, October 1949.

detailed analysis of the accounts of about 9,000 customers of a nationwide brokers' firm during the period 1925–34. These accounts reflected almost exclusively speculative transactions in grain futures, mainly by non-professional traders. The most striking results were that nearly 75 per cent of the speculators lost money and that in the entire sample total losses were about six times as large as total gains. Since in the futures market as a whole gains and losses cancel out (apart from commissions, which in futures trading are small), the question arises by whom corresponding profits were made. Although the coverage of Stewart's material was not wide enough to give much information on this point, he seems to have thought it difficult to account for these heavy losses and to have suspected some unknown bias in his sample.

There were, in fact, two possible sources of bias. In the first place, prices in 1934 were much lower than in 1925, while the customers tended to prefer the long side. This effect, however, does not explain a great deal, since the trading experience of the shorts in the sample was not much less disastrous than that of the longs. A second source of bias may have been that the firm with which the accounts were held went bankrupt, which casts some doubt on the reliability of the advice it presumably gave to its customers.

If no actual trading accounts are available estimates of gains and losses must be made from price movements and assumptions about commitments. This was done for speculators by Working[3] and for hedgers by Yamey[4] and others. The technique of the present paper is basically similar to theirs, but we were able to replace some assumptions about commitments by observed data and to consider a much longer period.

The method of estimating profits is based on monthly figures of open commitments and futures prices. The commitments are divided into three groups: (large) hedging, (large) speculative, and non-reporting. This division corresponds to the reporting requirements under the Commodity Exchange Act. Traders whose commitments in any one futures contract exceed the reporting limit (200,000 bushels in the case of wheat and corn and 5,000 bales for cotton) have to communicate their entire position to the Commodity Exchange Authority, which classifies futures commitments into hedging or speculative.[5] The remaining commitments are those of small traders, and it is commonly assumed that they are predominantly speculative in nature. It also seems clear that the reporting traders (both hedgers and speculators)

[3]H. Working, "Financial Studies of Speculative Holding of Wheat," *Wheat Studies*, vii (July 1931).

[4]B. S. Yamey, "Investigation of Hedging on an Organized Produce Exchange," *The Manchester School*, xix (1951).

[5]A special category of speculative commitments is "spreading" or "straddling" positions, in which a long position in one or more futures contracts is offset by a short position in one or more other contracts.

are almost exclusively professionals, and that the figures for non-reporting traders are representative of the small non-professional speculators.

To estimate profits and losses it was assumed that the commitments of a group of traders that existed at the end of a month were opened at the average price during that month and closed out at the average price during the following month. The profit or loss of that group was then found by multiplying the end-of-month position by the change in the average price. Thus if large speculators were long 10 million bushels of May wheat on March 31, and the average price of May wheat was $1.60 per bushel during March and $1.55 during April, then their loss on that position was put at $500,000. Commission charges have been ignored throughout. It need hardly be said that this estimation procedure is no more than approximate and could be improved in various ways, but it should be accurate enough for the purpose of this paper.

In the case of wheat and corn the calculation just described could be performed for each futures contract (i.e., delivery month) separately, thanks to a recent analysis of the Commodity Exchange Authority[6] which cross-classifies open contracts by future and group of traders.[7] Total profit or loss for each group was then found as the sum of the profits or losses in each futures contract, calculated by multiplying the position in a future by the change in the average price of that future. This procedure will be referred to as Method A.

For cotton Method A could not be applied because a cross-classification is not available. It therefore had to be assumed that the percentage distribution of open commitments between futures was the same for all groups of traders, and hence the same as the distribution of total open commitments between futures, which is known from Department of Agriculture data.[8] The price change used was a weighted average of the changes in the average price of each future, the weights being given again by the percentage distribution of total open contracts between futures. This procedure, to be called Method B, was also applied to corn and wheat as a check. As may be seen from Table 5 the results from Methods A and B are not grossly different, although there are systematic discrepancies which will be discussed below.

The price data used were monthly averages of daily closing prices in Chicago (for grains) and New York (for cotton), obtained by courtesy of the Commodity Exchange Authority. Results are given by crop years, which start on July 1 for wheat, August 1 for cotton, and October 1 for corn. Open

---

[6]U.S. Department of Agriculture, "Grain Futures Statistics 1921–51," Statistical Bulletin No. 131 (July 1953).

[7]Some minor problems connected with the use of these figures will be discussed in the monograph mentioned in footnote 1.

[8]U.S. Department of Agriculture, *Cotton Futures Statistics* (3 issues covering 1937–45), and *Commodity Futures Statistics* (annual).

contract data for grains in the crop years starting in 1937–39 refer to the Chicago Board of Trade only, for 1946–51 to all United States markets combined. The first six months of the crop year 1946–47 had to be omitted in wheat because futures trading was still restricted by the aftermath of wartime measures. Open contract data for cotton are based on New York and New Orleans together in crop years beginning in 1937–44; for the remaining years they also include the insignificant cotton futures market in Chicago.

Despite the considerable variability of the entries in Table 1 certain broad conclusions may be drawn. In all three commodities the large hedgers lost and the large speculators gained. The small traders lost in the grains but did quite well in cotton, although it will be noted that of their total computed profit of $130.9 million no less than $100.5 million was made during the period 1940–46, which was excluded in the grains because of lack of data. In the case of the hedgers, only profits and losses on futures commitments are shown, which have to be offset against profits and losses in the cash market.

Most conspicuous in these results is the consistent profitability of the large speculators' transactions. In cotton they made a net profit in every year observed, and although in corn and wheat they lost in a few years, they never lost much. A tabulation of the monthly figures underlying Table 1 is shown in Table 2. It will be seen that the large speculators had net profits in 59 per cent of all months for corn, 61 per cent of all months for wheat, and 68 per cent of all months for cotton. If, to make the period for cotton comparable to the period for the grains, the crop years beginning in 1940 through 1945 are omitted, the percentage for cotton becomes 65 per cent. These scores are sufficiently different from 50 per cent to provide *prima facie* evidence of forecasting skill; some tests of this hypothesis will be presented below.

Less forecasting ability is apparent from the results of the small traders. They gained in 55 per cent of all months for corn, 46 per cent of all months for wheat, and 64 per cent of all months for cotton. Again leaving out the period 1940–46 the score for cotton drops to 61 per cent.

The main purpose of Table 2 is to show to what extent gains and losses are connected with a net long or net short position. Both large speculators and small traders are net long most of the time and therefore stand to gain when prices go up. During the period of observation cotton prices rose fairly steadily; wheat and corn prices declined on balance during each of the two sub-periods, though in corn the number of months with price rises exceeded the number with price falls. This behavior of prices explains a good deal of the discrepancy between small traders' results for grains and for cotton, especially when it is considered that in each of the three commodities small traders were net short about 20 per cent of the time. The latter figure, incidentally, shows that the traditional picture of the small speculator as an

TABLE 1. *Net profits (+) or losses (−) of three categories of traders in commodity futures ($ million)*

Crop year§	Corn†			Wheat†			Cotton‡		
	Large hedgers	Large spec's	Small traders	Large hedgers	Large spec's	Small traders	Large hedgers	Large spec's	Small traders
1937–38	+ .46	+ .22	− .68	+21.93	+ .36	−22.30	− 3.43¶	+ .44¶	+ 2.99¶
1938–39	+1.68	− .81	− .88	+ 5.91	+ .45	− 5.46	− 3.80	+ .58	+ 3.22
1939–40	−1.67	+ .56	+1.11	− 2.59	+ 1.70	+ .90	− 8.04	+ 1.59	+ 6.45
Sub-total	+ .47	− .02	− .45	+25.26	+ 1.61	−26.87	−15.27	+ 2.61	+12.65
1940–41							−20.98	+ 2.04	+18.95
1941–42							− 9.39	+ 1.80	+ 7.59
1942–43							− 7.14	+ .82	+ 6.33
1943–44							− 1.84	+ 1.12	+ .72
1944–45							− 3.59	+ 1.41	+ 2.19
1945–46							−79.77	+15.06	+64.71
Sub-total							−122.72	+22.24	+100.48
1946–47	− .20	+ 6.12	− 5.92	+ 6.77#	+ 1.43#	− 8.20#	+11.00	+ 1.87	−12.86
1947–48	− .36	+ 1.28	− .92	−22.86	+13.39	+ 9.46	−12.80	+ 3.35	+ 9.46
1948–49	+3.58	− .55	− 3.03	+ .34	+ 1.56	− 1.22	+ 2.18	+ 1.85	− 4.02
1949–50	−6.06	+ 2.56	+ 3.50	− 5.44	+ 5.10	+ .34	−12.93	+ 7.28	+ 5.65
1950–51	−5.52	+ 2.50	+ 3.02	− .47	− .19	+ .66	−34.11	+ 9.25	+24.86
1951–52	+2.00	− .27	− 1.73	− 9.19	+ 4.24	+ 4.95	+ 1.20	+ 4.13	− 5.33
Sub-total	−6.56	+11.65	− 5.08	−31.53	+25.54	+ 5.99	−45.47	+27.73	+17.75
Grand total	−6.09	+11.62	− 5.53	− 6.28	+27.16	−20.88	−183.45	+52.58	+130.88

*Figures may not check downward or across because of rounding.
†Computed by Method A (see text). Prewar years Chicago Board of Trade only; postwar years all markets combined.
‡Computed by Method B (see text). Until August 1, 1945 New York and New Orleans only; thereafter all markets combined.
§Crop years start October 1 for corn, July 1 for wheat, August 1 for cotton.
¶Excluding first two months.
#Excluding first six months.

TABLE 2. *Number of months with profits and losses*

Months with:	Corn			Wheat			Cotton		
	Prices rising	Prices falling	Total	Prices rising	Prices falling	Total	Prices rising	Prices falling	Total
Large speculators' net profit	52	12	64	43	19	62	116	5	121
Large speculators' net loss	12	32	44	6	34	40	6	48	54
Small traders' net profit	51	8	59	38	9	47	99	15	114
Small traders' net loss	13	36	49	11	44	55	23	39	62
Total months	64	44	108	49	53	102	122	54*	178†

*Including one month in which large speculators broke even.
†Including two months in which prices did not change.

incurable bull, too ignorant to understand short selling, is incorrect. In fact, small traders do not appear to be less inclined to the short side than the large professional speculators. In cotton small traders were net short in 38 months as against only 11 for the large speculators. In grains the pattern, though opposite to that for cotton, is not very marked (20 against 25 for wheat, 21 against 24 for corn).

On the other hand it is clear that the small traders are rather less successful when net short than the large speculators in similar circumstances. Thus in wheat, although prices fell in 53 out of 102 months, the small traders were short mostly in months when prices were rising, whereas the large speculators in that market were remarkably accurate in their choice of the short side. There is some evidence, particularly from the early postwar years, that small traders were unduly cycle-conscious and therefore unwilling to believe that high prices could last for long. In the end this Cassandra attitude often turned out to be correct, but by then the initial losses had sometimes so undermined the small traders' courage or their margins that they were no longer able to reap the fruits of their badly-timed foresight. This happened for instance in the corn market during the boom of 1947. In the wheat market of 1947, too, small traders were initially speculating against the rapid price rise, but after a long period of losses they reversed themselves and made large profits from the tail end of the boom, only to lose again when prices broke early in 1948. If it is correct to explain the small speculators' actions by a belief that price rises will always be followed by falls, then the usual arguments about the destabilizing influence of speculation may require reconsideration.

In Table 3 the totals from Table 1 are analyzed by short and long positions. Apart from the difference in small traders' net profits noted previously, the general pattern is the same for the three commodities. The hedgers, who are nearly always net short in the futures markets, are the mainspring of profits for the other traders, who share in proportion to their net long position. In all three commodities the large speculators and small traders lost on balance on their short positions. It cannot be inferred from this that speculators would have done better to stick to the long side, for their short positions are often one half of a spread or straddle (i.e., they are offset by a long position in another delivery). Spreading is not only a means of saving on margin requirements[9] but it is helpful in distributing different maturities between speculators according to their preferences.[10]

The essence of futures trading, however, is the transfer of price risks

---

[9]Because the differences between the prices of various contracts (also known as "spreads") are less volatile than these prices themselves.

[10]J. M. Mehl, formerly Administrator of the Commodity Exchange Authority, ascribes the recent increase in spreading also to income tax considerations, since it permits the transformation of short-term into long-term profits. Cf. J. M. Mehl, *Futures Trading Under the Commodity Exchange Act* 1946–54, U.S. Department of Agriculture (December 1954), 20.

TABLE 3. *Profits (+) and losses (−) of three categories of traders on long and short positions* ($ million)

	Large hedgers			Large speculators			Small traders		
	Long	Short	Net	Long	Short	Net	Long	Short	Net
Corn									
1937–40	− .84	+ 1.31	+ .47	− .47	+ .44	− .02	− 1.67	+ 1.22	− .45
1946–52	+ 11.28	− 17.85	− 6.56	+ 27.97	− 16.32	+ 11.65	+ 34.74	− 39.83	− 5.08
Total	+ 10.44	− 16.54	− 6.09	+ 27.50	− 15.88	+ 11.63	+ 33.08	− 38.61	− 5.53
Wheat									
1937–40	− 4.79	+ 30.04	+ 25.26	− 8.68	+ 10.29	+ 1.61	− 40.98	+ 14.11	− 26.87
1947–52	+ 30.82	− 62.36	− 31.53	+ 41.99	− 16.44	+ 25.54	+ 57.20	− 51.21	+ 5.99
Total	+ 26.04	− 32.31	− 6.28	+ 33.31	− 6.15	+ 27.16	+ 16.22	− 37.10	− 20.88
Cotton									
1937–40	+ 9.99	− 25.26	− 15.27	+ 5.23	− 2.62	+ 2.61	+ 22.54	− 9.89	+ 12.65
1940–46	+ 49.30	− 172.01	− 122.72	+ 61.70	− 39.46	+ 22.24	+219.78	−119.31	+100.48
1946–52	+ 98.59	− 144.06	− 45.47	+ 98.83	− 71.10	+ 27.73	+250.77	−233.02	+ 17.75
Total	+157.88	− 341.34	− 183.45	+165.75	−113.18	+ 52.58	+493.09	−361.21	+130.88
Total all commodities	+194.36	−390.19	−195.82	+226.56	−135.21	+ 91.36	+542.39	−437.92	+104.67

*The footnotes of Table 1 apply also to Table 3.

from the hedgers to the speculators in return for a risk premium, and this is clearly illustrated in Table 3. Even in wheat and corn, where prices fell during the period of observation, a risk premium was produced. As it happened the whole premium went to the large speculators, who in addition obtained some of the small traders' funds. In cotton the risk premium went to both large and small traders. Of course a net risk premium accrues to speculators only in the long run, and not necessarily in any given period of time.

The exact mechanism by which the risk premium is transferred cannot be described in this paper. Its principal component is a tendency for the price of a futures contract to rise from the inception of trading to the delivery date. The existence of this tendency, which is implied by Keynes's theory of "normal backwardation,"[11] can be statistically demonstrated in various ways.

The main implication for the present analysis is that *in the long run* no great amount of skill is necessary to make a profit in the futures market: all one has to do is to maintain a long position. In this way a trader, if he has enough patience and capital to cover temporary losses, will sooner or later secure his portion of the risk premium. If, moreover, he can predict short-term price movements more accurately than other speculators, and adjusts his position accordingly, he may make a further profit at their expense. Conversely if he is outguessed by other speculators he may lose his share of the risk premium and more. There are consequently two kinds of skill: general skill, which consists only in being long and requires no information, and special skill, which involves a continuous adjustment to changes in current information. The two types of skill may be positive or negative: a negative general skill means a proclivity for the short side, whereas a negative special skill implies a tendency to be short when prices go up and long when prices go down.

The extent to which a category of traders possesses these two skills may be measured (*ex post*) from the following equation:

$$y_t = a + \beta x_t + \epsilon_t \tag{1}$$

in whicy y_t is the net position of that category, at a certain time t (here, the end of each month); x_t is an index of the change in prices around time t (more particularly the index used to estimate gains and losses by Method B described above); and ϵ_t is a random disturbance. The general skill is reflected in the constant term a: it is clearly positive when the group tends to be long irrespective of price changes. The coefficient β measures the special skill. What matters for our purpose is not the absolute magnitude of the estimates of a

[11]J. M. Keynes, *Treatise on Money* (London, 1930), Vol. II, 142–44. See also J. R. Hicks, *Value and Capital* (Oxford, 1939), 137–39; and the monograph announced in footnote 1.

TABLE 4. *Estimates of α and β in equation (1), with standard errors (in parentheses) and correlation coefficients*

	Number of observations	Large speculators			Small traders		
		α	β	r	α	β	r
Corn*							
1937–40	36	4.20	+.0318	.0235	9.56	+.0206	.0082
		(.77)	(.232)		(1.42)	(.430)	
1946–52	72	4.72	+.0416	.0927	7.58	−.2220	.2533
		(.52)	(.051)		(1.03)	(.101)	
Wheat †							
1937–40	36	4.87	+.2375	.3451	43.13	−.3370	.0462
		(.72)	(.111)		(8.18)	(1.250)	
1947–52	66	6.48	+.2024	.2950	10.51	−.0770	.0553
		(.84)	(.082)		(1.79)	(.174)	
Cotton †							
1937–45	94	62.2	+31.59	.3030	621.6	−90.56	.0879
		(5.3)	(10.42)		(54.4)	(106.99)	
1945–52	84	121.7	+16.57	.2646	153.2	+26.01	.0889
		(9.9)	(6.67)		(47.1)	(31.81)	

*Net position in millions of bushels, price changes in cents per bushel.
†Net position in thousands of bales, price changes in cents per pound.

and β, but rather their statistical significance, which can be found by comparing each estimate with its standard error.

It is important to realize that (1) is not a behavior equation; it is purely an *ex-post* relation. Estimates of α and β are given in Table 4, with standard errors in brackets. The number of observations and the correlation coefficient are also given. As an aid in judging significance we note that if α or β is "really" zero, its estimate has a 30 per cent chance of exceeding its standard error and a 5 per cent chance of exceeding twice its standard error. It is hardly necessary to go into further refinements since the results are rather clear-cut.

Table 4 shows that both speculators and small traders possess general skill, since all the estimates of α very considerably exceed their standard errors in all three commodities. A conspicuous difference appears in the measure of special skill, however. The estimates of β for the small traders all fall short of their standard errors and must therefore be regarded as insignificant, with the exception of postwar wheat where the small traders' special skill appears to be significantly negative. The special skill coefficients for the large speculators are significantly positive in wheat and cotton but not in corn, where they are positive but very small.

It seems clear, therefore, that there are real differences in the ability of large and small traders to forecast price changes. This implies also that the differences in profits and losses exhibited in Tables 1–3 are not wholly due to random causes.

We must now consider another aspect of relative skill. So far we have looked only at the total net position of a category of traders, that is to say at the net position in all futures contracts combined. Since, however, the prices of different deliveries do not usually move in an exactly parallel manner, there is also scope for skill in choosing the futures in which to be long or short; this might be called distributive skill to distinguish it from the sort of skill analyzed in Table 4.[12]

It is possible to estimate distributive skill by comparing results from the two methods used for estimating profits and losses in Table 1. Method A, used there for corn and wheat, was based on the actual distribution between futures of commitments of the three groups of traders, whereas Method B, used for cotton, was based on the assumption that the distribution between futures was the same for all three groups. By applying Method B to the grains, and subtracting the gains or losses it gives from those estimated by Method A, we will therefore obtain a measure of the gains and losses due to a more or less skillful distribution of a given over-all position between different deliveries.

Table 5 shows that Method B gives smaller profits (or larger losses) to the large hedgers and large speculators, and larger profits (or smaller losses) to the small traders. This would imply that the large traders have a positive distributive skill. The differences between the results from Methods A and B are not large, however, and the question arises whether they are not merely due to an accumulation of random errors. By way of a crude test[13] it was found that the large corn speculators showed evidence of positive distributive skill in 54 months out of 108, negative skill in 51 months, and equal results from Methods A and B in the remaining 3 months. The small corn traders showed positive distributive skill in 43 months, negative skill in 62 months, and zero skill in 3 months. In wheat the large speculators showed positive skill in 56 months out of 102, negative skill in 41 months, and a tie in 5 months; for the small traders these figures were respectively 42, 59, and 1. On the basis of these figures the apparent positive distributive skill of the large

---

[12]In principle this distributive skill might also be divided into general distributive skill, leading to a long position in those contracts which *on the average* tend to go up most, and special distributive skill, consisting in an ability to buy those futures which *in a given period of time* will go up most or sell those which fall most. It does not appear, however, that different deliveries have markedly different rates of average increase in the long run. There would consequently be no scope for general distributive skill, and the distinction between general and special skill would be redundant here.

[13]More refined tests could not be applied either here or in Table 2 because the distribution of gains and losses is not of the normal type.

TABLE 5. Analysis of distributive skill ($ million)

	Large hedgers		Large speculators		Small traders	
	Method B	Method A – Method B	Method B	Method A – Method B	Method B	Method A – Method B
Corn						
1937–40	+ .40	+ .07	– .07	+ .05	– .33	– .12
1946–52	– 7.49	+ .93	+11.32	+ .33	– 3.83	– 1.25
Total	– 7.09	+1.00	+11.25	+ .38	– 4.16	– 1.37
Wheat						
1937–40	+25.04	+ .22	+ 1.29	+ .32	–26.33	– .54
1947–52	–32.59	+1.06	+22.99	+2.55	+ 9.60	– 3.61
Total	– 7.56	+1.28	+24.29	+2.87	–16.73	– 4.15

speculators is not statistically significant; the apparent negative distributive skill of the small traders, on the other hand, cannot plausibly be attributed to random causes only.[14]

It appears, therefore, that the distribution between futures is one of the factors influencing the relative profitability of large and small traders' commitments. Further evidence on this point is provided by an analysis of the monthly profits and losses in corn and wheat for individual futures contracts. For this purpose futures have been grouped together according to their distance from maturity. Thus at the end of February the May future is regarded as 3 months distant from maturity, the July future as 5 months distant, and so on. The expiring future (in this case the March future) is consequently treated as one month away. Then the profits and losses on all futures one month distant from maturity, 2 months distant, and so on, were added up. The totals appear in Table 6.

TABLE 6. *Net profits and losses of three categories of traders by distance from maturity of futures contracts ($ million)*

Months from maturity	Corn			Wheat		
	Large hedgers	Large speculators	Small traders	Large hedgers	Large speculators	Small traders
1	−2.59	+ 4.37	− 1.78	− 1.04	+ 4.57	− 3.53
2	+1.47	+ 5.29	− 3.82	+ 8.90	+ 4.03	−12.93
3	+ .59	− .23	− .36	+16.01	+ 4.13	−20.14
4	+3.85	− 1.25	− 2.61	− 3.32	+ 5.25	− 1.93
5	− .54	+ 2.57	− 2.02	+ 5.73	+ 1.72	− 7.44
6	−2.63	+ 3.13	− .50	− 9.45	+ 5.00	+ 4.45
7	−1.87	+ .48	+ 1.39	− 5.68	+ 1.82	+ 3.86
8	− .84	− 1.08	+ 1.92	− 8.26	+ 1.33	+ 6.93
9	− .56	− .60	+ 1.16	− 9.06	+ .67	+ 8.39
10	− .03	− .77	+ .80	− .16	− .71	+ .86
11	− .01	− .27	+ .28	+ .06	− .67	+ .61
Total	−6.09	+11.62	− 5.53	− 6.28	+27.16	−20.88
1– 6	−2.79	+13.88	−11.09	+16.82	+24.71	−41.53
7–11	−3.30	− 2.26	+ 5.56	−23.09	+ 2.45	+20.65

Although the results are not as clear-cut as they might be we can nevertheless find some indication of a difference in success according to the distance from maturity. The large speculators do better in the near futures (those close to maturity) than in the very distant ones, and the opposite is true for

[14]If distributive skill were really zero, so that positive and negative skill was equally likely, the standard error for each of the grains would be about 5 months.

the small trader. The exceptions as regards the large speculators are the corn futures three or four months distant from maturity, in which they lose, in common with the small traders, and in which, consequently, the hedgers gain. The last two lines of Table 6 show that small traders lost twice as much in the near futures as they gained in the distant futures. It would be interesting to do the same analysis for cotton, but the data are not available.

It is not difficult to explain these differences. The price behavior of the near futures depends to a large extent on the magnitude and ownership of deliverable stocks at the relevant terminals (Chicago, Kansas City, and Minneapolis for wheat, Chicago for corn), and this is a matter on which non-professionals cannot easily inform themselves. Price movements in the more distant contracts, on the other hand, are influenced mainly by basic supply and demand factors such as crop prospects, the general economic outlook, or government policy. In evaluating the latter factors the professionals have no particular comparative advantage. Indeed it is often profitable for them to use their superior knowledge by taking a long or short position in the near futures, at the same time taking an opposite position in the more distant deliveries in order to limit their risks. We have already mentioned that such spreading accounts for a major part of the large speculator's operations. By taking the other side of the distant half of these spreads the small traders may then earn a risk premium from the professionals; the other side of the near half is more likely to be taken by hedgers, who rarely go into distant futures. This type of spreading is quite similar to hedging, which is based on hedgers' superior knowledge of the cash market.

Returning now to the question raised in the title we conclude that large speculators show definite evidence of forecasting skill, both in the long and in the short run. Since these large speculators are professionals whose existence depends on their skill, this finding is hardly revolutionary, edifying though it is to see virtue rewarded. The experience of the small traders indicates that they do quite well when they stick to the long side, where the theory of "normal backwardation" assures them of a profit in the long run, but they show no evidence of ability to forecast short-run price movements. It appears, moreover, that non-professionals would have done well to confine themselves to the more distant futures.

Corporate Insider Trading Profits and the Ability to Forecast Stock Prices*

Hsiu-Kwang Wu

[In accordance with the Securities Exchange Act of 1934, "every person who is directly or indirectly the beneficial owner of more than 10 percentum of any class of any equity security (other than an exempted security) which is registered on a national securities exchange, or who is a director or an officer of issuer of such security" is a corporate insider (editors).]

One of the basic assumptions of classical theory is that an insider with his inside information has better than average foresight and can predict future prices of his company shares. By buying the shares at relatively low prices and selling them at relatively high prices, he makes a profit and at the same time stabilizes price fluctuations. The classical theory and some objections to it have been discussed in detail . . . [elsewhere in the dissertation]; it is sufficient here to emphasize that, according to the theory, a stabilizing speculation is a profitable speculation; and the cardinal condition for a profitable speculation is the ability to forecast future prices correctly. Insider trading behavior during market movements has been examined in the last chapter, and there were some evidences that insiders did trade in accordance with the classical theory for the five year period as a whole under investigation. This chapter attempts to estimate the size of the insider profits (or losses) for the sample periods and also to determine whether insiders as a group have better than average foresight in regard to the future stock prices of their company shares.

*From "Corporate Insider Trading, Profitability, and Stock Price Movement," a Ph.D. dissertation presented to the faculty of the Graduate School of Arts and Sciences of the University of Pennsylvania, 1963, chap. 7, pp. 105–115. Some minor changes were made by the author. Reprinted by permission of the author.

SOME PREVIOUS FINDINGS

There have been three comprehensive studies of insider profits in the past. Both Smith[1] and Driscoll[2] were primarily interested in the size of insider trading profits; and O'Donnell[3] tested insider market performance by examining the relationship between insider transactions and subsequent price movements of their company shares. All these studies utilized the data provided by the Securities Exchange Act and its allied legislation. The Smith study covered roughly the period from 1935 to 1939 and included both the aggregate data and the data for a group of selected securities. By multiplying the appropriate monthly stock price indexes by the net insider monthly transactions, Smith estimated the weighted average price per share for the monthly net insider purchases and the monthly net insider sales. By comparison of these estimated prices of insider trading with the price index, he found no sufficient evidence to indicate that insider trading was superior in this period.[4] Driscoll, who used roughly the same method, found the same results for the management group for the more recent period of 1946–1955.

In the Driscoll study, insider trading behavior immediately before and after the announcement of a dividend reduction or omission was also examined. A sample of 17 companies which had unfavorable dividend action in the six months period prior to December 1955 was selected. From the sample, only a very few cases of large insider sales prior to the announcement and large insider purchases following the announcement were found. This lack of speculative interest of insiders in connection with unfavorable dividend action is certainly not surprising because of the publicity and the restrictions provided by Section 16 of the Securities Exchange Act of 1934. In fact, . . . , we have found that insiders on the average speculate very little during short-term price fluctuations.

The sample in the O'Donnell study included 349 insider market transactions effected between January 1 and March 10, 1958 on the New York Stock Exchange and the American Stock Exchange. These transactions consisted of 198 purchases and 151 sales. The subsequent prices of these securities involved in these transactions were examined at intervals of one month, three months and one year to determine whether these stock prices on the average increased (or decreased) at a greater rate than the Standard

[1]Frank P. Smith, *Management Trading, Stock-Market Prices and Profits* (New Haven: Yale University Press, 1941), Chapter VII.

[2]Thomas E. Driscoll, *Some Aspects of Corporate Insider Stock Holdings and Trading Under Section 16 (b) of the Securities Exchange Act*, An unpublished MBA thesis, Wharton School, University of Pennsylvania, 1956, Chapter VI.

[3]Thomas Michael O'Donnell, *The Stock Market Activity of the Corporate Insider, and Future Price Movements of His Stock*, An unpublished MBA thesis, Wharton School, University of Pennsylvania, 1960.

[4]Smith, *op. cit.*, p. 134.

and Poor stock price index. It was found that, for the securities involved in the purchase transactions, the majority of the prices increased to a greater extent than did the Standard and Poor index by the end of one year after the purchases had occurred. For the securities involved in the sale transactions, on the other hand, no definite trend of subsequent price movements can be found.

TRADING PROFITS
AND THE ABILITY TO FORECAST STOCK PRICES

One of the best methods of testing the ability of insiders to forecast stock prices would be to make a survey of the opinions of insiders in regard to the future prices of their company shares. These opinions then can be compared later with the actual price movements. A survey of such a nature, however, probably would not receive any response if there is no compulsion, legal or otherwise, for the recipients of the questionnaires to reply. Thus, in the present study, we shall rely on insider trading behavior and profits, which can readily be ascertained from the available data, to provide us with clues. There is another reason for using insider trading behavior and profits as indicators of insider forecasting ability. There is always the possibility that insiders in general refrain, for one reason or another, from using their company inside information for speculative gains in the market even though they are capable of forecasting future stock prices. Since our primary interest in this study is in the effects of insider market behavior, for our purposes then, profit and trading behavior variables are more meaningful.

The present study consists of three stages. The insider profits (or losses) for the sample periods will be estimated first. Secondly, the hypothesis that these profits or losses are the results of chance will be tested. Thirdly, we shall attempt to determine whether insiders have better than average foresight or whether insiders can outperform the market.

In determining the size of insider trading profit, we followed to some extent the Smith and Driscoll procedure. The sample is the same trading sample used . . . [elsewhere in this study], which consisted of 50 companies listed on the New York Stock Exchange. Under the present reporting procedure of the SEC summary, all insider trading data in a particular class of securities are reported monthly by individuals in aggregate form. The exact dates of the transactions and the exact number of shares in each transaction are not known. Consequently, the following method was used in estimating the average price per share at which insider net transactions for the sample period were effected. First, following the procedure established in the previous chapters of this study, only the data of monthly insider net sales (or purchases) were used. Secondly, the number of shares of each company in each month was multiplied by the appropriate monthly stock price average of the company. Thirdly, the resulting monthly values of insider net balances of these 50 companies over this period were summed separately for net sales and net purchases and each sum was divided by the corresponding total number of shares involved to obtain the weighted average price per share of insider net monthly sales and of insider net monthly purchases for the period.[5] The results are presented in Table 1. In interpreting the table, one point should be remembered; that is the insider trading data used are somewhat understated because insider trading (sum of purchases and sales) of less than one hundred shares in a given month is omitted by the SEC summary.

From our estimates, for the five year sample period from 1957 to 1961, both insider and management made profits. They on the average purchased at prices lower than the prices at which they sold their shares. For the insider group, the estimated average price per share of net monthly purchases was $36.7, and the estimated average price per share of net monthly sales was $53.8; a profit of $17.1 per share was realized. For the management group, the estimated average price per share of net monthly

TABLE 1. *Estimated weighted average price per share for insider net transactions in the 50 common shares listed on the New York Stock Exchange, 1957–1961*

	Estimated weighted average price per share		Average of the monthly stock price averages of the 50 companies*
	Net monthly purchases	Net monthly sales	
All insiders	$36.7	$53.8	$47.5
management only	34.7	54.6	

*The average is derived by dividing the total number of months of the period into the sum of the monthly stock price averages of the 50 companies.

purchases was $34.7, and the estimated average price per share of net monthly sales was $54.6; a profit of $19.9 per share was realized. Finally, the following fact should be noted: the average prices per share of both insider and management net purchases were lower than the average of the monthly stock price averages of the 50 companies; and the average prices

[5]The method used for estimating the weighted average price per share of insider net monthly sales for the period, for instance, can be expressed mathematically as follows: let P_{ij} = monthly stock price average of company i at month j; S_{ij} = the number of shares of monthly insider net sales of company i at month j; and $V_{ij} = P_{ij}S_{ij}$. Then, the weighted average price

per share of insider net monthly sales $= \dfrac{\sum_i \sum_j V_{ij}}{\sum_i \sum_j S_{ij}}$.

per share of both insider and management net sales were higher than the average of the monthly stock price averages of the 50 companies.

Now the question is whether these profits were the results of chance. Or in other words, were these profits the results of random insider trading behavior? If insiders traded randomly in this period, we would expect that, for each company, 50 percent of the shares involved in the net purchases (or sales) would have been purchased (or sold) at prices above (or below) the average over the sample period of the monthly stock price averages of the company. The sum of the number of shares involved in insider net purchases (or sales) of the 50 companies at prices below (or above) the appropriate averages of the monthly stock price averages of these companies, expressed as a percent of the total number of shares involved in the insider net purchases (or sales), is presented in Table 2. All these percentages were

TABLE 2. *The sum of the number of shares involved in the insider net purchases (or sales) at prices below (or above) the average of the monthly stock price averages of each sample company as percent of the total number of shares involved in the insider net purchases (or sales), 1957–1961*

	All insiders	Management only
Net purchases at prices below the averages	55.9%	57.8%
Net sales at prices above the averages	53.1%	52.3%

NOTE: All these percentages are significantly different from the 50 percent value at the .01 level.

tested by the statistical test of proportion and were found to be significantly different from the 50 percent value at the .01 level. Therefore, from these data, the hypothesis that the estimated insider profits were the results of insider random trading behavior should be rejected.[6]

From the above analysis, there is some evidence that insiders can forecast stock prices; on the average, they made profits in this period. In addition, both insiders and management did better in this period in net purchase transactions than in net sale transactions. In Table 1, for both the insider and the management group, the favorable differences between the average prices per share of the net monthly purchases and the average of the monthly stock price averages of the 50 companies are much larger than the favorable differences between the average prices per share of net monthly sales and the average of the monthly stock price averages of the 50 companies. In Table 2, the percentages of net purchases at prices below the averages for both insider and management group are larger than the per-

[6]It should be noted that this test is not a powerful test; it has a very strict definition of insider random trading behavior.

centages for net sales at prices above the averages. These results are certainly consistent with the evidence found in the previous chapters that there are more speculative reasons for insiders to purchase than to sell in the open market.

TABLE 3. *Insider transactions during a three month period (from October to December 1959) in the 50 common shares listed on the New York Stock Exchange and subsequent prices of these shares*

	Prices increased more than the SEC Composite Monthly Index	Prices increased less than the SEC Composite Monthly Index or declined	Total
(A) *Prices at June 1960*			
Purchase transactions	30	23	53
Sale transactions	38	22	60
	68	45	113
(B) *Prices at December 1960*			
Purchase transactions	26	27	53
Sale transactions	20	40	60
	46	67	113
(C) *Prices at December 1961*			
Purchase transactions	24	29	53
Sale transactions	18	42	60
	42	71	113

	Prices increased more than the monthly average stock prices of the 50 companies listed on the NYSE	Prices increased less than the monthly average stock prices of the 50 companies listed on the NYSE or declined	Total
(A) *Prices at June 1960*			
Purchase transactions	26	27	53
Sale transactions	38	22	60
	64	49	113
(B) *Prices at December 1960*			
Purchase transactions	25	28	53
Sale transactions	20	40	60
	45	68	113
(C) *Prices at December 1961*			
Purchase transactions	24	29	53
Sale transactions	18	42	60
	42	71	113

NOTE: chi-square value (with Yates correction of continuity) of these contingency tables is not significant at .05 level.

On the other hand, as was pointed out before, the market in the sample period can be characterized as a long-term bull market. Did insiders simply recognize the general market trend? Or did they really possess inside information and know that the prices of their company shares would go up (or down) more than the general market? In order to answer these questions, insider market transactions (purchases and sales) during a three month period from October to December 1959 were collected for the 50 companies in the trading sample. As in the previous chapter, a transaction is defined as the total net monthly purchases or sales of a single insider. The reason for using transactions rather than companies as units of study is that transactions give us more observations. Our primary interest is the market purchase transactions since insiders have more non-speculative reasons to sell than to purchase in the open market.

The 50 company stock price average during the three sample months was quite stable and declined generally thereafter until November 1960. If insider did possess inside information, we would expect that the subsequent prices of the shares purchased by insiders in these months would go up more than the general market trend. The relationships between these insider transactions in the 50 companies' shares and subsequent prices of these shares in relation to both the SEC composite monthly stock price index and the monthly stock price average of the 50 sample companies at six months, one year, and two years intervals are summarized in Table 3. Chi-square tests (with Yates correction of continuity) of independence were applied to these contingency tables, and the chi-square value was found insignificant at .05 level in all the cases. Therefore, from these data, there is very little evidence that a definite relationship exists between insider transactions and subsequent price movements in relation to the general market trend. In fact, six months after the purchases were made, the prices of the stocks involved in only 30 transactions out of total 53 increased more than the SEC composite index, and only 26 out of 53 increased more than the 50 companies monthly stock price average. At the end of the one year and the two year periods, less than 50 percent of the stocks purchased by insiders had greater increase of prices than either the SEC index or the 50 stocks price average. On the other hand, for the sales transactions, with the exception of the six month interval, the majority of the subsequent prices did increase less than the market trend. In conclusion, however, from these cross-section data, there is no sufficient evidence to prove that insiders in these 50 companies as a group had outperformed the market.

Stock Market "Patterns"
and Financial Analysis:
Methodological Suggestions*

Harry V. Roberts

INTRODUCTION

Of all economic time series, the history of security prices, both individual and aggregate, has probably been most widely and intensively studied. While financial analysts agree that underlying economic facts and relationships are important, many also believe that the history of the market itself contains "patterns" that give clues to the future, if only these patterns can be properly understood. The Dow theory and its many offspring are evidence of this conviction. In extreme form such theories maintain that *only* the patterns of the past need be studied, since the effect of everything else is reflected "on the tape."

A common and convenient name for analysis of stock-market patterns is "technical analysis." Perhaps no one in the financial world completely ignores technical analysis—indeed, its terminology is ingrained in market reporting—and some rely intensively on it. Technical analysis includes many different approaches, most requiring a good deal of subjective judgment in application. In part these approaches are purely empirical; in part they are based on analogy with physical processes, such as tides and waves.

In light of this intense interest in patterns and of the publicity given to statistics in recent years, it seems curious that there has not been widespread recognition among financial analysts that the patterns of technical analysis may be little, if anything, more than a statistical artifact. At least, it is safe to say that the close resemblance between market behavior over relatively long time periods and that of simple chance devices has escaped general attention, though the role of chance variation in very short time

*From the *Journal of Finance*, **14**, no. 1, March 1959, pp. 1–10. Back numbers can be obtained from the Kraus Reprint Corporation, New York. Harry V. Roberts is indebted to Lawrence West and Arnold Moore for help in the preparation of this paper.

periods has often been recognized. One possible explanation is that the usual method of graphing stock prices gives a picture of successive *levels* rather than of *changes*, and levels can give an artificial appearance of "pattern" or "trend." A second is that chance behavior itself produces "patterns" that invite spurious interpretations.

More evidence for this assertion about stock-market behavior is still needed, but almost all the fragmentary evidence known to me is consistent with it. The major published evidence from recent years is a paper about British stock indexes (and American commodity prices) by the British statistician, M. G. Kendall, which appeared in 1953.[1] I have done similar, though less comprehensive, work with recent American data, for both indexes and individual companies, which has been entirely consistent with Kendall's findings. If, for example, weekly *changes* of the Dow Jones Index are examined statistically, it is apparent that these changes behave very much as if they had been generated by an extremely simple chance model. The history of market *levels* behaves very much as if levels had been generated by a *cumulation* of results given by the chance model.

These general conclusions have been reached, probably repeatedly, long before Kendall's study. Thus Holbrook Working, writing in 1934, said:

> It has several times been noted that time series commonly possess in many respects the characteristics of series of cumulated random numbers. The separate items in such time series are by no means random in character, but the changes between successive items tend to be largely random. This characteristic has been noted conspicuously in sensitive commodity prices. . . . King has concluded that stock prices resemble cumulations of purely random changes even more strongly than do commodity prices.[2]

Indeed, the main reason for this paper is to call to the attention of financial analysts empirical results that seem to have been ignored in the past, for whatever reason, and to point out some methodological implications of these results for the study of securities.

From the point of view of the scholar, much more research is needed to establish more precisely the limits to which these generalizations can be carried. For example, do they apply to changes for periods other than weekly? (In my own explorations they have worked fairly well for both longer and shorter periods.) How well do they apply to individual securities? (Most work has been done on indexes.) What slight departures from the chance model are detectable? Perhaps the traditional academic suspicion about the stock market as an object of scholarly research will be

---

[1]Maurice G. Kendall, "The Analysis of Economic Time Series. I," *Journal of the Royal Statistical Society* (Ser. A), CXVI (1953), 11–25.

[2]Holbrook Working, "A Random-Difference Series for Use in the Analysis of Time Series," *Journal of the American Statistical Association*, XXIX (1934), 11.

overcome, and this work will be done.[3] This paper, however, is concerned with the methodological problems of the financial analyst who cannot afford to ignore evidence that is easily obtainable from the most casual

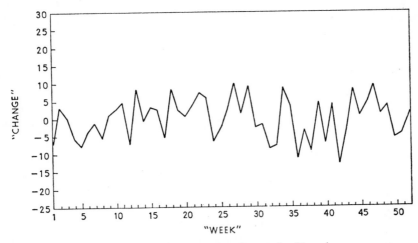

FIGURE 1   Simulated market changes for 52 weeks

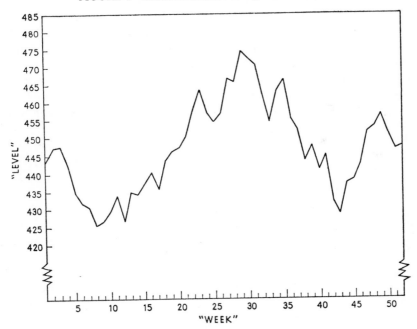

FIGURE 2   Simulated market levels for 52 weeks

[3]Holbrook Working has worked for many years on the behavior of commodities markets' and full publication of his findings is still forthcoming.

empirical analysis. From his point of view there should be great interest in the possibility that, to a first approximation, stock-market behavior may be statistically the simplest, by far, of all economic time series.

This paper will describe the chance model more precisely, discuss briefly the common-sense interpretation of the model, and outline a number of methodological suggestions for financial analysts.

THE CHANCE MODEL

Kendall found that changes in security prices behaved nearly as if they had been generated by a suitably designed roulette wheel for which each outcome was statistically independent of past history and for which relative frequencies were reasonably stable through time. This means that, once a person accumulates enough evidence to make good estimates of the relative frequencies (probabilities) of different outcomes of the wheel, he would base his predictions only on these relative frequencies and pay no attention to the pattern of recent spins. Recent spins are relevant to prediction only insofar as they contribute to more precise estimates of relative frequencies. In a gambling expression, this roulette wheel "has no memory."

The chance model just described insists on independence but makes no commitment about the relative frequencies, or probabilities, of different outcomes except that these must be stable over time. A frequency distribution of past changes is a good basis for estimating these probabilities, so long as the independence assumption holds. For concreteness in demonstration, we shall assume that weekly changes of a particular index behave as if they were independent observations on a normal distribution, with mean +0.5 and standard deviation 5.0. The details of constructing such a roulette wheel need not concern us here. We shall, in fact, employ for our purpose a published table of random numbers that can be modified easily to conform to the specifications stated above.[4] Assuming that the series starts at 450, we obtain a hypothetical year's experience graphed in Figures 1 and 2.

To even a casual observer of the stock market, Figure 2 is hauntingly realistic, even to the "head-and-shoulders" top. Probably all the classical patterns of technical analysis can be generated artificially by a suitable roulette wheel or random-number table. Figure 1 gives much less evidence of patterns, although intensive and imaginative scrutiny would undoubtedly suggest some. The only *persistent* patterns of Figure 1 (and its continuation beyond 52 weeks) are (1) the relative frequency of different outcomes and (2) the clustering tendency for similar outcomes. The clustering phenomenon runs contrary to intuitive feelings about chance and raises temporary hopes

---

[4]The RAND Corporation, *A Million Random Digits with* 100,000 *Normal Deviates* (Glencoe, Ill.: Free Press, 1955).

about predictability. These hopes, however, can be crushed by theoretical analysis that shows clustering to give no information beyond that contained in the relative frequencies.

Figures 3 and 4 give the corresponding diagrams for the Dow Jones Industrial Index for 1956. The general resemblance between Figures 3–4 and Figures 1–2 is unmistakable, although no pains were taken to devise a "roulette" wheel that would simulate closely the actual history of 1956. The major difference in detail between Figures 1 and 3 is that Figure 3 shows greater dispersion. We probably could have imitated Figure 3 more closely by using a somewhat larger standard deviation than 5 in constructing the artificial series. It is well, however, to avoid giving the wrong impression by showing *too* striking a parallel in all details. Two artificial series constructed by precisely the same method typically differ from each other just as would two brothers or two years of market history. To put it differently, the chance model cannot duplicate history in any sense other than that in which one evening in a gambling casino duplicates another. For relatively short periods of history like 52 weeks, there can be substantial differences. In fact, however, the dispersion of Figure 3 is almost surely greater than that of Figure 1 by more than we would expect from the same chance mechanism. We subsequently obtained a better simulation by using a standard deviation of 7 rather than 5.

MEANING OF THE CHANCE MODEL

There are two common reactions to this chance model: (1) while "chance" may be important in extremely short-run stock-market movements, it is inconceivable that the longer-term movement should be a cumulation of short-term "chance" development; (2) once one reflects on the situation, it is obvious that a simple chance model must hold. We shall discuss each reaction briefly.

The first reaction stems partly from a misunderstanding of the term "chance." The chance model of the previous section was meant to illustrate the possibility of constructing a simple mechanical device that would duplicate many of the characteristic features of stock-market movements. Even if the statistical behavior of the market and the mechanical device were completely indistinguishable, it might still be possible to attain a degree of predictability better than that given by knowledge of past relative frequencies alone. To attain such predictability, however, more would be needed than the past history of market prices: e.g., economic theory and knowledge of economic facts might suggest relationships of market prices with other economic variables that might be of predictive value. It seems more likely that economic analysis could give predictive insight into stock-market behavior than that physical analysis could help with a real roulette wheel. Even completely deterministic phenomena, such as the decimal expansions of irrational numbers (e.g., *e* and *π*), appear to be "chance" phenomena to

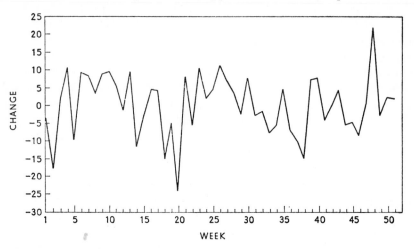

FIGURE 3   Changes from Friday to Friday (closing) January 6, 1956–December 28, 1956. Dow Jones Industrial Index.

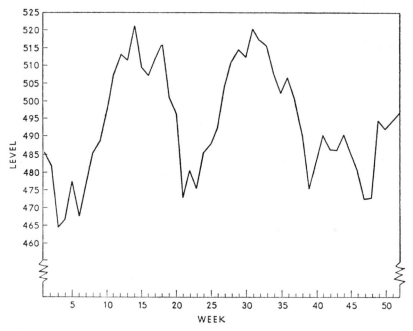

FIGURE 4   Friday closing levels, December 30, 1955–December 28, 1956. Dow Jones Industrial Index.

an observer who does not understand the underlying mechanism. Phenomena that can be described only as "chance" today, such as the emission of alpha particles in radioactive decay, may ultimately be understood in a deeper sense.

In another sense the reaction against "chance" is sound. Much more empirical work is needed, and it seems likely that departures from simple chance models will be found—if not for stock-market averages, then for individual stocks; if not for weekly periods, then for some other period; if not from the independence assumption, then from the assumption of a stable underlying distribution; etc. Indeed, the analytical proposals of this paper are based on the assumption that such departures will occasionally be found. Holbrook Working has discovered such departures in his commodity market research.[5]

As to the second reaction, that the chance model is obvious, there is a plausible rationale. "If the stock market behaved like a mechanically imperfect roulette wheel, people would notice the imperfections and by acting on them, remove them." This rationale is appealing, if for no other reason than its value as counterweight to the popular view of stock market "irrationality," but it is obviously incomplete. For example, why should not observation of market imperfection lead to greater imperfection rather than less? All we can do is to suggest the importance of the study of such questions.

SUGGESTIONS FOR FINANCIAL ANALYSIS

This section is devoted to statistical suggestions to financial analysts and others who make their living by the study of the market. The fundamental suggestion, of course, is to analyze price *changes* as well as price *levels*. Initially, the weekly change seems worth using, but other time periods may also be useful. This suggestion seems trivial, but it is not. If the simple chance hypothesis is correct, then the statistical behavior of changes, which are independent, is much simpler than that of levels, which are not. There already exists, for example, a body of statistical techniques for analysis of independent data: in fact, modern statistical theory has been largely built up on the assumption of independence. Much of it also assumes, as we did for convenience in the artificial example, that the underlying distribution is a normal distribution in the technical sense of that term. The assumption of normality usually seems far less crucial to the applicability of statistical methods than does that of independence, and some statistical techniques, called "non-parametric," do not make the normality assumption.

[5]Holbrook Working, "New Ideas and Methods for Price Research," *Journal of Farm Economics*, XXXVIII (1956), 1427–36.

If one graphs weekly changes without any formal statistical analysis, he will have taken the most important single step. So long as the stock or stock index behaves like a reasonably good roulette wheel, the visual impression will be similar to that of Figures 1 and 3. If there is a really fundamental shift in the underlying situation, it can be detected visually more readily by an analysis of changes than of levels. Conversely, if there has been no fundamental shift, a graph of changes will be much less likely to give the impression that there has been a shift.

There are formal statistical techniques to supplement visual analysis (though never to replace it entirely, since graphical study is always partial insurance against misapplication of statistical analysis). The most popular field of applied statistics—industrial quality control—draws on these techniques extensively. Though there would undoubtedly be many differences in detail, a financial analyst should find much of interest and relevance in methods of quality control.[6] We shall illustrate briefly how these ideas might be applied in financial analysis. For concreteness, we begin with the data given graphically in Figure 3.

1. The first question is that of independence: Can we regard these weekly changes as independent? Purely to illustrate one test of independence, we shall apply a test based on runs above and below zero. If we denote a positive change by "$+$" and a negative change by "$-$", Figure 3 yields the following sequence of $+$'s and $-$'s.

$- - + + - + + + + + + - + - - + + - - - - + - + + + + + +$
$- + - - - - + - - - + + - - + - - - + + - + +$

A "run" is a consecutive sequence of the same symbol: e.g., $- -$, $+ +$, $-$, and $+ + + + + +$ are the first four runs. We count 24 runs, which does not differ significantly from the expected number of 26.41.[7]

There are many tests for independence, and experience will show the most useful ones for this kind of application. I would guess that the mean-square successive difference[8] would prove useful. This has the virtue of providing a descriptive measure of the degree of independence or dependence, as well as a test that gives simply an all-or-none verdict or a significance level. A slight degree of dependence may not invalidate subsequent analysis of the kind proposed here, while substantial dependence may open the way for forecasts that exploit the observed pattern, just as one might do by careful study of a defective roulette wheel.

The idea of "rational subgroups" commonly used in industrial practice may be

---

[6]W. Allen Wallis and Harry V. Roberts, *Statistics: A New Approach* (Glencoe, Ill.: Free Press, 1956), chaps. 16, 18; A. Hald, *Statistical Theory with Engineering Applications* (New York: John Wiley & Sons, Inc., 1952), chap. 13; Eugene L. Grant, *Statistical Quality Control* (rev. ed.; New York: McGraw-Hill Book Co., Inc., 1952).

[7]For mechanical details see Wallis and Roberts, *op. cit.*

[8]*Ibid.*

[9]Grant, *op. cit.*

useful,[9] particularly in relating changes for different intervals of time, such as days and weeks.

2. If substantial dependence is found, it may be directly useful for forecasting, using the well-known methods of autoregression. Dependence may also suggest useful avenues for investigation. A sharp jump in the level of price changes for a particular stock, for example, might be found to coincide with a change in management. The company's history since that change would then be the object of an analysis like that described in the preceding paragraph.

3. If a close approximation to independence is found for any moderately large number of weeks (say at least 52, as a rule of thumb), set up "control limits" to aid visual analysis in the future. These limits can be calculated in many ways.[10] If a point falls outside the control limits, this gives a signal for the analyst to search for an explanation beyond the series itself: e.g., company developments, economic changes, governmental actions. So long as points stay within the limits, there is no need for special attention, although there may also be supplemental warning signals based on gradual shifts that cause trends but do not immediately throw points outside control limits. There will be risks of failing to search when a search is warranted and of searching when nothing is to be found. These risks can be evaluated and the control limits determined accordingly. The aim of the procedure is to economize the time of the financial analyst, who cannot possibly be simultaneously in close contact with the many individual companies that he must be familiar with. It should tend to avoid the numerous false signals that are so strongly suggested by examination of levels rather than changes.

This outline of statistical procedure is meant only to be suggestive. The general nature of the statistical attack is obvious, but the details will be supplied with practical experience guided by sound statistical theory. It may be found, for example, that it is wiser to analyze changes of logarithms or square roots of levels than absolute changes, especially when long periods of time are examined. But much is to be gained simply by viewing a familiar problem from a new vantage point, and minor statistical refinements or blemishes may not be crucial.

These statistical suggestions are only a preliminary to the real work of the financial analyst, which extends far beyond the tape itself and draws on knowledge and skills, including statistical knowledge and skills, that are not discussed here. There is every reason to believe, however, that this method of looking at the tape will facilitate all that takes place afterward. Further statistical analysis, such as multiple regression, will be sounder if based on independent changes rather than dependent levels. Judgment and intuition will proceed more soundly if not hindered by an unnecessary grappling with market "patterns."

[10]Wallis and Roberts, *op. cit.*; Hald, *op. cit.*; and Grant, *op. cit.*

Price Movements
in Speculative Markets:
Trends or Random Walks*

Sidney S. Alexander

There is a remarkable contradiction between the concepts of behavior of speculative prices held by professional stock market analysts on the one hand and by academic statisticians and economists on the other. The professional analysts operate in the belief that there exist certain trend generating facts, knowable today, that will guide a speculator to profit if only he can read them correctly. These facts are believed to generate trends rather than instantaneous jumps because most of those trading in speculative markets have imperfect knowledge of these facts, and the future trend of prices will result from a gradual spread of awareness of these facts throughout the market. Those who gain mastery of the critical information earlier than others will, accordingly, have an opportunity to profit from that early knowledge.

The two main schools of professional analysts, the "fundamentalists" and the "technicians," agree on this basic assumption. They differ only in the methods used to gain knowledge before others in the market. The fundamentalist seeks this early knowledge from study of the external factors that lie behind the price changes. In a commodity market he tries to estimate the future balance of supply and demand for that commodity. In the stock market he studies general business conditions and the profit prospects for various industries, and for the individual firms within those industries, with special attention to new developments.

The "technician" operates on the same basic assumption, that facts existing at one time will govern the prices at some future time, but he operates in a different manner. He leaves to others the study of the fundamental facts in the reliance that as those others act on their knowledge there

*From *Industrial Management Review*, **2**, no. 2, May 1961, pp. 7–26. The data gathering and processing underlying this research were supported by the Sloan Research Fund of the School of Industrial Management, Massachusetts Institute of Technology.

will be a detectable effect on the price of the stock or commodity. The technician, accordingly, studies price movements of the immediate past for telltale indications of the movements of the immediate future.

Both schools of analysts thus assume the existence of trends which represent the gradual recognition by the market of emergent factual situations—trends which, if they exist, must depend for their existence on a lagged response of the market prices to the underlying factors governing those prices. It might, at first blush, seem possible that the trends arise not from a lagged response of the market price to the fundamental circumstances, but rather from a trend in those underlying circumstances themselves. Thus, although a stock's price might at all times represent a given multiple of its earnings, its earnings might be subject to a long run trend. If, however, there are really trends in earnings, so that an increase in earnings this year implies a higher probability of an increase next year than do stable or declining earnings, the stock price right now should reflect these prospects by a higher price and by a higher ratio of price to current earnings. Consequently, if there is no lagged response there should be no trend in prices. By a trend in this connection we mean a positive serial correlation of successive changes or, more generally, a probability of future price change dependent on present price change.

The professional analysts would certainly not subscribe to the notion that the best picture of the future movements of prices can be gained by tossing a coin or a set of coins. Yet that is just what the academic students of speculative markets say is the best way. The academic students of speculative markets have come to deny the very existence of trends in speculative prices, claiming that where trends seem to be observable, they are merely interpretations, read in after the fact, of a process that really follows a random walk. A price can be said to follow a random walk if at any time the change to be expected can be represented by the result of tossing a coin, not necessarily a 50-50 coin, however. In particular, a random walk would imply that the next move of the speculative price is independent of all past moves or events.

This probabilistic view of speculative prices is consistent with the theoretical bent of economists who like to talk about perfect markets. If one were to start out with the assumption that a stock or commodity speculation is a "fair game" with equal expectation of gain or loss or, more accurately, with an expectation of zero gain, one would be well on the way to picturing the behavior of speculative prices as a random walk. But in fact, this picture of a speculative price movement is as much based on empirical findings as on theoretical predispositions. In a pioneer work Bachelier,[1] a student of the great French mathematician Poincaré, derived, in his doctoral

---

[1]M. L. Bachelier, Théorie de la Speculation, Gauthier-Villars, Paris, 1900.

thesis in 1900, a theory that speculative prices follow random walks, largely from the assumption of zero expectation of gain. He then compared the statistical distribution of price behavior expected from this theory with observed distributions of price changes of certain government securities (*rentes*) on the Paris *Bourse*, and he found a close correspondence between the observed distribution and that to be expected from his theory.

The most impressive recent findings confirming the random walk hypothesis are those of Kendall.[2] He calculated the first twenty-nine lagged serial correlations of the first differences of twenty-two time series representing speculative prices. Nineteen of these were indexes of British industrial share prices on a weekly basis. (See Table 1.) Two of the remaining three were cash wheat at Chicago, one weekly and one monthly, and the last was the spot cotton price at New York, monthly. Essentially, Kendall was asking with respect to each weekly series: How good is the best estimate we can make of next week's price change if we know this week's change and the changes of the past twenty-nine weeks and correspondingly for the monthly series?

Contrary to the general impression among traders and analysts that stock and commodity prices follow trends, Kendall found, with two or three exceptions, that knowledge of past price changes yields substantially no information about future price changes. More specifically, he found that each period's price change was not significantly correlated with the preceding period's price change nor with the price change of any earlier period, at least as far as he tested, up to twenty-nine periods. Essentially, the estimate of the next period's price change could have been drawn at random from a specified distribution with results as satisfactory as the best formula that could be fitted to past data. In the case of weekly wheat prices, that distribution was studied in detail and it turned out to be very close to a normal distribution.

There was one notable exception, however, to this pattern of random behavior of price changes. That was the monthly series on cotton prices in the United States since 1816 with, of course, a few interruptions for such events as the Civil War. For this series there did appear to be some predictability, and Kendall felt impelled to draw the moral that it is dangerous to generalize even from fairly extensive sets of data. For, from the behavior of wheat prices and the stock prices, one might have concluded that speculative markets do not generate autocorrelated price changes—and here was cotton providing a notable exception.

Alas, Kendall drew the wrong moral. The appropriate one is that if you find a single exception, look for an error. An error there was, for the cotton price series was different from the others investigated by Kendall.

[2]M. G. Kendall, "The Analysis of Economic Time Series—Part I: Prices." *Journal of the Royal Statistical Society* (*Series A*), Vol. 96 (1933), pp. 11–25.

TABLE 1. *Serial correlations of first differences of Kendall's stock price indexes, 1928–1938, for various intervals of differencing*

Kendall's No.	Industry group	First order serial correlations. Differences taken over interval of:					Second order serial correlations	
		1 Week	2 Weeks	4 Weeks	8 Weeks	16 Weeks	8 Weeks
1	Banks and discount companies	0.058	0.092	−0.067	−0.059	0.191	0.136
2	Insurance companies	.052	.048	− .056	− .169	− .035	.049
3	Investment trusts	.301	.450	.279	.020	.066	.064
4	Building materials	.125	.044	− .087	− .075	.345	.271
5	Coal	.148	.156	− .014	− .186	− .074	.032
6	Cotton	.087	.179	.036	− .227	− .075	.123
7	Electric light and power	.181	.145	− .024	− .130	.219	.232
8	Gas	.096	.235	.103	− .119	.360	.232
9	Iron and steel	.088	− .005	− .028	− .122	− .009	.057
10	Oil	− .013	.027	.015	− .015	.073	.061
11	Total industrial productive	.195	.155	− .016	− .149	.055	.110
12	Home rails	.010	− .030	− .002	− .162	.072	− .019
13	Shipping	.053	.032	− .017	.111	.388	.325
14	Stores and catering	.230	.145	− .082	− .218	.104	.199
15	Total industrial distributive	.237	.179	− .008	.033	.303	.241
16	Breweries and distilleries	.034	.102	− .046	.020	.152	.078
17	Miscellaneous	.200	.191	− .011	− .101	.267	.267
18	Total industrial miscellaneous	.177	.190	.033	− .069	.291	.252
19	Industrials (all classes combined)	.234	.207	.018	− .063	.279	.246

Almost all the others were series of observations of the price at a specified time—say, the closing price on Friday of each week. Each observation of the cotton series was an average of four or five weekly observations of the corresponding month. It turns out that even if the original data—the Friday closing prices—were a random walk, with successive first differences uncorrelated, the first differences of the monthly average of four or five of these weekly observations would exhibit first-order serial correlations of about the magnitude Kendall found for cotton.[3] So Kendall's exception vanishes, and we are left with the conclusion that at least for the series he investigated the serial correlations were not significantly different from zero.[4]

But the question immediately arises whether a week is not an inappropriate period of observation. The market analysts might protest that when they speak of a trend they are speaking of a smooth underlying movement on which is typically superimposed a lot of short-term fluctuation. With weekly observations the short-term fluctuations might very easily swamp the underlying trends. In particular, the give and take of the market leads to a phenomenon, recognized by all analysts, of reactions, usually called technical reactions, presumably associated with profit taking. These reactions are, of course, negatively correlated with the main price swings. That's what makes them reactions. Kendall's correlations, close to zero, could possibly be a consequence of the combination of the negative contributions of the reactions and the positive contributions of the trends.

The path of a speculative price might, accordingly, be represented by a sum of two components, a smooth underlying trend or cycle changing direction only infrequently, and a much shorter cycle of action and reaction. Under this hypothesis the first-order serial correlations of daily price changes might be negative, the first order correlation of weekly changes might be close to zero, while the first order serial correlations of monthly or bimonthly changes might be significantly larger than zero.

We can test this possibility by studying the first order serial correlations of Kendall's data using successively longer intervals of differencing. As we do so, and consider first the first order serial correlation of one week changes, then of two week, four week, eight week, and sixteen week changes, the influence of the reactions should become smaller and smaller and the trend effect, if there is one, should become dominant. The corresponding correlations, roughly calculated,[5] are given in Table 1.

[3]This point was independently discovered by the author and by Holbrook Working. The latter, however, had the pleasure of first publishing it in "Note on the Correlation of First Differences of Averages in a Random Chain," *Econometrica*, Vol. 28, No. 4, October 1960, pp. 916–918.

[4]Another possible exception may be noted for Kendall's Series 3, Investment Trusts, whose first five serial correlations were 0.301, 0.356, 0.158, 0.164 and 0.066. This series will be mentioned again below.

[5]Roughly, because they were computed, not from the original data, but from the serial correlations published by Kendall. Since successive serial correlations are based on fewer observations because of the necessity of sacrificing end terms, a certain "end term error" is introduced by this procedure.

While an occasional high value correlation occurs in Table 1 for intervals greater than one week, it must be remembered that for the given total time period under study, the number of observations drops in proportion to the length of the differencing interval. Since the variance of the correlation coefficient is inversely proportional to the number of observations, it is directly proportional to the length of the differencing interval. An occasional high computed value of the correlation becomes increasingly probable as the differencing period is lengthened, even if the true correlation is zero.

It must be concluded that the data of Table 1 do *not* give any substantial support to the hypothesis that, as differences are taken over longer and longer intervals, the first order serial correlations of the first difference generally increase.

Once again, Series 3, investment trusts, is an exception. It seems to have a particularly high level of serial correlation on a two-week period of differencing. Other occasional higher values among the various series, for changes at sixteen week intervals in particular, have to be seriously discounted although they suggest intriguing possibilities for further study.

These higher correlations for sixteen week changes (for Series 4, 8, 13, 15, and possibly 17, 18, and 19) proceed from a rather curious relationship that holds for 18 of the 19 series. The first order correlations on an eight-week basis tend to be algebraically smaller than the second order correlations (see Table 1). The implication of the existence of an eight week half cycle may be an interesting suggestion, although it could hardly be said to be established by the data.

One further attempt was made, in spite of Kendall's findings that the serial correlations were not significantly different from zero, to see if some nugget of systematic trend behavior might still be found in his data. It is possible that while the lagged autocorrelations of any series were not found to be significantly different from zero when taken one at a time, they might jointly form a pattern that is significant. A simple test of this possibility was attempted. A trend was fitted to the first differences of each stock price series by a Spencer 21-term moving average.[6] Then the ratio of the variance of the moving average to the variance of the first differences themselves was computed.

The variance ratios given in Table 2 are to be interpreted as follows. If each first difference lay exactly on the moving average trend line, that is, if the trend line were a perfect fit, the variance ratio would be unity. If on the other hand, all the serial correlations of order greater than zero were identically zero, the expected values for a random walk, the variance ratio

---

[6]See E. T. Whitaker and G. Robinson, *The Calculus of Observations* (4th ed.), London 1944, p. 290, for the formula used. Actually, it was not necessary to fit the trends to the series themselves, but the variance of the moving average, expressed in units of the variance of the first differences, could be computed by applying the smoothing coefficients of the Spencer formula directly to the lagged serial correlations.

TABLE 2. *Ratios of the variance of smoothed first differences to the variance of unsmoothed first differences. Kendall's stock price indexes**

Series	Industry group	Ratios
1	Banks and discount companies	0.161
2	Insurance companies	.158
3	Investment trusts	.525
4	Building materials	.162
5	Coal	.202
6	Cotton	.210
7	Electric light and power	.206
8	Gas	.230
9	Iron and steel	.158
10	Oil	.145
11	Total industrial productive	.212
12	Home rails	.138
13	Shipping	.151
14	Stores and catering	.212
15	Total industrial distributive	.219
16	Breweries and distilleries	.171
17	Miscellaneous	.221
18	Total industrial miscellaneous	.218
19	Industrials (all classes combined)	.232

*Smoothing performed by 21 term Spencer Moving Average.

would be 0.143, the sum of the squares of the coefficients in the smoothing formula. It is, of course, possible for the ratio to be even less than 0.143.

Except for Series 3, the trend variance is not a much larger proportion of the original variance of the first differences than would be expected in the case of a random walk. It must be concluded that, with this exception, if trends exist in the first differences, they are very weak.

All in all, Kendall's data do seem to confirm the random walk hypothesis. Further work by Osborne[7] strengthens the random walk hypothesis from a different point of view. While Kendall worked with serial correlations for each series separately, Osborne worked with ensembles of price changes. Roughly stated, he found that the changes in the logarithms of stock prices over any period in a given market, principally the New York Stock Exchange, constituted an ensemble which appeared to be approximately normally distributed with a standard deviation proportional to the square root of the length of the period. This proportionality of the standard deviation of price differences to the square root of the differencing period is

[7]M. F. M. Osborne, "Brownian Motion in the Stock Market," *Operations Research*, Vol. 7, No. 2, March–April 1959, pp. 145–173. See also comment and reply in *Operations Research*, Vol. 7, No. 6, November–December 1959, pp. 806–811.

a characteristic of a random walk and had been pointed out much earlier by Bachelier. In Bachelier's case, however, the differences were arithmetic, while in Osborne's they were logarithmic.

It must be noted that Osborne's measurements do not concern trends in the prices of stocks but merely the statistical distribution of the changes in the logarithms, which, as Osborne pointed out, correspond quite closely to percentage changes. That they do not correspond exactly to percentage changes has an important bearing on one of Osborne's principal findings, as we shall see.

Osborne also supplied a theoretical mechanism that *could* explain the observed pattern of price movements. The mechanism is a random walk in the logarithm of prices with each step being a constant logarithmic value, depending on the time length of the step. The basic step is a transaction of which there might be ten or a hundred a day. The compounding of such steps in familiar probability sequences would, over any period of time, yield a normal distribution of changes in the logarithms of price, with standard deviation proportional to the square root of the period over which comparison is made.

One peculiar result of Osborne's proposed mechanism merits further study. Bachelier, the pioneer in regarding speculative price behavior as a random walk, derived the theoretical properties of the distribution of changes in the prices of *rentes* on the assumption of a "fair game," that is a zero expectation of gain. A price change in either direction of a given amount was equally probable in Bachelier's model. Osborne made a somewhat different assumption with a radically different result; he assumed that a change in either direction of a given amount in the logarithm of price was equally likely, no longer a fair game.

Thus, under Bachelier's assumption, given an initial investment value, say $100, it would be equally probable, at the end of time T to be worth $100 + k or $100 − k. Exactly how large k would be for any stated probability would depend on the fundamental constant of the distribution and the square root of the length of time T. But whatever the value of k, so long as the probability of a gain of k is equal to the probability of a loss of k for all k within the permitted range, the expected value in any future period remains $100 and the expected gain 0.

Under Osborne's assumption, however, there will be an expectation of gain. Suppose, using logarithms to base 10 and starting from $100, a gain over some particular period of time, say five years, is equally likely to be a gain of logarithm 1 or loss of logarithm − 1. These would correspond to an equal probability that the price at the end of five years would be either $10 or $1,000. The mathematical expectation in this case would be $505, or an expected gain of $405. This example illustrates the familiar difference between the arithmetic and the geometric mean. Over the long run, then, it makes a great deal of difference whether there is an expectation of zero arithmetic gain or zero logarithmic gain. In the latter case there will be a tendency for an investment value to grow, independent of any growth in the economy other than the growth implicit in the existence of a random walk in the logarithms.

How clearly established an empirical finding is the logarithmic rather than the arithmetic step in the random walk? Osborne was led to the logarithmic form, while Bachelier was not, because Bachelier considered only a single type of security at a time, whereas Osborne considered an ensemble of prices, usually all the common stock prices on a particular exchange. Osborne assumed, without much explicit consideration, that it was appropriate to try to fit one distribution of expected change to all common stocks, whether priced at $100 or $10 or whatever. Very little empirical investigation is required to show that the relative frequency of price rises of $10 in one month is much smaller among stocks selling at $10 than among stocks selling at $100. On the other hand, it is quite reasonable to expect that the relative frequency of a $1 price rise in a month among $10 stocks would be about equal to the relative frequency of a $10 price rise in a month among $100 stocks. And rough empirical tests seem to be in accord with the latter case.

If then we have to choose a single distribution that will fit stocks of all different prices, and if our only choice were between equal probabilities of dollar amount changes and equal probabilities of proportional changes, we are necessarily led to choose the latter. The assumption of equal probabilities of given changes in the logarithm of price falls in the latter class.

But there are other possible models which yield equal probabilities of changes of given proportions. One is of particular interest to us in that it certainly fits the data as well as the logarithmic model and does not imply a built-in growth of values as does the logarithmic. It postulates equal probability of given percentage changes, almost the same as equal probability of given logarithmic changes, but not quite. On the tiny difference hinges the existence or nonexistence of the remarkable property of speculation being a game biased in favor of winning.

In both the logarithmic form and the percentage form of the hypothesis it is equally probable that a $100 stock rises by $10 in a month or that a $10 stock rises by $1. Under both schemes it is equally probable that a $100 stock declines by $10 in a month or a $10 stock by $1. But under the percentage form it is equally probable that a $100 stock goes to $101 or to $99 in a given time, whereas in the logarithmic form it is equally probable that a $100 stock goes to $101 or $99.01 in a given time. This difference of one cent in a dollar change from $100 spells the difference between zero expectation of gain and positive expectation.

If, then, the percentage hypothesis is adopted instead of the logarithmic hypothesis, the expectation of gain disappears. The difference between the distributions generated by the two hypotheses would, over most time periods of practical interest, be so fine that any test delicate enough to distinguish between them is likely to throw them both out.

In fact, both hypotheses would generate normal distributions of the changes in the logarithms of prices, differing only in their means and standard deviations. In testing various models of this sort we generally infer the mean and the standard deviation from the data and assume that the mean was influenced by general economic conditions separate from the random walk. Under these circumstances we can say whether the observed distribution is or is not close to normal, but we cannot say whether it is closer to the percentage hypothesis or to the logarithmic. To discriminate between these hypotheses we would need an independent measure of the random step, or of the standard deviation. Bachelier actually derived such an independent measure from the price of options, but Osborne merely showed that the distribution resembled a normal distribution and the standard deviation increased with the square root of the differencing period. To whatever extent his findings support the logarithmic hypothesis, they also support the percentage hypothesis.

But Osborne did not rigorously test the normality of the distribution. A rigorous test, for example the application of the chi-square test to some of the data used by Osborne, would lead us strongly to dismiss the hypothesis of normality. (See Table 3.) It yields a chi-square of over 60 for 8 degrees

TABLE 3. *Changes in prices of listed common stocks (NYSE) observed compared with expected**

	No. of issues	
Percentage price change	Observed†	Expected‡
+10% and over	54	21
+ 8% to +10%	30	30
+ 6% to + 8%	50	54
+ 4% to + 6%	71	87
+ 2% to + 4%	119	127
− 2% to + 2%	346	328
− 4% to − 2%	149	157
− 6% to − 4%	100	121
− 8% to − 6%	74	79
−10% to − 8%	31	43
−10% or over	51	28
Total	1075	1075

*Month ending November 15, 1956.
†SOURCE: *The Exchange* (NYSE), Dec. 1956, back cover.
‡On the assumption of normal distribution with mean equal to the median of the observed distribution, with standard deviation equal to the semi-interquartile range divided by 0.6745, and with total frequency equal to observed total frequency.

of freedom, although almost all of the discrepancy between actual and expected frequencies arises from the extreme classes of increases or decreases greater than 10 per cent.[8] It may be presumed that special factors operated to produce far more large price changes than are characteristic of a normal distribution. This sort of situation (leptokurtosis) is frequently encountered in economic statistics and would certainly overshadow any attempt to test fine points such as the difference between a logarithmic and a percentage scheme.

In any case the requirement that equal proportional gains for stocks of different prices should have equal probability does not imply a nonzero expectation. The nonzero expectation follows specifically from the assumption of unequal steps, measured in dollars, in the random walk, as between steps up and steps down. For small steps, equal logarithmic changes imply *almost* equal percentage changes, but the very small difference eventually grows to a very large one, another demonstration of the wonderful power of compound interest.

But more to the point than the difference between logarithmic and percentage schemes is the question: How far do Osborne's findings go to show that stock market prices really follow a random walk? Osborne, at best, merely showed that stock price changes might, to a rough approximation, have been generated by a random walk type of model. He suggests conditions that are sufficient to generate the observations, but not necessary. In plain language, he has a scheme which could have generated his observations; maybe it did and maybe it didn't.

It does seem that the principal clash between the analyst and the academic concerns not the nature of the statistical ensemble of price changes but rather the question of the existence of trends. For, if the implication of Kendall's findings are indeed general, it would make as much sense to try to predict the outcome of a coin toss as to predict movements of the stock market. The prime issue is, therefore, whether there is some way in which speculative price behavior is not random.

In order to attack this problem, the author ran off a set of simple tests of randomness of successive monthly or weekly changes of speculative prices. The technique may be illustrated by a weekly series on wheat (Wednesday closing prices of cash wheat over the period 1883–1934, excluding 1915–1920, a total of 2,379 weeks). Each week was classified as being a week of price rise or price fall, and the lengths of the runs were tallied. A run is defined as a sequence of successive weeks in which the price moves in the same direction. Table 4 shows the resulting table of runs and compares it with the distribution to be expected on the assumption of a random walk with equal probability of rise or fall. The correspondence is

[8]It should be noted that Osborne remarked that the tails of the observed distribution did not appear to correspond to those of the normal distribution.

TABLE 4. *Distribution of lengths of run of weekly cash wheat prices at Chicago**

Length of Run (Weeks)	Observed		Expected† Up or Down
	Up	Down	
1	280	295	297
2	147	132	149
3	86	77	74
4	38	42	37
5	15	18	19
6	13	12	9
7 or longer	7	8	9
Total	586	584	595‡

*1883–1934, Excluding 1915–1920. Source: Holbrook Working, "Prices of Cash Wheat and Futures at Chicago Since 1883," *Wheat Studies*, Vol. II, No. 3, November 1934, pp. 75–124. See also Kendall, op. cit., Table 1 for frequency distribution for these prices, of differences between week t and t + 1 against differences between weeks t + 1 and t + 2.
†Expected on assumption of 0.5 probability of rise or fall, and 2,379 monthly observations.
‡Expected total differs from sum because of rounding.

very close indeed, suggesting that at least the sequence of directions of changes in weekly wheat prices might have been produced by a random walk. Kendall[9] previously showed that, except for a few extreme items, the distribution of the size of these weekly wheat price changes is normal and independent of the movement of the preceding week.

The distribution of the runs of Standard and Poor's monthly composite index of stock prices,[10] 1918–56, is, however, inconsistent with the assumption of a random walk of equal probability of rise or fall. (Expectation 1 for 1918–56 in Table 5.) We may note, however, that for this stock average for the period 1918–56:

(a) The relative frequencies of rising and declining months were 0.58 and 0.42, respectively;
(b) The relative frequency of rising months among all months for which the preceding month was rising, $p\,(+\mid +)$, was 0.67, and the relative frequency of declining months for which the preceding month was declining, $p\,(-\mid -)$, was 0.50.

A new set of expected runs based on these contingent relative frequencies for 1918–56 did fit the observed runs quite well. (Expectation 2 for 1918–56 in Table 5.) Furthermore, expectations based on these relative frequencies derived from the 1918–56 data fit the 1871–1917 data for upruns quite closely, but downruns only fairly well. (Expectation 2 for 1871–1917

[9]Op. cit.
[10]The index is a monthly average of weekly observations.

TABLE 5. *Lengths of run of Standard & Poor's monthly composite stock price index,* observed (Obs) vs. expected (Ex)

	JANUARY 1918 TO MARCH 1956								JANUARY 1871 TO DECEMBER 1917					
	Up				Down				Up			Down		
Length of run (months)	Obs	Ex 1†	Ex 2‡	Ex 3§	Obs	Ex 1†	Ex 2‡	Ex 3§	Obs	Ex 2‡	Ex 3§	Obs	Ex 2‡	Ex 3§
							(number of runs)							
1	31	58	30	37	39	58	45	37	41	37	45	40	56	45
2	21	29	20	22	27	29	23	22	29	25	27	30	28	27
3	16	15	13	13	15	15	11	13	15	17	16	17	14	16
4	10	7	9	8	9	7	6	8	11	11	10	9	7	10
5	5	4	6	5	1	4	3	5	4	7	6	4	4	6
6 or longer	9	4	12	8	1	4	3	8	9	15	8	10	4	8
Total	92	117	90	93	92	117	90¶	93	109	112	112	110	112¶	112

*Monthly averages of weekly indexes. SOURCE: 1918–1956. Standard & Poor's *Trade & Securities Statistics* (Security Price Index Record). Number of Monthly observations: 467 for 1918–56, and 559 for 1871–1917.

†Based on probability of 0.5 for rise or fall, successive months independent, derived from *a priori* hypothesis.

‡Based on $p(+|+) = 0.67$ and $p(-|-) = 0.50$, derived from 1918–56 relative frequencies.

§Based on $p(+|+) = p(-|-) = 0.6$, derived from 1871–1917 relative frequencies.

¶Expected total, differs from sum because of rounding.

in Table 5.) Actually, the simpler hypothesis (Expectation 3) that the probability of continuation of a run is 0.6 and of termination 0.4 fits the 1871–1917 data very well and also the 1918–56 upruns. It does imply a much higher frequency of long downruns than was observed in 1918–56, however.

Unfortunately, this evidence of the probability of one month's movement depending on the previous month's is entirely the result of using an average of weekly prices for each month's observation. Distributions of runs of industrial stock prices for 1897–1929 and 1929–59 are given in Table 6, based on a single-point observation for each month, the last trading day of the month. These distributions are very close to those to be expected on the assumption of each month's change being independent of the previous month's, with a 0.57 probability of a monthly rise and 0.43 of a decline. (Expectation 4, Table 6.) The same probabilities seem to fit both periods equally well, and the hypothesis of trends seems to be blown sky high.

One notable exception to the rule that statisticians have not found trends in stock market prices is furnished by the work of Cowles and Jones.[11] They found an excess of sequences over reversals in stock market prices, but

TABLE 6. *Distribution of lengths of run of monthly Industrial Stock Prices,* * *Observed (Obs) vs. Expected (Ex)*

Length of run (months)	JAN. 1897–JAN. 1929				FEB. 1929–DEC. 1959			
	Up		Down		Up		Down	
	Obs	Ex 4†	Obs	Ex 4†	Obs	Ex 4†	Obs	Ex 4†
					(number of runs)			
1	42	40	58	53	38	38	49	50
2	24	23	18	23	22	22	19	22
3	16	13	14	10	9	12	10	9
4	6	7	4	4	7	7	4	4
5	1	4	1	2	3	4	2	2
6 or longer	7	6	1	1	8	6	2	1
Total	96	93	96	93	87	88‡	86	88

*End of month closing prices. Dow Jones Industrials, Jan. 1897 to Jan. 1929 with break from July 1914 to Jan. 1915 (379 months). SOURCE: *The Dow Jones Averages*, Barron's, New York 1931; Standard & Poor's Industrials, Feb. 1929–Dec. 1959 (362 months). SOURCE: see fn. (*), Table 5.
†Based on assumption of independence of successive monthly changes, and on the probability of 0.57 of a rise, and 0.43 of a fall, derived from entire period 1897–1959.
‡Expected total differs from sum because of rounding.

[11]Alfred Cowles and Herbert E. Jones, "Some a Posteriori Probabilities in Stock Market Action," *Econometrica*, Vol. 5, No. 280, July 1937, pp. 280–294.

they used, at least for monthly data, averages of weekly observations. Their findings presumably derive principally from this error, plus a second effect, the influence of more frequent movements up than down.

The first effect is illustrated by the data in Table 5, based on monthly averages of weekly observations. For these data there is a ratio of 1.56 of sequences to reversals for 1871–1917, and 1.54 for 1918–56. The ratio of sequences to reversals shrinks to 1.045 for the 1897–1959 end of month data of Table 6. The second effect can largely be explained on the basis of a 0.57 relative frequency of monthly rises and 0.43 of monthly falls for 1897–1959. For if each monthly movement were drawn independently at random with these probabilities of rise and fall, we should expect a ratio of sequences to alternations of 1.040, almost identical to that observed.

In a revision of his findings designed to eliminate the first effect, Cowles still found some evidence, though weaker, of the existence of an excess of sequences over reversals, a ratio of 1.07 for monthly one point observations as compared with an earlier figure of 1.33 for the monthly averages of weekly observations.[12] But he did not make any allowance for the effect of a higher relative frequency of rises than declines. If the relative frequency of monthly rises were between 0.59 and 0.60 in the period covered by Cowles' data, as is likely, the ratio of 1.07 would be expected even if monthly movements were independent.

It must be concluded that the month to month movement of stock prices, at least in direction, is consistent with the hypothesis of a random walk with about a 6 to 4 probability of a rise. Evidence to the contrary was spurious, arising from the correlations introduced by monthly averaging or neglect of the unequal probability of rise and fall.

Lest the reader take undue comfort from the bullish implication of the 6 to 4 probability of a rise, it must be noted that declines, though less frequent than rises, are sharper, so that the average decline is substantially larger than the average rise. Nevertheless, there has been a well recognized upward trend of stock market prices of the order of 5.6% a year over the period 1897–1959. (Table 7.)

One final test may be reported that should give great comfort to the analyst and encouragement to those who would use statistical studies to guide their speculative efforts, for it furnishes evidence that stock price changes could not have been generated by a random walk. Suppose we tentatively assume the existence of trends in stock market prices but believe them to be masked by the jiggling of the market. We might filter out all movements smaller than a specified size and examine the remaining movements. The most vivid way to illustrate the operation of the filter is to

---

[12]Alfred Cowles, "A Revision of Previous Conclusions Regarding Stock Price Behavior," *Econometrica*, Vol. 28, No. 4, October 1960, pp. 909–915. The data cover about 1,000 months over the periods 1834–1865, 1897–1922, 1928–1958.

translate it into a rule of speculative market action. Thus, corresponding to a 5% filter we might have the rule: if the market moves up 5% go long and stay long until it moves down 5% at which time sell and go short until it again moves up 5%. Ignore moves of less than 5%. The more stringent the filter, the fewer losses are made, but also the smaller the gain from any move that exceeds the filter size. Thus with a 5% filter there will be a loss on any move between 5% and 10.53% and a gain on any move larger than 10.53%. For if the move is just a 10.53% move, say from 100 to 110.53, then we would go long at 105 (100 plus 5%) and sell at 105 (110.53 minus 5%) and so just break even. With a 10% filter most of the moves which entailed a loss with the 5% filter would be filtered out. But a 20% move, which would yield a 9% profit with a 5% filter (computed on the lower vertex of the move, actually about 8.6% of the purchase price), would yield a 2% loss on a 10% filter.

Thus, as the filter size is increased, the number of transactions is reduced, and losses on small moves are eliminated, gains on large moves are reduced, and some moves which would yield gains with a small filter will yield losses with a large. This example illustrates the familiar tradeoff between reliability of the information and the cost of the information. The more stringent the filter, the higher the reliability, but the more of the move that is sacrificed in identifying it both in getting in and in getting out.

The results of the application of various filters to the Dow Jones and Standard & Poor's industrial averages from 1897 through 1959 are shown in Table 7. If stock price movements were generated by a trendless random walk, these filters could be expected to yield zero profits, or to vary from zero profits, both positively and negatively, in a random manner. Given an underlying long term trend, they might be expected to produce some profits, the greater profits being associated with the greater filter, but in any case, profits smaller than could be expected from just buying and holding.

In fact, medium filters uniformly yield profits, and the smallest filters yield the highest profits, and very high they are.

The retrospective gains from the filter rule (before commission) are compared in Table 7 with the gains that could be achieved over the corresponding period by just buying and holding. The results uniformly favor the smaller filters over the buy and hold method. Thus, the filter method derives its success from a characteristic of stock price behavior other than that implied by the upward long term trend alone. This conclusion is also confirmed by the fact, apparent from inspection of the work sheets, that the filter method made gains on the declines as well as on the rises.

From a practical standpoint these profits would be substantially reduced, but by no means eliminated, by the payment of commissions. I leave to the interested reader the computation of allowance for commissions.

It must be concluded that there *are* trends in stock market prices, once

TABLE 7. *Profits from filters of various sizes compared with buy and hold,* * 1897–1959†

| Period | Filter size‡ (percentages) | | | | | | | | | | | Buy & hold |
	5	6	8	10	12.5	15	20	25	30	40	50	
							Average move (%)§					
1897–1914	13.8	15.8	19.8	22.8	30.7	39.6	62.6	62.6	82.5	80.2	97.0	75.3
1914–1929	12.8	14.9	19.7	25.4	33.3	43.0	69.4	115.8	115.8	115.8	115.8	596.6
1929–1959	14.5	16.4	22.3	26.3	31.6	36.1	52.9	72.3	188.9	199.0	291.0	154.1
						Average profit per transaction (%)¶ (before commissions)							
1897–1914	2.9	3.0	2.7	1.5	3.2	5.4	12.2	4.0	7.7	(9.2)††	(15.5)	
1914–1929	2.0	2.2	2.6	3.6	5.2	7.8	16.3	32.5	24.7	9.6	(5.7)	
1929–1959	3.5	3.6	4.8	4.3	3.9	2.9	6.0	9.8	11.2	43.2	57.3	
						Number of transactions#							
1897–1914	117	95	67	53	32	22	12	12	8	7	7	1
1914–1929	112	93	59	40	28	19	10	6	6	6	6	1
1929–1959	274	228	144	113	86	70	40	26	20	8	6	1

*Based on Dow Jones Industrials, 1897–1929 and Standard & Poor's Industrials, 1929–1959. See fn. (*), Table 5, and fn. (*), Table 6 for source references.

†Periods: January 2, 1897 to July 30, 1914
December 12, 1914 to September 3, 1929
September 7, 1929 to December 31, 1959.

‡5% filter here designates 5% in either direction, others designate indicated percentages upward and equal *logarithmic* moves downward. E.g., 10% filter implies 10% upward or 9.09% downward.

§Calculated as follows: for each move, as defined by a specified filter, let the variable, M_i denote the difference between the logarithms of the upper and lower endpoints of the move. The figure given as the average move is 100 (antilog $\overline{M} - 1$) where $\overline{M}$ is the arithmetic mean of the M's.

¶Let $\overline{R}$ be the average logarithmic profit defined as $R = \overline{M} - 2F$. $\overline{M}$ is defined in fn. (§) and F is log $(1 + f)$ where f is the filter expressed as a ratio, e.g., f is 0.10 for a 10% filter. The quantity 2F corresponds to the portion of the move that is used up in getting in or out. On an upmove of average size $\overline{M}$ the percentage profit would be $P_u = 100(\text{antilog}(\overline{R} - 1)$; on a downmove, $P_d = 100 P_u /(100 + P_u)$.
The average profit entered in Table 7 is $\overline{P} = (100 + P_u)^{\frac{1}{2}}(100 + P_d)^{\frac{1}{2}} - 100$.

#A transaction is defined as a purchase and sale, so that each transaction would require two commissions. In each period there is one terminal transaction, such as for Dec. 31, 1959, terminated not by a filter signal but by the period limits. The corresponding terminal move was counted as half a move in the computation of $\overline{M}$, and of the number of transactions per year.

TABLE 7. Profits from filters of various sizes compared with buy and hold,* 1897–1959† (Continued)

Period	Filter size‡ (percentages)											Buy & hold
	5	6	8	10	12.5	15	20	25	30	40	50	
	Average transactions per year											
1897–1914	6.5	5.4	3.8	3.0	1.8	1.2	0.7	0.7	0.4	0.4	0.3	
1914–1929	6.6	6.3	4.0	2.7	1.9	1.3	0.7	0.4	0.4	0.4	0.4	
1929–1959	9.0	7.5	4.7	3.7	2.8	2.3	1.3	0.8	0.6	0.3	0.2	
	Average profit per year (%)** (before commissions)											
1897–1914	20.5	17.4	10.5	4.6	5.8	6.6	7.8	2.6	3.2	(3.3)	(3.9)	3.2
1914–1929	15.8	14.7	10.7	10.0	9.9	9.9	10.3	11.1	8.6	3.4	(2.1)	14.1
1929–1959	36.8	30.0	24.5	16.8	11.4	6.9	7.8	8.2	7.0	9.3	8.5	3.0

*Based on Dow Jones Industrials, 1897–1929 and Standard & Poor's Industrials, 1929–1959. See fn. (*), Table 5, and fn. (*), Table 6 for source references.

†Periods: January 2, 1897 to July 30, 1914
            December 12, 1914 to September 3, 1929
            September 7, 1929 to December 31, 1959.

‡5% filter here designates 5% in either direction, others designate indicated percentages upward and equal *logarithmic* moves downward. E.g., 10% filter implies 10% upward or 9.09% downward.

§Calculated as follows: for each move, as defined by a specified filter, let the variable, $\underline{M}$, denote the difference between the logarithms of the upper and lower endpoints of the move. The figure given as the average move is 100 (antilog $\overline{M}$ − 1) where $\overline{M}$ is the arithmetic mean of the M's.

¶Let $\overline{R}$ be the average logarithmic profit defined as $\overline{R} = \overline{M} - 2F$. $\overline{M}$ is defined in fn. (§) and F is log (1 + f) where f is the filter expressed as a ratio, e.g., f is 0.10 for a 10% filter. The quantity 2F corresponds to the portion of the move that is used up in getting in or out. On an upmove of average size $\overline{M}$ the percentage profit would be $P_u = 100(\text{antilog } \overline{R} - 1)$; on a downmove, $P_d = 100P_u/(100 + P_u)$.

The average profit centered in Table 7 is $\overline{P} = (100 + P_u)\frac{1}{2}(100 + P_d)\frac{1}{2} - 100$.

#A transaction is defined as a purchase and sale, so that each transaction would require two commissions. In each period there is one terminal transaction, such as for Dec. 31, 1959, terminated not by a filter signal but by the period limits. The corresponding terminal move was counted as half a move in the computation of $\overline{M}$, and of the number of transactions per year.

**Computed as $100[1 + (\overline{P}/100)]^{\overline{q}} - 100$, where $\overline{q}$ is the average number of transactions per year, and $\overline{P}$ is defined in fn. (¶).

††Numbers in parentheses signify losses.

the "move" is taken as the unit under study rather than the week or the month. That is, the nonrandom nature of stock price movements revealed by Table 7 proceeds not only from filtering out small moves, but also from transforming the measure over which changes are considered. The many statistical studies which have found speculative prices to resemble a random walk have dealt with changes over uniform periods of time. The filter operation, however, deals with changes of given magnitude irrespective of the length of time involved. In short, it substitutes the dimension of the "move" for the dimension of time.

The findings surveyed in this paper can be summarized by the statement that in speculative markets price changes appear to follow a random walk over *time*, but a move, once initiated, tends to persist. In particular, if the stock market has moved up x per cent it is likely to move up more than x per cent further before it moves down by x per cent. This proposition seems to be valid for x ranging from 5 per cent through 30 per cent. It will require further study to find out if it is valid for x smaller than 5%.

The riddle has been resolved. The statisticians' findings of a random walk over the time dimension is quite consistent with nonrandom trends in the move dimension. Such a trend does exist.

I leave to the speculation of others the question of what would happen to the effectiveness of the filter technique if everybody believed in it and operated accordingly.

5·9

Forecasting Interest Rates*

Roland I. Robinson

The forecaster of interest rates is one of the minor economic prophets. He lives in the shadow of the major prophets of production, income, and employment. For a while he was a victim of economic obsolescence: interest rates became the vassal of central banking and treasury policy. The interest-rate forecaster was reduced to being a mind reader of the policy-forming officials. This cloud has lifted, but his role is still circumscribed by the larger areas of general economic developments, public policy, and international politics.

In narrowly technical terms, interest-rate forecasting is a subcategory of

*From the *Journal of Business*, **27**, no. 1, January 1954, pp. 87–100. Reprinted by permission of The University of Chicago Press.

price forecasting. It uses the paraphernalia of supply-and-demand analysis; it leans on analysis of the market process and market characteristics. But it differs from other kinds of price forecasting, indeed from all other varieties of forecasting, in that the nature of the object being priced has been obscured by a variety of conflicting theoretical formulations. Interest has been most commonly and simply defined as the price for borrowed money. Economic analysis shows that the institution of borrowing and lending through the means of money is in reality a process of transferring the command of real economic wealth from those who own it to those who can use it more profitably or pleasurably. Had money been nothing but a passive and neutral agent in this process of transfer, interest as a price would be relatively simple conceptually. Money, however, has been neither passive nor neutral. The system of money generation (and extinction) and the habits of liquidity and money-holding have intervened to give interest rates an added dimension of complexity. When it is hard to determine what economic factors cause interest rates to be what they are, it is doubly difficult to frame a logical system for estimating what they will be in the future.

The obstacles to systematic forecasting of interest rates are such that no well-developed and recognized methodology prevails.[1] The interest-rate theory underlying most forecasting is intuitive, the methods sketchy, and the product often subjective. Furthermore, the published and identifiable forecasts of interest-rate changes reveal a sobering proportion of errors and misjudgments.[2]

But interest-rate forecasting, implicit or explicit, is almost unavoidable in the formation of both public and private policy. Some financial institutions are inclined to deny that forecasting plays a part in their portfolio operations. But this is often a kind of fiction; they usually follow policies so "conservative" that they clearly imply the expectation of great economic and interest-rate instability—itself a kind of forecast.

Interest rates appear explicitly on almost every direct lending transaction; they are mathematically derivable from the prices at which bonds, notes, or mortgages are sold. They are found in the small loans made to consumers, they are implicit in "time" prices of articles sold for deferred

---

[1]The literature on methodology for interest-rate forecasting is thin. I have been able to discover only one reasonably coherent discussion of the subject: Wilson Wright's *Forecasting for Profit* (New York: John Wiley & Sons, 1947), pp. 124–26. Most of Wright's discussion is limited to some observations about the control of interest rates by public policy and the obstacles that this presents to logical forecasting.

[2]This is not meant to reproach other interest-rate forecasters: the author has been guilty of his share of embarrassing boners. In June, 1950, he published an article (which he would prefer to let go uncited and forgotten) arguing that the Federal Reserve had weathered the heaviest pressures it was likely to experience, and that, in light of this, the 2½ per cent long-term rate seemed to be firmly intrenched. The outbreak of hostilities in Korea later that month can be used as an excuse for this grievous mistake; but the fact remains that the confidence expressed was not only the product of a too limited vision; it was bad economic judgment—as subsequent events have demonstrated. It is cold comfort that many others made the same mistake.

payment, they underlie the multiples by which ground rents or other fixed payments are capitalized. The dividend yields on high-grade preferred stocks are usually geared to the general level of long-term interest rates, sometimes closely and seldom without some discernible relationship. Some even aver that common-stock prices are materially influenced by interest rates.

If we should attempt to deal with the full range of explicit or implicit interest rates, we would exceed both our space and our competency. For the purpose of this article, we shall limit our purview; we will focus on interest rates that include little allowance for credit risk and small costs of investment or disinvestment. This means that we shall deal with the interest rates that prevail in large commercial lending and with the prices and yields on very high-grade bonds. Specifically, this excludes (1) all interest yields where cost of lending is substantial, such as in the consumer-credit market; (2) the differential yields between high-grade and lower-grade bonds;[3] (3) yield differentials due to differences in tax status, such as on state and local government bonds; and (4) yields on all classes of corporate equities. This reduces our purview to interest returns from large and almost riskless credit obligations with only one dimension of variation—maturity.

This means that we are also giving no consideration to one other forecasting aspect of interest rates: their use as a strategic indicator of general business developments. A generation ago, interest rates were thought by many to be an early indicator of changes in the level of business activity. It was thought that rates tended to advance late in a boom and thus that high rates signaled an early downturn.[4] Recently the idea has been revived, but consideration of it is not appropriate at this point.

INTEREST-RATE THEORY OF FORECASTERS

Every interest-rate forecaster operates from some basis of theory. In the practical world of loans, bonds, and mortgages this theory may be largely intuitive, but it is implied in the form of analysis used. Keynes, though anathematized by the financial community, furnished an interest-rate theory that was strikingly parallel to the intuitive theories of interest that prevailed in the money and capital markets for a considerable period.

[3] This differential was used as a forecasting index of "confidence" by Leonard Ayres in the *Monthly Bulletin* of the Cleveland Trust Company. See also his *Economics of Recovery* (New York: Macmillan Co., 1933).

[4] This view was largely abandoned after the Federal Reserve influence on rates became apparent, although there has recently been a revival of observations on this hypothesis. For a detailed exposition of this view see L. H. Haney, *Business Forecasting* (Boston: Ginn & Co., 1931), p. 305, and Elmer Bratt, *Business Cycles and Forecasting* (3d ed.; Chicago: Richard D. Irwin, 1948), pp. 416–18 and 432. Wilson Wright, *op. cit.*, pp. 102–3, also has a brief critical account of the use of interest rates as a forecaster of general business developments.

It may have been that Keynes, the successful college bursar, insurance and investment company executive, and personal investor, gave academic words to the ideas that had currency in the actions if not in the words of the financial community. But times change, and the ideas of Keynes about interest have been considerably modified by practice and by theorists. The explicit or implied theories of interest now held by many practicing forecasters of interest rates square remarkably well with what might be called the "modern synthesis" of interest-rate theory.[5] While agreement is by no means complete, the following points might be considered a fair summary of the theoretical foundations of practical interest-rate forecasting.

1. Most interest-rate forecasters assume the basic determinants of interest rates to be the rate of saving and the rate of capital demand. For reasons that will be more apparent in the next section, market forecasters are more disposed to look at personal saving than at business saving as a source of funds. The principal items of capital demand are the heavy capital expenditures of business, the demand for mortgage money, the business demand for working capital, and the borrowing demands of government. The relative importance of these factors varies widely from time to time.

2. While paying their respects to the economic primacy of saving and capital demand, a great majority of the practicing interest-rate forecasters nevertheless feel that the largest single influence on interest rates, both short-term and long-term, is central-bank policy—in the United States, Federal Reserve policy. They recognize that Federal Reserve credit actions sometimes buck the "natural" trend of the market, sometimes are neutral, sometimes work in sympathy with the market. But whether they are conflicting or complementary, people in the market tend to hold the view that interest rates will be, within rather wide limits, what the Federal Reserve wants them to be. They often dispute the wisdom, but not often the power, of the Federal Reserve.[6]

3. Practicing forecasters of interest rates generally hold the view that the saving rate is itself not very elastic with respect to interest rates. Market practitioners, however, are not quite convinced that capital demands are largely insensitive or inelastic to interest rates, as some economists have been since the Oxford surveys before World War II.[7] It is widely recognized that borrowers shop around among

---

[5]To my mind the best synthesis of such theory now available is in the remarkable little essay "Some Notes on the Theory of Interest," by D. H. Robertson. This was first published in *Money, Trade and Economic Growth: A Collection of Essays in Honor of John H. Williams* (New York: Macmillan Co., 1951), and later reprinted in a collection of Robertson's essays, *Utility and All That* (New York: Macmillan Co., 1952).

[6]It is very likely that this view of Federal Reserve power over interest rates is more strongly held in the market than by the Federal Reserve itself. The Federal Reserve has repeatedly said that credit policy is made effective through the availability of bank reserves and therefore of bank credit; interest rates are the indirect resultant of its credit actions, except in those cases of outright defense of a specific interest-rate and security-price level. Nevertheless, the Federal Reserve has at times attempted to set rates by "open mouth" as well as by open-market operations—an implied recognition of its position of leadership in the market.

[7]H. D. Henderson, *The Significance of the Rate of Interest* ("Oxford Economic Papers," No. 1 [1938]), pp. 1–13.

alternative sources of funds rather carefully. Modest differentials sometimes influence financing plans of the great corporations. It is recognized that higher interest costs may not wholly discourage capital outlays, but it is often observed that financing plans are delayed and modified by interest-rate market developments.

4. Interest-rate forecasters are well aware of the importance of changes in business and individual liquidity, particularly the former. This is not exactly Keynesian liquidity preference, since the market gives small weight to interest rates as a determinant of the decisions of businesses or individuals to invest or to hold idle cash. But the market recognizes that liquidity plans may change—something much more like a shift of liquidity-preference schedules than an elasticity of cash holdings with respect to interest rates.

5. One of the more common debates among interest-rate theorists has concerned the line of causation between long- and short-term interest rates. Keynes seemed to give primary recognition to the short-term rate and viewed the long-term rate as a summation of the expected short-term rates. Causation went from short to long.[8] Others, such as Robertson, feel that the long-term rate is the senior partner of the two. The argument for this second position is that, with free markets, the long-term interest rate is directly determined by the balance of (ex ante) saving and investment. While bank-reserve factors immediately influence short-term rates, their level cannot get far out of gear with prevailing and expected long-term rates without excessive pressure either to expand or to contract bank credit. In practical money and capital market forecasting, the more common view is that the two markets are somewhat separate; differences between long-term and short-term rates are moderated by a kind of arbitrage. Rates may differ, but the differences imply a pattern of rate expectations. Borrowers have some latitude in choosing which market they will patronize; investors vary their choices according to their individual expectations. But the question of causation between the two kinds of rates is seldom given much serious attention.

This explanation conflicts with the evidence of interest-rate history. During a large part of the nineteenth century, short-term interest rates appear to have exceeded long-term rates. On the other hand, short-term rates have been below long-term rates for the last twenty-four years. In other words, the implied forecasts of rate changes have been wrong a great many times—possibly a majority of the times in which such a differential prevailed. Either the forecasting of the market has been very poor, or arbitrage between the long-term and short-term markets is far from perfect.[9] We shall have more to say about this later.

---

[8]This position is best illustrated by chap. xv of Keynes's *General Theory*. Much of chap. xx, however, is based on a comparison of the long-term rate of interest with the marginal productivity of capital, and it often seems as if he implied that the long-term rate was directly responsive to changes in this productivity and did not come about through the causal action of changes in short-term rates.

[9]Interest-rate expectation can be derived from the shape of yield curves. See G. H. Evans, Jr., *Basic Economics: A Macro- and Micro-analysis* (New York: Alfred A. Knopf, 1950), pp. 226–41. Many illustrations of yield curves may be found in two studies of the National Bureau of Economic Research: David Durand, *Basic Yields of Corporate Bonds*, 1900–1942 ("Technical Papers," No. 3 [1942]); and David Durand and Willis J. Winn, *Basic Yields of Bonds*, 1926–1947 ("Technical Papers," No. 6 [1947]).

MONEY AND CAPITAL MARKET STRUCTURE
AND FORECASTING

The practicing forecasters of interest rates make allowance for a number of structural features in giving realistic details to their forecasts. Unfortunately, these features are not always spelled out explicitly; they are a part of the lore but not the literature of finance.

1. In the first place, the focus of money and capital market forecasting is on open-market rates: rates are determined by competitive bids and offers. Yields implied by the prices on Treasury securities are recognized as the standard of the market. Such interests are subject to considerable day-to-day and week-to-week variability. But open-market transactions in the full sense of the phrase are only a fraction of the whole money and capital markets. These markets really exist only for securities that are already outstanding. The bargains made by the original borrowers and lenders are in the past; these open-market rates apply to transactions between subsequent investors and disinvestors. The importance of this part of the market is easily exaggerated. For example, much of the activity in the government security market represents turnover after original placement. But, in spite of the vast size of the federal debt, the volume of transactions in the government security market, and particularly in the long-term end of it, is often small. In the late spring of 1953, the money market became rather tight; it has been called a period of "panic" or "crisis." For a part of one day during this period the prices of a few issues of long-term Treasury bonds were quoted below 90. But the purchases and sales at this price were negligible. And very soon the market recovered from this level. Quite obviously, little significance should have been attached to such a price; nevertheless, it set off an extensive controversy. Most sensible forecasters of interest rates claim no power to spot or measure such random swings.

Furthermore, the economic significance of brief and quickly reversed price swings in the market is not very great, *except as it may be a factor in financial sentiment.* The experience of brief price declines is no doubt remembered by many portfolio managers more vividly than more really important events. And it modifies their actions accordingly. For more than thirty years after the event, a quotation in the low 80's for long-term government securities in 1920 continued to be recalled far more frequently than any other single market experience.

This is not, of course, to belittle the importance of open-market rates but rather to put their role in proper perspective. Short-term securities, particularly Treasury obligations, are traded in large volume by banks in adjusting reserve positions. But this field is one in which central-bank leadership is probably more important (in most periods) than in the long-term market.

2. The new-issues market lies partly but not wholly in the open capital market. New issues are usually thought of as securities sold publicly by the investment-banking community. It includes a fair share of corporate obligations and almost all state and local government issues. Interest rates for the new-issues market are set by the tone of the open market. Investment bankers price the obligations as close to the market as they dare. In general, new issues sell at slightly higher yields (lower prices) than outstanding seasoned issues. To a considerable extent, the volume of offerings is "managed" by investment bankers, who fear a "congestion" of new issues. They are disposed to restrain marginal borrowers when they feel that their obligations may prove hard to sell and to feed out issues at about the rate at which they can be absorbed without disturbance to the market. The borrowing customers of investment bankers are often advised as to timing of offerings; this amounts to lining up or rationing prospective borrowers. High-grade borrowers, of course, can always crowd in at the top of the line (if they are willing to pay prevailing rates). But the volume of offerings is roughly geared to the flow of investment funds.

This practice sometimes results in a kind of uneasy stability of interest rates. New issues are fed out only at the absorptive rate, but if the line of borrowers becomes impatient and if investment buyers of securities sense that rate increases are imminent, then a rather sudden increase in rates is likely to take place. It will be reflected in the open-market yields of outstanding obligations, but it has been induced by the new-issues supply becoming "excessive," i.e., the market becoming "congested." As a result, increases in long-term interest rates often come as a series of jerks or sawtooth jumps. Decreases in interest rates, however, are likely to be slower—resisted by security buyers, but pushed gradually by the competition of money-seeking outlets. The forecaster of interest rates must often bring this into his calculations: an increase in yields may come quickly and can be no more than a change in market sentiment. But an increase in interest rates generally must be based on a real market imbalance at the old rates, if it is to endure. A decline in rates may require a longer period.

There are exceptions to this rule. If the market develops a belief that an interest-rate decline is in the making, interest rates can be driven down rather rapidly. This drive may be spearheaded by a decline in short-term interest rates. In the fall of 1953, the expected seasonal pressure on bank loans did not appear; Federal Reserve policy also seemed to be on the softer side. As a result, short-term rates declined considerably, the most conspicuous example being a great reduction in the weekly auction bids for Treasury bills. The yields on long-term obligations were also driven down rather rapidly (prices pushed up) as the market developed the conviction that lower interest rates were in the making. Investors hastened to cover their requirements, some of them for future periods. And this all happened in the face of the fact that at that time the demand for long-term funds was still rather heavy.

As Keynes pointed out in the famous chapter xii of the *General Theory*, the successful market forecaster is often the one who anticipates correctly the market judgments of other speculators. But this is only a rule of forecasting the short-term movements of the market. If the judgments of the market prove to be wrong, they will be quickly reversed.

3. Treasury borrowing plays a fluctuating role in influencing interest rates. When the Treasury is a big borrower, it may dominate the market. The federal government has been a big new-money borrower primarily during war or depression. Both are periods in which other borrowers are too weak to be good credit risks or reluctant to borrow or excluded by direct controls, as in time of war. During these periods the Treasury is virtually in the position of a monopolist (or monopsonist, if one prefers to view the Treasury as a buyer of services rather than as a seller of securities). The Treasury can go a long way toward naming its borrowing rates and making them stick even without Federal Reserve support. Although it was common to speak of interest rates as "controlled" during World War II, most of this control was exercised simply by Treasury decision. There was only one brief period in which outright Federal Reserve support of any importance was needed to keep rates at the level decided upon by the Treasury.[10]

When net new federal borrowing is small, the Treasury is less influential; it must follow the market except as the Federal Reserve intervenes on its behalf. The record shows that the Federal Reserve can intervene successfully even against the tide of economic events. Support purchases from the fall of 1947 to 1948—the largest of such operations by far in modern history—demonstrate that it can do so even with rather small net increase in bank reserves and consequent monetary expansion. The unanswered question would be how long they could buck the tide of the market without monetary expansion exceeding tolerable limits. Nevertheless, the market forecasters interested primarily in short-term prospects usually feel that the first fact to be determined is the nature of Federal Reserve policy and its likely short-term future.

4. A great many interest rates are "posted"; borrowers line up and present their qualifications and are accepted or rejected. The real economic

---

[10]This form of statement seems to belittle the part played by others, such as the Federal Reserve, in formation of Treasury borrowing policy. But for an account showing that it was not far from the truth see Henry Murphy, *National Debt in War and Transition* (New York; McGraw-Hill Book Co., 1951), and also the replies of the Secretary of the Treasury to questions 15, 17, 28, and 32 in the Patman inquiry (Joint Committee on the Economic Report, Subcommittee on General Credit Control and Debt Management, *Monetary Policy and the Management of the Public Debt*, Part I [Washington: Government Printing Office, 1952]).

change is in the variation with which marginal borrowers are accommodated or rejected and not in the rate they pay. Short-term loans of commercial banks to prime borrowers are usually made at the well-known and well-publicized "prime commercial loan" rate. Commercial banks may vary the customers that are accommodated at the prime rate, but the rate itself is likely to hold for a considerable period. In a year of transition, this rate may be changed two or three times; on the other hand, the prime rate has sometimes prevailed for several years. Even though the rates on term loans granted by insurance companies and banks are not generally explicitly posted, they tend to follow the prevailing pattern and fluctuate less than open-market rates.

Mortgage rates of many lenders are more nearly posted than negotiated. Borrowers, too, may be classified according to risk or type of mortgage; but, at the same time, there is a considerable degree of stability in the working rates. These rates are changed in sympathy with pronounced and sustained changes in open-market long-term interest rates, but the changes are not frequent.

To a limited extent, mortgages insured or guaranteed by the federal government have become quasi-open-market obligations, and they are sometimes quoted at prices above or below par; the yields computed from these shifting prices are more flexible than they formerly were. But this practice prevails for only a limited group of mortgages, and the record of yield changes implicit in such sales indicates that their range of variation is more compressed than that of true open-market rates.

5. A substantial fraction of saving never comes to the open market, and a substantial proportion of real capital outlays is self-financed. Corporate saving has financed a large fraction of corporate capital outlays. Most farmers and small businessmen self-finance a large fraction of their requirements. Both groups use some market credit—mostly short-term— but direct use of saving dominates their operations.

Although it has been somewhat overlooked, the proportion of non-market saving and investment fluctuates a great deal. For example, corporate net saving in the years 1947–49 can be estimated to have been from three-fifths to three-quarters of total saving; but in 1951–52 this proportion fell to about one-third. The difference was clearly evident in the flow of funds to savings institutions—they were small in the early group of years and large in the later group. It was probably this large flow of savings funds in the later period that kept open-market rates from going even higher than they in fact went.

6. Although financial institutions cannot "determine" interest rates, their earnings situations often give them courage either to push or to resist changes that affect their earnings positions. For example, life insurance companies accumulate legal reserves according to an explicit contractual

rate. During the 1930's, when the rate of actual earnings approached this contractual rate, life companies searched for alternative uses of funds, including direct investment in rental real estate—alternatives they probably would not have accepted if prevailing market rates had not forced them to do so. Thus interest-rate declines are sometimes resisted by a broadening of investment practices. Another example is the earnings pressures which pushed commercial banks into term lending.

7. Practical interest-rate forecasters are aware of the strategic importance of seasonal factors. If a change is in the making, the dating of it may depend on the normal seasonal pattern. Commercial banks are more likely to announce increases in prime loan rates when fall borrowings are approaching their seasonal high. And seasonal slack in the spring may bring about rate declines. Long-term mortgage rates are less likely to drop and more likely to increase in the spring and summer seasons of greater building activity. Seasonal factors do not create, but they may time, interest-rate changes.

8. In the days before World War I, when the international gold (or sterling) standard prevailed, money markets of the major nations were strongly influenced by developments in the City of London. Money rates tended to follow similar, if not parallel, patterns. The gold or sterling convertibility of the principal currencies furnished the cohesive force. Long-term interest rates were more scattered, but an observer of these rates might suspect that credit-risk differentials were more important in the scatter than were pure money factors.[11]

As a result of reduced intercommunicability among currencies by exchange control and related measures, money and capital markets are now more nearly national than international; interest rates can and sometimes do follow disparate courses in various nations. And varying policies of governmental control of rates have furthered these differences. Between closely related countries such as the United States and Canada, interest rates show a common pattern; but even in that case, it was not too close a one until 1951, when the Canadian dollar was made fully convertible. On the other hand, there is a certain amount of sentimental influence of international forces. As a recent example, United States Treasury security prices jumped sharply in the fall of 1953 when the Bank of England reduced its rediscount rate. Another example would be the bunching of recent central-bank rediscount rate reductions.

The impediments to passage of interest-rate influences from country to country do not lessen the importance of international politics on the course of interest. A truly ambitious interest-rate forecaster might aspire to the minds of the powerful men in the Kremlin. Probably the single greatest

[11]This idea is rather fully developed by Frederick R. Macaulay in chap. iii of his *Bond Yields, Interest Rates, and Stock Prices* (New York: National Bureau of Economic Research, 1938).

factor in the course of interest rates for the next decade will be whether we have outright war, have a tepid or cool war, or achieve the apparently remote goal of true world peace.

ANALYSIS UNDERLYING AN INTEREST-RATE FORECAST

As we said before, interest-rate forecasting does not follow any single widely accepted technique. Individual forecasters use various methods, ranging from those of intuitive introspection to systems of considerable complexity. The weights attached to various factors reflect the differences in views and judgments of the forecasters. The final forecast is often compounded mainly of intuitive judgment even when the preliminary analysis has been formal and detailed.

Most interest-rate forecasts can be broken down into four stages of analysis. First, a forecast of general business conditions is prepared. Second, the levels of *ex ante* saving and of investment implicit in the foregoing forecast of business are compared.[12] Third, a preliminary appraisal of technical money market factors is made. Fourth, the nature of Treasury financing needs and Federal Reserve policy are forecast. This final step is necessarily last in line because public policy itself is usually influenced by the state of business. But since policy is not necessarily consonant with the expected state of business, it is a separate and independent step.

General Business Forecast

The segments of the general business scene of most interest are those dealing with saving and investment. More specifically, the distribution of saving among the various groups is significant. An anticipation of large business saving does not mean a direct flow of funds to the capital markets; it does mean, however, a greater capacity for the self-financing of business capital outlays. In some circumstances, it is even worth while to break down the general forecasts of business profits, dividends, and capital outlays by line of business. For example, only a small fraction of the capital outlays of public utilities are financed by retained earnings; at the other extreme, the capital outlays of manufacturing concerns are financed in this way to a very great extent.

When estimating corporate saving for purposes of an interest-rate forecast, it is probably better to do so on a gross, rather than a net, basis.

---

[12]It should be noted parenthetically that if the first stage of general business forecasting has involved the construction of a model based on gross national product, the completed model will show an even balance of saving and investment, since this scheme presumes to forecast the *ex post* situation. The interest-rate forecaster is interested in the model during the stage of construction when independent and therefore unbalanced *ex ante* estimates of the various parts are being prepared.

The largest element in the difference between these two is, of course, allowance for depreciation, depletion, and other forms of capital consumption. Capital outlays are always estimated on a gross basis; in fact, capital outlays are seldom exactly parallel in nature to the existing capital equipment against which capital consumption charges are being made. It is therefore more convenient and probably more realistic to treat saving as well as capital outlays on a gross basis. Since prevailing national-income accounting practices also put individual saving on what is essentially a gross basis, this practice also tends toward consistency in pattern.

The interest-rate forecaster uses the standard sources for much of his data, but he is probably particularly interested in the surveys of planned capital expenditures by the Department of Commerce and by the McGraw-Hill economists. The less frequently cited parts of the surveys that show such outlays by industry categories are particularly important. The Federal Reserve annual survey of consumer finances and their economic expectations is also particularly relevant to the work of the interest-rate forecaster. These surveys can be used to prepare forecasts of saving, not only in general terms but by income groups and also by various economic categories. So far, the attitudes revealed by these surveys have been borne out remarkably well by subsequent developments.

The Balance of Saving and Investment

The part of the general business forecast of most use to the interest-rate forecaster is, of course, the balance between *ex ante* saving and investment. The important element is the degree of balance or imbalance. When the projected expectations are far out of balance, the forecaster of interest rates has a clear guide. A substantial excess of projected investment that is likely to require market financing means a substantial upward pressure of interest rates. A substantial deficiency means strong pressure in the downward direction. But if the margin between the projected levels of the two is not great, this margin is not only probably smaller than the likely error in forecasts; it is the kind of margin that can be resolved without material pressure on interest rates in either direction.

Technical Money Market Factors

At present, and for the foreseeable future, the Federal Reserve has ample powers to set the tone of the money market. It can offset gold flows, changes of currency in circulation, and the random shifts of Federal Reserve float as they occur. It can facilitate the normal seasonal variations in member-bank loans. It has considerable power over the level of member-bank reserve requirements. If the Federal Reserve did all these things fully and used all these powers regularly, the forecaster of interest rates could skip this stage of analysis and go directly to the question of what tone the Federal Reserve wants to set in the money market.

But, in practice, these factors are not precisely offset; nor does the Federal Reserve attempt to do so. Furthermore, these various factors may be allowed to press the market if they work in the direction desired by the Federal Reserve; it can make its policies effective without overt and evident credit action. If gold is flowing in when the Federal Reserve wants to ease the market, that is a convenient way of doing so; or an outflow may be allowed to tighten the market. The Federal Reserve can refuse to budge in the face of a fall increase in loan demand; it can let this demand tighten the market. Most interest-rate forecasters probably have overstressed the significance of technical money market analysis; but it cannot be omitted.

The sources of technical information on money market factors are ample: the weekly Federal Reserve statements of reserve factors and the balance sheets of leading member banks; the *Federal Reserve Bulletin*, for both statistics and occasional articles; the lead article in almost every issue of the *Monthly Review* of the Federal Reserve Bank of New York.

GUESSING PUBLIC POLICY

The concrete materials for judgment of public policy are relatively limited. The outlook for Treasury financing is outlined in each budget message, and forecasts of the major factors, announced by the President, are prepared for him by the Bureau of Budget or by the Council of Economic Advisers. In recent years, these messages and forecasts have presented not only the statutory basis for expenditures and receipts but have also converted federal operations to a cash basis—much more useful for the forecaster because the cash balance indicates the probable market operations of the Treasury. The interest-rate forecaster may wish to modify these public forecasts; he can substitute his own judgment of expenditure rates and tax collections if he feels the public forecasts either to be inaccurate or to be biased for reasons of propaganda. The balance of these corrected estimates will show the amount of Treasury new-money financing that will be required. A further judgment of the part to be played by the non-marketable or savings bonds sector will yield the net "new-money" position of the Treasury in open-market forms. The maturity schedule of the public debt provides a measure of the refunding problem of the Treasury. Since many outstanding Treasury obligations, mainly bonds, have optional call dates in advance of maturity, the exact schedule of refundings can be determined only by the extent to which the Treasury must issue advance notice of its intention to call and refund. But the likely calls can be forecast rather readily from a comparison of coupon rates with prevailing market yields.

A far greater uncertainty in this area is that of the general monetary and fiscal policy of the government. This means specifically the policies of the Treasury Department and the Federal Reserve; but at the same time it must include the general policy stand of the administration in office and the fiscal predispositions of Congress. The materials for judgment of policy are public statements, annual reports, speeches, and the record of prior action.

Guessing future public policy contains an even more nebulous element. Public authorities are dedicated to policies that will be consonant with the maintenance of good business conditions. This is based on sincere convictions as well as on political expedience. Therefore, what the public authorities think to be the business outlook is vitally important. Many government departments have established special economic services or departments for the study of business conditions. There is a certain amount of diffidence about publication in frank detail of the forecasting that is done by these agencies, but it is done, and the results are transmitted to the policy-forming officials. For these reasons almost all practicing forecasters visit Washington regularly. These visits may or may not influence their own forecasting, but what "Washington thinks" are data of great importance, even when the forecaster himself does not agree with these thoughts.

The character of congressional action is perhaps the most uncertain of all factors. Forecasting congressional action is a free and unrestricted sport, open to anyone brave enough to try. No rules and no formulas exist; but this factor often furnishes interest-rate forecasters with alibis when they fail to hit the mark.

SYNTHESIS OF AN INTEREST-RATE FORECAST

When the interest-rate forecaster has completed his collection of data, he must try to fit all the countless combinations and permutations of elements into usable general cases. The following are examples:

1. Business outlook is booming or inflationary. Projected private investment seems to outrun expected voluntary saving. The public authorities are expected to resist inflation by a hard money policy and by fiscal means to the extent possible. Under such circumstances, increases in interest rate, both long-term and short-term, are likely. And it is very possible that short-term increases will lead the way.

2. Business outlook is booming or inflationary, with projected private investment crowding saving as before. But in this case, the fiscal situation of the federal government indicates deficits, and the monetary authorities show a disposition to shelter the Treasury and to "underwrite" their financing needs. This is a case of conflict. Interest rates certainly will not decline; but the unresolved question is

whether the public authorities can resist an advance. Experience indicates that they can, if they are willing to pay the price of monetary expansion. But there is undoubtedly a limit to the period over which such a policy can be pursued.

3. Business outlook, saving, and investment are all in rough balance. There are several varieties of public policy that might prevail in such cases. A policy of hardening money rates seems very unlikely, but the choice is twofold: Will the public authorities accept prevailing rates and not try to drive interest rates down a little? Either is possible, but under these circumstances interest rate changes are likely to be small. And an easy-money policy will be reflected more in a softening of short-term rates than in long-term rates.

4. Business outlook is gloomy; saving promises to outrun the demand for funds. Under these conditions, public policy will almost certainly be on the side of easier money. While short-term rates will probably lead the way and may go very low, long-term rates will drift down after them.

There are, of course, quantitative differences and special circumstances, so that, rather than four cases, we really have a whole range of possibilities. The interest-rate forecaster, however, can usually expect to find that efforts to refine his results by a multiplication of variables will gain him very little accuracy. In the long run, the market for money and capital has many elements of internal stability. Short-term rates vary as a result of money market factors, but only a clear imbalance of saving and investment or a determined program of public policy will displace long-term rates substantially from their prevailing levels.

Range of Interest-Rate Movements

The forecaster of interest rates, of course, wants not only to point the direction of change; he wants to measure the range of change, at least approximately. In this section we shall suggest a few general rules for doing so.

Earlier we cast doubt on the interpretation of the differential of short-term and long-term interest rates as an implicit forecast by the market of expected rate changes. Let us explore an alternative explanation. The range of movement of long-term interest rates can be said to be limited by the following margins: On the low side, investors face such great risks of capital losses that long-term interest rates cannot be pushed far below the level that such investors feel to be a reasonable expectation of the future. Investors, as Keynes and many others have pointed out, will choose the alternative of holding cash or investing in short-term form rather than take the risk of such losses. Investors' expectations of the future are amorphous and change slowly. The bottom limits are real and almost inviolable, except as beliefs and convictions change; and they change slowly. Furthermore, the income requirements of some investors, such as life insurance companies, are such as to make them exhaust all other investment alternatives before accepting rates so low as to throttle their operations. The top limit is the paying limit of borrowers. This is not a clear limit, but it can be approximated by rough guides. The big borrowers, such as public utilities, are very conscious of the problems of fixed charges in relationship to expected earnings rates. For example, as long as public utility earnings are limited by service rate regulation, the interest rate they will pay the expansion is also limited.

Between these margins, rapid rate changes are resisted by a number of factors. Investors are quick to hold off if interest rates drop (bond prices rise) too rapidly. There is a considerable elasticity in short-term investment schedules. Borrowers are also rather quick to resist sudden increases; many borrowing corporations have alternatives, such as reducing cash balances, cutting projected investment plans, or reducing dividends (though this is done reluctantly).

The forecaster of long-term interest rates, therefore, must first judge whether prevailing rates are near the top or the bottom margins we have suggested. Then he judges the latitude of fluctuation between the prevailing rate and the margin toward which rates are tending. Allowing for the resistances to rate change, he must then guess the likely range of movement.

Short-term interest rates move between much wider margins. Short-term rates can and have approached zero.[13] For short periods of time they can go to very high levels. As recently as 1929, call-money rates averaged over 14 per cent per annum during the last week of March; even higher rates prevailed in 1919–20 and earlier periods. But the period over which short-term rates can be materially above long-term rates probably is limited.[14]

The forecaster has little chance of anticipating the range and timing of short-term rate movements anywhere near as accurately. Most of the time he can use the long-term rate as his upper margin (but not always), but there is no limit on the other side except a zero return.[15]

One general rule can be read from the record, although the logic

[13]For tax reasons certain special short-term yields have occasionally been negative. Treasury bills are used to avoid Illinois personal property taxes, and the issue that matured just beyond the assessment date had such negative yields in 1939 and 1940.

[14]Several have called attention to the fact that this seemed to be true for extended periods during the nineteenth century. See E. A. Goldenweiser, *American Monetary Policy* (New York: McGraw-Hill Book Co., 1951), p. 189, and Robertson, *Utility and All That*, pp. 110 ff. After some study of the data, it seems to me that this is a misinterpretation of the facts. The rates compared are not really comparable.

[15]An extreme example of an unpredictable short-term interest rate is that for federal funds. Since these funds are an alternative to Federal Reserve borrowing, the rate on them can never exceed the Federal Reserve discount rate. But since they are essentially one-day loans, they can and often do move between the discount rate and the nearest conventional fraction above zero (usually a sixteenth), all within a few days or weeks.

for it is far from clear: a sharp advance in rates is more likely than not to be followed by a sharp and quick decline. The decline from a rate that has advanced slowly or has been maintained for a long time usually seems to be slower.

AN EXAMPLE: 1954

The other articles in this issue will have presented both methods and forecasts that cover the more general areas of economic interest. Because of this, I shall not undertake to present a complex general business forecast. Furthermore, since these other articles are not available to me as I write, the assumptions I use here may not square with those the other authors use. The following, therefore, is to be treated more as an exercise in applying a general method than as a definitive forecast.

The assumptions used here are as follows: (1) General business activity in 1954 will be slightly below 1953 levels. (2) Further price declines of agricultural commodities will be resisted by some form of public action; the prices of industrial goods and of final goods for consumers probably will not drop at all and may rise a bit. (3) Saving of the kind that flows into the capital markets will continue at present levels. (4) Investment plans will slacken; however, the congestion of potential borrowers backed up during the recent tightness in the capital markets probably will not be cleaned up until well into 1954. (5) The Treasury will have rather modest new-money needs in 1954—mostly in the second half of that year—but its refundings will continue to be large. Long-term refunding will be attempted whenever the market shows signs of making this practically feasible. (6) The Federal Reserve will not feel the need for a drastic change in policy in either direction but will protect Treasury refunding operations rather more meticulously than it did in early 1953.

This amounts to the third of the general situations outlined above. The market has already anticipated slower business and lower interest rates. The question facing the forecaster is whether the market has fully discounted the probable nature of business developments or whether further reductions are to be anticipated. To develop our example further, the following strategic factors are expected to dominate the market: While a weaker demand for funds might tend to reduce long-term interest rates further, Treasury refunding of the federal debt into longer term will check such a decline. This possibility clearly limits the extent to which long-term rates can decline. The investment buyers will not fear a shortage of bonds as long as this Treasury policy prevails; they will not have to bid yields down very far to meet their portfolio needs. Thus the decline in long-term rates that has already taken place may not have much further to go—unless business recedes even faster than assumed here.

But slower business, the Federal Reserve assistance to Treasury refunding, and shrinkage in the supply of short-term Treasury obligations might tend to reduce short-term yields even further. Before the first half of 1954 is over, the money market may have reversed itself considerably, and funds may be quite "easy." In essence, this is a forecast of little further change in interest rates except for a possible widening in the spread between short-term and long-term rates.

Index

494